Consumer Economics

From identity theft to product recalls, from what we once thought of as unshakeable institutions to increasing concerns about sustainability, consumer issues are an integral part of modern life. This fully updated third edition of *Consumer Economics* offers students an accessible and thorough guide to the concerns surrounding the modern consumer and brings to light the repercussions of making uninformed decisions in today's economy.

This definitive textbook introduces students to these potential issues and covers other key topics including consumer behavior, personal finance, legal rights and responsibilities, as well as marketing and advertising. Combining theory and practice, students are introduced to both the fundamentals of consumer economics and how to become better-informed consumers themselves.

Highlights in this new edition include:

- New Critical Thinking Projects to encourage students to develop their critical thinking skills through analyzing consumer issues.
- Expanded coverage of social media and the impact of social influence on consumers.
- Revised Consumer Alerts: practical advice and guidance to help students make smart consumer decisions.
- A new Companion Website with a range of presentation materials and exercises related to each chapter.

Fully updated throughout, this textbook is suitable for students studying consumer sciences—what works, what doesn't, and how consumers are changing.

Elizabeth B. Goldsmith is Professor in the Department of Retail Merchandising and Product Development at Florida State University, USA.

"*Consumer Economics: Issues and Behaviors* by Goldsmith provides an all-encompassing introduction and overview to the study of consumerism. The detailed examples, discussion questions, and resources serve to engage students from varying disciplines in the exploration of their rights and responsibilities as a consumer."

Linda A. Bradley, PhD, Department of Family and Consumer Sciences,
California State University, Northridge, USA

"Goldsmith's latest edition of *Consumer Economics: Issues and Behaviors* contains all the elements of an excellent text. As an instructor, I use the quotes from each chapter as an introduction to each class session. The students connect with the practical nature of the case studies that reflect chapter content. The real-life examples and high interest topics connect easily with students and lead to lively discussion. I look forward to utilizing this updated text to enhance my classes."

Susan A. Reichelt, PhD, Chair and Associate Professor,
Sam Houston State University, USA

Consumer Economics

Issues and Behaviors

Third Edition

Elizabeth B. Goldsmith

Routledge
Taylor & Francis Group

LONDON AND NEW YORK

Third edition published 2016
by Routledge
2 Park Square, Milton Park, Abingdon, Oxon, OX14 4RN

and by Routledge
711 Third Avenue, New York, NY 10017

Routledge is an imprint of the Taylor & Francis Group, an informa business

First edition published by Pearson Education Inc., 2004
Second edition published by Pearson Education Inc., 2009

British Library Cataloguing in Publication Data
A catalogue record for this book is available from the British Library

Library of Congress Cataloging in Publication Data
Names: Goldsmith, Elizabeth B., author.
Title: Consumer economics : issues and behaviors / Elizabeth B. Goldsmith.
Description: Third Edition. | New York : Routledge, 2016. |
Revised edition of the author's Consumer economics, 2009.
Identifiers: LCCN 2015047046 | ISBN 9781138846586 (hardback) |
ISBN 9781315727363 (ebook)
Subjects: LCSH: Consumer education. | Consumption (Economics)
Classification: LCC TX335 .G585 2016 | DDC 640.73—dc23
LC record available at http://lccn.loc.gov/2015047046

ISBN: 978-1-138-84658-6 (hbk)
ISBN: 978-1-315-72736-3 (ebk)

Typeset in Bembo
by Keystroke, Station Road, Codsall, Wolverhampton
Printed in Great Britain by
Ashford Colour Press Ltd, Gosport, Hants

MIX
Paper from
responsible sources
FSC® C011748

Contents

Figures

Photos

Tables

Acknowledgments

With thanks and appreciation to Editor Elanor Best of Routledge for her hard work and determination. Thanks are also extended to the reviewers of the present edition:

Linda Bradley	California State University
Bonita Manson	South Carolina State University
Diann Moorman	University of Georgia
Jing Jian Xiao	University of Rhode Island

Also thanked are the reviewers of the previous edition:

Joyce Armstrong	Texas Women's University
Ruben Berrios	Clarion University
Barbara Briscoe	Morgan State University
Joyce Cantrell	Kansas State University
Thomas Dahlstrom	Eastern University
Pat McCallister	Eastern Illinois University
V. Ann Paulins	Ohio University
Patricia Pierson	Northwestern State University of Louisiana

Appreciation is also extended to the reviewers of the first edition:

John R. Burton	University of Utah
Jane Kolodinsky	University of Vermont
Julia Marlowe	University of Georgia
Patricia Scheeserd	Indiana University of Pennsylvania
Anita Subramaniam	Montclair State University (now in India)
Jing Jian Xiao	University of Rhode Island

Many thanks to the J. William Fulbright Scholarship Board (CIES) and the Bureau of Educational and Cultural Affairs of the US Department of State; the University of the West Indies; the University of Malta; my academic home, Florida State University; and to my family for their love and support.

Part **1**

Consumer Perspectives

Chapter **1**

Consumers in a Changing World

When we all think alike, then no one is thinking.

Walter Lippman

LEARNING OBJECTIVES

1. Understand the consumer.
2. Define consumer economics.
3. Explain the market economy.
4. Describe Adam Smith's contribution to consumer economics.
5. Explain the five steps in the consumption process.
6. Explain the three questions economies have to address.
7. Describe the three parts of the business cycle.

CASE STUDY

Buying Online and Data Tracking

The following quote illustrates three trends pervasive in today's consumer purchasing behavior. There is more buying online, more sophisticated data tracking, and a growing lack of privacy.

> "U.S. retailers are facing a steep and persistent drop in store traffic, which is weighing on sales and prompting chains to slow store openings as shoppers make more of their purchases online. Aside from a small uptick in April, shopper visits have fallen by 5% or more from a year earlier in every month for the past two years, according to Shopper-Trak, a data firm that records store visits for retailers using tracking devices installed at 40,000 U.S. outlets."
>
> Source: Shelly Banjo and Paul Ziobro (August 6, 2014).
> "Shoppers Flee Physical Stores." *The Wall Street Journal*, p. B1–B2.

Introduction

In 1905, Steverson wrote that "The world is so full of things, I'm sure we should all be happy as kings." With the advent of the Internet and mobile devices there is no question that consumers have more exposure to brands, prices, and products than ever before. What would Steverson make of today's world? He wrote that quote during the rise of the age of consumerism; Steverson's couplet highlights the importance of things and illustrates a childlike wonder about the possibilities set before us. If happiness is consumption, we should strive to acquire more and, if all goes well, in the end, live as kings. Unfortunately, it is not as simple as that; even the richest person cannot afford endless consumption. And, it is obvious that happiness is not so easily attained. What is the connection between happiness and consumption? What do consumers want? What motivates consumers to consume? How do they make choices? Consider these famous quotes:

> *Give me the luxuries of life and I will willingly do without the necessities.*
>
> *Frank Lloyd Wright*

> *When I was young, I used to think that wealth and power would bring me happiness . . . I was right.*
>
> *Gahan Wilson*

> *Money won't buy happiness, but it will pay the salaries of a large research staff to study the problem.*
>
> *Bill Vaughan*

Daniel Gilbert, author of *Stumbling on Happiness*, says that money itself doesn't make you happy—what makes a person happy is what is done with the money. Research suggests experiences such as travel (or even broader, relationships of all kinds) may bring more satisfaction than durable goods.

CRITICAL THINKING

Happiness and Consumption

Think about the last time you were really happy. Where were you? Who were you with? What were you doing? Was consumption involved? Do you agree or disagree with what Daniel Gilbert says?

This chapter introduces the fundamentals of consumerism and the changing world, including the steep rise in international business in which we live. Since we are all consumers, consumer economics is not esoteric; it is applicable every day. We live more and more in a knowledge economy filled with ever-changing technology. A revolution is taking place in social media.

Through understanding consumers, we have a better sense of:

- the multiple roles of consumers
- the roles of producers/manufacturers, suppliers, and retailers
- the government involvement in economic systems, and
- the decision-making process.

Consumer economics is the study of how people deal with scarcity, fulfill needs, and select among alternative goods, services, and actions. It provides an understanding of how the marketplace works, what our role is in it, and how our choices affect our lifestyles. Studying consumer economics:

- enriches our lives by helping us get the things we want
- enlarges our awareness of the impact of globalization on our living standards, lifestyles, and future opportunities
- increases our understanding of the factors influencing our choices and the choices of others
- improves our understanding of how the marketplace works
- increases our awareness of what is fair
- encourages us to think carefully about how we spend and invest our money.

An end result of studying consumer economics is improved decision making. Each person should be able to look back on decisions made and, for the most part, feel confident they were the right ones.

Why Study Consumer Economics?

> ### CASE STUDY
>
> **Jessica Wright**
>
> How do we learn about personal finance and consumerism? Consider the following quote by a young woman named Jessica Wright:
>
> > "When I was younger, my father would send me to the store to run his errands: 'Jessica is the only one who knows how to bring back change,' he would jokingly say. I learned about credit cards from my mother and cash from my father, but the most important lesson I learned from my parents is to take care of home first. With that being our family's golden rule, we understood that when money came in, we would take care of living necessities before spending on leisure activities. I grew up in a middle-class family with strong values in Mesquite, Texas. My mother was a free spender, but only when my brother and I needed clothes for school or we needed something for the house. I often remember hearing her say, 'Charge it,' but rarely did she splurge on herself. She used to take me with her to pay bills and sometimes let me give the teller the payment. I learned that if you use credit, you still need to pay more than the minimum amount before the due date.
> >
> > Source: "Lessons from Our Parents." *NEFE Digest*, September/October 2014, p. 7.

Did you have a similar upbringing to Jessica's in terms of family values and the allocation of money? Consumer economics is a discovery process driven by curiosity and impacted by our early socialization. The purpose of this text is to provide the reader with an increased understanding of consumer economics building on previous knowledge and experience. By following the principles in this book, you will:

- increase self-awareness
- understand others' consumption patterns and perspectives
- approach daily living with enthusiasm and a can-do spirit
- overcome limitations and weaknesses by knowing your rights and responsibilities
- improve your consumption and financial behavior
- participate in actions that bring fairness to the marketplace
- discover the rights and privileges provided to consumers by federal and state laws and regulations
- take control of your happiness (at least as far as consumption is concerned)

- find ways to make a profit and make your money stretch further
- discover career options and recognize opportunities as they arise.

Most students in consumer economics classes aspire to careers working with people in education, law, business, community development, the retail industry, management, health, merchandising, design, government, communications, human resources, or marketing. Specific examples of careers involving consumer economics will be given throughout the book. A combination available at some universities is consumer journalism, which combines the study of consumer economics with advertising, journalism, public relations, and communications. Internships in established business and startups, media, government, and non-profits provide opportunities to apply consumer economics theories and principles to the workplace.

The challenge that we, as educated citizens, face today is to overcome passivity and hesitation and to take the steps to join in; enter the marketplace; expect, receive, and provide fair treatment; and bring about improved lives. The main objective is to develop the ability to apply consumer economics knowledge to regulatory and social issues, as well as to personal buying decisions. Areas receiving a lot of attention are innovations in food buying and dining experiences. According to the National Grocery Association 2014 Consumer Panel, 87 percent of consumers regard availability of locally grown produce as a major influence when it comes to purchasing food. Most schools, hospitals, and companies would like to offer more locally grown produce, but it is not so easily

Photo 1.1
A young woman buying vegetables at a food market

Source: Thinkstock: Alexander Novikov

obtained in a consistent pattern due to growing seasons and local conditions. Making local sourcing more achievable is an ongoing but important challenge. These are some of the benefits:

- high-quality seasonal ingredients
- reduced carbon footprint by minimizing transport impact
- support for local farmers
- fresher food
- healthier lifestyles.

The desire for fresher food shows a passion for a better life and environment, a sense of hope and renewal that one brings to consumerism; it is not all reason and dry theory. Abundant food and a clean water supply are fundamental to human survival. Caring about the rights of others is central to the field. The consumer advocates and reformers such as Erin Brockovich and Ralph Nader, whom you'll read about, were passionate about making people's lives better and safer. They gave stirring speeches and wrote popular books that changed the way cars and other goods were made in this country, and they crusaded for a cleaner environment. Brockovich exposed pollution in California and became famous in a 1990s movie directed by Steven Soderbergh for which Julia Roberts, playing the role of Brockovich, won an Academy Award. Brockovich and Nader symbolize how one person can make a difference, which is another key concept in consumer economics. There are groups, individual leaders, and politicians who have led or fostered the consumer movement by exposing fraud and corruption. We have all benefited from their efforts. To summarize the role of passion in economic behavior, Alexander Pope wrote in *Moral Essays, I*:

> *On life's vast ocean diversely we sail,*
> *Reason the card, but Passion is the gale.*

CONSUMER ALERTS

Too Much Food Waste

Besides eating better quality food, we need to reduce food waste. According to the US Environmental Protection Agency/Municipal Solid Waste Characterization Report (2014), 35 million tons of food waste reaches landfills each year in the United States. Consumers today around the world are interested in reducing food waste and making more eco-friendly choices. Some solutions include reusable to-go-containers and water bottles, trayless dining, less use of drinking straws or using paper ones versus plastic, and fryer-oil recycling. The trend is on to promote a better environment, conserve energy and resources, and eliminate unnecessary food waste.

Who Consumes and Why?

We need to consume to exist. **Consumers** are individuals or groups such as families who obtain, use, maintain, and dispose of products and services to increase life satisfaction and fulfill needs. Consumers are not always efficient in this process.

Brian Wansink of Cornell University is a leader in food waste research. In his book *Slim by Design: Mindless Eating Solutions* (2014), he details the positive changes we can make to approach and merge our diets, resulting in healthier eating. He suggests innovative and inexpensive design changes for homes, grocery stores, and schools. He has found having healthier food visible, such as a bowl of fruit on a counter, will encourage more people to eat fruit versus keeping it in the crisper drawer in a refrigerator. In one of his co-authored shopping studies, the researchers found that many grocery products (usually ones bought for specific recipes or occasions) were never used (Wansink, Brasel, & Amjad, 2000). The usual reason given by respondents was that products were not used immediately after purchase and were slowly pushed to the back of the cabinet and forgotten. They called these products "cabinet castaways." It is estimated that about 12 percent of purchased products are never used and eventually thrown out (Wansink & Deshpande, 1994), and 80 percent of new products fail. Part of the reason for this is that preferences change as people learn and change, and some products are ill-conceived. One of the subtopics in consumer economics is how to increase the awareness of purchase and usage habits in order to save money and reduce waste. For example, information search is a good idea, but it can be costly.

About 12 percent of purchased products are never used and eventually are thrown out.

Consumerism has many definitions. Sometimes the word is used to refer to the positive efforts of the consumer movement (essentially the consumer interest), while other times it refers to runaway materialism. For an excellent description of the word and all its permutations, see Roger Swagler's "Evolution and Applications of the Term Consumerism: Theme and Variations" listed in the reference section at the end of this chapter. For the purposes of this book, **consumerism** refers to the belief that goods give meaning to individuals and their roles in society. This combination of consumption, social roles, and politics was first voiced by Adam Smith (1723–1790), the founder of modern economics. He argued in his book *An Inquiry into the Nature and Causes of the Wealth of Nations* (1776), found in Heilbroner's *Essential Adam Smith* (1986), that the essential task of coordinating national economies should fall to consumers. He wrote:

> *Consumption is the sole end and purpose of all production; and the interest of the producer ought to be attended to only so far as it may be necessary for promoting that of the consumer. This maxim is so perfectly self-evident that it would be absurd to attempt to prove it. But in the mercantile system, the interest of the consumer is almost constantly sacrificed to that of the producer. (Heilbroner, 1986, p. 284)*

CRITICAL THINKING

Adam Smith Inspires

The father of modern economics did not come up with his approach to economics overnight. He wrote an earlier book entitled *The Theory of Moral Sentiments* in which he states that charity alone will not help provide the essentials of the good life to all. Rather, he stressed the importance of trade and functioning, competitive markets. What is your opinion about how ideas evolve? Ideas can have consequences, so discuss the impact of Adam Smith from this book to his more famous one, *An Inquiry into the Nature and Causes of the Wealth of Nations*.

As a professor of moral philosophy at the University of Glasgow in Scotland, who taught classes several days a week (some as large as 90, with students ages 14 to 16), Smith knew consumers well. He did not sit isolated in a country mansion, and although he never married, he traveled and had many friends. He said his 3,000 books (a very sizable collection in that time) were his companions in life. Smith knew that consumers could make mistakes, but he thought for the most part that they could be counted on to be conscientious and careful spenders since this was in their best interest. He proposed that consumers be given freedom and authority in running their own economic affairs, and in the long run he felt this would benefit the nation as well. His doctrine, considered

Photo 1.2 Adam Smith (1723–1790) published *An Inquiry into the Nature and Causes of the Wealth of Nations* in 1776, laying the foundation of economics. He argued that the wealth of nations came from the goods and services produced and consumed

Source: flickr: Surfstyle

revolutionary in its time, was resisted by the English king and the businesspeople of the day who dominated national decision making about trade. Across the ocean, his book was well received by many of the founders of the United States who were looking for more democratic ways to do things. They liked the idea of the consumer as king; it fit well into building a new country, welcoming new settlers, and encouraging expansion. In Smith's philosophy, the wealth of nations was not based on gold and silver but rather on the goods and services produced and consumed by people. His philosophy of the "invisible hand" was directed as much against monopoly as government. He extolled the virtues of the acquisitive process and competitive markets. To put his philosophy into one phrase, Smith's understanding of human nature was that "to be human is to exchange freely."

In more modern times, consumerism expresses the cardinal political ideals of liberty and democracy because being able to choose among a vast array of commodities gives people a sense of freedom (Heilbroner, 1986). David Harris, author of *Cute, Quaint, Hungry and Romantic: The Aesthetics of Consumerism* (2000), writes:

> *What, after all, would a world without consumerism be like?*
>
> *Surely not one that I myself would choose to live in. There would be no cities because cities are dependent on trade, nor money because there would be nothing to buy. There would be no insurance companies because there would be no possessions, no realtors because there would be no houses, no lawyers because hunters and gatherers rarely have to untangle the red tape of copyright infringement or haggle over joint stock agreements or fax each other angry letters to cease and desist. To imagine a world without consumerism is to erase oneself. (p. 265)*

Goods and Services

Would you like a nicer car or apartment? Most of us aspire to a better life. Buying or using goods and services is an act of faith—one assumes when purchasing something that the goods (e.g., a sandwich) or services (e.g., dry cleaning) will provide satisfaction or fulfill a need. **Choice** is the act or process of selecting between alternative goods and services. Goods are tangible objects: things you can see and feel, such as a car. Services are intangible actions: work done to satisfy or provide for others, such as a catering service. **Resources** (inputs necessary to produce goods and services) can be categorized by type:

- Human resources: Knowledge, skill, ability, and strength.
- Natural resources: Oceans, rivers, lakes, land, mineral deposits, and air.
- Capital resources: Human-made resources such as tools, machines, buildings, and money.

Because the general economic meaning of consumer goods encompasses consumer services, in this book when the word *goods* is used, it implies both goods and services. In recent years, the growth in the number of new consumer goods has been astounding—online classes, mobile phones and Internet access, specialty coffee shops, emails, and so forth. As an explanation, one author wrote:

> *Consumer goods became a language, defining, redefining, and easing relationships between friends, family members, lovers, and strangers. Cars and clothes gave identity to young and old, female and male, ethnic majority and minority, telling others who they were and how they expected to be treated. Cosmetics and candy expressed both rebellion and authority, thus providing people with an understanding of themselves in an otherwise indifferent and sometimes unfriendly world. Moreover, goods redefined concepts of the past and future and gave a cadence to the rhythms of daily life when people purchased antiques and novelties and when Christmas became a shopping "season." (Harris, 2000, p. 265)*

Not all our memories of consumption are such good ones. Consumerism is not always nostalgic. Have you ever purchased something that disappointed? What was it that did not bring you the degree of satisfaction that you had hoped? Was it a ticket to a lousy movie or a printer that was always breaking? Perhaps most frustrating of all is a car that is constantly in the repair shop.

Not only does consumption not guarantee happiness, but it can also bring misery, as the car in the repair shop example shows. The dark side of the marketplace exists. For example, according to government estimates, there are over 14,000 fraudulent tele-marketing firms in the United States, bilking consumers (usually the elderly) out of $40 billion a year. This illustrates that consumerism is a multifaceted experience: It is attractive and pleasurable, but at the same time it can be fraught with deception. **Injurious consumption** happens when individuals or families make consumption decisions that will have negative consequences, affecting their quality of life in the long run.

> *Every year over 10 million American consumers suffer financial losses from their addiction to gambling. There are currently 10 million alcoholics and 80 million cigarette smokers in the United States. Every year 25,000 people die as a result of alcohol-related traffic accidents. All of these disturbing and disturbed behaviors result from consumption gone wrong. (Hirschman, 1991, p. 4)*

Caveat emptor, translated as "May the buyer beware," is an integral part of the study of consumer economics, and you will see sections of chapters devoted to problems in the marketplace. Even knowing the pitfalls, consumers forge ahead, looking for new and better products and enjoying the discovery of the latest fashions and electronics. A case in point is the refrigerator from LG, a Korean company, that has multifunctions such as a television screen and a keypad built in with Internet capabilities. Why should a refrigerator, an appliance using energy 24 hours a day, have only the purpose of keeping food cold? Constant striving for improvement is part of consumer behavior.

Human Needs

In thinking about changes in families and households, it is important to place families within the context of changes in the distribution of households. Most Americans still marry and have children, but the timing and the percentages are changing so that there are more singles living alone or with one child or a pet. For example, Samantha is getting her PhD in Economics from the University of Missouri, and she is interviewing for teaching positions at several universities. Because she is in her late twenties and single, one would assume she would want an apartment or a condominium, but she says she has three dogs and wants a single family house with a big fenced-in backyard and therefore is looking for positions that would offer that type of housing at an affordable price with a short commute to campus.

In the US, 25 percent of all households are two-parent families with children, and 10 percent are single-parent families.

According to psychologist Abraham Maslow, humans have basic needs that have to be met before moving to higher-order needs (see Figure 1.1). In his hierarchy of needs, physiological needs such as hunger and thirst have to be at least partially met before safety, love and belongingness, esteem, and self-actualization can be fulfilled (Maslow, 1954). Multiply these levels of needs across the population and you begin to realize the enormity of human demands and needs.

According to Mark Oleson (2004), there is a relationship between money attitudes and Maslow's hierarchy of needs. In fact, each level of needs (as shown in Figure 1.1)

Figure 1.1 Maslow's Hierarchy of Needs. In this hierarchy of needs, basic physiological needs such as hunger and thirst have to be met before higher-order needs

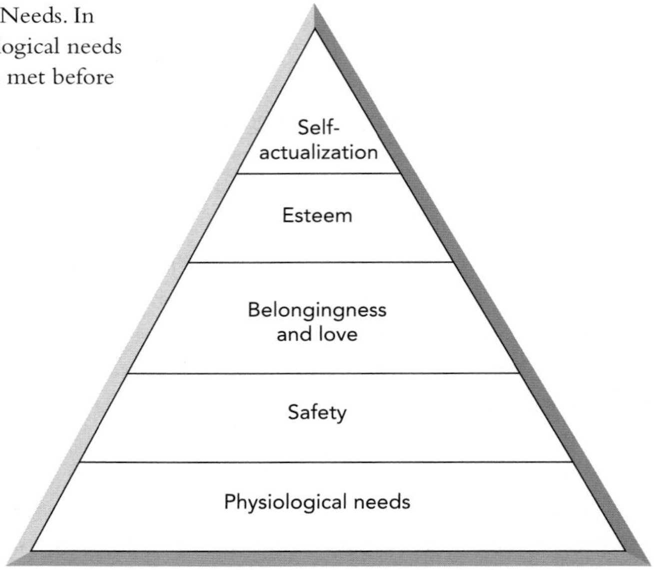

```
Self-
actualization

Esteem

Belongingness
and love

Safety

Physiological needs
```

has a specific money attitude related to it; for example, having money affects our needs for esteem and safety. But Oleson (2004) points out that "not all individuals will have the same needs, or combination of needs, at the same time" (p. 91). In his research he found that men's money attitudes were more related to safety needs, whereas women's money attitudes were more linked to esteem. He makes the practical observation that a financial planner or counselor could mix needs with money, for example, by providing lunch or dinner and a comfortable setting during a personal finance workshop with those struggling with lower-order needs such as physiological and safety/security needs.

The last census revealed there are over 316 million people in the United States and over 80 million households. Less than half of all households have a married couple, so unmarried is more common than married, or the household has another configuration such as a single mom and child. By the US Census Bureau definition, a **household** includes the related family members and all the unrelated persons who share a housing unit. According to the census, "traditional" households, consisting of a husband, wife, and children under age 18, make up less than 35 percent of all US families. Regardless of household type, consumerism is an integral part of every household. The world population is over seven billion.

Although consumerism received a boost in the twentieth century and into our current century, it is not a time-bound concept since, as previously mentioned, humans need to consume to exist. Advertisements etched in stone in ancient Rome, Greece, and Egypt indicate that consumers have desired comfort and style for centuries. What has happened is that the rapid increase in worldwide populations and the market's response to meeting their needs have spurred the current surge in the growth of consumerism. Technological developments have played an important role as well, but it would be limiting to say that consumerism is merely a result of increased populations and subsequent responses from merchandisers and advertisers. Consumerism is a way to define self, family, and community through the ownership, the use, and, ultimately, the disposal of goods. Owning a Lexus sends a far different message than owning a Kia.

Demography and Demographics

Trying to calculate changes in human needs is an ongoing problem for marketers, educators, advertisers, public policy makers, and manufacturers. In the United States, the idea of a melting pot was popular in the twentieth century. During the twenty-first century, the concept still exists but embraces a more holistic frame of mind, encompassing radically and ethnically diverse groups, both native and foreign born (Frey, 2006). Patterns of groups and their movements have important implications for consumer and voter behavior, economic development, and race relations in metropolitan areas both large and small (Frey, 2006). In the United States, historic ports of entry for Hispanics and Asians have been Miami, New York, Tampa, Los Angeles, San Francisco, and Chicago, and also states bordering Mexico for Hispanics. Friends, relatives, and universities, in addition to location, affect network patterns, employment, and the settling of minorities in certain areas. The largest US state in population is California followed by Texas and Florida.

Demography is the study of human populations, including characteristics such as size, growth, density, distribution, movement, and other vital statistics. The world population is over seven billion, and the ten most populous countries in 2014 are listed in Table 1.1.

The term **demographics** refers to data used to describe populations or subgroups. To show how populations change in even a five-year period, here are the shifts in the US population from 2000 to 2005:

Table 1.1 Ten Most Populous Countries. In order by population so that China is the country with the largest population in the world

China
India
United States
Indonesia
Brazil
Pakistan
Nigeria
Bangladesh
Russia
Japan

- Population grew 4 percent overall.
- African American population grew 5 percent.
- Asian American population grew 15 percent.
- Hispanic/Latino population grew 10 percent.

The demand for products is strongly influenced by population shifts. Consider trends in use of toys and types of sports and leisure equipment as age groups wax and wane.

Demographics are often applied to the study of consumers who are grouped by age, race, gender, income, educational level, marital status, zip code, rented versus owned housing, and number of children in the household. Marketers find these useful ways to segment consumers so they can reach them better than a scattershot approach would provide, but they do not limit their advertising and distribution to demographic characteristics alone. Personality, taste, and lifestyle (in essence, individuality) play a role in consumer behavior as well as in statistical groupings. Consumption of products gives people a way of identifying themselves in groups—displays, advertising, packaging all have ways of attracting certain groups based on the identity that they have or seek. For example, a travel agency specializing in tours for those over age 55 may place ads in publications of the American Association of Retired Persons (AARP) or may find that direct mailings or email alerts to repeat customers work best. Another example is that short skirts sell better to younger women than to older women; if the demographics change so that there is a shortage of young women, then it would be prudent to consider this in cloth-ing design in order to reach the masses or to sway fashion in general. Failure to realize changes in demographics has been the downfall of many businesses.

Consumption Process

Consumer economics, since it has everyday uses for the individual, the family, and the household, is considered an applied social science. Something is going to happen rather than an idea that is merely discussed; in other words, consumer economics is not purely philosophical but is a reality-based, action-oriented discipline. We are all consumers, we all have experiences, and we all want to get better at this practical life skill. Because there are so many aspects to consumption, it can be thought of as a process. In terms of the individual making purchase decisions, the consumption process can be broken down into five parts (see Figure 1.2):

1. Awareness
2. Thinking
3. Planning
4. Implementation/action
5. Evaluation

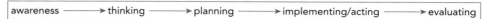

Figure 1.2
Consumption
Process

The consumption process begins with an awareness that something is needed or desired. Perhaps the stimulus is that something has broken and needs to be replaced, or an occasion or event is coming up that requires new things or actions, or a new product has come on the market that could solve a problem or fulfill a need, want, or goal. Problems are questions or dilemmas and provide a stimulus to act. **Needs** are things that are deemed necessary, such as food, and **wants** are things wished for or desired, such as an expensive car. When consumers become aware, they begin to wonder about the benefits of a purchase and if certain services are better than others. For example, cars are not chosen simply to provide transportation; they provide status, identity, or prestige for their owners. Needs are few in number and very general (such as needing something to eat or a car to drive), but wants are limitless and often specific (such as a certain kind of food or car). The basic economic problem is how to distribute limited resources among competing uses. Economic theory says that human wants are limitless, although this concept can be challenged by individuals who say that the simpler life is better and that there is a level of contentment that can be reached with that approach. In other words, more is not always better. For instance, have you ever had too many clothes and needed to clean out your closet? Needs and wants are usually more immediate than goals. **Goals** are end results, things you are striving for, and are based on values. The value of a good or service is subjective, meaning that preferences differ dramatically among individuals.

After awareness of the need, want, or goal is complete, the process follows these next four steps:

1. *Thinking.* Thinking is a mental exploration of the possibilities: weighing pros and cons and gathering information. Product image or features may be important at this stage.

2. *Planning.* Deciding on an ordered set of steps or activities involves planning. Whom do I need to call? Where do I need to go?

3. *Implementation/action.* To implement means to put plans into action, to do something, or to go somewhere. This may include sampling a product, visiting websites, getting an estimate, or actually buying.

4. *Evaluation.* Evaluation is a time for reflecting on outcomes. Individuals may ask, "Am I happy with what happened?" To be specific, "Do I like this brand of whole wheat bread or another brand better?" If someone likes another brand better, that person will act differently the next time he or she goes to the grocery store. From the business point of view, evaluation can lead to repurchase behavior. Profitability increases with repeat business, such as multiple haircuts over the course of several months versus a single visit, so a customer may notice extra special treatment during the first visit because the wise barber or stylist tries to establish a relationship or rapport with the customer so that he or she will both return and recommend the place to friends.

This relationship can reduce choice for the consumer and makes purchasing decisions easier. By going to the same barber or stylist, a customer simplifies

> *the cognitive work and mental effort required for buying. . . . The benefits of choice reduction are especially prevalent when the product category is complex, where there is some risk associated with purchase, or if it is time-consuming or difficult for the consumer to specify his or her preferences. (Hofacker, 2002, p. 46)*

To discuss the consumption process further, the steps of thinking and planning may seem like the same thing, but they are not. Thinking is a random set of thoughts involving the accepting and rejecting of inputs and ideas, whereas planning is a more advanced stage of decision making when a specific course of action is chosen. It is possible for someone to get stalled in the thinking stage and not move on to the others. Also, the process may be stopped at the awareness level if individuals are too busy to take the time to think or plan about a consumption decision and decide to wait before taking further steps.

Place of Consumption

Let us think back in time. Three hundred years ago life was very tough, and most people spent the better part of their day on getting food, shelter, and clothing. Animals (horses) were used for transportation, or one used boats/ships or walked. According to English philosopher Thomas Hobbes in his writing titled *Leviathan* (seventeenth century), life was "solitary, poor, nasty, brutish, and short." The first thought about consumption is that it takes place in a store between buyer and seller, but actually consumption takes place in a variety of settings, including at home, at school, at work, in the community, on trips, and over the Internet. During the course of the day, you may consume water in several places: before leaving home, while walking or driving in the car, when having lunch or dinner, and while working or being in school. Think how bottled water has revolutionized the places water can be consumed—even to the point that an etiquette columnist was asked if it was all right for a guest to swig water from a bottle during a wedding. What do you think was the answer the columnist gave?

Businesses and governments consume, as do individuals and households. There are all sorts of levels of consumption, from the humble to the grand. It explains why in the marketplace there are bath towels that sell for $5 each and others that sell for $75: different markets, different consumers, different needs, different incomes.

Influences on Consumer Style

Consumers have a characteristic way of prebuying, buying, and postbuying that could be called their **consumer style**—patterns of behaving or ways of making financial decisions and acting on them. Seven factors that influence consumer style follow:

1. *Economics.* The condition of national and worldwide economies during times of decision making affects consumer style. The economy is said to follow a business cycle (described in the next section).

2. *History.* The background of a person influences the way his or her decisions are made and acted on. This includes immediate and past family history and the history of the area or region or society in which the individual resides. Why is history an influence? The answer is that we can learn a great deal about consumer behavior from our past and from our general cultural past. In the *Life of Reason,* Santayan wrote, "Those who cannot remember the past are condemned to repeat it."

3. *Culture.* Groups and their behaviors or traditions that surround the individual or family also impact consumer style. This group may be the overall culture and subcultures, including a consumer culture. Do you know what the manufacturer Lea & Perrins makes? You probably know it is Worcestershire sauce, a condiment. Can you even picture what the bottle looks like? It is a glass bottle wrapped in brown paper. This is part of a shared consumer culture.

4. *Personality.* The sum total of an individual's enduring traits, ways of relating, and characteristics, including reaction to risk and opportunity, likes and dislikes, determines consumer choices. Are you between the ages of 25 and 50 and interested in "natural" or environmentally friendly products? If so, the Origins line of the Estee Lauder brand was created for you (Koehn, 2001).

5. *Biology or environment.* The physiology of individuals (such as thirst or hunger) and the environment in which they live influence consumer style. You can see that the Origins line speaks not only to personality but also to environment. Successful products fulfill several areas of consumer needs or spheres of influence.

6. *Technology.* Technology, a broad term that encompasses machines, techniques, material objects, and processes, is used by individuals to get what they want. Certain individuals are more fascinated by technology than others; entrepreneurs and inventors tend to lead in this area. Henry Ford led in automobiles, and Michael Dell led in personal computers; both were fascinated by new technology, constantly taking machines apart and reassembling them (Koehn, 2001). "From lighter aircraft to electric knickers, flexible filaments raise a wider range of interesting possibilities. . . . With a glance at their smartphones, wearers will see statistics on, among other things, their 'Zen Index'" (An Uncommon Thread, 2014).

7. *Politics.* Voters, politicians, organizations, and bureaucrats affect the decisions that alter public policy.

To apply these influences to a specific purchase area, consider clothing. The style, color, and quality selected are affected by what is affordable and available (economics), what has fit or has proven serviceable in the past (history), what others think or what friends wear (culture), what attracts (personality), what keeps a person warm or comfortable (biology or environment), what the cut or weave is (technology), and what sales tax is placed on the garment (politics).

Although, as stated earlier, consumers have a characteristic way of consuming, in recent times more variance in style has been observed by postmodernists. Whereas consumers in the past may have been fairly consistent in purchasing behavior (partly because they had fewer choices), in the twenty-first century there has been a more eclectic mix of goods that may sometimes seem inconsistent to outside observers. This mixing is called **cross-selling**.

> *People do not always remain true to type. Depending on shifts of mood or shifts of situation, the same individual will behave like an upscale achiever one moment, like a downscale bargain hunter the next. The same consumer will buy part of her wardrobe at Bloomingdales and part at K-Mart. (Oglivy, 1990)*

Economics and the Business Cycle

So far the chapter has focused on introducing consumerism and some beginning concepts about consumer behavior. Now the chapter moves into the more economic side of consumption.

In 2000, there were 15 square feet of retail space for every man, woman, and child, up from 11 square feet in 1980.

Most simply stated, economics is about the choices we make. More formally we say that **economics** is the study of or science of production, distribution, and consumption. It concerns itself with how wealth is created and managed in households, businesses, regions, and countries. Consumers participate in and react to movements in the economy, and their spending habits affect growth. One of the changes has been a decreased preference for shopping at malls: At least 300 older malls, each with one or two anchor stores, shut down between 1995 and 2001 (Greene, 2001). Another 300 to 500 such malls will follow suit. For a specific example, a mall named Woodville opened in 1969 and was torn down in 2014. Why are so many malls closing and so few being built? Besides the economic problems the country was going through with the depth of the recession at 2009, another reason may be the glut in retail space. In 2000, the United States had 15 square feet of retail space in shopping centers for every man, woman, and child, up from 11 square feet in 1980, according to National Research Bureau data (Greene, 2001).

Periodically, fluctuations occur in the **real gross domestic product (real GDP)**, which is a measure of the value of all the goods and services newly produced in a country during some period of time, usually a year or a quarter, adjusted for inflation. **Inflation** is a steady increase in prices. **Deflation** indicates falling prices.

As a way to illustrate the usual expansions and contractions in the economy, there is a **business cycle** (see Figure 1.3). This cycle is made up of three stages:

1. **Expansion** (the preferred stage in the business cycle) is a period of prosperity, growth, higher output, low unemployment, and increased retail sales and housing

starts. In general, economic activity, including investing, is growing, and interest rates are low or falling. With low interest rates, consumers find it easier to buy cars, homes, and other expensive goods on credit. For most of the 1990s, the United States was in a time of expansion.

2. **Recession** is a temporary moderate decline or downturn in the economy. It is classically defined by the Bureau of Economic Research as a recurring period of decline in total output, income, employment, and trade, usually lasting from six months to a year, and is marked by widespread contractions in many economic areas. From 2001 to 2003, the United States experienced an economic slowdown. Consumer confidence declined, and there were many layoffs; unemployment rose to 6.1 percent in June 2003. A very deep or prolonged recession is called a depression, and these are rare. The most notable one was the Great Depression of the 1930s, which reached its greatest depth in 1933. Another economic slowdown started in 2007 and reached its depth in 2009.

3. **Recovery**, the period in the business cycle when economic activity picks up, leads to expansion. Economic indicators show that when things are getting better, production and spending rise, consumer confidence improves, and employment picks up. Sometimes this stage includes a rise in interest rates. Signs of recovery are in evidence, with unemployment dipping to 4.5 percent in 2006 and again at 5 percent in 2014 with a burst of hiring taking place.

As illustrated, these three stages run in a cycle, but no one knows for sure how long each stage will last or how high or low the swings will go. Changes in the GDP are the main indicators, but unemployment, interest rates, business growth, and other factors play a role.

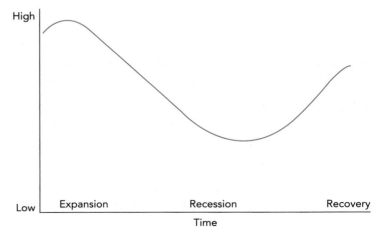

Figure 1.3 Business Cycle. The economy goes through stages that tend to be cyclical. The stages reflect changes in employment, production, and consumption

Scarcity

Unlimited wants combined with limited supplies create **scarcity**, a condition in which there is an insufficient amount or supply, a shortage. Scarcity lies at the heart of production and consumption. A product may be in short supply, and the manufacturer cannot make enough of the product to meet consumer demand. For example, after the September 11, 2001, destruction of the World Trade Center in New York City and a section of the Pentagon in Washington, DC, there was a shortage of American flags in the United States. Demand far exceeded supply; it took several weeks for manufacturers and suppliers to catch up.

Scarcity exists on the consumer side as well. A consumer may not have enough money to buy what he or she wants. Scarcity often exists because we have unlimited wants but limited resources to pursue those wants. Scarcity is not the same as poverty. It can exist in a time of abundance and prosperity and is relative to the individual. As we all know, some people are content living on very little, whereas others feel deprived if they cannot immediately get everything they want.

In economic theory, as long as a human need is not satisfied, there is scarcity. In summary, scarcity is a normal part of life, unavoidable and individually defined, and it cycles and flows.

Supply, Demand, and Equilibrium Price

The American flag shortage mentioned earlier is an example of supply and demand. A worldwide shortage example is that of broadband Internet access: The demand far exceeds the supply, and suppliers are hurrying to catch up. Over two billion people are online, and the number keeps going up according to Nielsen Global Online. More than 85 percent of these have purchased online. There are over 500 million online users in China; this number is higher than the US population.

Over two billion people are online around the world.

In economics, there are a number of theories that partially explain consumer reaction to prices. Some of these theories are elaborated upon in upcoming chapters, but for this introductory chapter, the most basic theory is that of **equilibrium price**, which is reached when supply and demand are equal (see Figure 1.4). Scarcity affects supply. According to the **law of supply**, as the supply of a good or service goes up, the price comes down. This principle states there is a direct relationship between the price of a good and the amount offered for sale. In the **law of demand**, as the price of a good or service rises, the quantity demanded of that good or service falls. The price paid for goods and services reacts to these laws. For example, when a color goes out of style in furniture upholstery, goods in that color are less desired and the price decreases (the goods go on sale). Figure 1.5 gives more details about supply and demand, in particular what causes shifts in each. Supply represents the firms' side of transactions; demand represents the consumers' side of transactions. As the price of a product increases with

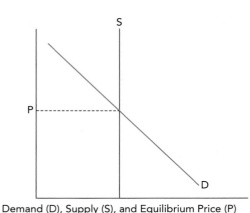

Figure 1.4
Links among
Supply, Demand,
and Price.
A change in one
affects changes in
the others

Demand (D), Supply (S), and Equilibrium Price (P)

Supply represents the firms'
side of transactions.

Supply shifts are due to:
• Number of competitors
• New inventions, "new and improved"
  driving out old
• Price of goods needed for production
• Future price expectations
• Government taxes, subsidies, legislation

Demand represents the customers'
side of transactions.

Demand shifts are due to:
• Preferences
• Access: Ease of purchase
• Prices
• Number of competing buyers
• Consumers' ability to pay
• Expectations of shortages or rising prices
• Price of related goods that could be substituted
  (example, lamb chops cost more so person buys
  pork chops instead)

Figure 1.5
Supply and
Demand Shifts

other things remaining constant, producers will increase production—trying to get
more supplies to market.

Prices based on supply and demand may be on actualities or only on perceptions. For
example, in a natural disaster there may be plenty of gasoline available, but people may
assume that is not the case and rush to the pumps to fill up. Word of mouth and news
media can have a tremendous effect on people's perceptions: An announcement of
crop failures in peanuts will motivate consumers to buy whatever they perceive will
be in short supply, such as peanut butter. Figure 1.6 shows a diagram of how consumer
demand affects supply and eventual resource use.

Figure 1.6
Impact of
Consumer
Demand on
Supply and
Eventual
Resource Use

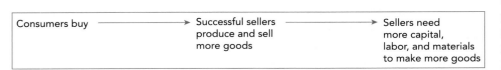

Supply, Demand, and Demographics

What distinguishes echo boomers from previous generations is their ease with computers.

Population changes affect consumption patterns. Demand can be explained as the relationship between the price and the quantity demanded by consumers. If the number of consumers increases, then it follows that demand will increase; where populations choose to cluster makes a difference as well. Figure 1.7 shows an example of the spillover effect.

A successful supplier not only responds to changes but also anticipates buyers' changing preferences and, in the case of population shifts, responds to changes in movement patterns. Regarding US population trends, during the first years of the twenty-first century there was a surge in the number of undergraduate students going to college, which affected demand for classes, dorm rooms, apartments, and types of goods that people in their late teens and twenties buy.

Many readers of this book belong to Generation Y, the millenials, and the exact birth years are in dispute, but most sources would say born between 1977 or 1980 and 2000 (see Figure 1.8). (Unless otherwise noted, the population figures given in this section are from the United States.) The Gen Y group peaked in 1988 when 3.9 million babies

Figure 1.7 Spillover Effect: Ways that Moving Affects Others

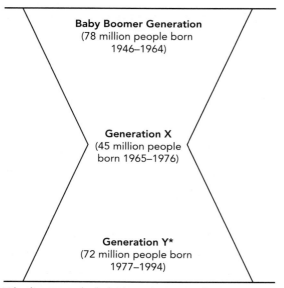

Figure 1.8
US Age
Distribution.
Adapted from
Kotler and
Armstrong (2013)

*Also known as the baby boomlet generation.
This group is still forming their preferences and behaviors.

were born (the highest number since 1964). They are bringing another wave of high consumption through the nation as they go through their teen years and into early adulthood. What most distinguishes this group from previous groups is their computer fluency. Unfortunately, this group was coming of age when the country was going through tough economic times and more young American adults over age 18 were returning to the family nest. These young adults, called "boomerangers," were most likely to return home because they were experiencing financial pressures (student loans, credit card bills, unemployment) or because they were marrying later. Nearly four million or 10.5 percent of the 25- to 34-year-old age group (and 12 percent of those ages 25 to 29) were living in the family home (Greider, 2001). This follows an historic trend: The number of boomerang kids rises when the economy sours. A November 2001 survey by Monstertrak.com found that 60 percent of college students planned to move back home after graduation, and more than 20 percent will stay a year or more (Greider, 2001).

The group called Generation X is composed of the 45 million people born between 1965 and 1976. Generation X is a smaller group representing a shorter span of time than the groups before and after. This group cares about the environment; they like lower prices and a more functional look.

A marked upswing or downswing in the economy can change patterns overnight. If people in any age group feel vulnerable, they will change their spending and saving behaviors immediately.

Risk and Opportunity Costs

Two other economic concepts that greatly affect consumer purchasing behavior are risk and opportunity. Consumers weigh the risks and opportunities associated with decisions. An individual may be risk averse, risk attracted, or risk neutral.

Risk is the possibility or perception of harm, suffering, danger, or loss. In financial risk, this may include the fear of losing money in the stock market or of buying an inferior product. Most people are risk averse, especially when it comes to their money, which is why discussions about how Social Security money should be invested or whether consumers should be allowed to have more say in how their Social Security money should be invested turn into heated debates. Retirement is a time when people want to be secure and comfortable—they don't want surprises.

The psychologist Abraham Maslow said that at any one time people are torn between growth and safety and that safety has the stronger pull, so when given a choice, individuals are more drawn to the familiar and predictable. This is, of course, an overgeneralization, and it is difficult to completely typecast a person as risk averse, risk attracted, or risk neutral because much risk-taking behavior is situational. Someone may be experimental when it comes to trying new food but be predictable when it comes to music or clothing. Usually, a risk-averse person would be attracted to a financial arrangement such as one that has a fixed-rate mortgage of 5 percent on a house versus an adjustable-rate mortgage that varies from 4 to 9 percent because he or she may be more worried about losing money than excited about the prospect of gaining money. Risk-attracted individuals may be more drawn to the adjustable-rate mortgage, figuring the economy will go in their favor and the mortgage will stay at the lower end of the range and therefore be less costly than the fixed-rate mortgage. A risk-neutral individual could go either way: He or she is indifferent toward risk and uncertainty and would be drawn to expected rates of return.

Research indicates that women avoid risk more than men when it comes to investments. Women are more likely to say they are "careful with money" (31 percent of women versus 24 percent of men), which is probably why they pick safer investments and let banks handle their accounts rather than keeping them with brokerages or mutual fund managers (Whelan, 2001). In the same nationwide study of 31,576 Americans, it was found that female college grads are more likely to put their money in investment products than those who graduated from high school.

In addition, there is true risk and there is perceived risk. What may be pleasurable to one person, such as a thrill ride at an amusement park, may be perceived as a dangerous risk to be avoided by another. In order to reduce perceived risk, individuals diminish their fears by finding out all they can about a product before purchasing it. For example, a person unsure about a thrill ride may watch it go around a few times and talk to others about it before standing in line to get on the ride; another example is that people read about new car model ratings in *Consumer Reports* or *Motor Trend* and talk with friends before purchasing a car. An additional commonly used search mechanism to reduce risk is to gather information on the Internet.

There are other types of risks:

- *Time risk.* Consumers do not want to waste time in finding and purchasing products.
- *Security risk.* Consumers may fear being a victim of crime, perhaps involving their credit card number or Social Security cards.
- *Privacy risk.* Consumers may fear that their buying behavior or personal information is being reported and sold to companies.

Opportunity refers to a favorable outlook, a chance for progress, advancement, and action. Economics assumes that people will try to increase their satisfaction by taking advantage of opportunities. However, it is not always easy to tell when something is a risk or an opportunity, such as a job offer in Idaho when you have lived all your life in Alabama. Is this the opportunity of a lifetime, or is it a risky venture that will be regretted? Every choice made means that something else is given up. This is referred to in economics as **opportunity cost**: One alternative is selected over another, and

Photo 1.4 Volleyball player/actress Gabrielle Reece appears on the set of *Cloud Nine* on May 12, 2004, at Will Rodgers State Beach, in Pacific Palisades, California. Her decision to change her career path is an example of opportunity costs, selecting one alternative for another

Source: Getty Images: Stephan Shugerman

there is a cost attached to this choice. For example, Tiger Woods decided to drop out of Stanford University because he did not have the time to pursue his studies full-time and play golf full-time. He joined the Pro Tour in 1996. He stunned the golfing world with huge victories in 1997; by 1999 he was the top prizewinner on the Pro Tour. In Tiger's case, his scarce resource was time, and taking a risk paid off. Another example is Gabrielle Reece, who left being a star volleyball player in college to be a supermodel on the cover of *Vogue*.

Opportunity cost is related to the concept of **trade-offs**. To get something that is desired, it is necessary to sacrifice something else because of scarcity (of time, of money, of energy).

Three Questions

Many of the previously mentioned examples are of an individual or personal nature, but large-scale economies tackle similar issues. There are three problems or questions that economies must find a way to solve:

1. What is to be produced? Examples are trucks, television shows, computers, ice cream, and health care. A **product** is anything a consumer acquires or perceives to need. Over 15,000 new or improved products are introduced each year in grocery stores, but not many will succeed.

2. How are these goods produced? Examples include what companies, what types of factories, and how much equipment, material, and labor are needed. International agreements such as the North American Free Trade Agreement (NAFTA) have changed the level of competition and reduced international trade barriers. The Internet has also opened up exchange across borders. The general trend is toward freer exchange and less trade restraints, which is usually a good thing for consumers. One of the few negatives is the problem of quality control since many countries in the world do not have strong consumer protection laws (e.g., copyrights, trademarks). Gucci purses, Louis Vuitton luggage, or CDs purchased abroad may be fakes.

3. For whom are the goods produced? Examples can range from the young to the old, from domestic markets to international ones.

Market Economy and Competition

Most economically developed countries, including the United States, Canada, Australia, Japan, and Western European countries, are referred to as consumption societies, where consumers have a great deal of freedom to buy and sell products as they choose. In fact, people in consumption societies spend more time in consumption than nearly any other activity, including working and sleeping (both of which involve consuming). This is part of being a **market economy**. In a market economy, exchanges are controlled by marketplace forces of demand and supply rather than by outside forces such as government control. This goes back to Adam Smith's philosophy that the market is a self-correcting mechanism—if left alone, it will function well. These exchanges do not exist in a vacuum, however, because untold numbers of dollars are spent on activities that encourage consumption, such as attractive store environments, catalogs, and websites.

A market economy is characterized by the free exchange of goods and services in markets and by freely determined prices. This is contrasted with the **command or centrally controlled economy** wherein most decisions about what, how, and for whom to produce are made by those who control the government. An example would be the Soviet sphere for much of the twentieth century. In a total or absolute market economy, there would be no restraints placed on the economy by outside forces, which would result in perfect competition and market sovereignty. Perfect competition means that many businesses could offer the same product at the same price. No company could be so large nor its brands so popular that the company could ask a higher price.

Photo 1.5
Robots prevent people from doing heavy or dangerous work. In the car manufacturing industry, robots can weld reliably and safely

Source: Thinkstock: supergenijalac

The Importance of Property Rights

Connected to the market economy is the concept of **property rights**—the legal rights over the use, sale, and proceeds from a good or resource. Property rights are important to economic progress because they allow people to buy and sell goods. If there were no property rights, anyone could take what you own and sell it. Imagine someone coming into your home, removing everything, and conducting a yard sale on your front lawn. Private property rights include the exclusive right to use, the right to protect, and the right to transfer use or ownership. These rights, however, are within the context of the greater society. For example, a homeowner cannot park a giant boat in his front yard if the homeowners' association of the street he lives on prohibits it, but if he lives in a rural area where there are no such rules, he can do what he wants. To summarize, private owners bear the cost of ignoring the wishes of others when they try to sell their home if they chose to have unusual colors or decorations on the exterior. Here are some features of private ownership:

- Private owners have an incentive to maintain property owned.
- Private owners expect property values to increase.
- Private owners have to pay for damages to the property, or persons involved in its use are held accountable.

Consumer Sovereignty

Consumer sovereignty refers to the premise that consumers decide which goods will survive and that producers cannot dictate consumer tastes. Products do fall in and out of favor. Take the example of ketchup made from tomatoes. Today, we are used to that kind of ketchup, but in the mid-nineteenth century, walnut ketchup and mushroom ketchup (as well as tomato ketchup) were established seasonings in the United States (Koehn, 2001). Why did walnut ketchup and mushroom ketchup fall out of favor? Will they come back in style? As another example, people change their minds about what type of leisure activities they want to pursue. It is important to forecast trends in leisure because it generates $535 billion a year and affects fitness clubs, theme parks, marine and cruise industries, and motorcycle and motor sports businesses (Paul, 2001). Research indicates that leisure activities on the rise include swimming, hiking, running, weight training, fishing, and using aerobic machines. When people are at home, the biggest leisure activities are reading, watching television, spending time with friends and family, exercising, and being on the Internet, according to a 2012–2013 Harris poll on top leisure activities. When they go out, the vast majority of Americans say that eating out is their favorite leisure activity and that they plan to do more.

The concept of consumer sovereignty is based on Adam Smith's philosophy that consumers should guide the economy—the consumer is king. In many cases the consumer is king, but in looking at the total marketplace environment, consumer sovereignty does not always exist because of outside intervention such as government support for schools and postal services or government controls on imports and exports. For example, recent newspaper reports showed that the United States imports and sells far more Mexican beer than it exports because of consumer preferences and policies making it difficult for US beer to be delivered to and sold easily in Mexico. Each country sets up its own trade agreements and policies regarding imports and exports, which greatly affects what the consumer can purchase. We do not live in a world where the only interaction is between the consumer and the market.

Sometimes, the government steps in to aid industry. For example, in 2001 the federal government gave billions of dollars to airlines to help bail them out when there was a decline in air traffic. During the Obama administration, there was a major bailout to General Motors (GM) to aid the auto industry. In regional or national disasters, the normal balance of supply and demand is disrupted, and the government steps in to restore order and provide funds for rebuilding. This intervention is regarded as necessary for the good of the overall economy as well as for the good of the industry, employees, residents, or region.

Monopolies

Government also becomes involved in the market economy by discouraging the growth of monopolies. The word *monopoly* comes from two Greek words meaning "single seller." A **monopoly** exists when there is only one producer and there is no substitute, such as there being only one airline or cruise ship line. There are two reasons monopolies are discouraged: Without competition, consumers may have no choice but to pay higher prices, and a monopoly may discourage new inventions or the growth of new companies (new businesses are discouraged when there are high barriers to entry). Rather than being absolute, a monopoly can be thought of as incremental since it is rare for a monopoly to totally control a product or market. An example of a monopoly may be an electricity service in a particular area, but it may not be practical to have competitors in this situation.

Oligopoly refers to a market situation in which a small number of sellers controls the entire market or industry. Examples can be seen in retail groceries and car manufacture. Large sale operations take advantage of economies of scale by charging minimum costs for a unit by buying materials in bulk. There is an interdependence among the leading companies in an oligopoly so that if one raises prices, the expectation is that the others will follow suit. However, if agreed upon ahead of time (for example, setting oil prices among the leading oil producers in the world), then it can be considered **collusion**. This means they joined together to control prices, and this can be illegal under the antitrust laws of the US.

Price is the amount of money a person pays to buy or use a product. Setting the right price is essential in the consumer–market exchange. If a price is too low, it may indicate low quality; if it is too high, there will be few buyers. Price is affected by demand. For example, there is a higher demand for eggs at Easter than at other times of the year. Sellers can decide whether to raise prices or to use increased holiday consumption as a ploy of attracting customers by reducing the price on eggs in the hopes they will buy other products in the store.

> ## CRITICAL THINKING
>
> ### Car Shopping
>
> Have you ever noticed that car prices are similar across manufacturers for a similar size and style car? It could be Ford, Honda, Toyota, or GM. How do these companies set prices? Have you noticed end-of-year or other types of sales events advertised on television, online, or on the radio? Discuss.

In consumer economics, there is a widely held principle: Competition in the marketplace is good for consumers. Sometimes it may not seem like much of a problem if a monopoly exists; a consumer may think "I simply won't buy any more of that type or brand of product" (such as a food or drink item), but there are situations in which consumers have no choice, such as a particular medicine that their doctor prescribes. If there are other brands or generic products, it would give the consumer a better range of choices and prices. In recent years, one of the most publicized monopoly cases in the United States involved Microsoft.

A successful business has to have a thorough understanding of competitors' goods, capabilities, and strategies. Part of a business's strategy may be to provide superior service so that other businesses will have to upgrade their customer service to compete.

Economic Systems

To summarize the key point of the previous sections, it can be said that for the most part the United States has a market economy. In many ways, we are free as consumers to choose the products and services we want. If we want to go to the store or go online to trade on eBay, we do; if we choose not to purchase new clothes because we don't like the season's fashions, that is also our choice. A market economy is also referred to as **capitalism**, an economic system characterized by open competition in a free market. The ownership and control of resources and businesses are largely held by private individuals, and the forces of supply and demand are relied on to control the production of goods and services. Adam Smith called this perfect liberty, which later became known as laissez-faire capitalism (loosely translated, laissez-faire means "hands off").

Socialism is an economic system in which the government (also referred to as the state) centrally plans, owns, and controls most of the capital and makes decisions about prices and quantities. In socialism, government has more control over prices and supplies than in market economies. Capital refers to factories, stores, farms, and equipment. The degree of socialism varies by country; for example, Scandinavian countries are generally regarded as more socialistic than the United States. Also, a country could have socialized medicine (such as is found in Canada or the United Kingdom) but have a capitalistic structure in general. **Communism** is a social or economic system in which nearly all capital is collectively owned, and examples (as of the writing of this book) are North Korea and Cuba.

Since most of the world functions as a market economy, this economic system will form the backbone of this book. Today, most people and most nations prefer a high degree of consumer sovereignty.

Internet and E-commerce

The main trend in the shift to online sales has prompted retailers to scale back on store openings and pare back on unprofitable stores. When this book went to press, Amazon (Internet retailer) overtook Wal-Mart as the world's largest retailer.

> *Growth in store counts at the 100 largest retailers by revenue has slowed to less than 3% from more than 12% three years ago according to Moody's. The pressure*

comes as consumer tastes are changing. Instead of wandering through stores and mak-
ing impulse purchases, shoppers use their mobile phones and computers to research
prices and cherry-pick promotions, sticking to shopping lists rather than splurging on
unneeded items. Even discount retailers are finding it harder to boost sales by lower-
ing prices as many low-income consumers struggle to afford the basics regardless of the
price. (Banjo & Ziobro, 2014, p. B1–B2).

CRITICAL THINKING

Less Wandering Through Stores

Have you noticed a change in shopping behavior among your family and friends?
Is there less wandering through stores and less impulse purchasing? Have you
used mobile phones while you shop in a grocery store or other type store in
order to compare prices or to ask someone else what you need to buy?

Discuss your answers.

Consumers are responding to the fact that economic systems cannot remain as isolated
as they once were due to the high degree of internationalization of business and the proliferation of the Internet. There is no question that the Internet has revolutionized the
worldwide marketplace in terms of communication, entertainment, and exchange and
provides an interactive medium as opposed to the conventional modes of mass media
such as TV, magazines, billboards, and radio. Mass media are unidirectional (or one-
to-many) communication processes (Hofacker, 2000), whereas the Internet provides
a wide array of communication patterns between consumers and between consumers
and firms.

A term used in consumer marketing research is **consumer-mediated environment
(CME)**, which refers to buying and selling over the Internet. **E-commerce** is a general
term referring to exchange transactions that take place on the Internet, such as buying
and selling goods, services, and information. This is in contrast to more conventional
modes of exchange transactions, such as in person, over the telephone, or by surface
mail. Characteristics of e-commerce include pervasiveness of technology, speed, and
globalization.

Many goods and services are sold on the basis of convenience and speed, and buying
over the Internet fulfills these needs. For example, at most universities you can buy your
textbooks from the campus bookstore and have them delivered to your door or have
them available for pickup rather than having to wait in long lines to find the books
and purchase them. Campus bookstores had to do this in response to competition from
Amazon and other online booksellers that were delivering books straight to dorm
rooms and apartments.

E-commerce is such a huge concept that it is useful to break it into two parts:

1. *E-merchandise.* Selling goods and services electronically and moving items through distribution channels, such as Internet shopping for groceries, cars, tickets, music, clothes, hardware, travel, books, flowers, or gifts, are examples of e-merchandise.
2. *E-finance.* Banking, debit cards, smart cards, banking machines, telephone and Internet banking, insurance, loans, financial services, and mortgages are all done online and represent e-finance (Goldsmith & McGregor, 2000).

Chapter 11 on the Internet, technology, and identity theft discusses how much things have changed. The top category in terms of percent of traffic (visits) on the Internet is health and medical, followed by education.

Many stores have buildings and Internet sites. An example would be Britain's famous Harrods department store, which has a large building in London and an Internet site (www.harrods.com). Internet retailers are referred to as e-tailers.

Although e-commerce has opened up new ways of trading, it is not without its risks, drawbacks, and critics. Some of the concerns center on the collection and dissemination of consumer information by marketers who participate in online retailing. Specific issues pertain to the privacy and security of consumer data and consumers' perception of such risks: 37 percent of online consumers say they would buy more online if they were not so concerned about privacy issues (Forrester Research, 2001). More recent research shows millenials have fewer fears of buying online and will use credit cards or debit cards for small purchases like gum and candy moreso than older generations who are used to using cash for small purchases. Previously, it was revealed in a survey by the UCLA Internet Project that 94.5 percent of consumers express some concern about credit card security online, a number that actually rose from 91.2 percent the previous year (Weber, 2001). An innovation is the growing use of passwords and codes:

Issue: Should the government regulate online privacy?

When shoppers buy at a participating site, they will be prompted for the password. But the site won't ever see the secret code. Instead, it will be beamed to the credit card bank, which will then give the retailer an all-clear on the transaction. If it catches on, the approach could cut down on online fraud. (Weber, 2001, p. B1)

A related concern is how much government should be involved in regulating online privacy. A nationwide survey revealed that 54 percent of respondents say government should regulate online privacy; this represented a decrease from the previous year of 61 percent (Forrester Research, 2001). Another issue is about the control of airspace. This has come to light in the discussion of airborne drones to deliver packages to homes, a suggestion of Amazon and other online retailers.

As may be expected, research studies indicate that higher levels of Internet experience lead to lower risk perceptions regarding online shopping (Miyazaki & Fernandez,

2001). In other words, those regularly using the Internet often perceive fewer risks than less frequent users or nonusers. Frequent users have found that their transactions have been protected and that the goods they ordered were delivered as expected. Much Internet shopping takes place during office hours, and this phenomenon is being tracked internationally.

In the third chapter of this book is more coverage on different types of media; later in the book there is more information on legislation and regulations regarding privacy and security when buying and selling over the Internet. For this introductory chapter, the main points are that the use of the Internet is growing and that consumerism as we once knew it is rapidly changing. Economic growth increasingly depends on innovation and the spread of technology.

Summary

Now is an exciting time to study consumer economics with all its global implications. Political campaigns focus on getting workers back to work, on health care, taxes, and economic reform. An understanding of the consumer is fundamental to the study of consumer economics. This field of study is practical, personal, and involves critical thinking. It covers how people deal with scarcity and choose between alternative goods, services, and actions. Our task is to decide how to allocate limited resources to different competitive uses. Consumption has a purpose: It fulfills a need or want or is used to fulfill or reach a goal. Consumerism is the belief that goods and services give meaning to individuals and their roles in society. According to Adam Smith, founder of modern economics, consumers guide the marketplace, and the goods and services they produce and consume have more to do with the wealth of nations than silver and gold. This consumer power can be referred to as consumer sovereignty.

The chapter addressed the following questions:

- Why consume?
- Who consumes?
- What affects consumption?

Consumption was explained as a process. The ever-changing nature of the marketplace and consumer demands has made consumer economics an increasingly necessary and important field to study. Given the demographic, economic, social, and technological changes in the world, the need for skilled consumption practices (more efficiency, less waste, risk minimization, increased Internet access) at all levels has never been greater. Monopolies and oligopolies were discussed. The goal of this chapter is to help the reader understand that part of the economy, to learn to think like a consumer economist (e.g., to understand why competition is good for consumers), and to get an intuitive feel for how scarcity, choices, and economic systems interact.

KEY POINTS

1. We are all consumers.
2. Consumption is a multistep process.
3. Everyone experiences scarcity (usually of time or money).
4. Scarcity leads to choice; a choice requires consideration of opportunity costs or trade-offs.
5. Three questions that economies face are what, how, and for whom production takes place.
6. The business cycle has three parts: recovery, expansion, and recession.
7. The United States (and most of the world) has a market economy (also referred to as capitalism). A market economy involves freely determined prices, individual property rights, and the freedom to trade, produce, and consume, and it also includes a role for government.

KEY TERMS

business cycle

capitalism

caveat emptor

choice

collusion

command or centrally controlled economy

communism

consumer economics

consumerism

consumer-mediated environment (CME)

consumers

consumer sovereignty

consumer style

cross-selling

deflation

demographics

demography

e-commerce

economics

equilibrium price

expansion

goals

household

inflation

injurious consumption

law of demand

law of supply

market economy

monopoly

needs

oligopoly

opportunity

opportunity cost

price

product

property rights

real gross domestic product (real GDP)

recession

recovery

resources

risk

scarcity

socialism

trade-offs

wants

DISCUSSION QUESTIONS

1. Consider the Duchess of Windsor, who said, "I've been rich and I've been poor; rich is better." What do you think about that sentiment? In your opinion, what is the connection between happiness and consumption?

2. Gabrielle Reece, a star college volleyball player, gave up her scholarship and her studies to be a supermodel, appearing on the cover of *Vogue* magazine. Would you have done the same in her place?

3. Give an example of an opportunity cost in your own life. Why did you make the choice that you did?

4. A former head of Revlon said, "In the factory we make cosmetics; in the store we sell hope." What does this quote tell you about consumer needs?

5. Author Daniel Gilbert (2006) says that experiences may bring more happiness than durable goods. Do you agree or disagree? Describe two experiences that made you happy.

REFERENCES

An uncommon thread (March 8–14, 2014). *Economist*, 22–23.

Banjo, S., and P. Ziobro (August 6, 2014). Shoppers flee physical stores. *Wall Street Journal*, p. B1–B2.

Forrester Research. *Privacy issues inhibit online spending* (October 3, 2001), www.nua.ie.

Frey, W. (2006). Diversity spreads out: metropolitan shifts in Hispanics, Asian, and Black populations since 2000. The Brookings Institute, Washington, DC, 1–17.

Gilbert, D. (2006). *Stumbling on happiness*. New York: Alfred A. Knopf.

Goldsmith, E., and S. McGregor. (2000). E-commerce: consumer protection issues and implications for research and education. *Journal of Consumer Studies and Home Economics,* 24 (2), 124–127.

Greene, K. (December 12, 2001). What a bleak Christmas may mean for older malls. *Wall Street Journal,* pp. B1, B8.

Greider, L. (December 2001). Hard times drive adult kids "home." *AARP Bulletin,* 42 (11), Washington, DC.

Harris, D. (2000). *Cute, quaint, hungry, and romantic: the aesthetics of consumerism.* New York: Basic Books.

Heilbroner, R. L. (1986). *The essential Adam Smith.* New York: Norton.

Hirschman, E. (1991). Secular mortality and the dark side of consumer behavior. In *Advances in consumer research XVIII,* ed. R. Holman and M. Solomon. Provo, UT: Association for Consumer Research, 1–4.

Hobbes, T. (1651). *Leviathan.* Part I, Chapter 13.

Hofacker, C. (2000). *Internet marketing.* Dripping Springs, TX: Digital Springs, Inc.

Hofacker, C. (2002). *Internet marketing,* 3rd ed. New York: John Wiley.

Koehn, N. F. (2001). *Brand new: how entrepreneurs earned consumers' trust from Wedgwood to Dell.* Boston: Harvard Business School Press. Also quoted in Michael Dell with Catherine Fredman, *Direct from Dell: strategies that revolutionized an industry.* New York: HarperCollins, 1999.

Kotler, P., and G. Armstrong. (2013). *Principles of Marketing.* Upper Saddle River, NJ: Prentice Hall.

Maslow, A. (1954). *Motivation and personality.* New York: Harper & Row.

Miyazaki, A. D., and A. Fernandez. (2001). Consumer perceptions of privacy and security. *Journal of Consumer Affairs,* 35 (1), 27–44.

Oglivy, J. (1990). This postmodern business. *Marketing and Research Today,* February 4–21. See also E. C. Hirschman and M. Holbrook (1992), Hedonic consumption: emerging concepts, methods, and propositions. *Journal of Marketing,* 46, 92–101.

Oleson, M. (2004). Exploring the relationship between money attitudes and Maslow's hierarchy of needs. *International Journal of Consumer Studies,* 28 (1), 83–92.

Smith, A. *An inquiry into the nature and causes of the wealth of nations,* 1776, as edited by Robert Heilbroner in *The essential Adam Smith.* New York: Norton, 1986.

Swagler, R. (1994). Evolution and applications of the term consumerism: theme and variations. *Journal of Consumer Affairs,* 28 (2), 347–360.

Wansink, B. (2014). *Slim by design: mindless eating solutions.* New York: HarperCollins.

Wansink, B., and R. Deshpande. (1994). Out of sight, out of mind: pantry stockpiling and brandage frequency. *Marketing Letters,* 5 (1), 91–100.

Wansink, B., A. Brasel, and S. Amjad. (2000). The mystery of the cabinet castaway: why we buy products we never use. *Journal of Family and Consumer Sciences,* 92 (1), 233.

Weber, T. (December 10, 2001). What do you risk using a credit card to shop on the net? *Wall Street Journal,* p. B1.

Whelan, D. (November 2001). Investing with care. *American Demographics,* 12–13.

Chapter **2**

The Consumer Movement

In the 19th century novels we first see the caricature of capitalism: the individual who lives for no other purpose than maximizing his profits. How far this all is from Adam Smith.

William McGurn

1. Trace the beginnings of the consumer movement.
2. Identify key economists, presidents, writers, and scientists and their contributions to consumer protection legislation and reform.
3. Describe how the consumer movement changed from 1880 to the present.
4. Give examples of worldwide consumer concerns.

> ### CASE STUDY
>
> **Italy's Crackdown on Raw-Milk Machines**
>
> "Andrea Verlicchi, an Italian Web designer, used to leave his apartment in the mornings, stroll to a nearby vending machine and fill his recyclable glass bottle with fresh raw milk. 'The milk is great,' said Mr. Verlicchi, like drinking it 'directly from the cow.' Vending machines that dispense fresh, unpasteurized milk have proliferated in Italy and throughout much of Europe in recent years. The stainless steel mechanical fridges can be found in supermarket parking lots, town square and on roaming milk-mobiles. According to a 'milk map' website designed by Mr. Verlicchi there are currently around 1,300 machines in Italy alone. But even in Europe, where stinky cheese, steak tartare and snails are all cheerfully scarfed down, the machines are under siege. In Italy, regulators have cracked down on the sales, suspending or shutting down machines that don't meet exacting hygiene standards. Those that remain must carry big warning signs in red letters, advising buyers to boil their milk before drinking it."
>
> Source: Sarah Kent (October 21, 2014). "Lactose Intolerance: Crackdown on Raw-Milk Machines Steams Fans." *The Wall Street Journal*, p. A1.

Introduction

This chapter traces the developmental stages of the consumer movement and legislation and as such begins with an exploration of economic thought and practice. The beginning case study on the crackdown on raw milk in Italy by regulators is an example of the worldwide nature of consumer protection.

As we learned in the last chapter, Adam Smith lived in eighteenth-century Scotland; by the nineteenth century, his writings about rational self-interest, freedom, and the marketplace were being challenged by a less noble approach to consumerism: Buy more to get ahead. There was also an element of speed in expanding nations such as the United States. In 1835, Alexis De Tocqueville, French political theorist and historian, wrote in the *Democracy of America* that "It is strange to see with what feverish ardor the Americans pursue their own welfare, and to watch the vague dread that constantly torments them lest they should not have chosen the shortest path which may lead to it." In analyzing the nineteenth century, Josephson (1962) wrote, "The expanding America of the post–Civil War era was the paradise of freebooting capitalists, untrammeled and untaxed. They demanded always a freehand in the marketplace, promising that in enriching themselves they would 'build up the country' for the benefit of all people. . . . Theirs is the story of a well-nigh irresistible drive toward monopoly" (p. v).

In the early nineteenth century, English economist David Richardo developed the **law of comparative advantage**. It states that individuals, firms, regions, or nations can gain by specializing in the production of goods that they can produce as cheaply as possible. In other words, one should strive for the lowest opportunity costs. Trading partners should use their time and resources prudently, leading to mutual gain and higher levels of income. "Once one thinks about it, the law of comparative advantage is almost common sense. If someone else is willing to supply you with a good at a lower cost than you can produce it yourself, doesn't it make sense to trade for it and use your time and resources to produce more of the things for which you are a low-cost producer" (Gwartney, Stroup, Sobel, & Macpherson, 2003, p. 43).

Through the nineteenth century in the United States there was an incredible expansion in the production of goods and services to meet the needs of the newly launched society. There was a move to produce within the country. Mary Elizabeth Sherwood wrote that by 1897, "the tendency to vulgarity is the great danger of a newly launched society." Another author stated, "Waves of immigrants brought their own manners to America, and on the frontier a spoon and fingers were sufficient for a tasty repast" (Crossen, 2001). In short, money and taste did not always go hand in hand, "as was demonstrated during the Gilded Age when wealthy American men collected diamond-encrusted daggers, and women carried 2,000 violet bouquets" (Crossen, 2001). In 1895 the largest home in the United States was open to the guests of George W. Vanderbilt in Asheville, North Carolina. With 250 rooms and Renoir paintings, the Biltmore, a visible example of splendorous nineteenth-century consumption, is owned by descendants of Vanderbilt and open to the public today.

Adam Smith promoted **rational self-interest**, meaning that people make choices that will give them the greatest amount of satisfaction at a particular time based on information they have at their disposal. As mentioned in the previous chapter, not all consumption is based on reason; other factors such as status come into play. At the end of the nineteenth century, Thorstein Veblen offered his withering assessment of **conspicuous consumption** (Barber, 2007). Conspicuous consumption occurs when someone pays an extremely high price for a product for its prestige value, leading to a much higher demand than a simple price–demand relation would indicate. Material plenty overrides sense. A modern-day example is when a consumer pays $500 for a designer pair of shoes versus paying $59 for a store brand pair of shoes.

One of the difficulties in understanding rational self-interest is that there is a difference between it and selfishness. People acting in their own rational self-interest are not necessarily selfish, nor is conspicuous consumption necessarily a bad thing (depending on your point of view). Is it a form of expression and individual freedom, or is it to be reviled? Some would say that the more stuff one has, the less important it becomes because it is easily replaced. At a certain point individuals begin to search for more meaningful uses for their money, such as helping others through philanthropy and public service, and seek satisfaction from intangibles, such as memorable experiences and self-realization, rather than tangibles. Of course, this usually takes place after people have met their own basic needs for food, clothes, and shelter and their spending becomes more discretionary. This partly explains why very rich people run for Governor, Senator, or President—they want to give back or lead; they may crave fame or adulation; they no longer have to worry about providing for themselves or their families.

In the nineteenth century, there was an explosion of consumer choice: a more pragmatic view of consumerism was evident. Many espoused that the main purpose was, as the opening quote shows, to maximize profits. These times were exciting but at the same time harsh. People relied less on families for support as they moved across the ocean and across the country in their quest to establish new lives. The gap between the poor and the rich was growing, and as a means of distinguishing rich from poor, conspicuous consumption gained in importance, especially in clothing and homes. In cities, things were more crowded; people felt more competitive. Of course, in the nineteenth century you could find individuals who would not fit these generalizations, but an examination of novels and diaries in the nineteenth century reveals a decided switch in attitude from earlier times. Consider the importance of dress in a novel such as *Gone with the Wind* in order to establish status and pecking order during the 1860s.

The reason it is important to begin this chapter on the consumer movement with a discussion of the nineteenth century is to provide a bridge between what Adam Smith and his contemporaries thought in the eighteenth century and what came about in the twentieth century. What we shall see is that the twentieth century brought both another attitude change and historical events that necessitated increased government intervention in the form of subsidies and consumer protection. These previous developments and events led to the consumer climate in the twenty-first century, which like all preceding centuries is filled with risks and opportunities.

Demographic and Consumption Shifts

In 1776 the population of the 13 colonies was about 2.5 million (compare this with over 319 million today in the United States), and people were highly self-sustaining and individualistic. In the eighteenth century, most lived in rural areas, but by 1890 nearly 40 percent lived in cities. In 1776, pioneers wanted freedom and independence and were mostly self-sufficient, but by the 1890s, citizens had less personal control over the production of goods and relied more on big companies for basics like food and soap. While this transition was taking place, there was a period when dangerous untested products were being sold to unsuspecting consumers, which led to the consumer protection legislation discussed in this chapter.

The trend toward reliance on outside companies and businesses for our basic needs continues. Buyers today are more removed from the production of goods than ever before and are confused by the array of products that are available and most specifically an understanding of how they work. Consider this perspective given by Daniel Harris, author of *Cute, Quaint, Hungry and Romantic: The Aesthetics of Consumerism*:

My life is suspended above an abyss of ignorance. Virtually nothing I own makes sense to me. What happens when I flick on my light switch? Why does my refrigerator keep my food cold? How does my answering machine record the voices of my friends? When I delete a paragraph on my word processor, what makes it disappear and where in the world does it go? In the interest of saving time, as well as out of pure laziness, I, like most people, have deliberately chosen to leave these questions unanswered. . . . I live quite happily hemmed in on all sides by an impenetrable wall of technological riddles. (2000, p. ix)

During wartime, concerns about consumerism tend to take a backseat as the focus shifts from domestic policy to foreign policy. But during other times, a health crisis such as the West African-based Ebola scare of 2014 rallies the call for more consumer protection. As other examples, well-publicized safety problems or court cases also put the spotlight on the need for regulation. In addition, consumer behavior shifts such as more attention to organic and green living affect consumer-related regulations and legislation. The Environmental Protection Agency (EPA) is a regulating body with a key role in reducing pollution, and the Department of Energy has a mandate to reduce energy use. Consider the following case study.

CASE STUDY

The Greenest Generation

Some people have called today's college-age students the greenest generation. Do you agree or disagree? Green can mean riding a bicycle to campus instead of driving a car. Other commute alternatives are public transit, carpooling, and walking. According to the last census, 78 percent of all trips to and from work are drive-alone.

Campuses are holding green transportation rallies with free bike tune-ups, bike races, and entertainment. Companies and campuses are participating in the ENERGY STAR Change a Light, installing compact fluorescent lightbulbs (CFLs) that use up to 75 percent less energy, produce 75 percent less heat, and last up to ten times longer than incandescent. On Earth Day, the Home Depot gave away one million CFL bulbs. This alone equals the removal of 70,000 cars from the road and resulted in a total greenhouse gas reduction of 196 million pounds.

Do you have a digital camera? They require fewer chemicals and less paper than film, and you can delete unwanted shots before printing or share photos through the Internet.

Source: Adapted from www.energystar.gov and www.eere.energy.gov (the US Department of Energy's Energy Efficiency and Renewable Energy Network for sources of energy savings for homes).

Consumerism and the Consumer Movement Defined

As explained in Chapter 1, consumerism is defined as the understanding of self in society through goods. The **consumer movement** refers to policies aimed at regulating products, services, methods and standards of manufacture, selling, and advertising in the interests of the buyer. Regulations can be voluntary, by industry initiative, or mandatory, due to written laws or statutes. The movement involves not only policies but also issues and leaders who brought to the public the need for regulations. The objective of the consumer movement is to ensure that consumers pay a fair price for safe, effective, environmentally sound, satisfying goods and services.

"A narrow definition of the consumer interest might deal solely with safe, reasonably priced and accurately labeled products. To its credit the consumer movement has never defined the consumer interest so narrowly" (Aaker & Day, 1982, p. 32).

Consumer Movement Worldwide

For simplicity's sake, most of the coverage in this chapter is on the consumer movement in the United States, which is a recognized leader in consumer legislation, product testing, and advocacy. However, most other countries also have a consumer movement history (meaning a progression of legislation designed to protect consumers and promote fair dealing in the marketplace) so that to be most accurate the consumer movement should be described as a worldwide movement.

One of the linkages between countries is that the substances most likely to be regulated in any country are food and drugs. Another common thread is legislation regarding labeling; for example, the Swedish system of labeling requires labels to describe the main characteristics of the product in easily understood language in under 200 words. Another link between countries is that legislation adopted in one country often leads to the adoption of similar legislation in another. As an example of this, in 1893 England passed a general law entitled the Sale of Goods Act stating that whenever a buyer expressly or by implication makes known to the seller the particular purpose for which the goods are required, there is an implied expectation that the goods sold will be reasonably fit for their intended purpose. England also passed the Adulteration of Food and Drugs Act in 1872, many years before a similar act was passed in the United States. The United Kingdom continues to be a leader in safe food regulation and consumer protection in general.

Another connection between countries is that news of a consumer fraud or health risk spreads from one country to another—information (and infection) is borderless. Also, consumer courses are commonly taught in many schools and universities around the world. The European Union (EU) made consumer education part of the general objective of consumer protection by the Treaty of Amsterdam in 1997. Consumer education is a legal right of European consumers to be fulfilled jointly by the European

Community and the Member States (Nordic Council, 2009; Goldsmith & Piscopo, 2013). A further linkage is that countries that share borders (such as the United States with Canada and with Mexico) usually set up cooperative agreements because so many goods transverse borders and workers cross borders for employment. In Europe there are many examples of cooperation between countries, especially those that share borders (which may include rivers or coastlines), regarding water quality/pollution, fishing rights, and transportation issues.

As the global market grows and more goods transverse borders and are manufactured in several countries, more international cooperation and agreement will be sought on quality, labeling, trademark, copyright, finance, and safety issues. An example of international cooperation is the adoption of euro coins and notes replacing the mark, franc, and other currencies as legal tender in European countries.

International consumer conferences and world trade conferences are held regularly to discuss issues, research, and policies. The *International Journal of Consumer Studies* based in the United Kingdom is a leading academic journal with authors and subscribers throughout the world.

CASE STUDY

Global Consumer

Cheers

Consumer regulation puts more power in consumers' hands. Producers ruled in the nineteenth century and into the twentieth century, but gradually consumer rights emerged, making it easier to get money back and have avenues for redress. With the Internet, consumer choice has increased and markets and producers have become more accessible worldwide. Our knowledge of companies and countries has increased. A case (yes, there is a joke there) is the production of champagne.

Where would you assume most champagne in the world is produced? You are right if you guessed France. Three in four bottles of champagne sold in the US [are] bottled by industry leader LVMH Moet Hennessey Louis Vitton.[1] LVMH dominates the $5.4 billion global market with 18.6 percent of the global market for champagne by volume according to Impact Databank.[2] The LVMH conglomerate is controlled by Bernard Arnault, the richest man in France. His empire also owns Fendi (handbags, leather goods) and Guerlain (perfume). The global demand for champagne is increasing, especially in China and Russia.

Who regulates champagne? The European Commission (EU) is the governing body regarding price and opening up competition. Ninety percent of the vineyards in France are owned by independent farmers, and LVMH is the biggest buyer of their grapes.

Notes

1. Christina Passareillo, "To Rule Champagne Market, LVMH Courts Grape Growers," *Wall Street Journal*, January 2, 2008, p. A1.
2. Ibid.

Decades of Consumerism

In the following sections, information is given about the lifestyles of the times and the consumer legislation that was enacted. The growth of the consumer movement is evidenced, as are leaders and issues.

1880–1900

What stands out the most in these two decades is the passage of the Sherman Antitrust Act (1890), which prohibited monopolies and price-fixing and encouraged competition. It is heavily cited still today in court cases. Why was it necessary? In the United States, the early nineteenth century was a time of great promise called "the gilded age." Railroads, appliances, and indoor plumbing became more common. Immigrants came in droves— the flow of immigrants after 1880 came from the Orient and Mexico as well as from Eastern and Southern Europe and Russia, adding diversity to all aspects of American life, including religion and diet. An American style of manners, home design, and cuisine distinct from Western Europe developed. Life became easier for most, but not for all. To name just a few of the problems: Coal miners worked under appalling conditions, gold rushes and land rushes often left people broke and stranded, and the Native American nations were systematically moved against their will farther west to reservations.

> From 1880–1900, the middle class grew. It was not unusual for middle class households to have servants or at least a hired girl in to do the laundry once a week. Domestics who lived in received a room usually in the attic or near the kitchen, board, a small wage, and sometimes used clothes. (Schlereth, 1991)

There was no income tax, so a few very wealthy families emerged unfettered. As described earlier in the chapter, they built palatial mansions such as the Biltmore, owned by the Vanderbilts. The Vanderbilt fortune was built on steamships, railroads, coal mines, and securities. Other famous rich and powerful men included J. P. Morgan (railroads, finance, and banking), Andrew Carnegie (steel), and John Rockefeller (oil). Their influence on the rise of industry and capitalism in this country cannot be overestimated. These captains of industry were also active in politics, educational and humanitarian causes, and the arts, funding museums, libraries, foundations, and universities such as Carnegie-Mellon University in Pittsburgh.

Photo 2.1
The expansion of the United States: Conestoga wagons pulled by horses in a land rush circa 1910s

Source: Getty Images: Charles Phelps Cushing/ ClassicStock

There were a lot of food fads and **hucksterism** (extreme promotion) from 1880 to 1900. Food fads, including diet fads such as fasting, miracle foods, and Fletcherism (ritual over-chewing of food), abounded. Fletcherism is named after Horace Fletcher, who believed that chewing food 30 times or more would help people digest their food more easily and use it more effectively. Many patent medicines contained alcohol, which is why they gave patients "a lift." Through school and community classes, home economists and dietitians stepped in to give a sensible voice to nutrition. With the growth of railroads, American consumers had far more access to a variety of fresh fruits and vegetables, so in time the American diet became broader, relying less on meat. John Harvey Kellogg and C. W. Post launched their breakfast cereal empires in Battle Creek, Michigan: Kellogg recommended large doses of bran, granola, and graham crackers, and Post developed Grape-Nuts (1898) and Post Toasties; Kellogg challenged Post Toasties with his own version, named Kellogg's Toasted Corn Flakes.

Early 1900

The start of the twentieth century was exciting. The fashions and attitudes of the previous century were questioned, with materialism and consumerism becoming more complex as inventors and businesses brought many new goods to the market. There was less domestic help, and women's roles began to change. Suburban and small-town

Photo 2.2 Harvey Wiley, the founder of the consumer movement, was a pure food reformer. He encouraged the packaging of food to keep it clean

Source: flickr: Courtesy of The US Food and Drug Administration's photo stream

living began replacing rural living for the masses. As the twentieth century progressed, the former manners and ways of living of the nineteenth century faded: "[C]alling cards, debutante balls, morning coats and finger bowls gave way to backyard barbecues, cocktail buffets and BYOB parties" (Crossen, 2001). Perhaps a sense of elegance was also lost.

In the consumer realm, early consumer protection legislation centered on the control of trade and monopoly and of products closely related to the home (namely, food and drugs). It is difficult to put consumer protection legislation into categories by decade because often the groundwork is laid in one decade and the legislation comes about in the next or even a later decade.

A case in point is the fight for better food quality led by Harvey Wiley—Wiley is often called the founder of the modern consumer movement. To give you some idea of his background, he began his career as a chemistry professor at Purdue University and then resigned that post to go to work for the Indiana Department of Agriculture. While there, he tested the ingredients in bags of chemicals purchased by farmers to improve soil. From this experience he went a step further and thought that consumers should also have food products tested and took this quest to the US Department of Agriculture. His role was to determine the safety of the US food supply. In the 1880s he circulated his findings among other professionals; in the 1890s he went public with his research, urging consumers to join in a campaign aimed at getting Congress to initiate laws on food quality.

Historical Perspective. To set Harvey Wiley and his work in historical perspective, in the early twentieth century things were developing so fast that there were very few regulations to manage production and distribution in a consistent way. Food was the largest expense for the factory laborer and for many middle-class families, which is different from today when housing is usually the most expensive item. So the cost and purity of food were especially critical to the well-being of individuals and families. Inventions that we now take for granted had their start during these times: the airplane, the automobile, motion pictures, electric lights and appliances, radio, canned soups, detergents, and bottled soft drinks. Let us take, for example, the evolution of Coca-Cola:

On May 8, 1886, the soft drink was invented by the Atlanta druggist John Pemberton, primarily as a headache cure. He and a partner named it Coca-Cola because its ingredients included extracts derived from Peruvian coca leaves and African cola nuts (Schlereth, 1991).

By 1891, it was one of the most popular soft drinks in the United States, and Asa Candler bought controlling shares.

Between 1891 and 1929, Coke gained national distribution, selling for a nickel a bottle.

By 1929, Coke was sold in 66 countries.

In the late 1930s, Pepsi-Cola became a serious challenger. The main way Pepsi challenged Coke was by selling at a lower price.

Coke and its competitors raised the question: Are brand names and advertising important? Yes, they are. "Coca-Cola stands today as the second most widely understood term in the world, after okay" (Tedlow, 1990, p. 24). The basic goal of the advertising campaign was to make consumers think of Coke when they were thirsty and to assure them that Coke was the best choice to quench that thirst (Tedlow, 1990).

When Coca-Cola came of age, the timing could not have been better: Prosperity, affluence, and expansion ruled. Americans had more purchasing power than ever before and a growing array of goods to choose from, and they also had more free time. The six-day workweek was common in 1900. Between 1900 and 1930, Americans extended their time in school by going beyond the eighth grade; finishing high school became more the norm, and more students went on to college. Additional time in school meant more time for leisure, increased exposure to peer pressure, and a better educated citizenry. Home economists taught food and consumer classes in schools and in communities and prepared pamphlets for the poor, based on the theory that educated consumers could combat high prices; they publicized food purity concerns in their classes (Strasser, 1989).

Another invention, the automobile, liberated middle-class youth as well as families. In short, in the early twentieth century, to consume took on whole new meanings, and luxury was part of it (Cross, 2000). One author states, "Materialism became Americanism" (Schlereth, 1991, p. 302).

However, before we go any further, it should be pointed out that laboratory testing methods in the late nineteenth and early twentieth centuries were primitive compared with those of today. In 1902, in order to test food additives, Wiley set up a group called the "Poison Squad." The squad was made up of healthy young adults, mostly college students, who ate unadulterated food and also ate the same diet with food additives over a five-year period. He compared their weight and physical condition and found that preservatives readministered continuously in small doses negatively affected their digestion, appetite, and general health.

The men, of course, knew they were eating potential poisons. They didn't know, however, which foods contained the substances. At first, borax was added to butter, to which the men developed a sudden distaste. Wiley then tried it in milk, meat, and coffee. Borax is a hydrated sodium borate (borate is a salt of boric acid used as a preservative). Evidently, as the men determined which food contained the substances, they began eating less of it and eventually avoided that food altogether (Lewis, 2002, p. 14).

Not everyone backed Harvey Wiley's quest for better food safety. Some business groups said his work was antibusiness— even anti-American.

Wiley, observing this, eventually started putting preservatives inside gelatin capsules. The Poison Squad became a sensation with the press and the public (reporters were interviewing the chef through a basement window). Wiley decided he had better cooperate, so he ended up sharing the details of the experiments with reporters. The experiments stopped when the men couldn't function or work. Wiley's efforts led to the regulation of food additives. What happened to the Poison Squad? There are no scientific reports, but anecdotal reports indicate that none were harmed. William O. Robinson of Falls Church, VA, a member of the Squad, lived to be 94 years old.

Wiley became the symbol of food and drug reform. Reformers were interested in two main issues: fraud and poison. The kinds of frauds included the extension of flour, mustard, and ground coffee with cheap fillers, including sawdust and chalk (Strasser, 1989). Besides the alcohol already mentioned, patent medicines were found to contain cocaine and opium.

The Pure Food and Drugs Act of 1906 was the first federal law in US history specifically enacted to protect consumers.

Wiley's results caught the attention of the American Medical Association (AMA), which began analyzing drugs and medicines. Not everyone rallied behind Wiley and the AMA; many business groups said the research was antibusiness and even anti-American. Business was a tremendous force during this era, and improvements were made in transportation, advertising, packaging, machinery, and corporate growth and coordination (Cross, 2000). It was the golden age of national name brands such as Ralston Purina and Quaker Oats. As an example, cereals were no longer just breakfast foods but were promoted as having all kinds of health benefits, including inspiring confidence and providing a good start to one's day. So Wiley was up against a formidable enemy, but he persevered, and his work paved the way for the Pure Food and Drugs Act of 1906, which was considered the first federal law in US history specifically enacted to protect consumers. This act dealt with the production, transportation, and sale of food and drugs in the United States.

Upton Sinclair and President Theodore Roosevelt. Another piece of legislation came to the forefront whose source was not the laboratory but a stirring novel written

Photo 2.3
The Poison Squad

Source: flickr: Courtesy of The US Food and Drug Administration's photo stream by a journalist. In 1906, public uproar over the exposé of the Chicago meatpacking industry depicted in the novel *The Jungle* by Upton Sinclair led to the passage of the Meat Inspections Act. Sinclair graduated from the College of the City of New York in 1897 and went to graduate school at Columbia University. He supported himself by journalistic writing, and *The Jungle* was his sixth novel. His purpose was to write about immigrant families and their struggle, but his story of the squalor and impurities in processed meats aroused widespread public indignation. He said, "I aimed at the public's heart and by accident I hit it in the stomach." Here is a passage from the book:

> *There was never the least attention paid to what was cut up for sausage; there would come all the way back from Europe old sausage that had been rejected, and that was mouldy and white—it would be dosed with borax and glycerine, and dumped into the hoppers, and made over again for home consumption. There would be meat that had tumbled out on the floor, in the dirt and sawdust, where the workers had tramped and spit uncounted billions of consumption germs. . . . [R]ats were nuisances and the packers would put poisoned bread out for them, they would die, and then rats, bread, and meat would go into the hoppers together. (Sinclair, 1905, p. 136)*

Photo 2.4 American author Upton Sinclair writing by the light of his desk at home in California. His most famous book was *The Jungle*, which exposed wrongdoing in the meatpacking industry

Source: Getty Images: Murray Garrett

Sinclair became known as a **muckraker,** a term for writers, politicians, journalists, and public speakers who search out and expose political or commercial corruption. *The Jungle,* which is still in print today, was first published at Sinclair's own expense and became a best-seller. He wrote more books, including *Oil!* (1927), based on the Teapot Dome Scandal, and *Boston* (1928), based on the Sacco-Vanzetti case, but none had the enduring impact of *The Jungle.* His works were popular abroad, including in Russia before and after the Revolution of 1917. In later years he ran as Democratic candidate for governor of California and lost. He was known throughout his life as a fighter for social causes. Sinclair was not alone in his crusade and was joined by many others, who formed the first Consumer's League in 1891; in 1899, this was followed by the National Consumers League, which fought for justice in the marketplace. What was happening was the development of a consumer consciousness. There is no question that consumer consciousness—through organizations, books, the press, and word of mouth—was raised during this era.

President Theodore Roosevelt, writer, rancher, explorer, and soldier whose years in office were 1901 to 1909, was outraged by *The Jungle* and called for an investigation, just as he had earlier by assigning eminent chemists to review Wiley's work (Strasser, 1989). Food reformers had a friend in Roosevelt, who had testified before a Senate investigating committee that he would just as soon have eaten his old hat as the canned food that, under a government contract, had been shipped to the soldiers in Cuba during the Spanish-American War (Downs, 1963). The investigation of the Chicago meatpacking industry revealed that the book did not exaggerate; in fact, conditions were worse than Sinclair had reported. Based on this, Roosevelt joined Congress in calling for federal legislation to correct the matter. On June 30, 1906, he signed both the Pure Food and Drugs Act and the Meat Inspection Act.

Theodore Roosevelt, a Republican, is known as a president who expanded the powers of the federal government on the side of public interest in conflicts between big business and big labor. In 1902 he established a Bureau of Corporations with powers to inspect the books of all businesses engaged in interstate commerce. He was also a trust-buster, bringing suit against 44 major corporations during his presidency.

Roosevelt's most successful suit was against the Northern Securities Company using the Sherman Anti-Trust Act, which was passed in 1890 but was largely ignored until Roosevelt invoked its power. **Antitrust laws** prevent business monopolies and are aimed at establishing and maintaining competition so that consumers get fair prices as well as goods in adequate quantities. The rights of buyers and competitors fall under the general category of **common law,** which is based on custom and is the unwritten system of law that is the foundation of both the English and US legal systems (excluding Louisiana whose laws are based on the Napoleonic Code). The Sherman Anti-Trust Act made monopoly and price-fixing illegal so that firms were prevented from unfairly harming their competitors. Roosevelt was first and foremost a crusader, a person who

Photo 2.5 Theodore Roosevelt, the twenty-sixth president of the United States, was a champion of consumer rights and an antimonopolist

Source: Thinkstock: Photos.com

overcame physical weakness in his youth to become a lifelong competitor and adventurer, but he is also considered a leader in the modern concept of consumer protection.

In 1908 the first court case using the Pure Food and Drugs Act was tried. The product under investigation was deemed worthless: It did not cure headaches as it was supposed to do, nor did its usage make consumers more intelligent. The manufacturer was ordered to change the label and was charged a $700 fine. As was common, this fine was a mere slap on the wrist because the manufacturer had already made millions of dollars. This is an ongoing problem in consumer protection today—the fines are often minuscule compared with the profits. By the time advertisements are pulled or companies are sent to court, they have already made all the money they set out to make. Another problem is that corporate lawyers are usually better paid and have more staff support than government lawyers, which makes for uneven battles.

1910s

In 1914, two key pieces of legislation were passed:

- The Clayton Act restricted price discrimination, exclusive dealing, and tying contracts.
- The Federal Trade Commission (FTC) Act prohibited deceptive advertising and unfair and deceptive trade practices.

The FTC Act was passed to enforce antitrust laws. The FTC, for example, can issue a **cease-and-desist order**, an administrative or judicial order ordering a business to cease "unfair or deceptive acts or practices." For a listing of key consumer laws passed between 1880 and 1929, see Box 2.1. Also in 1914, Christine Frederick published *The New Housekeeping: Efficiency Studies in Home Management*, which extolled the virtues of an orderly labor-saving home and the need for more packaged goods and for fairer deals in the marketplace. She testified before Congress on behalf of consumers.

Box 2.1 Key Consumer Legislation 1880–1929

During this time period, over 50 consumer laws were passed in the United States. Here is a sample:

Year	Act	Description
1887	Interstate Commerce Act	Power to regulate commerce was reserved to the states.
1890	Sherman Anti-Trust Act	It prohibits monopolies and price-fixing and encourages competition.
1906	Pure Food and Drug Act	It prohibits adulteration of food and drugs and mislabeling of such sold in interstate commerce, requires disclosure of narcotics and alcohol contents on patent medicine labels, and prohibits manufacturers from claiming ingredients that are not present.
1906	Meat Inspection Act	It provides for meat inspection. There had been an earlier act in 1891 that set up the Federal Meat Inspection Service.
1914	Federal Trade Commission Act	It prohibits deceptive advertising and unfair and deceptive trade practices. The FTC Act was used in the battle against trusts. Examples of early trusts (combinations of firms that got together to reduce competition and control supplies and/or prices in an industry or region) included sugar, whiskey, matches, and fuel.
1914	Clayton Act	Restricts price discrimination, exclusive dealings, and tying contracts.

The Federal Bureau of Standards established a national system of weights and measures; as its name implies, it standardized how goods were weighed and sold. To raise consumer awareness, at food expositions and state and county fairs consumers were shown measuring devices with false bottoms and non-regulation-size milk bottles and bushel baskets (Strasser, 1989).

Other developments include the establishment of Better Business Bureaus (BBBs) in 1912 that discouraged dishonest business practices. In 1913 the Sixteenth Amendment to the US Constitution was passed, giving Congress the right to collect income taxes. The amendment stated, "The Congress shall have the power to lay and collect taxes on income." The first tax was only 1 percent of income. By 1915, to be middle class meant to have electricity, and the expression "chain store" came into being. Chain stores that bought in bulk passed savings on to consumers. It was more common for people to eat cereal out of a box for breakfast instead of the previously home-cooked breakfast of beefsteak, bacon and eggs, fried potatoes, wheatcakes and sausage, porridge, donuts, and fruits (Schlereth, 1991).

In 1917, the United States became involved in World War I, so concern switched from domestic to international affairs. The war led to a quiet period in the consumer movement.

1920s

The 1920s began with relief that the war was over. Parties, extravagant lifestyles, gambling, bobbed hair, and flapper dresses marked the first years, and consumer incomes rose steadily while prices remained stable. However, by 1928 discontent was expressed in *Your Money's Worth* by Stuart Chase and F. J. Schlink, who exposed false advertising and high-pressure sales techniques. They called for more testing of products and improved standards. As a result, in 1929 Consumers' Research, Inc. (of which Schlink became technical director) was formed to perform testing work. Although there was a dearth of consumer protection legislation during this decade, the government was actively involved in testing the effectiveness of "germ-killing" products and enforcing the 1906 Pure Food and Drugs Act, seizing defective food and drugs before they were shipped. In October 1929 the stock market crashed in the United States, and a depression began not only in this country but also worldwide. A **depression** is characterized as a drastic and long-lasting decline in the economy, with high unemployment, falling prices, and decreasing business activity.

1930s

The lowest point of the Great Depression was in 1933. Although there was a panic and a run on the banks in late 1929, no one really knew what was happening until well into the 1930s; more importantly, at first no one really knew what to do about it. There was no question that people lost faith in American industry and in American banks.

The Depression hit America like a typhoon. One half the value of all production simply disappeared. One quarter of the working force lost its jobs. Over a million urban families found their mortgages foreclosed, their houses lost to the bank. Nine million savings accounts went down the drain when banks closed, many for good.

Against this terrible reality of joblessness and loss of income, the economics profession, like the business world or government advisers, had nothing to offer. Fundamentally, economists were as perplexed at the behavior of the economy as were the American people themselves. (Heilbroner & Thurow, 1998, p. 30)

Economist John Maynard Keynes. During these troubled times, English economist John Maynard Keynes (pronounced "canes") published *The General Theory of Employment, Interest, and Money* (1936), a more complicated and technical book than Adam Smith's *Wealth of Nations*. It had a central message that was easy to grasp: Economic activity in a capitalist system is determined by the willingness of its entrepreneurs to make capital investments (Heilbroner & Thurow, 1998). Sometimes this willingness is blocked, and the import of Keynes' theory was that if there is no self-correcting property in the market system, such as prolific business investment to keep capitalism growing, other solutions have to be found. The solution in this case was increased government spending on public works. Since his book was published during the Great Depression, it influenced President Franklin D. Roosevelt, his economic/political advisors, and their policies. He founded a school of thought called Keynesian economics that emphasizes the role government plays in stabilizing the economy, and his influence extends to today.

FDR signed into law the 44-hour workweek in 1938 and reduced it to 40 hours in 1941.

President Franklin D. Roosevelt. Franklin Delano Roosevelt (FDR), a Democrat who became president in 1933, rose to the challenge that the Depression presented. As evidence of his popularity and effectiveness, he is the only president to be reelected three times; his years in office were from 1933 to 1945. He used the federal government's powers to bring about a national economic recovery, which was called the New Deal, and he was president during World War II. Therefore, during his administration his policies were not the hands-off kind of government recommended by Adam Smith because Roosevelt thought that the crisis demanded a more hands-on approach, and Keynes' book provided the theoretical background for much of the approach that was taken. Examples of Roosevelt's policies include signing the Fair Labor Standards Act in 1938, which established the 44-hour workweek; in 1941 this was reduced to the standard 40-hour workweek that we use today. Also in 1938, the Wheeler Lea Act was passed, providing the FTC more jurisdiction over misleading or false advertising.

By way of background, Roosevelt went to Harvard and studied law at Columbia University. In 1905, he married Eleanor Roosevelt, an outspoken consumer advocate and the niece of Theodore Roosevelt. In 1910 he was elected to the New York Senate and later became governor of New York. He rose up through the ranks, and as president he promoted sweeping economic programs that provided relief, loans, and jobs through federal agencies.

Photo 2.6 President Franklin D. Roosevelt raises his hat while riding in a convertible with his wife, Eleanor Roosevelt. They were both consumer activists who fought for better working conditions and product safety

Source: Getty Images: Fotosearch

During his years in office, many consumer laws were passed, including the Food, Drug, and Cosmetics Act of 1938. This act amended the 1906 act by adding cosmetics and allowing inspectors to remove dangerous products from store shelves while tests were being completed. Congressional leaders and Roosevelt were horrified by the disfigurements and the nearly 100 deaths caused by the new sulfa wonder drug named Elixir Sulfanilamide.

There were other problem products as well. The respectability in the use of cosmetics and beauty salons grew tremendously in the 1930s, but with it came abuse in the form of face creams that burned and dyes that caused hair to fall out: "[A] once pretty matron was blinded by Lashlure, an eyelash dye" (Aaker & Day, 1982, p. 27). Adding fuel to the fire was the 1933 *100,000,000 Guinea Pigs* by Arthur Kallet and F. J. Schlink when they introduced the public to a number of cosmetic, food, and drug problems, including the use of a well-known rat poison as the active ingredient in the depilatory cream Koremlu. The book gave the following case, first documented in the *Journal of the American Medical Association*, about a woman, age 24:

> *[She] came to the Cleveland Clinic complaining of severe pains over the soles of both feet and ankles, weakness of both feet and legs, and intense burning of both feet. . . . Four and one-half months prior to entering the clinic, the patient had first noticed intermittent epigastric [abdominal] pains which gradually increased in severity to sharp, cramp-like pains throughout the entire abdomen. . . . The patient had become very nervous, cried easily, had lost about ten pounds, and felt continually tired. . . .*
>
> *It was discovered that she had been using a depilatory cream, "Koremlu," nightly for the preceding five months, beginning its use two weeks before the appearance of the first symptoms. A quantity sufficient only to cover the upper lip and the chin had been used on each occasion. (Kallet & Schlink, 1933, p. 82)*

Kallett and Schlink (1933) went on to make the following point:

> *Purchasers of ordinary foods and drugs have little enough assurance of safety, despite the control (as some term it) provided by the Federal Food and Drugs Act and by various state agencies. The purchaser of cosmetics has no protection whatever. No Federal agency has jurisdiction over cold creams, depilatories, skin lotions, hair dyes, or any other substance intended for external use and not for the treatment of disease. (p. 78)*

Although it was still the Depression and news of fraudulent products abounded, consumers bought what they could. Inexpensive treats such as nickel movies and gum sold well. The Snickers candy bar was introduced in 1930.

> *There were signs of downscaling. Sales of men's suits dropped sharply. . . . Thin wallets led to record sales of glass jars for home canning. The "live at home movement" meant foregoing the night on the town and instead listening to the radio. . . . As common as cutting back, however, was a very different response—a refusal to retrench. Many Depression-era Americans were unwilling to abandon the "luxuries" of the 1920s. Cigarette smokers could not give up the habit. . . . Americans held on to their old Model Ts. (Cross, 2000, p. 69)*

Economist John Kenneth Galbraith. John Kenneth Galbraith (1908–2006) was a Canadian who lived most of his life in the United States. A prolific writer, one of his most famous books was *The Affluent Society*, published in 1958. In this book he called for less emphasis on production and more emphasis on public service. He was a key advisor to John F. Kennedy and served as ambassador to India (1961–1963) before returning to Harvard.

Earlier during the FDR years, Galbraith also served in several government posts. FDR rode out the storm very well and was highly regarded by contemporaries and the general populace. John Kenneth Galbraith, the Paul Warburg professor of economics emeritus at Harvard University, at age 93 had this to say: "Franklin D. Roosevelt was good on great issues or small. A great war. A great depression. He presided over both. No question about it—he's the person who most impressed me. In my life, he had no close competitor" (Fussman, 2002, p. 60).

1940s

World War II turned everyone's attention to the war front, and interest in consumer legislation faded. Food and gasoline were rationed here and abroad, so people were more interested in getting goods than worrying about their quality. "Here is a partial list of what you could not get for Christmas in 1943: beer mugs, bird cages, cocktail shakers, radios, doll carriages, rubber boots, bicycles or tricycles, typewriters, griddles, toasters, hair curlers, phonographs, alarm clocks or balls that bounced. America's armed forces, fighting overseas, needed all the metal, rubber, chemicals and food they could get" (Crossen, 2002, p. B1). Because household income had grown substantially from the depression years, for many men and women working at jobs in the United States this was the first time they could not buy something they were able to afford. According to recorded oral histories and exhibits at the D-Day Museum in New Orleans, this was the first time many women went to work outside the home, becoming welders and shipbuilders, thus earning their own wages. The economic freedom this provided was unprecedented and set the groundwork for the future expansion of women's employment.

Because of the wartime shortage of gasoline, travel was curtailed. The lack of basics such as eggs, milk, and butter led to the development of recipes for cakes such as fruitcakes that used none of these ingredients. With shortages came a growing black market. To lessen hoarding and to provide commodities fairly, the federal government instituted rationing and price limits.

> *Every man, woman and child received a monthly ration book, giving them a certain number of red points (for meat, cheese, and oil) and blue points (for canned goods). A person might get 64 red points a month, but a pound of butter could require as many as 24. . . . So strict were the rules, that government employees would scan newspaper death notices and send letters to families asking them to return ration books. (Crossen, 2002, p. B1)*

Another response to the shortages was provided by the advertising industry. Instead of promoting consumption, they came up with slogans such as "Use it up, wear it out, make do or do without" (Crossen, 2002, p. B1).

Homeowners were encouraged to grow victory gardens for personal consumption so that foods canned in factories could be shipped overseas. Nylon was used in the war effort, so it could not be used for stockings, and women drew pencil lines up the back of their legs to simulate stocking seams. "In 1943, the season's most coveted gifts were a carton of cigarettes or a pair of nylon stockings" (Crossen, 2002, p. B1).

American homes were growing more technologically complex: Flush toilets were considered standard, telephones were owned by 36 percent of families, and refrigerators were in 91 percent of households (Cross, 2000). Even though there were shortages, the average household improved substantially during the war years and immediately afterward. The teen market was also growing and paving the way for resurgence of bobby sox power in the 1950s. *Seventeen* magazine was introduced earlier in 1944.

Box 2.2 shows that no major federal consumer legislation was passed in the 1940s and only a few laws were passed during the 1950s. On the marketplace side of things, during the 1940s and 1950s advertising surged, and demand for consumer goods was never higher. Production was more important than protection, with cigarette smoking glamorized.

Box 2.2 Key Consumer Legislation 1930–1979

1938 Wheeler Lea Act	Provided FTC with jurisdiction over false and misleading advertising.
1938 Federal Food, Drug, and Cosmetics Act	Extended coverage of the earlier act added cosmetics and gave federal agencies the power to remove untested products from stores.
1938 Federal Trade Commission Act	It updated the 1914 act and prohibits deceptive and unfair trading practices.
1939 Wool Products Labeling Act	It requires accurate labeling of wool products.
1951 Fur Products Labeling Act	It requires proper labeling of fur products.
1953 Flammable Fabrics Act	It prohibits selling highly flammable clothes.
1957 Poultry Products Inspection Act	It requires inspection of poultry.
1958 Textile Fiber Products Identification Act	It covers advertising and labeling of all textile products not covered in the Wool and Fur Products Labeling Acts.
1960 Hazardous Substances Labeling Act	It requires warning labels on dangerous household products.
1964 Civil Rights Act★	It guarantees consumer choice, the "full and equal enjoyment of the goods, services, facilities, privileges, advantages, and accommodations of any place of public accommodation."
1965 Cigarette Labeling Advertising Act	Warning labels are required of possible health hazards (this act grew out of growing evidence that tobacco caused cancer).

1965	Immigration and Nationality Act	It opened up the United States to large numbers of immigrants from Latin America and Asia.
1966	Child Protection and Toy Safety Act	It bans dangerous toys and requires childproof devices and special labeling.
1966	Fair Packaging and Labeling Act (more commonly known as Truth in Packaging Act)	It requires that weight and content information be given on product labels (thus enabling consumers to comparison-shop).
1966	Child Protection and Toy Safety Act	It requires childproof devices and labeling.
1966	National Traffic and Motor Vehicle Safety Act	New car dealers must be informed by manufacturers of any safety defects found after the manufacture and sale of autos.
1967	Wholesale Meat Act	It updates 1906 legislation and provides for higher standards in slaughterhouses of red-meat animals.
1967	Federal Cigarette Labeling and Advertising Act	Cigarette packaging must carry health warnings.
1968	Interstate Land Sales Full Disclosure Act	It requires accuracy of information on interstate land sales.
1968	Consumer Credit Protection Act (Truth in Lending Act)	It protects and regulates credit transactions, demands that lenders inform debtors of annual interest rates, and limits the practice of garnishing wages.
1970	Public Health Cigarette Smoking Act	It prohibits cigarette advertising on television and radio.
1970	Fair Credit Reporting Act	It protects consumers' credit reports.
1970	Clean Air Act	It authorizes the Environmental Protection Agency to establish national air-quality standards and requires states to develop plans for reducing pollution emissions by 90 percent in five years.
1970	Bank Secrecy Act	It establishes record-keeping and reporting requirements for national US banks and federal branches and agencies of foreign banks.
1972	Consumer Product Safety Act	It establishes the Consumer Product Safety Commission; regulates hazardous items, especially those related to the home such as toy, baby, and play equipment and household products; and provides for a continuous review of products.
1972	Odometer Act	It protects consumers by stating that used-car odometers cannot be rolled back or disconnected.
1972	Water Pollution Control Act	It endeavors to make major waterways clean enough for fishing and swimming by 1983.
1973	FTC** Door-to-Door Sales Rule	The FTC regulates door-to-door sales contracts.
1973	FTC Rules of Negative Options	It spells out FTC rules regarding book and record clubs.
1974	Real Estate Settlement Procedures Act	It requires the disclosure of home buying costs.
1974	Equal Credit Opportunity Act	It prohibits discrimination regarding credit.
1974	Fair Credit Billing Act	It protects against billing errors and establishes procedures for resolving mistakes on credit card bills.

| 1975 | Magnuson–Moss Warranty Act | It governs content of warranties, including full and limited warranties. Warranty information must be given to the consumer before he or she makes a purchase. |
| 1977 | Fair Debt Collection Practices Act | It limits debt collectors and their methods and prohibits abuses such as harassment. |

*This is far more than a consumer protection law. It was directed at ending racial discrimination, the humiliation of segregated facilities, and the denial of access by minorities to consumer choices.

**Federal Trade Commission.

Advertisers gained respect when they produced effective propaganda for the war effort. More important, they shaped popular opinion by addressing the critical question: "What are we fighting for?" Their answer was well summarized by one ad: "For years we have fought for a higher standard of living, and now we are fighting to protect it against those who are jealous of our national accomplishments." A Nash–Kelvinator ad showed a paratrooper affirming, "We have so many things, here in America, that belong only to a free people . . . warm, comfortable homes, automobiles and radios by the million" (Cross, 2000, p. 84).

1950s

When the war ended in 1945, everyone wanted new houses, cars, furniture, washing machines, and every other kind of consumer good imaginable. The emphasis was on increasing production to meet these needs, and modern American and European business was born. In the United Kingdom, rationing continued longer than in the United States, but when it was over, it was replaced by an upsurge in choice and availability (Lyon, Colquhoun, & Kinney, 2004). Both in the United States and abroad, modern grocery stores and shopping plazas replaced corner mom-and-pop stores; checkout lines and counter service became the wave of the future. Everyone wanted to buy what was new and to put the war behind them.

For homeowners who already had washing machines, they upgraded from wringer washers to automatic washers and from clotheslines to electric dryers. Television grew tremendously during this decade, and the Mickey Mouse Club premiered in 1955. College towns and campuses grew substantially during the late 1940s and the 1950s, as the GI Bill allowed returning soldiers to go to college, swelling enrollments in universities. There was renewed interest in science and invention that would benefit homes and industry.

By 1954, Frigidaire was selling ten kinds of appliances; demand was high, and consumers wanted choices (Tedlow, 1990). Some of the innovations—especially the early dishwashers—were less than successful. To make them appear more useful, they were sold

Photo 2.7 Ken and Barbie are displayed during the Toy Industry Association (TIA) 108th American International Toy Fair 2011 in New York, on February 16, 2011. Barbie revolutionized the toy market and is still a top-seller worldwide, though she now comes in countless variations

Source: Getty Images: Bloomberg

as multifunction appliances: For example, it was suggested that meat could be defrosted and cocktails (in shakers) could be mixed in the dishwashers while washing dishes.

The 1950s was a decade of private consumption, capitalism gone full tilt. To consume was to be free (Cross, 2000). In the mid- to late 1950s, loud was in—loud colors, loud television westerns, loud fashion, and loud music with rock 'n' roll and Elvis Presley. Food preferences changed too, with chips and dip replacing sandwiches for when guests dropped by (Cross, 2000). The split-level house was introduced as a change from the rectangular ranch; inside, unlikely combinations of the old and the new, such as knotty-pine cabin-like paneling and kitchen cabinets mixed with plastic formica tables and counters, occurred. The decade ended with the introduction of Mattel's Barbie in 1959.

Businesses became more sophisticated in their understanding and use of market research. By the end of the decade, a new muckraker emerged: Vance Packard. His 1957 book *The Hidden Persuaders* exposed the manipulative methods that businesses use to stimulate sales. The book stated that "supermarket operators are pretty well agreed that men are easy marks for all sorts of impulse items and cite cases they've seen of husbands who are sent to the store for a loaf of bread and depart with both their arms loaded with their favorite snack items" (Packard, 1957, p. 95). Packard (1957) also related the following:

> An Indiana supermarket operator nationally recognized for his advanced psycho-logical techniques told me he once sold a half ton of cheese in a few hours, just by getting an enormous half-ton wheel of cheese and inviting customers to nibble slivers and cut off their own chunks for purchase. They could have their chunk free if they could guess its weight within an ounce. The mere massiveness of the cheese, he believes, was a powerful influence in making the sales. "People like to see a lot of merchandise," he explained. "When there are only three or four cans of an item on a shelf, they just won't move." (p. 94)

In 1959, the Food and Drug Administration (FDA) seized boxes of Pillsbury blueberry pancake mix for misbranding. The ingredients list and the picture on the box included blueberries, but there were none in the product. Also, in 1959 a cranberry crop scare shook the nation. Cranberries were being sprayed with chemicals that caused cancer, so the FDA called for the end of distributing cranberries until this problem was solved. By the end of the 1950s, with books like Packard's and the cranberry exposé, there was a return to interest in consumer protection, and the groundwork was being laid for advances in the consumer movement in the 1960s.

1960s

Health and environmental concerns move to the forefront in this decade. Cigarette packages were required to have health warning labels under the Federal Cigarette Labeling and Advertising Act of 1967. Earlier, in 1962, American biologist Rachel Carson, founder of the modern environmental movement, exposed other environ-mental pollution problems in her book *Silent Spring*. **Pollution** refers to any undesirable change in biological, chemical, or physical characteristics of air, land, or water that harms activities, health, or survival of living organisms. Carson advocated the use of natural pests or deterrents rather than chemicals and questioned the soundness of runaway con-sumption. She is an important symbol of the powerful impact and leadership provided by many women in government, business, and activism, such as Susan B. Anthony and Elizabeth Cady Stanton before her.

Since the 1960s, **environmentalism** (defined as concern for the environment) has become a very important part of the modern consumer movement. Extensive media coverage of both environmental ills and disappearing species and a growing appreci-ation of the natural world spurred interest in environmentalism. There may be another reason as well:

Photo 2.8 Rachel Carson (1907–1964) is considered the founder of the modern environmental movement. She was an American biologist who wrote *Silent Spring,* an exposé on pollution

Source: Getty Images: CBS Photo Archive

> *Most consumers lack the scientific background to understand many environmental issues and few have relevant previous experience to guide them in assessing the relative environmental merits of market-place alternatives. Thus, the potential for consumer fraud and deception is great. (Cude, 1993, p. 207)*

President John F. Kennedy, a Democrat, read Carson's *Silent Spring* and decided to take action. His interest in her work led to his Consumer Message to Congress in March 1962; in the preamble, Kennedy gave the famous Consumer Bill of Rights:

1. The right to safety (to be protected from hazards to health and life).
2. The right to be heard (to be protected from fraud, deceit, or grossly misleading information including advertising and labeling).

3. The right to choose (to have access to a variety of products and services at competitive prices).

4. The right to information (to be assured of fair and expeditious treatment from government and in policy formation).

He particularly cited the need for revision of laws pertaining to food and drugs. Later presidents added the following three rights:

1. The right to a decent environment (influenced by several presidents).

2. The right to consumer education (added by President Gerald Ford).

3. The right to reasonable redress for physical damages suffered from using a product (added by President Richard Nixon).

In January 1964, President Lyndon B. Johnson, a Democrat, created the new White House post of special assistant for consumer affairs and appointed outspoken consumer

Photo 2.9 President John F. Kennedy, shown here with his wife, Jacqueline, was a pro-consumer leader

Source: Getty Images: National Archives

advocate Esther Peterson to fill it. He also promised he would support new consumer legislation. The 1965 Immigration and Nationality Act and landmark civil rights laws opened up the United States in many ways, including new job and educational opportunities and an influx of newcomers from Latin America and Asia.

The 1960s was the age of dominance of large national general merchandise and department stores over small local mom-and-pop stores as well as the spread of fast-food brands. In 1965, the leader in sales and profits was Sears, Roebuck & Company, followed by J.C. Penney and Montgomery Ward (Tedlow, 1990). Ray Kroc bought out the McDonald brothers in 1960 and franchised McDonald's restaurants. In the 1960s the FDA also seized bogus bust developers such as Lady Ample.

Any discussion of consumer protection in the 1960s would be incomplete without recognizing the enormous contribution that muckraker Ralph Nader made in his 1965 book *Unsafe at Any Speed*, which highlighted the need for more auto safety, including cushioning and seat belts. "The automobile had been around for seventy years before Ralph Nader got general recognition of the fact that autos included unsafe design features and sometimes were ill-engineered," according to authors David Aaker and George Day (1982, p. 31). A series of horrendous accidents caused by poorly manufactured cars led to a call for reform. Nader spoke out against industrial pollution and the abuse of corporate power not only in the car industry but also in the home repair industry, the food industry, and securities, to name a few. He testified extensively before Congress and still advocates on behalf of consumers, particularly regarding environmental concerns, and he founded consumer groups that are still active.

In 1968, Paul Erlich's *The Population Bomb* made the case that there are too many people, too many cars, too much of everything and that if the trend continued unchecked, then famines and other catastrophes would occur. His book influenced the debate on the use of birth control methods and a reconsidering of optimal family size.

Another important book in 1968 was *The Dark Side of the Marketplace* by Senator Warren G. Magnuson and Jean Carper, who explained how the consumer movement had vastly expanded its scope "from sales deceptions and safety standards to concern over the environment—air and water pollution—and the ominous trend toward economic concentration which threatens consumers' welfare" (1968, p. 2). In the first chapter, the authors discussed how elderly couples were being bilked out of thousands of dollars by con men selling aluminum siding door-to-door. This influenced the passage of the 1973 FTC Door-to-Door Sales Rules Act. Magnuson and Carper asserted that deceptive selling by the unscrupulous few cheated Americans out of more money than is lost to "robbery, burglary, larceny, auto theft, embezzlement, and forgery combined" (1968, p. 13). Their disturbing conclusion was that the public is not being adequately protected, including not knowing enough about the hazards of smoking. Their book influenced the passage of the 1970 Public Health Cigarette Smoking Act (see Box 2.2); also notice the 1975 act that bears Magnuson's name.

1970s

As Box 2.2 shows, there was a great deal of consumer protection legislation in the 1970s led by Presidents Richard Nixon (Republican), Gerald Ford (Republican), and Jimmy Carter (Democrat). Nixon, a lawyer by training, signed numerous pieces of consumer legislation into law and led the way to the development of small claims courts throughout the United States, while Gerald Ford promoted consumer education. Carter called for conservation and reduction of energy consumption. He was personally interested in solar power and other environmental technologies and appointed numerous strong consumer advocates to government posts, including Esther Peterson as special assistant for consumer affairs. Because of this and the legislation he supported, Carter is considered a strong pro-consumer president.

Other developments during this decade included the end of the Vietnam War and changes in consumer buying patterns. Discount stores and malls grew, and with them the growth in credit cards, and more stores were open on Sundays.

Photo 2.10 Lifelong consumer activist, author, and former presidential candidate Ralph Nader speaks at the DC Full Democracy Freedom Rally and March in Washington, DC, Saturday, October 15, 2011. His famous book, *Unsafe at Any Speed*, revolutionized car safety

Source: Getty Images: MCT

Faux exercise devices, including different models of the Relaxacizor, were seized by the FDA several times during the 1970s. The FDA has a museum with collections of these types of devices, as well as cosmetics that came under regulation, biological agents, foods, medical devices, and quack products of every sort. The museum is part of the FDA History Office, whose mission is to increase knowledge of the history, mission, and activities of the FDA and its predecessor, the Bureau of Chemistry of the US Department of Agriculture. Besides this Washington-based museum, objects are on loan to the St. Louis Science Center, the Science Museum of Minnesota, and also Washington's Smithsonian Institution.

Many of the 1970s acts, because they are landmark legislation, are still influential today (for example, the Equal Credit Opportunity Act and the act establishing the Consumer Product Safety Commission). Especially significant was the previously mentioned 1973 FTC Door-to-Door Sales Rule, which came about because high-pressure salespersons were rushing consumers into buying things they did not want, such as encyclopedias, magazine subscriptions, vacuum cleaners, and home improvements. Because consumers were approached at their homes, many people, particularly women and the elderly, felt threatened if they didn't sign for the product or felt vulnerable in some other way. With the legislation, a consumer could cancel within a three-day cooling-off period. The problem, as the Consumer Alert box shows, is that not all types of contracts were covered. This is often the case with consumer legislation: It stops some of the blatant abuses, but while it is well intentioned, it only covers certain problem areas; additionally, over time it becomes dated as new situations and products arise that were not anticipated and covered in the original legislation.

1980s

With President Ronald Reagan, a Republican, at the helm from 1981 to 1989, there was a renewed look at consumer protection in this country. Agencies were reorganized, and some would say they became less powerful. As an advocate of supply-side economics, Reagan mostly took the view that the market should regulate itself. He thought his predecessors may have been overzealous regarding reform, and there was evidence that citizens in the 1980s were tired of restrictions and conserving. The general attitude was that consuming, after all, is fun for most people, most of the time. Movies about greed and Wall Street abounded, college students flocked to business schools, video games came into style for children, the term *yuppie* was used to describe trend-setting dual-earner childless couples, and name brands such as BMW and Ralph Lauren promised prestige.

Consumers were encouraged to use the laws already on the books. Nevertheless, quite a bit of consumer protection legislation was passed during the Reagan term, as shown in Box 2.3. According to public opinion polls, Reagan was a popular president. He was followed by George Bush (1989–1993), also a Republican, who took a similar consumer protection stance.

Box 2.3 Key Consumer Legislation 1980–Present

1981 FTC★ Used-Car Rule	It requires used-car dealers to disclose to consumers specified types of information.
1984 FTC Funeral Home Rule	It requires disclosure of prices and services.
1984 Counterfeit Access Device and Computer Fraud and Abuse Act	It prohibits counterfeit credit cards and other unauthorized access to credit.
1984 Automobile Restraints	It requires all new cars sold after September 1, 1990, to have restraints (seat belts).
1984 Toy Safety Act	By this act, CPSC★★ can more quickly recall hazardous toys and equipment for children.
1984 Generic Drug Act	It allows the FDA to speed up acceptance of generic drugs on which patents have expired on original drugs.
1986 Smokeless Tobacco Act	It requires labeling of hazards on smokeless tobacco products and prohibits advertising of these products on television and radio.
1988 Home Equity Loan Consumer Protection Act	It requires fuller disclosure of loans and prohibits lenders from changing contracts after signage.
1990 Clean Air Act	It updates the 1970 act and establishes new pollution limits and standards for automobile, power plant, and cancer-causing substance emissions.
1990 Children's Advertising Act	It directs the FCC† to limit TV advertising directed at children.
1990 Food Labeling Act	It establishes new labeling standards.
1993 Truth in Savings Act	It requires that financial institutions report APY (annual percentage yield) in the same way.
1994 Dietary Supplement Health and Education Act	It requires manufacturers to provide product safety information to the FDA.‡
1994 Fair Credit Reporting Act (Amended)	It increases access to credit.
1994 NAFTA (North American Free Trade Agreement)	It gradually eliminates tariffs among Mexico, Canada, and the United States on most products. Agreement is in full force in 2008. Included is a dispute-resolution program.
1998 The Digital Millennium Copyright Act	It adapted US legislation to the WIPO treaties. The World Intellectual Property Organization (WIPO) had two treaties, laid down in Geneva, that adapted copyright rules for e-commerce. Copyright laws cover physical copies, broadcasting, books, songs, and films distributed online. The treaties, ratified by 41 countries, went into effect in 2002.
1998 Children's Online Privacy Protection Act	It establishes rules governing online activities.
1999 Anticybersquatting Protection Act	It prohibits the act of cybersquatting.
2001 USA PATRIOT Act	It requires every bank to adopt a customer identification program.

★Federal Trade Commission.
★★Consumer Product Safety Commission.
†Federal Communications Commission.
‡Food and Drug Administration.

CONSUMER ALERTS

There is no universal three-day cooling-off period. Do not be misled into thinking that you have an automatic three-day or other cancellation period for all purchases. Only a few types of contracts give you a right to cancel. Federal law, for example, gives you the right to cancel certain door-to-door contracts within three days, and some states provide cancellation periods for such things as health and dating club contracts. Check with your state and local consumer office for more information about cancellation rights.

Source: Federal Consumer Information Center.

During the 1980s, there was a corporate thrust behind consumer education because for-profit companies preferred consumer education to more legislation. Increased consumer education is worthwhile if it hits the right audience at the right time, but there is only so much it can do, as the following quote makes clear: "Even genuine consumer education cannot, of course, solve consumer problems by itself. If all meat prices go up it's little help to tell consumers to buy the lower-price cuts. These usually go up the most. Nor can consumer education help much in restraining high mortgage interest rates or high medical and hospital fees" (Margolius, 1982, p. 56).

1990s

With the growth and spread of the Internet, this decade sees the emergence of Internet or computer fraud legislation such as the Anticybersquatting Consumer Protection Act of 1999.

Cybersquatting is a practice wherein deceptive individuals attempt to purchase and control websites that look like commercial legitimate sites. Consumers are harmed because they don't know if they are on a legitimate site or not. They may purchase products or give to a charity from an unreliable source. **Desirable products and services** deliver high utilitarian (usefulness) and **hedonic** (pleasant or pleasing) **value** and benefit consumers and society.

President Bush, the forty-first president, was followed by Bill Clinton, a Democrat, who held office from 1993 to 2001. Although it is not considered consumer protection legislation per se, Clinton signed the North American Free Trade Agreement (NAFTA), which greatly impacted trade, employment in certain industries, and prices. His vice president, Al Gore, was known for his interest in environmental and family issues and wrote the book *Earth in the Balance*, which is about environmental problems. In 2007, Al Gore was awarded the Nobel Peace Prize for his environmental efforts. A modern-day muckraker, Erin Brockovich, was in the news, and there was an award-winning movie about her investigative work on exposing health-endangering pollution in a small town in California.

This was a decade of affluence, expansion, and low unemployment. The stock market rose steadily, hitting century highs near the end of the decade. The Dow Jones Industrial Average of 30 major American companies hit a twentieth-century high when it closed at 10,000 in 1999. At the same time there were a number of books, magazines, television shows, and writers advocating a simpler, less materialistic life. A book entitled *Affluenza* and public television documentaries *Affluenza* and *Escape from Affluenza* recommended that people go hiking, spend time with their families, or volunteer rather than go to the mall. Although not everyone chose to scale down their consumption, some did, and there was a nationwide switch to more recycling. Schoolchildren were encouraged to participate. It became the American way in this decade and into the twenty-first century.

Holders of wealth changed greatly in the 1990s. By the time Sam Walton, founder of Wal-Mart, died in 1990, he was the richest man in the United States, but within a few years the richest man in the world (not just in the United States) was Bill Gates, founder of Microsoft. The consumption story of the 1990s cannot be told without a nod to computers and the Internet, the growth of email and online buying, and the trend toward working and shopping at home. Few consumer goods have become obsolete so fast: The "286" processor was replaced by the "386," then the "486," and then the Pentium in 1993, advancing to the Pentium IV and an operating system introduced by Microsoft called Windows XP—the list goes on. To meet demand, office-supply, computer, and electronic stores grew. As an alternative, consumers could buy computers online, customizing the system they wanted and getting home delivery.

To stay competitive, by the late 1990s most leading store chains, including department stores and gift shops, offered both **bricks and clicks**, meaning a physical store and an online store. More recently, retailers or marketers would use the terms **online shopping** and/or **offline shopping**. The Mall of America opened in suburban Minneapolis in 1993, showing that entertainment, tourism, leisure, and shopping could all happen underneath one roof; it sports two indoor lakes and an amusement park. Across the country, old malls were closing, there was a partial return to free-standing stores, grocery stores had their own delis and bakeries, and there were more superstores open 24 hours a day. Large mass-market and department stores regrouped; others (such as Kmart) filed for bankruptcy and closed many of their stores. This trend continued into early 2000, with other store chains cutting down on the number of their stores, such as Sears in 2014 announcing the closing of 70 of their stores.

The Twenty-First Century

The twenty-first century brought a new dawn of successes, growth, recessions, tragedies, and disasters. A recession (defined as a temporary downturn in the economy) and various ups and downs occurred. Unemployment reached 6.1 percent in June 2003 and dropped to around 4.5 percent in 2007 and rose up again in 2009. The depth of the recession was reached in 2009. The recession affected the types of jobs that college grads could readily get, so many added greatly to their student loans as college tuition increased significantly. A study released by Collegiate Funding Services found that more than 30 percent of college graduates said they had to take a job other than the one they really wanted in order to pay off their loans, whereas a year earlier the percentage was 20 percent (Kim, 2003). The average debt ranged from $10,000 to $40,000, with some students reporting being over $120,000 in debt in 2015, particularly students attending private colleges and those going on to graduate school, medical school, or law school. Discussions took place from President Obama and the Congress on down to the family level about what should be done about student loan debt.

In 2000, the 66-year-old consumer activist Ralph Nader ran as the presidential candidate of the Green Party, garnering about 3 percent of the vote. To learn more about his views on politics, read his book *Crashing the Party: How to Tell the Truth and Still Run for President* (2002). A theme running throughout is that both major political parties "routinely savage the interests of the American people by ignoring such fundamental concerns as corporate control, environmental pollution and the widening gap between rich and poor" (Nader, 2002, p. A12). He ran again in 2004 and in 2014, now in his 80s, said he would not run for presidential office again.

As of the writing of this chapter, it was too soon to give a full report on the legacy of consumer protection legislation under Barack Obama, the forty-fourth president.

Photo 2.11 President Barack Obama speaks at the Rutgers University-Newark S. I. Newhouse Center for Law and Justice on November 2, 2015, in Newark, New Jersey

Source: Getty Images: Andrew Burton

What stands out the most during his initial years in office is the Affordable Care Act (nicknamed by some "Obamacare"), which provided broader access to underserved populations to affordable health care. During the previous administration of George W. Bush, much of his attention was drawn to the war on terrorism, the war in Iraq, and related security issues. The USA PATRIOT Act of 2001 required every bank to adopt a customer identification program as part of its compliance with the Bank Secrecy Act. His early years as president were marked by business scandals about financial mismanagement and improper reporting of funds. Corporate responsibility to employees and stockholders was questioned, as well as the adequacy of outside auditing procedures, and in response, the Securities and Exchange Commission strengthened rules about reporting procedures and increased investigations.

During the George W. Bush administration, there were waves of mergers and turnovers in economic advisors. His Council of Economic Advisors noted that merger activity was well above average levels and had been growing for several decades. Mergers escalated for several reasons:

- Antitrust legislation was less enforced.
- Deregulation spread.
- Large companies benefited from mergers.
- A weakened economy made smaller companies more vulnerable and willing to sell.

Here are some examples of mergers taken from a February 25, 2002, article titled "Why the Sudden Rise in the Urge to Merge and Form Oligopolies?":

> Twenty years ago, cable television was dominated by a patchwork of thousands of tiny, family-operated companies. Today, a pending deal would leave three companies in control of nearly two-thirds of the market. In 1990, three big publishers of college textbooks accounted for 35% of industry sales. Today they have 62%. . . . In 1996, when Congress deregulated telecommunications, there were eight Baby Bells, today there are four, and dozens of small rivals are dead. (Wall Street Journal, p. A1)

The proliferation of cell phones and fraud related with them led to the 2006 Consumer Telephone Records Act, which prohibited the sale of consumer cell phone records. Privacy issues regarding the use and tracking of smart phones escalated.

The growth of the Internet as an information and selling source is a hallmark of the twenty-first century. Evidence of this was apparent in the passage of international legislation and the signing of treaties between countries regarding legalities and the Internet. The globalization of the economy continued with the spread of factories and sales.

Conclusion of the Decades of Consumerism

The more recent legislation and issues discussed in this chapter may ring a bell. Perhaps you heard about them on television or learned about them in school or through the Internet. Most of you probably do not remember a time when seat belts were not required or when food labels were not as extensive as they are today, nor do you remember presidents much before Presidents Clinton and George W. Bush. To avoid fatiguing the reader, the chapter ends at this point with the intention of exploring the most current legislation and related issues further in upcoming chapters. It should also be noted that for brevity's sake not all persons and organizations that contributed to consumer protection are mentioned. The consumer movement, much as the Internet, is borderless, free-ranging, and growing. Health and food crises continue, with outbreaks of infectious diseases such as Ebola to illnesses derived from contaminated spinach, peanut butter, and pet food. It gets to the point where people ask, "What next?" One of the values of studying the history of the consumer movement is to increase awareness of past crises and to learn how regulation helps prevent future outbreaks. When food crises occur, food regulation and inspection and places like the Center for Disease Control (CDC) come to the forefront.

Crises such as threats to our health draw attention to faulty products, inspections, health systems, or services that need correcting. The range of problems includes everything from faulty tires to improper food processing. The FDA has been enormously important in testing foods and seizing misbranded food (such as blueberry pancake mixes with no blueberries in them), with many of these seizures being well publicized. We become aware of crises or misrepresentations through the news and the Internet. In the past, newspaper articles and books written by muckrakers rallied support for product or financial reform. Sometimes, reform has arisen out of invention or a natural evolution of things—new scientific discoveries disclose new ills, or inventions such as computers or credit cards require new rules for handling their potential abuse.

This chapter focused on consumer rights and legislation, but this is only one side of the coin. Chapter 4 explores consumer responsibilities. The government cannot be everywhere, so how do consumers look out for themselves? What is their responsibility in the marketplace?

Summary

Economic theory advances with the principle known as the law of comparative advantage in the nineteenth century. Production exploded in the US and in other developing and expanding countries. By the twentieth and twenty-first centuries affluence continued. But with affluence came abuses in the marketplace that necessitated more consumer protection. The twenty-first century began with a rocky start as the national and worldwide economy experienced a slowdown, and a series of corporate scandals led to a loss of faith in the dependability of business standards and practices. Through it all, the consumer movement has been active. In the United States, the modern consumer movement can be traced from the 1880s. The earliest concerns were about food quality, but over time many more product areas came under scrutiny, including medicine, cosmetics, toys, and broader social, technological, and financial concerns. The consumer movement embraced the environmental movement, and they are so coupled today that it is difficult to separate them. The late 1960s and early 1970s and 2000s were spiked with environmental concerns spurred by well-publicized oil spills or leaks that wrecked coastlines and killed wildlife. Ever present are concerns about food and health safety.

Certain decades produced more consumer protection legislation than others; particularly active decades were the 1930s and the 1960s through the 1980s. Presidents from both the Republican and Democratic parties have provided leadership in consumer protection. Senators, scientists, writers, corporate employees, and organizations have stirred the public interest by bringing to light shoddy and questionable practices and products. Ralph Nader and other consumer activists provided leadership and put the spotlight on food, environmental, and car problems. Some may question whether the phrase "consumer movement" is the best term since it is no longer an ideological movement because consumerism is a regular part of our everyday experience. If a product breaks or causes injury, we expect remedy or justice—consumer protection is a given in our daily lives. We rely on regulations to facilitate our reasoned choice and, in particular, to protect the young, elderly, and defenseless from unscrupulous practices.

Consumer protection needs arise in response to:

- new technological developments (an example would be cybersquatting)
- changing conceptions of the social responsibilities of consumers, businesses, and nations
- exposés of the dishonest, greedy, and selfish fringe that break the rules and take advantage.

In conclusion, as long as there are consumers, there will be a need for consumer protection.

KEY POINTS

1. From 1776—the year of the publication of Adam Smith's book—to the present, there has been a growing trend of consumer reliance on business to provide goods. With the decrease in self-production of goods comes the necessity to rely on business or government to ensure quality and safety.

2. In the early nineteenth century, English economist David Ricardo developed the law of comparative advantage about trade, producing cheaply (efficiently), and exchange.

3. Abuses in the marketplace lead to the need for consumer protection legislation.

4. The consumer movement refers to policies aimed at providing regulations and standards.

5. Harvey Wiley, chemist, is the founder of the consumer movement, and some would say the founder of the FDA. He is famous for his Poison Squad experiments on the effects of food additives.

6. Food reformers were most concerned about fraud and poison.

7. World War II brought shortages and rationing. Consumer legislation took a backseat to concerns about obtaining goods. Immediately after the war, increased production for houses, household goods, and cars became paramount.

8. Rachel Carson, biologist and author of *Silent Spring*, is the founder of the modern environmental movement.

9. Muckrakers such as Upton Sinclair, author of *The Jungle*, led to reforms in meat processing, and others such as Ralph Nader, author of *Unsafe at Any Speed*, led to reforms in car safety.

10. Two economists—John Maynard Keynes and John Kenneth Galbraith—and their contributions were introduced in this chapter. Keynes, whose book *The General Theory of Employment, Interest, and Money* was important during the Depression, made the case for more government intervention. Galbraith, author of many books including *The Affluent Society*, served in various government roles during World War II; later, as an advisor to John F. Kennedy and ambassador to India, he influenced public policy and promoted public service.

11. Several presidents were key figures in influencing consumer legislation. Particularly noteworthy is John F. Kennedy, who, in his Consumer Message to Congress, outlined the four basic principles of consumer protection—the rights to be safe, to be heard, to choose, and to have information.

12. Consumer legislation is necessary and well intentioned. However, loopholes nearly always exist, and the acts or rules do not cover everything. For example, the 1973 FTC Door-to-Door Sales Rule only allows a consumer to cancel a few types of contracts within three days. In all cases, caveat emptor (meaning "May the buyer beware") holds true.

KEY TERMS

antitrust laws	cybersquatting	law of comparative advantage
bricks and clicks	depression	muckraker
cease-and-desist order	desirable products and services	offline shopping
common law	environmentalism	online shopping
conspicuous consumption	hedonic value	pollution
consumer movement	hucksterism	rational self-interest

DISCUSSION QUESTIONS

1. If President John F. Kennedy was alive today, would he be pleased with the state of consumer protection in this country? List his four consumer rights, and give a current example of each from your own life or from a friend's or relative's experience.

2. After reading the excerpt from *The Jungle*, do you think reforms were necessary in the meat-processing industry in 1906? Explain your answer. What was President Theodore Roosevelt's role in meat-processing reforms?

3. It isn't easy being a reformer. Who did not support the work of food safety reformer Harvey Wiley?

4. Select one of the e-resource websites listed next. What did you find on the site?

E-RESOURCES

Consumers Union
www.ConsumerReports.org

Consumers Union, the publisher of *Consumer Reports,* is a nonprofit organization chartered in 1936 that provides information on consumer goods such as toothpaste, toys, toasters, and cars and conducts tests.

Center for Science in the Public Interest
www.cspinet.org

A nonprofit membership organization that conducts research, education, and advocacy on food safety, nutrition, health, and related issues.

FDA History Office
http://www.fda.gov/oc/history/resourceguide/. office.html

The office provides information about its evolution, function, the oral history program, the museum collection, and the staff.

Federal Trade Commission
www.ftc.gov and www.consumer.gov

This government commission offers consumer information on many subjects, including labeling, advertisements, and monopolies.

North American Free Trade Agreement (NAFTA)
www.mac.doc.gov/nafta/

Issues and information are given on this website, which is of use to exporters, public policy experts, and economists.

Consumer WebWatch
www.consumerweb watch.org

A Consumers Union site, it helps make websites more accountable for accuracy and provides research results and news alerts for consumers.

REFERENCES

Aaker, D., and G. Day. (1982). *Consumerism: search for the consumer interest,* 4th ed. New York: Free Press.

Barber, B. R. (2007). *Consumed.* New York: Norton.

Carson, R. (1962). *Silent spring.* Boston: Houghton Mifflin.

Chase, S., and F. Schlink. (1928). *Your money's worth.* New York: Macmillan.

Cross, G. (2000). *An all-consuming century: why commercialism won in modern America.* New York: Columbia University Press.

Crossen, C. (December 28, 2001). Etiquette for Americans today. *Wall Street Journal,* p. W13.

Crossen, C. (December 18, 2002). In wartime holidays of the past, patriots curbed their spending. *Wall Street Journal,* p. B1.

Cude, B. (1993). Consumer perceptions of environmental marketing claims: an exploratory study. *Journal of Consumer Studies and Home Economics,* 12, 207–225.

Downs, R. B. (January 1963, 4th ed.). Afterword in Upton Sinclair's *The Jungle.* New York: New American Library, 343–350.

Erlich, P. (1968). *The population bomb.* New York: Ballantine Books.

Frederick, C. (1914). *The new housekeeping: efficiency studies in home management.* New York: Doubleday.

Fussman, C. (January 2002). Interview with John Kenneth Galbraith. *Esquire,* p. 60.

Galbraith, J. (1958). *The affluent society.* Boston: Houghton Mifflin.

Goldsmith, E. B., and S. Piscopo. (2013). Advances in consumer education: European initiatives. *International Journal of Consumer Studies,* 38 (1), 52–61.

Gore, A. (1992). *Earth in the balance.* New York: Penguin Books.

Gwartney, J., Stroup, R., Sobel, R., and Macpherson, D. (2003). *Economics: private and public choice,* 10th edition, Mason, OH: Thomson/South-Western.

Harris, D. (2000). *Cute, quaint, hungry and romantic: the aesthetics of consumerism.* New York: Basic Books.

Heilbroner, R., and L. Thurow. (1998). *Economics explained.* New York: Simon and Schuster.

Josephson, M. (1962). *The robber barons.* New York: Harcourt, Brace & World.

Kallet, A., and F. Schlink. (1933). *100,000,000 guinea pigs.* New York: Grosset & Dunlap.

Keynes, J. (1936). *The general theory of employment, interest, and money.* London: Macmillan.

Kim, J. (September 2, 2003). More college graduates postpone their "dream jobs" to pay loans. *Wall Street Journal,* p. C1.

Lewis, C. (November–December 2002). The "poison squad" and the advent of food and drug regulation. *FDA Consumer,* 36 (6), 12–15.

Lyon, P., A. Colquhoun, and D. Kinney. (2004). UK food shopping in the 1950s: the social context of customer loyalty. *International Journal of Consumer Studies,* 28 (1), 28–39.

Magnuson, W., and J. Carper. (1968). *The dark side of the marketplace.* New York: Prentice Hall.

Margolius, S. (1982). The consumer's real needs. In *Consumerism: search for the consumer interest,* 4th ed., David A. Aaker and George S. Day. New York: Free Press, 48–56.

Nader, R. (1965). *Unsafe at any speed.* New York: Pocket Books.

Nader, R. (2002). *Crashing the party: how to tell the truth and still run for president.* New York: Thomas Dunne Books.

Nordic Council of Ministers (2009). Teaching consumer competences: a strategy for consumer education. Proposals of objectives and content strategy for consumer education, Nordic Council of Ministers, Copenhagen (accessed on December 20, 2012).

Packard, V. (1957). *The hidden persuaders.* New York: Pocket Books.

Schlereth, T. (1991). *Victorian America: transformations in everyday life 1876–1915.* New York: HarperCollins.

Sinclair, U. (1905). *The jungle.* New York: New American Library of World Literature.

Smith, A. (1776). *An inquiry into the nature and causes of the wealth of nations,* as edited by Robert Heilbroner (1986) in *The essential Adam Smith.* New York: Norton.

Strasser, S. (1989). *Satisfaction guaranteed.* New York: Random House.

Tedlow, R. (1990). *New and improved: the story of mass marketing in America.* New York: Basic Books.

Why the sudden rise in the urge to merge and form oligopolies? (February 25, 2002). *Wall Street Journal,* p. A1.

Chapter **3**

Consumer Theories and Models

If we do discover a complete theory, it should in time be understandable in broad principle by everyone, not just a few scientists.

Stephen Hawking

LEARNING OBJECTIVES

1. Explain different theories and models and their relevance to the study of consumer economics.
2. Describe the components of the Consumer Power Model of Consumer Economics.
3. Explain factors that affect the model.
4. Explain how consumer well-being is defined and measured, including consumer confidence.
5. Describe the basic functions of business and the nature of entrepreneurship.

Rationality Involved in Buying a Laptop

The following question was put to Daniel Ariely, the *Wall Street Journal* columnist and Duke University psychology professor:

> "Dear Dan, I'm about to buy a new laptop—definitely a larger-than-usual purchase for me. I've found that when the base item is expensive, I'm much more likely to indulge in complementary ones, such as a new laptop case or software that I don't really need but would be fun to play with. Why is it that I think twice about buying good beer on a night out but have no problem spending another $60 on a computer mouse I don't need?—Andrew"

Dan's answer:

> "Here's another example to help think through your question. Imagine that you're going to buy a new car for $30,000 and the salesperson tells you that you can get leather seats for $2,000 more. How expensive would those luxury seats seem to you? How likely would you be to go for the upgrade? Now imagine instead of going to buy a car, you're buying a new chair for your home office, at a cost of $500—and the furniture store tells you that you can get the chair in leather for $2,000 more. How likely would you be to go for it? Most people would feel much better about the car upgrade than the chair upgrade. That's because we think about money in relative terms: Relative to $30,000, that $2,000 doesn't look that bad, but the same amount feels outrageous relative to $500."

> Source: Dan Ariely (October 2–26, 2014). "Ask Ariely.
> He Knew He Was Right." *Wall Street Journal*, p. C12.

Introduction

We learned in the first chapter that the founder of modern economics, Adam Smith, believed that "to be human is to exchange freely." That idea—of humans wanting the freedom to exchange unrestricted by outside forces—is a theory that Adam Smith espoused. He believed in an orderly, progressive, and harmonious commercial society. We learned about rational self-interest in Chapter 2, and the introductory case study in this current chapter speaks to the concept of rationality in consumer purchasing.

Economists generally agree that consumers have **rationality** (the ability to reason) and **acquisitiveness** (a strong desire for things, ideas, and information). In today's world, many economists follow the teachings of Adam Smith (summarized as faith in the market), while others believe, as did John Maynard Keynes, that the more complicated world we live in necessitates more government intervention and regulation. Most agree that ideally there is some balance between the two main theorists and theories.

Recent developments in economic theory and research have questioned the nature of rationality. For example, the 2002 Nobel Prize in economics went to Daniel Kahneman and Amos Tversky, who published an article highlighting the irrational nature of people when it comes to consumption. They represent a growing area of economics called **behavioral economics** or **behavioral finance** or **neuroeconomics**, which is "pushing the frontiers of research by introducing psychologically realistic models of economic agents into economic theory" (Robinson-Brown, 2002, p. 1). Their particular contributions about judgment, attitudes, and decision making are discussed in this chapter. Economics is about studying choices and decisions. Neuroeconomics is a subset focusing on personal choices (versus those of firms and institutions) and the mental changes that affect choice selection, and it confirms that emotions are important factors in selection (Glimcher, 2003). It extends the beginning theories on choice by adding observations of the nervous system so that, for example, full brain scans or other such measures may be performed to understand economic decision making (usually some recording mechanism is involved).

Regarding the acquisitive nature of human behavior, Harvard University Professor Juliet Schor (1998) wrote that what we acquire is tightly bound to our identity. Theories such as these form the bulk of this chapter, which explores the nature of theories and their roles in consumption. The chapter ends with discussions of consumer well-being, including measures of consumer confidence.

Theory, Exchange Process, and Utility

Theories are useful for guiding research and explaining consumer behavior. A fundamental consumer theory backed by research is that past purchasing behavior is a strong predictor of future purchasing behavior.

A **theory** is an organized system of ideas or beliefs that can be measured. Theories are essentially systems of principles or assumptions, and because of the measurement aspect, theories are useful in guiding research and explaining behavior. A research project may start with questions or hypotheses that are predictions of future occurrences; for example, a researcher might predict that if a consumer has bought Tide detergent for the last ten years, he or she will likely continue to do so. In consumer research it has been proven many times over that past behavior is a strong predictor of future behavior. Knowing this, many companies work hard at building brand loyalty in young people. As an example, consider the number of credit cards that have been offered to you during your college years. Even though you may not have much money now, the credit card companies know that you will soon and that you are unlikely to change credit cards once you graduate.

In the following pages, we explore various theories about how people plan, decide, buy, and exchange goods given scarce resources. Several theories exist because many factors or groups impact different kinds of consumers, and as time goes on, new theories are formulated to describe behavior. Consumers come in all shapes, sizes, ages, nationalities, income levels, and so forth, although discernible patterns and statistics are useful in determining these groupings. For example, in the United States, women account for about 80 percent of consumer spending (Allon, 2001). That makes gender a factor in consumption behavior. A specific example of this is that in the United States most women use body wash, but only 45 percent of men use body wash and "most are using women's products and half are using them secretly. Their partners typically do not know that they're using it" (Neff, 2002, p. 8). Hoping to change this behavior and directly market to men, Procter & Gamble Co. launched Old Spice High Endurance body wash in January 2003 and marketed it to men. This is called a **brand extension** because Old Spice already comes in aftershave, antiperspirant, and deodorant. Note also the words "high endurance," which sounds masculine rather than feminine.

Since consumer economics can be described most simply as the study of exchange activities, it is important to define what this encompasses. The **exchange process** occurs when people (as individuals, family members, employees, members of religious groups, etc.) negotiate with a goal of reaching an agreement, such as an agreed-on price or date of delivery. When the exchange is fulfilled, it is called a **transaction**. A successful transaction will result in more exchange involving the same consumers and businesses.

CRITICAL THINKING

Give-and-Take Principle

React to this quote by Mark Twain, American novelist and humorist. He said, "Every man is a suffering-machine and a happiness-machine combined. The two functions work together harmoniously with a fine and delicate precision, on the give-and-take principle."

Source: Mark Twain (1908). *The Mysterious Stranger.*

Another useful consideration in consumer economics is the concept of **utility**, which generally refers to the usefulness of a product, service, or idea. In economics, **diminishing marginal utility** means that in a given time period, a consumer will receive less satisfaction from each successive unit (such as a food item) consumed; for example, a second piece of chocolate cake is less satisfying than the first.

In summary, consumer economics and behavior are affected by many variables. To make the study of these variables more organized, this chapter will incorporate theories and models, and they serve as guides to explaining consumers' choices and the influences on their behavior.

Theory of Reasoned Action

Although consumers are generally considered to be rational (as explained in the Introduction), here is more evidence of irrationality. Consider this example from the past:

> In the late 19th century, teacher-turned-snake-oil-seller Lydia E. Pinkham used her image and signature to help sell her eponymous vegetable compound as a cure-all for faintness, flatulence, depression and other "female" complaints. While her product may have been suspect—a main ingredient was alcohol—her marketing strategy was sound. Ads that appeared in newspapers and on barns were so persuasive that women wrote her detailing their aches and pains. They always received a letter back signed by Lydia—even long after the lady died, thanks to those who kept the company going. (Well, 2001, p. 124)

Was it rational for women to think of Lydia Pinkham, a person they never met, as a friend? Do women think of modern-day media moguls Oprah Winfrey, Rachel Ray, Suze Orman, and Martha Stewart as friends? Do their companies promote these relationships much as Lydia Pinkham's did? This connection between attitudes, social relationships, and consumer behavior has been explored by several theorists. Probably the most commonly cited theory of this kind is the **theory of reasoned action** developed by Martin Fishbein and Icek Ajzen (Ajzen & Fishbein, 1980). Their theory states that behavioral intentions are based on a combination of the attitude toward a specific behavior, the social or normative beliefs about the appropriateness of the behavior, and the motivation to comply with the normative beliefs (Sheppard, Hartwick, & Warshaw, 1988). In the theory of reasoned action, what is important is the consumer's attitude toward behaving a certain way and the consumer's subjective norm, which is his or her belief about others' evaluations of his or her actions.

Regarding this second point, what the consumer believes to be a rational or reasonable purchase or course of action may or may not be shared by his or her family, coworkers, or friends. For example, if a 55-year-old bald man buys a red sports car, he may or may not wonder what others think. If he senses disapproval (for example, he is perceived as having a midlife crisis), he may select another color or a pickup truck instead. This middle-aged man is not alone. "Many of us are continually comparing our own lifestyle and possessions to those of a select group of people we respect and want to be like, people whose sense of what's important in life seems close to our own" (Schor, 1998, p. 3). The theory of reasoned action shows that consumption is based on beliefs and attitudes, that it has consequences, and that it takes place within a social context.

Prospect Theory and Theory of Mental Accounting

As mentioned in the Introduction, economists for the most part follow a central tenet that people are logical with their money and that the market operates sensibly. The problem is that when the stock market reverses and companies go bankrupt, economists and others wonder how sensible the market really is. It appears to be capable of irrational behavior, and the corollary to this is that consumers also act in illogical ways. When people do not have all the answers or ways of systematically approaching decisions, it does not stop them; they proceed and do what they can. In other words, they do not let uncertainty get in the way of making decisions.

In 1979, an American psychologist named Daniel Kahneman (noted for his pioneering work in behavioral finance) and Amos Tversky (who died in 1996) published "Prospect Theory: An Analysis of Decision Under Risk" in *Econometrica*, a journal of economics. In this article, "[they] argued that people's degree of pleasure (their 'utility' in social science-ese) is more dependent on the change in their condition than on the absolute level. In other words, a rich man who loses $10 is apt to feel bad, whereas a poor man who wins $100 is apt to feel rich. This concept broke ground with classical economics, which held that rich always feels better than poor" (Lowenstein, 2003, p. 42). This was called **prospect theory**. It is an economic theory that explains choice under uncertainty and led to the idea of loss aversion. This idea holds that people feel more pain from loss than pleasure from profit. This explains why people hold on to stocks that are performing poorly (they are doing so to avoid pain even if they can afford the loss), although it would probably be more rational to sell the stocks and put the money into a better-performing investment. Prospect theory describes decision-making processes

Photo 3.1 Lydia Pinkham's Vegetable Compound. Marketed to women, the compound had alcohol as its main ingredient

Source: flickr: Courtesy of the Boston Public Library

and includes the steps of editing and evaluating: We are exposed to countless advertising pitches a day that we have to edit and evaluate, we subjectively frame messages, and we determine the utility we expect to receive from our decisions.

An outgrowth of prospect theory is the impact of **message framing**. For example, an advertising or marketing campaign may indicate you will be happy if you buy this product or sad if you do not. Think of all the advertisements that use these approaches. Consider the saying "At these prices, run in before everything is gone." This is an example of a *negatively framed message* since it says you will be sorry if you pass up this deal. *Positively framed messages* let consumers know the benefits to be gained from the purchase: "You will smell better and have more friends if you use this deodorant." Both types of messages are about purchasing behavior, and the messages connect risk or negative consequences if consumers do not act. Initially it appears that negative framing of a choice has more impact than positive framing, but a warning or negative message can act as a boomerang by making the risky behavior more attractive. This is referred to as **reactance**. A warning sign posted outside a rollercoaster ride might stimulate more desire to experience it than if there was no sign at all. Likewise, a group of golfers might be stimulated to hit their balls harder if they see a sign posted at a swampy area on the course that says "Beware of snakes and alligators"; in other words, they need to hit their balls over this swampy area or they will lose them. Playing this risky hole may be more challenging to them than hitting in an open fairway or chipping up to a pretty azalea-lined green.

In regard to Kahneman's contribution, his department chairman, Gene Grossman, said, "He's challenged the basic model of how individuals behave economically. The standard model is that everybody is rational, self-interested, calculating; he's suggested that more psychological motives determine people's behavior and that these motives are important for economic phenomena . . . I think there is now a broader range of thinking about certain issues, especially savings behavior and participation in the stock market" (Robinson-Brown, 2002, p. 2).

Kahneman and Tversky were collaborators with Richard Thaler. Thaler, who teaches at the University of Chicago, studied with Kahneman (a Princeton professor who teaches Psychology 101 and has never taken or taught a course in economics) and came up with the **endowment effect**. In experiments, Thaler found that "[s]ubjects who have been given a present—they used a coffee mug—will demand a higher price to sell it than people who don't have the mug would be willing to pay for one" (Lowenstein, 2003, p. 42). This finding contradicts the widely held classical economist view that in a free market, one price fits all. Again, human behavior (in this case, a sense of ownership) affects what people set as an appropriate price. Thaler took this a step further and developed the **theory of mental accounting** in which people frame or put into context their buying and selling: "[P]eople who obsess over saving $5 on groceries will happily blow $1,000 on a vacation because they account for it differently" (Lowenstein,

2003, p. 42). They are, therefore, uneven in their response to money. Thaler, other economists, and family and consumer economists around the country are exploring other dimensions of saving and spending behavior through surveys and experiments.

Innovation Theory

Innovators or early adopters of new products and services are of interest to consumer economists and marketers. Research surrounds certain questions:

- Who are these first people to buy?
- Why do they do it?
- Does the trend toward buying first affect all product categories, or is it product-specific?

Innovators are the earliest buyers of new brands, services, products, and store or other market offerings, and they like new ideas and technologies as well. They are attracted to grand openings of stores, advertisements of new products, door prizes, and excitement. Does this describe you or someone you know? The theoretical background for this phenomenon was provided by E. M. Rogers, author of *Diffusion of Innovations*:

> He defined a process through which an individual . . . passes (1) from first knowledge of an innovation, (2) to forming an attitude toward the innovation, (3) to a decision to adopt or reject, (4) to implementation of the new idea, and (5) to confirmation of this decision. (1995, p. 161)

An innovative consumer is highly involved and wants to know what is happening. He or she may be an avid reader or follower of the news or may talk with friends about new products and services. Online consumer communities are central to creating and spreading the buzz. As mentioned in the Introduction, economists believe that people are acquisitive—they need to know what is going on in the marketplace and to acquire (or at least to think about or look at) new things such as cars, houses, or electronic items (digital cameras, flat-screen televisions). Rogers posited that there is a theme in consumer behavior of adoption and diffusion of innovations.

What is curious about innovation adoption is that a person can be an innovator in one category, such as wearing the latest fashions, but a laggard in another category, such as going to see the latest movies. This makes sense because it would be very expensive, time-consuming, and exhausting to be an innovator in all areas of consumption, so people make choices about where to put their time, effort, and money. Many choose to ignore the latest ideas or products altogether and prefer the tried-and-true. One thinks of the expression, "If it ain't broke, don't fix it." One example involves a nutrition professor who has a 1980s Amana microwave oven in her home kitchen; the oven is huge, and family and friends kid her about it, but it still works, she is used to it, and she sees no reason to change.

There are behavioral self-control issues as well. Innovators can be nonconformists since they don't follow the crowd, they lead the crowd. A form of not following the crowd or an authority is that people do not always follow doctor's orders (Makarem, Smith, Mudambi, & Hunt, 2014). Innovators tend to be highly self-directed and independent risk-takers. An innovator is more likely to take risks (for example, on a new product or idea) and be more venturesome than later buyers.

If marketers can find the innovators in a particular product class, promotion and distribution should be directed to them first. Marketing researchers would want to know what magazines and newsletters innovators read, what clubs they belong to, what sporting events or arts events they attend, and so on. Innovators are drawn to grand openings. Generally, innovators are more upwardly mobile and less price-sensitive than later adopters.

A product class that attracts innovators is computers and computing services. A public relations approach could involve announcements, advertising, and direct marketing, such as holding a launch party for magazine editors or hosting exhibit booths at conventions to display new wares. More subtle approaches include such things as sponsoring community or cultural events or sports teams, contributing to high school yearbooks, and buying tickets to charity events. The parties or events may involve gift bags with the new product or a discount coupon on its purchase.

An innovation may be new to one social or cultural group or country, whereas it may not be perceived as new by another. It can be said that the innovation diffuses, or moves through, a social system over time—some pick it up early, some pick it up late, and the vast majority fall somewhere in between. People in the middle are interested in what is new but are wary of things that are brand new. They may think that if they wait, the kinks will be worked out of the new product (such as a car model) or that the price will come down. Rogers developed a bell-shaped curve to illustrate the rate at which new products, services, or ideas are typically adopted. At the beginning is 2.5 percent of the population, designated as the innovators. They are followed by 13.5 percent, who are the early adopters; 34 percent, who are the early majority; 34 percent, who are called the late majority; and ending with the last group to adopt, who are called the laggards and are estimated as 16 percent of the population. The nutrition professor with the old microwave oven would be a laggard.

Scientific Method

At this juncture, it would be useful to describe the scientific method that consumer researchers follow (as do biologists and chemists). Following are the five steps in the scientific method:

1. Describe what is happening (recognize the problem or opportunity).

2. Explain why it is happening (make assumptions).

3. Develop a model.

4. Predict what will happen in the future.

5. Control, check, or test what is happening.

The problem may be "I need shoes." The opportunity may be "I need new shoes even though I already own 30 pairs." Assumptions are commonly held beliefs or statements that are accepted as true without proof. Someone may assume that the new pair of shoes will give more wear, satisfaction, and status than the shoes already owned. He or she may predict or imagine what will happen when wearing the shoes, what compliments will be received, what outfits the shoes will go with, and so on.

In step five of the scientific method, the word *control* refers to the things people do to check their course of action or to test what they have purchased. Checking, tests, or trials are used to determine whether a theory is consistent with the facts or the outcomes. For example, if someone theorized that saving money was better than spending it, he or she could set up an automatic deduction of $50 from his or her paycheck that goes directly into a savings account. The control aspect would be checking on how the savings account is building. Did it bring the desired effect? Did the person feel too limited by having the $50 deducted from each paycheck? When individuals make purchase or financial decisions, they are trying to predict what will happen (how much pleasure or pain they will derive from the decision); on the basis of that analysis, they change or alter their behavior accordingly.

Some of us are more visual learners than others and enjoy things being drawn or demonstrated. An example in a work setting would be seeing a flow chart of the officers' or administrators' names and titles. With drawings, plans, and charts, one can instantly visualize relationships. **Models** are representations or schematics or illustrations of relationships. They take abstractions from the real world and allow us to visualize the connections between ideas or between people or institutions. A common model is a blueprint, which is a flat drawing of a house. Another way to visualize the building of a new house or the remodeling of an existing home is to use computer simulations of floorplans and elevations. In the next section of the chapter, frameworks (which are outlines or connections of ideas) are discussed first, followed by more theories and models. In the course of this discussion, a new consumer model is proposed and illustrated.

Basic Framework for Model Development

Exchanges

Consumer economics involves processes of exchange between two or more parties. The process occurs when parties negotiate (this can be verbal or nonverbal) and reach an

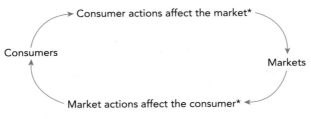

Figure 3.1 Exchange Process between Consumers and Markets

agreement. The fulfillment of the exchange process is called a transaction (as mentioned earlier) and is illustrated in Figure 3.1.

An everyday example of this is when a person goes to the grocery store to buy a gallon of milk and then pays for it—the exchange is completed. This is what happens on the surface, but the exchange process is not really that simple. Behind the scenes, there are many forces and parties. The cows produce milk, and the farmers and suppliers get the milk to market; then come the regulators, grocers, marketers, and promoters. Public policy may also be involved in the form of taxes, farm subsidies, exports, or regulations so that prices or supplies are affected. A government agency may reinforce the rules that regulate product dating, and the stores will have to stamp the appropriate pull date on the milk. Government inspectors make sure this is done correctly and consistently.

Other relationships are also formed in exchanges, such as market-to-market transactions (businesses selling to each other) and consumer-to-consumer transactions (such as people buying and selling at yard sales or college students selling used textbooks to each other). Consumer-to-consumer relationships are often communicated by word of mouth or referral networks such as local newspapers or signs. Because this book is about consumer economics, the focus is on where and how the majority of consumer transactions take place, which is between consumers and markets.

While most consumer–market exchanges are satisfactory, meaning that both sides are satisfied, sometimes things go wrong, creating a **consumer–market conflict**. Getting an agreement or reconciling differences may be difficult. Here is where public policy steps in: It anticipates potential areas of conflict and deals with them before, during, and after they have happened, and as such it plays a very important role in the consumer–market exchange and deserves a place in our model (see Figure 3.2).

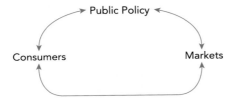

Figure 3.2 Consumer Exchange. This model shows the interaction between three fundamental components in the consumer exchange: consumer, public policy, and markets

Public Policy

Figure 3.2 shows a traditional view of the consumer–market exchange wherein public policy serves as a moderator or mediator. The role of public policy is to make sure the exchange is fair in terms of competition, labeling, access, advertising, and pricing. The arrows in the Figure 3.3 Consumer Power Model indicate relationships. As an example, the market (through for-profit and nonprofit organizations) may hire lobbyists to sway public policy in its favor, and this lobbying effort may lead to fewer restrictions on the organization, reduced taxes, or advertisements in new mediums.

Consumers want useful, safe, environmentally sound products at fair prices, and they also want selection. The next chapter will delve into specific consumer complaint categories and the government response through the Consumer Product Safety Commission, for example. This section provides an overview or introduction to **public policy**, which is a plan or decision by government to act in a certain way or go in a particular direction, such as to keep products safe, open up competition, eliminate poverty, allocate more money to medical research or the space program, or clean up the environment. This is in contrast to private matters or concerns, such as how an individual or family acts. Public policy makers exist at all levels, from the smallest town to the federal government, and they work in the executive, legislative, and judicial branches. Individuals and families get

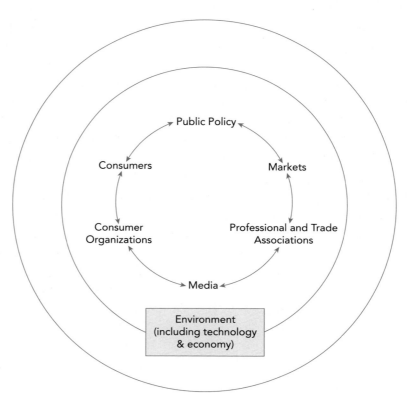

Figure 3.3
Consumer Power Model of
Consumer Economics

involved in public policy through an aspect of their consumer well-being referred to as political well-being, which is a reflection of each individual's internal sense of power and autonomy and of what is right and wrong. Freely making decisions, voting, and choosing products in the marketplace are part of political well-being.

Public policy responds to issues, problems, causes, and influences such as those of voters, activist citizens, consumer organizations, and lobbyists. At any given time, one set of constituents' goals may be in conflict with those of another set of constituents, or they may not agree or support proposed policies or actions. When conflicts occur, difficult decisions have to be made, usually in the interests of the greater good. Most public policy is designed to promote the general public interest but is influenced by politics and the support of certain individuals, groups, and organizations.

A common role of government is regulation. Through regulation, society allows a bureaucracy to promote certain public or community interests, causes, or goals. An ongoing debate is how much regulatory power government should have versus allowing the market to exist unhampered. In the final analysis, it comes down to a series of trade-offs involving decisions about both how much regulation is in the best interest of consumers and whether the costs involved in regulation are worth the money spent.

Consumer Organizations

Besides consumers, regulators, and markets, other groups of consumer organizations come into play and include the Consumers Union, the National Consumers League, and the American Association of Retired Persons (AARP) (see Box 3.1 for a sample list of organizations). As their names imply, consumer organizations may cover a wide range of interests or may specialize in one area such as senior citizens' concerns. They may push for the passage of legislation in the public interest, they may send staff members to testify before Congress, or they may hire lobbyists or support people to run for political office in order to sway public policy their way.

Consumer organizations assist, protect, and advocate for consumers.

The main mission they have in common is to assist and protect consumers and provide consumer advocacy. Most try to improve the health and safety of consumers and better their lives, including improving their financial health and promoting their fair treatment in the marketplace. In the model, they could be placed under consumers as a subgroup, but not all consumers support or appreciate the work of consumer advocacy groups. In many ways, they are a force in and of themselves, so they deserve their own spot in the model. An updated and revised model includes other influences and groups such as trade and professional associations, which are discussed next.

Box 3.1 Examples of National Consumer Organizations*

Alliance Against Fraud in Telemarketing and Electronic Commerce (AAFTEC)

American Association of Retired Persons (AARP) (Consumer Issues Section)

American Council on Consumer Interests (ACCI)

American Council on Science and Health

Center for Science in the Public Interest

Center for the Study of Services

Coalition against Insurance Fraud

Community Nutrition Institute

Consumer Action

Consumer Alert

Consumer Federation of America

Consumers for World Trade

Families USA Foundation

HALT: An Organization for Americans for Legal Reform

Health Research Group

Jump$tart Coalition for Personal Financial Literacy

National Association of Consumer Agency Administration

National Coalition for Consumer Education

National Community Reinvestment Coalition

National Consumer Law Center

National Consumers League

National Fraud Information Center/Internet Fraud Watch

National Institute for Consumer Education

Public Citizen, Inc.

Self Help for Hard of Hearing People (SHHH)

Society of Consumer Affairs Professionals in Business (SOCAP)

United Seniors Health Cooperative

US Public Interest Group (US PIRG)

*This is not a comprehensive list. More national organizations exist, and some come and go. Local, state, and international organizations also exist.

Trade and Professional Associations

Companies that manufacture similar products or offer similar services often belong to trade and professional associations that serve to resolve problems between consumers and member companies and that also provide consumer information and education through websites and publications. One example is the American Bankers Association (www.aba.com), which provides consumer education materials; another is the Food Marketing Institute (www.fmi.org), which conducts programs in research, education, industry relations, and public affairs on behalf of its members (grocery retailers and wholesalers). Both of these associations are located in Washington, DC, as are many others. They offer career opportunities for those trained both in consumer economics and in public policy. Since trade and professional associations are most associated with markets, they are placed under markets in the model being developed in this chapter.

Besides these organizations, more has been added to the model (shown in Figure 3.3), such as the influence or impact of the environment and technology on the economy. Both of these are discussed in the following sections.

Environment

CASE STUDY

Environment and College Students

Consumer organizations, including college activist groups specializing in protecting the environment, are exploring the varied dimensions of consumerism. Eco-reps are students encouraging eco-friendly lifestyles among their peers. About 40 colleges including Harvard University have eco-reps and more colleges are participating.

"One unseasonably warm morning in late October, the University of Vermont paid a group of students to do something kind of rowdy on the Burlington campus: spread 680 pounds of trash on the ground in front of the David Student Center for all to see and smell. The effort worked." Passersby demanded an explanation, and they got it along with a discussion of how two tons of food waste goes from the center to the landfill every week. When it comes to consumer issues, drama often works.

The goal of the eco-reps is to show students how to lessen their environmental footprint. Administrators like it because it saves them money and shows social awareness. Harvard University saved $170,000 yearly in electricity costs because of a five-year campus energy saving program. Sustainability is the name of the game. Can you give examples on your campus of energy saving or recycling programs? This is all about behavior change, and sometimes it happens in small steps. Peers tend to be more effective in bringing about change than higher-ups, hence the success of the eco-reps. "Students can't change out a boiler or negotiate an electricity contract or erect a large wind turbine," says Sarah Hammond Creighton of the Tuft's Office of Sustainability, "but they can turn their lights off."

Source: G. Jeffrey MacDonald (November 5, 2007). "Students Teach Students to Waste Less on Campus." *USA Today*, p. 4D.

Sometimes the word "environment," as in the case study, refers mostly to our physical environment and being green. It can be used this way in the Consumer Power Model, and it can refer to the space in which all transactions (trades) or potential transactions occur. Probably the best way to think of an environment is its all-encompassing external conditions. To give a specific example, a shopping mall is a consumer environment. An individual or family may window-shop or may actually buy a specific good, with pre-buying, buying, and postbuying all being part of the consumption process. Environments affect what is being offered and how well it is received, so attractive displays and pleasant music are important. Consumption, therefore, takes place in an environmental context. Think of sitting in a dentist's chair or shopping in a grocery store and the music you hear—probably a preprogrammed tape with soothing instrumental music from old movies such as *The Sound of Music* or *Sleepless in Seattle*.

Regional subcultures exist in the United States due to differences in the natural environment and resources, characteristics of immigrant groups, and other social forces, including history and traditions. Beer consumption, advertisements, and formulas vary widely, resulting in the rise of microbreweries. To compete, large firms such as Anheuser-Busch have regional formulas and **targeted advertising**. For example, Anheuser-Busch divided Texas into regions and developed unique advertising for Budweiser in each: In the northern part of the state, it used a cowboy image, while in the southern part a Hispanic identity was stressed (Hawkins, Best, & Coney, 2001). As other examples of environmental effects, hot donuts and coffee sell better in cold climates than in warm climates, and iced tea is on the menu year-round in the South but may be a summer-only item in New England and Canada (around the world, partly because of the huge populations in Asia, tea is the most consumed beverage).

There are over 50,000 products in the average grocery store, and one out of four of these products is only bought once a month (think of a rarely used barbecue sauce or spice). If consumers do not like or need a product, they will not buy it or will try it once and reject it. It is estimated that 90 percent of new products (speaking generally, not just grocery products) fail. When the second edition of this book went to press, it was yet to be seen if Old Spice High Endurance body wash would succeed or fail, even though it had a better chance than average since it is a product extension and the product launch was backed by an estimated $15 million to $20 million in marketing support (Neff, 2002). It is still on the shelves, so Old Spice High Endurance body wash proved to be a success.

Failed products are an enormous expense to companies, so every effort is made for them to succeed, but even very successful companies make mistakes. Examples of failed products by established businesses include Harley-Davidson wine coolers, Levi Strauss tailored suits for men, Life Savers gum, and Country Time apple cider (Hawkins, Best, & Coney, 2001). Each of these major product launches was an expensive loss. A new movie, for example, could cost millions of dollars to distribute, advertise, and merchandise. Why products fail is a subject of consumer research. One finding is that products

Tea is the most consumed beverage in the world.

About 90 percent of new products fail.

are not pretested to the degree they should be; another is that manufacturers do not take into account regional differences or shifts in consumer preferences. Whatever the reason, a company has to be well capitalized to withstand the wins and the losses. In 1968 when Estee Lauder launched Clinique, a new line of skin care products and makeup, it lost money for several years before it became one of the market leaders that it is today (Koehn, 2001).

Sometimes companies reinvent themselves. The restaurant chain Boston Chicken changed its name to Boston Market and became a wholly owned subsidiary of McDonald's Corporation, operating more than 650 company-owned restaurants in 28 states. It also sells a line of frozen entrees and jarred gravies and broths, manufactured by H. J. Heinz Co. The newer restaurants or remodeled restaurants have booths and softer colors and lighting. Alyson Kim, communications manager for the Golden, Colorado-based chain, said, "Customers said they loved our home style food, but the dining experience didn't match it. . . . They wanted a warm, homey atmosphere" (Sams, 2001).

Photo 3.2 Technology has allowed for a proliferation of ways to listen to music

Source: Thinkstock: m-gucci

To conclude, the term *environment* is used in the model in its broadest sense, referring to the environment in which consumer–market interactions take place. Environment encompasses the natural environment and human-made environment and includes the following: cultural, educational, technological, physical, social, political, economic, situational, chemical, and biological influences. It is a view of the world in which we live and everything contained in it, including measures of time and place and all other external conditions affecting our lives.

Since environment is such a large concept, some theorists have divided it into two parts—microenvironment (meaning close to the home and the individual) and macro-environment (everything that surrounds the microenvironment). It used to be that the microenvironment was the context in which most production and consumption took place, but with the proliferation of world trade, radio, television, and the Internet, consumption even at the individual level is very much influenced by both parts of the environment. For example, you may buy a Hostess cupcake at the local convenience store, but the ingredients (wheat, sugar, and flavoring) and the packaging may have come from anywhere in the world (ingredients are listed on the package label, but not sources).

Technology

In Chapter 1, the subject of technology was introduced as a theme throughout this book. What drives a lot of consumer commerce is the desire for the latest technology. Mobile phones and Netflix use all sorts of new technologies. **Technology** is the application of scientific knowledge to useful purposes. In the model, technology is considered part of the environment. Besides mobile phones, other examples of technologies that have revolutionized peoples' lives were the introduction of machine-read bar codes on products that are used in grocery and discount stores and the introduction of automatic teller machines (ATMs) used in financial transactions. Netflix went from 7 to 25 million users in three years.

A paradox exists in technology—a specific technology may save time but may also require time or take time away from using other technologies or being involved in other behaviors. Paradoxes increase conflict in decision making; in other words, they make life more complicated. Here is an example of a technology-based decision situation: Should you use a dishwasher to wash six dinner plates, glasses, and forks, or should you wash them by hand? What is the best use of your time? The trade-off between using a computer and cell phone versus other means of communication or information search is another example. Research shows that time spent on the Internet and emailing (in the evening especially) is taking away from time spent watching television. As another example, at the turn of the century American cell phone users ages 25 to 34 were more than four times as likely to use their mobile phones as their primary phones than those over age 35 (Gardyn, 2001a).

If a product becomes outdated soon after purchase or before it is worn out, a consumer experiences **technological obsolescence**. Products such as computers and cameras lose value because they so rapidly become technologically out-of-date. No one can anticipate every new product or upgrade, so the best someone can do is to keep abreast of changes and/or buy equipment or devices that can be upgraded with add-ons. As seen in the previous case of the nutrition professor, another option is to hold on to old technologies and let the new technologies pass you by—new is not always better or necessary.

Media

Media is a term for a means of mass communication, such as newspapers, magazines, television, or the Internet, that revolutionizes human life in developed and developing countries. To get an idea of the impact of different media, it is useful to look at earlier technologies such as radio and television.

In 1947 there were 200,000 TV sets in the United States; by 1949 there were two million.

Radio exposed listeners to mass advertising, and television let them see it as well as hear it. The heyday of radio was from the 1920s through the 1940s, but by the late 1940s it had a competitor in the form of television. By 1947, 200,000 US homes had black-and-white television sets; in 1948, there were enough viewers to make a national audience for *The Ed Sullivan Show* and *The Milton Berle Show*; and by 1949, there were two million television sets in the United States, showing a very rapid adoption of this form of technology (Goldsmith, 2002). Although available in the 1950s, color television did not become common until the 1960s. In the late 1970s, a device for projecting television onto a large screen became widely available, and this technological advance was followed by videocassette recorders (VCRs). Presently, over 95 percent of US homes have televisions.

The first radio shows often had only one sponsor, and the show was often named after that sponsor. Several early television shows also were named after their sponsor (such as the 1940s and 1950s *The Texaco Star Theater*), but eventually television shows were so expensive to produce that they had multiple sponsors, which is the format we are familiar with today. If we watch a televised football game, we expect to see many different advertisements (razor blades, cars, snack foods) rather than advertisements from a single company. The reason this is important to point out is that with only one sponsor the advertiser had quite a bit of control over program content as well as the show's stars and guests, but multiple sponsors provide more freedom of expression and a greater differentiation between the ads and the show.

Today, radio and television can provide background noise, and the listener or viewer may only really notice it when a special song or an interesting show or announcement comes on. In this way, radio and television are different from print forms such as books and magazines that require more focus and usually require the reader to sit down. An exception to this is audiobooks, which people listen to while driving.

With the advent of the remote control, people gained even more options because television and radio advertising could be muted and channels could be changed more quickly without getting up. Similarly, Internet users can mute certain messages and ignore others or create musical tapes of only the songs they want to hear. The Internet is different from radio and television in that it is still undergoing vast experimentation. Advertisements can be changed every few seconds, whereas a television advertisement may take months to create and may be repeated for months. Can you think of any advertisements that you are tired of or that you find irritating?

Growth of the Internet. The development of the Internet is just part of the development and proliferation of computers. The Internet can be seen as part of media. No one planned the Internet, and it still has few controls. Since no one company or government controls it, it is difficult to set policies or to screen what information is put on the World Wide Web, the information retrieval system.

Internet Interactivity. The Internet is useful in providing services and information, a communication exchange between customers and providers. It is interactive to a greater degree than most other forms of media, which is partly what makes it more fun and useful. Billboards, magazines, radio, and television are mostly one-way exchanges from the publication, station, or program to the reader, listener, or viewer. An exception to this is that magazines have added the interactive feature of providing aftershave, perfume, or grapefruit samples (to increase grapefruit juice sales) that can be smelled; the addition

Photo 3.3 Computers have opened up the world to commerce and communication
Source: Thinkstock: LuminaStock

of smell (usually in scratch and sniff samples) was a true innovation in print medium. Children's books have had similar interactive experiences for years (think of *Pat the Bunny*) before the magazines found a way to inexpensively mass-market an interactive experience. Other examples of more interactivity are radio or television call-in or email-in shows or shows with email messages being sent and responded to on the air.

An interesting mix of Internet and television can be experienced in shows such as *Good Morning America* that continue after the show goes off the air via *Oprah.com*, where viewers can go online and follow the discussion that takes place after the show is over. But most typical television shows are one-way exchanges, and you usually can't call-in during the program and talk with the actors and suggest plot changes, although some shows broadcast live, and some stage plays have experimented with this format. In these plays, the characters are presented to the audience at the beginning of the show, and the audience votes as to who shall play what roles. Internet games allow for these types of interactivity, so the general trend is for most forms of media to move to more interactivity. Higher involvement usually leads to more sales, so sponsors and advertisers want to encourage as much interactivity as possible. This is why they hand out perfume samples in department stores—if you try it, you are more likely to buy it. Besides being a source for information and communication, the Internet is a useful tool for buying and selling financial services, software, tickets, collectibles, and computers.

Internet Buying Trend: Upward. Internet sales go up each holiday season. Consumers report that the main reason they shop online is that it is easier. In the United States in 2006, 6 percent of November/December holiday purchases were made online; this jumped to 40 to 50 percent in 2014.

Illustrative of a one-year change, the number of Americans shopping online was about 65 million in 2001 compared with 49 million in 2000, according to Jupiter Media Matrix Inc., a market research firm. The total number of dollars was over $34 billion in 2001 compared with $24 billion the previous year (Landau, 2001). Since the numbers are constantly changing, memorizing the numbers is less important than witnessing the phenomenon—the upward trend in buying online.

Media and the Model. The purpose of media is to inform consumers about goods, services, news, and events and to provide purchase opportunities. Figure 3.4 illustrates the information transaction process. Negotiations may include price, conditions, model, quantity, and delivery. The transaction is completed when both sides are satisfied and a purchase is made with an order, money, or a contract.

The process can be diagrammed as:

information sent ⟶ information received ⟶ transaction negotiated ⟶ transaction completed

---

Figure 3.4 Information Transaction Process

There are two major media categories:

1. *Print.* Print media include magazines, direct mail, newspapers, mass transit (that is, signs in subways, buses), billboards, and dealer promotions such as free calendars.
2. *Broadcast.* Broadcast media encompass the Internet, cable, television, and radio.

The newspaper is the most basic of print media. Many national and international newspapers and magazines have regional editions so that advertising and stories can be targeted to certain markets. Inserts in newspapers are targeted for a certain area where stores and restaurants exist. Newspapers or magazines may have special teen editions, such as *Teen People* or *Teen Vogue.* In economically developed nations, the most pervasive forms of media are radio and television and the Internet. In some countries, radio and television are state-run and accept no advertising but may run government-sponsored spots announcing programs or events.

Consumer Power Model

So far, the chapter has built a model of consumer economics that focuses on the transactions that take place between consumers and markets, given other conditions and players. Consumer economics can be described as a collection of activities, situations, or exchanges among several parties that take place within an environment. It assumes that individuals seek to maximize their satisfaction from the decisions they make and that they seek fair trade and justice in the marketplace. It also assumes that, for the most part, consumers will gather information (a type of resource) before making decisions. The **Consumer Power Model** shows how all the pieces fit together. A circle is used instead of a square because the process involves a fluid motion, a feeling of constant motion rather than an angular or linear beginning-and-end exchange. Relationships are indicated by the arrows that serve as channels or mediums for exchange.

Theory, research, and common sense suggest that consumers select what messages to receive and process.

The model incorporates theories from many areas. For example, consumers are bombarded daily with hundreds of messages. They cannot evaluate every message, so they selectively choose the ones to listen to or read about. Much of this selection is automatic as new perceptions are made to fit comfortably with existing knowledge or cognition (Foxall, Goldsmith, & Brown, 1998).

Consumers

Although the model shows consumers as only one player in a series of players, they are the most important part. The consumer drives the system, or to use the wording from Chapter 1, the consumer is king. This is true, for the most part, but even kings don't always get their way. For example, a consumer may go to a store to buy a certain product and then learn that the store no longer carries that product nor does anyone

---

CRITICAL THINKING

The Power of Social and Consumer Networks

The Consumer Power Model illustrates in a diagram all the main players in the consumer domain. A growing field of study explores the impact of social and consumer networks. The focus in consumer economics is on how information influences the decision process, examples of which are online social or consumer networks such as eBay, MySpace, and Facebook. These have opened up consumers to more opportunities to be influenced and to influence than ever before through discussion boards and reviewer comments as well as private conversations. Do you have online friends (ones you have never met in person)? Have you asked them about a product or service? If so, give an example. Do you think this widening of information is a good or a bad thing? What are the implications for the marketplace and for the way people search for information and ultimately purchase? What types of advertising have you noticed on network sites? Should there be limits on advertising? For example, should sites directed toward children have limits on the type of advertising allowed? Who should regulate the advertising?

---

else in town; in this situation, the consumer feels more like a pawn than a king. Given that it is an imperfect and complicated world and that the demands of the mass market have to be considered in the mix of goods that are offered, the individual consumer is shown as a player in an interactive environment rather than being placed at the center of the process.

In the model, consumers are placed directly across from markets because, as the first illustration in this chapter shows, the primary relationship or exchange is between consumers and markets. Consumers participate when they spend, save, barter, trade, and invest; they are involved in public policy when they vote or act to influence public policy in some other way; and consumers use and dispose of goods, gather information and opinions, and react to media and other forms of communication. By behaviors such as voting and gathering information, consumers hope to improve their **quality of life**, which is their perception of and satisfaction with their lives. During lean economic times, Americans focus more energy and money on keeping their homes and families secure (Gardyn, 2001b).

Consumption refers to the using up of goods. Consumers have a **level of living**, which is the way they are actually living, but they aspire to a **standard of living**, which is a certain quality of life. The difference is between how one actually lives and how one would like to live—actual versus ideal. This is connected to one's self-concept, and self-concept is important in all cultures. There is the private self (how someone sees himself or herself) and the public or social self (how others see that person). A strong disconnect between the private and public self can cause confusion. Public figures, such as actors and politicians and their families, are confronted with this all the time, but the majority of people experience it to a lesser degree. **Lifestyle** is how one lives and includes patterns of time use and living space; it also involves what one thinks is important and how one spends money. Have you ever heard the expressions "contented housewife," "business tycoons," or "social climber"? These are phrases that describe lifestyles. "Researchers have speculated that our happiness is influenced not by what our absolute level of wealth and income is but rather by how our financial situation compares with that of friends and colleagues (Clements, 2006).

Much of consumption behavior is directed toward improving one's lifestyle, which is linked to self-concept. For example, someone may say, "Next year I'm moving into a better apartment" or "Someday when I'm working full-time, I'm going to buy Ralph Lauren clothes." When millions of consumers make similar choices, this is called **mass consumption**, which has a tremendous impact on the general economy.

Consumer Decisions and Experiences

The relationships within the Consumer Power Model are based on the fact that consumers hope to increase their well-being through consumption (something they have to do to exist) and that there are various indicators of well-being. One of these is environmental well-being. In consumer economics, we are concerned about the quality of the natural environment and the sustaining of it for future generations. Environmental well-being refers to a concern for society's role in the earth's diminishing resources, which affect the overall well-being of individuals, families, and communities.

Our consumer life is also influenced by our experiences. Think of all the experiences you have had visiting restaurants, hotels, theme parks, bakeries, national parks, grocery stores, schools, and friends' homes. As a specific example, what have you observed about birthday cakes? At birthday parties, were the cakes store-bought or homemade? Which do you think is better? What is the tradition in your family? Do you blow out candles on the cake? Do you sing happy birthday? Or, do you completely ignore birthdays? Many of our traditions and consumer experiences have their roots in our early life.

Based on our childhood experiences, we make assumptions about how other people live. College is often a real awakening to the differences in how people live—what they eat, what they consider cleanliness, what their bathing and sleeping habits are, and so forth. For instance, one male student reported that his roommate bought a sack of potatoes and existed almost exclusively on baked potatoes. He said, "It freaked me out." Another male student reported that he ate cereal and bananas 90 percent of the time because it was an easy meal to fix. An 18-year-old boy coming home from two college friends' apartment told his mother that all they had in the refrigerator was water and milk. He said, "Doesn't everyone at least have orange juice?" His assumption was based on his home refrigerator, which was well stocked.

Another area to look at is the type of experiences that businesses provide (for example, Carnival describes itself as "The Fun Ship" or "The Most Popular Cruise Line in the World"). Many companies are not only selling products or services but also selling experiences or entertainment. Consider theme restaurants such as Rainforest Cafe, Hard Rock Cafe, and McDonald's. Note the use of the word *café*. What images does that word conjure up? Compare those with images for the words *tearoom*, *roadhouse*, and *diner*. When stores decorate for the holidays, they are also providing a fun shopping experience and are getting customers in a shopping mood. Spas try to get their guests to relax through massages, creams, lotions, aromatherapy, and soft lighting and music.

How do experiences relate to public policy and consumer organizations (the remaining parts of the model)? Nearly everyone has experiences with rules and regulations, with government, with elections and politics. Out of these experiences come policy opinions about who should be US president, what is the right and wrong way to do things, and what would be best for the greater good. Consumer organizations provide consumer education and advocate for change on behalf of consumers. In terms of public policy, most legislation is based on previous laws and regulations, but as the economy and consumers change, legislation and the causes that consumer organizations take up need to be updated.

Consumer Well-Being

As mentioned earlier, a key aspect of consumers' lives is their well-being. Well-being is made up of a variety of factors, including material, social, and spiritual dimensions (Chambers, 1999). In the Introduction we said that consumers are acquisitive, which means they want more things, ideas, and information, and they have to replace things that are worn out or used up. People consume or spend money to take care of basic needs such as food, clothing, and shelter and to take care of future needs through investing in retirement plans, by making estate plans or setting up trusts, and by buying insurance. Through such activities, they are providing for their own well-being and that of their family members.

Consumer well-being is an umbrella term encompassing the following six areas:

1. *Economics or financial well-being.* The degree to which individuals and families have economic adequacy and security reflects their financial well-being. It is the desire for or extent of protection against the economic risks people face in their daily lives (such as loss of employment, illness, bankruptcy, bank failures, poverty, destitution in old age). Economic well-being also includes an overriding sense of economic equity or economic justice and involves the concept of fairness, not only within one's own

community and nation but also internationally. The setting of a minimum wage is an example of economic equity or justice; another is child labor laws.

2. *Physical well-being.* Personal safety and goods and services that provide one's physical needs impact physical well-being. Threats to physical well-being include, but are not limited to, unsafe or irresponsible personal conduct as well as unsafe or irresponsible actions of others; illness, disease, and malnutrition; lack of or inappropriate exercise; dangerous and hazardous products; adulterated foods; incompetent and irresponsible service delivery; and environmental degradation (McGregor & Goldsmith, 1998).

3. *Social well-being.* The social space of the family or the group provides for a sense of emotional well-being, caring, and working together. "The crux of social well-being is interpersonal relationships and the dynamics of familial interaction to fulfill six basic functions: procreation, socialization, economic consumption and production, social control, physical care and maintenance, and love and emotional support" (McGregor & Goldsmith, 1998, p. 4). **Socialization** refers to the process of learning to interact with others, forming cooperative relationships, participating in society, and learning the ways of daily life. Parents and family are very important in the socialization of children. As social beings, we have a need to belong, which leads us to join groups, form families and circles of friends, buy certain brands, or wear certain types of clothes or adornments.

4. *Psychological or emotional well-being.* The mental state of an individual within the family or other groups reflects the degree of that person's psychological or emotional well-being. The emphasis in social well-being is on the group, whereas the emphasis in psychological or emotional well-being is on the individual. Emotions are strong feelings that affect one's behavior and attitudes, general temperament, and demeanor. Consumer socialization is part of emotional well-being as well as part of social well-being. Consumer and family life specialists are interested in how well people are socialized to be consumers—how they process information and make decisions, how they react to advertising, and how they seek remedy or recourse when a consumer difficulty arises. When something goes wrong, do they fly into a rage, or do they follow the steps necessary to get a refund? Psychological or emotional well-being is associated with thought and reflection, a sense of self and self-preservation.

5. *Environmental well-being, political well-being, and spiritual well-being.* The first two realms (environmental and political) were introduced in previous sections; spiritual well-being "captures a layer of well-being, a sense of insight, and ethereal, intangible evolution not readily imparted by either social or psychological well-being as conventionally defined" (McGregor & Goldsmith, 1998, p. 5). A very broad definition of spiritual well-being encompasses the joy and sense of completeness associated with a connectedness with the world as well as peace, hope, and faith gained from insights and moments of growth and enlightenment. It is not simply about organized religion, although many people experience spiritual well-being in this way. Nearly 90 percent of Americans claim a religious affiliation (Kosmin & Lachman, 1993).

6. *Philosophical well-being.* This is "the healthy state of one's ability to think, reason, acquire, critique, and apply knowledge and paradigms. To live in a state of harmony, each individual must regularly attempt to define what life is about. Professionals must also ask themselves, 'Why am I doing what I do, and what is the impact of my actions? What are the underpinnings of my practice? Am I philosophically sick or well?'" (McGregor, 2006, p. 297).

If we consider the concepts of trade-offs and opportunity costs introduced in Chapter 1, we can see that individuals may choose to spend their time in different ways, such as in church or as a choir member, in a mall, at a movie, or in the woods communing with nature; they may give to charities or choose a more consumption-oriented activity such as buying another $10 T-shirt. This is not to imply that spiritual well-being and consumption activities are always opposites. Someone may find looking at a beautiful Christmas display at a store to be a joyful, spirit-lifting experience, while another may get a lift from singing the school song or the national anthem at a football game. Spiritual well-being may include beauty or aesthetics, music, patriotism, appreciation of nature, and all sorts of other qualities or reactions, individually defined and appreciated.

Discussing well-being or the qualities that make up human welfare is one thing, but measuring it is another since so much depends on people's attitudes and responses. The

Table 3.1 Human Development Index (HDI) and Its Components

HDI rank	Country	Human Development Index (HDI) value, 2013	Life expectancy at birth (years), 2013	Mean years of schooling (years), 2012a	Expected years of schooling (years), 2012a	Gross national income (GNI) per capita (2011 PPP $), 2013	Human Development Index (HDI) value, 2012
	Very high human development						
1	Norway	0.944	81.5	12.6	17.6	63,909	0.943
2	Australia	0.933	82.5	12.8	19.9	41,524	0.931
3	Switzerland	0.917	82.6	12.2	15.7	53,762	0.916
4	Netherlands	0.915	81	11.9	17.9	42,397	0.915
5	United States	0.914	78.9	12.9	16.5	52,308	0.912
6	Germany	0.911	80.7	12.9	16.3	43,049	0.911
7	New Zealand	0.91	81.1	12.5	19.4	32,569	0.908
8	Canada	0.902	81.5	12.3	15.9	41,887	0.901
9	Singapore	0.901	82.3	10.2b	15.4c	72,371	0.899
10	Denmark	0.9	79.4	12.1	16.9	42,880	0.9

http://hdr.undp.org.table1. Human Development Index and its Components.

United Nations Development Programme's **Human Development Index (HDI)** puts a number on (quantifies) well-being by combining several measures of human well-being. The HDI is broader than consumer well-being per se but touches on it. The HDI compares the progress of nations by using the same measures of quality of life across the globe, and it uses an adjusted measure of real per capita gross domestic product (GDP) as one component of an index that includes school enrollment ratios, adult literacy, and life expectancy. Notice that Norway ranks number one on the Human Development Index in Table 3.1.

Consumer Price Index and Consumer Expenditure Survey

Consumer durables last three or more years.

The Consumer Price Index (CPI) provides a statistical measure of the nation's economic well-being.

Connected to the discussion of well-being are other factors that consumer psychologists and economists look at as indicators of the strength of the economy. Consumers need confidence to buy high-ticket items such as consumer durables and homes, and because of the lasting nature of these products, consumers look for quality. **Consumer durables** are products bought by consumers that are expected to last three years or more and include automobiles, appliances, and furniture. Companies such as Maytag and Electrolux that make these types of products are considered consumer durables manufacturers. In contrast, consumer nondurables manufacturers make more immediately consumable items such as food or medicines.

The **Consumer Price Index (CPI)** measures prices each month of a fixed list ("market basket") of 400 goods and services (durables and nondurables) bought by a typical consumer. The market basket on which the CPI is based includes shelter, transportation, tires, utilities, entertainment, health care, clothing, and services. The CPI is published by the Bureau of Labor Statistics (BLS) in the Department of Labor and is based on a score of 100 in 1982. The following information is taken from the BLS website (www.bls.gov):

> *The process by which the Bureau measures price changes to consumers each month requires the efforts of hundreds of BLS employees and the patient cooperation of thousands of individuals in households and retail outlets throughout the country. The cycle begins during the first week of the month when BLS data collectors (called economic assistants) gather price information from selected department stores, supermarkets, service stations, doctors' offices, rental units, etc. For the entire month, about 80,000 prices are recorded in 87 urban areas. During these monthly visits, the economic assistant collects price data on a specific good or service. If available, the economic assistant records the price. If not available or if there are changes in the quality of an item, the assistant selects a new item or records the quality change. This sampling technique is used because it would be impossible to gather the price of every good or service bought each month in the United States. The entire process takes about 20 days for the reviewing, analyzing, and publishing of the data.*

The CPI is widely held as a cost-of-living benchmark that affects adjustments in Social Security payments and other pay schedules and tax brackets. The thinking is that if it costs more to live, then the government should respond by increasing payments, for example, to the elderly. The president, Congress, and the Federal Reserve Board note trends in the CPI and use them for formulating policy. The CPI is used to adjust wages and payments, such as to keep pensions, rents, royalties, alimony, and child support payments in line with changing prices. At the headquarters in Washington, DC, and in regional offices, specialists check the incoming data for accuracy and consistency, and computer programs calculate the weighted changes in prices. By the time the CPI is reported on the television news, the process has started all over again, and the next month's data are being gathered.

The CPI is actually a series of interrelated samples. These include the **Consumer Expenditure Survey** collected from a national sample of over 30,000 families that provides detailed information on spending habits. According to the BLS website (www.bls.gov), "This enables BLS to construct the CPI market basket of goods and services to assign each item in the market basket a weight or importance based on total family expenditures. Another national sample of about 16,800 families serves as the basis for a Point-of-Purchase survey that identifies the places where households purchase various types of goods and services." The BLS uses census data to determine which urban areas are selected for price checks. BLS job openings, including positions for economic assistants, economists, and administrators as well as internships and summer employment, are listed on its website, www.bls.gov.

Consumer Confidence

Another measure of consumer well-being is consumer confidence. **Consumer confidence** is measured and nationally reported by two organizations:

1. Conference Board (a New York-based organization).
2. Survey Research Center (at the University of Michigan in Ann Arbor).

The monthly Consumer Confidence Survey is based on a probability-design random sample, and it is conducted for The Conference Board by Nielsen, a global provider of information and analytics around what consumers buy and watch. The Conference Board specializes in consumers' plans to buy cars, houses, and appliances and to participate in activities such as traveling. According to The Conference Board, consumer confidence was declining in October 2001, dropping to 85.5 from 114 in August—the steepest fall since October 1990. According to the survey, fewer than 1 in 5 consumers rated business conditions as favorable, down from more than 1 in 4 the previous month (Paul, 2001). To give a more recent statistic, in November 2014 The Conference Board Consumer Confidence Index stood at 88.7, down from 94.1 in October.

During the same August to October 2001 period, the Survey Research Center found a similar drop in consumer confidence. The Survey Research Center measures a sample of 500 consumers' expectations about the economy and their own personal finances and tries to determine attitudes about consumption and changes and trends therein. Both these organizations seek to determine how consumers view the health and direction of the economy and how they are responding to it, so the measures are very much about perception; for example, optimism about the economy makes the consumer feel more confident about spending and more willing to acquire debt (credit cards and loans). Consumer confidence levels are reported in the news and used by government and business so they can make better policies and plans of action.

To provide more figures, The Conference Board reported a high of 110.2 in March 2002 compared with the previous six months (Eisinger, 2002). Likewise, the US Commerce Department reported that in March 2002, personal income, savings, and spending rose. The general thinking is that if consumer confidence appears to wobble, consumer spending will fall; if confidence is up, then spending goes up. Investors watching these figures react in terms of what companies they will invest in and what stocks they may sell. A large reported gain or dive will impact investor reaction more strongly than a slight rise or dip.

When consumer confidence is down, how might consumers and businesses respond? This is the type of question investors would ask themselves. During times of uncertainty, familiar brands such as Procter & Gamble's Ivory Soap provide reassurance. An article published after the economic downturn caused by the September 11, 2001, tragedies put it this way:

> *Marketing messages should be straightforward, honest and down-to-earth. This is not the time for messages about luxury or indulgence, which can come across as insensitive and irrelevant. Neither is it the moment for cheap solutions and quick fixes. People want to feel confident that what they're getting is the "right" product, something they can count on, something that will deliver on its promise. (Paul, 2001, p. 23)*

In contrast, how should businesses respond when consumer confidence is up? In 2002, consumers were marching to a different drummer than they were in 2001. Luxury became attractive again, and consumers were buying upscale appliances, cars, electronics, travel, and homes. "Millions of Americans who once made up the vast middle of the nation's $7 trillion consumer market migrated upscale toward premium and luxury goods" (White & Leung, 2002, p. A1). Helmut Panke, an executive at German automaker BMW, stated that "today's auto market is increasingly shaped like an hourglass," meaning there are many high-end and low-end purchases and not many in the middle. When interviewed, many consumers say for a few thousand more they would rather have a premium car than an ordinary car (White & Leung, 2002). For another example of this trend toward high-end consumption, consider the following:

During uncertain times, consumers are drawn to familiar brands.

Who would pay $2,200 for a washer-dryer set with stainless-steel drums, 12 different wash cycles, rounded styling, baby-blue trim and room for 22 bath towels? Whirlpool Corp. thought it knew the answer when it introduced its Duet line last year: a niche of affluent laundry-doers willing to pay about three times the price of the company's midrange machines. Whirlpool expected the Duet would make up only 5% of its North American washer and dryer sales. Instead, in its first six months on the market, the Duet line is on track to double Whirlpool's projections. (White & Leung, 2002, p. A1)

As an example of a typical family who bought a Duet, the Boyd family with four children, who live in suburban Chicago (the mother is a substitute teacher, and the father is a field manager in a construction company), said they bought the Duet because "we find in the long run it's more cost-effective to have high-quality products," because they perform better and last longer (White & Leung, 2002, p. A8). As this book went to press, consumer confidence was rising and luxury goods in many categories were selling well.

Businesses and Markets

As the preceding quotes illustrate, today's businesses need to be sensitive to consumers' perceptions and actions at any given point in time. The goal of businesses is to maximize profits, and they pursue this goal while cooperating with government, listening to consumers, and watching sales figures closely.

The goal of business is to maximize profits.

Businesses cannot get so stuck on current conditions and issues that they lose the bigger picture—planning for the future. For example, Albertson's, a food and drug retailer based in Boise, Idaho, updates its grocery stores' appearance every ten years. When the retailer plans its redesigns, it has to imagine what future grocery stores will look like: Will there be the usual 21-aisle store with freezer cases? Will people still push carts up and down the aisles, or will groceries be ready for customers at the door of the store or delivered directly to their homes? Experiments with both are taking place, but it is not yet clear what the future holds except that history shows that we can expect changes, not just in store design and layout but also in products. The typical 1950s North American grocery shopper would not have known what zucchini squash or sushi or pesto was.

In ancient times, markets were actual places where consumers and producers came together to trade.

Going back several steps into our past, in ancient times most markets were physical locations where consumers and producers came together to make trades, and they set prices by arguing over what would be the right price. In many countries today, including the United States, Northern Ireland, France, Finland, and Mexico, farmers' markets coexist with modern grocery stores. Some markets allow or encourage bargaining, but most have set prices. Other examples are the New York Stock Exchange and tobacco and cattle markets where buyers and sellers come together to buy and trade. The Internet and other modern telecommunications services and devices have made being in the same location less important than it was in the past.

Typical Company Functions

In the old markets, selection was limited by season and availability. With modern transportation and growing methods, seasons are less important in terms of what is offered. A concern for the future is deciding how much choice consumers can handle. For example, most large grocery stores and Home Depot supply stores offer 50,000 products, and some of the superstores go as high as 100,000. How much more selection do consumers need? Is there an optimum number of products or size of store?

Average-size grocery stores have 50,000 products.

To handle these sorts of questions, a typical company that markets to consumers has various divisions, including top management, marketing, finance, human relations, research and development (R&D), purchasing, manufacturing, and accounting as well as product design and in-house public/media or consumer relations and investor relations. Here are their functions:

- Top management sets the goals, missions, objectives, and strategies and often answers to a board of directors.
- Marketing promotes, sells, conducts survey research (or conducts focus groups to gather consumer opinions), and distributes goods. (The next section provides additional information on marketing and consumer psychology.)
- Finance balances current funds and procures more funds. A chief financial officer (CFO) may visit banks to get loans for factory expansion or may give presentations to mutual fund managers in hopes that they will buy substantial numbers of shares in the company.
- Human relations departments take care of employee needs such as hiring and benefits.
- R&D focuses on developing new and exciting, yet safe and effective, products. An example is Post-it notes used in offices that were developed in the R&D Department of 3M (Minnesota Mining and Manufacturing).
- Purchasing gets supplies and materials, such as raw materials, at a good price.
- Manufacturing oversees the production of a quality product and handles decisions on quantity.
- Accounting watches the books and checks costs and expenditures. Sometimes a head tax accountant moves into the finance department, and there may be other movements among different groups within companies noted in this section.
- Product design may be part of marketing or R&D or may be free-standing.
- For major public relations campaigns, including advertising, large companies usually hire outside firms, but they may have an in-house division to handle day-to-day media inquiries such as a newspaper columnist asking for a media kit with press releases and photos or slides.
- Consumer relations departments in large companies that sell consumer goods or services have to handle consumer inquiries and complaints and report consumer

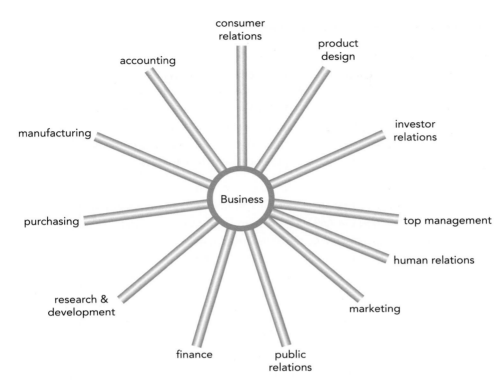

Figure 3.5
Components of
Typical Consumer
Product
Companies

trends to higher management. Thousands of companies, from airlines to toy and food manufacturers, have such departments. Choose nearly any packaged food product off a shelf at the grocery store or at home, and on the label there will be the toll-free number and address of the consumer relations department. For example, on the back of a Progresso French Onion soup can it says: "Questions or Comments? Call 1–800–200-9377 weekdays 8–6 CT. Information from label on end of can will be helpful. Consumer Relations, P.O. Box 555, Vineland, NJ 98360."

- An investor relations department is usually found if the company has stock that is publicly traded (in other words, the stock is available in a stock exchange). An investor owning stock or thinking of buying stock can contact the investor relations department to find out more about how the company is doing and in particular inquire about the influences on stock. Figure 3.5 shows all these components.

Note that in a smaller company, many of these functions may be performed by one employee or outsourced to another company. For example, accounting, public relations, or marketing may be done by an outside firm, and manufacturing may take place in another country. In a large multinational company, top management and many other functions may be spread throughout the world.

Marketing and Consumer Psychology

Throughout the book we're talking about consumer psychology, but let's pause for a few minutes here to revisit the topic, given changes in the global economy and technology. Reaching consumers is easier in some ways than before with the Internet, but in some ways it is harder because there is less personal interaction. People report spending more time at home than in the last few decades, so reaching them has to be done differently. The likelihood they will come into a physical store is diminishing; consequently, retailers are shifting gears. Let's take the example of cereal maker Kellogg Company.

To help sell Frosted Flakes, Kellogg offers a website where kids can send emails or make trading cards featuring Tony the Tiger. On another site, the company offers behind-the-scenes clips of *American Idol* stars on tour. Beyond the Internet, Kellogg has tried word-of-mouth campaigns, where the company taps loyal customers to tell others about new products, and in-store marketing (Steinberg, 2006, p. R1).

Note the use of the practice of making original cards and the words "word-of-mouth campaign." In the quote, Kellogg has made loyal customers part of a campaign. This is part of the **consumer-in-control movement**, meaning consumers want more say about products and services. They want to design ads, products, and packaging; send emails; and let others know about their input, their insider's knowledge of what is available or what is to come. **Customization**, specifically designed products such as shirts with logos or custom-made drapes and coordinating pillows in another fabric, is a result. Companies can encourage this (as seen in the Frosted Flake example). Children especially enjoy creating original designs. We can also envision the consumer-in-control movement as part of the Consumer Power Model, as more and more consumers have control of the marketplace.

Related to this is the concept known as **market mavens**, opinion-leading consumers who are very involved in the marketplace. They are enthusiastic, energetic buyers and shoppers who talk about what is for sale. They may not be wealthy, but they are more involved than usual consumers. For example, they may enjoy knowing that a new grocery store or Starbucks is opening in their community, and they will visit early and tell others about their experience. Was the food good or bad? How was the service? What was the atmosphere like? Consumer researchers are intensely interested in the way these people disseminate information through frequent interactions with other consumers. Market mavens have a willingness to try new things. They are unique and willing to seek social status through consumption (Goldsmith, Clark, & Goldsmith, 2006). Are you a market maven? If so, in what category are you most interested and knowledgeable? Examples would be fashion, cars, shoes, travel, movies, sporting events, hunting, fishing, technology, organic food or gardening, store openings, and restaurants. Do you know any market mavens? "As consumers increasingly use the marketplace to express their self-concepts and to show their status, they come more and more to *seek out unique products*. This behavior can be studied via uniqueness theory, which proposes that individuals vary in the extent to which they wish to be different" (Goldsmith, Clark, & Goldsmith, 2007). Uniqueness theory is further discussed in Chapter 7.

Entrepreneurship

Businesses don't exist without leadership. Unique industry-changing leaders are called **entrepreneurs**. Entrepreneurs pursue new business opportunities relentlessly without becoming deterred by the limited resources they initially controlled (Stevenson, 1985). Few are called and even fewer succeed. Entrepreneurs such as Bill Gates and Michael Dell are rare, and timing is everything. When they started their computer businesses, only a small number of people owned a personal computer, let alone one that was made to order or designed for individual purposes. Many students enrolled in consumer economics classes are interested in some day forming their own business, selling a product, or offering a service. The opportunities are limitless.

The concept of entrepreneurship is not new. In 1759 in the midst of the Industrial Revolution, Josiah Wedgwood founded his own pottery workshop with the idea of making affordable but well-designed dinnerware for the masses. He noticed that with the improved economy, more people wanted consumer goods, including china, linens, clocks, tea, tobacco, chocolate, window curtains, books, and cutlery (Koehn, 2001). China was fast replacing the wood and pewter dishes that Britons had used for centuries. Within a few years the Wedgwood brand was well established and continues to be a leading brand of quality china, housewares, and giftware today. Besides developing new methods of production, Wedgwood was a master at organizing, and he established good public relations by making special sets for royalty that were displayed at special events and exhibitions.

How did Josiah Wedgwood become a successful entrepreneur? What qualities or characteristics does one need to succeed in today's competitive business environment? In her study of six entrepreneurs documented in *Brand New: How Entrepreneurs Earned Consumers' Trust from Wedgwood to Dell* (2001), Nancy Koehn writes that each entrepreneur "intended to make the most of the moment to construct a name, brand and organization that would endure, and each succeeded brilliantly, in substantial measure" (p. 320). She lists the following five reasons (Koehn, 2001, p. 320):

- They had deep knowledge and personal experience of their product or service.
- They learned quickly from their mistakes and made rapid adjustments.
- They created meaningful brands that distinguished their offerings and responded to consumers' changing priorities.
- They initiated a process of reciprocal learning with their customers that resulted from ongoing two-way communication with them.
- They created a range of organizational capabilities that delivered on the promises of their respective brands.

Photo 3.4 A portrait of English industrialist Josiah Wedgwood

Source: Thinkstock: Photos.com

Their efforts have important consequences for businesses and for consumers. Without their energy, foresight, and sheer drive, products may have remained unchanged and needs gone unfulfilled for many years.

Women as Entrepreneurs

Women start businesses at 1.5 times the rate of men and are at least half-owners of 46 percent of privately held firms (Schiffman, 2014). Most of these businesses are small with only 2 percent of women-owned businesses making $1 million in revenue. The march is on to change this last statistic. As recently as 1973, women owned just 4.6 percent of the US businesses. Between 1987 and 2000, the number of women-owned businesses doubled from 4.5 million to 9.1 million in the United States (Allon, 2001). These businesses employ more people than the Fortune 500 companies; in other words, businesses run by women are flourishing, and part of the reason may be that women understand the needs of female consumers better. This is important because (as mentioned in the Introduction) women account for 80 percent of consumer spending in this country. Go to the grocery store and who do you see? Go to the mall and who is shopping? Go to a Gap Kids store and who is there? One might assume most shoppers in Home Depot or Lowe's are male, but recent surveys show that about one-half the shoppers in Home Depot and Lowe's are women. If knowledge is power, then shopping knowledge should be an asset for someone wanting to lead any consumer-related business or start one up.

CASE STUDY

Naomi Whittel

"Naomi Whittel, CEO of nutritional supplement manufacturer Reserveage recalls a ski instructor who once encouraged her to fall again and again, an experience which inspired her to be brave, be bold, take risks and never be afraid to fail, because it will ultimately lead to success. 'Anything you can believe,' she says, 'you can make happen.'"

Source: Lisa Schiffman. (December 3, 2014). "Women Entrepreneurs Act As The Role Models They Never Had." *Forbes*. http://www.forbes.com/sites/ey/2014/12/03/women-entrepreneurs-act-as-the-role-models-they-never-had/#57c1c6024bb9.

Summary

Adam Smith, founder of modern economics, said that "to be human is to exchange freely." This chapter explored theories that explain or provide insight into consumer behavior and presented a multifaceted Consumer Power Model. It was also stated that consumer researchers follow the scientific method, a five-step method of analyzing issues: They recognize problems, make assumptions, develop models, make predictions, and check, control, or test facts or outcomes. Researchers are concerned about scarcity and how consumers make transactions in a complex market involving public policy and other input. Theory and the exchange process were also defined, and examples of various theories that explain consumer behavior and the variances thereof were given.

Consumer decisions take place in an overall environment, including technology, and are based on experiences. When someone makes a new purchase, it is influenced by past purchase experiences as well as media and other factors. Public policy serves as a mediator or rule maker, and consumer organizations seek to protect, educate, and advocate for consumers. Consumer well-being was introduced as an umbrella term referring to many aspects of life, including economic, psychological or emotional, environmental, political, spiritual, and philosophical well-being. Measures of consumer well-being include the Human Development Index (HDI), the Consumer Price Index (CPI), and consumer

Consumer economists are curious about why people behave as they do.

confidence. In business, unique leaders called entrepreneurs emerge who substantially change industries; examples include Michael Dell, Bill Gates, and Josiah Wedgwood.

The Summary section in Chapter 2 challenged you to think like a consumer economist. Here is another facet this chapter has added: Consumer economists are curious—they want to know why people spend money and behave as they do. This is what consumer economics is all about. Given scarce resources, why do people buy what they do? Who are market mavens? What is the impact of the consumer-in-control movement? How much are consumers influenced by family and friends? How can they become better consumers? How can consumer well-being be improved as part of the greater picture of improving human welfare? Theories help us predict future behavior, and models help us visualize the interplay among various groups and influences, including individuals' real and perceived self-concepts.

KEY POINTS

1. The objective of consumer economics is to understand the real world and how it operates, how exchanges or transactions take place, and what factors (such as environment and experiences) influence them.

2. Theories and models are abstractions of the real world; they are used to organize and visualize thoughts and connections or relationships.

3. The theory of reasoned action is a consumer behavior theory that states that one's own attitudes and those of others matter when it comes to a purchase decision.

4. Prospect theory argues that people make consumption decisions even when they are uncertain. They are not always rational, self-interested, and calculating. Kahneman and Tversky, authors of prospect theory, won the Nobel Prize in recognition for their work integrating psychology with economics and in so doing laying the groundwork for behavioral economics and behavioral finance.

5. Innovation theory is a consumer behavior theory that indicates that innovations diffuse through social systems and that some people are innovators (early buyers or adopters), whereas others are late adopters or laggards. Research indicates that the differences vary by product category.

6. The Consumer Power Model was introduced. In this model, the key players are consumers, business, public policy, media, and consumer organizations interacting within an environmental and experiential context. The growing field of study of social and consumer networks is a result of more people going online to discuss everything (including goods and services).

7. Consumer economics is an applied social science. Perceived wants are unlimited, and resources to satisfy them are limited, so consumers make decisions about how to allocate scarce resources.

8. Level of living (actual) is different from standard of living (ideal). Much of consumption behavior is directed at raising one's level of living. The Consumer Price Index (CPI), calculated monthly by the Bureau of Labor Statistics (BLS), is a leading measure of inflation and buying power.

9. Consumer confidence is tracked each month by two main organizations: the Conference Board of New York and the University of Michigan's Survey Research Center. Consumer confidence fluctuates, and to be successful, markets have to be responsive to changes in how consumers feel and act.

10. There are several components of consumer well-being. The United Nations has attempted to compare human welfare conditions (including PPP$, which refers to purchasing power of goods in relation to income) across many nations using the Human Development Index (HDI).

11. In ancient times, markets were physical locations where buyers and producers haggled over prices. Some markets of this type (such as farmers' markets) still exist, but for the most part, consumers and producers do not physically meet—there are many middlemen in between. Modern businesses have numerous divisions that have specialized functions.

KEY TERMS

acquisitiveness

behavioral economics

behavioral finance

brand extension

consumer confidence

consumer durables

Consumer Expenditure Survey

consumer-in-control movement

consumer–market conflict

Consumer Power Model

Consumer Price Index (CPI)

consumption

customization

diminishing marginal utility

endowment effect

entrepreneurs

exchange process

Human Development Index (HDI)

innovators

level of living

lifestyle

market mavens

mass consumption

media

message framing

models

neuroeconomics

prospect theory

public policy

quality of life

rationality

reactance

regional subcultures

socialization

standard of living

targeted advertising

technological obsolescence

technology

theory

theory of mental accounting

theory of reasoned action

transaction

utility

DISCUSSION QUESTIONS

1. Select one of the six main types of well-being and discuss how it impacts consumer behavior.

2. What do you think of prospect theory? Give an example of when you were uncertain but went ahead and made a consumption decision anyway. Describe the outcome (positive or negative) of the decision.

3. Give an example of a product that you were an innovator in (an early buyer) and an example of a product that you have been a laggard or in the late majority in buying. Describe why you were an early buyer in one case but a late buyer (or nonbuyer) in another.

4. According to Pamela Paul, "Americans want good quality and good value from good companies doing good things." Do you agree or disagree? Explain your answer. How does a declining economy affect consumers' behavior, especially their need for value?

REFERENCES

Ajzen, I., and M. Fishbein. (1980). *Understanding attitudes and predicting social behavior.* Englewood Cliffs, NJ: Prentice Hall.

Allon, J. (2001). *Turn your passion into profits.* New York: Hearst Books.

Chambers, R. (1999). *Whose reality counts?* London: Intermediate Technology Place.

Clements, J. (August 16, 2006). Money and happiness: here's why you won't laugh all the way to the bank. *Wall Street Journal,* p. D1.

Eisinger, J. (April 30, 2002). Ahead of the tape: today's market forecast. *Wall Street Journal,* p. C1.

Foxall, G., R. Goldsmith, and S. Brown. (1998). *Consumer psychology for marketing,* 2nd ed. London: Thomson Business Press.

Gardyn, R. (December 2001a). Phone home. *American Demographics,* 18–19.

Gardyn, R. (December 2001b). The home front. *American Demographics,* 34–36.

Glimcher, P. (2003). *Decisions, uncertainty, and the brain: the science of neuroeconomics.* Cambridge, MA: MIT Press.

Goldsmith, E. (2002). Colgate Palmolive. *Encyclopedia of Advertising,* 1, eds. John McDonough and Karen Egolf. New York: Fitzroy Dearborn.

Goldsmith, R., R. Clark, and E. Goldsmith. (2006). Extending the psychological profile of market mavenism. *Journal of Consumer Behaviour,* 5, 411–419.

Goldsmith, R., R. Clark, and E. Goldsmith. (2007). The desire for unique consumer products and innovativeness. Proceedings of the Academy of Marketing Science Annual Meeting, Coral Gables, FL.

Hawkins, D., R. Best, and K. Coney. (2001). *Consumer behavior,* 8th ed. Boston: Irwin McGraw-Hill.

Kahneman, D., and A. Tversky. (1979). Prospect theory: an analysis of decision under risk. *Econometrica,* 47, 263–292.

Koehn, N. F. (2001). *Brand new: how entrepreneurs earned consumers' trust from Wedgwood to Dell.* Boston: Harvard Business School Press.

Kosmin, B., and S. Lachman. (1993). *One nation under God.* New York: Harmony Books.

Landau, M. D. (October 22, 2001). Holiday hints. *Wall Street Journal,* p. R4.

Lowenstein, R. (January 2003). A salute to the irrational. *SmartMoney,* 42–43.

Makarem, S., M. Smith, S. Mudambi, and J. Hunt (Fall 2014). Why people do not always follow the doctor's orders: the role of hope and perceived control. *The Journal of Consumer Affairs,* 48 (3), 457–485.

McGregor, S. (2006). *Transformative practice: new pathways to leadership.* A Kappa Omicron Nu publication.

McGregor, S., and E. Goldsmith. (Summer 1998). Expanding our understanding of quality of life, standard of living, and well-being. *Journal of Family and Consumer Sciences*, 122.

Neff, J. (December 30, 2002). P&G shores up Old Spice with body-wash extension. *Advertising Age*, 8.

Paul, P. (December 2001). Pulse: a critical look at American views. *American Demographics*, 23 (9), 22–23.

Robinson-Brown, L. (December 19, 2002). Daniel Kahneman wins Nobel Prize. *News from Princeton University*, Office of Communication.

Rogers, E. M. (1995). *Diffusion of innovations*, 4th ed., New York: Free Press.

Sahlman, William A., Howard H. Stevenson, Michael J. Roberts, and Amar Bhide, eds. (1995). *The entrepreneurial venture*. Boston: Harvard Business School Press.

Sams, R. (December 13, 2001). Third Boston Market on the way. *Tallahassee Democrat*, p. E1.

Schor, J. B. (1998). *The overspent American*. New York: Harper Perennial.

Sheppard, B., J. Hartwick, and P. Warshaw. (December 1988). The theory of reasoned action. *Journal of Consumer Research*, 324–343.

Steinberg, B. (July 10, 2006). The marketing maze. *Wall Street Journal*, p. R1.

Stevenson, H. (1985). A perspective on entrepreneurship. In *New Business Ventures and the Entrepreneur*, ed. H. H. Stevenson, Michael J. Roberts, and H. Irving Grousbeck. Homewood, IL: Richard D. Irwin, 2–15.

Well, M. (December 10, 2001). Less than perfect pitch. *Forbes*, 122–124.

White, G., and S. Leung. (March 29, 2002). Middle market shrinks as Americans migrate toward the high end. *Wall Street Journal*, pp. A1, A8.

Part **2**

Consumer Protection

Chapter **4**

Consumer Protection and Law

Why should there not be patient confidence in the ultimate justice of the people? Is there any better or equal hope in the world?

Abraham Lincoln

LEARNING OBJECTIVES

1. Identity theft has been the number one fraud complaint for over a decade according to the FTC.

2. Explain consumer responsibilities.

3. Discuss consumer service problems.

4. Explain the steps to follow before buying.

5. List the steps to follow to complain effectively.

6. Discuss how small claims courts work.

Introduction

> ### CASE STUDY
>
> **Vetting Crowdfunding**
>
> "This summer, a unique bracelet promising to project digital information on the back of a person's hand appeared on Indiegogo, a website where people can raise money from the public to build their projects. Dubbed Ritot, the $120 bracelet quickly raked in hundreds of thousands of dollars in contributions. But during the fundraising, it drew flags online from some in the growing crowdfunding community, such as: How could such a perfect display be projected from such a small device? Why was there no working prototype? And who were the founders, whose names couldn't be found anywhere? Many backers began asking for refunds, while the founders admitted to using fake names and country of origin because they feared a backlash over their association with Ukraine due to its current conflict with Russia . . . . The Federal Trade Commission, which oversees consumer protection laws, said it has received a 'few hundred' complaints involving crowdfunding last year but declined to comment whether it is actively looking into them. Complaints have also prompted little legal action."
>
> Source: Nick Shchetko (November 26, 2014). "There's No Refunding in Crowdfunding." *Wall Street Journal*, p. B1.

If it sounds too good to be true, it probably isn't.

Chapter 2 documented the growth of the consumer movement, and the emphasis was on consumer protection legislation that was passed to remedy or curtail abuses in the marketplace. This chapter discusses the other side of the coin: the responsibilities that consumers have in the marketplace. For example, it is their responsibility to spend and invest wisely and to consider the environmental implications of their consumption not only for themselves but also for future generations. It is also their responsibility to shop wisely. The chapter also builds on consumer protection offered through the government, media including call-in radio programs, and other sources.

> ### CRITICAL THINKING
>
> **Rebates Attract Consumers But Do They Redeem Them?**
>
> What is your response to the following? "Fewer than 50% of consumers tend to mail in their rebates and the redemption rate drops as the size of it falls." For example, "A $50 rebate on a new consumer electronic device is much more likely to be redeemed than a $2 rebate on a box of kitty litter, he said." The "he" in this case is John Gourville, a Harvard Business School professor.
>
> Source: Suzanne Kapner (November 26, 2014). "The Making of a 'Doorbuster': Behold the $5 toaster at Kohl's." *Wall Street Journal*, p. B1

Consumers have a responsibility to carefully examine products and avoid falling victim to fraudulent schemes. This is easier said than done because consumers are exposed daily to get-rich-quick schemes, miracle diets, and mechanical belts that shake off fat. Who buys these things, such as pharmaceutical-grade, industrial-strength olive oil pills to build muscles, especially when they know that they don't work? Nearly all of us are vulnerable to sales pitches, some more sophisticated than others, that promise improved appearance or increased bank accounts. If we can take a pill rather than exercise to build muscles, that is pretty attractive, and maybe it is true that people in the Mediterranean have the secrets to a long life and now their secret (olive oil) can be ours! Hope often triumphs over experience or common sense. This is not to say that hope is bad—a certain amount is important, as the opening quote by Abraham Lincoln illustrates—but hope has to be tempered with a degree of skepticism. One of the sayings in consumerism is that if it sounds too good to be true, it probably isn't.

What complicates the process of sorting the legitimate from the fraudulent is that often fraudulent products are sold by legitimate stores such as drugstores or pharmacies and that the fraudulent products may have some basis in fact, although greatly exaggerated. Another complication is how the avenues of trade have changed. Consumers are taking more chances in direct consumer-to-consumer sales and trades. In the following case study, the trade was successful.

CASE STUDY

Some French Guy Has My Car

"He seemed nice enough—a little sweaty from walking up the hill to my house, but I've got faux leather seats that are easy to wipe clean. I'm renting it to him for $27 a day through RelayRides, a company that facilitated my transition from 'dude with a car' to 'competitor with Hertz.' The French guy visited me a day early on a practice walk to make sure he could find my place, which is tucked away up a bunch of steep, winding roads. When I saw his sweaty face, I just gave him the keys to my yellow Mini Cooper convertible instead of having him hike back the next day. He returned the car with a full tank and left $27 in cash in an envelope to pay me for the extra day, even though I told him not to. Afterward, the French guy and I rated each other five out of five on the RelayRides app."

Source: Joel Stein (February 9, 2015). "Baby,
You Can Drive My Car." *Time*, p. 34.

> ### CRITICAL THINKING
>
> **Trusting People**
>
> The author of the article in the case study who owned the car says that the key (no pun intended) is that "We totally distrust strangers but we totally trust people—significantly more than we trust corporations or governments. Many sharing company founders have one thing in common: they worked at eBay and, in bits and pieces, recreated that company's trust and safety division" (Stein, 2015, p. 34). What do you think of the sharing concept? Do you agree we trust people? Companies that facilitate sharing have grown wildly. Why do you think this is?

In this chapter, the steps to follow if a person becomes a victim of any kind of fraud or buys a faulty product will be covered as well as ways to reduce the chances of it happening. This chapter also discusses the more general topic of customer service and the steps to follow in the complaint process regardless of the nature of the complaint. When all else fails, the last resource is the court system.

Top Consumer Fraud Complaints

Poor-quality products need to be differentiated from fraud. **Fraud** is an intentional deception perpetrated to deprive another person of his or her assets. Consumers deal with many frauds, but the fraud area rising the fastest is identity theft, which is the leading consumer fraud complaint, far exceeding gripes about Internet auctions and services. Of the two million complaints compiled by the Federal Trade Commission (FTC), 18 percent were identity theft. The hijacking of a person's identity information, such as Social Security numbers or credit card numbers, to steal money or commit fraud is one of the fastest-growing crimes in the United States. The number of people victimized is increasing. Most victims do not know how or when their identity was stolen. It costs the average victim more than $1,000 in expenses to cope with the damage to accounts and reputation. "This is a crime that is almost solely on the shoulders of the victim to resolve," said Beth Givens, director of the Privacy Rights Clearinghouse. "They're beleaguered, they're tired, they're angry, and it takes them a good deal of time to recover." In some cases, recovery of one's financial identity, getting bank accounts and financial records straightened out, can take as many as five years. The most likely use of another person's identity is for credit card fraud, but other major categories include fraudulent bank and cell phone accounts. The top consumer fraud complaints compiled by the FTC (percent of complaints) are as follows:

- Identity theft (18 percent)
- Debt collection (10 percent)
- Banks and lenders (6 percent)

- Shop-at-home and catalog sales (6 percent)

- Prizes, sweepstakes, and lotteries (5 percent)

- Imposter scams (4 percent)

- Internet scams (4 percent)

- Auto-related complaints (4 percent)

- Telephone and mobile services (4 percent)

- Credit cards (3 percent)

Identity theft tops the list of frauds.

Obviously, new methods of protecting one's identity are needed. Retailers, credit card companies, and bank companies are devising better methods of protecting their clients' identities.

CRITICAL THINKING

Protecting ATM Cards

Have you ever complained about a product or a service? Have you ever been ripped off? Has your identity been stolen? Have you lost credit cards or had them stolen? If you follow the news, most likely you have seen reports of someone stealing someone's ATM (automated teller machine) card and going to the machine to remove cash. The problem from the criminal's point of view is the need for the password code or number to get into the account. Have you noticed how banks are trying to track and limit this sort of crime? Cameras on the machines taking photos of those using cards is one way, and more sophisticated means of identifying cardholders are in development.

Consumer Responsibilities

As discussed in Chapter 2, President John F. Kennedy gave a list of consumer rights to Congress. Unfortunately, a formal list of consumer responsibilities does not exist, but over the years it has become evident that consumers can look out for themselves in several ways. It should be noted that besides consumers, someone may be referred to as a client, patient, expert by experience, customer, or user (McLaughlin, 2009):

Consuming takes time, but complaining takes even more time.

1. *Be honest with merchants and manufacturers.* For example, consumers should be honest when filling out job applications, mortgage applications, warranty information, sales of used cars, returns of purchased clothing, and so forth.

2. *Be realistic in possible outcomes and expectations.* Cologne or toothpaste will not dramatically change one's life regardless of what advertisements say.

3. *Avoid nuisance or frivolous lawsuits.* File complaints or lawsuits only when necessary.

Complaining takes time, and Americans have less time today than they had 30 years ago (De Graaf, Wann, & Naylor, 2001; Schor, 1992). What is frivolous is in the eye of the beholder (or more specifically, in the mind and body of the sufferer and the lawyers who represent them). A widely publicized case dealt with overweight people suing fast-food restaurants, charging that their weight gain was a result of eating the fattening food served. See the case box about a particular lawsuit that was thrown out. Many people reading or hearing about this case thought it was frivolous since the decision to eat in these restaurants and what to choose to eat were personal responsibilities rather than a corporate responsibility. In another case it was the restaurant chain's responsibility when it said it fried potatoes in vegetable oil when it turned out there was beef lard in the frying oil, which was not in keeping with the diet requirements of vegetarians. The restaurant had to own up to the practice and change its oil immediately to vegetable oil only. A very controversial legal area is asbestos (used in fireproofing, electrical insulation, and building materials) and its harmful effects. In 2002, 90,000 new asbestos claims were filed—triple the number filed in the two previous years. Asbestos lawsuits (usually about lung abnormalities) now run more than $200 billion, and the amounts awarded are increasing. The claimants (some of whom are sick, while others are neither sick nor impaired) and the tort lawyers are pitted against an ever-widening group of defendants (corporations, builders, and owners of buildings, including schools and businesses). When it is not a legitimate claim (no illness or injury), it can be considered a fraud in and of itself. In response, some law professors are calling for Congress to limit fraudulent claims, putting a cap on how much can be awarded (Brickman, 2003). Others would say this is not a good idea and would like to continue the present system wherein the courts decide on the amount of awards.

4. *Be aware that complaint behavior varies by age group.*

5. *Keep within the law when protesting or boycotting products or companies.* Safety is paramount, and there are many ways to effect change. Consumers have the right to be heard and informed but not to injure themselves or others in the process as they exercise the First Amendment right to free speech.

6. *Report faulty goods.* Producers want to know when a product doesn't work because they want satisfied customers. And there is a larger aspect to this; for example, if cars or tires are faulty, reporting problems may save lives. In recent years, there were terrible problems with several car models that led to the sudden death of the occupants. The CEOs of the companies involved were brought before Congress to explain what they were going to do about it.

7. *Report crime and wrongdoing.* It is important to report crime and wrongdoing to the proper authorities or government agencies as a way to protect oneself and others.

8. *Take responsibility for ill-conceived actions.* If the garment label says to dry clean only and the consumer washes a sweater in hot water in a machine, the maker cannot be held responsible. Likewise, if signs at a national park tell tourists not to go into

certain areas because of lava or geysers, tourists should obey or possibly suffer negative consequences.

9. *Recognize that consumption has an effect on the environment and future generations.* According to Juliet Schor (1998), "A necessary first step toward becoming an educated consumer is to learn about the impact your consumption has on the environment. Only then can you make responsible and informed choices" (p. 156).

10. *Get referrals before signing a contract.* Check out a contractor's recommendations with local consumer protection agencies and the Better Business Bureau (BBB). A rule of thumb is the more substantial the investment or cost is, the more time should be spent investigating the business.

11. *Get estimates from at least two companies.* In such areas as making home improvements, removing trees, or moving furniture, a consumer should get more than one estimate and should have a firm understanding of all charges, licenses, and potential liabilities.

12. *Lessen the chances of identity theft.* By not leaving credit card receipts where they can be found and not writing Social Security numbers or home phone numbers on checks, consumers can lessen their chance of becoming victims of identity theft. Also be careful about what gets put in a mailbox that anyone can get into (for example, checks can be stolen out of letters). Even locked US postal boxes have been broken into and checks removed. In this case, surveillance cameras revealed who the thief was. More and more surveillance cameras film criminals in action.

13. *Deal with reputable, socially responsible companies.* More and more consumers expect companies to take **social responsibility**, a broad-based term referring to caring about the community and the environment (Mohr, Webb, & Harris, 2001).

What do all these consumer responsibilities add up to? They are really about using common sense; being aware of surroundings, business dealings, and potential victimization; and thinking about others as well as oneself.

CASE STUDY

Youthquake

Peter is a millennial, a member of a group ages 18 to 29, and they are fed up with the economy and politics as usual. They want change, and they are not afraid to complain about issues or under-performing products. According to the Census, nearly 43 million people fall in this age category or about 20 percent of registered voters. "I think about the costs of having a family, and it's going to be so difficult," says Edward Summers, 25, assistant to the president of Marist College in Poughkeepsie, NY.

This generation has watched corporate scandals and their parents lose jobs. They are keenly aware of how difficult it is to stay secure. "They saw their parents get burned," says Claudia Tattanelli, CEO of Universum Communications, a research firm that specializes in millennial workplace issues. "They watched 401(k)s that never got paid, parents losing health plans."

"As the government and employers shift more responsibility for benefits like health care and retirement onto the shoulders of individuals, many millennials see themselves as unwitting victims. Although that trend has been building for decades, this may be the first generation to fully feel the great shift of risk in their bones." "This is a group of people who understand what it means to have no safety net," says Elizabeth Warren, a Harvard University School of Law professor. Note, as of this writing she is a Senator from Massachusetts. Wielding their power for change is the hallmark of the millennial generation.

Source: Michelle Conlin (January 21, 2008).
"Youthquake." *Businessweek*, pp. 32–36.

CASE STUDY

McDonald's

In 2003, a federal judge dismissed a class action lawsuit filed on behalf of New York children that claimed McDonald's food caused them to suffer health problems, including diabetes, high blood pressure, and obesity. "One necessary element of any potentially viable claim must be that McDonald's products involve a danger that is not within the common knowledge of consumers. Plaintiffs have failed to allege with any specificity that such a danger exists," stated US District Court Judge Robert Sweet in a 65-page ruling.

Source: McDonald's (January 23, 2003). *Tallahassee Democrat*, p. E1.

Customer Service

The consumer experience includes not only what someone actually buys but also what happens during the entire shopping experience. Potential areas of complaint include problems with delivery and in-store customer service.

> *Clueless clerks roaming the aisles at Home Depot. Flight attendants in need of "anger management" counseling. Telemarketers calling promptly at dinner time to sell long-distance service. These are just some of the consumer gripes that proved costly to companies in the third annual corporate reputation survey conducted. Source: Harris Interactive Inc., an online market-research firm. (Alsop, 2002, p. B1)*

Consumer gripes are costly to companies because dissatisfied shoppers can take their business elsewhere. "When a company provides great service, its reputation benefits from a stronger emotional connection with its customers, as well as from increased confidence that it will stand behind its products," said Joy Sever, a senior vice president at Harris. Harris surveys tens of thousands of consumers about corporate reputation. Amazon ranked number one in 2013 followed by Apple (see Table 4.1). Johnson & Johnson has been in the top five for many years in the Harris polls. It cultivates a powerful image as "the caring company" and being associated with products for cuddly babies. Quality products and services play into how people responded in the survey.

Besides Amazon and Apple, the Walt Disney Company and Google scored high. Since this survey is taken every year, the names on this list shift around, but the point is that customer service is part of the consumer experience and that an individual's buying experience as well as the company's reputation play into customer satisfaction and expectations.

Smart companies react to these types of polls. When Home Depot dropped to nineteenth place in 2001 from fourth in 2000, it made some changes, such as having salespeople unpack merchandise at night so they could help customers during prime shopping hours and putting more employees on the floor on weekends. Table 4.1 lists the top fifteen companies and their reputation rankings.

Table 4.1 Corporate Reputation Rankings of the Most Visible Companies—Top 15 Companies, 2013

1. Amazon

2. Apple

3. The Walt Disney Company

4. Google

5. Johnson & Johnson

6. The Coca-Cola Company

7. Whole Foods Market

8. Sony

9. Procter & Gamble Co.

10. Costco

11. Samsung

12. Kraft Foods

13. USAA

14. Nike

15. Microsoft

Source: Harris Interactive, 2013. Reputation Quotient Survey.

Steps to Follow Before Buying

In subsequent chapters, there will be information on specific products and services such as buying houses or leasing cars. But here are some general buying guidelines that consumers can follow to avoid potential problems:

1. Decide in advance what is needed and affordable.

2. Research the product or service by using resources (including the Internet) to comparison-shop or to find out rules and regulations governing goods or businesses. Also find out if a company has a complaint record through the BBB or local consumer affairs offices.

3. Ask friends, family, and coworkers for recommendations about companies and products.

4. Shop around in person and online, compare quality and prices.

5. Read and understand contracts and warranties, labels and tags; check licenses. For example, if you are hiring a contractor to repair your roof, you would make sure first that he or she is properly licensed to do roof repairs.

6. Find out about refund and return policies.

7. Get things such as receipts in writing, and keep credit card receipts.

8. Be wary of buying from door-to-door salespeople, at the side of the road, out of a motel room, or from any other type of business without a permanent address. Be wary about buying over the Internet from unknown companies or private individuals. For example, a woman felt bad for two men who stopped at her front door in early December selling steaks door to door from the back of their truck. One of the guys kept saying, "Help me out; I need to make this sale for my bonus." . . . "It was before Christmas," the woman said. "I did feel sorry for him" (Rosica, 2003, p. B1). She wrote a check for $329.50, and the men filled her freezer with steaks. She paid for 120 steaks and got 117, but the main problem was the quality: Some of the cuts could not be identified, and much of the meat was hamburger patties and thin steaks rather than the steaks the men had shown her initially. When she complained, she could not get her money back. Their out-of-town company would not return phone calls. The men did not have a license to sell in her county, and she discovered from the BBB in the company's city that it had an "unsatisfactory record . . . of no response to customer complaints brought to [the Bureau's] attention," according to the bureau's website. As of the writing of this book, she was continuing her efforts, but it was not promising because she waited a month before filing a complaint and the state has a three-day cooling-off rule in which contracts can be cancelled from day of purchase. "The best thing to tell people is 'caveat emptor'—Latin for 'let the buyer beware,'" said Dr. James Varley, a food safety specialist with the state's Department of Agriculture and Consumer Services. When it comes to buying meat, he said, "You'd

do better at a name-brand grocery store" (Rosica, 2003, p. B1). In those stores, they pay attention to cleanliness and keep the meat properly frozen. The woman said she learned a valuable lesson. "Shut the door," she said. "There's no point in trying to be polite to these people. And they are very aggressive" (Rosica, 2003, p. B1).

9. Do not sign contracts until all blanks or changes are properly initialed or filled in.

10. Know which areas are complaint prone. Besides the identity theft already discussed, there are a number of other prominent fraud areas. Every year the Consumer Federation of America and the National Association of Consumer Agency Administrators survey government consumer protection offices to find out what transactions generate the most complaints. Following are those commonly on the list:

- sales of new and used cars
- auto repairs
- home improvements
- retail sales
- credit and lending
- mail-order and online orders
- auto leasing.

Steps to Follow After Buying

Consumer Redress

Before using any new product, read the instructions or labels, send in the warranty card, and keep all contracts, sales receipts, cancelled checks, owner's manuals, and warranty documents. If, even after acting in this responsible manner, there are problems with a product or service, consumers have the **right to redress**, which is the right to seek and obtain satisfaction for damages incurred through the use of a product or service. Consumer redress means that consumers could not foresee or protect themselves against faulty goods or services and after the fact can seek satisfaction for damages incurred. **Consumer satisfaction** is a construct or idea that performance perceptions and service expectations are met or, better yet, exceeded. For example, the brakes on a car should work because if they don't, the driver will not be safe.

Consumer redress is complicated because it is not always easy to determine fault and to decide who to approach for redress. Accidents may be the fault of many parties or manufacturers as well as the consumer himself or herself. The *Statistical Abstract of the United States* has been published since 1878. It is an authoritative and comprehensive guide to key government and industry data. It lists the number of home accidents per year connected to consumer products, and they are in order:

1. Stairs, ramps, landings, and floors

2. Bicycles

3. Knives

4. Beds★

5. Doors

★You may wonder how one get hurts by a bed; a common accident is a child getting hurt from falling off or jumping off of a top bunk bed.

Routine activities also causing injuries are barbecuing, bicycling, bowling, and, of course, driving. The following is a true story. Zelda and Ray who lived in a small town invited guests over for their first barbecue using a huge new outdoor grill. It touched the back outdoor wall of their garage, causing a fire and a call to the fire department. The firefighters put the fire out, the ribs were salvaged, no one was injured, and Zelda and Ray invited them to stay and eat, which they did.

Ways to Complain Effectively

Before hiring an attorney or running off to court, there are less time-consuming and less expensive remedies to try first. Figure 4.1 gives the order of steps to follow when seeking redress. The following sections provide descriptions of each step.

Local Business. The first step is to go back to the local business where you bought the product, such as returning rotten strawberries immediately to the store where you bought them and getting a refund. Before taking this step, make sure you have the receipt or paperwork. Go to the customer service desk at the grocery store, and get a cash refund. Many stores won't even require the receipt because the bar code on the plastic container has the needed price information. A more expensive product, such as a car, is going to require more documentation, but still, the first step is to contact the business that sold you the item or performed the service. Most consumer complaints can be resolved at this level.

Business Headquarters. If the local business does not provide satisfaction, you may want to go directly to the headquarters of the company. For example, if the local department store does not provide satisfaction, you would contact its headquarters by letter, online, or by phone. To find a company's headquarters and customer service office, go to www.companyname.com, click on customer service or a similar name,

Figure 4.1
Steps to Follow
when Bringing a
Complaint

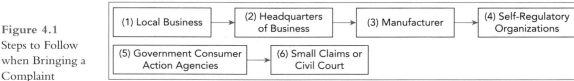

and report the problem or Google the company name. Calmly and concisely, describe the problem and what action you would like, such as a refund, repair, or replacement. If you file a complaint online, there will be a form to fill out or a place to type in your complaint, which is easier than composing a formal letter and mailing it. Online has the advantages of being free and 24/7. Many complaint toll-free phone lines are only open during normal business hours Monday through Friday. Increasingly, more people are going online directly to the company to file complaints with companies or with government agencies. Companies and the government prefer online inquiries because they can manage them better than having employees responding to a surge of phone calls flooding the phone lines at certain times of the day.

Manufacturer. Another option is to go to the manufacturer or maker of the product. Let's say an electric ceiling fan does not work right and the local home supply store where it was purchased will not give a refund. Besides going to the supply store's headquarters, an option would be to contact the manufacturer directly. There may be a regional office (rather than a central office) that will help you. Most products have a consumer complaint toll-free phone line or online address on the box or product label. Telephone companies and libraries can also be of assistance, or check *standardandpoors. com* for a registry of manufacturers. At a manufacturer's main offices (just as at retail stores' headquarters), there is a chain of command going from the entry-level person you first contact all the way up to the president or chief executive officer (CEO) of the company. A last resort would be to send a letter and copy of receipts and/or correspondence to the president or CEO.

Over 1,500 companies have consumer affairs departments in the United States and Canada.

Consumer affairs or consumer relations departments are set up within companies because they want to hear from consumers. Many of the companies are members of the **Society of Consumer Affairs Professionals (SOCAP)**. Founded in 1973, this international professional organization offers training, conferences, and publications to encourage and maintain the integrity of businesses in their transactions with consumers and in communications with government regulatory groups and agencies. Their goal is to improve the marketplace for consumers through addressing their concerns with corporate structures. Examples of companies belonging to SOCAP are AAMCO Transmissions Inc., American Express Company, Ball Park Brands, and Campbell Soup Company.

As consumers go through these levels of complaint steps, they should keep a record of efforts to resolve the problem. When you write to the company, describe the problem, what you have done so far to resolve it, and what solution you want. See Figure 4.2 for a sample complaint letter. When you call, keep notes of whom you spoke with and what they said, and include dates.

An additional piece of advice is to allow time for the person you contacted to resolve your problem. Save copies of all letters to and from the company. Don't give up if you are not satisfied—there are self-regulatory organizations (discussed next), trade associations,

Figure 4.2
Sample
Complaint
Letter

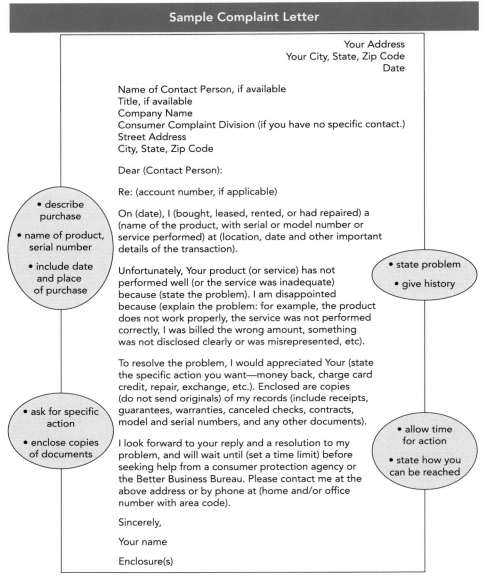

Sample Complaint Letter

Your Address
Your City, State, Zip Code
Date

Name of Contact Person, if available
Title, if available
Company Name
Consumer Complaint Division (if you have no specific contact.)
Street Address
City, State, Zip Code

Dear (Contact Person):

Re: (account number, if applicable)

- describe purchase
- name of product, serial number
- include date and place of purchase

On (date), I (bought, leased, rented, or had repaired) a (name of the product, with serial or model number or service performed) at (location, date and other important details of the transaction).

- state problem
- give history

Unfortunately, Your product (or service) has not performed well (or the service was inadequate) because (state the problem). I am disappointed because (explain the problem: for example, the product does not work properly, the service was not performed correctly, I was billed the wrong amount, something was not disclosed clearly or was misrepresented, etc).

- ask for specific action
- enclose copies of documents

To resolve the problem, I would appreciated Your (state the specific action you want—money back, charge card credit, repair, exchange, etc.). Enclosed are copies (do not send originals) of my records (include receipts, guarantees, warranties, canceled checks, contracts, model and serial numbers, and any other documents).

- allow time for action
- state how you can be reached

I look forward to your reply and a resolution to my problem, and will wait until (set a time limit) before seeking help from a consumer protection agency or the Better Business Bureau. Please contact me at the above address or by phone at (home and/or office number with area code).

Sincerely,

Your name

Enclosure(s)

Keep all copies of your letter, fax, or e-mail, and all related documents
For information about federal programs and services, call 1(800) FED-INFO or visit www.firstgov.gov.

media programs, national consumer organizations, and legal assistance programs listed throughout this book that may be able to assist you.

Self-Regulatory Organizations. There are self-regulatory groups, which may be known as **third-party complaint-handling sources** or dispute resolution groups. The reason they are called "third party" is because consumers are involving someone besides themselves and the source of the complaint. A third party is necessary when the local business, company headquarters, or manufacturer refuses to do anything to resolve the complaint. Nonprofit third-party organizations exist to resolve disputes between buyers and sellers, and probably the best known of these is the Better Business Bureau (BBB), which has offices in 112 communities in North America (the United States and Canada). According to their website, their mission is to be the leader in advancing marketplace trust. How do they do this? They list the following:

- setting standards for marketplace trust
- encouraging and supporting best practices by engaging with and educating consumers and businesses
- celebrating marketplace role models
- calling out and addressing substandard marketplace behavior
- creating a community of trustworthy businesses and charities.

(Source: www.bbb.org, Mission & Vision, February 2, 2015).

BBBs are nonprofit organizations supported mostly by business members. In other words, citizens are not paying taxes to run these organizations; rather, legitimate businesses in the community pay to run them because they know it is good business to support an ethical marketplace and to provide an alternative place for dispute resolution. To find the office in your area, go to www.*bbb.org*. Generally, BBBs offer the following:

- consumer education materials that encourage honest advertising and selling practices and expose scams
- answers to consumer questions
- information about a business, including whether there are unanswered or unsettled complaints or other marketplace problems
- help in resolving buyer/seller complaints against a business, including mediation and arbitration services
- information about charities and other organizations that seek public donations.

What won't BBBs do? They do not judge or rate individual products or brands, handle employer–employee wage disputes, or give legal advice.

How do BBBs work exactly? The consumer calls or contacts the BBB; the BBB takes the consumer's records and takes up the complaint with the company involved. The company gets to tell its side of the transaction and what went wrong. A company could choose not to respond, but this is unusual because the company does not want to have a bad record at the BBB and does not want to have its membership dropped in the BBB. If the call or letter from the BBB does not settle things, then the BBB may offer mediation or arbitration. **Mediation** is the process of negotiating to resolve differences, an attempt to bring about a peaceful settlement or compromise between the consumer and the business through the intervention of a third party. **Arbitration** is the process by which the parties in the dispute submit their differences to the judgment of an impartial person or group appointed by mutual consent. The arbitrator is the person who is chosen to settle the disagreement and who has the ability or power to make authoritative decisions. Mediation and arbitration are less expensive than legal proceedings.

So far the emphasis in this section has been on BBBs, but there are other organizations that offer mediation and arbitration. Another option is the consumer action panels (CAPs) that many industries have set up to handle industry-wide complaints.

Besides mediation and arbitration, there is a third type of dispute resolution program: conciliation. **Conciliation** means to reconcile, to make things pleasant again. A consumer offered a choice of these programs should select the one most appropriate by asking for a copy of the rules of the program before filing a case. The ruling may be binding for both the business and the consumer, or it may apply only to the business. If the program turns down your request, then the next step may be contacting consumer protection agencies or going to court.

Government Consumer Protection Agencies. Some people may go to agencies before they go to third-party dispute resolution organizations because they feel it is more appropriate or there is no BBB in their community, as well as for a variety of other reasons. Which level of government is appropriate varies by location and type of complaint. State, county, and city government consumer protection offices do the following:

- mediate complaints
- conduct investigations
- prosecute offenders of consumer laws
- license and regulate a variety of professions and professionals (this varies by state but may include banking, insurance, securities, utilities, doctors, lawyers, home improvement contractors, auto repair companies, debt collection agencies, and child day care businesses)
- promote strong consumer protection legislation
- provide educational materials
- advocate in the consumer interest.

County and city offices may have a better idea of local problems and businesses, so that would be the place to start; however, if a consumer does not have access to these, the next step is to contact the state consumer office or agency. Often these offices are part of the attorney general's office (this is the case in Arizona, Arkansas, Michigan, and Minnesota, to name a few) or the governor's office, but other times they are either separate entities or part of another unit. See Box 4.1 for a list of the primary state offices dealing with consumer complaints. For example, Florida has a Division of Consumer Services within the Department of Agriculture and Consumer Services, and they handle over 25,000 consumer complaints a month, so that gives you an idea of volume. Florida also has other areas of state government that handle complaints, including the Department of Insurance and the Attorney General's Office. To keep the list in the box manageable, only one main source is given for each state; for example, for California, the Department of Consumer Affairs is listed because it is the leading consumer department in a large and complex state with many consumer relations areas.

Box 4.1 State Consumer Protection Offices

Please note: Although states may have many consumer protection offices, the primary one for each state (located in the state capitol), Puerto Rico, and the District of Columbia is listed here as a beginning contact. A Google search (or other search engine) will get you there.

Alabama
Consumer Affairs Division
Office of the Attorney General

Alaska
Consumer Protection
Office of the Attorney General

Arizona
Public Advocacy Division
Office of the Attorney General

Arkansas
Consumer Protection Division
Office of the Attorney General

California
Department of Consumer Affairs

Colorado
Consumer Protection Division
Attorney General's Office

Connecticut
Department of Consumer Protection

Delaware
Fraud and Consumer Protection
    Division
Office of the Attorney General

District of Columbia
Office of the Attorney General

Florida
Consumer Services
Department of Agriculture and
    Consumer Services

Georgia
Governor's Office of Consumer Affairs

Hawaii
Office of Consumer Protection
Department of Commerce and
    Consumer Affairs

Idaho
Consumer Protection Division
Office of the Attorney General

Illinois
Office of the Attorney General

Indiana
Consumer Protection Division
Office of the Attorney General

Iowa
Consumer Protection Division
Office of the Attorney General

Kansas
Consumer Protection Division
Office of the Attorney General

Kentucky
Office of Consumer Protection
Office of the Attorney General

Louisiana
Public Protection Division, Consumer
  Protection/Environmental Section
Office of the Attorney General

Maine
Attorney General's Office
Consumer Protection Division

Maryland
Consumer Protection Division
Office of the Attorney General

Massachusetts
Consumer Protection and Antitrust
  Division
Office of the Attorney General

Michigan
Consumer Protection Division
Office of the Attorney General

Minnesota
Consumer Services Division
Minnesota Attorney General's Office

Mississippi
Consumer Protection Division
Office of the Attorney General

Missouri
Attorney General's Office
Consumer Protection Division

Montana
Department of Justice
Consumer Protection

Nebraska
Attorney General's Office
Consumer Protection Division

Nevada
Bureau of Consumer Protection

New Hampshire
Office of the Attorney General
Consumer Protection and Antitrust
  Bureau

New Jersey
New Jersey Division of Consumer
  Affairs
Office of Consumer Protection

New Mexico
Consumer Protection Division
Office of the Attorney General

New York
New York State Consumer Protection
  Board

North Carolina
Consumer Protection Section
Office of the Attorney General

North Dakota
Office of the Attorney General
Consumer Protection and Antitrust
  Division

Ohio
Attorney General's Office
Consumer Protection Section

Oklahoma
Oklahoma Attorney General

Oregon
Financial Fraud/Consumer Protection
  Section
Department of Justice

Pennsylvania
Office of the Consumer Advocate

Puerto Rico
Departmiento de Asuntos del
    Consumidor

Rhode Island
Consumer Protection Unit
Department of Attorney General

South Carolina
Department of Consumer Affairs

South Dakota
Office of the Attorney General
Consumer Protection Unit

Tennessee
Division of Consumer Affairs

Texas
Attorney General of Texas

Utah
Division of Consumer Protection

Vermont
Consumer Assistance Program
Office of the Attorney General

Virginia
Office of the Attorney General
Consumer Assistance

Washington
Office of the Attorney General

West Virginia
Consumer Protection and Anti-Trust
    Division
Office of the Attorney General

Wisconsin
Department of Agriculture, Trade, and
    Consumer Protection

Wyoming
Attorney General's Consumer
    Protection Unit

When contacting a state department or office about a consumer complaint, the first contact should be a phone call on their toll-free line or go online. The consumer hotline person or responder will know how to direct your call or tell you what steps to take in filing a complaint. Investigators may be put onto cases involving several complaints such as travel fraud, auto repair, or health fraud. They are interested in helping the consumer who has filed a complaint and also in preventing similar problems from happening.

How often do people file complaints? Although toll-free lines or websites gather tens of thousands of complaints a month in populous states, this is only the tip of the iceberg. An American Association of Retired Persons (AARP) study found that 75 percent of victims age 55 and over did not report their experiences with fraud (Don't Fall Prey to These Senior Scams, 2014). Why? The two most likely reasons are they don't want to bother or don't know where to turn for help.

State consumer protection agencies may license and regulate a variety of professions and professionals. They may oversee boards that issue rules and regulations; prepare and give examinations; issue, deny, or revoke licenses; bring disciplinary actions; handle consumer complaints; and provide referral services. The agency may contact a professional on your behalf, may conduct an investigation, and may take disciplinary action, which may include probation, license suspension, or license revocation for that business.

Regarding identity theft, state governments and the FTC's consumer protection agency are actively investigating consumer complaints in this area, trying to lessen their occurrence and changing laws and procedures in the process. For example, in Florida, a statewide grand jury that is searching for ways to stop identity theft recommended tighter restrictions on the distribution of personal data, more frequent in-person driver's license renewals, and a swifter response from law officials. Although identity theft is a growing national problem, certain areas are reporting more complaints than others: The District of Columbia had the highest rate of identity theft in 2001, with 77 victims for every 100,000 people; California and Nevada followed, with 45 and 41 victims, respectively (Ho, 2002).

As mentioned previously, besides the general consumer protection office in the state, certain divisions may have their own toll-free lines or websites to handle complaints in specific areas, such as auto repairs or insurance. For example, if a consumer was having problems with a repair shop or an insurance agency or policy, after trying to remedy the problem with the local company, its headquarters, and the BBB, the consumer could call the Auto Repair Division or the Department of Insurance in his or her state and find out what to do next. If there is a specialized agency, the consumer should contact it first rather than the general consumer complaint agency.

The federal government may handle individual complaints in certain areas, such as investment fraud on a national scale, but more likely the consumer should start at the city, county, or state level. For information and complaints regarding investments, a consumer could contact the Securities and Exchange Commission (SEC) Office of Investor Education and Assistance at www.sec.gov.

Besides government agencies, on occasion private consumer organizations will try to help a member with a complaint, but generally consumer groups do not assist individual consumers with their complaints and encourage members to go through the steps previously outlined. For example, a group such as AARP has a consumer issues section that is mainly charged to examine those consumer problems and issues that impact the financial security of people 50 years of age or older and to help its members protect themselves from marketplace fraud and deception. AARP employs a variety of strategies to keep members informed of wrongdoings but does not pursue individual complaints on a regular basis.

To avoid unnecessary duplication of effort, state consumer protection offices meet regularly to inform each other about scams that are drifting through the United States. It is common for states to form coalitions leveling charges of fraud or deception against a repeat-offender company. For example, the attorney generals of several states may charge a company with false and misleading claims. An out-of-court settlement may be reached wherein the company stops making such claims and pays each state an amount of money to cover the costs of their investigations and legal efforts. In so doing, the company is stopped, and the states bring issues to federal attention. It also takes the load off the courts.

Another way states have taken the load off the courts is by instituting systems of ombudspersons. The office of the **ombudsperson** mediates disputes, offers counseling and mediation services, and uses other out-of-court means to resolve conflict. Ombudspersons work with the court system to accelerate the bureaucratic process.

States also work together through the **Uniform Commercial Code (UCC)**, whose main purpose is to set a standard by which merchants operating in more than one state can more easily comply with that state's laws. This statute has been adopted at least partially by all states and regulates most sales of goods. It makes it easier for sellers to conduct business in several states.

Small Claims Courts or Civil Courts. When all the previous steps have failed, a consumer can go to **small claims court** (in some places it is called conciliation court or magistrates court). This is a form of civil court that allows **litigants** to claim damages or resolve disputes that involve modest amounts of money. Each state sets the maximum allowed; in some states the maximum is $5,000. In small claims courts, consumers speak for themselves, the business also gives its side of the story, and a judge listens and decides the outcome. It is rare, but some states have juries instead of judges. Usually the consumer wins. Often businesses do not show up or try to settle out of court because they can't spare the court time (usually there is some waiting time involved). A business owner's time may be worth more than the amount of money in dispute. Typical cases involve ruined clothes at dry cleaners, landlord–tenant disputes, and faulty home repairs. The judge, for example, may have the dry cleaner give a newlywed $1,000 for a ruined wedding dress. Cases involving more than the maximum allowed amounts or more complications would go to another civil court. The process that is usually followed in a small claims court is given in Box 4.2.

CASE STUDY

Small Claims Court

This is a real story about a student and what happened to her in small claims court. The student was a middle-aged female who was an American citizen born in Mexico. Her husband worked for the US Post Office, and she was very proud of her family and American citizenship. One Christmas she was shopping for gifts at a store and left the gifts to be wrapped at the gift wrap department. On her return, the gifts were missing, and the store insisted that she had made it all up and that she had not purchased anything. As the argument escalated, the store managers used racial epithets. On the basis of her consumer economics class, she decided to go to small claims court. While waiting outside for her case to be called, the store managers said they wanted to settle out of court and would give her the money. She said, "No, I want my day in court" and went in. Not only was she awarded the money, but it turns out she exposed a ring that was working in the gift wrap department. They had an accomplice outside the backdoor whom they would give the merchandise to when a shopper's back was turned. The judge awarded her the money she had lost. The student said that had it not been for the class, she would not have known what to do nor had the courage to do it. When she reported what had happened to her classmates (she did not tell anyone at the time, including her family, because she did not know what would happen), they applauded and congratulated her. As a prevention technique, classmates also mentioned that shoppers should get proof that their gifts are being wrapped if they leave them (often stores have a ticket for this purpose) or should keep their purchase receipt or stay and wait for the gifts to be wrapped. (In the case of this student, the wrappers not only took the gifts but also took her receipt, so she had no proof of purchase.)

Photo 4.1 Consumers have their day in court

Source: Thinkstock: moodboard

Civil vs. Criminal Cases

Civil court involves the hiring of attorneys, more formality, and more money than small claims court. If the litigant loses, there are routes of appeal within the court system that go all the way up to state supreme courts. This is a costly and time-consuming process. If a person cannot afford a lawyer, he or she may qualify for free legal help from the office of a legal aid agency or a Legal Services Corporation (LSC) office or may receive help on a contingency basis which usually means the attorney will take a percentage of the awarded amount if the case settles in favor of the complainant. The LSC was created in 1974 by Congress to provide financial support for legal assistance in noncriminal proceedings for low-income consumers; it has offices in all 50 states, as well as Guam, Puerto Rico, Micronesia, and the Virgin Islands, and the website is www.lsc.gov.

Box 4.2 Typical Small Claims Court Process

- First, the "wronged" consumer initiates the process by speaking with the clerk of the court (usually the consumer must live, work, or do business in the locale in question).

- If the clerk advises the consumer to proceed, he or she files a claim and becomes known as the **plaintiff** (the initiator of the lawsuit). Everything on the forms must be accurate. There may be a small fee for filing a claim, and businesses as well as consumers can file suits.

- Once the plaintiff files suit, the court issues a **summons**, which is a notice to appear in court as a juror, defendant, or witness, or a **subpoena**, which is a legal writ requiring an appearance in court to give testimony. The **defendant** is the person required to answer the lawsuit. Upon receiving the summons, about one-quarter of the cases will be settled out of court; in such an occurrence, the consumer should get the agreement in writing and file it with the court.

- If the case goes on and the defendant does not show up at court, then the court will often grant the claim by default. Usually there are no lawyers unless there is a substantial amount of money involved. Some states prohibit lawyers from presenting at these cases because generally the setting is informal, and plaintiffs should be able to represent themselves. In preparation for a case, college students can often get free legal advice at their university (call student services to find out if your college offers legal services to students). A common student problem is landlord–tenant disputes.

- If both sides show up at the court case, then they both give their sides of the story and present evidence in the form of photos, receipts, letters, contracts, cancelled checks, and so on. A calm, simple explanation is advised. Visitors, friends, and families can watch cases in progress.

- The judge usually decides the outcome right then; occasionally the judge may wait a few weeks and send the verdict by letter.

> **Advice on Finding an Attorney**
>
> To find a lawyer, ask family and friends for references, and check with the lawyer referral services in your area such as the bar association. As mentioned earlier, as a college student you may have access to free legal help on your campus; contact student services.

Sometimes if the litigant wins and is awarded the money, the defendant refuses to pay, which may necessitate going back to court. **Civil cases** involve the settling of private conflicts between people or between businesses. Common cases involve landlord–tenant disputes, contract disputes, and ruined products; usually the wrongdoer is asked to pay or remedy the situation in some way, so compensation is involved. A **tort** is a civil wrong that causes either emotional or physical injury (or both). Torts can be intentional or negligent.

Crimes are acts that society forbids or punishes through legislative bodies or courts. **Criminal cases** involve prevention, punishment, and rehabilitation. In criminal cases, a violation is deemed to have taken place or an injustice committed against the government, which brings charges against the person or persons who committed the crime. A person committing a crime is prosecuted, and if found guilty he or she is punished by the government according to its statutory laws.

Photo 4.2 A bailiff swears in a witness in court

Source: Thinkstock: Fuse

Consumer Law

The law provides safeguards to buyers. Laws pertaining to consumers can be broken down into statutory law, regulatory law, common law, and constitutional law. There are hundreds of federal statutory and regulatory laws related to consumers. **Statutory laws** are enacted by the legislative branch of government, which at the federal level means the US Congress. **Regulatory laws** are laws, rules, or regulations enacted to protect consumers through agencies of the federal or state government. At the federal level, the FTC is often the agency that protects consumers, but there are over 100 federal government regulatory laws, and these involve many agencies, from food safety to airline safety. Examples of other agencies are the Department of Agriculture and the Food and Drug Administration. At the state level, the most likely agencies or offices are the state attorney general's office or consumer affairs departments or divisions (listed in Box 4.1).

Common law is based on judicial decisions and embodied in reports of decided cases that have been administered by the common-law courts of England since the Middle Ages. These laws evolved into the type of legal system we now have in the United States and Canada, for the most part. The trend is away from common law to statutory law. **Constitutional law**, as the name implies, is based on the US Constitution, which is the fundamental law of the US federal system of government. An example of a right discussed in the Constitution that affects consumers is the right to a fair trial.

Licensing Boards

Much of the state consumer protection activity takes place through state licensing boards before something reaches the complaint level. The boards issue licenses to professionals such as barbers, physicians, attorneys, and funeral directors. When you have had your hair cut, you have probably seen the license of the barber or cosmetologist prominently displayed. The boards have the power to issue and revoke licenses and charge fees, and in so doing, they protect the consumer from deceptive, harmful, or ineffective services. Critics of boards feel that some are not as consumer-oriented as they ought to be (depending on the makeup of the board members and the kinds of information they are given, this may or may not be true) and that they are inclined to be more in favor of the professional. Most boards try to do the right thing, and they perform important preventive services. Aren't you glad that someone has checked out your barber or cosmetologist before he or she takes scissors or a razor to your head or uses chemical dyes?

Warranties and Guarantees

Many products offer warranties or guarantees. The terms *warranty* and *guarantee* can be used interchangeably according to the Magnuson-Moss Warranty Act, which became law in 1977. This act requires that consumers be given warranty information, if it exists for a particular product or part of a product, before making a purchase. The act does not

Photo 4.3 Car warranties guarantee that the condition, character, and quality of the car are as represented by the manufacturer

Source: Thinkstock: Jirsak

require that manufacturers give warranties, but if a warranty is given, it must be clearly stated as either a full or a limited warranty. See Box 4.3 for a list of what a full warranty promises and what a limited warranty means according to the act. A product such as a washing machine can have a full warranty on some parts and a limited warranty on others. Violations of the act should be reported to the FTC (www.ftc.gov).

Besides full and limited warranties, there are also implied and express (or written) warranties. Automobile manufacturers issue **written warranties**, which are written promises that the character and quality of the product are as the manufacturer represents them. Usually the guarantee specifies what is covered for a specific number of miles or years (when leases are involved) or months. **Implied warranties** are not written but are inherently understood in the transaction. The **implied warranty of fitness** for a particular purpose means that the warranty holds for the correct use of the product; for example, the seller guarantees that a shampoo will clean hair, but he or she does not guarantee that it will clean car seat covers. The **implied warranty of merchantability** is more open than the implied warranty of purpose and simply means that the product should work, that it is salable and fit for the market; as an example, a blender that doesn't blend would be unmerchantable. Products delivered to your home should be as merchantable as they were in the store. The seller is obligated to deliver the product in a reasonable amount of time ("reasonable" means what an average responsible adult would expect given the circumstances). A **reasonable person** is rational, attentive, knowledgeable, and capable of making judgments in his or her best interest.

Contracts

Agreements or promises that are legally enforceable are called **contracts**. Most significant contracts in consumer law are written, but they may also be oral or implied. Obviously, written contracts are more easily defended in court and in the complaint process. A contract is an understanding reached between parties having the legal capacity to agree and when something of value is exchanged between them, and a contract is formed when the parties involved may be held liable or responsible. Contracts are made for the present and the future—not the past. The pros and cons of service contracts or extended warranties are covered in Chapter 10; the present chapter's coverage serves as an introduction and emphasizes the legal ramifications of contracts.

Box 4.3 Magnuson-Moss Warranty Act

The Magnuson-Moss Warranty Act is the federal law passed by Congress in 1975 that governs consumer product warranties. It requires manufacturers and sellers of consumer products to provide consumers with detailed information about warranty coverage. In passing this act, Congress specified a number of requirements that warrantors must meet. The act affects the rights of consumers and the obligations of warrantors under written warranties. The following is a description of parts of the act and its objectives (for further information, go to www.ftc.gov).

Below is a list explaining the act's contents:

- It enables consumers to comparison-shop for warranties.
- It encourages warranty competition.
- It promotes timely and complete performance of warranty obligations.
- It does not compel the consumer to be given a written warranty. (The act does not apply to oral warranties; only written warranties are covered.)
- It does not apply to warranties on services.
- It says that a product is "merchantable," meaning it is supposed to do what it claims. For example, one assumes that an oven will bake food at a controlled temperature selected by the buyer, so if it does not heat or heats improperly, an implied warranty of merchantability would be breached.
- It implies warranty of fitness for a particular purpose, which means that customers rely on sellers to make a product for a specific use. An example given on the

---

FTC website is that if an appliance manufacturer says that a washing machine will handle a 15-pound load, it should be able to handle 15-pound loads.

- It implies a standard or level of performance at time of purchase. Implied warranties do not cover problems caused by abuse, misuse, ordinary wear, failure to follow directions, or improper maintenance. However, the normal durability of an appliance, for example, would be considered. Used merchandise may have implied warranties when the seller is a merchant who deals in such goods, not when a sale is made by a private individual.

- It discusses the concept of selling "as is." You cannot sell "as is" in some states; in others, merchandise has to be clearly marked as defective or damaged. Sellers have to be careful when selling a product "as is" because they may be liable if it is dangerous or causes personal injury to someone.

- It distinguishes between a full warranty (and the promises thereof) and a limited warranty. In short, a limited warranty lets consumers know that the warranty offers less than a full warranty. Caution is advised because limited may mean that only certain parts will be replaced for free or that the buyer may have to pay for labor costs.

A legally binding contract requires the following:

- There must be a mutual agreement.
- Competent participants are involved. For example, the people must be of age (usually 18 years or older). A person who is intoxicated or in some other way incapacitated is usually not legally held to a contract signed under those conditions.
- The subject matter is legal.
- There must be consideration (an exchange of goods, money, or services, that is, something involved beyond just words).
- A legal form is required. The form varies by state; in some states, contracts have to be written.

Consumer Legal Terms

The chapter has already introduced some legal terminology and provided some basic information about courts. Naturally, there is much more, and Box 4.4 lists other basic definitions of legal terms. The intent of this chapter is not to turn you into an attorney but to expose you to "legalese" relevant to the study of consumer economics. Many students who have found this part of the course interesting have gone on to law school or to graduate school in public administration or public policy; others work in businesses or nonprofit settings where they interact with lawyers, so it is useful to have a beginning understanding of legal terminology.

Media Sources for Redress

At any point in the complaint process, a consumer may seek help from a media source. In most cities, there is a hotline or action-line column in the newspaper or a consumer reporter or a consumer segment on the radio or the television news programs. Many of the columnists or reporters will go to bat for wronged consumers and try to get answers. To find these services, contact the local newspaper (usually the business section editor will know whom to contact), or call radio or television stations. Media are most likely to take up your cause if they feel that it affects other viewers or readers and that it would be a public service. Newspapers and television news shows also perform a valuable public service by providing information about current fraud schemes, telling what is happening and how to avoid being victimized. A well-known, long-standing national television program is *60 Minutes*, which for years has broadcast investigations into wrongdoing, much of which is consumer-linked, such as health fraud investigations or telemarketing and investment schemes.

Another media resource is Call for Action, Inc. (www.callforaction.org). Several decades old, it is an international nonprofit network of consumer hotlines operating in conjunction with broadcast partners. Its purpose is to educate and assist consumers and small businesses with consumer problems. Box 4.5 gives a list of its hotlines in major markets that are staffed with trained volunteers who offer advice and mediate complaints at no cost.

Box 4.4 Consumer Legal Terms

Here are some legal terms relevant to the study of consumer economics that have not already been defined in this chapter. These will not be listed in the Key Terms section at the end of the chapter because they are given mainly as a reference.

action: a judicial proceeding; a lawsuit contested in court.

adversary proceeding: a legal procedure involving opposing parties, such as a plaintiff and a defendant.

adversary system: a system with a trial where the truth will emerge (the system we are used to in the United States).

answer: the defendant's written response to the plaintiff.

breach of contract: the failure (without legal excuse) to fulfill any promise that is part of a contract.

---

class action: an action brought by a group or class of plaintiffs or defendants who share the same interests in the litigation.

complainant: the group or person who files a complaint.

complaint: the initial pleading that begins a lawsuit and includes allegations and remedies sought.

default: the failure to do something (such as pay a loan or show up in court); the failure to comply.

deposition: a statement or testimony made under oath.

discovery: the methods used to obtain information held by the other party that can be used in civil or criminal actions.

dismissal: the termination of an action or claim; the end of a lawsuit.

enjoin: to impose, constrain, attach; to stop a person from a specific act.

fiduciary: a person acting on behalf of another (such as managing money or property); a person acting in good faith (such as being an executor of a will or a guardian of a minor).

garnishment: a device used by creditors to get back money owed to them (a third party, such as an employer, can garnish wages of an employee and send that money through the court to creditors).

injunction: a remedy by a court order compelling a party to do or refrain from doing a specified act (such as the court ordering a person to leave a celebrity alone).

joint and several liability: a joint liability imposed on all the parties involved, and if one party does not pay, the other parties must (liability may vary by jurisdiction and considerations of fault).

joint tenancy: two or more parties being held equally responsible; a form of legal co-ownership.

liability: the position of being answerable according to law, of being held responsible (such as being an accomplice in a crime).

negligence: the failure to exercise the right amount of care in protecting others.

rebuttal: the giving of evidence or argument that rebuts or refutes previous testimony or evidence given by an adversary.

settlement: an agreement reached that terminates the lawsuit.

verdict: the decision of the jury for the plaintiff or the defendant; in criminal actions, the finding of guilty or not guilty.

Box 4.5 Call for Action, Inc. Hotlines in Major Markets (TV and Radio)

Altoona, PA: WTAJ-TV, www.wearecentralpa.com, 814-944-9336

Atlanta, GA: WAGA-TV, http://www.fox5atlanta.com/, 404-879-4500

Augusta, GA: WRDW-TV, www.wrdw.com, 803-442-4550

Birmingham, AL: WBRC-TV, http://www.wbrc.com/, 205-583-4321

Boston, MA: WBZ, www.wbz.com, 617-787-7070

Buffalo, NY: WIVB-TV, www.wivb.com, 716-879-4900

Cincinnati, OH: The Enquirer, www.cincinnati.com, 513-768-8833

Cleveland, OH: WJW-TV, http://fox8.com/, 216-578-0700

Colorado Springs, CO: KKTV-TV, www.kktv.com, 719-457-8211

Columbus, OH: WSYX-TV, www.abc6onyourside.com, 614-481-6848

Detroit, MI: WXYZ-TV, http://www.wxyz.com/, 248-827-3362

Fort Myers, FL: WINK-TV, http://www.winknews.com/, 239-334-4357

Greensboro, NC: WFMY-TV, www.wfmy2.com, 336-379-5618

Kansas City, MO: KSHB-TV, www.kshb.com, 816-932-4321

Las Vegas, NV: KTNV-TV, www.ktnv.com, 702-368-2255

Madison, WI: WISC-TV, www.channel3000.com, 608-270-2833

Milwaukee, WI: WTMJ-TV, www.touchtmj4.com, 414-967-5495

Philadelphia, PA: WPVI-TV, abclocal.go.com/wpvi, 866-978-4232

Phoenix/Flagstaff, AZ: KPNX-TV and KNAZ-TV, http://www.12news.com/, 602-444-1212

Providence, RI: WPRI-TV 12, www.wpri.com, 401-228-1850

St. Louis, MO: KTVI-TV, http://fox2now.com/, 636-282-2222

Toledo, OH: WTOL-TV, www.wtol.com, 419-255-2255

Washington, DC: WUSA-TV, www.wusa9.com, 301-652-4357

For phone number updates or any other changes, go to www.callforaction.org.

Summary

The study of consumer economics includes learning how to effectively complain and how to avoid fraud. Identity theft tops the list of consumer fraud complaints according to the Federal Trade Commission.

Legitimate businesses want satisfied customers (because they are more likely to return and provide good word of mouth to friends and family and through online reviews), so for the most part they will seek to remedy problems. This chapter gave a list of consumer responsibilities and steps to follow when seeking redress. The chapter addressed the following questions:

- What do I do first if I have a faulty product or get poor service?
- When is it appropriate to contact a third-party complaint-handling organization such as a Better Business Bureau or a government consumer agency?
- When is it appropriate to go to small claims court or civil court?

The goal of this chapter is to help the reader feel in charge, to know what to do when a purchase goes wrong, how to complain effectively, and who to turn to for help.

Most consumers do not complain to authorities. An AARP study found that 75 percent of victims age 55 and over did not report their experiences with fraud.

Knowing legal terminology and understanding basic consumer rights and responsibilities are useful consumer skills. Reading online reports and newspapers, listening to the radio, and watching television programs that expose fraud help keep consumers abreast of current scams. These are examples of knowledge being power. A lot of consumer complaints can be avoided by being wary (for example, not buying from door-to-door salespeople or from people at the side of the road) and by making wise purchases and seeking redress when necessary (for example, by immediately returning faulty products or cancelling a contract within three working days if necessary).

KEY POINTS

1. Consumers have responsibilities (for example, to be honest in their dealings).
2. There are steps to follow in the complaint process. The recommended first step is to talk to the people at the place the faulty product or service was purchased.
3. More people are using the Internet as a way to alert potential consumers and as a way to contact manufacturers and resolve complaints.
4. Most companies want good customer relations and will try to resolve complaints.
5. In most small claims court cases, lawyers are not necessary, and there is usually a judge who decides the case instead of a jury.
6. Warranties, of which there are several kinds, protect consumers.
7. State government consumer protection departments and related units and media sources are ready to help consumers in their quest for complaint resolution.

KEY TERMS

arbitration

civil cases

common law

conciliation

constitutional law

consumer satisfaction

contracts

criminal cases

defendant

fraud

implied warranties

implied warranty of fitness

implied warranty of merchantability

litigants

mediation

ombudsperson

plaintiff

reasonable person

regulatory laws

right to redress

small claims court

social responsibility

Society of Consumer Affairs Professionals (SOCAP)

statutory laws

subpoena

summons

third-party complaint-handling sources

tort

Uniform Commercial Code (UCC)

written warranties

DISCUSSION QUESTIONS

1. Regarding the list of consumer responsibilities in the chapter, does it make any difference to you if a company that you buy from is socially responsible? Explain your answer.

2. What has been your experience with customer service? Name one company that provided good service and one that did not. What happened in each case?

3. Do you know anyone who went to small claims court? If so, what was the case about, and what was the outcome?

4. Find the Better Business Bureau nearest your campus. Select a business or charity and see what the BBB says.

5. Go to lawyers.com and either click on "Ask a lawyer" to try a question out or click on legal resources and find out more information beyond what the chapter covered.

REFERENCES

Alsop, R. (January 16, 2002). Reputations rest on good service. *Wall Street Journal*, p. B1.

Brickman, L. (January 6, 2003). The great asbestos swindle. *Wall Street Journal*, p. A18.

De Graaf, J., D. Wann, and T. Naylor. (2001). *Affluenza: the all-consuming epidemic.* San Francisco, CA: Berrett-Koehler Publishers.

Ho, D. (January 24, 2002). Identity theft tops list of frauds. *Tallahassee Democrat*, p. E1.

McDonald's. (January 23, 2003). *Tallahassee Democrat*, p. E1.

McLaughlin, H. (2009). What's in a name: "client," "patient," "customer," "consumer," "expert by experience," "service user"—what's next? *British Journal of Social Work*, 39, 1101–1171.

Mohr, L., D. Webb, and K. Harris. (2001). Do consumers expect companies to be socially responsible? The impact of corporate social responsibility on buying behavior. *Journal of Consumer Affairs*, 35 (1), 45–72.

Rosica, J. (January 7, 2003). Freezer full of unwanted steaks has woman steamed. *Tallahassee Democrat*, p. B1.

Schor, J. (1992). *The overworked American: the unexpected decline of leisure*. New York: Basic Books.

Schor, J. (1998). *The overspent American: why we want what we don't need*. New York: Harper Perennial.

Chapter **5**

Government Protection, Consumer Groups, and the Media

Nothing is easier than spending the public money. It does not appear to belong to anybody. The temptation is overwhelming to bestow it on somebody.

Calvin Coolidge

LEARNING OBJECTIVES

1. Explain how to contact an elected official.
2. List the functions of government agencies most involved with protecting the consumer interest.
3. Discuss the reasons for regulation and deregulation.
4. Describe the three primary interests of consumer groups.
5. Explain the mission of consumer media.

> ### CASE STUDY
>
> **Rotten Apples**
>
> "A Missouri company is recalling packaged caramel applies that may be linked to a listeria outbreak that has hospitalized 29 people and killed at least three in 10 states. Happy Apples of Washington, MO., recalled caramel apples carrying a best-use date between Aug. 25 and Nov. 23 that were sold in grocery, discount and club stores in packs of one, three, four and eight. In a statement Wednesday, the company said an apple supplier, Bidart Brothers, had notified it that 'there may be a connection between this outbreak and the apples that supplied' to a Happy Apples facility in California. On Friday, the Centers for Disease Control and Prevention warned consumers to stop eating prepackaged caramel apples while it investigated the outbreak of *listeria monocytogenes*, a bacterium that causes the rare but sometimes fatal infection."
>
> Source: Lenny Bernstein (December 25, 2014). "Missouri company recalls caramel applies that may be linked to listeria outbreak." *Washington Post*, *To Your Health* blog. Available online at www.washingtonpost.com/news/to-your-health/wp/2014/12/25/missouri-company-recalls-caramel-apples-that-may-be-linked-to-listeria-outbreak.

Introduction

Government is underfunded for the job they are assigned to do to protect consumers. An example is the US Consumer Product Safety Commission (CPSC), which has 21 people working at select ports. There are over 300 ports of entry in the United States.

> *The CPSC cannot fight a fair fight with just 21 people to screen $700 billion worth of consumer products coming into our ports annually. The CPSC's presence at the ports is just one-half of one percent of the number of FDA inspectors located at ports around the country. (Tenenbaum, 2014, p. 650)*

On that discouraging note, this chapter begins the discussion of government protection of consumers and the functions of the main agencies. In looking back, a researcher wrote:

> *When consumer and corporate spending declines in difficult times, government spending acts as a buffer for the economy. And currently, the federal government has a major budget surplus, helping to ensure government spending can continue, even when tax receipts decline. (Lynch, 2001, p. A5)*

CRITICAL THINKING

Government's Role in Consumer Protection

Do you have an opinion on government spending or the role of government in the economy that you would like to share with other students or with an elected official? Explain your answer.

This chapter shows how to reach elected officials, including the president and vice president. Although President Coolidge in the beginning quote criticized those who loosely spend government money, we all need some of the services government provides, including consumer protection. When we use a product, we assume it is safe.

In an American customer satisfaction survey conducted by the University of Michigan, consumers were just as satisfied with services they received from federal government agencies as they were with services from private companies (Jones, 2002). A striking example was that respondents were more satisfied with the service from the Internal Revenue Service (IRS) than from McDonald's. If that survey was taken today, what might be the results?

This chapter builds on topics introduced earlier in the book: government, consumer groups, and media—all parts of the circular power model of consumerism (see Figure 5.1).

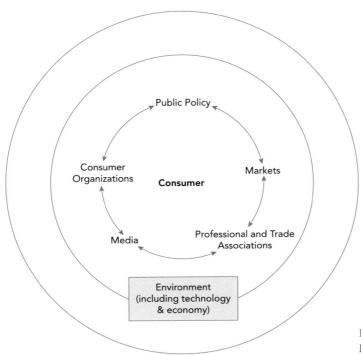

Figure 5.1 Circular Power Model of Consumer Economics

We are living in an information economy. Use it here as well.

Some of the topics to be covered include product recalls, regulation and deregulation, and websites for information. This latter point is important because we are living in an **information economy**—those who produce, have access to, and influence the spread of information have power in the global society. **Informational influence** refers to how consumers use their reference groups for information and as a basis on which to make decisions.

Ways to Contact Elected Officials

It takes only a few minutes to write to an elected official, but it can make a difference if there is an issue you care about. When elected officials receive enough letters from constituents or even a single stirring letter, it may sway their vote or stance on an issue. Often elected officials will read parts of the letters when they give testimony or make other types of public pronouncements. For greatest impact, follow these six guidelines:

1. Use your own paper and your own words; write clearly and concisely. Of course, now a more typical way is to send your request online.

2. State your problem or issue. Focus on one subject per letter or email.

3. Refer to specific legislation by name and/or number.

4. Request a specific action, such as voting in a particular way, or suggest public hearings. Allow time for action or response. State how you can be reached.

5. If you work or live in the elected official's district, say so.

6. Insulting words or lack of courtesy will not work; polite wording will get more of the kind of attention and action you want.

7. Enclose copies of documents or receipts (do not send originals).

To find addresses of state and local representatives, check your phone book. US senators and representatives can be reached at the following addresses:

The Honorable _____	The Honorable _____
[name]	[name]
US Senate	US House of Representatives
Washington, DC 20510	Washington, DC 20515

"The Honorable" in front of a person's name is a title of respect in the United States and is reserved for those who hold or have held high office at the federal, state, and city levels. Members of Congress also have local addresses in their districts as well as email addresses and websites. The salutation on the letter should be Dear Senator _____ or Dear Mr. _____ or Ms. _____ for a US representative (putting the person's last name in the blank).

You can email the president at president@whitehouse.gov and the vice president at vice.president@whitehouse.gov. Emails or letters should have the following salutation: Dear Mr. President or Dear Mr. Vice President. In the event of a female president or vice president, it would be Dear Ms. President or Dear Ms. Vice President unless she announces another choice.

The correct salutation for a governor is Dear Governor or Dear Governor _____ (add the last name). An email or other form of online contact or letter to a state governor would be addressed:

> The Honorable
>
> _____ [name]
>
> Governor of _____ [state]
>
> Address

For the closing of a business letter, "Sincerely" is always appropriate; for the president or another high official, it is appropriate to use "Respectfully yours." In a letter, skip three spaces down and then type in your name. In the space above, handwrite your signature.

Agencies and Commissions

Federal Consumer Protection

The federal government is empowered to act on behalf of consumers through a series of acts, rules, regulations, and legislation. Several federal government agencies provide recall information, perform product tests, conduct research studies, and enforce product safety regulations. The agencies most involved with consumer protection are the Federal Trade Commission (FTC), the Consumer Product Safety Commission (CPSC), the Food and Drug Administration (FDA), the US Department of Agriculture (USDA), the Department of Justice (DOJ), the Securities and Exchange Commission (SEC), and the National Highway Traffic Safety Administration (NHTSA). Also included in this section is the Federal Consumer Information Center (FCIC), which announces recalls and distributes the *Consumer Action Handbook* as well as booklets and pamphlets on specific consumer topics.

Federal Trade Commission (FTC). At the federal level, the FTC is the government's most aggressive agency in rooting out fraud, violations of consumers' privacy, and deceptive marketing practices in the emerging point-and-click marketplace (Simons, 1999). The FTC was established in 1914 by the Federal Trade Commission Act, and since then its powers have broadened.

CASE STUDY

Do Not Call Registry

A major consumer problem is receiving unwanted calls. If you have a problem with unwanted calls that cannot be solved by asking the company to stop, you can file a complaint at www.donotcall.gov using the File a Complaint page. Do Not Call complaints are entered in the FTC's Consumer Sentinel Network, a secure online database available to civil and criminal law enforcement agencies. The FTC does not resolve individual consumer problems, but a complaint will lead to an investigation of the company and could lead to law enforcement action.

In 1938, the Wheeler Lea Amendments clarified the FTC's role in regard to including "unfair or deceptive acts or practices," and by these amendments, deceptive advertising came under the FTC's jurisdiction. Warranties and other trade regulations were added under the 1977 Magnuson-Moss Warranty Act, which also extended FTC's ability to enforce its rules (previously it had to go through the Department of Justice). In the 1980s, the FTC established an Office of Consumer and Competition Advocacy to identify and respond to issues regarding government intervention in the market. The FTC is continually balancing the need to protect legitimate business while going after fraudulent businesses (as shown in the Consumer Alert).

CONSUMER ALERTS

"Retirees! Moms! Earn extra cash while working at home!" We have all seen these classified ads that promote work-at-home scams in newspapers. The person answers the ad by sending money or charging a toll call to a credit card to get details. And what does he or she get in return? He or she receives instructions for running more ads or setting up a business, a box of trinkets for assembling, or envelopes for stuffing, after which the person mails the items back at his or her own expense and supposedly earns a fee. Often the person's work is then said to be shoddy, so the company offers more expensive kits—or more likely the company then disappears. Common sense should tell people that they will not be paid huge sums of money to sit at home and do simple work. This is where the FTC steps in: It warns people about misleading advertisements. To learn more about scams and how to spot them, log on to the FTC's website (www.ftc.gov) and search for consumer tips and advice related to working from home opportunities.

The FTC pursues Internet-related enforcement actions including fraud cases such as get-rich-quick pyramid schemes and miracle weight-loss drugs. The FTC is responsible for the laundering instructions sewn into every piece of clothing sold in the United States and also wrestles with regulating television advertising and curbing telemarketing fraud. The agency has enforcement powers based on its statutes; for example, it can insist that advertisers run **corrective advertising**. This type of advertisement disclaims previous false advertising claims and is run by a firm to cause consumers to "unlearn" inaccurate information from prior advertisements. Here are two examples of corrective advertising messages (Hawkins, Best, & Coney, 2001, p. 728):

- "Do you recall some of our past messages saying that Domino sugar gives you strength, energy, and stamina? Actually, Domino is not a special or unique source of strength, energy, and stamina. No sugar is, because what you need is a balanced diet and plenty of rest and exercise."
- "If you've wondered what some of our earlier advertising meant when we said Ocean Spray cranberry juice cocktail has more food energy than orange juice or tomato juice, let us make it clear: we didn't mean vitamins and minerals. Food energy means calories. Nothing more."

Although the effectiveness of corrective advertising has been questioned, the FTC continues in this effort as a means to bring accurate information to the public. In order for the FTC to insist on corrective advertising, the false impression that is made has to be very strong. Indirect effects or flattering words are difficult to define, so puffery and fluff in advertising are legitimate and pervasive.

The FTC enforces consumer protection laws against any illegal acts that are considered unfair methods of competition or unfair or deceptive practices. It was considerably strengthened in terms of enforcement power by the Magnuson-Moss Warranty Act.

One of FTC's biggest challenges is enforcing labeling and trade violations from overseas. With the advent of the Internet, more and more problems are coming from other countries where consumer laws are usually weaker. For example, websites abroad are offering prescription drugs without doctors or licensed pharmacies being involved.

One of its newer realms of coverage is dealing with telemarketers. As mentioned earlier, the FTC runs the National Do Not Call Registry. The states are involved in this as well. Florida established the first state no-call list in 1991. To give you an idea of how "do not call" legislation comes about, this particular law was supported by Carl Carpenter, a state legislator whose elderly disabled mother could hardly get to the phone, and when she did get to it, the call would be from some firm selling aluminum siding or bulk beef. She told him there should be a law to protect people from unsolicited sales calls, so Carpenter fought for it and won.

Since the FTC's jurisdiction is so vast, it has divided its functions into several divisions with different responsibilities:

- advertising
- marketing
- credit
- enforcement
- service industries.

The FTC looks for a pattern of complaints and then decides which ones to investigate. Complaints can come from a variety of sources, including consumers or consumer organizations, whistleblowers, congressional leaders, and scholars and institutes. If after an investigation the FTC believes that a business has violated the law, it will ask the business to stop a specific action and/or issue a complaint. If the business will not stop and no settlement is reached, the case may go forward. Formal hearings may take place, and then an administrative law judge may issue a decision. Decisions can go all the way to the Supreme Court. Along the way, an FTC rule may be challenged in a US Court of Appeals. The rules or trade regulations are the FTC's most effective means of protecting consumers and legitimate businesses.

Another area of jurisdiction of the FTC is that of monitoring mail-in rebate offers. For example, the FTC has taken action against electronics makers, such as manufacturers of scanners, that routinely paid out rebates months later or not at all (Spencer, 2002). More valuable rebates are the ones that most often come into question. Some offer as much as $400 off computer purchases. For example, a charcoal rebate offer on a $4.99 bag of charcoal may be for only $1 (when you take off the cost of the stamp, that isn't much of a rebate). For the low-end offers, the percentage of consumers mailing in rebate coupons, known as **claim rates**, may be only 5 percent, but for the high-end electronics offers, the percentage may go as high as 40 percent (Spencer, 2002). The rebates attract customers and move merchandise, but they can trip up a company that does not plan wisely. One dot.com filed for bankruptcy court protection because it owed customers $90 million in rebates; one particularly enthusiastic shopper was owed $90,000 (Spencer, 2002).

The FTC also issues sets of guidelines such as voluntary guidelines for green claims (the word *green* meaning environmentally sound), and Box 5.1 offers examples of these guidelines.

> ### Box 5.1 Examples of Environmental Guidelines Issued by the Federal Trade Commission
>
> An ad calling a trash bag "recyclable" without qualification would be deemed misleading because bags aren't ordinarily separated from other trash at incinerators and landfills.
>
> A shampoo advertised as "biodegradable" without qualifications wouldn't be deceptive if there is reliable scientific support showing it will decompose in a short time.
>
> A "recycled" label on a bottle made from recycled material wouldn't be considered misleading even if the cap isn't made from recycled material.

Consumer Product Safety Commission (CPSC). The CPSC, headquartered in Bethesda, Maryland (outside Washington, DC), was created in 1972 by Congress under the Consumer Product Safety Act; it began operating in 1973. It has regional offices. It recently opened the National Product Testing and Evaluation Center in Rockville, Maryland.

According to Inez M. Tenenbaum, former Chairperson of the Consumer Product Safety Commission (2009–2013), "the CPSC is stronger, more proactive and better at protecting the consumer especially children" (2014, p. 648). Here are the initiatives from recent years:

- "Developed a new five-year strategic plan which set forth a 21st century mission and vision for the CPSC, made the agency more proactive, more focused on injury prevention, and moved the agency into being the global leader in consumer product safety;
- Increased its number of employees by 175—now an agency with more than 500 diverse employees;
- Implemented the landmark Consumer Product Safety Improvement Act (CPSIA) that establishes the lowest allowable lead limits in children's products, provides for a mandatory federal toy standard, and provides for new rules on infant-durable equipment. The United States can now say that it has the safest, strongest crib standard in the world" (Tenebaum, 2014, p. 648).

Its basic function is to protect consumers against injuries and deaths associated with consumer products; the kinds of products most often involved are toys, baby and sports equipment, and household products such as coffeemakers and lawn mowers. The CPSC does not have jurisdiction over some categories of products such as automobiles, tires, boats, drugs, food, cosmetics, pesticides, and medical devices. The CPSC website lists its activities:

- To develop voluntary standards with industry.
- To issue and enforce mandatory standards for consumer products (or ban them if no feasible standard would adequately protect the public).
- To obtain the recall of products or arrange for their repair.
- To conduct research on potential product hazards.
- To inform and educate consumers through the media, state and local governments, private organizations, and responses to consumer inquiries.

One of the problems involved in monitoring the safety of babies and young children is that because they live with adults and older brothers and sisters, they are exposed to products that are not made for them. The worst-case scenarios result when babies suffocate in water beds, swallow parts from their older siblings' toys, and get strangled in window blind cords. Toy and household product manufacturers that are aware of such risks do what they can to reduce the risks; for example, one leading window manufacturer places the blinds between two panes of glass and in so doing removes the blind cords as a safety measure for children. Parents and other caregivers have a responsibility to watch over children and to remove potential hazards. Seemingly safe products such as a bucket with wash water for floors can turn deadly if a toddler puts his or her head in it, can't get out, and drowns.

CRITICAL THINKING

Alerting the Public

During a Super Bowl ad in 2015, there was public criticism of Nationwide Insurance presenting several possible child dangers, including drowning in a full bathtub. They responded that these things happen and it was a public service to alert viewers. If you saw or heard about the ad, what did you think?

Childproofing a house, yard, and pool area, coupled with active supervision, is essential. The CPSC offers suggestions on how to prevent accidental injuries in its publications and on its website.

A product is recalled if it presents a significant risk to consumers because the product either is defective or violates a mandatory standard issued by the CPSC. If a product is recalled, you should stop using it and find out from the CPSC what to do next. If a toy, for example, is found to be unsafe, the recall may only apply to products manufactured and dated at a specific time. When you check into a recall order, sometimes you get your money back, and sometimes you don't. The CPSC regularly updates recall information on its website.

Typical product recalls by manufacturers in cooperation with the CPSC have included those for strollers, activity gyms, baby clothes, electric ranges, glue guns, dishwashers, and pull toys. Regarding these particular problems and their remedies, the strollers, for example, often collapsed and injured children who fell. To remedy this, the manufacturer sent a free repair kit so that the parent could make the stroller safer. In the case of activity gyms that had detachable rattles that posed a choking hazard, refunds were offered from the stores where the activity gyms were purchased. The baby clothes had a zipper pull that posed a choking hazard, so a refund was offered. When sparks or flames from the electric range were possible, a free in-home repair was offered. For glue guns that overheated, causing burn risks, a refund was offered. With the dishwashers in question that could ignite, free rewiring or rebates were offered from the company. For the pull toys that had plastic connectors on a string that could detach and put children at risk of choking, the manufacturer offered replacement.

The CPSC has a publicly searchable database on consumer products at saferproducts. gov which allows consumers, government officials, and others to share experiences with consumer products. It receives more than 200,000 visits per month.

Food and Drug Administration (FDA). The FDA, located within the Department of Health and Human Services, is an influential federal agency designed to protect consumers. Its mission is to promote and protect the public health by helping safe and effective products reach the market in a timely way and by monitoring products for continued safety after they are in use (see the example shown in the case study and the Consumer Alert).

CASE STUDY

Aloha's Premium Protein Products

The FDA posted a press release entitled Aloha Voluntarily Recalls Line of Premium Protein Products Due to a Possible Health Risk (www.fda.gov/Safety/recalls/ucm432558.htm).

"All sizes of Aloha's Vanilla and Chocolate Premium Protein blends are being volunatrily recalled. This product is packaged and sold in both 14-serving steel tins and single-serving pouches. . . . To date, Aloha has received 17 complaints from customers who have reported transient gastrointestinal symptoms consistent with staphylococcal food poisoning. This voluntary recall is a result of an extensive testing program, which Aloha began immediately following individual customer complaints of gastrointestinal issues. Aloha is working closely with its manufacturer, co-packers, ingredient suppliers and distribution partners to determine the source and cause of the contamination. Aloha has temporarily ceased production and distribution of the Premium Protein products until further analytical testing can confirm the specific source of the contamination."

CONSUMER ALERTS

Shock your wrinkles away? Yes, this was a product promoted by actresses as the secret for younger-looking skin. Put this battery-operated device on your face every day, and the companies making the device suggest that the appearance of wrinkles will be reduced. The device sold for between $99 and $250, depending on the company. Testers who tried it said they felt pain and tingling. The FDA said the devices weren't authorized for removing wrinkles and sent warnings to the companies. The bottom line was that muscle stimulation may produce temporary swelling, but according to dermatologists, it cannot permanently remove wrinkles (GH Institute Report, 2001).

Photo 5.1 The FDA looks out for the safety of the US food supply

Source: Thinkstock: artisteer

The FDA considers its work as a blending of law and science aimed at protecting consumers. FDA-regulated products account for about 25 cents of every consumer dollar spent in the United States.

Every day, every American comes in contact with products that the FDA regulates.

Most countries have similar food safety agencies because, as discussed earlier in the book, food is one of the first categories of consumer protection. People getting sick and dying from foodborne illness is hard to ignore.

According to the FDA website, from the beginnings of civilization, people have been concerned about the quality and safety of foods and medicines. In 1202, King John of England proclaimed the first English food law, the Assize of Bread, which prohibited adulteration of bread with such ingredients as ground beans or peas. In the United States, regulation of goods dates from early colonial days (Chapter 2 of this text highlights legislation passed in the twentieth century). Remember the discussion of Dr. Harvey Wiley, the father of the Pure Food and Drugs Act of 1906? He unified a variety of groups, including the media and the public, behind this federal law to prohibit the adulteration and misbranding of food and drugs.

Federal controls over the drug supply began with inspection of imported drugs in 1848. For example, in 1998 the Federal Food and Drug Administration Act, which offered gravely ill patients easier access to experimental drugs and cut the waiting period for approval time, was passed. More on the history of food, drug, and cosmetic controls, with a focus on health, is found in Chapter 8. The emphasis in this chapter is on the present and the ways these agencies function and affect our daily lives.

As the Consumer Alert shows, the FDA has jurisdiction over human drugs, but as its name ("Food and Drug") implies, it also oversees most food products (other than meat, poultry, and egg products). In addition, the FDA is in charge of animal drugs; therapeutic agents of biological origin; medical devices; radiation-emitting products for consumers and for medical and occupational uses; cosmetics; and animal feed. Agency scientists evaluate applications for new human drugs and biologics, medical devices, food and color additives, infant formulas, and animal drugs (Swann, 2002).

CONSUMER ALERTS

"They claimed their products could bolster the immune system and treat several serious diseases, including AIDS and cancer. But Allen J. Hoffman of Finksburg, Maryland, and a Virginia physician are now serving prison terms for fraudulently peddling an intravenous mixture containing aloe vera to treat autoimmune and other conditions." They billed up to $18,000 for a two-week treatment of intravenous aloe vera. Patients traveled from the United States to the Bahamas and Mexico for treatments. The investigator's report stated that "it is clear that some people were misled and defrauded into trying dangerous, unapproved and ineffective alternative treatments."

Source: Michelle Meadows (May–June 2002). "Maryland man, Virginia physician sentenced for illegally marketing aloe vera 'treatments.'" *FDA Consumer*, p. 34.

To give a broader picture, listed next are the types of products that the FDA regulates and the issues it is involved in:

- food: foodborne illnesses, nutrition, and dietary supplements

- drugs: prescription, over-the-counter, and generic

- medical devices: pacemakers, contact lenses, and hearing aids

- biologics: vaccines and blood products

- animal feed and drugs: livestock and pets

- cosmetics: safety and labeling

- radiation-emitting products: cell phones, lasers, and microwaves.

To give specific examples, in a press release on January 30, 2015, the FDA announced a nationwide recall of the Stone Mountain Pecan Company "Pecanettes" sold in 8-ounce packages because the product had potential for contamination with salmonella. A few years earlier, Susie Brand-imported cantaloupe was recalled due to salmonella (rod-shaped bacteria that can cause illness). It should be noted that poisoning, much of it from food sources, is the nation's third most common form of unintentional death; other sources are household cleaning products and medicines (usually swallowed by children).

Department of Agriculture (USDA). The USDA, headquartered in Washington, DC, has offices and testing centers throughout the United States (examples of some centers or divisions are given in Box 5.2). The USDA began in 1862 under President Abraham Lincoln when 48 percent of the people were farmers who needed good seeds and information to grow their crops. With less than 2 percent of the American population now living on farms, the mission and outreach of the USDA have broadened to include all segments of the population. Its range of activities has grown to include food and water safety, research, education, and conservation, as well as oversight of a number of programs such as food stamps and school breakfasts and lunches.

Regarding food, the USDA is responsible for the safety of meat, poultry, and egg products, which falls under Food Safety, a division that administers the federal meat and poultry inspection system and educates industry and consumers about food safety. Inspection of meat products is required by federal law. In 1996 the Meat and Poultry Rules were passed that allowed inspectors to use microscopes to detect E. coli and salmonella bacteria, making it much easier to determine if products carry these potentially deadly organisms. Another area of the USDA, the Food, Nutrition, and Consumer Services, runs the federal food assistance programs and coordinates nutrition research and policy.

Box 5.2 Centers and Divisions within the USDA Most Related to Consumer Issues

- Animal and Plant Health Inspection Service, Riverdale, MD; www.aphis.usda.gov
- Center for Nutrition Policy and Promotion, Washington, DC; www.usda.gov. cnpp
- Cooperative State Research, Education, and Extension Service, Washington, DC; www.reeusda.gov (you may also consult county government listings in local telephone directories for the number of local Cooperative Extension Service offices)
- Meat and Poultry Hotline, Washington, DC; www.fsis.usda.gov

The mailing address for the USDA and all its agencies is US Department of Agriculture, 1400 Independence Avenue, SW, Washington, DC 20250.

CONSUMER ALERTS

WASHINGTON, Jan. 28-2015 – Washington Beef, LLC, a Toppenish, Wash., establishment, is recalling 1,620 pounds of boneless beef trim product that may be contaminated with E. coli O157:H7, the U.S. Department of Agriculture's Food Safety and Inspection Service (FSIS) announced today . . . Consumers with food safety questions can "Ask Kean," the FSIS virtual representative available 24 hours a day at AskKaren.gov or via smartphone at m.askkdaren.gov.

Source: USDA Food Safety and Inspection Service (January 28, 2015). "Washington firm recalls boneless beef trim product due to possible E. coli O157:H7 contamination." Available online at http://www.fsis. usda.gov/wps/portal/fsis/topics/recalls-and-public-health-alerts/ recall-case-archive/archive/2015/recall-022-2015-release.

The Cooperative State Research, Education, and Extension Service of the USDA has been a source of information and assistance to consumers for over a century. Educators are located in nearly every county to bring research-based knowledge directly to families and communities with programs that include personal finance issues, such as budgeting and retirement, as well as programs on food and nutrition and safe housing. College students who have completed coursework in consumer economics and related areas can consider the Cooperative Extension Service, as well as the other agencies and commissions covered in this chapter, as a place for internships and employment.

Department of Justice (DOJ). The mission of the DOJ, according to its website, is to enforce the law and defend the interests of the United States based on the law, to provide federal leadership in preventing and controlling crime, to seek just punishment for those guilty of unlawful behavior, to administer and enforce the nation's immigration laws fairly and effectively, and to ensure fair and impartial administration of justice for all Americans. The part of the DOJ most connected to consumer economics is the Antitrust Division, which promotes and protects the competitive process through the enforcement of antitrust laws. A more common way to refer to the antitrust function is "trust busting." The following are practices that restrain trade:

- price-fixing conspiracies
- corporate mergers likely to reduce the competitive vigor of particular markets
- predatory acts designed to achieve or maintain monopoly power.

Mergers are business combination transactions involving the combination of two or more companies into a single entity. Besides the Department of Justice, others involved are the Securities and Exchange Commission and state laws requiring mergers to be approved by at least a majority of a company's shareholders if the merger will have a significant impact on the acquiring or target company. Mergers can be classified by economic function: horizontal, vertical, market, product, or conglomerate. A **horizontal merger** combines direct competitors in the same product lines and markets, with an example of a horizontal merger being two department store chains merging. A **vertical merger** combines supplier and company or customer and company, an example of which is when a producer of a raw material also manufactures and wholesales the material. A **market extension merger** combines firms selling the same products in different markets; for example, one grocery store distribution company buys another, increasing the area to which it distributes. A **product extension merger** combines firms selling different but related products in the same market, as when a soft drink company acquires a snack food company and thus extends or expands the product line. The catch-all merger category is the **conglomerate merger**, which combines companies with none of the previously mentioned relationships or similarities; an example of a conglomerate merger would be a beer manufacturer joining with a furniture company. Sometimes the federal government blocks or slows the growth of mergers, but other times it lets them go by or only focuses on certain types. Many mergers involve small companies that do not have much consumer impact, and because cases are usually costly in terms of personnel and money, the emphasis is on larger companies or precedent-setting cases. There are a number of other factors as well, such as the general economic climate and the presidential administration. Now and then, Congress steps in (usually in response to a company scandal or consumer uproar) and insists on the need to strengthen antitrust laws.

Monopolies occur when there is only one producer (a single firm) that controls or dominates an industry and for which there is no substitute. Because we live in a market economy, we want to be free, as consumers, to choose the products and services we want—we like selection and value competition. Adam Smith, founder of economics, recognized the desire of businessmen to monopolize trade by joining forces, and "although he was not able to specify what the monopoly price would be, he recognized that monopolists would extract a higher price by restricting output" (Landreth & Colander, 2002, p. 83). In other words, monopolies would ultimately result in higher costs to consumers, so he encouraged competition. "He saw competition as fundamentally requiring a large number of sellers; a group of resource owners who were knowledgeable about profits, wages, and rents in the economy; and freedom of movement for resources among industries" (Landreth & Colander, 2002, 82–83).

Historically, the goal of antitrust laws is to protect economic freedom and opportunity through promoting competition. What are the benefits of competition?

- Competition provides businesses with the opportunity to compete on price and quality, on a level playing field, in an open market, unhampered.

- It tests and strengthens companies at home, making them better able to succeed abroad.

- Competition leads ultimately to lower prices, better quality, and greater choice for consumers.

The Antitrust Division prosecutes serious and willful violations of antitrust laws by filing criminal suits. Possible outcomes include fines and jail sentences. Civil action, which would forbid future violations of the law, is also possible. These statutes are enforced by the Antitrust Division:

- *Sherman Antitrust Act*. This 1890 act is about restraining trade and monopolies. The main purpose of this act is to maintain a competitive economy. It was named after Senator John Sherman, who was quoted on the Senate floor as saying, "If we will not endure a King as a political power, we should not endure a King over production, transportation, and sale of the necessaries of life." The first case tried under this act decided by the Supreme Court was *United States* v. *E. C. Knight Company* (1895). The American Sugar Refining Company controlled 98 percent of the US sugar-refining industry. Cases since then have included monopolies in aluminum, oil, tobacco, steel, telephone, and computer industries.

- *Clayton Act*. This act, passed in 1914, includes statements about discrimination in price, services, or facilities. It discusses corporate mergers, exclusive contracts, and other processes that lessen competition.

- *Wilson Tariff Act*. This act encompasses imports and fairness of trade. There are also codes and statements regarding falsifying, concealing, or covering up, by any trick, scheme, or device, a material fact or in any other way using misrepresentation, including frauds and swindles by mail, wire, radio, or television. Defrauding through the mail became a federal crime under the Mail Fraud Act of 1872.

Securities and Exchange Commission (SEC). The SEC, headquartered in Washington, DC, is the investor's advocate. Its primary mission is to protect investors and maintain the integrity of the securities (a word referring to stocks and bonds) markets. This agency was created by the Securities Exchange Act of 1934 to administer that act and the Securities Act of 1933, formerly under the jurisdiction of the FTC. The SEC is composed of five commissioners who are appointed by the president on a rotating basis for five-year terms; the chairman of the SEC is designated by the president, and no more than three members of the commission may be of the same political party. The SEC supports full public disclosure and protects the investing public from malpractice in the securities market.

As the quote from the SEC website in the Consumer Alert indicates, millions of Americans and foreign investors have money invested in the stock market, either directly through individual stocks or mutual funds or through retirement accounts, so the work of the SEC is crucial to people's financial future. The SEC watches for fraud and deception in the securities market and provides investor education. It may also investigate allegations of wrongdoing on its own or join with other groups. In 2002 the SEC, the New York Stock Exchange, and the regulatory arm of the National Association of Securities Dealers launched a joint examination of Wall Street compliance that was spurred by a broker in Cleveland who took an estimated $125 million from clients (see the Consumer Alert). Since other brokers were found to have committed similar fraud, the joint examination included a plan to canvass nearly 6,000 registered brokers to see if there were other gaps in monitoring the actions of brokers.

The laws and rules that govern the securities industry in the United States require public companies to disclose meaningful financial and other information to the public. The SEC promotes a steady flow of timely, comprehensive, accurate information so that investors can make sound decisions. The SEC oversees stock exchanges, broker-dealers, investment advisors, mutual funds, and public holding companies.

CONSUMER ALERTS

"As more and more first-time investors turn to the markets to secure their futures, pay for homes, and send children to college, these goals are more compelling than ever. The world of investing is fascinating, [is] complex, and can be very fruitful. But unlike the banking world, where deposits are guaranteed by the federal government, stocks, bonds and other securities can lose value. There are no guarantees. That's why investing should not be a spectator sport; indeed, the principal way for investors to protect the money they put into the securities markets is to do research and ask questions."

Source: US Securities and Exchange Commission.
"What We Do." Available online at www.sec.gov.

CONSUMER ALERTS

"Frank Gruttadauria, a star Lehman Brothers broker in Cleveland, siphoned an estimated $125 million from clients over 15 years, covering his tracks with forged account statements, federal regulators say. Where was the local Lehman official who was supposed to monitor his conduct? He reported to Mr. Gruttadauria. In Miami, R. Christopher Hanna used strikingly similar methods over 10 years to steal $15 million from his clients at Credit Suisse First Boston (CSFB), regulators say. The former CSFB branch manager who was supposed to be overseeing Mr. Hanna may not have noticed because he was busy as a broker in his own right, handling accounts for wealthy customers."

Source: C. Gasparino and S. Craig (May 23, 2002) "Broker watchdogs face scrutiny as investor complaints mount." *Wall Street Journal*, p. A1.

National Highway Traffic Safety Administration (NHTSA). The NHTSA, in the Department of Transportation (DOT) headquartered in Washington, DC, works to reduce injuries and develops minimum performance standards by enforcing safety standards on motor vehicles, including bicycles, motorcycles, automobiles, trucks, buses, mopeds, and recreational vehicles, as well as all accessories for these vehicles (for example, safety belts come under their jurisdiction). The NHTSA's goal is to reduce highway deaths, injuries, and property losses. Defects may require recalls so that corrections can be made. Visit www.nhtsa.gov for information on air bags, auto safety, child seat inspections, crash statistics, and crash tests.

Federal Consumer Information Center (FCIC). The FCIC, located in Pueblo, Colorado, is part of the US General Services Administration. This center was established to help federal agencies and departments develop, promote, and distribute useful consumer information to the public. The center can also tell consumers whom to contact for help with problems. The FCIC enables consumers to send complaints directly to companies and agencies through its website, but it does not handle consumer complaints. One of the ways it disseminates information is by publishing a *Consumer Information Catalog*. Its catalog lists more than 200 free or low-cost booklets on topics such as these:

- Cars (what to look for when buying new and used cars).
- Computers (how to avoid Internet investment scams).
- Education (how to financially plan for college).
- Employment (how to create resumes and cover letters).
- Family (how to find resources for aging parents and for black family research).
- Federal government (how to find out about public land for sale and disability rights laws).

- Food (how to locate diabetes recipes and reports on food allergies).
- Health (how to find out about drug interactions).
- Housing (how to buy a new home and find information on indoor air hazards).
- Money (how to save for a rainy day).
- Small business (where to get small loans).
- Travel (how to get national park system information and maps and how to get a passport).
- Records (how to obtain vital records on births, deaths, marriage, and divorces).

For a free catalog, go to www.pueblo.gsa.gov. At the website, search for topics of interest or the latest consumer news, and use the links to other federal agencies and consumer offices.

This concludes the federal government section of this chapter, but it should be noted that there are many other federal departments and commissions that affect consumers. For brevity's sake, not all of them can be covered here, but many are covered in other areas of the book. For example, the Commodity Futures Trading Commission and the Federal Reserve System (the "Fed") will be covered in Chapter 13 on banking.

State Consumer Protection

Information about preventing injuries and other forms of consumer protection may come from the state as well as federal government. As mentioned in previous chapters, state governments provide consumer protection through agencies, commissions, boards, attorney generals' offices, Departments of Insurance, and Offices of Consumer Affairs, as well as other units such as Departments of Families and Children. They serve an important role in handling consumer complaints in their states; some states have better protection measures than those of federal government agencies, and in some cases, states handle the same sorts of complaints and cases as the federal government.

CONSUMER ALERTS

According to a brochure entitled "Keep Your Kids Safe" by the Florida Department of Children and Families, "protecting children is a community responsibility. The Florida Department of Children and Families teamed with community partners throughout the state to educate Floridians about ways to ensure safe environments for children to live and grow. These campaigns provide parents and caregivers with resources that build awareness about risks that endanger children and tools that empower them to better protect their children." Here are some of the recommendations in the brochure:

- Make sure baby's crib meets Consumer Product Safety Commission standards.
- The mattress should be firm and fit snugly in the crib's frames.
- Crib sheets should fit tightly around the mattress.
- Place baby on his or her back to sleep in order to reduce the risk of suffocation.
- Keep baby's sleep area clear of strings, cords, and wires.
- For more information, resources, and referrals visit myflfamilies.com/safesleep.

In an earlier section, it was noted that the FTC can go after companies that are consistently late in paying rebates; likewise, state government attorney generals can go after companies slow to pay up. Examples are Texas, which settled with CompuServe, and Florida, which filed a complaint against the same company for failing to pay $400 rebates to dozens of customers who had signed up for three years of Internet service (Spencer, 2002). Box 5.3 gives a list of places to turn to if your rebate does not arrive in a reasonable time.

Certain fraudulent and deceptive practices tend to occur more often in specific areas of the country more than in others, so in many cases localized solutions make more sense than federal intervention. There is also a history in the United States of states' rights. Regarding targeted fraud, in Florida, California, and other states in the Sunbelt, state governments are well aware that their high concentration of elderly makes them attractive to fraudsters, so additional protections are needed. Con artists may come in the form of telemarketers, nursing home salespersons, financial planners, sellers of gold coins and foreign lottery tickets, roof repairers, and fortune-tellers. It is difficult to track financial crimes against the elderly because those crimes are less obvious than product purchases, and the elderly are less likely to report fraud than the general population. Sometimes the elderly simply don't know what happened to them; other times they are too embarrassed to speak out. Other types of fraud common in the Sunbelt, desert areas, Hawaii, and mountain resort areas are phony land deals and tourist scams.

Box 5.3 Where to Turn When Your Rebate Fails to Come

To move merchandise, companies are offering record numbers of rebates for everything from computers to charcoal. If your rebate is late beyond a reasonable amount of time, here are places to turn:

- You can contact your state attorney general's office. To find the address and phone number, go to www.naag.org, which is the phone number of the National Association of Attorneys General.
- You can file a complaint online by going to www.ftc.com.

Besides the obvious consumer units, states have public health commissions that provide information on health care and look out for the health of citizens. They have other divisions that test foods (such as citrus fruit) grown within the state for diseases. States also have human rights commissions, boards of review, departments of transportation, and other departments similar to those at the federal level that handle consumer concerns. State and local courts also handle consumer cases, especially those involving contracts.

Local Consumer Protection

Counties, cities, small towns, and military bases have their own consumer affairs, financial, or police departments that investigate consumer complaints, hear tenant–landlord disputes, conduct investigations, prosecute offenders of consumer laws, and advocate in the consumers' interest. If there are criminal acts involving finances, threats, and scams, the police become involved. Crimes of this type investigated by police may come under the category or division called bunco or, more commonly, **bunko**, referring to swindles in which an unsuspecting person or group of people is cheated. Police departments in recent years have had to spend more time on these types of crimes, a trend that has been shaped by economic, legal, technological, and social forces along with the perennial problem of runaway greed. There are always people who want to get rich quick or to get rich without working for it.

As readers of this book know by now, fraud is not new. "Old scams never die—they just change hands, passed along from one grifter to the next" (Adams, 2002, p. 240). A **grifter** is someone who uses his or her position to derive profit or advantages by unscrupulous means. **Extortion** is the illegal use of position, power, or knowledge to obtain money, goods, funds, or favors. In nineteenth- and twentieth-century novels, the main type of extortion was blackmail. The plot would revolve around the blackmailer holding a scandalous letter or photograph of a person, and the blackmailer would then threaten to show the letter or photograph to interested parties unless he or she was paid money or given a position. With advances in printers, this type of blackmail no longer makes sense since there can easily be more than one copy in circulation so that the victim would never know if his or her secret was safe by burning the original letter or photograph. More recently, tape recordings and emails have been used by blackmailers.

CASE STUDY

Consumer Rights on the Ski Slopes

Consumer rights and regulations include all sorts of issues, including the rights of snowboarders versus skiers. In the US, Taos Ski Valley in New Mexico was one of the last places of snowboard-free skiing, and that changed in 2008. Snowboarders are now allowed on the slopes. "Relations between skiers and riders (as snowboarders are known) have never been chillier. An age gap helps put the group at odds. The majority of skiers who skied more than a day at a U.S. resort this past year were older than 25, according to the National Ski Areas Association; the majority of snowboarders weren't old enough to rent a car."[1]

Skiers say boarders are reckless and boarders say skiers are old and stuffy. What do you think? Can these two groups co-exist and use the same areas? Besides the managers of the slopes, real estate developers and restaurants/hotels are involved. Many think real estate will take a downturn if riders are allowed. "They bring their lunch to the mountains instead of buying it," says Liz Jamison, a real estate agent and ski instructor at Taos for 22 years."[2] Can you think of another consumer rights issue where there is an age divide?

1. Hannah Karp, "Snowboarders invade another ski shrine," *Wall Street Journal*, December 22–23, 2007, p. W1.
2. Ibid.

CONSUMER ALERTS

"In 1848 William Thompson came up with a disarmingly simple trick for separating New Yorkers from their assets. Well-dressed and polite, he approached a genteel-looking stranger on the street. After a bit of conversation, he asked, 'Have you confidence in me to trust me with your watch until tomorrow?' When a sucker did, Thompson walked off richer by a watch. This dodge gave birth to a new term: 'Confidence man' or con man for short."

Source: S. Adams (June 10, 2002). "May I hold your watch?" *Forbes*, p. 240.

The term **con artist** (or confidence man or con woman) refers to a person who carries out a particular type of swindle in which victims are defrauded after their confidence has been won. The confidence or con game may take minutes, weeks, or years to pull off, based on the amount of money involved and the complexity of the fraud. Movies such as *Ocean's 11* (with George Clooney) and *The Sting* (with Paul Newman and Robert Redford) have glamorized con games, but in reality con games are not glamorous and can result in years in prison. A common crime occurs when female housekeepers or caregivers steal either from the households they are hired to clean or from the people they are hired to care for, especially the elderly. Besides stealing jewels and money, these people may get hold of the elderly person's checkbook or credit card and scam undetected for a long time. Banks are on the lookout for any unusual movement of large amounts of money and may report suspicious activity to the account holder. Before leaving the subject of con games, it should be pointed out that they occur in business as well as in personal life; accountants or bookkeepers can siphon off company funds for a long time before they are caught. On a national scale, rigged television game shows and fake company sweepstakes have been exposed in the past. As a result, con games can be petty or involve millions of dollars. Regarding fraud directed at individuals, it is becoming more common for con artists today to be less personal than the example in the Consumer Alert, with contact with the victim more likely coming through advertisements in newspapers or television or over the telephone or on the Internet.

In summary, as the marketplace becomes more complex, so does the need for protection. It behooves all of us to pay more attention. We need to be curious about what is going on, what we are buying, and what we are eating and drinking. Being present in the moment will help us avoid injuries and fraud by being more careful of the environment that surrounds us, which leads us to the next subject to be discussed—injurious consumption.

Injurious Consumption

The government agencies described in this chapter actively work to reduce injuries caused by consumer products and their use. **Injurious consumption** occurs when individuals or groups make consumption decisions that have negative consequences or misuse products in such a way as to cause injury to themselves or others. These injuries can occur anywhere; see the Case Study on India.

CASE STUDY

Bootleg Liquor Kills at Least 23 in India

"NEW DELHI – At least 23 people died and 200 others were seriously sickened after drinking contaminated moonshine in the northern Indian state of Uttar Pradesh, the authorities said on Tuesday. 'People started getting sick Sunday night,' said H.D. Kaul, a spokesman for the city of Lucknow, the state capital. The police arrested a man they identified as Jugnu and accused him of manufacturing and selling the deadly beverage. Local government officials were also suspended and accused of neglecting their duties, Mr. Kaul said."

Source: Hari Kuman (January 13, 2015). "Bootleg liquor kills at least 23 in India." *New York Times*. Available online at http://nyti.ms/1XWTfAO.

Every year in the United States, 25,000 people die as a result of alcohol-related traffic accidents; some of these people were drunk or alcohol impaired, and others were innocent victims. There are about 10 million alcoholics and 80 million cigarette smokers in the United States (Faber, 1985; Hirschman, 1991). Companies promoting such products are often the culprit, but the government is not immune if one considers the number of state-sponsored gambling activities, including lotteries and companies that make potentially harmful products that are given subsidies or tax breaks.

In summary, consumers often engage in harmful activities, and businesses and even the government can be the source of injurious consumption. "Economics is about events in the real world" (Landreth & Colander, 2002). So even though it is difficult to point out that people consume for reasons that are not always healthy or in their best interest, it has to be done. The Landreth and Colander quote points out that economics (and especially consumer economics) is about the real world, and the outcomes of consumption are not always attractive.

Regulation and Deregulation Issues

So far, this chapter has talked about rules, legislation, and agencies to protect consumers as well as some types of fraud and injuries that may befall consumers. Government, through its policies on taxes (such as placing high taxes on cigarettes) and spending, affects consumer behavior. It decides how schools will be funded and what sidewalks and roads will be built. Congress decides each year if Social Security recipients will receive a raise. Once an agency is created, it has the authority to develop rules and regulations. It is usually easier to have rules and regulations set up than to have legislation pass through state legislatures and Congress. Besides developing rules, agencies have to see that they are enforced. In terms of consumerism, a **rule** or **regulation** is an attempt by government to control the workings of the marketplace. Rules and regulations are necessary because policy makers believe that it is in the best interest of consumers and the overall economy as well as the development of certain industries if monopolies are held in check because they reduce competition in the marketplace. This reduction could lead to price fixing, poor service, and scarcer choices. This stance, of course, is opposed to the general philosophy of Adam Smith, who argued that government interference, for the most part, is undesirable because it infringes on the natural rights and liberties of individuals. However, his greatest concern was about the regulation of international trade rather than domestic trade (Landreth & Colander, 2002).

Rules and regulations relevant to consumer economics do the following:

- educate consumers
- protect consumers
- regulate sellers
- discourage unfair, deceptive, or dangerous business practices
- change the relationship between buyers and sellers, making certain practices or products illegal.

Many rules protect children in terms of the advertising content and images targeted at them. For example, in 1996 the Federal Communications Commission (FCC) issued new rules under the Children's Television Act that required stations to air three hours of educational programming targeting children 16 years old and under per week and tightened the definition of what constitutes educational programming. Most people would agree that children need protection in the marketplace.

Regulations placed on products aimed strictly at adults are more controversial. Some economists and many corporations (especially those that are under investigation and those who represent them) feel that government intervention has gone too far and would argue for more public choice. They believe that government regulation is ineffective or too restrictive of trade and agree with Adam Smith's philosophy of laissez-faire (let the marketplace run itself). Given the countless numbers of products and services available, it is safe to say that for the most part the marketplace is not regulated. For example, "supplements are largely unregulated by the federal government and are not monitored for potency, purity or correct dosage; older adults on other medications may be particularly susceptible to overdoses or adverse reactions" (Pope, 2002). Many in the population applaud government intervention and would like more of it, especially as new problems crop up. When it comes to the unknown and the untested, the public looks to government to serve as a protector.

CRITICAL THINKING

Amount of Government Protection Needed

What do you think (what is your judgment) about how much government protection of consumers is needed? Explain and justify your stance.

To summarize and extend the arguments already presented, as the marketplace becomes more impersonal, as small local stores disappear and consumers deal with sellers in an impersonal environment, fraud is more easily promulgated. Product complexity has also grown, requiring more knowledge of companies, products, and services, and advertising is more intrusive. All these factors make a case for the necessity for regulation.

Below is a list of several areas of regulation:

- *Pricing.* A maximum price may be set for a product or service.
- *Licensing.* A license may be required to be an interior designer, a nail technician, or a barber.
- *Standard setting.* Safety standards can be set in factories, as can standards regarding how much beef should be in a can of beef noodle soup.
- *Subsidies.* Government can become involved in regulating supplies of imports, such as oil, and provide incentives or subsidies for growing specific crops or developing certain businesses.
- *Privacy.* Standards regarding privacy in financial transactions can be determined.

In the 1970s, proponents of reform and some lawmakers began to question the wisdom of too much government regulation of industry. They argued that too much regulation was restricting trade and that in the long run consumers may gain from deregulation. **Deregulation** removes or reduces government intervention and allows the free market to operate. Below are examples of deregulated industries:

- *Airlines.* Deregulation of airlines in 1978 covered fares, schedules, and routes. Under discussion is a passenger bill of rights as well as better airfare disclosures.

- *Banking.* Deregulated in the 1980s, banking practices affect savings rates, fees, and lending standards. When some banks failed in the 1980s, they were bailed out by the government; mergers ensued. The opening up of interstate banking came in 1994. In the United States, the top 25 banks controlled 51 percent of deposits in 1998, compared with 29 percent in 1980 (Deregulated, 2002). Under discussion is more protection from unreasonable rate hikes, especially in the area of ATM charges.

- *Cable television.* The cable television industry was regulated and deregulated throughout the 1980s through to today, affecting choices, rates, and services. This industry often ranks low in consumer satisfaction surveys.

- *Electricity.* Deregulation of electricity providers in certain areas in the 1990s was controversial. Problems with blackouts in California, for example, caused that state to suspend deregulation in 2001.

- *Telephones/cellphones.* In 1984 telephone equipment was deregulated; long-distance service was partly deregulated in 1984, and domestic service began to be deregulated in the 1990s and is continuing. There are problems with customer confusion over billing, rates, and services.

Box 5.4 provides a list of criteria to use in judging how well deregulation has worked.

If it works as intended, deregulation should lead to more competitive pricing, product and service innovations, and more options for consumers. In deregulation, sometimes smaller companies rise to the top; for example, Southwest Airlines, once a small regional airline which is now nationally known, has consistently high consumer satisfaction ratings on service and prices. When deregulation does not work out well, there are problems, such as the blackouts in California noted previously. In deregulation, services may suffer, prices may not decrease, and the number of choices can lead to customer confusion. An example of this is the confusion of many consumers over which cellphone company or computer server to choose and arguments over improper or misleading charges. Because of the variance in industries and in consumer needs, each deregulated industry has to be judged individually. Traditionally it was assumed that, for the most part, the positive aspects (in particular, better prices) far outweighed the negative aspects, but there have been articles that question how much consumers really benefit from deregulation (Deregulated, 2002). If an industry is deregulated, it does not mean that the government is no longer involved because government is watching for abuses in the

Consumers need government protection through regulations and legislation, but they also can benefit from deregulation because of more competitive pricing.

Box 5.4 Deregulation Criteria

There are arguments for and against deregulation. The reason a clear-cut pro and con list cannot be given is that deregulation in certain industries may be better for urban dwellers living in concentrated high-profit centers because they experience increased service and more competitive prices, whereas people in rural areas may experience less service and higher rates. In this chart, the usual criteria listed are used to decide if deregulation is working from a consumer point of view (adapted from Deregulated, 2002):

- *Choice.* Are consumers given more choices?
- *Consumer rights.* Are consumers given more rights, or are the rights they already have upheld?
- *Innovation.* Are better products offered? Are new ways of manufacturing and production encouraged?
- *Safety.* Have security and safety increased?
- *Savings.* Are consumers saving money? Are prices lower?
- *Service.* Are consumers being served better? Are services dependable?

system, such as runaway rate hikes or discrimination, and is prepared to step in when things get out of hand or existing laws are violated.

Another type of deregulation is when government turns to **privatization**, which means turning over some of the functions of government to business. The trend in many states is toward more privatization or outsourcing of formerly government-based work. This may involve government workers losing their jobs, being offered early retirement, or shifting from government to business occupations. There is debate on both sides (government and business) as to whether privatization leads to better service and (in the long run) to more efficiency and cost savings for citizens.

Special Interests

Businesses, organizations, and government do not operate in a vacuum—they influence and are influenced by many groups. **Special-interest groups** are units of two or more persons who have a common interest and seek to influence government policy and enforcement. They may do this by lobbying. **Lobbyists** represent special-interest groups. A study by the Center for Public Integrity found that lobbyists vastly outnumber and overwhelm elected state officials and are also a significant presence in Washington, DC. Lobbyists may represent an entire industry such as insurance or oil and gas or they may be specific to a company such as General Electric or AT&T. There are different opinions about the worth and the functioning of lobbyists, with some calling them swarming locusts and others calling them useful resources. They definitely serve a function—to influence legislation on behalf of their client, which may be an organization, education, industry, or employer—and are another voice in the legislative process. According to a study titled *The Fourth Branch* by the Center for Public Integrity, lobbyists spend more than $600 million per year influencing legislation in states across the country. States have laws regulating how much legislators can accept from lobbyists; for example, in Florida, the limit is $100 per occurrence that a lobbyist can spend on a lawmaker, and this money can go for dinners, hunting trips, and sporting events tickets.

Enlightened Companies and Consumer Protection

The activities of lobbyists as well as new laws and regulations will continue to grow, but enlightened companies encourage their managers to look beyond what the rules say and simply to "do the right thing." In other words, well-run companies will self-regulate. Socially responsible firms actively seek ways to protect the long-run interests of their consumers and the environment (Kotler & Armstrong, 2002). They do not rip off consumers by selling products that stop or reverse the aging process, for example. Since this reversal is not currently possible, anyone who sells such products is lying, even if he or she is a doctor, according to S. Jay Olshansky, a demographer at the University of Chicago (Pope, 2002).

How businesses run themselves as well as the products they produce has come under public scrutiny. For example, recent well-publicized corporate scandals have drawn the public's attention to the pitfalls of poor business practices, including shoddy accounting. Businesses more than ever before are being expected to use common sense and to be above reproach. Many industries and professional associations have adopted a code of ethics or a set of guidelines for standards of behavior and accountability. The development of the Internet has pushed this agenda even further, and privacy issues have moved center stage. Legislators and company managers are asking: What are the rules in cyberspace? Written laws from the government have often not kept pace with this fast-moving technology, and existing laws are often difficult to apply or enforce in cyberspace.

If companies don't self-regulate, the government can and does step in. An example is the 1998 case of America Online (AOL), which paid a $2.6 million penalty and agreed to update its business practices to settle a deceptive-marketing complaint brought forward by 44 state attorneys general. AOL failed to notify consumers clearly that the "50 free hours" in its online service's much-touted trial memberships must be used within a one-month period and that users would incur subscription fees after the first month (Kotler & Armstrong, 2002). Unethical marketing tactics are part of an area called social marketing. In **social marketing**, marketing strategies and tactics are applied to alter or create behaviors that have a positive effect or that try to reverse negative outcomes for individuals, society, and the environment. For example, social marketing could be used to encourage recycling or to reduce smoking (in the case of smoking, this could be done through dramatic advertisements showing close-ups of the ruined teeth, wrinkled skin, or blackened lungs of lifelong smokers).

Leading corporations support social marketing by considering their own business practices and by advertising to try and help the communities in which they are located. They want consumers to have the information they need to make sound choices. Successful businesses know that good products, information, and word of mouth are essential to their continuing success in the marketplace, and smart consumers look for reliable companies they can trust. Legitimate businesses know it is in their best interest to have good relations with consumers, and that is why they get involved in issues of consumer protection. They provide full disclosure through warranties and labels, especially for health care products both because they want to have happy customers and repeat business and because they want to drive out illegitimate or quasi-legitimate businesses that give business in general a bad name. They may join Better Business Bureaus (BBBs) or associations whose primary goal is to help legitimate businesses maintain good reputations in communities by accepting consumer complaints.

As mentioned in the previous chapter, over a thousand companies (such as Dial Corporation and Delta Air Lines) belong to the Society of Consumer Affairs Professionals (SOCAP), which provides training, conferences, and publications. SOCAP exists to encourage and maintain the integrity of business in transactions with consumers; to encourage and promote effective communication and understanding among businesses, government, and consumers; and to define and advance the consumer affairs profession.

Nongovernmental Pro-Consumer Groups

There are literally thousands of nongovernmental pro-consumer groups, ranging from Centers for Economic Justice to Legal Aid Societies. Some have the word "consumer" in their titles and others don't, which makes some of them difficult to identify or classify without closely examining the issues or the people they represent. For example, the American Cancer Society would not be thought of primarily as a consumer organization, but it is a research and consumer advocacy group on the specific subject of cancer prevention and the search for cures. To summarize the main emphases, consumer groups are concerned with three things:

1. Do consumers have full knowledge of what they are buying?
2. Are products safe?
3. Are products environmentally sound?

Chapter 3 provided information about leading national organizations that look out for consumers' interests. One of the oldest, largest, and most visible is the Consumers Union (CU), which publishes *Consumer Reports*, a magazine, as well as other publications and media. The CU researches and tests consumer goods and services and publishes the results. CU is an independent nonprofit organization.

The Consumer Federation of America (CFA), founded in 1968, is a large, nationally recognized advocacy organization working to advance pro-consumer initiatives. CFA focuses much of its advocacy on several areas:

- financial services
- utilities
- product safety
- transportation
- health care
- food safety.

Located in Washington, DC, it mainly serves as a lobbying federation. Staff members testify before Congress, the White House, federal and state regulatory agencies, and the courts on consumer issues, and their testimony is based on facts gathered and issues analyzed. CFA also is an educational organization and coordinates the efforts

Table 5.1 Consumer Groups

Group	Function
American Association of Retired Persons (AARP)	Information (especially for those 50 years and older), lobbying, research, publications
American Council on Consumer Interests (ACCI)	Academic-based organization, information, journal
American Standards Association (ASA)	Research on products, standard setting
Better Business Bureaus (BBBs)	Business-supported organizations, consumer protection
Center for Auto Safety	Car complaints, testing, lobbying
Center for Science in the Public Interest	Legal-based organization, lobbying, nutrition
Center for Study of Responsive Law	Legal-based organization, lobbying
Consumer Federation of America (CFA)	Coordination, lobbying
Consumers Union (CU)	Testing, publications
Tax Reform Research Group	Subgroups such as Congress Watch
Public Interest Research Groups (PIRGs)	Lobbying, research, presence on some college campuses
Public Citizen	Legal defense, lobbying, information

of hundreds of organizations, including trade unions, credit unions, and rural electric cooperatives, and in so doing serves as a clearinghouse of information. Because of this, CFA represents a wide constituency and range of interests versus some groups that are more focused. CFA is especially concerned about the needs of the less affluent and less educated consumers who have little discretionary income and are especially vulnerable to deceptive or fraudulent sales. A partial list of some of the thousands of nongovernmental pro-consumer groups and their primary functions is given in Table 5.1. There are other organizations that are primarily academic in nature such as the American Council on Consumer Interests (ACCI), which publishes the *Journal of Consumer Affairs*, and the Association for Financial Counseling and Planning Education, which publishes *Financial Counseling and Planning*.

Consumer Publications

Media mix refers to the combination of media vehicles, nontraditional media, and marketing communication tools whose mission is to reach a targeted audience (Wells, Burnett, & Moriarty, 2000). In consumer economics, messages could include how to stimulate shopping or search behavior or how to be more cautious and selective in purchasing behavior. A successful media campaign should deliver on its objectives, which may be to:

- increase sales
- increase awareness
- change attitudes.

Consumers can be divided into two groups: those who buy the product or service, and those who use the product or service. For example, parents buy baby food, but the baby eats the food. In terms of consumer protection, a parent may be interested in putting screens or limits on Internet access to certain sites for their teenager; the user would be the teenager, but the purchaser of the product or service would be the parent. In both cases, the parent is the targeted consumer.

A major source of consumer information is the many newspapers and magazines published about health; about personal finance, such as *Money*; or about the results of product tests, recalls, travel bargains, or other consumer news, such as car testing results in *Motor Trend* magazine. These publications, combined with radio, the Internet, and television throughout the world, reach millions of consumers and perform a great public service.

Consumer Reports

As mentioned previously, there are generalized consumer groups and sources of information, and there are also specific publications with "consumer" in the title. The most famous of these is *Consumer Reports* (and Consumer Reports Online and Consumer Reports on TV in the United States and Canada) published by Consumers Union, an independent nonprofit testing and information organization. CU's mission since its inception in 1936 has been to test products, inform the public, and protect consumers. Its Consumer Policy Institute and testing and research center is in Yonkers, New York, and is the largest nonprofit education and consumer product testing center in the world. All the products are tested off the shelf, meaning the staff buy them just as a consumer would (but the staff do send back free products sent by manufacturers). What do they test? In more than 50 labs, the staff test appliances, autos, chemicals, electronics, food, home environment products, public service, and recreation and home improvement products. Cars and trucks are tested at the auto-test facility in East Haddam, Connecticut. The staff also survey readers to find out about repair reliability and to rate services. The Consumer Policy Institute conducts research and education projects on such issues as air pollution, food safety, biotechnology, and right-to-know laws. It calls itself "America's #1 Consumer Product Test Center." *Consumer Reports* does not take advertising but does engage in sales of its own services, products, and publications, such as the *Consumer Reports Travel Letter*, and uses inserts for new subscriptions or subscription renewals. Further, inside the magazines there are statements and advertisements that encourage subscribers to remember CU in their wills. The following was found on paper wrapped around an issue mailed to a subscriber:

> *Your next issue will be your last issue! It's alarming, but true . . . unless you renew now! You're about to lose the money-saving, safety preserving, rip-off preventing independent research results and recommendations compiled in every issue of* Consumer Reports. *So, quick! Check the term you prefer on the postage-free card and mail it today. (*Consumer Reports, *October 2002)*

So it could be said that *Consumer Reports* meets the three media objectives listed earlier: increased sales, increased awareness, and changed attitudes.

CU has three advocacy offices in Washington, DC, San Francisco, and Austin, Texas. Advocacy staff testify before federal and state legislative and regulatory bodies on issues such as health care, financial policies, and food and product safety, and they also petition government agencies and file lawsuits on behalf of consumers. This brings us back full circle to the beginning of the chapter, which stressed that we are living in an information society. As consumers, we need to know what is going on, what the results of product tests are, and how we can make the best choices.

Summary

Pro-consumer government websites such as saferproducts.gov and media are important elements in our information economy. The US Consumer Product Safety Commission's saferproducts.gov receives over 200,000 visits a year and has more than 15,000 incident reports for consumers to review. The mission of media is to inform. *Consumer Reports*, published by CU, is an example of a nongovernmental, consumer-oriented publication. Government is one of the main gatherers, sorters, producers, and monitors of information and produces many useful publications, including the more than 200 publications about everything from buying cars to making wills found in the *Consumer Information Catalog* by the FCIC. The federal government is empowered to act on behalf of consumers in a number of ways, such as rules and regulations.

The chapter began with a description of how to contact elected state and federal officials about issues and concerns and moved on to explain the workings of the main federal government agencies related to consumerism. Because their jurisdictions differ, it is not always easy to differentiate one from the other. For example, the USDA handles meat, poultry, and egg product testing, whereas the FDA handles other food sources. Some agencies test products and others don't, and some have more investigation and enforcement powers than others. The different agencies also cooperate with each other and may each have a say in a particular part of a case or investigation. All are involved in providing consumer information to the public through their websites. State and local governments are also active in consumer protection, as are some corporations, associations, and nongovernmental consumer groups (such as the CFA).

As the marketplace becomes more complex, the need for more consumer protection increases, but it was also pointed out that consumers often engage in injurious or risky behaviors such as drinking bootleg liquor. It is impossible to remove all consumer risks, but reducing risks and providing better consumer information are goals of government agencies and consumer organizations.

KEY POINTS

1. The Federal Trade Commission (FTC), established in 1914, is responsible for handling complaints of false advertising, fraud, and product safety and administering antitrust and consumer protection legislation. The FTC looks for patterns of noncompliance, fosters free and fair business competition, and prevents monopolies and activities that restrain trade.

2. As the name implies, the Consumer Product Safety Commission (CPSC) handles consumer product safety, mainly in the areas of toys, baby and sports equipment, and household items. They are a prime example of how many of the government agencies and commissions provide updated publicly searchable databases for consumers.

3. The Food and Drug Administration (FDA) has as its mission to promote and protect public health by helping safe and effective products reach the market in a timely way and by monitoring products for continued safety after they are in use.

4. The US Department of Agriculture (USDA) helps farmers and ranchers and leads in the food stamp, school lunch, and school breakfast programs. It researches human nutrition; encourages stewardship of the land, conservation, and community development; and monitors the safety of meat, poultry, and egg products.

5. The Department of Justice (DOJ) enforces antitrust laws and promotes competition.

6. The Securities and Exchange Commission (SEC) advocates for the investor and provides investor education. It looks for fraud and deception in the securities markets.

7. The Department of Transportation (DOT) oversees highway safety and monitors seat belts and other safety devices.

8. State and local governmental units, including police, get involved in consumer protection.

9. There are pros and cons to deregulation. In theory, the pros may include lower prices, expanded choices, and enhanced services, but in practice this has not always been the case when industries are deregulated.

10. Thousands of nongovernmental consumer groups look out for the consumer interest.

11. The media, including *Consumer Reports* published by the Consumers Union, inform consumers about product quality, possible fraudulent schemes, and recalls.

KEY TERMS

bunko	horizontal merger	privatization
claim rates	informational influence	product extension merger
con artist	information economy	
conglomerate merger	injurious consumption	regulation
corrective advertising	lobbyists	rule
deregulation	market extension merger	social marketing
extortion	media mix	special-interest groups
grifter	mergers	vertical merger

DISCUSSION QUESTIONS

1. Why does the Department of Justice get involved in the violation of antitrust laws?

2. How do the police get involved in consumer protection? What sort of cases might they investigate? What is extortion, and why would the police become involved in investigating extortion?

3. What is an example of injurious consumption? Why do consumers engage in activities that put themselves and others at risk?

4. Consumer advocacy comes in many forms. Go to the Consumer Federation of America website at www.consumerfed.org, and list the current issues that they are working on.

REFERENCES

Adams, S. (June 10, 2002). May I hold your watch? *Forbes*, p. 240.

Bernstein, L. (December 25, 2014). Missouri company recalls caramel applies that may be linked to listeria outbreak. *Washington Post, To Your Health* blog. Available online at www.washingtonpost.com/news/to-your-health/wp/2014/12/25/missouri-company-recalls-caramel-apples-that-may-be-linked-to-listeria-outbreak.

Deregulated. (July 2002). *Consumer Reports*, 30–35.

Faber, R. (December 1985). Two forms of compulsive consumption. *Journal of Consumer Research*, 22 (3), 296–304.

Fourth Branch, The (2002). Center for Public Integrity. Washington, DC.

Gasparino, C., and S. Craig. (May 23, 2002). Broker watchdogs face scrutiny as investor complaints mount. *Wall Street Journal*, p. A1.

GH Institute Report (August 2001). Shock away your wrinkles? *Good Housekeeping*, 16.

Hawkins, D., R. Best, and K. Coney (2001). *Consumer behavior: building marketing strategy.* Boston: Irwin McGraw-Hill. Examples cited from I. Teinowitz, FTC faces test of ad power, *Advertising Age*, March 30, 1998, 26.

Hirschman, E. C. (1991). Secular mortality and the dark side of consumer behavior, in *Advances in Consumer Research XVIII*, eds. R. Holman and M. R. Solomon. Provo, UT: Association for Consumer Research, 1–4.

Jones, D. (December 17, 2002). More consumers give government services thumbs-up. *USA Today*, p. A1.

Kotler, P., and G. Armstrong. (2002). *Principles of marketing activebook*. Prentice Hall. Available online at www.prenhall.com/myactivebook, 19.

Kuman, H. (January 13, 2015). Bootleg liquor kills at least 23 in India, *New York Times*. Available online at http://nyti.ms/1XWTfAO.

Landreth, H., and D. Colander. (2002). *History of economic thought*, 4th ed. Boston: Houghton Mifflin Company.

Lynch, P. (October 15, 2001). What's next? *Wall Street Journal*, p. A5.

Meadows, M. (May–June 2002). Maryland man, Virginia physician sentenced for illegally marketing aloe vera "treatments." *FDA Consumer*, p. 34.

Pope, E. (June 2002). 51 top scientists blast anti-aging idea. *AARP Bulletin*, 3–5.

Simons, J. (July 30, 1999). FTC has a committed foe of Internet fraud. *Wall Street Journal*, p. A20.

Spencer, J. (June 11, 2002). Rejected! Rebates get harder to collect. *Wall Street Journal*, pp. D1–2.

Swann, J. P. (May 14, 2002). History of the FDA. Available online at www.fda.gov. Adapted from George Kurian, ed. (1998). *A historical guide to the U.S. government*. New York: Oxford University Press.

Tenenbaum, I. M. (2014). The US consumer product safety commission a global leader in consumer product safety. *Journal of Consumer Affairs*, 48 (3), 648–652.

US Securities and Exchange Commission. "What we do." Available online at www.sec.gov.

USDA Food Safety and Inspection Service (January 28, 2015). Washington firm recalls boneless beef trim product due to possible E. coli O157:H7 contamination. Available online at http://www.fsis.usda.gov/wps/portal/fsis/topics/recalls-and-public-health-alerts/recall-case-archive/archive/2015/recall-022-2015-release.

Wells, W., J. Burnett, and S. Moriarty. (2000). *Advertising: principles and practice*, 5th ed. Upper Saddle River, NJ: Prentice Hall.

Part **3**

Consumers in the Marketplace

Chapter

Brands, Buying Process, and Product Development

Nothing ventured, nothing gained.

Geoffrey Chaucer

LEARNING OBJECTIVES

1. Explain types of brands and brand development.

2. List the six steps in the buyer decision process.

3. Discuss the four stages in product development.

4. Explain population trends, including changes in families and households.

5. Identify the four stages in the household life cycle.

> ### CASE STUDY
>
> **Who Buys What and Why?**
>
> "To prepare for the fashion week debut of Banana Republic, Marissa Webb, the brand's creative director, was in the showroom doing what she often does – scrunching, adjusting and rolling collars, waistlines and cuffs on the outfits the two models were wearing. . . . 'We're in a business where it's about romancing the product,' says Art Peck, Gap Inc.'s newly appointed chief executive. . . . In some ways, Banana's struggles reflect a broader problem in this slice of the apparel market. Office attire isn't the uniform it used to be and no longer relies heavily on dress slacks, shirts and suits. The line between weekday and weekend is blurring."
>
> Source: Elizabeth Holmes (February 18, 2015). "The art of making even a cardigan stand out." *Wall Street Journal*, pp. D1 and D3.
>
> Note to the reader: Gap Inc. owns Banana Republic.

Introduction

Why do we care about what to wear? Why do we fall for deals? Why do sale signs attract us? Why does a new brand or style capture our imagination? Consumer behavior is about the "why" of consumerism. It is a field of study strongly allied with consumer economics, but not identical. In economics, the maximization of utility is stressed with the assumption that rational buyers seek to maximize economic gains from a purchase transaction. Consumer behaviorists know that economic gain (or finding the lowest price) is only one factor in what goes on in consumer decision making. Adam Smith (1723–1790, founder of economics) saw numerous connections between many areas of society—things that today are studied by economists, political scientists, philosophers, sociologists, marketers, and family and consumer scientists—particularly in consumer behavior. *Consumers seek value* in many ways, but it is not all about price, novelty, or economic conditions. **Consumer behavior** refers to the complex buying behavior of consumers—the individuals, families, and households that buy goods and services for personal consumption. What are their motivations? And what motivates companies?

Our task in this chapter is to build on Smith's contribution by continuing to explore the interconnectedness of the economy, with a particular emphasis on behaviorism and the connections between consumers and businesses. "One of the fundamental premises of the modern field of consumer behavior is that people often buy products not for what they do, but for what they mean. This principle does not imply that a product's basic function is unimportant, but rather that the roles products play in our lives go well beyond the tasks they perform. And the deeper meanings of a product may help it stand out from other, similar goods and services" (Solomon & Rabolt, 2004, p. 27). The chapter begins with the steps consumers go through in the buying decision.

Steps in the Buyer Decision Process

Consumers go through six steps in the buying process (shown in Box 6.1) that are part of prepurchase, purchase, and postpurchase behavior.

Box 6.1　Steps in the Consumer Buying Process

Prepurchase

1. Assessing need
2. Searching for information
3. Evaluating alternatives
4. Selecting a product or service

Purchase

5. Buying

Postpurchase

6. Evaluating after purchase through use and comparisons

Prepurchase

Purchase intentions are one of the most studied areas in consumer behavior. Of particular interest is **prepurchasing**, which focuses on what consumers are thinking about and how they are behaving in leading up to an actual purchase. One of the factors of note is perceived quality, which has a direct effect on purchase intentions and involvement (Tsiotsou, 2006). If someone believes a product or service is best, he or she is more inclined to buy it. If the individual is truly involved, he or she may talk about it with others, sharing knowledge and information. This person would be a market maven (a type of consumer discussed in Chapter 3). Marketers want to know consumer purchase intentions so that they can make a **forecast** of sales of existing products or demand for those in development. According to Box 6.1, prepurchasing involves four steps: assessing needs, searching for information, evaluating alternatives, and selecting a product or service, and each of these will be discussed.

Assessing Needs. In prepurchasing, the consumer tries to determine how much pleasure or pain will be derived from a product or service. What is the anticipated performance? How much enjoyment can be expected? The first step, *assessing need*, results when problems or decision situations are recognized because people sense a discrepancy between their current state and a desired state. Need recognition can emerge internally

("I am thirsty") or externally ("There is no milk in the refrigerator"). The difference between needs and wants was presented in earlier chapters, which included the discussion of Maslow's hierarchy of needs that begins with the importance of fulfilling our most basic physiological needs (hunger, thirst, shelter) before moving on to more advanced needs. Table 6.1 shows examples of needs and wants.

In terms of employment, most people need work skills, people skills, benefits, transportation, a gathering place and/or communication system, and, of course, pay. Wants can include nearly anything—the sky is the limit. Examples would be corner offices, special phones, designer clothing, boats, private jets, sports cars, state-of-the-art computers and sound systems, swimming pools, vacations, and fitness equipment.

Consumers can fall for a deal even if it appears to have little utility. Our houses and closets are full of items that were bought because they were good deals rather than because the objects were really needed (Liu, 2014). Consider the contents of most gift stores. Some consumers are more deal-prone than others.

In marketing, the term **need set** is used to reflect the fact that most products satisfy more than one need. For example, a house offers more than shelter: At a minimum, it offers storage for possessions and a place to sleep and eat, besides serving as a shelter from the wind and weather; it also offers status and services, which can be seen as an extension of the self. For instance, a homeowner told an interior designer who was suggesting a brown sofa and beige walls, "I need color. I cannot live without color." For the homeowner, color is a need—not simply a want—she cannot live in a brown world. Someone else may not care about color if a sofa is needed immediately and the price is right. Another way to look at needs is to consider the types of relationships that individuals form with products, according to Susan Fournier (1998). Following are four relationships:

1. *Self-concept attachment.* Products help establish the user's self-concept and identity (for example, a professor carrying a briefcase or a student carrying a backpack).

2. *Nostalgic attachment.*

3. *Interdependence.* A product that is part of someone's daily routine, such as a specific soap and shampoo or a certain brand of orange juice, creates interdependency. Most people also have a favorite seat in the family room, so they and the chair or sofa are interdependent. This connection is shown on the television show *The Big Bang Theory* where the character Sheldon Cooper has a specific place on the sofa he always sits in and if anyone else sits there they are asked to move.

4. *Love.* The product may elicit love, warmth, passion, or another strong emotion from the consumer. Examples would be stuffed toys, lingerie, or red roses at Valentine's Day. Expressions of love can be conventional, like red roses or a heart-shaped box of candy, or unique. One husband gave his wife a jar of honey every Valentine's Day.

Table 6.1 Differences between Needs and Wants

Needs	Wants
Basic clothes for school, leisure, and work	Stylish clothes for special events
Transportation for school and work	Brand-new high-end car
Apartment or room	House with a pool, a tennis court, and a view
Healthy, affordable food	Maine lobster (5 lb.), steak (16 oz.), loaded baked potato, and cheesecake

Marketers take an individual's basic needs a step further by grouping consumers with similar need sets because they do not want to offer products that appeal only to one customer but to many. Once this group or segment is determined through research and/or demographics, then marketers focus their attention on the **target market**—the largest, most likely group to purchase. Once this market is determined, then **marketing strategy** is formulated that addresses the question "How can we give excellent customer value to this target market?" The question is answered by providing the proper **marketing mix**, which includes communications or information (to be discussed next) as well as product, price, distribution, and service.

Searching for Information. The second step in the consumer buying process is searching for information. In this step, information is accessed either internally or externally. Non-risky behavior, such as choosing what flavor of iced tea to buy, requires less search behavior than a riskier purchase, such as which car to buy. Information search involves sorting behavior. Consumers search for information before they buy: They may conduct an **internal search**, going over in their minds what they know about a product based on past searches or personal experiences, or they may conduct an **external search**, looking at advertisements, reading articles, going on the Internet, or asking others what they think about a product. An internal search is easier than an external search because an external search requires activity such as talking with individuals or groups, reading marketing information, or experiencing the product itself (for example, test-driving cars or sampling foods at the grocery store).

Convenience plays a large part in consumer decision making.

Advertisers and businesses want to reach today's consumers who are actively conducting internal searches, and they also want to influence consumers' external searches. This is a challenging task because consumers don't always have the time, energy, or money to conduct extensive searches, either internal or external. Have you ever heard someone say, "I just don't have time to think about that right now"? This means that an internal search would take more time than he or she currently has. Regarding external searches, if a carload of people is running out of gasoline, they will drive into the nearest gas station regardless of cost or brand. But if they come to an intersection with two gas stations, then they may choose the one they prefer because of cost or brand preference

Photo 6.1 Consumers will likely conduct both an internal and external search when buying items such as camping equipment

Source: Thinkstock: bodu9

or may select the one on the "right" side of the street. Convenience plays a large part in consumer decision making, which explains how two Starbucks (coffee shops) or Circle K or 7-Eleven convenience stores located only a block from each other can succeed. It also explains how a college science library which was only slightly used by students went to maximum capacity overnight when a large Starbucks was added, so much so that the university librarians were concerned how everyone would find seats during upcoming finals week.

CRITICAL THINKING

How much do you value convenience when you shop or go for coffee? Give an example of your usual behavior in this regard.

The following are part of external searches:

- *Opinions, attitudes, and behaviors of others.* Influence from friends, family members, neighbors, club members, television personalities, and strangers, such as reviews online.
- *Direct experiences.* Consumers' searches are also based on their own product inspections, trials, or observations. For example, an attorney could observe that in her law firm the attorneys drive BMWs and the secretaries drive Toyotas or KIAs.

- *Reading materials.* Articles and professional publications provide consumers with external search information.
- *Marketing communications.* External searches are impacted by advertising, public relations, coupons, labels, packaging, billboards, in-store displays, and other signals and messages that a company provides about itself and its products, which are termed **marketing communications**. To reach the target market, the products and the communication mode should match—you wouldn't expect to see the giant purple Barney swigging down liquor or Spiderman eating fast food.

When consumers conduct a search, sometimes it is deliberate and sometimes it is not. For example, if someone needs an airplane ticket immediately, he or she will go on the Internet and search for airplane routes, availability, and prices. If there is more time, then the search may be less deliberate, and the person may think, I wonder what flights there are between New York and London and what they are going for; then he or she may search the Internet out of curiosity. There are many competing online travel companies and consolidators offering discount fares. They advertise heavily on television.

CASE STUDY

Jittery Times for Magazines

"These are jittery times for magazine publishers as readers and advertisers dance between the companies' once-dominant publications and relatively new but powerful competitors such as Twitter, Facebook and Instagram. For Joe Ripp, chief executive of Time, Inc., the competitive landscape has translated into the sale of once-prized real estate, and a coming move to lower Manhattan that will save on rent. Two bets on video startups, the Daily Cut and 120 Sports, pit the publisher of People, InStyle and Sports Illustrated against rivals such as Google Inc.'s YouTube, Yahoo, Inc. and AOL Inc. for viewers and advertising dollars." Ripp says, "We've got a legacy business that is shrinking and it's going to continue to shrink."

Source: Jeffrey A. Trachtenberg (February 23, 2015). "Is *People* magazine relevant in a digital age?" *Wall Street Journal*, p. R2.

Another way to look at search behavior is to consider an **ongoing search**, which is conducted to acquire information for possible later use. One person, for example, may enjoy paging through fashion magazines or Internet websites with an intention of future clothing purchases, while another individual may like going to open houses or looking at housing or building magazines for ideas. Camping equipment, cars, clothes, shoes, computers, boats, recreational vehicles, and trips may all be part of ongoing searches.

Searching for information takes time and energy. The **information search rule** states that a consumer will search as long as the cost of the search is less than or equal to the expected savings from the search. Businesses help reduce search costs by locating near each other (for example, auto dealerships and malls). The cost of the information search should be mentally added to the total cost of the product.

Experience goods refer to those about which the consumer gets relevant information after purchasing them, such as food and entertainment. Until consumers eat the food or see the movie, how can they tell if it was a pleasurable experience or not? Often with these types of goods, free samples or taste tests of food are given, and previews provide partial experiences of movies. **Credence goods** are those for which consumers can never get all the needed and relevant information and/or cannot evaluate the goods themselves, so these goods are often under government regulation and protection. An example of credence goods would be drugs.

Because so much consumer information exists and information overload is a distinct possibility, consumers make decisions about what types of information to access. They may use the following criteria:

- *Attractiveness.* Are they drawn to the information? For example, does the cover of a magazine attract? Does a movie preview look promising?
- *Appropriateness.* Does the information fit their lifestyle? If they never climb mountains, it is unlikely they will read books about climbing or go to mountain climbing websites.

Photo 6.2 Food is an "experience" good

Source: Thinkstock: Andreas Rodriguez

- *Existence of various alternatives.* Does one form of information fit better than another?
- *Performance characteristics.* What features (including cost) are provided? Is the information free or readily available? If a magazine costs $7.99, is it worth buying for the information and entertainment value that it contains?
- *Usefulness or caring.* Do they care what the information is about? If an article is about foot care for diabetics, it is unlikely that a ten-year-old would be interested.

Information may be passively or actively acquired. **Passive information** is encountered when one is doing something else. For example, many people listen to music when they are jogging, working at a desk, driving a car, or doing housework, but they do not just sit and listen to music. If the source of the music has advertising (such as a radio station) the ads have to break through consumers' inattention. Passive information is provided by websites and by billboards at the side of the road. **Banner ads** come up at the top of a website, and there is debate in the communications and marketing literature about how successful (or how irritating) banner ads are. **Actively acquired information** is sought after for its own sake (for example, test-driving a car or going to a fashion show). If you are planning a Disneyland or Disney World vacation, you could ask your friends and family, go on the Disney website, call the Disney phone number, read about Disney in books or travel magazines, or use a travel agent or go to a general travel website—all are methods of actively seeking information about the trip using a variety of sources. Marketers are very interested in how an active external search goes and may use surveys ("How did you hear about us?"). Other sought-after information includes how many stores or websites the person visited, the number of alternatives considered, the number of personal sources used, and the overall combination of measures and factors that influenced the final choice. Another way that marketers can target consumers is by asking for their zip code at the time of purchase because the zip code information will show them where to send circulars and catalogs. This area is fast moving. The data collected is incredible, as you can see if you go information searching—suddenly it pops up on your screen when you are reading Yahoo.com news or other general sources. How do they know you were looking at swimsuits at a company website a few minutes ago?

Evaluating Alternatives. In the third step, the person evaluates the alternatives based on the information search. Likes and dislikes, beliefs about the product or brand, on-site visits to several stores or websites, pricing, and availability help the consumer narrow the choices. In the case of which flavor of iced tea to buy, a consumer could eliminate all flavors with lemon in them if he or she doesn't like lemon, which narrows the field. Another evaluation involves sorting behavior—picture someone looking at the products on the shelf or reading labels or warnings.

Price, the amount of money one pays to obtain the right to use a product, is very important in alternative evaluation. An individual paying a price can own a product outright or may pay to rent or lease a product or service. One may assume that a lower price would sell more products, but price is also an indicator of quality. Would you feel comfortable paying $250 a month for a one-bedroom apartment, or would you feel suspicious, thinking something must be wrong with an apartment that could be rented at such a low price? The same could be said for the pricing of any other object or service. For example, retailers have witnessed the phenomenon of a bin of the same sale-priced sweaters selling better at $49.99 than they did at $25.00. Setting a price requires a thorough knowledge of not only the product but also the potential market for that product and how odd-end numbers attract more than round numbers, at least for US consumers.

Potential buyers will also consider the **consumer cost**, which is the total cost involved in owning or using the product; this is also called the nonprice cost. For example, if someone buys a car, the consumer costs include the cost of gasoline, repairs, parking fees, depreciation, tire replacement, and so forth. A car that gets good mileage with regular gasoline will cost less to run than a car that uses a lot of premium gasoline. Sellers of products often will promote the cost savings.

Availability has an effect in the alternative evaluation. If the product is not readily available, a substitute product may be offered in its place or the purchaser may decide to wait until more selection is available. This relates to the marketing concept of **distribution**, that is, products being available in places near target customers. A truckload of snow tires in Miami will just sit there, but in January they may be a "hot" item in Boston. This is an obvious example, but less obvious examples are differences in food preferences throughout the United States, which successful grocers have to be aware of or they are stuck with slow-moving produce.

Consumers will also evaluate **service**, any activity performed to enhance and sustain the primary product or service. For example, when consumers buy from a local distributor of appliances, they may inquire whether the seller will also service an appliance when it breaks down. If they buy appliances over the Internet, they may wonder who will install and service the appliances. Other service considerations may be free pickup and delivery. Will the company take away the old appliances and install the new appliances, all at no cost? With people's busy lives, as has been said before, convenience becomes more and more important. Amazon Prime delivering groceries to the door is a "prime" example.

Information is a key input into the alternative evaluation, but there are other factors such as resources and product characteristics. Resources include time, energy, and money, as well as anything else that is useful to the decision and subsequent planning and action. Resources can be current or anticipated.

Since it would be impossible to taste every food in the grocery store, consumers evaluate the alternatives based on the amount of their shopping time and on a product's characteristics (such as sweet or sour, highly caloric or low-fat, bitter or smooth). Does chunky peanut butter taste better than regular? What is your preference? Consumers evaluate product characteristics based on the following:

- cost
- accessibility or availability
- features
- style
- perceived risk.

All day long we make consumer decisions—we have to if we are to eat and drink and stay alive. We also consume to fulfill social functions since we are social beings. For example, a mother may be baking a birthday cake from a mix at home that requires two eggs, but when she opens the refrigerator, she finds there is only one egg. Should she bake the cake using one egg (taking a risk), should she go to the store for more eggs, or should she forget baking and go to a bakery or grocery store bakery? Her final decision will rest on energy, time, money, availability of the store and bakery, transportation, desired features or style of the cake, and so on. A connected decision is the candles, which are another resource, as are the matches to light the candles.

One consumer decision builds on another, forming a chain of decisions.

Selecting a Product or Service. To return to the prepurchase process, the fourth step is selection. The consumer takes the product off the shelf and puts it in his or her shopping basket; if it is a large purchase, he or she may tell the salesperson when and where to deliver it. If shopping online, the consumer clicks the desired selection and puts it in his or her virtual shopping basket or shopping bag. What if consumers see something they like better on the way to the checkout? They may change their minds, put the object back, and proceed to the next step.

Purchase

The next phase is the actual purchase—the consumer buys the product. At the point of purchase, consumers think they have made the best choice by weighing all the factors, and the item or service is purchased, with money being spent or a trade being made. Things usually go smoothly, and the consumer can relax—unless his or her credit card isn't accepted, there isn't enough money to cover the purchase, or a computer is down.

> ## CRITICAL THINKING
>
> ### Slow Check Outs
>
> Have you ever had trouble at check out? Has the person ahead of you slowed things down? How can stores move the purchase end of things along better? Compose three strategies.

Postpurchase

After the purchase, buyers evaluate their purchase and seek reinforcement. Was the best decision made? This third phase, called postpurchase behavior, encompasses the consumer deciding if it was a good or bad purchase by comparing the expected performance internally and externally. For example, internally a postpurchase consumer may decide that a food tastes good or bad. External reactions may include what others say or how they react to the consumer's new product; at the gas pumps, for example, he or she may notice the make of other cars and talk to owners who own the same car to see if they like the way their car is performing.

Cognitive dissonance is the tendency to accentuate the benefits (in other words, look for reinforcing information that the consumer made a good purchase) and downplay the deficits. Consumers look for reinforcement and seek acknowledgment of the characteristics that are important to them. Being reassured brings pleasure to the decision-making process because a right decision removes doubt and uncertainty. It is generally more profitable for companies to retain customers than to replace them with new customers, so it behooves them to be concerned with factors such as cognitive dissonance as part of overall **customer satisfaction**, which is a function of the prepurchasing, purchasing, and postpurchasing experience (including that derived from the value of the product while it is in use).

Companies knowing all this seek to build loyalty in their customers. Ways to do this include frequent-flyer programs, discounts on future purchases, gifts, discount coupons, and loyalty points, such as those offered by Nordstrom. As an example, a woman may be given a bottle of free shampoo at the salon she frequents or a 10 percent discount on her next beauty treatment. Another way to do this is to give the purchaser a consumer satisfaction survey (at the time of purchase, at the end of a service such as a cruise or hotel stay, or immediately upon his or her return home by a survey sent in the mail). Accompanying the survey may be a newsletter with discounts or other encouragement to buy again.

If things go wrong, the final evaluation of a product or service is an important step that many consumers choose to ignore because they want to avoid pain or negative thoughts. They don't want to revisit bad clothing decisions, so they will put ugly clothes at the back of their closet or get rid of them. The problem with an unworthy product may be its style or other characteristics, the brand, unrealistic expectations, or the place where the purchase was made. In order to avoid wasting money again, the postpurchase step is a necessary part of the consumer process.

Motivations of Marketers

In previous chapters we've discussed how businesses interact with consumers and government, but how do they operate internally? What are their motivations and concerns?

Specifically in terms of marketing, what are their goals? We know that consumers want the best products at the best prices. Businesses want to participate in this process by bringing these sought-after goods to market and in so doing maximize profits. Marketing is key to this outcome.

Effective consumer complaint handling is a way to keep customers and maintain good word of mouth.

Listed below are four things marketers want to maximize:

1. They want you to notice their brands, goods, and services, their promotions and advertisements. There will be more about advertising in Chapter 7.

2. *Consumption.* They want you to try their products and buy more the next time. From the business perspective, greater levels of consumption are seen as a way to better things for both the consumer and the seller. As covered in previous chapters, not everyone agrees with this perspective (the scornful indictment of consumerism expressed in *The Overspent American* by Juliet B. Schor), but this section of the chapter is about how firms view consumption and their place in it.

3. *Loyalty.* As mentioned in the last section, marketers want to see you again. For example, you could be invited to join a loyalty club such as a university football boosters club or the Crown and Anchor Society for repeat Royal Caribbean International cruisers. With the Crown and Anchor Society, you are a gold member after completion of one cruise and a platinum member after five cruises; the incentives go up with each category, and there are separate cruises just for repeat customers. Fund-raisers for universities, sororities, fraternities, and charities often distinguish levels of givers, and the names or titles provide prestige. Metals and gems may denote different levels (it is better to be gold than silver and platinum than gold), and often at the top are diamond categories (such as 5-diamond). The word "loyalty" is not always easily defined for a company or for a brand and varies by customer (see Case Study: Millennials and Loyalty).

4. *Consumer satisfaction.* Although marketers want repeat customers, they want not only volume but also quality. They want to know that consumers like what they buy and that their product or service satisfies a need in a style or way that is pleasurable or comfortable. This is less easily measured than the number of products sold, but it is important to the long-running success of a business. Handling consumer complaints promptly and efficiently falls under this category (as well as the previous one of loyalty).

CASE STUDY

Millennials and Loyalty

The following is an interview with Hyatt Hotels and Resorts CEO Mark Hoplamazian that appeared in *USA Today* on February 23, 2015, p. 6B.

USA Today: Studies have shown that Millennials don't actually have brand loyalties. So why do all this—Create brands and social spaces and improve technology—if they are not loyal?

Hoplamazian: First of all, we are talking about an age group of 16 or 17 years in breadth. There is a big difference between how an 18-year-old is behaving and a 34-year-old is behaving. . . . I actually don't agree necessarily that Millennials are not brand-loyal. They develop and evolve their brand loyalty in very different ways than the Boomers did or Gen Xers.

Companies and Competition

In order to meet customer needs, companies have to efficiently manage their finances, production, research and development, delivery, human resources, facilities, technology, and image and reputation. Managing the company image and reputation goes beyond producing effective advertising because image and reputation include other areas such as displays in stores or at conventions and news stories about managers and the health of the company, including present and future worth, growth, community leadership, treatment of employees, and environmental friendliness. If a scandal (such as a tampered-with consumer product) breaks out, how does the company handle it? Does it act like nothing happened, or does it quickly try to remedy the problem? Often positive news is sent out to counteract bad news: When one drug fails in a pharmaceutical company, management puts out news about a promising drug that is undergoing research and development; in a movie production company, a failed movie is pushed aside, and the promotion effort switches to the next upcoming film. Where to put time and how much energy and resources to expend are continual issues for companies, but making those decisions is what managers are paid to do.

CASE STUDY

Case Study: Dead Ladybug in Salad Mix

The following happened to the author of this book. I found a dead ladybug in a bag of prepackaged salad mix bought at the grocery store. The bug was found after half the salad mix had been eaten, to which my family replied, "Oh, gross!" I called the manufacturer's toll-free number and got the Consumer Care line. After explaining what happened and reporting that no one had gotten sick, I was offered a check for $15 or coupons worth about that much for future purchases. The Consumer Care person said that the salad mix is chlorinated in California and then shipped, so the bug was chlorinated as well and posed no health threat to anyone. However, she said that she would report the bug to quality control and thanked me for providing the code on the label information so she could track the place of origin. She also said I could take the complaint further and possibly get more money, but she said that rarely works. She advised me to take the $15, which I did. The check arrived, along with an apology letter, a few days after the call. The letter writer's title was "Consumer Response Specialist." In the second paragraph she wrote, "We are concerned when a product does not meet our high quality standards. Ready-to-use items, such as our pre-cut salads, are triple washed. The process should remove field debris or insect material. We informed our Quality Assurance staff of your report. The information will be helpful to prevent this in the future."

Competition is a continual threat and a stimulator. If companies are to succeed, they need to keep up with or surpass as well as anticipate competition. They can respond to competition in several ways:

- reduce prices
- increase advertising or change ad placement
- introduce a new product
- buy out the competition through mergers
- develop a new strategic plan
- improve customer service, giving better value such as offering free gift wrap or delivery
- improve product quality.

Across the United States and in many other places in the world, a common phenomenon is when a big-box store such as Wal-Mart or Home Depot comes into a small community and disrupts the existing mix. Since they deal in such large volumes, they often offer lower prices than smaller dealers can, so in order to stay alive, the smaller stores have to make themselves distinctive by offering easier parking, more services, or unique products. In the long run, competition allows companies to grow to be more efficient and profitable and serve customers better. Government policy plays a part in this competition through changes in zoning and in treaties or trade agreements such as the North American Free Trade Agreement (NAFTA), which greatly reduced trade barriers and increased the level of competition.

CASE STUDY

Global Consumption of Coffee

Keeping established brands fresh and competitive [is an] ongoing concern of businesses. "Howard Schultz, whose vision 25 years ago took Starbucks from a handful of stores to an international behemoth with 15,000 locations worldwide, has returned as its CEO with this promise: Starbucks is returning to its roots. 'I am dissatisfied more than anyone else where we sit today,' he said in a hastily called conference call with industry analysts. 'We have a lot to do.' Starbucks' competitive map has changed drastically. The CEO change came the same day that McDonald's began to detail aggressive plans to invade Starbucks' turf by selling—at lower prices—such Starbucks favorites as cappuccino and lattes."

For Starbucks, the plan is to return to the basics, [removing] some of the non-coffee products and adding new "better for you" products. Boosting international growth is also on tap.

Source: Bruce Horovitz (January 8, 2008).
"Starbucks orders an extra shot." *USA Today*, p. B1.

Customers and Brand Loyalty

The basic ambition of using a brand is to distinguish a product or service from other competing products. Thus, through branding efforts, brand managers hope to get consumers to identify the product with a specific identity, to influence the consumers' ability to recall and recognize the product (among other products) . . . To accomplish these goals, brands must engage a larger number of our mental systems, including perception and awareness, memory and cognition, and emotion. (Ramsoy & Skov, 2014, p. 1)

A **brand** is a distinctive name identifying a product or a manufacturer; an example of a popular brand for a product would be Apple, and a popular company would be Johnson & Johnson or Gillette. Sometimes the product or object is so popular that it becomes synonymous with a brand name—someone may be more likely to say "Hand me a Kleenex" than "Hand me a tissue." Examples of famous brands (besides those already named) are Gucci, Campbell, Crayola, Hilton, Nabisco, Marriott, Chevrolet, Ford, Maytag, and Macy's. As you can see from this list, brands can originate with manufacturers (such as Nabisco) or with retailers (such as Macy's). Sometimes manufacturers and dealers are one and the same or have a close relationship through a franchise or partnership. You can also see on this list competitive brands such as Hilton and Marriott and Ford and Chevrolet.

Photo 6.3 Times Square in New York City is full of advertising. Can you think of other places in the world with highly visible advertising?

Source: Thinkstock: RalphPuglieseJr

Companies use **product positioning** to give brands a specific and unique image or position in the minds of consumers within a target segment (Foxall, Goldsmith, & Brown, 1998). Their goal is to make their brand the most popular with the group they are trying to reach. It involves "creating the appropriate image of a product in the minds of consumers in the targeted markets" (Echtner & Ritchie, 1993). Generally, the greater the match is between a consumer's image of a product and the self-concept of the individual, the greater the likelihood the individual will have a favorable attitude toward the product and the more likely that he or she will purchase it (Sirgy & Su, 2000). To do this, a company such as Unilever makes many kinds of toothpaste (including Aim and Pepsodent) that are positioned for different markets. As another example, tourist destinations can be marketed by product or image positioning (Sirgy & Su, 2000). Marketing managers determine the best product positioning through research, testing, and experience.

From a customer's point of view, familiar brands make it easier to shop—a sure thing is easier than experimentation each time one shops. For example, if a family is on vacation looking for a place to stop for lunch, they know the menu, quality, and prices they can expect from a Cracker Barrel restaurant versus an unfamiliar local "home-cooking" restaurant. Another aspect of branding is that given economies of scale, widespread distribution of certain brands should save money for producers and sellers, and the savings should be passed on to the consumers.

When the same brand name is given to several products, it is termed a **family brand**, examples of which are Tom's Snacks and Frito-Lay. A family brand makes the most sense when the brands are of the same category, such as a food or a household cleaning product line. Unique packaging promotes and protects products.

As mentioned in earlier chapters, the Federal Fair Packaging and Labeling Act of 1966 requires that consumer goods be clearly labeled in easily understood terms. There are ethical issues regarding packaging: The picture on the label on the front of a can or package should be similar in appearance to the product within, labels of competitive brands should be different enough so that consumers are not confused about which product they are buying, and the size of the package should be similar to the amount of contents found inside. The latter is particularly a problem with potato chips and cereals that settle, but manufacturers remedy this by stating ounces and giving a warning on the label that contents may settle in transit.

Product Development

Products go through four stages in their development:

1. *Introduction.* In the introductory stage, the product is developed and introduced to the market.

2. *Growth.* In the growth stage, easily recognized brands are aggressively marketed, such as using product placement in movies or increasing advertising to keep sales growing, and gimmicks, including coupons, games, add-ons, and giveaways, may be used. An example of an add-on is when a popular shampoo is bundled with a conditioner; a giveaway takes place when a bank gives $500 to every five-hundredth new customer.

3. *Maturity.* In the mature stage, the product is well known and accepted (for example, Crest toothpaste), but it may be reenergized with new formulas or packaging.

4. *Dormancy/decline (and possibly revitalization).* A product in the last stage may no longer be manufactured (for instance, a book may be out of print and available only on the used-book market). Cartoon characters or fairy tale characters such as Cinderella and toys such as Paddington Bear can become popular again and be remarketed.

To explain further, let's look at how new products in stage one are introduced:

- A product could be new. An example of a totally new product would be chocolate-flavored French fries (although it could be said this is an off-shoot of chocolate-flavored or –dipped potato chips or pretzels that already exist). It is difficult to come up with a totally new product.

- A product could be a line extension, such as Coke Vanilla. (If it sells, will they try Coke Cinnamon?) A new flavor of potato chip could be developed by an existing potato chip company.
- A product could be a brand extension, such as Mello Yello candy.

Since new product development is costly, it is critical that extensive consumer research takes place before the product is introduced to the market. Research shows that certain individuals are more likely than others to quickly try something new—these people are called innovators. An **innovation** is something that is perceived as new or different. Those attracted to innovations are important from a company perspective because they are heavy users of new products, often paying full price or a premium for newness. They may drive hours to see a car or boat show or buy a new product, or they may book an exotic trip to go somewhere none of their friends have gone. Usually people choose their innovative categories, such as computer equipment, software, cameras, music, clothes, or restaurants. Innovators give valuable feedback to companies through their buying habits and their reactions to specifics about product features; in the marketplace, they encourage future sales through positive word of mouth (the consumer innovation curve was described in Chapter 3 and more about it follows).

Although so far the discussion has been about products, there can be innovators in other areas:

- ideas
- sources
- brands
- practices
- strategies, plans, or actions.

Following innovators are the early adopters; then the early majority, the late majority, and the laggards, who are the last people to adopt an innovation. They may want to wait until all the information is in before they make a decision or may be waiting for the price to fall before purchasing. Since people pick the category or categories they are innovators in—an individual can be a laggard in clothes but an innovator in electronics.

Innovativeness is linked to personality. A broad personality trait may be an affinity for trying something new versus having a more cautious outlook. Innovators are more likely to be risk takers than later adopters. Innovativeness is also linked to socioeconomic class since it takes discretionary income (extra money) to buy new products. Innovators are usually exposed to more media than laggards.

Everett M. Rogers, a leader in innovation theory, defined the innovation decision process as "the process through which an individual . . . passes (1) from first knowledge of an innovation; (2) to forming an attitude toward the innovation, (3) to a decision to adopt or reject, (4) to implementation of the new idea, and (5) to confirmation of this decision" (1995, p. 161).

To put this into a list, think of these as stages in the process (Foxall, Goldsmith, & Brown, 1998):

- knowledge
- persuasion
- decision
- implementation
- confirmation.

To demonstrate how this works, take a magazine about shopping, such as *Lucky*, or a lifestyle magazine, such as *Real Simple*. Your introduction to it may be through a friend or family member or through a store display or at the dentist's office. You would form an opinion of whether it is right for you or not and then decide to page through it or not. If you like it, you may buy a copy or a subscription, and after a while you could decide if the purchase was a good decision or not. If you do not like the magazine, you might just give it back or put it back on the display.

Brands, Counterfeiting, and Pirating

Brand names can be trademarked, which means they can be protected by law. A **trademark** is a legal term that includes words, symbols, or marks that are legally registered for use by a company. An example of a trademark is Big Mac for McDonald's; no other competing fast-food restaurant uses the term *Big Mac*.

Counterfeiting refers to making a look-alike copy, and counterfeiters sell knockoffs, products that look like the real thing but aren't (for example, counterfeit copies of Gucci handbags, Levi's jeans, or Rolex watches). Most consumers know that if the item is being sold on the street or at an extremely low price, then the item is probably a copy. If someone buys the product with this understanding, that is one thing, but if it is bought without this knowledge, then a deception has taken place, as has a rip-off of the legitimate manufacturer, artist, company, or designer.

Counterfeiting is especially common in countries that do not honor international trademark or copyright laws or that have a culture in which counterfeiting is not considered unethical. In recent history in China and South Korea, there were many counterfeit products and few protections for internationally known brands in such areas as clothing, music, and books (including the Harry Potter books). This is changing.

However, it is important to point out that low-income nations steal from other low-income nations, so it is not a question of the products of richer nations being pirated by poorer ones. A case in point is the Ghana textile industry (the average annual income in Ghana is very low) that continually combats cheap knockoffs by China, Pakistan, Nigeria, India, and the Ivory Coast. These other countries make cheap copies of the most popular Ghana textiles, smuggle them back into Ghana, and snatch sales from potential customers of the original high-quality fabrics (Phillips, 2002). "The fakes aren't hard to spot. They tend to be made of flimsier, less regular fabric, often synthetic such as rayon, instead of cotton. The colors don't always line up with the shapes" (Phillips, 2002, p. B1).

Pirating means stealing an original idea or product and selling it. Currently, "entertainment companies have a variety of techniques at their disposal to make it harder for people to share music, movies and software over the Internet" (Wingfield, 2002, p. D3). Following are some examples of these techniques:

- *File spoofing.* In file spoofing, a song or movie is labeled as something else. The user often experiences bursts of static or hears only part of a song's chorus.
- *Redirection.* Redirection happens when instructions are inserted into a bogus file; a possible outcome is the sending of the user to a commercial music site.
- *Interdiction.* Interdiction overloads a computer, jamming the computer with traffic.

Obviously these techniques are controversial and could be considered extreme or anti-consumerist. Pirating is not a new concept—ever since the advent of tape recorders, music could be taped and copies shared, and with equipment and cameras, movies can be copied. Because only a few people used to be involved in swapping activity, it was hard to prosecute or to work up much energy over the practice, but the Internet has made it much easier and more pervasive through file-swapping websites. Traditional industries are fighting back. "We think copyright owners ought to be able to do whatever they can that's lawful to protect their rights and their artists' careers," says Cary Sherman, president of the Recording Industry Association of America (Wingfield, 2002, p. D1).

Brand Perception and Image

Many researchers have measured brand perception. Of particular note is a study by Magda Nenycz-Theil and Jenni Romaniuk (2014), who found that the real difference between consumers' perceptions of **private label brands (PLs)**, also called store brands, and national brands was that consumers know more about **nationally advertised brands (NBs)**. Makes sense doesn't it? The consumer may pay more for that knowledge through higher prices. PLs are brands owned by retailers and distributed in their stores.

"When a brand appears in a television show or movie, it often becomes part of the consumer's experience" (Coker, Altobello, & Balasubramanian, 2013, p. 102). This is called **product placement**. When the show or movie is watched with friends it adds the component of social context, and this shared experience may reinforce the product placement even more.

Brand perception refers to how consumers view or rate a brand: How do they classify the brand? Do they think the brand is reliable or untrustworthy, innovative or old-fashioned? "An **image** of a product, person, brand, or place is formed when people develop beliefs, ideas, perceptions, or impressions about a product, person or place" (Deslandes, Goldsmith, & Bonn, 2002). An individual can have an image (an impression or attitude) about a vacation destination, for example, without having ever been to that place, and this image can come from the general media, educational sources, family, friends, travel agents, or brochures. It is widely assumed that an appropriate image can make or break a vacation destination; for example, news of terrorism or civil unrest can wreak havoc with a country's tourist industry, but visions of swaying palm trees, beautiful beaches, and cool drinks attract tourists. To be more specific, **brand image** refers to the set of perceptions that consumers have formed about a brand, such as a brand being perceived as targeting the young. Mello Yello soft drink is marketed to young people, with its advertisements showing shirtless teenage boys swinging on ropes out from cliffs, letting go, and dropping into a lake or pond. One would assume that a brand extension, such as Mello Yello candy, would appeal to a similar group. Since consumers tend to resist change and keep buying the same brands or brand extensions, firms especially like to attract young people because once young people like a brand, they have a lifetime of buying ahead of them. It often takes a crisis such as nonproduction of a good or a true innovation to move someone away from his or her established brand preferences.

Early brand perception is part of the socialization process in families. Think about any brands that your family routinely buys (a particular detergent, soap, toothpaste, or cleaning product). Assume your family buys Lysol, a brand that was introduced in the 1800s. What is your perception of Lysol? Will it get things clean? Will it be strong? Usually one of the earliest consumer experiences outside the home is the child accompanying parents to the grocery store—think of all the babies and toddlers you have seen in their carriers in grocery carts. This, among other reasons, is why it is important to turn our attention next to families and households in terms of population trends.

Socio-Demographic, Psychographic, and Population Trends

Socio-demographic variables include gender, age, education, income, and family size, and these can be compared with **psychographic measures** such as idealism, deal proneness, end-of-aisle display proneness, impulsiveness, brand loyalty, price/deal proneness, and smart-shopper self-perceptions. Psychographics refers to consumer lifestyles (how a person lives) and how they are measured. There is a relationship between consumer psychographics and the attitude towards private label brands (Shukla, Banerjee, & Adidam, 2013). This relationship can have an effect on display strategies. Higher-income and higher-educated consumers are generally less impulsive according to these researchers.

Demographics refer to statistical aspects or characteristics of populations. Data are used to describe populations (see Chapter 1). For example, the global population is growing more urban. Worldwide growth is uneven and impacts market demand and the use of resources. Population trends are important to study in consumer economics because one has to know where the humans are now and where they are likely to be in the future. By 2050 the US population could be more than 500 million. Rather than being overwhelmed by this number, it is important to remember that this country has been growing steadily since colonial times and that solutions will be found to accommodate everyone. There are vast spaces in this country that are wilderness areas; other areas are actually losing or barely maintaining their population.

Here are some population trends in the US and worldwide:

- In the United States, the five largest states in population are California, Texas, Florida, New York, and Illinois. Great growth relative to current population is expected in the West in states such as Alaska, Arizona, Colorado, Idaho, Nevada, New Mexico, Utah, and Wyoming. North Dakota and other oil-producing states experienced growth spurts and changes in their economies. Technology clusters or corridors are also affecting employment and population patterns.

- In the United States, much future growth will come from immigration.

- Europeans, Americans, and Japanese are having fewer children, meaning that more money will be spent per child and that there will be more demand for smaller homes, out-of-home food and entertainment, travel, and smaller food packages in grocery stores.

- The average age in the US is 37.6 years and rising. For males it is 36.3 years and for females 39 years.

- In the US, there are more empty nesters (those between 50 and 64 years old whose children have grown) as well as senior citizens (those over age 65) and elders, affecting health care, cars, food services, finances, housing, and tourism.

- Life expectancy in the United States is rising with 75.96 being the national median. It varies by state:

  Minnesota: 78.32

  Hawaii: 78.23

  Utah: 78.11

  New York: 77.80

  California: 77.80

- There are more teens now. Over 30 million US teens will influence sales of electronics, clothing, recreation, cars, and music.

- Recent studies report that the preferred residential area for most Americans is suburban. Since World War II, the most popular move has been to the suburbs, affecting transportation (cars and mass transit are necessities), jobs, stores, and homes. In the twenty-first century, there is a move back to cities, where people are renovating homes and rejecting long commutes. Although there is a return to urbanism and planned developments, with access to green spaces, there is also a segment of the population favoring "the new ruralism," a return to small-acreage farms or homes with two acres or more of land. Organic farming and raising chickens and beekeeping are growing in popularity.

- Mobile populations are higher consumers than people who stay in one place because each move necessitates consumption of products and services. In the retired population, the main choices are to stay put, move permanently to a new location (usually in a more economical place or a warmer climate), or be nomads, living permanently in RVs criss-crossing the country or changing homes every three to five years while looking for the best location near family, friends, and services such as health care, recreation, shopping, airports, restaurants, and entertainment.

- There is increased diversity. About 1 in 10 US homes is non-English-speaking (or combined English- and non-English-speaking), and the percentages are much higher in certain areas than others, which affects education and all sorts of consumer preferences from food to entertainment.

- Households increasingly have two primary income providers.

Changing Families and Households

Japan has been experiencing negative growth since 2004. So, the main thing to say about this section is that families and households are indeed changing and the changes are occurring worldwide. As noted in Chapter 1, a household is made up of one or more persons; a family is made up of two or more persons. Since 1980 the percentage of households that are families has declined. The household is the most basic consumer unit. Households drive the consumer market in their selection of housing, food, transportation, entertainment, financial services, and clothing. The US Census Bureau defines a **household** as comprised of all persons who occupy a "housing unit," that is, a house, an apartment or other group of rooms, or a single room that constitutes "separate living quarters." A household can contain related family members as well as unrelated persons such as foster children, lodgers, wards, or employees who share the same housing unit. A household may be made up of one person or many, but the trend is for household size to be smaller.

By US Census Bureau definition, a **family** consists of two or more persons related by birth, marriage, or adoption and residing together in a household. It should be noted that some groups and family specialists do not like this definition of family because it does not include gay couples or other groups such as young heterosexual couples or unmarried elderly couples who live together. The American Red Cross has a much broader definition of family, which they used when they determined who was eligible for aid after the September 11, 2001, tragedy. As another example of a broader definition, an advertisement intoned that family is whoever is around the dinner table, and for many this is a better definition than the Census Bureau's. Numbers show that **nonfamily households**, made up of householders who live either alone or with others to whom they are not related, are a growing group, accounting for almost 30 percent of all households in 2000. Another phenomenon is extended families, which may include a core family and aunts, uncles, grandparents, in-laws, or other family members. Extended families living together are more common in China, India, and South Korea than they are in the United States.

Since 1980, the percentage of people living alone has risen. Single women represent 11 percent of home buyers. There are more households than ever before, but household composition is changing. Fewer households have two parents and children under the age of 18 years living at home. Americans are also marrying later. Cities such as Boston, New York, San Francisco, and Washington, DC, have large populations of singles.

What does all this mean for consumerism? For one thing, advertising has to reflect changes in households and families. If the marketer is trying to attract extended families, then a grandmother should be in the television advertisement and should have lines to say along with the two parents and children. Appealing to families can be tricky because members of the same family have differing tastes and desires. For a family vacation destination or cruise line, the advertisement should show fun activities for children and adults. For example, the Disney and Carnival cruise lines use advertisements that show a variety of activities for the whole family. The family emphasis may have to be toned down to attract the more than 30 million unmarried men and women living alone in the United States. What sort of vacations would single, working 35-year-olds like? Will they travel alone, or are they more apt to travel with friends or family or with a tour group?

Basically, product developers and advertisers want to know details such as the size and structure of the household, age of the youngest child, and family income. These are all **life stage** variables. In terms of housing, several questions arise: How many bedrooms and bathrooms should the featured home have? How large should the garage or the master bedroom suite be? Are supersize stainless-steel refrigerator/freezers with four doors/compartments preferred over two-door models?

Households can be segmented into four life stages. Each poses problems and opportunities:

- *Stage 1.* The first group consists of unmarried and married individuals under age 35. This can be further subdivided into those under age 25 and those between 25 and 35 years. In the younger group, the persons may have recently graduated from high school or college and may be starting work and setting up households. Movement is common in this age group. For those age 25 to 35 years, more stability sets in regarding employment, friends, and family. Marriage and divorce may occur in this stage; children may be born or adopted. In the United States, the average age at first marriage is 26.5 years for women and 28.7 years for men, and higher-educated individuals tend to marry later than national averages. Whether married or not, younger people spend more money than other groups proportionally on movies, take-out food, alcoholic beverages, and clothes.

- *Stage 2.* The second group encompasses married or single parents with young children. Whether by adoption, birth, or remarriage, adding children brings with it changes in lifestyle and consumption. Housing needs increase; baby clothes, furniture, and equipment are bought; televisions are tuned to kid shows; and restaurant and food choices change. Hamburgers, pizza, macaroni and cheese, and chicken nuggets take the place of quiet romantic dinners, and noisy restaurants or restaurants with overhead televisions are preferred. This is one of the most expensive stages in terms of what needs to be bought. If one parent does not work, reduced income is another outcome, but if they both work, child care costs go up. This can be a time of high debt and other financial problems, so advertisements on television about consolidating debt services are directed at this age group, which spills over into stage 3. Since people are having children later in life than earlier generations, it is difficult to separate stages 2 and 3, so no age range is given for stage 2.

- *Stage 3.* Security, safety, and a sense of community are high priorities. So what we see in the marketplace, for example, is the State Farm insurance slogan "Like a good neighbor State Farm is there."

Middle-aged single or married individuals, with or without children, make up stage 3. These people are between 36 and 64 years of age and comprise the middle years of life, although some prefer to start the clock of middle age ticking at age 45 or 50. Putting a number on an age or stage is not an exact science because age is not only a chronological issue but also a frame of mind or attitude. Since the midyears represent such a wide time span and remarriages or blended families are common from age 35 to age 64, there may be young children or children in the middle, teen, or college years or the family may be experiencing the empty nest syndrome. Households with teens and children in their early twenties experience high costs associated with car insurance and college tuition.

Middle-aged singles without children generally live alone and have higher incomes and fewer expenditures than those with families, yet they still need dishwashers, cars, and so forth. Single-person households tend to have the same equipment as multifamily households, but singles' preferences may include condominiums or homes with small yards, expensive restaurants and wine, luxury automobiles, jewelry, and travel. They tend to be heavy gifters; they also contribute to charitable groups and organizations.

People in middle age may also be part of the **sandwich generation**, meaning they are supporting or taking care of children as well as aging parents; consequently, the time and energy and strain may be enormous. Vacations, maid services, yard services, pet care, and other types of services may target them.

Middle-aged marrieds with no children travel extensively, prefer dining out, and buy time-saving services (such as housecleaning, yard care, laundry, and shopping) and luxury items (such as expensive haircuts or spa treatments, jewelry, sports bikes, or fitness club memberships). They may take up tennis, yoga, or golf and may be interested in long-term care insurance because there are no children to take care of them in their old age.

- *Stage 4.* Older married persons and singles in the 65 years and older group are in stage 4. Most are now on their own, with the exception of grandparents who are taking care of grandchildren full-time and those elders who are living with adult children. Most are not working full-time (although 1 in 5 men and 1 in 10 women work full-time after the age of 65), so they have extra time for travel and recreation. They may be interested in part-time work, volunteer positions, or seasonal jobs. As long as their health holds out, they may favor retirement communities or new multiage developments (with walking paths or other recreational facilities), vacations, and recreational vehicles. Many elders are active Internet users. The consumption patterns of young retirees (those ages 65 to 75 years) are quite distinct from those of older retirees: Often the younger ones are heavier travelers and users of recreation than the older ones; elders tend to follow the news and the weather more than younger groups. Since people are living longer and staying healthier than ever before, the age range of active retirement keeps getting pushed upward, so what may be considered a young retiree could expand upward to age 80 and beyond. In the later years, estate planning, insurance issues, health care, and assisted living and retirement homes become important.

Groups and Market Segmentation

In the last section, the discussion was mainly about households and families, but people belong to other groups as well. One of these is **reference groups**, which are collections of people that influence your decisions and behavior. The family stands out as the most important reference group because of its longevity, emotional attachments, shared genetics, and intensity. Other than family members, reference groups can include teachers, neighbors, religious groups, political parties, racial or ethnic organizations, clubs, colleagues, and students. If there is frequent contact, then the reference group is considered primary; if contact is infrequent or in the past, it is considered secondary. In consumerism, reference groups exchange information, offer advice and guidance, provide identity, and serve as a measuring stick or as a means of comparing. Belonging to certain groups may require uniforms or other forms of appearance. For example, college students usually dress casually, so if a student shows up for class in a suit, the other students will assume that student is giving a presentation or going to a job interview.

Thus, group members engage in usual ways of behaving and may share other characteristics such as age, gender, education, social class, lifestyle, occupation, income, religion, and race and ethnicity. Depending on source there are various definitions but generally speaking about 10 percent of Americans are upper class (referring to annual income), 70 percent are middle class, and 20 percent are working or lower class. Going beyond strictly income, a widely used determinant is the **socioeconomic index (SEI)**, an index based on education level and occupation. For example, in the SEI, bartenders and stevedores are rated lower than engineers and dentists (Stevens & Cho, 1985). Studies have shown that income does not cause direct consumption nearly to the extent that education and occupation do (Hawkins, Best, & Coney, 2001). Americans are becoming more educated and taking more white-collar positions.

75 percent of Americans visit a mall (or large shopping center) at least once a month.

Household consumption takes time as well as energy and money. Working women are important sales generators in malls (Fetto, 2002). Shopping malls and restaurants/coffee shops are often places of **boundary time**, meaning transition time between home and work. Other community places include libraries and fitness/recreation centers. Shopping is often a social experience; 81 percent of Americans shop with someone else.

Photo 6.4 Shopping with others offers social benefits

Source: Thinkstock: Purestock

Companies as well as families have a social and cultural context. According to Charles Holliday, CEO of DuPont, "It's part of our culture to think about doing the right things and we're not going off on any short-term whims" (Hymowitz, 2002). He says he feels responsible to four distinct stakeholders: employees, investors, customers, and the public. He adds, "We're not changing our core values, including concern about the safety of our products and our people" (Hymowitz, 2002).

Businesses and the media study what groups exist and who belongs to which **market segment** (a specific group of consumers). A market segment is a portion of a larger market whose needs differ somewhat from the larger. The segment has to be sizable enough to generate enough sales.

To determine a market segment, consumers are first grouped by similar needs; for example, young families may be interested in backyard swing sets. In order to establish this need, a company may conduct focus groups, interviews, or surveys, with questions being asked about features, such as how many swings are needed, whether a slide is desired, and which building materials and colors would be preferred. Once this need set is delineated, then attention turns to the most likely consumers. What is their lifestyle? Where do they live? What media do they use?

Everyone belongs to a dominant culture as well as subcultures. People identify with their core culture and their subcultures, each of which has values, norms, and customs. Holiday celebrations and foods are often connected with cultures and subcultures. Ethnic subcultures include members with shared behaviors and beliefs based on a common language, background, or race.

In a directive from the federal Office of Management and Budget, all federal agencies are to report statistics according to the following recommended race and ethnicity categories: American Indian or Alaska Native, Asian, Black or African American, Native Hawaiian or Other Pacific Islander, White, and Hispanic or Latino. The different groups have different consumption patterns and store preferences. According to Simmons Market Research, whites shop at home improvement stores more than African Americans, Asians, or Hispanics (Frequent Shoppers, 2003). But for the most part, profession or income may be more of an indicator of consumption than race or other criteria. For example, "African American, Hispanic and Asian American cable households are significantly more likely than their non-cable counterparts to be luxury car owners, homeowners, and college graduates with annual incomes exceeding $75,000, according to MRI research. . . . Consumers in these groups are also more likely to have professional/managerial jobs" (Karrfait, 2003, p. S4).

In the 2010 census, many Americans refused to pick a race or ethnicity category. Some people object to being classified in categories; others find making a selection difficult, especially if they are of mixed heritage. In the 2010 census of the US population, the percentages were as follows:

Whites/Caucasians: 77.7 percent

Hispanics/Latinos: 17.1 percent

Blacks/African Americans: 13.2 percent

Asian: 5.3 percent

American Indian/Native American: 1.2 percent

Hispanics/Latinos. The term *Hispanic* is used to describe an ethnic group with Spanish-speaking heritage. In the last census, respondents were asked if they were Spanish/Hispanic/Latino. After responding yes, they could select a nationality group of Mexican/Mexican American/Chicano, Puerto Rican, Cuban, or Other. Hispanics are the largest ethnic group in areas of Arizona, Florida, New Mexico, and Texas and one of the fastest-growing groups nationwide due to a high birthrate as well as immigration, making them an attractive consumer segment. Their households are larger (3.5 people) than those of the general population (2.7 people). By the year 2050, the US Census predicts Hispanics will comprise 23 percent of the nation's population.

Hispanic populations are spreading out from traditional metropolitan centers. In 2004, 23 percent of the nation's Hispanic population lived in the Los Angeles and New York metropolitan areas; in 1990, it was 30 percent.

Hispanic advertising is a hot area. Given the results of the last census, advertising firms, many of which are owned and staffed by Hispanics, are catching up. According to

Photo 6.5 Hispanics and Latinos are the largest minority groups in the United States

Source: Thinkstock: Huntstock

Hispanic Business, the total ad budget for Hispanics is about $2.2 billion a year, compared with $234 billion for the mainstream market (Raymond, 2002). The number of radio stations for Hispanics is lower than the number for African Americans.

Hispanics are known for being more brand loyal than other groups. One of the best-known brands directed at the Hispanic market is the food powerhouse Goya, whose products include Mexican chilies, Caribbean fruit juices, and Spanish olive oil. It is the fourth-largest Hispanic-owned company in the United States (Bianchi & Sama, 2002). Competitors include Unilevers' Iberia Foods and La Cena Fine Foods Ltd. as well as smaller companies. According to Marino Roa, vice president of sales at Le Fe Foods Inc., "Latinos are very loyal to their brands" (Bianchi & Sama, 2002). Latinos visit grocery stores an average of 4.7 times a week, compared with 2.2 times for the average American, and also outspend other Americans $117 to $87 per week (Bianchi & Sama, 2002).

Since Hispanics are a growing market and high food spenders, grocery stores such as Albertson's Inc. are considering all-Hispanic stores; Kmart and Wal-Mart are considering similar initiatives. Meanwhile, retailers are expanding the number of products that they offer in their current stores that are attractive to Hispanics. This group is often called a sleeping giant because although retailers have been slow in the past to market to this group, that is rapidly changing.

Hispanics eat out less often than most Americans, averaging only 1.2 times per week. At home, meals are prepared mainly from scratch. Convenience foods are less important than foods made with care. In urban markets, there are television channels and magazines devoted to Hispanics, and with cable television nearly everyone gets at least one Hispanic channel. Hispanics' incomes and education levels are rising dramatically. The Hispanic market is not homogeneous, meaning that being Hispanic may be less important than country of origin, so care must be taken in how they are approached in terms of products (such as food) and music and media messages. Hispanics also pay more for phone services, furniture, and apparel and spend a higher proportion of their income on housing and transportation than the general population (Karrfait, 2003).

M. Isabel Valdes, in her book *Marketing to American Latinos: A Guide to the In-Culture Approach, Part 2* (2002), emphasizes the "in-culture" approach, which is a philosophy that encourages marketers to thoroughly understand consumers' culture and origin before attempting to court them. She says there are vast differences in spending power and consumer viability among Hispanics based on age, geographic distribution, and country of origin.

Blacks/African Americans. In general, African Americans use the Internet less frequently than do Caucasians, but more frequently than Hispanics; however, the African American community has increased its usage since 2008. Online usage among African Americans increased when Barack Obama's candidacy began to soar, and websites such as NewsOne.com and TheRoot.com began to attract significant audiences . . . Internet usage among Asian Americans is extremely high, making Asian media outlets move aggressively online (Diamond, 2011, p. 91).

When it comes to grocery shopping, African Americans spend slightly more per week than the total US market but less than Hispanics. The US Census estimates they will make up 14 percent of the population in 2050. Currently, they are somewhat younger than the general US population; their household incomes range from low to high, but overall their incomes place them in the middle between Caucasians and Hispanics. Many of their consumer preferences are linked more to SEI than to race. Generally, they spend less on housing and more on clothing, personal care items and services, and shopping trips to upscale malls and retailers (Fisher, 1996). On average, the African American woman spends three times as much as a Caucasian woman on hair-care products (Soloman & Rabolt, 2004), and companies such as Clairol, L'Oreal, and Alberto-Culver have extensive ethnic lines.

Magazines such as *Essence, Jet, Black Enterprise*, and *Ebony* are directed at the African American market. For example, *Jet* claims to reach 90 percent of the black male market (Soloman & Rabolt, 2004). Advertisements in these magazines include product categories such as skin and hair care, cosmetics, and food and beverages. Another marketing approach is to offer promotions or sponsor events targeted to African Americans, such as sporting events or concert tours. African Americans tend to view shopping as more recreational than other groups and appreciate a pleasant and fun shopping environment, and they have more buying power than any other ethnic group. They watch 40 percent more TV than the general market; what they watch differs from programming for general audiences (Karrfait, 2003). "Because many more African American men love sports than any other group, they have purchased more large screen TV sets, with price tags of $500 or more," according to Willis Smith, principal researcher of the *Urban Market Report* (Karrfait, 2003, p. S4).

The largest percentage of Asian Americans are Chinese.

Asian Americans. As with all groups, sensitivity is needed when appealing to Asian Americans. A mistake was made when an American company used a Chinese model in an advertisement for a Korean product, which demonstrates that even though this section is discussing different racial and ethnic groups, within these groups there are vast differences. There is not a single Asian American market, just as there is not one for Hispanics. Asian American children and adults are often seen with groups of people in ads especially for fashion, toys, electronics, food, and bars.

Asian Americans are more highly educated and have higher household incomes than the general population. At 5.3 percent of the population, they are smaller in number than Hispanics or African Americans, but they are slated to grow to 10 percent by the year 2050. The largest numbers are Chinese and Filipinos, followed by Koreans, Vietnamese, and others. They are mostly concentrated in urban areas, especially Chicago and New York, as well as California and Hawaii. One of the challenges to reaching this group is the diversity of languages: Chinese (25 percent), Filipino (18 percent), Indian (17 percent), Vietnamese (11 percent), Korean (11 percent), and Japanese (8 percent). About 70 percent of the 12 million Asian Americans in the United States are foreign born, compared with 44 percent of Latinos (Karrfait, 2003).

Grocery stores devote sections to foods used exclusively by Asian Americans and to those of the general population who like Asian cuisine. Some Asian Americans (estimated at about 49 percent) strongly identify with their original culture, and about half of them know their native language (Hawkins, Best, & Coney, 2001). Younger groups and those brought up in the United States have less traditional associations. Asian Americans are stronger savers than the general population, are quality oriented regarding the goods they seek, and are heavy users of computers and the Internet. Name brands and status appeal to a sizable number of Asian Americans, who prefer BMW, Mercedes Benz, and other premium car brands, as well as designer handbags and clothes. They are generally affluent and the best educated of the major ethnic groups. Asian Americans and Hispanics spend more than other groups or the general population during visits to the mall (Fetto, 2002). Although their current numbers are small, this is a fast-growing segment of the US population. According to Simmons Market Research, they are more likely to shop in home electronics stores and home furnishing stores than whites, African Americans, or Hispanics (Frequent Shoppers, 2003).

> *Young Asian Americans are also displaying a new ethnic pride in their heritage, helped by role models such as the seven foot, six inch Yao Ming of the Houston Rockets, who beat out Shaquille O'Neal in fan votes to start in this year's NBA All Star game (Ming appears in commercials for Visa and Apple Computers and just signed a five-year deal to represent Gatorade). It's never been so hip to be Asian, as kids across all demographics are learning. (Karrfait, 2003, p. S5)*

Gays and Lesbians. Because some people may be offended by or feel uncomfortable with images of gay lifestyles if they are portrayed in general audience publications, many companies, including American Express, Sony, and Subaru of America, make specific advertisements designed for the gay media. Many of the ads are for prosaic products and services such as financial planning. One reason this is a special concern for gays and lesbians is that employers may not provide benefits or coverage for partners to the extent that they do for heterosexual married couples. The ads may show same-sex couples embracing, holding hands, or looking off into the distance.

Research shows that homosexuals tend to be more highly educated than the general public; are dedicated to their careers; have more discretionary income; enjoy change, humor, and trends; and are more informed politically and socially. "A Simmons study of readers of gay publications found that compared to heterosexuals, these consumers are almost twelve times more likely to hold professional jobs, twice as likely to own a vacation home, and eight times more likely to own a computer notebook" (Solomon & Rabolt, 2004, p. 157). They are heavy users of the Internet. They also use other media:

> *[They] prefer to read newspapers targeted at them and more upscale sections of the newspaper; the same is true for magazines. [They] prefer more intellectual and upscale TV and radio programs [and] use catalogs, 800 numbers, and online forms of direct marketing. (Wells, Burnett, & Moriarty, 2000, p. 99)*

High-profile gay figures in advertising include athletes, actors, comedians, and singers. Gays and lesbians are more likely to be urban dwellers than rural dwellers. Advertisements even for general audience publications often show homosexual relationships, so watch for changes in how and where this group is depicted. The exact proportion of the population that is gay or lesbian is difficult to say; the numbers vary based on source and location.

Summary

This chapter explored the meaning of consumption and brands. For example, it was shown that individuals have relationships with products and brands that go beyond mere function. How functional are a dozen red roses? Why is an $8,000 man's suit from Brioni desirable? Consumer behavior refers to the buying behavior of individuals, families, and households that buy goods and services for personal consumption. Consumers go through six steps in the buying process: assessing needs, searching for information, evaluating alternatives, and selecting a product or service (prepurchase); buying (purchase); and evaluating the product or service afterward (postpurchase). In this last step, companies or organizations want to build loyalty and relationships and to enjoy positive word of mouth.

Companies compete with each other for consumer dollars and use product positioning to give brands specific and unique images. Products go through four stages of development: introduction, growth, maturity, and dormancy/decline.

Some consumers are more innovative than others. Innovativeness is linked to personality.

Brand names can be trademarked. Counterfeit means look-alike copies, and pirating refers to stealing an original idea or product and selling it.

The household is the most basic consumer unit. Households can be segmented into four stages, beginning with young adults and ending with older singles and married persons.

KEY POINTS

1. Consumers go through six steps in the buying process.

2. Businesses want to maximize profits by offering sought-after goods.

3. A brand, such as Nike or Under Armour, is a distinctive name identifying a product or manufacturer.

4. Using annual income as a metric, about 10 percent of Americans can be considered upper class, 70 percent middle class, and 20 percent working or lower class. A more broadly used determinant of population segments is the socioeconomic index (SEI). Studies indicate that income does not cause or direct consumption nearly as much as education and occupation.

5. The trend is toward smaller family size in Europe, Japan, and the United States.

6. Media and business study market segments and life stages which are groupings of people.

7. The three largest ethnic/racial groups in the United States are Hispanics/Latinos, African Americans, and Asian Americans. Each group has individual characteristics and consumption needs that differentiate them from the general population. Marketers are increasingly aware of ethnic groups' consumption needs and market to them. New networks are springing up to serve a growing demand for multicultural fare.

KEY TERMS

actively acquired information

banner ads

boundary time

brand

brand image

brand perception

cognitive dissonance

consumer behavior

consumer cost

credence goods

customer satisfaction

distribution

experience goods

external search

family

family brand

forecast

household

image

information search rule

innovation

internal search

life stage

marketing communications

marketing mix

marketing strategy

market segment

nationally advertised brands (NBs)

need set

nonfamily households

ongoing search

passive information

pirating

prepurchasing

price

private label brands (PLs), also called store brands

product placement

product positioning

psychographic measures

reference groups

sandwich generation

service

socio-demographic variables

socioeconomic index (SEI)

target market

trademark

DISCUSSION QUESTIONS

1. Why would State Farm have as its slogan "Like a good neighbor, State Farm is there"? What family or household stage might they be targeting?

2. What is the main difference between consumers' perceptions of private labels (store brands) and nationally advertised brands?

3. What are the steps in the prepurchase process? Why is so much time taken before purchase?

4. What are the stages in product development? Give an example other than those in the chapter for each stage.

5. Go to the Procter & Gamble website (www.pg.com) and navigate to P&G brands. Find out the brand names of different laundry detergents or shampoos. Why would the same company offer different products at different price levels that essentially perform the same function?

6. Select a life stage (households) and predict what products or services they would most likely need.

REFERENCES

Bianchi, A., and F. Sama. (July 9, 2002). Goya Foods leads an ethnic sales trend. *Wall Street Journal*, p. B4.

Coker, K., S. A. Altobello, and S. K. Balasubramanian. (2013). Message exposure with friends: the role of social context on attitudes toward prominently placed brands. *Journal of Consumer Behaviour*, 12, 102–111.

Deslandes, D., R. Goldsmith, and M. Bonn. (2002). Measuring destination image: do the existing scales work? A working paper, Florida State University, Tallahassee, FL.

Diamond, J. (2011). *Retail advertising and promotion*. New York: Fairchild.

Echtner, C. M., and J. E. B. Ritchie. (1993). The measurement of destination image: an empirical assessment. *Journal of Travel Research*, 31 (4), 3–13.

Fetto, J. (March 2002). Mall rats. *American Demographics*, 10.

Fisher, C. (September 1996). Black, hip, and primed to shop. *American Demographics*, 52–59.

Fournier, S. (March 1998). Consumers and their brands: developing relationship theory in consumer research. *Journal of Consumer Research*, 24, 343–373.

Foxall, G. R., R. Goldsmith, and S. Brown. (1998). *Consumer psychology for marketing*, 2nd ed. London: Thomson Business Press.

Frequent shoppers. (May 2003). *American Demographics*, 8.

Hawkins, D., R. Best, and K. Coney. (2001). *Consumer behavior: building a marketing strategy*, 8th ed. Boston: Irwin McGraw-Hill.

Holmes, E. (February 18, 2015). The art of making even a cardigan stand out. *Wall Street Journal*, pp. D1 and D3.

Horovitz, B. (January 8, 2008). Starbucks orders an extra shot. *USA Today*, p. B1.

Hymowitz, C. (July 9, 2002). CEOs must work hard to maintain faith in the corner office. *Wall Street Journal*, p. B1.

Karrfait, W. (May 2003). A multicultural mecca. *American Demographics*, pp. S4–S6.

Lui, M. W. (2014). Utility blindness: why do we fall for deals? *Journal of Consumer Behaviour*, 13, 42–49.

Nenycz-Thiel, M., and J. Romaniuk. (April 2014). The real difference between consumers' perceptions of private labels and national brands. *Journal of Consumer Behaviour*, 13, 262–269.

Phillips, M. (July 12, 2002). Pilfered patterns. *Wall Street Journal*, p. B1.

Ramsoy, T. A., and M. Skov. (2014). Brand preference affects the threshold for perceptual awareness. *Journal of Consumer Behaviour*, 13, 1–8.

Raymond, J. (March 2002). ¿Tienen numeros? *American Demographics*, 22–25.

Rogers, Everett M. (1995). *Diffusion of innovations*, 4th ed. New York: Free Press.

Schor, Juliet B. (1998). *The overspent American*. New York: HarperCollins.

Shukla, P., M. Banerjee, and P. T. Adidam. (2013). The moderating influence of socio-demographic factors on the relationship between consumer psychographics and the attitude towards label brands. *Journal of Consumer Behaviour*, 12, 423–435.

Sirgy, J., and C. Su. (2000). Destination image, self-congruity, and travel behavior: towards an integrative model. *Journal of Travel Research*, 38, 340–352.

Solomon, M., and N. Rabolt. (2004). *Consumer behavior in fashion*. Upper Saddle River, NJ: Prentice Hall.

Stevens, G., and J. Cho. (1985). Socioeconomic indices. *Social Science Research*, 14, 142–168.

Trachtenberg, J. (February 23, 2015). Is *People* magazine relevant in a digital age? *Wall Street Journal*, p. R2.

Trejos, N. (February 23, 2015). Hotel CEOs talk wi-fi, millennials and mobile keys. *USA Today*, p. 6B.

Tsiotsou, R. (2006). The role of perceived product quality and overall satisfaction on purchase intentions. *International Journal of Consumer Studies*, 30 (2), 207–212.

Valdes, M. I. (2002). *Marketing to American Latinos: a guide to the in-culture approach, part 2*. New York: Paramount Market Publishing.

Wells, W., J. Burnett, and S. Moriarty. (2000). *Advertising principles and practice*, 5th ed. Saddle River, NJ: Prentice Hall.

Wingfield, N. (July 11, 2002). Behind the fake music. *Wall Street Journal*, p. D1.

Chapter 7

Decision Making and Advertising

You can have any color as long as it's black.

Henry Ford, referring to his automobiles in 1914

LEARNING OBJECTIVES

1. Discuss decision making in consumer behavior.

2. Explain three main types of decision making.

3. Understand advertising in relation to buying decisions and sustainable behavior.

4. Know the pros and cons of advertising in relation to consumers.

5. Describe the government agencies that impact advertising.

6. Understand the value of social marketing and public service announcements.

CASE STUDY

FTC Charges Gerber with Falsely Advertising Infant Formula

"The Federal Trade Commission has charged Gerber Products Co., also doing business as Nestle Nutrition, with deceptively advertising that feeding its Good Start Gentle formula to infants with a family history of allergies prevents or reduces the risk that they will develop allergies.

The agency also alleges that Gerber has falsely advertised Good Start Gentle's health claims as FDA-approved. Through its federal court enforcement action, the Commission is seeking to prohibit Gerber from making the alleged false and unsubstantiated allergy-prevention claims.

'Parents trusted Gerber to tell the truth about the health benefits of its formula, and the company's ads failed to live up to that trust,' said Jessica Rich, Director of the FTC's Bureau of Consumer Protection. 'Gerber didn't have evidence to back up its claim that Good Start Gentle formula reduces the risk of babies developing their parents' allergies.'"

> Source: Federal Trade Commission (October 30, 2014). "FTC charges Gerber with falsely advertising its Good Start gentle formula protects infants from developing allergies." Available online at ftc.gov/news-events/press-releases/2014/10/ftc-charges-gerber.

Introduction

Consumers make decisions every day. They are solving problems and fulfilling needs like getting gasoline for the car or yogurt for lunch. Decisions follow about where to buy the gasoline and what brand and flavor of yogurt to buy. This chapter builds on the last one on the buying process, brands, and product development. It delves further into how consumers make decisions and how advertising influences those decisions. We discuss why people buy what they do, why they want to be unique, and how they react to advertising. We also explore how advertising works and in particular why those irritating jingles stay in our minds. The secret is called "locking power." The chapter also discusses the influence of cultural or societal groups and lifestyles in relation to consumerism and social marketing, which influences behaviors that benefit individuals and communities for the greater social good, such as more green or sustainable behavior.

Decision Making Takes Time

Decisions are conclusions or judgments about some issue or matter. **Decision making** is a choice between two or more alternatives. The decisions made and consumption behaviors determine what type of society we live in. We make choices considering scarcity—scarcity in time, money, and energy. Consumers can feel rushed to make quick decisions. In the last chapter, we discussed the steps that consumers go through in the buying process, including prepurchase, purchase, and postpurchase behavior. Another way to say this is that consumers are involved in pre-selection, selection, and post-selection. This process can be applied to services as well as goods.

CASE STUDY

Spear Fishing

New evidence suggests that consumers value (find happiness in) experiences over things, but that they buy things anyway to fulfill more than basic needs. For example, Clay Shaw likes to go spear fishing and he also likes to fly his seaplane to get to remote islands. He values extreme sports but needs things to get him there, and he works hard running a business in order to afford the experiences he likes.

Consumers try to make good decisions, but this is becoming more difficult because (1) time is limited, (2) the number and complexity of products and services have increased, (3) the Internet and off-shoots such as Netflix have expanded choices, and (4) consumers have become further and further removed from the origin or basis of products although there is a move back to origins as evidenced in publications like *Organic Life*. Since the last edition of this book, yogurt and almond milk have soared in popularity. The dairy aisle at grocery stores has been reconfigured to meet these changing preferences.

There is a decided trend by millennials (young adults born in the 1980s through early 2000s, making up 24 percent of the US population) to buy organic food and products produced locally. Stores and farmers are responding to this. Millennials are also said to value a big life over a big house. This affects the real estate market. They also move more often than the general population. They move for better jobs, further education, and more attractive lifestyles.

CASE STUDY

Target and Millennials

"Target Corp. plans to lean on Greek yogurt, bagged coffee, and craft beers in an effort to make its grocery aisles feel less like Wal-Mart Stores Inc. and to attract younger shoppers. Target has zeroed in on seven grocery categories—from granola and yogurt to candy and snacks—where it thinks it has the best chance of standing out to urban dwellers, younger families and Hispanics, to people familiar with the matter said. Along with a proclaimed goal of adding more organic, natural and gluten-free foods, Target is showing signs that its food direction will become less reliant on packaged and processed foods that are out of favor with many millennial consumers."

Source: Paul Ziogro (March 3, 2015). "Target thinks 'millennials' in its revamp of groceries." *Wall Street Journal*, p. B2.

Regarding time as a scarce resource, we all have to make decisions about the best way to manage time. In consumption, there are countless examples of time and consumption trade-offs, such as cooking a meal from scratch that would take several hours versus popping a preprepared frozen dinner in the microwave that will take minutes to heat. Another time-saver is using the Internet to search for products. For example, a recent search for a certain brand of popcorn popper revealed that none of the local stores had one and that the only way to get the popper was by ordering online direct from the company. The good part was that ordering online saved time and could be done at 11 o'clock at night when stores were closed, and it also saved gasoline; the negative was the shipping charge (versus buying in person).

Parkinson's law states that a job expands to fill the time available to accomplish the task, such as finding and purchasing a product. A person who has all day to shop will view the shopping task differently than a person who has to buy something quickly on his or her lunch hour. Thus, Parkinson's law shows the elasticity of time and consumption behavior. It was named after an English historian, C. Northcote Parkinson, who studied the Royal Navy and found that the more people hired, the more work was created without increasing output. So in consumption, the analogy would be that more time spent in shopping does not necessarily mean there will be increased return for that effort. There is a point at which comparison shopping (and the time and energy that it involves) is wasteful, and going to several stores a day could become a full-time occupation.

Another law or principle relevant to consumption is the **Pareto principle**, also known as the 80–20 rule, which states that 20 percent of the time expended produces 80 percent of the results and that 80 percent of the time expended results in only 20 percent of the outcomes. Essentially this means that people waste a lot of time on nonproductive activities, so again the message would be to use time wisely, to seek information and shop efficiently. This principle was named after Vilfredo Pareto, a nineteenth-century Italian economist and sociologist who found that in any series of elements to be controlled, a select small fraction of the elements accounted for a large fraction of effectiveness.

Three Types of Decision-Making Styles

As has been evident throughout the book, consumers make decisions in different ways. These ways can be put into three broad categories.

1. *Habitual Decision Making.* In this category falls routine decision making where choice making is a habit. The consumer goes to the same store and buys the same products or services without thinking about it. They may be brand loyal (deeply held commitment) or have **brand inertia**, meaning buying something without real attachment.

CRITICAL THINKING

Critical Thinking: Brand Loyalty and Brand Inertia

Name a product you buy out of brand loyalty and a product you buy out of brand inertia.

---

2. *Extended Decision Making.* This is when the consumer searches for more information before making a decision. They want to be sure. Usually costly items like homes and cars lend themselves to extended decision making.

Photo 7.1 Apple is a popular brand that people across the world demonstrate loyalty to, buying multiple Apple products

Source: Getty Images: Andrea Kamal

3. *Limited Decision Making.* This involves limited search behavior (may be internal or external) and low amounts of product risk or involvement such as browsing in a new store or trying out a sample in a grocery or warehouse store. Time-stressed consumers often engage in limited decision making.

Theory and Style Preference

The role of **self-concept**, the totality of thoughts and feelings that an individual has about himself or herself, is a strong driver of consumer behavior. Consumers use their self-concept to reduce the amount of thoughts and options. **Self-esteem** refers to the positive nature of our self-concept. Consumers often use **rules of thumb**, principles that guide purchases (such as only buying certain brands, only shopping in certain stores, or only buying certain styles). **Style** refers to the distinctive qualities of a product that set it apart from others of its kind. Consider the following in regard to consumers and style:

Buying style. Consumers can be rational, slow, comparative, or impulsive, and they have certain preferences, maybe choosing bargains rather than new merchandise at full price and shopping at small stores instead of large ones.

Preference for certain styles and colors. A person may like or dislike the color red, stripes, polka-dots, or plaids. Think of your favorite clothes. What do they look like?

Desire for either conformity or uniqueness. People vary in whether they want to stand out from the crowd or fit in. The appeal of owning something that is one of a kind

Photo 7.2
Some purchases are driven by fashion

Source: Thinkstock: Sky View

is often the driving force behind auction bidding. Scarcity or uniqueness explains why someone would pay $145,000 at an auction for John Travolta's leisure suit from the movie *Saturday Night Fever*. When the auctioneer was asked later if the price seemed excessive, he remarked graciously, "Well, it certainly was a record for polyester" (Cialdini, 2001, p. 227). Another example of a high payment for memorabilia was $807,000 paid for the black dress worn by actress Audrey Hepburn as Holly Golightly in the 1961 film *Breakfast at Tiffany's*. A charity had received the dress from the designer, and the proceeds of the auction went to the City of Joy Aid, which helps India's poor.

Uniqueness theory proposes that individuals vary in the extent to which they wish to be different. This can be measured by the Desire for Unique Consumer Products (DUCP) scale by Michael Lynn and Judy Harris (1997). For example, the DUCP scale can be used to measure general innovativeness, innovativeness for fashionable clothing, and conformity (Goldsmith, Clark, & Goldsmith, 2007). In the expanding global marketplace, consumers are exposed to an ever growing array of products and brands. What they select is connected with their self-realization, identity manifestation, and self-expression (Solomon, 2003). Utility or usefulness for some may be less of a draw than **authenticity**, the quality of being genuine and trustworthy. Consumers want authenticity and have "a desire for original, innovative, and distinctive products and services" (Lewis & Bridges, 2000, p. 4). A monogram, for example, is a way to make a product unique to the owner; other examples are the purchasing of memorabilia (such as the Travolta suit or the Hepburn dress), each a famous one-of-a-kind item. In summary, uniqueness stimulates people to embrace new things, defy convention, and pursue rare and unusual objects.

To go back to the second point on the above list, having a preference in either a buying style or the color of a product or design is common to all of us. We like certain types of shopping experiences and colors and fabrics. Preferences save a lot of time and anxiety. A person who hates crowds would be well advised to avoid malls on Black Friday, the Friday after Thanksgiving in the United States which is the kick-off of the holiday buying season. Likewise, an individual who hates used or damaged goods would be well advised to stay away from antique stores or flea markets, used-book stores, or consignment shops. If conformity is appealing, in department stores a male consumer can pick from a display of dozens of the same blue shirts. When it comes to apparel, style is "a particular combination of attributes that distinguishes it from others in its category" (Solomon & Rabolt, 2004, p. 6). Examples would be styles of shirts, pants, dresses, and skirts (dress or skirt length used to be a determinant of the latest style, a way of being fashionable).

Technological Advances and Obsolescence

Technological advances go hand and hand with technological obsolescence. The first (which we usually welcome as progress) drives the other one out. How long should products or certain technologies last? For example, how long should televisions, refrigerators, and batteries last? Are they purposely timed to fail at a certain time? Or, are discovery and replacement totally random?

As discussed in Chapter 3, technological obsolescence means that a product loses value even though it is not worn out yet because it can be replaced with a more technologically advanced product. Examples are fax machines, printers, landlines versus cell phones, cameras, and computers. Technological advances may be in design as well as function.

> *GoPro Inc., the popular maker of tiny video cameras, is making them even tinier. How tiny? The new GoPro Hero4 Session is the size of an ice cube, about half that of previous GoPros. It can fit into the spikes of a bike, hang onto the end of a fishing pole or turn a toddler into a documentary film-maker. (Fowler, July 7, 2015, B1)*

The more rapid the advances, the more quickly the product will undergo **depreciation**. Not only do you not want the product anymore, but it is not worth very much to anyone else. New cars depreciate around $2,000 right after they are driven off the lot by the owner; however, over time, the rate of depreciation slows or else the car could be worthless in a month. So what should you do? First, accept technological obsolescence and depreciation as facts of life. Second, think before you purchase—ask yourself if it would be better to wait. Third, realize that sometimes you cannot wait before making a purchase (such as a drug for a life-threatening disease or a business suit for an interview).

Computer companies are particularly aware of how rapidly computers are changing and have been very forthcoming with information about new releases to prospective buyers. For example, a college student ordered an Apple laptop and was called by the company to tell him that if he waited two weeks, he could have a newer model at a similar price. Now that is customer service. Because he was a long-time Apple user, the company wanted to keep him happy, so it gave him the choice of going with the model he ordered or getting the newer model with more bells and whistles. What would you do?

CRITICAL THINKING

Who Owns Music?

The following quote comes from 2008, but the battle rages on as to who owns music and how it is marketed and sold. Singer Taylor Swift brought this controversy up again in 2015. What is your opinion on access to music and the costs involved?

"The battles over who owns music and how much consumers should pay continue. Sony BMG Music Entertainment says it is selling digital albums, similar to gift cards, without copyright protection. The estimated price is $12.99 at retailers. This allows consumers to download MP3 files onto their home computers, making it easier to play music and transfer songs to various equipment. Other companies are changing the way they offer music as well, such as Warner Music Group who have a deal with Amazon.com's download store and Universal Music Group. The EMI Group was the first major company to remove the protection in a deal with iTunes."

Source: Bloomberg News (January 8, 2008). "Sony BMG will sell music without copyright protection." *New York Times*, p. C13.

Impulse Buying

Impulse buying means to walk into a store (offline) or go to a webpage (online) and immediately buy something without taking the time to think about the ramifications, such as cost, benefits, values, or needs. Sellers exploit impulse buying by putting displays at the front of the store or the checkout counter. Online websites may offer an add-on at the end; for example, if you spend $10 more, you will receive a bonus or a discount. Impulse items are often inexpensive or fun, like a candy bar or magazine. Buying a refrigerator is rarely an impulse item, but a GoPro camera or a set of golf clubs may be. Style is often more important than substance in product categories such as clothing, jewelry, restaurants, furniture, and architecture, and it certainly is in packaging. This is why a hamburger ranges in price from $0.99 to $30 depending on the restaurant.

Packaging and logos (like the Nike swoosh or Under Armour symbol) attract the impulse buyer and adds to image and branding. If you are going to throw out a package or display item anyway (such as a cardboard box for cosmetics or those tiny hangers used to display socks in stores), why would the style of the package or display matter? Packaging does matter because it conveys messages. It attracts your attention, helps you differentiate the brand from those of competitors (for example, the light green boxes of Clinique cosmetics versus other brands), and is useful for other aspects of display. In many cases, part of image is aesthetic appeal and status, but beyond that it is personal expression. For example, no one really needs a $1,000 glass bathroom sink embedded with copper, but it may be more pleasing to look at and certainly more unique than a typical $100 white porcelain sink. Both of the sinks function the same; the difference is in the style. Other examples are $600 antique door knobs and $7,000 custom-made copper range hoods when ordinary ones would cost much, much less.

Can an expensive item be an impulse item? Most definitely! Many time-shares, jewelry pieces, art, and boat purchases are impulse items, as are services and gifts. Jason, a millionaire, decided spontaneously to treat a hundred friends to a barbecue lunch at a marina.

Photo 7.3 Would you pay $145,000 for John Travolta's suit? Someone did

Source: Getty Images: ullstein bild

As in Jason's case, if a product makes consumers feel good and they can afford it, it can be thought of as a **consumer payoff**, an impulse or a positive result from searching and making the best choice. The optimum behavior is to seek the highest quality at the lowest price (the essence of consumer economics), but as we have discussed, this is not always the case. Sometimes to get the highest quality, one has to pay the highest price because there is no alternative, such as when you live in an isolated place or when purchasing a piece of art, an antique, or a collectible. Emerson lived on an island where there was no fresh milk, only powdered milk. To connect this with the section on decision making and time at the beginning of the chapter, a consumer would seek the largest expected payoff from the least time and energy expenditure, especially given the price of the item. For example, one would assume a consumer would spend less time selecting a mouthwash than a computer. A truly busy person with a high income may send out a personal assistant to search for information or make the purchase. For example, an owner of a horse farm/estate sent her personal assistant to look at fabric for drapes; the assistant reported back what she had found, and then the owner went to the store. Most of us do not have personal assistants, but we may have little time and find other ways to cut corners such as using shopping online or going through the drive-through on the way home from work.

Consumers reach a point where the cost of searching further is greater than any possible benefit that can be derived from this practice. Comparison shopping over a distance for a single can of soda does not make financial sense.

Price variation refers to a situation when a single seller may charge the same consumer different prices at different times for the same item. In the case of a large, heavy antique armoire, an antiques seller will probably be willing to sell it at a lesser price the last hour of a three-day antiques show than at the beginning—the reason being the problem and expense of packing it up and taking it to the next show. More common examples of **price discrimination** (different prices for the same product or service based on purchaser and/or date) include the different prices charged by hotels, airlines, and cruise lines, depending on when the trip is booked, by whom it is booked (meaning a travel agent versus a private individual), and the days on which the travel will take place. Price discrimination can be illegal if it is proven that an individual or a group is discriminated against in an unfair manner. For example, if a hotel charged a different price for the same room on the same day to people of different races or ethnicity, that could be grounds for claiming discrimination.

Another rule of thumb is that people use seals of approval or trademarks as guides. Sometimes a new competitor will use only a slightly different brand name than a successful, established product, but if it is too close, the established brand may sue over name rights. Quasi-fraud charities are notorious for using names that are very close to those of legitimate charities. An additional rule of thumb involves price. For example, if peaches are on sale for $.99 a pound, the consumer will buy, but if they are $5 a pound, then he or she will pass and substitute another fruit. However, price is not the only guide (as noted in earlier chapters).

Consumers may ignore a rule of thumb if they are in a hurry and really need a product, such as disposable diapers. This explains why they will pay twice the normal price for milk at a convenience store than at a full-service grocery store or twice what they would normally pay for a hotel room if they are exhausted, are in the middle of a snowstorm, and want to get off the road. Because of **budget constraints** (the relationship between what someone can spend and what someone will spend), most people can afford to pay double the price on a gallon of milk whereas they could not afford to pay twice as much for a desired house. This is impacted by the **ability to trade**, meaning trading one good for another. Let's say it is a new development of houses, all very similar, and the houses are lined up in a row. House A is right next to House B and is essentially identical; the prices differ by $5,000, so the preference will be for the less expensive house. Things get a little more complicated when the trade is between slightly dissimilar items, such as lamb chops for pork chops or watermelon for cantaloupe, and get much more complicated when choosing between vastly dissimilar items, such as ham and lobster or rutabaga and lettuce. In the case of dissimilar items, the consumer will have to decide how to maximize satisfaction given the conditions (price, quality, selection) that exist and then trade or purchase accordingly. Information will be part of the transaction—consumers will not buy a rutabaga if they do not know what to do with it or are unsure of the taste, whereas a choice between iceberg lettuce and romaine lettuce may be easier to make.

Besides the purchase price of the item, there are additional expenses such as cost of use, maintenance, sales taxes, or end-result preparation. Examples of after-purchase expenses are property taxes for homes and land or gasoline and repairs for cars. There are even added-on costs for simple things like food. Take, for example, the choice of buying a pound of hamburger: This could be a low-budget item or a mid- to high-priced meal, depending on the going price of different grades of hamburger, where it is consumed, and what goes with it.

Reading Customers' Minds: Can It Be Done?

Consumers use rules of thumb (price, time, style, etc.) to guide decisions, but research and testing are underway that may totally change how we think about and certainly how we measure consumers' decision-making process. Gerald Zaltman, the author of *How Customers Think* and a marketing professor at Harvard Business School, "uses brain scans, psychotherapy-like interviews and his patented Zaltman Metaphor Elicitation Technique (ZMET) to help the likes of Procter & Gamble, Pfizer, General Motors, and Coca-Cola get inside the consumer's head" (Useem, 2003, p. 48).

Zaltman says that at least 95 percent of the thinking that drives our behavior occurs unconsciously. Much of what we think were the steps we went through are actually after-purchase constructions—in short, people are buying products for reasons they are not fully conscious of. The brain scans involve monitoring blood flow in the brain and seeing cortices light up. A new product can be shown to a subject, and the person experiences it negatively or positively; the brain scan picks up his or her reaction. To bring this out of the laboratory into a larger setting, new technologies are being developed, such as caps that people can wear. So far, Zaltman and his colleagues have studied positive responses (joy and happiness) rather than negative reactions (disgust and turnoff). In the long run, you have to know what repels consumers as well as what attracts them. Zaltman sees many applications of the new technology and testing, particularly in certain industries such as cosmetics and personal appearance.

Another testing method that Zaltman uses involves asking people to bring in eight-by-ten pictures that represent their thoughts and feelings about something such as snack foods. One person brought in a picture of someone covered with bees. The trained interviewer asked what the bee picture meant, and the woman responded that she had a lot of confidence that she wouldn't get stung—"that she could safely indulge in snack foods without running the risks of harm that everyone else talks about. So there was a bit of defiance to it" (Useem, 2003, p. 48). You can see from this example that this method is in the experimental stages (and some would question the interviewer's

Price often serves as a rule of thumb guiding selection and purchase.

interpretation), but it is presented as a wave of the future, a consumer research area that will draw attention and will grow. What Zaltman would say is that simply asking people why they buy what they do falls far short of what really happens.

Consumerspace

Michael Solomon, director of a consulting firm called Mind/Share, a professor, and the author of *Conquering Consumerspace*, differentiates marketspace (a commercial system in which companies sell to us) from consumerspace (a commercial system in which they sell *with* us). His concept is that business no longer calls the shots—consumers do. He describes a trend called **identity marketing** that fuels the fire of consumerspace. In identity marketing, consumers wear or display in their homes product logos (for example, T-shirts and shoes with Nike on them or lamp shades with a university name on them). In Great Britain, an ad agency paid students to wear temporary tattoos of product logos on their foreheads. Would you do this? And if so, at what price and for how long?

According to Solomon, branding provides security and clarity in a complicated world where nationalities are less important. To summarize, the bedrock of our identities is formed by allegiance to common value systems, often expressed concretely through affiliation with common product sets. In the preface he writes: "Welcome to consumerspace. Where reality is branded. Where we avidly search for the products and services that define who we are and who we want to be. Where we are what we buy—literally" (2003, p. xiii). Not everyone in consumer economics will be comfortable with this notion, feeling it is going too far and believing that people are much more (their identities are much more) than what they purchase and use. But he is expressing a point of view that business listens to, and anything that might become a trend nature is interesting to watch. He wonders what consumerspace will look like and what firms will help build it and even control it, and he posits that people will move seamlessly between offline and online worlds, something which in many ways is already happening. Have you ever searched for a product online and then bought it at a store? Or have you found something in a store that you liked but that was not available in the right color or size or model so you went online to purchase it or to find a lower price?

According to Solomon, "People hunger for unique products that help them express their individuality in an impersonal world. We have what psychologists call a *need for uniqueness*" (2003, p. 128). We can add that to the list of needs that Abraham Maslow posited in his hierarchy of needs. Solomon says that everyone needs to feel special, and perfumes are often marketed as smelling differently on each person. This leads us to our next section on advertising where mass-marketed products boldly carry the messages "as individual as you are" or "making you feel your best."

Advertising and Social Influence

The world of advertising has been turned upside down by mobile devices, the Internet, social media, and societal changes, including a surge in pro-social, pro-environmental, and pro-organic lifestyle changes and causes. Advertisers are responsive to these changes. According to *Social Influence and Sustainable Consumption*, advertisers are social influences—their messages influence us or at least try to influence us (Goldsmith, 2015).

CASE STUDY

Organic Food for Babies and Young Children

"She serves her children organic food. She swears she would never open a can of soup for a toddler's lunch. She is Plum Organics' core customer. And Plum hopes she will buy its new pouches of organic tomato meatball soup with kale and spinach even if it got help from owner Campbell Soup Co. to make them. Plum used Campbell research to learn children's favorites are chicken noodle and tomato and then reworked recipes 'in a Plum way,' adding more vegetables," says Neil Grimmer, co-founder and chief executive of Plum.

Source: Sarah Nassauer (March 18, 2015). "What if we all bought organic?" *Wall Street Journal*, p. D1.

Advertising is defined as a "form of communication intended to convince an audience (viewers, readers or listeners) to purchase or take some action upon products, information or services etc. The purchase process is a decision-making process under risk" (Kumar & Raju, 2013, p. 37). Simply put, advertising is an announcement. Mass media forms, such as newspapers, websites/webpages, radio, and television, are used to transmit messages to reach large groups. The message may be sent to an anonymous audience who does not respond back to the source of the message or it may be an interactive environment such as an advertisement that is clicked on or responded to on social media.

The first role of advertising is to gain attention. Advertising is part of the promotional mix that sellers use to reach customers. It can be produced in-house, a separate advertising agency may be hired, or the promotional mix could involve a combination of both. Advertising could also be self-generated by an individual, such as an announcement of a product trend on a blog.

Table 7.1 Advertising Research Model

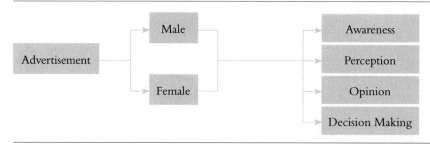

Note: In the Kumar and Raju model, their research design examines the relationship between the advertisements directed towards males and females and the effect of advertisements on their purchase decision making. Source in references p. 39.

Advertising as a form of mass communication can be classified in several ways:

- *National advertising.* National advertising is the biggest category; some of the largest consumer brand advertising budgets belong to Proctor & Gamble and General Motors.
- *Retail and local advertising.* Examples of retail and local advertising would be fitness clubs and local restaurants.
- *Political and cause-based advertising.* Political slogans and public service announcements would come under political and cause-based advertising.
- *Direct-response advertising.* In direct-response advertising, the customer reads the information and can choose to buy direct from the company.
- *Industrial advertising.* Business and health care publications would be grouped under industrial advertising.
- *Professional advertising.* Professional advertising targets groups such as doctors, teachers, and lawyers.

Advertising is based on the goals of the advertisers. What do they want to achieve? Most likely one or more of these would be on the list:

- increased sales
- attitude or perception change
- increased product and brand awareness
- provision of reminders and reinforcements.

To achieve these types of goals, the advertisements have to be attractive, creative, well executed, and placed in the right form of media. Familiar advertisements for familiar products reinforce past purchases and remind people to buy again. The message can be simple, such as "Got Milk" from the American Dairy Association, or complex and multileveled. Notice that simple messages have mental staying power. The message can be broken down into five parts: perception, awareness, understanding, persuasion, and retention/memorability (Wells, Burnett, & Morarity, 2000). In this way the message can be seen as a multilevel process, and it is only part of developing the total end-result advertisement.

An effective advertisement encompasses the following:

- memory (the consumer remembers it)
- exposure (the right consumer sees and/or hears it)
- attention-grabbing power (the consumer notices it)
- interpretation or understanding (the consumer gets the message).

Advertisers can determine these factors in a number of ways, including recall reports, recognition tests, diary reports, and sales figures (after an ad has been shown). More intrusive measures would be wiring people and putting them in a special research room as they watch ads to measure eye pupil dilation or using brain wave analysis or brain scans (as in the Gerald Zaltman studies mentioned earlier).

Usually there is a link between the cost of the advertisement space and the potential size of the market. Thus, one ad during the Super Bowl game (usually airing the last Sunday in January) costs over a million dollars but has the potential of reaching more than 500 million people because the game attracts not only the US audience but international viewers as well. Originality counts, so many advertising firms and companies try to show off with their best talent, to the point that many viewers remark that the ads are better than the game. About 48 percent of the viewers are women, so it is not strictly a male market. Some start-up companies only advertise on the Super Bowl, putting their entire advertising budget on that one opportunity; they would be focusing on building awareness, making a first impression. Most companies, such as giant, established beverage manufacturers and carmakers, would use the Super Bowl as only one venue among many, and their goal would be to keep the public interest alive in their brands and maybe to push a new flavor, model, or version.

CASE STUDY

Timing of Television Advertising with DVRs versus Live Audiences

Higher ad rates are charged for highly rated shows. This makes sense and reflects supply and demand. Broadcast networks used to pit popular shows against each other so that consumers had to pick a show and watch it along with the commercials. This traditional practice is being challenged by DVRs (digital video recorders). More viewers are opting to record rather than watch live. Television programmers are forced to rethink their strategy since DVRs allow viewers to skip through commercials.

"The latest Nielsen figures have been eagerly anticipated: They represent the first look at how many people actually watch the commercials during the fall primetime season, when advertisers spend the most on ads. Previous Nielsen data looked only at viewership of the shows. Six of the top 10 most-recorded shows during the first three weeks of the fall season air on Thursday night, according to Michael Mellon, senior vice president of research for Walt Disney's ABC. One example is ABC's hit *Grey's Anatomy*."[1]

Grey's Anatomy according to the data was recorded by 20 percent of its viewers; the overall audience is growing, but the live audience is dropping. Similar viewer behavior is evident for CBS's *Survivor* show. Analysts say that the move away from live viewership and toward playback has not affected ad rates for specific shows yet, but it is simply a matter of time.

Complicating the matter further is that owners of DVRs are more upscale. They are an attractive market to advertisers.

"One of the things you've seen this year is there are really no breakouts of new programs, in part because people capture the shows they already know they like on DVR, and they're leaving live shows to watch DVR shows,"[2] says Michael Nathanson, a senior analyst at Sanford Berntein. Mr. Nathanson calls this a "logjam" effect.

1. Rebecca Dana (October 31, 2007). "Latest ad challenge: must-record TV." *Wall Street Journal,* p. B4.
2. Ibid.

Placement and timing of advertisements are important. The most expensive ads on the Super Bowl come at the beginning of the game when viewership is highest. Depending on how the game goes, viewership may remain constant or drop off, a factor on which advertisers take a risk. Besides the large audience, another reason that the Super Bowl is so popular as a showcase is because of **association**—advertisers use association to build or maintain images. Big worldwide sporting events such as international contests of golf, soccer, and cycling (such as the Tour de France) draw enormous amounts of viewers and, subsequently, advertising. The advertising takes place before, during, and after the event.

With the opening up of global markets, advertisers have to address global markets as well as local markets. Naming products is difficult because an acceptable name in the United States may not be acceptable elsewhere. Similarly, settings or environments and types of

Photo 7.4 The US women's soccer team in the New York victory parade: (L–R) Carli Lloyd, Megan Rapinoe (with trophy), and coach Jill Ellis on July 10, 2015

Source: Getty Images: Yana Paskova

models used have to be appropriate to the market. Advertising has to be adaptive and accountable and accurate to succeed.

Advertising push is uneven. Some products, such as food and beverages (that is, goods that are used often and used up), are heavily advertised, but other products are rarely advertised and then only in small targeted markets. Candy may be advertised only at Halloween, Christmas, and Easter. High-volume flower purchasing is also seasonal. Because of economies of scale, large advertisers have an advantage—they are already known and accepted by markets. It is difficult for a new smaller firm to break into established, heavily branded markets such as cereals, which are dominated by three major brands. Going organic has helped some smaller brands make a sizable dent in the cereal market.

It is also necessary to point out that some ads don't work even if they are advertising a good product. The ad may be inappropriate or offensive. Have you ever watched an ad and wondered what it was about? Obviously, the sales point was not made. Probably the least effective advertising is direct mail that goes to mass markets: It is estimated that 98 percent of junk mail is thrown out. Examples of this are high-rise apartment dwellers receiving circulars for tires, middle-aged women without children receiving catalogs for children's clothes, and rural Midwesterners receiving reviews of the latest restaurants in Manhattan.

A home freezer may not be about keeping food cold or saving money; it may be about security, warmth, and safety.

Is Advertising Necessary?

The answer to the section title is yes. Advertising can be as simple as word of mouth. There is evidence that advertising in drawn or written form is as old as recorded history. It is an important part of trade, production, and consumption.

Do you recall the discussion in Chapter 2 of muckraker Vance Packard, author of *The Hidden Persuaders*? At the beginning of his book, he wrote:

> This book is an attempt to explore a strange and rather exotic new area of American life. It is about the large-scale efforts being made, often with impressive success, to channel our unthinking habits, our purchasing decisions and our thought processes by the use of insights gleaned from psychiatry and the social sciences. Typically these efforts take place beneath our level of awareness; so that the appeals move us are often, in a sense, "hidden." (Packard, 1957, p. 1)

There is no doubt that, as Packard suggests, advertising can be manipulative and that it uses psychology for profit and advantage. He says some of the manipulating is amusing because it is so obvious (for example, beautiful models draped on cars or rock stars drinking colas). But he says some of it is disquieting, intense, and potent. For example, the Weiss and Geller Advertising Agency became suspicious of the reasons people gave for buying home freezers because economically it didn't make much sense considering the initial cost, the added utility costs, and the amount of frozen leftovers thrown out. Researchers, whom Packard called "probers," found that families filled freezers because they were trying to fill their inner anxieties brought on by the uncertainties in their lives. The probers concluded that a full freezer is reassuring because it means there will always be food in the house, which means security, warmth, and safety. Economics had very little to do with the real reason for a home freezer purchase, so the advertising and sales pitches were adjusted accordingly (Packard, 1957).

Packard goes on to say:

> [Probers have found out] why we are afraid of banks; why we love those big fat cars; why we really buy homes; why men smoke cigars; why the kind of car we drive reveals the brand of gasoline we will buy; why housewives typically fall into a hypnoidal trance when they get into a supermarket; why men are drawn into auto showrooms by convertibles but end up buying sedans; why junior loves cereal that pops, snaps, and crackles. (1957, p. 2)

Of course, consumer behavior and advertising research have come a long way since the 1950s, but the basic premise he puts forth has merit.

The industry would counter by saying that advertising is important for consumer information—it lets the consumer know what is out there and by doing this stimulates choices and competition. Advertising also communicates availability by saving consumers the time of comparison shopping and needlessly shopping at stores that do not carry certain brands or products. For example, a television ad for a new movie says that it opens on March 3. This is useful information, saving the filmgoer the trouble of going to the theater in February.

Advertisers would also say they are primarily recommenders, for example, offering samples as a way to try something out. They would say they do not create needs but rather help to fulfill them. In the transaction process, advertisers and marketers cannot create demand, so they try to fill the demand that is already there. So is advertising necessary? Yes, because it fulfills a function in the marketplace.

The power of samples can be explained by the **rule of reciprocation**. In a classic psychology study, a university professor sent Christmas cards to perfect strangers. He was amazed at the number of people who sent holiday cards back addressed to him, and most did not inquire into his identity (Kunz & Woolcott, 1976). They appeared to have some sort of automatic drive—get a card, and send a card. The rule of reciprocation means that we try to repay what someone has given us. A free sample will often encourage people to buy the full-size product, and individuals receiving samples may feel obligated to the salesperson or the company. Samples or free gifts are often for food or shampoo but also may be higher-priced items such as certificates for free T-shirts or scarves, accompanied with a letter from the company president appreciating their business, given to frequent buyers at a national clothing chain. The rule of reciprocity has been tested and found to be true in many societies around the world. Sociologists and anthropologists theorize that our ancestors developed networks of sharing and learning, so this feeling of indebtedness is deeply ingrained in us.

The dark side to the rule of reciprocation is explained by Robert Cialdini in his book *Influence: Science and Practice*. What he says is that some people take this too far and may make a person feel uncomfortably indebted by expecting a favor in return. This could be a tactic of door-to-door salespeople or charities; for example, a common tactic is to receive unsolicited gifts such as address labels or notecards from charities or nonprofit organizations. A person may also try to get someone to comply with a request. There are two approaches to dealing with unwanted samples, gifts, or favors: reject them outright, or see the offers for what they are and not for what they are represented to be. Cialdini states, "We should accept initial favors or concessions in good faith, but be ready to redefine them as tricks should they later be proved as such. Once they are redefined in this way, we will no longer feel a need to respond with a favor or concession of our own" (2001, p. 50). It all boils down to a need for self-regulation when it comes to advertising—the informed consumer knows when to respond and when not to respond.

Advertising and Color

Are you attracted to black-and-white photos of pizza? No, the advertisement or circular that comes in the mail or in your newspaper needs red for the tomato sauce and yellow for the cheese to be effective. Color has the power to create brand imagery, convey moods, and stimulate taste buds. Red is a common color in political advertising because it attracts attention, and red, white, and blue is a popular combination for a patriotic appeal. The attractions of certain colors vary by intended message, targeted age group, and other classifications. Parkay margarine in electric blue and shocking pink targeted to children was a surprise to many doubting adults who asked, "Who would eat that stuff?"

Blue is the most favored color overall, but the second most popular color varies by ethnicity and race. Whites like green, Latinos/Hispanics and blacks lean toward purple, and Asian Americans prefer pink. Shades of colors matter too. Older people like sky blue much more than younger people. Silver cars sell well, but the most favored car colors vary by area of the country. It used to be there was more impact based on gender, but increasingly men and women are agreeing on house paint colors and car colors (Paul, 2002). Reasons given for this trend are that gender roles have loosened up and that men are being exposed (through the world of sports) to masculine men wearing uniforms of purple and teal. There are limits; for example, you can't put GI Joe in pink, according to Richard Brandt of Landor Associates (Paul, 2002).

Another trend is toward brighter and more complex colors. Crayola crayons come in 120 different hues, so children are exposed early to a wide range of colors. When marketing to Latino/Hispanic children, the emphasis is on warmer tones of yellow and red, according to Margaret Walch of the Color Association of the United States (Paul, 2002). But any generalization can vary around the country since a consumer's palette is dependent on light, temperature, and location as well as on how he or she spends time. Mexican Americans favor reds, blues, and blacks, whereas Florida Hispanics like pastels, pinks, and salmons for fashions and interiors (Paul, 2002). African Americans experiment with colors from chartreuse to brown; they are also attracted to yellows and reds. To be effective, advertising needs to keep up with trends in ethnic and racial preferences. There are advertising agencies that are run by or specialize in minority or ethnic groups.

Although this section is on color, it should be pointed out that typeface, font, size, and legibility also affect how ads are perceived; for example, elderly people cannot and will not read small print. On television, advertising can use motion, so Old Navy and Target ads often feature people dancing while wearing those companies' products.

Value of Repetition and Consistency

A successful advertisement can stay in our heads for decades. Baby boomers can sing the Mickey Mouse Club song from their younger days, and the elderly remember jingles and slogans from their youth for products that no longer exist. Memorability or **locking**

power is a goal that advertisers strive for. Advertising plays on two forms of memory—recognition (sight) and recall (more complex associations). For example, shoppers who see hot dog buns realize they do not need the buns, but seeing them is a cue that they need hot dogs or mustard or ketchup. Likewise, a Krispy Kreme ad triggers a memory that causes a consumer to say, "Oh yes, I need to remember to stop by and get donuts on the way to work tomorrow."

Repetition can be used as a memory-jogging device over many years or over a short time span. For example, during the 2003 Super Bowl, an advertisement for Anheuser-Busch (the world's largest brewery) featuring singer Tim McGraw promoting responsible drinking was shown in all four quarters of the game. Is it worth the expense to be repetitive? Usually, the answer to this is yes. Many people will ignore a first or second ad, but it is difficult to ignore the fourth ad shown during a single event or evening. And when it comes to the major TV broadcasting advertising event of the year—the Super Bowl—the timing becomes even more complicated. "These days, PepsiCo releases its commercials about a week in advance of the game 'to capitalize' on the buzz surrounding Super Bowl," says Dave DeCecco, senior manager of public relations for Pepsi-Cola North America. "The beverage and bottling concern got an estimated $10 million in free publicity for a 90-second Britney Spears performance it used to promote Pepsi soda last year" (Vranica & O'Connell, 2003, p. B1).

Memory devices include **jingles** (music), **slogans** (short phrases), and **taglines** (end messages) and consistently feature models or actors. Repetition thrives on rhyme, catchy melodies, and repeating sounds. An example of a repeating sound is the sound of an Alka-Selter tablet dissolving in a glass of water accompanied by the jingle "Plop, plop, fizz, fizz, Oh what a relief it is." Can you sing the Oscar Mayer Wiener song? Characters such as cartoon characters or animals can also assist with repetition and locking power; for example, the AFLAC duck promotes insurance, a product that is difficult to visualize or make attractive. Progressive insurance features humorous situations and a character named Flo who wears a wig and a hairband. She is consistent in the ads and represents that brand.

Economics and Advertising Pros and Cons

Advertising is part of the free market system. It encourages competition and fosters economic growth, which is good for consumers. New products are developed and offered, stimulating the economy. Volume sales can lead to lower production costs, and those savings should be passed on to consumers in the form of lower prices. These are all pros. The main negative is that advertising adds to the cost of marketing goods, and this cost is also passed down to consumers. The debate about the economic value versus the possible negative effects of advertising may never be resolved. Some economists take a negative view of advertising, others feel that "it depends on your point of view," and still others are very positive. Consumer economists are not critical of advertising per se but may be critical of techniques or type of appeal. All agree that advertising is a powerful institution integral to the workings of the market and the Internet. "There's the simple argument that without ads, there would be no Gmail, no Facebook, no countless other services on which we all rely every day" (Mims, 2015, p. B1).

From an economic standpoint, advertising provides information about alternatives and provides consumers with recall cues that help them make substitutes at the time of purchase. The more alternatives that consumers can think of, the greater is the price elasticity. They may say that they can't afford this product but can afford another that will easily substitute. Advertising succeeds best in environments where choices exist and there is disposable income. The basic economic role of advertising is to let people know what is available, and that helps them make consumption decisions.

Deceptive Advertising

Among other things, advertising should be accountable, it should be accurate, and it should give a fair portrayal of the product or service. But advertising can be deceptive or misleading. How much so is difficult to pinpoint; it is also difficult to know where to draw the line between persuasiveness and manipulation. In political advertisements, mud-slinging occurs and misleading statistics are presented, both of which alter people's perception of the truth. There have been studies that decisively show both that purchases are consumer driven based on needs and that advertising is simply an information source. Other studies show that consumers become aware of a new product and then the need or want follows. Critics say vulnerable groups, such as young children, teens, and the elderly, too easily succumb to marketing messages and that businesses take advantage of their vulnerability. Evidence to prove this is shaky, except in the area of very young children who cannot distinguish between an advertisement and a cartoon show.

Puffery is legal.

Accuracy or accountability refers to whether the advertising message, either direct or subtle, is accurate. Most watchers of television know that a new face cream will not improve their social life, but where do you draw the line? **Puffery** refers to advertising that exaggerates the characteristics of a product. If an advertiser said its face cream would remove all wrinkles, that would be misleading, but it is okay for the company to say a moisturizer used as directed will reduce the "appearance of wrinkles." Puffery is legal. A common phrase of puffery is "the world's best pizza." The Uniform Commercial Code (UCC) is a set of laws about sales and other commercial matters that in essence says it is okay for ads to make general statements praising a product or service. Therefore it is all right for Silversmith's to advertise that it is the area's leading jeweler, but it is not okay for the store to advertise that "all our gold jewelry is 18 karat gold" when it also sells gold of lesser quality.

The Federal Trade Commission (FTC) says an advertisement is unfair if it causes or is likely to cause substantial consumer injury which is not reasonably avoidable by consumers themselves and is not outweighed by countervailing benefits to consumers or to competition. The FTC says an ad is deceptive if it contains misrepresentation or omission. It also uses the average man rule, which is based on whether an average person would be deceived by the advertisement; if that is true, then the ad is ruled misleading. As has been discussed in other chapters, there are other groups besides the FTC that monitor advertising messages and images.

Here are more examples of deceptive advertising:

- Puffed-up packaging (container or packaging makes the consumer believe the contents are more plentiful than they really are).
- A hamburger is made to look large by putting it on a very small plate or in the hands of a small child.
- A toy race track set appears to have cars that go fast by using camera tricks and angles when in reality the cars putter around a dull oval-shaped track.
- Vegetables and beef are added to a bowl of vegetable beef soup for a TV ad so that it looks like there are more vegetables and beef than would be found in an actual can. (An old trick was to put weights in the bottom of the bowl so that the vegetables and beef floated to the surface.)
- Cars are driven off-road by professionals, a practice that would actually wreck the cars if they were driven by ordinary people. In an effort to be more truthful, some television ads have small print on the bottom of the screen that says "driven by professional drivers."
- People appearing to be doctors give testimonials or are supporters of diet products when in fact they are not medical doctors or are doctors whose specializations have nothing to do with diets.
- Someone says a product is low in calories when it is actually high in calories.

Examples of ethical concerns (morals, principles, or values) include the sharing of buyer lists and personal information about consumers by companies, the promotion of harmful substances such as tobacco and alcohol to teens, and questionable or rigged sweepstakes and contests. When it comes to court action against companies, it often boils down to figuring out if the advertisers were deliberately untruthful or misleading. This can be proved by emails, letters, and employees' testimony. Legitimate companies and advertisers want to eliminate flagrantly deceptive advertising because shady advertising of any kind reflects poorly on the advertising industry as a whole.

Does advertising encourage materialism (a preoccupation with material things)? It is hard to argue that this is not the case. After all, it encourages consumption and also affects our sense of what constitutes status, success, and achievement. For example, a wine campaign could equate wine with elitism and elegance. Drinking wine could say, "I've arrived."

Does it create dissatisfaction? Many consumer economists would give a resounding yes in response to this question. They would say that advertising encourages the throwing out of the old in favor of buying something new. In the world of advertising, "new" is almost always better, the exception being eBay and similar websites. Advertisers say that they did not create materialism—they are simply providing information, supplying a service. They think advertising has become a scapegoat for all of society's ills, as a maker of values rather than as a reflector of values. They will also say that no amount of advertising can sell a lousy product. Since products fail all the time, there is some merit to this argument—people will not buy what they don't like or can't use.

Does advertising portray an unreal world, a world of perfection? Yes, it often does. The models have perfect teeth and hair; everyone in the ad is happy and secure. Viewers or readers accept this because they want a better life and like attractive people and settings.

Advertising also preys on people's insecurities: fear of being a victim of theft (to sell home security systems), fear of dying penniless (to sell funeral burial policies and financial products), and fear of smelling bad (to sell deodorants, soaps, shampoos, body washes). Baldness remedies are sold to men on the basis of fear—of losing their youth and of what other people are saying about them. The basic message is that if you buy this product, you will look younger or feel better. Current events play into the type of advertising that is run and the products that sell. Following the September 11, 2001, tragedies in the United States, life insurance sales skyrocketed. War news curtails foreign travel and has the effect of increasing domestic travel, especially destinations within easy driving distance of home.

Does advertising pay for television, websites, and radio shows? The answer is yes. The web banner ad debuted in 1994. Huge amounts of money and many job opportunities exist in the world of advertising from the smallest firm to the largest. Sheryl Sandberg, author of *Lean In* and chief operating officer of Facebook, headed Google's ad products for seven years prior to joining Facebook.

The web banner ad debuted in 1994.

When I say the word "commercials" what probably pops to mind first are television commercials. The commercials are most obvious on commercial television and radio and are more subtle but nevertheless present on PBS (public broadcasting) when company names such as Ralph Lauren or Viking Cruises splash across the screen. PBS television and radio also rely on viewer and listener contributions and federal government support. According to the PBS Annual Report, leading corporate underwriters of shows that target kids, such as *Sesame Street*, include over $1 million from Playskool, W. K. Kellogg Foundation, General Mills, Lego Co., and LookSmart Ltd. There are ethical issues involved in corporate support, with some feeling it has gone too far. "It used to be 'the following program is brought to you with support from Mobil,'" says Robert Thompson, director of the Center for the Study of Popular TV at Syracuse University in Syracuse, New York. "Now it is a moving video and some of it is pretty substantial—it's longer, it's a full-fledged commercial. It's no longer a mention. It's a commercial pure and simple and sometimes not so pure and not so simple" (Beatty, 2002, p. B1).

For television viewing in general, experiments have been conducted where people paid for television shows without commercials, but these experiments failed. We have become accustomed to "free" television and radio. With the advent of mute and fast-forward buttons on remotes, we are paying less of a price. Netflix and competitors have opened up whole new ways of viewing and pricing.

Not all advertisements are difficult to watch. Some are entertaining, using the latest music, or amusing as well as informative, especially on the first exposure; repeated exposure lessens the pleasurable effect. Curiously, though, some of the dullest commercials sell the most products.

Bait and switch as a fraudulent sales practice was discussed earlier in the book, but it needs to be added here because it is a common advertising fraud. A person reads an ad for a digital camera selling for $125, and since that is a very low price, he or she goes to the store wanting to buy it. The store says the camera is sold out and tries to switch the customer to a $500 digital camera. State attorney generals' offices or other consumer affairs areas can look into bait-and-switch fraud, and consumers can file individual or class-action suits demanding compensation.

The Subconscious and Subliminal Advertising

Advertising is a combination of marketing and science, or neuromarketing, according to Martin Lindstrom, author of the New York Times *best-seller* Buyology: Truth and Lies About Why We Buy, *which details his story of how ads affect consumers. Advertisements operate on two tracks; the conscious, using information you can read and understand, and, more commonly,* the subconscious, using information and techniques that you are not clearly aware of. *'Seventy-five percent of everything you and I do every day takes place in our subconscious mind.' Lindstrom says. 'In my opinion, advertising industries are doing pretty well in terms of drawing us in. Most of us think we are deeply rational but we are really not.' Subconscious advertisement techniques can include making soda poured over ice in a glass have a high amount of bubbles or increasing the noise of a steak sizzling on a grill. 'It triggers our craving instinct,' Lindstrom says. 'It's the same spot in your brain that's activated when you are gambling, hungry for chocolate or jogging.' (Kossman, 2013)*

To target our subconscious mind, subliminal advertising can have embedded images for a product that aren't noticed on a conscious level. We assume that advertising is seen and/or heard, and in the case of radio it is totally heard and in television it is mostly heard as one passes through a room or while doing something else waiting for the show to begin or proceed.

Subliminal advertising operates below the level of consciousness. It refers to messages "transmitted in such a way that the receiver is not consciously aware of receiving it" (Wells, Burnett & Moriarty, 2000, p. 41). The symbols or words may be too faint or too fast for the conscious mind to pick up. The often agreed upon standard is that most people will not be consciously aware they've seen a stimulus that is presented for .003 seconds (that is, three one-thousandths of a second). Many would say this is foul play, whereas others would say this fear is largely unfounded like the creature Big Foot—it does not exist. Comedian Steven Wright has a joke that goes something like this: "I saw a subliminal advertising executive the other day, but only for a second."

Subliminal advertising is a favorite topic in psychology and consumer classes. It opens up a fascinating set of questions about what influences the human mind and behavior. The central question is: Is it possible to manipulate the mind of consumers with faint or hidden messages? In experiments when psychologists or communications experts have tested subliminal advertisements that they designed, it appears that they do not work. Consumers will not buy products they do not need regardless of either overt or subliminal advertising messages. The advertising industry does not like the insinuation that its members use subliminal advertising and says that accusations of its use are damaging and false. Common accusations target movie theaters, which are said to use subliminal messages in pre-movie advertisements to increase popcorn and soda sales.

Author Wilson Keys suggested that most embedded ads appeal to sexuality (Weir, 1984). An example is that of an attractive woman's body embedded in ice cubes in a print advertisement for an alcoholic beverage. Research indicates that an advertisement such as this may trigger a like or dislike for the product, but it appears unlikely that a subliminal advertisement will cause someone to drink whiskey if they do not normally drink whiskey. Although subliminal advertising may not exist, it has been shown to be largely ineffective in experiments. It may be possible in the future for more sophisticated forms to be developed that may be capable of manipulating consumers. This is the reason that this subject is worth mentioning in a book on consumer economics, and given the previous section on the Zaltman research studies, perhaps there is more merit to studying unconscious thought regarding consumption than previously assumed.

CRITICAL THINKING

Consumer Reactions to Advertising

What can consumers do? Educate themselves of what to look for or sense. Beware of a sense of urgency in advertising. Scrutinize, process information properly. Can you think of an advertisement that pushed urgency or that you felt was deceptive or trying to appeal to your subconscious? Discuss. Did you watch an ad for food and then get something to eat or plan to buy that food next time you were out? Breakfast fast foods are advertised the night before probable purchase.

Distasteful Advertising

Massively deceptive advertising is one thing; what constitutes good or bad taste is another. Table 7.2 gives a list of ethical and/or taste issues facing advertisers.

CRITICAL THINKING

Painting Sides of Cows and Baby Carriages

In Europe, an advertising firm painted advertisements on the sides of cows standing in fields (with the permission of and payment to the owners), and animal rights activists objected, saying it was in bad taste because it took advantage of the cows. Do you agree or disagree? Also in Europe, a baby carriage manufacturer had a contest, and the winners received expensive baby carriages with company advertising on the side of the carriages. People said this was in bad taste, too. Do you agree or disagree?

Taste, as a value-laden word, is in the eye of the beholder, and this includes reactions based on where the viewer or consumer lives. Taste can refer literally to what tastes good. For example, cheese flavor is not appealing to most Chinese, so to sell Frito-Lay Cheetos in China, the company tried out over 600 different flavors in taste tests. Although the end product is still called Cheetos, the flavor we are used to in the United States cannot be found in most of China. What flavors is the company selling? American Savory and Japanese Steak are two of the favorites. In regard to advertising, what passes for bad taste in one country or area of the world may be considered appropriate in others. In Australia and Western Europe, women's breasts are shown in television commercials, whereas in the United States this is considered poor taste and not allowed. In the United States, the time of day and the type of show that beer ads can appear on are regulated. Beer ads are not allowed on Saturday cartoon shows, but it is okay to have them on Saturday afternoon football games. Since children may be watching the games or playing in the room while their parents are watching the games, they are exposed to beer commercials. So although there are some guidelines to protect children, this example shows that they are exposed to adult product advertising on a regular basis.

Some parents have made the decision not to have television in their homes to protect their children from advertising, tasteless shows, and distressful news programs. This is not easy to control because children visit their friends' or relatives' houses and see television there. On a driving trip, children see roadside billboards for adult entertainment clubs and other adult fare.

Table 7.2 Ethical and/or Taste Issues Facing Advertisers

Issue	Types or examples
Controversial products and ads	Should alcohol, tobacco, lotteries, and gambling be advertised?
Personal products or medicine	How should ads sell erectile dysfunction treatments, feminine hygiene products, and underwear?
Advertising to children	Should there be guidelines for ads targeting children in terms of type of ad, placement of ad, and time of day?
Bias or stereotyping	What should be done about offensive depictions in ads of racial/ethnic groups, the elderly, the disabled, or other groups?
Puffery	What is legal exaggeration in an ad, and does it include the use of the word "best"?
Social responsibility	Do ads hurt or help causes? Do some ads go beyond legal lobbying rules?
Use of models and spokespersons	Does the model or spokesperson really use the product? Is proof of use necessary?
Use of former public figures	Should former presidents, sports figures, governors, legislators, or generals endorse products? Which products are off-limits?

US consumers complain that much advertising, regardless of whom it is directed to, is in poor taste. They say it is irritating, repetitive, insulting to their intelligence, and humorless, as well as degrading to certain individuals and groups. Beer ads and advertising for bars are often degrading to women. Asian Americans, African Americans, Latinos/Hispanics, and the elderly have also been the target of stereotyping. The kinds of ads said to be obnoxious often have to do with personal care, such as deodorants, dandruff shampoos, and denture creams. Irritating ads can have close-ups of dogs crunching dog food or a doorbell or cellphone ringing that gets someone up off a couch to answer the door or find their cellphone. Nauseating ads may have close-ups of people chewing with their mouths open, little children smearing food all over their faces (some find this cute), or women spooning cat food from a can. Repetitive music or jingles can be especially irritating.

Infomercials are program-long advertisements that can run an hour or more for cooking products, cosmetics, hair products, tools, and diet programs/supplements. Traditionally, these were shown late at night when airtime was inexpensive, but increasingly infomercials are airing at noon during the week and on Saturdays and Sundays. Some people find these irritating, while others enjoy the advice, demonstrations, and comfortable conversational style. Infomercials go in and out of style, with some dropping off the air and being replaced with others and some seasonal.

Marketing to Children

A lot has already been said in this chapter about the issues surrounding advertising to children. Marketing is a broader category. The Internet and electronic devices have opened up a whole new set of problems involving marketing to children and the need (or not) for parental guidance.

Mobile devices have changed entertainment options for children and parents. Samantha, age 29, said, "My two-year-old was entertained on the whole flight playing a game and watching a movie on his iPad, I don't know how we would travel without it."

Games like Monopoly and other games like Electronic Mall Madness by Milton Bradley encourage children to be acquisitive, aggressive, and shrewd in their spending decisions. The objects of the games are to make the most money or to have the money spread as far as it will go. In the case of Electronic Mall Madness, the object is to get the most stuff and then get back to the parking lot first. It is quite an introduction to the world of credit cards, consumption, and competitiveness. Some would say this is too much for nine-year-olds; others would say it is good life training since grown-ups are exposed to a continuous barrage of sales ads, credit card offers, and car salesmen screaming at them from the television set about new, low prices.

Games involving money or gambling aimed at children are nothing new, nor are advertisements aimed at children. In 1912, Cracker Jack was offering a toy inside so that children would ask for it. Before television, children were saving box tops for prizes; the practice of putting toys in cereal boxes to attract children has been going on for

Photo 7.5
Today, children play computer games at a younger age than in the past

Source: Getty Images: Bloomberg

decades, although lately coupons for products or discounts are becoming more common. McDonald's has had Happy Meals for years, as have competitors (using slightly different names for their meals), with prizes marketed to children. In the summer of 2015, McDonald's was giving away $250,000 each week online by playing Minion Mania (keyed to a popular movie for children).

Children are exposed to about 200 television commercials a day, and the commercials have changed considerably from the ads that their parents viewed (DeGraaf, Wann, & Naylor, 2001). In earlier ads, parents were shown as authority figures, people who would help the children out by explaining how products worked or who could be relied on to put products together. Newer ads often leave out parents and are more likely to show peers or cartoon-type characters showing children how products work—in other words, a mom and dad are no longer shown as the wise figures (value setters) that they used to be.

Government and Advertising

Government agencies, such as the Federal Communications Commission (FCC) and the FTC, and legislation both affect the advertising industry and its practices (see Table 7.3).

Role of FCC in Advertising. As this chapter and previous ones have shown, the government and the advertising industry are often at odds, but sometimes they cooperate and work together. For example, on October 6, 2000, President Clinton signed an executive order at the White House that included language to establish the first multicultural advertising guidelines for federal government departments and agencies. The main point was to encourage inclusiveness and fairness throughout the marketing and advertising processes, from employment and career advancement to competition and compensation for creative services. The American Advertising Federation (AAF) and the AAF Foundation formed a committee that drafted the *Principles and Recommended Practices for Effective Advertising in the American Multicultural Marketplace*; 26 companies, such as DaimlerChrysler and Kraft General Foods, and agencies have committed to adopting the principles laid out.

Role of FTC in Advertising. In an earlier chapter, there was a lengthy description of the oversight and powers of the FTC, but here is a review with a focus on advertising.

> *Section 5 of the FTC Act declares unfair or deceptive acts or practices unlawful. Section 12 specifically prohibits false ads likely to induce the purchase of food, drugs, devices or cosmetics. Section 15 defines a false ad for purposes of Section 12 as one which is "misleading in a material respect." Numerous Commission and judicial decisions have defined and elaborated on the phrase "deceptive acts or practices" under both Sections 5 and 12. Nowhere, however, is there a single definitive statement of*

> the Commission's view of its authority. (James C. Miller, Chairman, FTC Policy
> Statement on Deception, October 14, 1983)

The FTC states that marketing and point-of-sales practices can be misleading and deceptive as well as written and oral misrepresentations of product claims. The FTC receives complaints and inquiries each month about advertising; it investigates problems and may take action, depending on the case. A first step is a **consent decree** in which the FTC notifies the advertiser that its ads are deceptive and asks the advertiser to sign a consent decree saying it will stop the deceptive practice. Most do sign it and thus avoid a possible fine of $10,000 per day and the bad publicity for refusing to do so. Recent cases have to do with cellphone companies and service providers. As one example, "The Federal Trade Commission filed a federal court complaint against AT&T Mobility, LLC, charging that the company has misled millions of its smartphone customers by charging them for 'unlimited' data plans while reducing their data speeds, in some cases by nearly 90 percent" ("Company 'Throttles' Many Consumers Who Had Signed Up for Unlimited Data," FTC release, October 24, 2014). The FTC often works in conjunction with other government agencies such as the Food and Drug Administration (FDA) as in the case at the beginning of the chapter about baby formula claims.

Table 7.3 Government Agencies Affecting Advertising

Agency	Effect
Bureau of Alcohol, Tobacco, and Firearms (AFT) (a division of the US Treasury Department)	Regulates advertising of alcohol; can revoke permits for distillers, wine merchants, and brewers
Federal Communications Commission (FCC)	Issues and revokes licenses for radio and television stations; can eliminate deceptive or poor-taste ads
Federal Trade Commission (FTC)	Regulates advertising, labeling, and packaging; issues warnings; requires advertisers to validate claims, recent cases on "unlimited data" from telecommunications companies
Food and Drug Administration (FDA)	Regulates labeling, packaging, and manufacture of food and drug products including company claims about baby formulas as well as safety and purity of cosmetics
Library of Congress	Watches over copyright protection issues such as coined phrases and well-known slogans in ads
US Patent Office	Watches over trademark and patent registrations and infringements
US Postal Service	Controls advertising through the mail; handles complaints of unsolicited ads and products that come in the mail (such as obscenity, contests, fraud)★
State agencies	Regulate unfair and deceptive trade practices within states (often including advertising)

★Consumers who receive sexually offensive material in the mail can request that no more mail be delivered from that sender. The postmaster general has the power to stop offensive mail or questionable offers sent through the mail such as get-rich-quick schemes.

Role of Legislation in Advertising. For consumer redress, one of the strongest pieces of legislation is the **Magnuson–Moss Warranty–FTC Improvement Act of 1975**. It empowers the FTC to obtain consumer redress when a person or firm engages in deceptive practices such as false or misleading advertising. This includes the ad agency as well as the manufacturer of the product. For example, one case of misleading advertising of a shaving product ended with both the company and the agency paying $1 million each to the government, and they had to halt the advertising campaign. On behalf of consumers, the FTC can order any of the following:

- cancellation or reformation of contracts
- refund of money
- return of property
- payment of damages
- public notification.

One of the strongest actions that the FTC can take is **cease-and-desist orders**. A hearing, similar to a trial, takes place in which the company presents its defense. An administrative law judge presides, and FTC staff attorneys represent the commission. If the FTC succeeds in proving that an ad is unfair or misleading, then it issues a cease-and-desist order requiring the ad to stop; if the company does not do so, it is given a stiff fine. The advertiser can appeal.

Counteradvertising, also called corrective advertising, is new advertising that is undertaken pursuant to an FTC order for the purpose of correcting false claims about the product. The new ad can be on radio, in print, or on television and gives information to correct former misinformation. The purpose is not to punish the advertiser but rather to act in the best interest of consumers. A classic case was Warner–Lambert's Listerine campaign that ran for nearly 50 years. In this ad campaign, the claim was that the product prevented colds or reduced the severity of colds and sore throats. The cost of the corrective advertising was $10 million and ran for 16 months, mostly on television (Wells, Burnett, & Moriarty, 2000).

Whether counteradvertising works or not (whether it changes consumer behavior) is questionable. For example, Warner-Lambert found that after the corrective advertising was ended, 42 percent of Listerine users still believed that the mouthwash was being advertised as a remedy for colds and sore throats, and 57 percent of users rated cold and sore throat effectiveness as a key reason for purchasing the brand (Wilke, McNeil, & Mazis, 1984).

Social Marketing and Public Service Announcements

It is fitting to end this chapter on a positive note about **social marketing** which seeks to benefit individuals and communities for the greater social good.

> *Social marketing is the use of marketing to solve a social problem, to promote a social good, or to benefit society. Some social marketing strategies make use of social influence to direct and change individual behavior. . . . Using social media to promote sustainable behavior is just one element of a coordinated strategy. (Goldsmith & Bacile, 2015)*

An example is that we have all benefited from **public service announcements (PSAs)**, defined as messages on behalf of some good cause such as stopping drunk driving (Mothers Against Drunk Driving) or preventing forest fires. A leader in creating these announcements is the Ad Council, a private nonprofit organization whose mission is to identify a select number of significant public issues and stimulate action. The Ad Council often teams up with government agencies or nonprofit organizations to get a message out to the public. For example, the Ad Council and the US Department of Health and Human Services had a joint campaign to inspire healthier lifestyles. One of the first Ad Council campaigns was during World War II, using the slogan "Loose Lips Sink Ships." Here are some slogans that you were brought up with that were developed by the Ad Council:

- McGruff the Crime Dog's "Take a Bite Out of Crime"
- Smokey Bear's "Only You Can Prevent Forest Fires"
- "Keep America Beautiful"
- "A Mind Is a Terrible Thing to Waste"
- "Friends Don't Let Friends Drive Drunk"

According to the Ad Council's website, 68 percent of Americans exposed to the "Friends Don't Let Friends Drive Drunk" advertisements say they have personally stopped someone who had been drinking from driving. The United Negro College Fund's slogan "A Mind Is a Terrible Thing to Waste" helped raise more than $1.9 billion, which helped 300,000 minority students graduate from college.

Summary

This chapter explored further the question: Are we deeply rational or not? The pursuit of happiness and security, self-concept, self-esteem, and positivity drives much of consumer behavior. Time, technological advances and obsolescence, and depreciation affect buying decisions. Gerald Zaltman of Harvard University has conducted research that indicates that much of consumer decision making may be unconscious. More research is underway to determine the extent to which this is true. In 1957, Vance Packard's *The Hidden Persuaders* exposed the advertising industry and its manipulative ways. Government agencies and the advertising industry are often at odds with each other, but sometimes they cooperate on social advances and initiatives. A positive side of the advertising industry is the public service announcements (PSAs) that they create, often in cooperation with government agencies or nonprofit organizations, to bring about positive social change.

Price often serves as a rule of thumb—a guide for narrowing down choices. A $200 cashmere sweater may be out of the question, but one marked down to $69 may be considered. Scarcity plays a part as well and explains why famous oil paintings go for $75 million and John Travolta's leisure suit from the movie *Saturday Night Fever* sold for $145,000 at auction.

Researcher Michael Solomon, author of *Conquering Consumerspace*, suggests that the traditional way of doing business in which companies call the shots is obsolete; the trend now is for businesses to work with consumers. He describes a world where boundaries between branded commodities and everyday life are blurred and nationalities are less important. More and more people will move seamlessly between the offline and online domains.

Advertising is part of the free enterprise system. It provides exposure to choice and competition; in the long run it is added on to the price of consumer goods. There are many levels or steps in advertising—getting the message across is an underlying purpose. Advertisers like their products or services to be associated with pleasant experiences or attractive lifestyles. Because of economies of scale, large advertisers have an advantage over smaller ones or beginners in a market. It is debatable whether subliminal advertisements exist or not, but there is no question that we are exposed to obnoxious and distasteful advertising. The Federal Communications Commission (FCC) has the authority to issue and revoke licenses to broadcasting stations and works closely with the Federal Trade Commission (FTC). The FTC is the government's main watchdog on deceptive advertising. It can issue consent orders and cease-and-desist orders and can request counteradvertising (also known as corrective advertising). Research studies question whether counteradvertising is effective. The positive effects of social marketing were addressed.

KEY POINTS

1. Consumers vary in their decision-making style and in their ability to trade, based on the amount of time and the amount of money they have (budget constraints). Some seek bargains; others are content to pay full price. Design, authenticity, quality, and appearance matter to some and not to others; price usually serves as a strong guide (but not the only guide) to purchasing.

2. Millennials (1980s–early 2000s) make up 24 percent of the US population and buy more organic products and move more than the general population.

3. Uniqueness theory proposes that individuals vary in the extent to which they wish to be different.

4. Technological advances and technological obsolescence both play a part of what is offered and what is replaced.

5. Impulse buying is encouraged by sellers by various means such as checkout displays of candy or magazines or add-ons from catalog or Internet sales. Impulse items can be expensive items.

6. Advertising encourages competition and fosters economic growth, but it also ultimately costs the consumer. Consumers often find advertising irritating, objectionable, and in bad taste, but this varies by consumer, by region, and by country.

7. Puffed-up packaging and other techniques can deceive or disappoint consumers. The FTC can fine companies for deception.

8. Puffery, exaggerated claims such as "the world's best pizza," is legal.

9. Children are exposed to about 200 television commercials a day.

10. Public service announcements (PSAs), developed on a volunteer basis by advertising and communications professionals, inform the public about critical social issues such as drunk driving and forest fires.

KEY TERMS

ability to trade

advertising

association

authenticity

brand inertia

budget constraints

cease-and-desist orders

consent decree

consumer payoff

counteradvertising

decision making

decisions

depreciation

identity marketing

impulse buying

infomercials

jingles

locking power

Magnuson-Moss Warranty–FTC Improvement Act of 1975

Pareto principle

Parkinson's law

price discrimination

price variation

public service

announcements (PSAs)

puffery

rule of reciprocation

rules of thumb

self-concept

self-esteem

slogans

social marketing

style

subliminal advertising

taglines

uniqueness theory

DISCUSSION QUESTIONS

1. Why is advertising part of social influence? Think of an advertisement that you have seen or heard and how it made you aware of a product or service. Explain your answers.

2. What do you own that has depreciated in value? Do you accept this depreciation or not? Explain your answer.

3. Select two print ads and compare their messages. What are they selling? Who is their audience or target market? How effective are the ads in grabbing your attention?

4. Do you think there should be more or less government regulation of advertising? Support your answer with examples.

5. Go to the FTC website and see what it says about advertising. What are the current issues they are involved in?

REFERENCES

Beatty, S. (July 11, 2002). PBS and corporate underwriters: too close for comfort? *Wall Street Journal,* p. B1.

Bloomberg News (January 8, 2008). Sony BMG will sell music without copyright protection. *New York Times*, p. C13.

Cialdini, R. (2001). *Influence: science and practice.* Boston: Allyn and Bacon.

Company "Throttles" Many Consumers Who Had Signed Up for Unlimited Data. For release from TCS, October 28, 2014. Available online at www.fc/gov/news-events/press-releases/2014/10.

Dana, R. (October 31, 2007). Latest ad challenge: must-record TV. *Wall Street Journal,* p. B4.

DeGraaf, J., D. Wann, and T. Naylor. (2001). *Affluenza: the all-consuming epidemic.* San Francisco, CA: Berrett-Koehler Publishers.

Federal Trade Commission (October 30, 2014). FTC charges Gerber with falsely advertising its Good Start gentle formula protects infants from developing allergies. Available online at ftc.gov/news-events/press-releases/2014/10/ftc-charges-gerber.

Fowler, G. A. (July 7, 2015). GoPro shrinks the camera again. *Wall Street Journal*, p. B1.

Goldsmith, E. (2015). *Social influence and sustainable consumption.* International Series on Consumer Science, New York: Springer.

Goldsmith, R., and T. Bacile. (2015). Guest chapter entitled "Social influence and sustainable behavior," in E. Goldsmith, *Social influence and sustainable consumption.* International Series on Consumer Science, New York: Springer.

Goldsmith, R., R. Clark, and E. Goldsmith. (2007). The desire for unique consumer products and innovativeness. Proceedings of the Academy of Marketing Science Annual Meeting, Coral Gables, FL.

Kossman, S. (July 22, 2013). The truth about false and deceptive advertising. *U.S. News & World Report*. Available online at http://money.usnews.com/money/personal-finance articles/2013/07/22.

Kumar, D. P., and K. V. Raju. (November–December 2013). The role of advertising in consumer decision making. *IOSR Journal of Business and Management*, 14 (4), 37–45.

Kunz, P. R., and M. Woolcott. (1976). Season's greetings: from my status to yours. *Social Science Research*, 5, 269–278.

Lewis, D., and D. Bridges. (2000). *The soul of the new consumer.* London: Nicholas Brealey Publishing.

Lynn, M., and J. Harris. (1997). The desire for unique consumer products: a new individual differences scale. *Psychology and Marketing*, 14 (6), 601–616.

Miller, J. C. (October 14, 1983). *FTC Policy Statement on Deception* given by FTC Chairman Miller to the Honorable John D. Dingell, Chairman Committee on Energy and Commerce, US House of

Representatives, Washington, DC. Available online at www.ftc.gov/public-statements/1983/10/ftc-policy-statement-deception.

Mims, C. (July 6, 2015). Why ads are the best thing ever to happen to the Internet. *Wall Street Journal*, p. B1.

Nassauer, S. (March 18, 2015). What if we all bought organic? *Wall Street Journal*, p. D1.

Packard, V. (1957). *The hidden persuaders.* New York: Pocket Books.

Paul, P. (February 2002). Color by numbers. *American Demographics*, 31–35.

Solomon, M. (2003). *Conquering consumerspace.* New York: American Management Association.

Solomon, M., and N. Rabolt. (2004). *Consumer behavior in fashion.* Upper Saddle River, NJ: Prentice Hall.

Useem, J. (January 20, 2003). This man can read your mind. *Fortune*, 48.

Vranica, S., and V. O'Connell. (January 21, 2003). For immediate release! *Wall Street Journal,* p. B1.

Weir, W. (October 15, 1984). Another look at subliminal facts. *Advertising Age*, 46.

Wells, W., J. Burnett, and S. Moriarty. (2000). *Advertising principles and practice*, 5th ed. Saddle River, NJ: Prentice Hall.

Wilke, W., D. McNeil, and M. Mazis. (Spring 1984). Marketing's "scarlet letter": the theory and practice of corrective advertising. *Journal of Marketing*, 48 (2), 26.

Zaltman, G. (2003). *How customers think.* Cambridge, MA: Harvard Business School Press.

Ziogro, P. (March 3, 2015). Target thinks "millennials" in its revamp of groceries. *Wall Street Journal*, p. B2.

Chapter **8**

Food and Water Issues

Some old-fashioned things like fresh air and sunshine are hard to beat.
Laura Ingalls Wilder

LEARNING OBJECTIVES

1. Discuss food and water/beverage consumption patterns and issues.

2. List the agencies and laws that protect our food and water.

3. Explain what organically grown means.

4. Compare the different points of view regarding genetically altered foods.

5. Discuss health and legal issues as well as government protection of food and water.

Grocery Stores Weigh In

"Whole Foods Market® is working more closely than ever with farmer partners who support our commitment to quality, human health and the environment. We are excited to introduce our Responsibly Grown rating system for produce and flowers. Just like the other tiered rating systems we use in our stores—such as the 5-Step™ Animal Welfare Rating System and the third-party wild-caught seafood ratings—Responsibly Grown is designed to help you make informed shopping decisions."

Source: Whole Foods Market (2014). "Get to know responsibly grown." Available online at wfm.com/responsiblygrown.

Introduction

This chapter explores a specific area within consumer economics—that of changes in food and water consumption and government regulations. For example, in the United States, sales of packaged goods are stagnating and fresh produce and organic sales are up.

Shannon Blankenship and Honest Tea

"Food giants such as Coca-Cola Co., General Mills Inc. and Kellogg Co. are looking to the smaller food brands they've purchased such as Honest Tea, Annie's Inc. and Kashi, which sell food perceived as healthy or labeled organic. Their goal: to drive sales to this desirable, loyal consumer willing to pay up in the name of organic or natural, as sales of soup, soda and cereal stagnate. These shoppers are easily offended by too much sugar, artificial ingredients or brands that ignore seemingly niche issues like concerns about genetically modified ingredients or artificial food dyes. In the age of social media, one perceived misstep can quickly dent sales. Big companies need to tread carefully to bring in more shoppers without losing the base. . . . Shannon Blankenship, a human resources manager from Raleigh, N.C., says she stopped drinking Diet Coke three years ago, but buys Honest Tea's organic root beer every week. Ms. Blankenship switched after deciding to stop consuming aspartame, a sweetener in Diet Coke. Organic root beer is still a treat and more expensive than a Coke, she says, but 'if I know I'm not putting a whole can of chemicals in my body I feel a little better.'"

Source: Sarah Nassauer (March 18, 2015). "What if we all bought organic?" *Wall Street Journal*, p. D1.

International companies like McDonald's have to adjust their advertising and products to each country. Consider the Critical Thinking example that follows.

CRITICAL THINKING

McDonald's Japanese Style

When you have traveled have you noticed changes in food choices and advertising? Discuss the following:

> "In Asia, McDonald's follows cultural habits and uses celebrities. [One ad features] a young woman putting on all sorts of different hats and in the end eating a ham burger. What is special is that her name is Yuri Ebihara. McDonald's Japan annually has a special filet-o-fish with shrimp inside, which is called *ebi filet-o*. *Ebi* means shrimp in Japanese. Since Ebihara is such a famous model, and her name is actually a bit strange, including the word *ebi*, anybody in Japan can easily relate Ebihara to *ebi filet-o*, even without saying anything about the ham burger. Consumers easily got influenced by this ad and productivity for McDonald went high as compared to other brands with even less or similar price. It reflects the behavioral change in consumers due to advertisements."
>
> Source: Naveen Rai (April 2013). "Impact of advertising on consumer behaviour and attitude with reference to consumer durables." *International Journal of Management Research and Business Strategy*, 2 (2), p. 77.

As mentioned in Chapter 2, food is usually the first area of consumption that is government regulated because it is such a fundamental human need and people can get extremely ill or die from contaminated food. Since *the first food and drug law was enacted in 1906 in the United States*, the federal government has taken an active role in ensuring the quality of our food supply. Food and drink are such integral parts of our daily lives that they are important areas to single out in terms of discussions about consumerism. We may buy only a few cars in the course of our lives, but we will buy endless quantities of food and drink.

Eating and drinking with friends and family scores high on happiness rating scales. People generally have a positive view of food, farms, and agriculture, including organic foods (Gifford & Bernard, 2006). Not all is well, though, when it comes to food; there are many issues. For example, **trans fats** have been under scrutiny. They are made when manufacturers add hydrogen to vegetable oil in a process known as hydrogenation. The average American consumes about five pounds of trans fats a year, a number that should go down because many fast-food chains, theme parks, school systems, and in some cases entire cities are eliminating trans fats.

Technology has provided the means for great advances in food and beverages. Did you know the Defense Department's combat-feeding program has come up with a barbecued chicken sandwich that has a shelf life of three years? Military rations (now called MREs, for Meals Ready to Eat) have come a long way from the tinned foods and Spam of World War II. Speaking of Spam, did you know that the number one state in Spam consumption is Hawaii? Products sold to the general public such as powdered milk, freeze-dried coffee, and processed cheese have their origin in GI rations. The military found a way to keep lettuce and tomatoes fresh for 50 to 60 days at room temperature. One of the main developers of MREs is the feeding director for combat troops, Gerald Darsch, who has been described as a wry man with a great deal of intestinal fortitude. He is a modern-day example of the Poison Squad you read about in Chapter 2. "His distinguished combat-food record includes taste-testing 12-year-old canned ham and lima beans. 'It was ugly' is all he'll say about it, apparently trying to forget" (Stipp, 2003, p. 46). Another technological advance is our ability to track tainted food through DNA matching. This advance, which has enormous health and legal implications, is covered later in this chapter.

Although eating is one of life's greatest pleasures, nearly all Americans are on a diet or concerned about their weight, so people enjoy eating but worry about it at the same time. The concern about weight gain is so great that it has been called a national obsession. "The single most important issue in nutrition right now is gaining weight, and that's a matter of calories," says Marion Nestle, chairwoman of the Department of Nutrition and Food Studies at New York University. "It doesn't matter if they're healthy calories or unhealthy calories—calories are calories" (Parker-Pope, 2003, p. D1).

Several individual states and the US government as a whole were implementing legislation to have the required listing of calorie counts by food items in restaurants such as on menus and message boards. Part of the reason for this is that menu names alone can be misleading as to calorie and nutrient content.

According to the Centers for Disease Control and Prevention (CDC), more than 60 percent of US adults are either overweight or obese, but the question is what to do about it, if anything. Is it a problem that government and business should get involved in, or is it a matter of individual choice? Consumers have to sort through lots of fads, misinformation, and downright fraudulent information coming from innumerable sources. Who should they believe? What should they do? Seemingly low-calorie, healthy-sounding foods are often not either; for example, a Fresh City Chicken Teriyaki Wrap has 968 calories and 33 fat grams, and Baja Fresh Ensalada Chicken contains 857 calories and 57 fat grams. What drives up the calories and fat grams are the sauces and dressings. A ham sandwich at Fresh City only has 547 calories by comparison, but most consumers would assume this is higher in calories than a Chicken Teriyaki Wrap. Nutritionists would like calorie information available at the counter or on the packaging. "Nobody can tell how many calories are in food they haven't prepared themselves," says Dr. Nestle.

"Even a trained nutritionist can't tell, not even a really good one" (Parker-Pope, 2003, p. D1). Restaurant chains such as Wendy's International that owns Baja Fresh say that consumers can always get wraps or salads without the sauces or dressings and that they offer low-cal items like mahi mahi tacos, with 216 calories and 11 fat grams. In short, nutritionists, consumer economists, and health advocates want to educate the public about food and health risks, encourage participation in healthy behaviors, and make sure that useful and valid information is available to the public.

Casual dining or fast-food consumption varies greatly by country. According to *Euromonitor*, the United States leads in per-person spending on fast food, followed by Canada, the United Kingdom, and Australia. In some countries there are great divides between rural and urban consumption and shopping patterns; as may be expected, choices may be more limited in rural areas, but fresher produce may be available. In a study in Scotland, the researchers found that consumers living in rural areas accepted a lack of shops and more expensive products, and they concluded that distance from retail centers strongly influenced shopping behaviors (McEachern & Warnaby, 2006). Have you noticed differences in food availability in the different places you have lived?

Writing about food and beverage issues has its share of pitfalls because it is such a fast-moving area, making it difficult to be absolutely accurate and up-to-date. Every effort has been made to provide balanced and current coverage, but because of the rapid pace of discoveries, the best advice is for readers to keep up with new developments from reliable sources and consult with their own physicians. Government sources are heavily relied on for the information provided in this chapter.

Food and Water Consumption

Basic Terminology

Foods are products from plants or animals that can be taken into the body for energy and nutrients to sustain life and growth. The food and beverages consumed are one's diet. **Nutrition** is the science of foods and nutrients and their actions within the body. The six classes of nutrients are carbohydrates, lipids, minerals, proteins, vitamins, and water. Your body obtains nutrients through the digestive process, in which foods are broken down in the gastrointestinal tract into compounds that the body can absorb. A kilocalorie is a measure of energy content in food.

Brief History

In early Colonial America, food often consisted of whatever came out of a large pot set above the flames of the fireplace, and food was plain (except for the rich). Alcohol consumption (beer, wine, liquor, and cider) was high, estimated at six gallons per year for Americans over the age of 15. Around the time of the American Revolution, the most common main dish served was ham, except in the South, where it was chicken. Accompanying these were breads and desserts, cheese and other dairy products. Vegetables, seafood, and fruits depended on the season and consumer location, although importing was beginning from the Caribbean. By the 1820s, finer dining and restaurants were in evidence in the cities, and manners, etiquette, and utensils improved; by the 1830s and 1840s, extensive menus were available. Dining out became high fashion from New Orleans to Boston. Railroads and ships brought fine cuisine to the West. A famous dinner at New York's Delmonico's held in 1868 to honor English author Charles Dickens involved nearly 40 sumptuous dishes (Mariani, 1991). By the end of the 1890s, with advances in refrigeration and transportation, nearly any food was available anywhere. Americans went oyster mad, with an average consumption of 660 oysters per year, compared with 120 in the United Kingdom and only 26 in France (Mariani, 1991). This points out how consumption has changed over the years and how it varies by country. Do you normally eat 660 oysters a year?

In 1900 the hamburger patty on a bun was introduced, followed immediately by a hot dog in a bun. In the 1920s the widespread use of refrigerators revolutionized food and beverage storage, and dairy products, including pasteurized milk, became popular. In 1924 Clarence Birdseye sold the first frozen food—fish. Snack foods and candies prospered during the 1930s depression, with the Twinkie being introduced in 1930.

The first TV dinner was sold in 1954 by C. A. Swanson & Sons. The first affordable home microwave oven was introduced in 1965, and it became a common household appliance by the 1980s. In 1990 Oscar Mayer launched Lunchables, packs of meat, cheese, and crackers, leading the way to more individualized servings. In 2000 Smucker's introduced Uncrustables, packages of frozen peanut-butter-and-jelly sandwiches. Throughout the twentieth century, baking from scratch became less and less common. Prepackaged, prewashed salad mixes made their debut in the 1990s. Look in any large grocery store and notice how much space is devoted to salad mixes versus heads of lettuce. Changes in shelf space are good indicators of changes in American shopping habits. Another development in the twentieth century was the increase in snack food space: What once occupied a back corner of the store now has a whole aisle. Other changes include a wider variety of foods from other cultures and a greater variety of fruits and vegetables.

The twenty-first century has brought more research on organic versus non-conventional foods. Consumers are concerned about:

- hazards—sources of danger
- toxicity—the ability of a substance to harm living organisms
- risk—a measure of the probability and severity of harm
- safety—the condition of being free from harm or danger.

Today's Practices and Habits

What are Americans eating and drinking today? Ready-to-drink coffee and bottled water are the fastest growing non-alcoholic beverages in the United States. Figure 8.1 shows the daily beverage consumption of Americans. Water is the highest category, followed by coffee and bottled water, then soft drinks and milk, and on down the list. Probably most surprising in recent years is the explosive growth of sales in bottled water. This may seem like a new phenomenon, but water has been bottled and sold far from its source for thousands of years. The Food and Drug Administration (FDA) regulates bottled water products that are sold interstate under the Federal Food, Drug, and Cosmetic Act. Under this act, manufacturers are responsible for producing safe, wholesome, and truthfully labeled food products, including bottled water products (Buller, 2002). Box 8.1 gives the FDA classifications of bottled water.

Food and beverage choices and practices constantly change for individuals, families, households, communities, and nations. A good example of this is that carrying individually sized bottled water was a rarity until the 1990s in the United States. Some

Photo 8.1
A young man drinking a sports drink after exercise

Source: Thinkstock: George Doyle

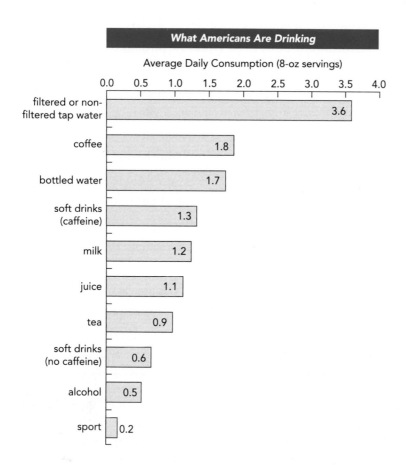

Figure 8.1 What Americans Are Drinking

Courtesy of International Bottled Water Association.

consumers, especially parents, are careful about what water bottles are made of and limit their use of them to emergencies or remote locations.

People decide what to eat and drink and when and where to do it. Several things determine their choices:

- personal preferences and tastes
- habit
- background, ethnicity, heritage, and history
- convenience, availability, and location
- emotions (comfort foods, positive and negative associations)
- values (religion, vegetarian, fresh versus prepared foods)
- cost (for example, hamburger versus steak)
- body image
- nutrition and health benefits
- innovation and marketing including brand names.

Box 8.1 FDA Classifications of Bottled Water According to Its Origin

Artesian well water. Artesian well water comes from a well that taps an aquifer (layers of porous rock, sand, and earth that contain water). According to the Environmental Protection Agency (EPA), water from artesian aquifers is often more pure.

Mineral water. Water from an underground source that contains at least 250 parts per million of total dissolved solids is called mineral water. Minerals and trace elements must come from the source, not be added later.

Spring water. Spring water comes from an underground formation from which water flows naturally to the earth's surface.

Well water. Water obtained from boring or drilling a hole into the ground and tapping an aquifer is classified as well water.

Tap water. Tap water comes from municipal sources and is usually treated.

Sparking water, seltzer water, soda water, tonic water, and club soda are not included as bottled water under the FDA's regulation; historically these have been considered soft drinks.

As an example, coffee consumption fell 50 percent over four decades until Starbucks Corp. made a brand out of a commodity; coffee consumption has inched upward since 1995 (Kilman, 2002). Another example of a food with a consumption history is chocolate. A nineteenth-century gourmet, Jean-Anthelme Brillat-Savarin, said that Spanish ladies in the New World were so enamored with hot chocolate that they sometimes had it brought to them in church. Chocolate consumption has been rising steadily in the United States. In 2000 total US chocolate consumption rose to 3.3 billion pounds, up almost 7 percent from 3.1 billion pounds in 1996, which amounts to almost 12 pounds for every man, woman, and child (Constant Cravings, 2002). Other items increasingly consumed are salty snacks like chips, popcorn, and pretzels. According to a report released by Chicago-based Mintel Consumer Intelligence, 17 percent of Americans report they "can't help snacking on salty snacks" (Junk-Food Nation, 2001).

Different colors and taste combinations keep being developed. H. J. Heinz Co. introduced an Ore-Ida line extension called Funky Fries. This kid-oriented product, found in the freezer section of grocery stores, has new colors and flavors, including Cocoa Crispers (chocolate fries). This product comes on the heels of the success of neon-colored ketchup by the same company.

Unusual uses for foods also are on the horizon. Four football players at Sacramento State applied ConAgra Foods' Pam nonstick cooking spray to one another during a game with the University of Montana. They lost the game, but the Big Sky Conference launched an investigation into the "slippery actions of the players."

Waiting for fruits and vegetables to be in season is a thing of the past. We get kale, apples, grapes, and lettuce year round. When it is winter in the United States, it is summer in New Zealand and Chile. With transportation and shipping advances, anything can be brought fresh to market.

US Spending on Food Consumed

In the typical family's budget, the most expensive monthly item is housing, followed by transportation and then food. Low-income families spend a higher proportion on food than high-income families, so rising food prices hit low-income families harder than high-income families. The **food stamp program**, which is also called SNAP or supplemental nutrition assistance program, helps low-income people buy food. Assistance approval is based on gross income, assets, eligibility rules, and the number of people in the household. If a household is approved, an electronic benefit transfer (EBT) card is issued to the family that can be used to purchase food in most grocery stores and some farmers markets.

According to the US Department of Agriculture (USDA), food expenses consist of food and nonalcoholic beverages purchased at grocery, convenience, and specialty stores, including purchases with food stamps, dining at restaurants, and household expenditures on school meals. Consumer spending on food dropped 10 percent between 1990 and 2000 (Weiss, 2002). The Food Marketing Institute says that was because there were a lot more places to buy food, which means competitive pricing. In the present day, it is more complicated than that; for example, items such as health care and cellphones are taking a larger share of the family budget.

Those under the age of 25 spend more on fresh fruit than other age groups. Across the whole population, in the decade from 1990 to 2000, spending went up for poultry, fish, and seafood and down for beef, eggs, and dairy. Think of the appearance of sushi display counters in grocery stores in the 1990s; they weren't there in the 1980s. Beef consumption has been declining over the last 25 years, but the fresh meat counter is still a major money maker for grocery stores, ringing in over $60 billion in sales each year (Kilman, 2002). New attempts are being made to remarket beef as precooked microwaveable roasts. In 2001, 474 new beef products were launched, compared with 70 in 1997 (Kilman, 2002).

Over the next decade, there are several probable trends:

1. More convenience.
2. More healthy foods.
3. Smaller packages for smaller households.
4. More flavor (watch for words such as *zesty* and *spicy*).

5. More dollars spent in restaurants and bars than in grocery stores. In 2015, American dollars spent at restaurants and bars outstripped those spent in grocery stores, according to the Census Bureau, who has been tracking this data since 1992.

6. Increased food safety.

7. More ethnic foods and regional distinctions (especially watch for more Latino/Hispanic/Cuban and Asian foods).

Household Food Waste

Money lost on food not consumed is an enduring problem. It is estimated Americans throw out 25 percent of the food they buy. Some estimates go as high as 33 percent when you figure in loss before it gets to the household. To find the latest data, go to the US Department of Agriculture website and similar websites in other countries. See Figure 8.2 to see the share of each commodity that ends up in consumers' trash.

USDA MyPlate

The United States Department of Agriculture develops different plans or guides regarding food consumption. The latest is called USDA MyPlate (go to ChooseMyPlate.gov) and it:

- explains what/how much to eat and why
- provides a Supertracker tool that lets you track what you eat and plan your diet; also lets you track exercise
- proves a BMI calculator
- provides daily food plans
- provides a detailed section on physical activity and tells you how many calories certain activities burn
- gives a Food-A-Pedia with food searches and nutritional information
- provides printable resources for teachers and other individuals
- gives general and detailed healthy eating tips.

Fish and seafood	33%
Roots and tubers	30%
Fruits and vegetables	28%
Cereals	27%
Milk	15%
Meat	11%

Figure 8.2 Household Food Waste by Category

Source: Beth Kowitt (September 22, 2014). "Waste not, want not." *Fortune*, p. 14.

Figure 8.3
MyPlate

Source: Courtesy of
US Department of
Agriculture

Crossover Between Food and Drugs

Consumers are increasingly aware and educated about food sources and farming practices. Over five billion pounds of pesticides are used worldwide each year. The move is on to prohibit the most harmful chemicals and to measure and reduce the rest. Over the last hundred years, the lines have become more blurred about what a food is and what a drug is. Fresh fruits and vegetables are most likely to still be classified as foods, but what about a "healthy" flaked cereal, which is a grain product that has been sprayed with vitamins, or a prepackaged frozen lasagna with over 40 ingredients, many of which have lengthy chemical names on the label? Foods that have additives and supplements are more expensive and may be somewhere between a food and a drug. Manufacturers say that foods have been engineered to promote health, and if the alternative is rapid spoilage or fewer nutrients, they have a point. But consumers are very much on their own to determine, for example, if a candy bar full of sugar and fat is healthy because it also contains herbs.

Labels

Labels provide information about nutrient content and compare similar foods, so they are useful up to a point. Usually they do not tell the amounts in products, however; they simply give a list. The first item on the list is the one with the highest amount, so if the first ingredient listed in a candy bar is sugar, then sugar is the leading ingredient, but the consumer will not know if it makes up 80 percent or 20 percent of the product or if it is organic or not. In soft drinks, the first ingredient is water. Consumer advocacy groups, weight-loss groups, and those with certain diseases have been asking for years that amounts be put on labels, but manufacturers insist they have the right to have "secret formulas" or recipes and that lengthy labels are impractical and ultimately costly to the consumer.

The labels on food products should show the quantities per serving in the following easy-to-read format:

- total food energy (kcalories)
- food energy from fat (kcalories)
- total fat (grams)
- saturated fat (grams)
- cholesterol (milligrams)
- sodium (milligrams)
- carbohydrates, including starch, sugar, and fiber (grams)
- dietary fiber (grams)
- sugar (grams)
- protein (grams).

Also, labels must present vitamin A, vitamin C, iron, and calcium information. Sometimes, the manufacturer chooses to add other nutrient information. To encourage consumers to read labels, various campaigns have been launched through alliances with the food industry, government agencies, consumer advocacy groups, and educational and health organizations. Notice that some foods such as fresh fruits and vegetables do not have labels; part of this is practicality—it does not make sense to have a tiny label on every cherry or grape.

Can all labels be believed? The answer is no. When nutrition experts heard about a product called Poi English Muffins that had only 70 calories each, which is about half the amount in other standard-size brands, they did some testing. The muffins had taro root, a Hawaiian delicacy, and weight-loss magazines were raving about the muffins as a speedy low-calorie breakfast. The Good Housekeeping Institute sent two bags to an independent laboratory. The report came back that each muffin actually contained

160 calories and 30 grams of carbohydrates, equivalent to two slices of bread (*Good Housekeeping*, 2001). The Poi English Muffins were definitely not a weight-loss food and should not be marketed as such.

Activity, Diet, and Eating

Dr. William Dietz of the Centers for Disease Control and Prevention (CDC) says that we should opt for smaller portions, turn off the TV, walk rather than drive, and don't make cleaning the plate a requirement for kids and that if a child refuses a healthy meal, it's not up to the parents to prepare something else. The thinking here is that a hungry child learns to eat what is served; if the child is not hungry, he or she should not be forced to eat.

The percentage of the American population that is obese has more than doubled in the last 40 years. Obesity is the number two cause of preventable death in the United States (after smoking) and accounts for almost 10 percent of the money spent on health care. Some people blame the growing preference for fast food and snacking, but as Dietz mentions, there is more to it than that. The solution cited in source after source is that it is not just about food—inactivity and cultural practices play a part. As the next section points out, some are questioning the wisdom of our practices and preferences.

Fast Food or Quick Service

Fast food (also called quick service) has changed a lot since the last edition. Some new restaurant chains (pizza, Asian rice bowls, barbecue, organic, mostly hamburgers or mostly chicken) have joined the competition, and existing players are changing what they offer to keep up with customer demands. Younger customers want fresher food (Nassauer, 2015). The challenge to restaurant chains is how to keep prices low while keeping quality high.

About 14 percent of Americans consume a diet comprised almost entirely of fast food.

CASE STUDY

Inside Chipotle's Kitchen

"Workers at each restaurant chop onions every morning . . . after the chain found machines made onions watery. Employees spend 4 hours prepping before the doors open, right. Salsa is mixed with tomatoes diced by machine. . . . Workers shred meat cooked off-site into two-inch long pieces. . . . At Chipotle, if a customer asks for more, employees will generously oblige. They'll add rice, beans or salsa. But they are trained to be stingy with the 'critical seven,' expensive foods such as meat, cheese and guacamole. If pressed for more, they explain that a full scoop of meat is an extra charge. This is part of Chipotle's formula to balance made-by-hand and

> automation, giving diners quick meals they feel are lovingly prepared. . . . At Chipotle, guacamole is made from scratch in each of its almost 1,800 outlets.
>
> Source: Sarah Nassauer (February 26, 2015).
> "What's made from scratch?" *Wall Street Journal*, p. D1.

A little history: fast food came into vogue in the twentieth century because of the frantic pace of life, multiple roles, and the need to pick up a quick meal. Today, about 50 percent of Americans visit a fast-food restaurant each month, and 30 percent go six to ten times (Addicted to Grease, 2002). It is estimated that about 14 percent of Americans consume a diet comprised almost entirely of fast food; the ones most likely to say this are between the ages of 18 and 24 (Junk-Food Nation, 2001).

The term *fast food*, popularized in the 1960s in the United States, referred to something quite specific—the preparation and service of hamburgers, French fries, milk shakes, fried chicken, and pizza at a chain restaurant where people order their meals from a cashier who sets the prepackaged order on a tray with a regimented, almost robotic quickness that sends the customer on his or her way without further ado (Mariani, 1991). Today, fast food is joined by a category called casual dining, which has table service—examples are Chili's, Applebees, and Olive Garden.

Probably the origin of what we call fast food originated with the McDonald brothers, who led the way by firing carhops, cutting their 25-item menu to nine choices, minimizing the number of employees, getting rid of china and metal flatware, and passing their savings on to customers (Mariani, 1991). McDonald's hamburgers sold for 15 cents, French fries for 10 cents, and milk shakes for 20 cents in the late 1940s and early 1950s. The first McDonald's with the trademark arches opened in 1953 in Phoenix, Arizona. In 1961, Ray Kroc bought out the McDonald brothers for $2.7 million and expanded the business, experimenting with drive-through windows that are the staple of many fast-food restaurants today (Mariani, 1991).

> *There is no question that McDonald's led the charge for fast food and that all other competitors—even those that had been in business before McDonald's—followed that lead. . . . There were fast-rising Mexican restaurants like Taco Bell of Irvine, California, and Chi'Chi's (Louisville), roast beef and steak restaurants like Arby's (Atlanta), Roy Rogers (Bethesda, Maryland), and Ponderosa (Dayton, Ohio), and pizzerias, which in the 1980s registered astounding growth, led by Pizza Hut (Wichita, Kansas), Little Caesar's (Farmington Hills, Michigan), Godfather's (Omaha), and Domino's (Ann Arbor, Michigan), whose selling point was the delivery of its pizzas to the customer's door. And there were fried chicken restaurants like Bojangles (Charlotte, North Carolina), Popeye's (Jefferson, Washington), Church's (San Antonio), and the granddaddy of them all, Kentucky Fried Chicken. (Mariani, 1991, p. 172)*

The cities of origin or headquarters are given to show how the fast-food movement is spread across the United States; there is no one place or one corporation that owns it all. Also, it is curious to see how Western-sounding restaurant names like Roy Rogers or Ponderosa are headquartered in the East and Midwest.

Coming back to the cultural changes that led to the popularity of fast food, Roxburgh (2002) found that heavy time pressures are related to the number of roles consumers occupied. In answer to the question "Who are the time pressured?", she found in a study of 734 full-time workers that they were the affluent, parents, caregivers, and those with high-demand, low-control jobs. She concluded that time pressure is experienced by both men and women.

Slow Food and Buy Local

Nearly everyone knows what fast food is, but fewer are aware of the expression "slow food." Slow food is about enjoying local cuisine including wine and going to micro-breweries, slowing down, and buying locally produced products. Slow food is definitely on the upswing.

Social commentators have argued that life has accelerated because of capitalism and that people are engaged in the relentless pursuit of consumer goods to the point that the true pleasures of life, such as fine dining, have been all but ignored (Schor, 1992). Overloaded schedules and being busy have become cultural ideals that symbolize economic and social success (Daly, 1996; Hochschild, 1989).

In the twenty-first century, people around the world began to question the value of this increased pace. *The slow food movement started in Italy* (now it is worldwide) as a way to defend endangered local foods, and as the name implies, it serves as a counterpoint to the trend toward mass-produced fast foods and the range of foods offered in modern supermarkets. Slow food advocates favor local cheeses, wines, and meat products such as sausages and disdain the commercial over-processing that is commonly done for shipping and storing purposes. Fresh is the emphasis; genetically modified food is reviled. The movement embraces organic methods of agriculture to produce foods more slowly even though it may cost more to do so. Many hail it as a return to taste and regional differences. The slow food movement supports authentic regional cuisine and the turning away from generic international cuisine. Guides for tourists are published indicating local wines, restaurants, and food stores. The headquarters of the slow food movement is in Italy, and its website is www.slowfood.com. The United States also has a slow food association.

The slow food movement can be likened to the "buy local" movement. They both inspire consumers to get more of their food from local sources and resist an increasingly globalized agriculture industry. For example, a study by the Leopold Center for Sustainable Agriculture found that grapes make an average trek of 2,143 miles before arriving on Americans' plates. Produce shipped such long distances can lose freshness and flavor along the way, and there are also concerns about the environmental costs (electricity for cooling, gasoline for transportation). Driving the system is consumers' demand for a consistent marketplace where locally or even nationally out-of-season fruit is available year round, which is possible with worldwide growing and shipping practices. If we are trying to get people to eat healthier, a wide range of foods is usually preferable, but this is in itself an issue. A takeoff on the slow food and buy local movements is the 100-mile diet (or something similar), whose underlying principle is that people should try to eat only foods that are grown within a 100-mile circle drawn around where they live; following this practice, people only eat locally and seasonally available foods. Depending on where someone lives, this is easier to do for some than for others.

In summary, food fads, diets, and trends are in continual motion, and the slow food movement is one approach that is gathering advocates. It combines tourism, community development, environmental awareness, and foods in an interesting way.

Organically Grown Foods

Organically grown foods are crops grown and processed according to USDA regulations. Many of the foods have gone mainstream and are sold not only at natural or local-emphasis grocery stores such as Trader Joe's and Whole Foods Markets but also at the more conventional grocery chains such as Kroger and Publix and big-box discount or warehouse stores like Costco, Sam's, Target, and Wal-Mart. The products may be displayed in a separate section or may be integrated throughout the store (for example, organic canned vegetables on the shelf with the other canned vegetables). Usually the color green is associated with organic products and labels. The most accurate term is *organically grown food*, but often the word *organic* is used for simplicity's sake. An advertisement for Publix promoted its "greenwise market" and a "naturally tasty night" complete with tastings and natural/organic foods gift basket door prizes. Here is some copy from the ad:

> *Publix knows you're trying to live healthier. By eating natural and organic foods. Using products that are environmentally sound. And taking a more wholesome approach to raising your family. Now we've made it easy, with our extensive selection of quality health products—in Produce and in Frozen Foods, on our Grocery aisles and in our Dairy case, in our Deli and our Seafood departments. If you know what's good for you—and especially if you don't—join us for our naturally tasty night, Thursday, January 16, 4 until 7 P.M. (Tallahasee Democrat, January 12, 2003, insert)*

Manufacturers of conventional foods also sell organically grown versions (for example, Heinz sells organic ketchup).

Organic food has grown from a niche market to mainstream in the space of a few years in the United States, Canada, Europe, and Asia. A study of Norwegian consumers showed a positive attitude toward the consumption of organic food (Honkanen, Verplanken, & Olsen, 2006). In the United States, organic food has gone well over the $15 billion mark in sales per year. One can see the growth in the number of products lining grocery store shelves and in the marketing of basic foods like cereals in organic forms. The USDA established the USDA National Organic Program in 2002 with specific, detailed national standards. University departments of agriculture are offering organic food classes, and the University of Florida has one of the nation's first organic-agriculture growers associations. Growers, farmers, consumers, and megafirms like Kellogg's are devoting more attention to anything organic—there is organic milk, organic beef, and nearly every other organic food product imaginable.

Why would someone choose organically grown foods?

1. To enjoy improved taste.
2. To avoid artificial ingredients (this includes synthetic colors and flavors).
3. To reduce "bad" foods in a diet (artery-clogging partially hydrogenated oils are not allowed in organic food).
4. To limit exposure to pesticides.
5. To be more environmentally friendly.

Under the USDA rules, organically grown produce cannot be treated with synthetic pesticides, but this does not mean that organically grown foods are pesticide free because chemicals linger in the soil and the air. This can happen if an organic farm is next to a conventional farm that uses pesticides. One study found organically grown foods contain a third of the residues present on conventional produce. Another reason some consumers prefer organically grown foods is to protect the environment; organically grown foods reduce spraying and water contamination, improve soil quality, and enhance wildlife habitats.

Many consumers are willing to pay more for organically grown foods. These foods may cost 15 to 50 percent more than nonorganic. This potential for additional profit makes them attractive to manufacturers, farmers, and grocery store owners. Conventionally grown bananas might be sold alongside organically grown with signs for both types about price per pound.

Why do consumers pay more for organically grown foods? The main answers have already been suggested, but in the end it comes down to individual choice. Cheryl Rezendes Rulewich became a big believer in organic foods when her five-year-old son's food allergies cleared up when she switched him to an organic diet (de Lisser, 2002, p. D4). She also believes organic foods are healthier and taste better for the whole family. "Conventional fruit and vegetables, with their bright colors and waxy, unblemished surfaces, look unnatural to her eyes. 'They look like Play-Doh food,' she says" (de Lisser, 2002, p. D4).

Not everyone would agree, so the debate continues as to whether organic foods are truly healthier or even preferred given the greater price. "Nelda Mercer, a registered dietitian and spokeswoman for the American Dietetic Association, says there is no scientific evidence showing that organically produced foods are nutritionally better than their conventional counterparts" (de Lisser, 2002, p. D4). What does this mean for consumers? Most agree that organic and sustainable foods are better for the planet, and because organic foods use fewer pesticides, it follows that people who eat organic will have lower levels of pesticides in their bodies. Partly what weighs in is cost and how we respond to advertising messages and images of what is healthy and what isn't. Consumers have to consider the costs and the benefits about organic versus conventional food, just as they do in other consumption areas. Another issue is whether or not to buy meat or milk from cloned animals and how these products should be labeled. Should they be mixed in with the more conventional products, or should they be displayed separately?

USDA regulations define the use of synthetic fertilizers, herbicides, insecticides, fungicides, preservatives, and other chemical ingredients. Organic products cannot have been irradiated, genetically engineered, or grown with fertilizer made from sewer sludge (Whitney & Rolfes, 2002). Dairy and meat products may be called organic if the livestock have been raised according to USDA regulations, which include grazing conditions and the use of organic feed, hormones, and antibiotics.

Foods that have met USDA standards may have a seal on their label. To get this green-and-white USDA seal, a product must be at least 95 percent organic. Examples of products with the seal are fruits and vegetables and cereals that are 100 percent organic, but if a product is at least 70 percent organic, the label can say, for example, "made with organic corn." Another label designation states that the product contains "organic ingredients," which means that less than 70 percent of the product is organic. In this latter case, "organic" cannot be used on the front of the package, but the manufacturer can list organic ingredients on the back.

Implied in the marketing of organically grown foods is that they are healthier than foods grown by conventional methods—this may or may not be the case. There are advantages and disadvantages to both, and consumers have to ask questions about pesticide and fertilizer use and other conditions. These can be difficult questions because the use of fewer chemicals is inherently appealing, but properly used pesticides can yield more crops. If pesticides are used improperly, they can be hazardous to human health; for example, organic fertilizers such as unprocessed animal manure can have ill effects. In the home, consumers can remove or reduce pesticide residues by peeling fruits and vegetables, washing fresh produce in warm water, using a scrub brush, and rinsing thoroughly.

Genetically Modified Foods

CRITICAL THINKING

Should Companies Be Required to Label Genetically Modified (GMO) Foods?

Consumer advocates are pushing for rules requiring companies to label foods that contain ingredients that have been modified, such as resistance to herbicides. Opponents say the risks of GMOs are overblown and that foods are safe. It is possible that the labeling would increase the price to the consumer without any added benefit. What do you think about this issue?

One of the hottest controversies worldwide is the topic of genetically modified foods (GMOs). Some consumers feel uneasy about the possible risks associated with genetically engineered foods, and others don't see the problem because foods have always been altered genetically either by nature or by man. "One theory of the origins of agriculture holds that domesticated plants first emerged on dump heaps, where the discarded seeds of the wild plants that people gathered and ate—already unconsciously selected for sweetness or size or power—took root, flourished, and eventually hybridized. In time people gave the best of these hybrids a place in the garden, and there, together, the people and the plants embarked on a series of experiments in coevolution that would change them both forever" (Pollan, 2001, p. 186).

Genetic engineering is defined as the use of biotechnology to modify the genetic material of living cells so that they will produce new substances or perform new functions (Whitney & Rolfes, 2002). According to the USDA, the genetically engineered share of all corn, cotton, and soybeans planted in the US has grown considerably since the year 2000. In the year 2014, each of these crops had reached over 90 percent genetically engineered.

One of the first foods to be genetically engineered was the tomato, introduced into the market in 1994. Prior to this development, tomatoes did not last long on the shelf, and because they were somewhat fragile, many did not make it to market. Experiments have been carried out on potatoes. "NewLeaf" is the name of a genetically engineered potato by the Monsanto Corporation (Pollan, 2001). This potato produces its own insecticide. What might the future hold? Possibilities include potatoes that are genetically modified to absorb less fat when fried, corn that can withstand drought, lawns that don't ever have to be mowed, "golden rice" rich in vitamin A, and bananas that deliver vaccines (Pollan, 2001). **Biotechnology** is the use of biological systems or organisms to create or modify products. Examples of biotechnology include the use of bacteria to make yogurt, of yeast to make beer, and of cross-breeding to enhance crop production (Whitney & Rolfes, 2002). Plant engineering, a type of biotechnology, is being conducted worldwide. China's bioengineers have worked with more than 50 species of plants, adding genes for traits such as resistance both to viruses and to insects to everything from peanuts to papayas; as a consequence, they are reporting major fiscal and public health gains (The Shape of Biotech to Come, 2002, p. 130).

The reason that the controversy has heated up in recent years is that the twenty-first century has brought very rapid advances in agriculture and food production, and the public is more aware than ever before about these dramatic changes. Through genetic engineering, scientists can introduce a copy of a specific gene that will produce a desired trait, with the goal of improving crops or livestock. So the process has been speeded up, and this worries some people because it does not feel "natural"—it is tampering with nature. Others would argue that ever since crop rotation, selective breeding, and grafting, nature has been tampered with. The beginnings of agriculture and food production can be traced to before 8000 BC in Southwest Asia (the Fertile Crescent) and soon spread to Europe and North Africa (Diamond, 1999). But there is no question that genetic engineering is speeding up the changes in how farmers farm and how foods and drugs are processed. On the plus side, genetic engineering improves the nutrient content in foods, lengthens shelf life, usually means less use of pesticides, and makes land more usable. In terms of government control, much of the approval responsibility falls to the FDA, the EPA, and the USDA.

Consumer advocacy groups want GMOs labeled as such so that consumers know what they are buying. The problem with this is what to say and how much to say. In recent years, some foods have been pulled from the market when the public felt misled regarding contents. This dispute is not settled yet. For the most part, the scientific community (and this includes the FDA) contends that biotechnology can deliver a safe and better food supply and needs to continue, and that genetically altered food will serve more people and reduce hunger around the world. It is estimated that one person in every five in the world suffers from persistent hunger, and tens of thousands die every day from starvation.

What do consumers think about GMOs? According to a Nielsen study of 1,133 consumers in May 2014, many people say they avoid eating GMOs (43 percent yes, 53 percent no) and 61 percent have heard of GMOs ("Should Companies Be Required to Label Genetically Modified Foods?" *Wall Street Journal*, July 13, 2015, p. R1).

Irradiated Foods

Exposing any food to radiation for commercial purposes is called **food irradiation**. To say this another way, "Food irradiation is the treatment of foods with gamma rays, X-rays, or high voltage electronics to kill potentially harmful pathogens, including bacteria, parasites, insects, and fungi that cause food-borne illness. It also reduces spoilage and extends shelf" (Insel & Roth, 2002, p. 348). For example, irradiated strawberries can last unspoiled in the refrigerator for up to three weeks versus the usual three to five days for untreated berries. Lengthening the shelf life of products has great value for grocers and ultimately consumers because it cuts down on the amount of food thrown out. Irradiated foods are very useful in situations such as camping, space exploration, and military operations when people are away from fresh sources of food for long periods of time. Since 1963, the government has allowed certain foods to be irradiated, starting with wheat and flour and now including fruits, poultry, herbs, vegetables, and meats. Irradiation is also used on contact lenses, medical supplies, teething rings, milk cartons, and plastic wrap. Although irradiation has been endorsed by the CDC, the American Medical Association (AMA), and the World Health Organization (WHO), the general consuming public is skeptical. They have the following concerns (legitimate or not):

- Essential nutrients may be destroyed.
- Eating irradiated foods may cause cancer or other ill effects.
- Employees exposed to irradiation or who live near factories that use irradiation could be hurt.
- Foods treated with irradiation may taste different or odd.

The bottom line is that the foods are tampered with, and many consumers feel this is unnatural. Irradiated spices or ingredients embedded in complex products do not have to be labeled as irradiated, but primary goods such as fruits, vegetables, and meats that have been irradiated should carry a flowerlike radura symbol and a brief information label. Studies show that when consumers are given information about irradiation and its benefits, most want to try the foods (Insel & Roth, 2002).

Food Additives

Additives are substances added to food either intentionally (such as sugar added to soda or tea) or by accident. Examples of "by accident" are bits of conveyer belts and packaging, soil, feathers, rocks, pesticide residues, or insects that can fall into products during processing or while in storage. If, for example, rocks being in food sounds absurd, notice the packaging on dry split peas or beans; often it will say to sort and rinse the peas or beans before use, looking out for rocks and stones. Since rocks and stones can look and weigh the same as beans, no machine can completely sort them out, so the consumer must do this before making split-pea or bean soup or forget the whole thing and buy already-prepared or canned soups.

"Today, some 2800 substances are intentionally added to foods for one or more of the following reasons: (1) to maintain or improve nutritional quality, (2) to maintain freshness, (3) to help in processing or preparation, or (4) to alter taste or appearance" (Insel & Roth, 2002, p. 348). These substances make up less than 1 percent of our food, however. Most additives are preservatives that help prevent spoilage; others make food taste or look better.

Preservatives are antimicrobial agents, antioxidants, and other additives that retard spoilage or maintain desired qualities, such as softness in baked goods (Whitney & Rolfes, 2002). Regarding appearance, think of the colors in M&M candies—they are the result of color additives that make the candy look better. Color is also added to margarine, cheeses, pastas, soft drinks, and baked goods. Nutrient additives include iodine in salt, vitamins A and D in milk, calcium and vitamin C in fruit juices, and thiamin in bread.

Additives are approved by the FDA, but the manufacturer has to show that the additives are effective (do what they are supposed to do), detectable and measurable in the final product, and safe. Additives have initial and periodic re-reviews. Regarding safety, the risk of cancer is not tolerated. The **Delaney clause** (a clause in the Food Additive Amendment to the Food, Drug, and Cosmetic Act) states that no substance that is known to cause cancer in animals or human beings at any dose level shall be added to foods. Over time, this tough clause has been difficult to administer, a case in point being the popular artificial sweetener saccharin. When animal tests in the 1970s revealed a possible cancer hazard, leading to talk of removing it from the market, there was a public outcry, and it is still on the market. The key problem is the phrase "at any dose level" because it has been shown in animal testing that huge amounts of a single additive may prove harmful, but very few people would consume the necessary amount to cause the problem (for example, people would not normally drink 50 cups of coffee sweetened with saccharin daily). Instead of zero risk, a more likely standard that the FDA uses is "negligible risk" or minimal risk.

The food additives that have long been in use and are believed to be safe are on the **GRAS List**, which stands for "generally recognized as safe." Examples are sugar, salt, and herbs.

CRITICAL THINKING

Taxing Sugary Drinks

Does it make sense to tax a single additive such as sugar? The argument for such a tax is that sodas and other sugary drinks lead to obesity and other health problems that ultimately cost everyone. So, a higher tax would help cover medicine and other health costs. The argument against is individual freedom and that other things would make more sense to tax. Cities and states are debating these issues. What do you think?

Calories, Weight, and Diets

Calories are units by which energy is measured. Food energy is measured in kilo-calories (1,000 calories equal 1 kilocalorie), abbreviated kcalories or simply kcal. You can lose weight by eating fewer calories and increasing physical activity. Just because a product is fat-free does not mean it is calorie-free—it can be loaded with sugar and other sweeteners. There is also a tendency for consumers to eat more of a food that is low-fat or fat-free, thinking this will save them calories, but if the portion size is larger than normal, any potential calorie savings may be lost.

The surgeon general says that only one in five US adults gets the recommended amount of physical activity. Overweight and inactivity affect the rate of coronary heart disease and increase the risk of developing diabetes, hypertension, and colon cancer. About 30–40 percent of US women and 20–30 percent of men consider themselves overweight, and about 5 percent of US adults are underweight.

Questionable Claims

The market for weight-loss diets and books is estimated at $33 billion a year in the United States (Whitney & Rolfes, 2002). There is no doubt that some diets will provide short-term weight loss, but improved health and long-term weight loss (or maintenance of a preferred weight) are rarer. Consumers need to watch out for common fad diet claims:

- You can lose weight by eating only at certain times of the day.
- Certain combinations of foods will help you lose weight.
- Some diets energize the brain.
- Certain products can rewire your genetic code.
- There are surefire remedies for weight problems.
- Millions of people have been successful at permanent weight loss using this plan.

Also consumers should beware of programs that insist on large sums of money up front. Regarding the role of genetics, genes may not cause obesity, but genetic factors may influence the food intake and activity patterns that lead to it and the metabolic path-ways that maintain it (Heitmann et al., 1997). Studies have shown that adopted children tend to be similar in weight to their biological parents, not to their adoptive parents. In experiments it has been shown that some people gain more weight than others even given the same energy intakes. Clearly, genes play a role in gaining and losing weight, but what can be done about this is still under investigation. To conclude this section, given that people are saying obesity is a major health problem in many countries and study after study stresses the importance of not being overweight, there are certainly benefits to maintaining a healthy weight.

FTC's Fight against "Miracle" Weight-Loss Products

CASE STUDY

Refund Checks

"The Federal Trade Commission is mailing 11,585 refund checks totaling more than $464,000 starting today to consumers who lost money buying dietary supplements deceptively marketed as 'fat burning' and 'calorie blocking.' These are legitimate checks and the FTC encourages consumers who receive them to cash them before they expire on April 21. The refunds are being made from funds collected through a July 2014 settlement with Canadian marketers who falsely claimed that their Double Shot pills would cause rapid, substantial, and permanent weight loss without diet or exercise. According to the FTC's complaint, Manon Fernet and the company she controls, which did business as the 'Freedom Center Against Obesity,' marketed Double Shot to U.S. consumers from 2012 through October 2013. The company falsely claimed that users could eat as much of any food as they wanted and lose 15 to 20 pounds a week, just by taking the pills."

Source: FTC Press Release (2015). "Marketers of 'fat burning' and 'calorie blocking' diet pills to pay $500,000 for making deceptive weight loss claims." Available online at ftc.gov/news–events/press–releases/2015/02/ftc–sends.

The case study about refund checks is just one of many cases that the FTC pursues on fake weight-loss claims. They crack down on deceptive advertising and products such as green coffee beans that really do not reduce weight. One FTC study analyzed 300 ads for products and services that promised quick fixes for shedding weight and found more than half featured at least one claim that was very likely to be false or that lacked adequate proof. Howard Beales III, director of FTC's Bureau of Consumer Protection, said, "'Lose weight while you sleep' [and] 'Exercise in a bottle' are claims that editors and publishers ought to be able to recognize as problematic. . . . Most newspapers don't run pornographic ads and it's not by accident. It's because they looked. That same level of looking should identify the kinds of [weight-loss] claims that are clearly not true" (December, 2002, p. D7). In a magazine directed to the elderly, weight-loss claims included foods that make you sleep sounder (if you are not awake, you can't eat). As a counterpoint to this argument, publishers and broadcasters would say that it is difficult to verify advertisements, meaning newspapers and TV stations do not have scientific laboratories to conduct experiments on advertised products.

CONSUMER ALERTS

Examples of fad diets are those involving one particular food or type of food. The food may be cabbage or grapefruit or a group of foods, such as high-protein items. Although there is initial weight loss, these are hard diets to maintain for a lifetime, and there are potential negative health effects to concentrating on only one food or type of food for long periods of time.

So-called magic pills are to be avoided, but the FDA has approved prescription drugs that may help obese people who have difficulty losing weight through diet and exercise alone. Before trying any radical diet or medicine for weight reduction, a person should contact his or her doctor to discuss treatment, options, and possible side effects.

CONSUMER ALERTS

The days when a wagon would wheel into town and the huckster would get up on the top and extol the virtues of his new food, miracle drink, or cooking device to anyone who would listen are long gone. In its place are other forms of misinformation and unproven products: the Internet, glossy magazine advertisements and articles, "health" magazines, television infomercials, in-home sales, and so on. The Internet is a particular problem because in many countries of the world there are few (if any) controls on what is sold and advertised in terms of health-related products. More than ever, remember the words "may the buyer beware."

There is also the question of profit incentives. Full-page ads for weight-loss products bring in a lot of revenue to magazines and newspapers, as do infomercials on television. Publishers and broadcasters also hesitate to compromise freedom of speech and think that they have the right to run ads with the idea that the reader or viewer will be smart enough to read between the lines. The FTC is intent on promoting stricter media self-policing of obvious fraudulent claims.

Where are these ads placed? The FTC found fraudulent ads in broadcast and cable television, infomercials, radio, magazines, newspapers, supermarket tabloids, direct mail, commercial email, and websites. When the FTC compared current ads with ones from a decade earlier, it found weight-loss ads not only appeared more frequently but also promoted 159 percent more products and carried a dramatically different tone. Box 8.2 shows some of the common advertising claims used by weight-loss ads.

> ## Box 8.2 Questionable Ad Claims for Weight Loss
>
> Common advertising claims and techniques are used by weight-loss ads. Here is a list of the FTC's examples of questionable ad claims:
>
> "The fastest all-natural diet known for rapid weight loss without a prescription!"
>
> "Amazing fat-fighting diet pill produces an extremely fast weight loss . . . even if you cheat or refuse to diet."
>
> "It can make a delicious, juicy hamburger as low in fat as a lean turkey sandwich."
>
> "Major weight loss breakthrough: New carb-killer lets you cheat and eat like crazy and still get skinny lightning fast!"
>
> "Our amazing 'Herbal Bullet' blasts fat and flushes it out of your body!"

In summary, the FTC goes after fraudulent marketers, advertisers, and manufacturers. Some media outlets have said that it is easier to determine what is wrong in liquor, tobacco, and gambling ads than it is for food and beverage ads (that is, what is misleading and what isn't) and that copyeditors are not trained in nutritional analysis.

Foodborne Diseases

The most common foodborne **pathogen** is salmonella, which enters the GI tract in contaminated foods such as undercooked poultry and unpasteurized milk. Symptoms include abdominal cramps, fever, vomiting, and diarrhea (Whitney and Rolfes, 2008, p. 664).

It used to be when people got sick from tainted food, it was difficult to trace the source. Although it is not foolproof, DNA analysis (genetic testing) is an objective way to link each sick person with a particular food or product. For example, the CDC found that a 68-year-old woman's death was caused by a strain of E. coli bacteria with a DNA fingerprint that matched a strain found 1,300 miles away at a meat-processing plant; tainted ground beef was probably the culprit. "For epidemiologists, the genetic match was a powerful illustration of the role DNA fingerprinting can play in food safety and public health. Plaintiffs' lawyers, meanwhile, say the technique has become a formidable legal weapon in product-liability cases against food companies. The number of lawsuits stemming from food-borne illnesses is small, but the implications of using genetic fingerprinting are huge" (Abboud, 2003, p. B1). If an attorney can prove that a person became seriously ill or died from a food and the source is known, the only question is how much the settlement should be. Consumers will benefit because the food industry will be even more aware than usual of the importance of food safety.

A totally risk-free food supply is a goal to shoot for, but the reality is that the most that can be hoped for is increased risk reduction. Canned and packaged goods sold in grocery stores are largely controlled, and sources of problems can be traced through codes. Accidents occur, for example, when contaminated foods make their way to market or when seals or packages are broken, intentionally or unintentionally. Consumers should immediately report any concerns they have to the store where the item was purchased and to the toll-free consumer complaint number on the package or can. Everyone—from producers to suppliers to consumers to parents (especially)—should be involved in maintaining a safe food supply.

In recent years, E. coli outbreaks have been traced to contaminated spinach and lettuce, and a fast-food chain had to close several restaurants for over a month due to consumers getting sick. Responding to public outcry, several US senators introduced legislation that would form a central food agency. Another problem was contaminated imported wheat used in pet food, which caused illness or death of many pets in 2007.

In summary, foodborne diseases can cause illness or even death. The estimates are that annually there are 76 million illnesses, 325,000 hospitalizations, and 5,200 deaths in the United States from foodborne illnesses (Landro, 2002). Especially at risk are infants, small children, and the elderly. The FDA's Food Safety and Applied Nutrition website has useful information. According to the Partnership for Food Safety Education, there are many bugs to look out for:

- Botulism caused by botulinum toxin, found in canned goods and luncheon meats.
- Campylobacteriosis caused by *Campylobacter jejuni*.
- Listeriosis caused by *Listeria monocytogenes*.
- Perfringens food poisoning caused by *Clostridium perfringens*.
- Salmonellosis caused by salmonella bacteria, found in raw meats, dairy products, and shrimp, and as said earlier, often the source is undercooked poultry and unpasteurized milk.
- Shigellosis (bacillary dysentery) caused by shigella bacteria, found in milk and dairy products, poultry, and potato salad (the food becomes contaminated when hands aren't washed).
- Giardiasis caused by *Giardia lamblia*.
- Hepatitis A caused by hepatitis A virus, found in oysters, clams, mussels, scallops, and cockles (usually when their beds are polluted by untreated sewage).
- Staphylococcal food poisoning caused by *Staphylococcus aureus* bacteria, found in bacteria that grows on food left at room temperature.

Other Food Concerns

To eat meat or not is an issue. Besides a question of individual taste and choice, some researchers defend the use of animals in achieving food security in terms of their valuable contributions to agricultural sustainability, especially in developing countries, and the high nutritional value of animal products in the diet (Reynolds, Wulster-Radcliffe, Aaron, & Davis, 2015). Food insecurity affects children especially.

Another food issue is whether research should be conducted on animals. The degree to which animal testing is necessary is controversial, and some activists call for no further testing on animals. Regarding research using animals, some researchers would say that it is better to run tests on animals than on humans, so the lesser of the two evils is to only conduct animal testing when absolutely necessary to protect human health. Some would differentiate between types of animals, feeling more comfortable with experimentation on mice and rats than on larger animals. The general consensus is that animals should be treated in as humane a way as possible and that testing should be done only when absolutely necessary.

A **food allergy**, which is a bodily reaction to a substance that is more severe than food intolerances such as lactose intolerance or reactions to food coloring or MSG, is another issue. "A true food allergy is a reaction of the body's immune system to a food or food ingredient, usually a protein. The immune system perceives the reaction-provoking substance, or allergen, as foreign and acts to destroy it" (Insel & Roth, 2002, p. 349). The reaction (hives, swelled tongue, cramps, asthma, or in severe cases a loss of blood pressure called anaphylaxis) can occur in minutes. Trigger foods such as nuts, milk, eggs, wheat, fish, and shellfish must be avoided, and people at risk should carry medications to treat their reactions. Many infants outgrow food allergies, but it is estimated that about 2 percent of the adult population has food allergies (Insel & Roth, 2002). A good first step in determining whether you have a food allergy or just an intolerance is to keep a diary or log of foods eaten and reactions to determine a pattern, with consultation with a physician being the next step.

A final food concern to discuss is use of a **boycott**, a (usually group) decision to avoid purchasing a product or doing business with a company. Stated another way, a boycott is "an attempt by one or more parties to achieve certain objectives by urging individual consumers to refrain from making selected purchases in the marketplace" (Friedman, 1999, p. 4). No one knows when boycotts began, but there is evidence of them throughout history, from boycotts in England and Ireland long ago to the 1773 Boston Tea Party to the beef boycotts in 1973 (when protestors stood in front of selected grocery stores and asked people not to buy beef). There are commodity boycotts (for example, against beef) or boycotts against a company or a single product (for example, StarKist tuna). Boycotts can last a couple of days to several months. Techniques range from boycotters with signs to sit-ins, call-ins, mail-ins, emails, and signed petitions; they may also include more drastic measures such as obstruction—using physical presence or obstacles and not allowing people to shop at stores or to work at their jobs (such as harvesting grapes or unloading boats of fish). Examples of food companies that have been boycotted include Bumble Bee Seafoods and Heinz (the company that makes Starkist tuna, with the issue being dolphin-safe tuna). The media are involved through coverage of events. The subject of consumer boycotts is much more comprehensive than food only; for a classic guide to the subject, read Milton Friedman's *Consumer Boycotts* (1999).

Junk Food and Legal Issues

How much should food and beverages be regulated is a central issue in this chapter. Junk food is of particular concern. Many consumer advocates are fighting to keep snack and soft drink beverage vending machines out of elementary, middle, and high schools. The question can be asked: Does this work, or do children bring snacks in their lunches from home or go off school grounds to buy snacks at neighboring convenience stores, thus enhancing their risk of being hit by cars, being late for school, or skipping classes? These are not easy questions. It is all about freedom of choice, as well as what children prefer to eat versus what they should eat. What were the rules in the schools you attended? Were vending machines available on school grounds?

One approach to lessening the availability of snacks and soft drinks is to bring lawsuits against the industry (similar to the way the anti-tobacco lobby conducted itself). A drawback is that snack food is less easily defined than tobacco products because a wide range of foods can be considered snacks. Most of the lawsuits have been directed at fast-food restaurants rather than at food and beverage manufacturers. The most newsworthy was the July 2002 lawsuit in which a "272-pound New York City man sued four fast-food chains, alleging that their food contributed to his obesity, heart disease and diabetes" (McKay, 2002, p. A1). One of the restaurants in the lawsuit was Kentucky Fried Chicken. The National Restaurant Association came out with a statement dismissing the lawsuit as "senseless, baseless, and ridiculous" (McKay, 2002, p. A10). But ridiculous or not as a defensive maneuver, fast-food chains are responding by using healthier oils.

Trans fats, discussed earlier, are no longer used in many restaurants and products. For example, a package of baked snack crackers or cheese-flavored crackers with peanut butter filling may have on the label 0g trans fat or zero grams trans fats.

Steven Reinemund, chairman and chief executive officer of PepsiCo, says, "The trend is clear: More consumers are concerned about nutrition, and 'we need to be prepared to deal with it.' Already, low-fat snacks such as baked potato chips and pretzels account for 20% to 25% of Frito-Lay sales" (McKay, 2002, p. A10). In the case of PepsiCo, some of its less caloric products have succeeded, but some (like Wow! Chips with their unpleasant side effects) were less successful. Salt sprinkled on the surface of chips and pretzels helps with "flavor delivery" because salt is one of the first elements to hit the tongue, meaning that many products contain less salt than a lot of people think because salt is just on the surface while the products seem to taste best. Attempts to reduce salt have been less than successful; in some cases, low-salt products have sold, but no-salt products have not.

Besides using better oils, what else can fast-food or snack manufacturers do to produce healthier foods? PepsiCo is experimenting with adding broccoli, carrot, and tomato flecks to chips, and more snacks may have oats, soy, and/or dairy products. It is tricky to find the right combinations because as Reinemund says, "The consumer wants a balance of indulgence, as well as 'better for you.' And if we overreact . . . in either direction, we won't get the balanced growth that we want" (McKay, 2002, p. A10).

Navigating the Grocery Store

The typical grocery store has a grid layout with parallel aisles with merchandise on shelves on both sides of the aisles. This layout works well for customers in a hurry. Full-line discount stores use the same grid layout. The checkouts and customer service desks are at the front of the store; fresh, perishable foods are around the periphery of the store.

Grocery stores seek to develop and maintain long-term ties with their customers because they know loyal customers return again and again. Loyalty is often based on familiarity, availability of desired products, and good customer service. In a study of large-format retailing, Morganosky and Cude (2000a) found that attending to the details of the food retail business (accurate pricing, product availability, continuity of personnel) is a way to improve the consumer experience. But there are problems such as misleading promotions and advertisements as well as scanning errors at the checkout and coupons and rebates that don't always work.

End-of-aisle displays may feature products at a higher cost than similar products placed mid-aisle. For example, grape juice may be $3.99 on the end of the aisle and $2.99 on the shelves where there is a less expensive competitive name brand or a store brand. **Tie-ins**—where complementary products are placed side by side, with one price jacked up to compensate for the **loss leader** (a very-low-priced advertised special to bring shoppers in)—are common. For example, hamburgers may be on sale, but the price on the buns or ketchup next to it may be jacked up. Food and wine samples also encourage sales, as do the pleasant aromas circulating from the bakery; sometimes, the aromas from the deli or bakery are piped out the front door so that the sensory experience starts before customers enter the store. Bananas are the number one food item sold in US grocery stores, so where they are located (usually at the back of the store) will draw customers.

Bananas are the most sold US grocery product.

Most stores are set up so that a consumer has to go around the perimeter or, as said earlier, the periphery to get the basics such as poultry, meat, milk, cheese, bread, fruits, and vegetables, with the frozen-food aisles in the middle of the store. *The longer the customers stay in the store, the more they will spend*, hence the perimeter layout (which encourages them to go up and down all the aisles), free samples, relaxing music, and

Photo 8.2
A woman
shopping in the
frozen dinner
section of a
grocery store

Source: Thinkstock:
Minerva Studio

tantalizing aromas. The addition of precooked foods, pharmacies, in-store restaurants, floral section, cards, magazines, books, and deli areas also slows consumers.

At the checkout area, there are the last-minute impulse items: candy (at child height), magazines, tabloids, small gadgets, gum, and other sundries. Checking the foods you have at home, reading the advertisements, clipping coupons, and making a list before shopping will save you money in the store, but studies show that fewer and fewer people are doing these things. One way stores are responding to this is by having coupons placed right on the products or in a coupon dispenser attached to the shelf.

Unit pricing refers to the presentation of price information on shelves on a common basis such as per ounce, which is valuable information for making price comparisons within brands and between brands. Sometimes unit pricing reveals that the middle-size box of cereal or tube of toothpaste is actually less expensive per ounce than a larger size.

Open dating is a system of placing a date on perishable products that indicates when the product should be sold or consumed. Other dates are the **pull date** (the last day the product should be sold), **expiration date** (the last day the consumer should use the product), **quality assurance date** (the last day when the product is at its peak), and **pack date** (when the product was packaged or manufactured). Quality assurance dates or statements may be found on bread wrappers: "The quality of this product is best if purchased by September 1." Sometimes consumers know these dates, such as an open date stamped on a gallon of milk, and sometimes they do not. For example, a loaf of bread may have a green, blue, or red twist tie that tells the person stocking the shelves when to remove the bread, but the color means nothing to the consumer who doesn't know the code. The tendency is for shoppers to pick the freshest product (in other words, the one with the freshest date), so if milk is set out with dates of July 31 and August 1, shoppers will take the August 1 date even if it is July 24 and they intend to use the whole gallon that day.

Not everyone shops at large grocery stores; convenience stores do a lot of business and their prices are generally higher, but like anywhere else there are sales and deals to be had if one reads ads and compares shelf prices. Drug stores increasingly sell food and beverages.

A technology called **radio frequency identification (RFID)** puts a tiny chip in products that allows for the automatic tracking of products. It was test-marketed in a prototype grocery store in Germany and is spreading to other countries, including some in the United States. RFIDs would replace barcodes on products. RFID tags fall into three broad categories: passive, semiactive, and active. Passive tags are the simplest and least expensive; they obtain power from the radio frequency field of the reader and therefore do not require an integrated power source. Semiactive and active tags use an on-board power source to achieve a greater range or the ability to record data from a sensor. There are several reasons why RFIDs are favored by grocery stores: The main one is faster, more detailed inventory, which makes stocking and ordering easier, and others include more accurate pricing and less shoplifting. Consumers worry about a loss of privacy. Will their products be tagged all the way to their homes? Technology exists for consumers to have their goods detagged before leaving the store, but this may involve standing in another line—not an attractive option. Since this is such a new technology, all the pros and cons have not been worked out yet, but it is something to watch unfold.

The largest US grocer is Wal-Mart.

The largest grocer in the United States is Wal-Mart Stores, Inc. This is an amazing story of the growth of a business because Wal-Mart started selling food in 1988 and in 2002 became the nation's largest grocer with more than $53 billion in grocery sales:

> Wal-Mart sells groceries in at least 1,258 supercenters, 180,000 square foot grocer/discount store combinations and in 49 small Neighborhood Markets. Most of the stores are in the South and Southwest. If Wal-Mart's supercenters continue to expand at their current pace, within this decade, more than three-quarters of the nation's Krogers and Albertsons Inc. stores and more than half the Safeway Inc. outlets could be within 10 miles of a Wal-Mart supercenter, according to Trade Dimensions, a market-data provider. (Callahan & Zimmerman, 2003, p. B1)

Wal-Mart offers organic produce to keep up with consumer demands. It is known for competing by offering low prices. "Studies show that items at Wal-Mart cost 8% to 27% less than at Kroger, Albertsons or Safeway, including discounts from these competitors' loyalty cards and specials" (Callahan & Zimmerman, 2003, p. B1).

Grocery Shopping Online

Various grocery stores and major retailers in the United States, Canada, and Europe have experimented with online grocery sales. Some experiments have worked and some have failed. It tends to work best in urban areas where people live close to the stores so delivery costs are low. There are online grocery retailers and online grocery shopping services such as offered by Amazon. Charges can be a percentage, a monthly flat rate, or a minimum charge per delivery, but some services waive the delivery fee if the order is above a specified amount (such as $75). Another way to avoid a charge is for consumers to place their grocery order by computer and pick up the preselected groceries (all bagged) on their way home. This works well for branded prepackaged foods such as crackers, cookies, and canned goods that are always the same but does not work so well for meat, fruit, and vegetables because shoppers might like to see these products before buying them.

Regarding home delivery, the concern is having someone there to receive the groceries or having a unit in the garage or a housing unit where a delivery person can leave frozen or refrigerated food. Naturally, there are also security concerns. Delivery of groceries and other products by drones (in the air) is under experimentation.

Convenience is the most-cited reason why a consumer uses online shopping (Morganosky & Cude, 2000b). Shopping online is also a boon to customers with physical constraints, such as disabilities or injuries, or lack of transportation.

Bottled Water Consumption

The difference in the quality (taste, consistency, safety) of tap water versus bottled water is controversial. Tap water may smell or look different from bottled water, but you can't always tell by that because most of the dangerous contaminants are those consumers cannot see, smell, or taste (Buller, 2002). Tap water is constantly tested for harmful substances. One of the controversies is the addition of fluoride to tap water; fluoride is added to drinking water to promote strong teeth and prevent tooth decay. There is a concern that children who drink only bottled water will have more dental problems. Again, this is controversial, and if you are concerned, you should ask your dentist or your children's dentist. To complicate things, some bottled water products contain fluoride and some contain vitamins. To find out if the bottled water you drink has fluoride in it, you need to contact the individual company directly.

Why do consumers, especially young health-oriented people, buy bottled water? Jeremy Buccellato, age 31, of Ramsey, Minnesota, says he's heard the arguments "that tap water is just as good if not better than bottled water. A glass from his own tap, however, provides water that's discolored, chlorinated, and tastes like 'pool water.' Buccellato says the extra money he spends on bottles of Dasani water is worth it" (Buller, 2002, p. 18). Portability is certainly also a plus.

Photo 8.3
Water is
important
when exercising
and bottled
water makes it
convenient

Source: Thinkstock:
AmmentorpDK

Does bottled water ever go bad? No, according to the International Bottled Water Association, assuming that it has been treated by the bottler according to guidelines set by the FDA coupled with state and industry standards. Bottled water should contain nothing to attract and grow pathogens that pose a threat to human health. To preserve taste, it is recommended that bottles should be stored in cool, dry places away from odors and toxic substances. Some bottles have two-year expiration dates stamped on them, but this has nothing to do with product safety; it is a number that store owners use to rotate bottles on the shelves.

"Generally, over the years, the FDA has adopted EPA standards for tap water as standards for bottled water," says Dr. Henry Kim, a supervisory chemist at the FDA's Center for Food and Safety and Applied Nutrition, Office of Plant and Dairy Foods and Beverages. "As a result, standards for contaminants in tap water and bottled water are very similar" (Buller, 2002, p. 16). Box 8.1, found earlier in this chapter, shows the FDA classifications of bottled water based on origin. Bottled water sales are growing at a faster pace than soft drink sales.

In bottled water consumption, there is the battle of the brands. Top leaders are the inexpensive store brands and nationally advertised brands such as Aquafina by PepsiCo Inc. and Dasani by Coca-Cola Co. Competitors include regional and imported bottled waters. In recent years bottled water has grown at a faster pace than soft drink sales, with annual supermarket sales of over $13 billion for soft drinks and over $3 billion for bottled water.

Agencies and Laws

In an earlier chapter, you learned that the FDA regulates food, including the areas of foodborne illnesses, nutrition, and dietary supplements; drugs, including prescription, over-the-counter, and generic; medical devices and biologics; and cosmetics, including safety and labeling issues. The FDA monitors websites for products that may endanger the public health. In 1994, the Dietary Supplement Health and Education Act established specific labeling requirements and authorized the FDA to promulgate good manufacturing practice regulations for dietary supplements. This act defined the terms *dietary supplements* and *dietary ingredients* and classifies them as food; it also established a commission to recommend how to regulate claims.

Box 8.3 lists the government agencies (including the FDA) that monitor the food supply. The USDA has a Food Safety and Inspection Service (FSIS), which inspects meat and poultry and monitors slaughterhouses and processing plants. States also monitor parts of the food supply, particularly the wholesomeness of foods grown in their own state; for example, California and Florida actively test and look out for problems in their citrus industries.

Both the FDA and USDA are active in consumer education, spending millions of dollars each year on education (and in the case of the USDA, on promotion of agricultural products). The USDA has government-sponsored trade associations, including the Egg Board, the National Pork Board, the Cattlemen's Beef Promotion and Research Board, and the National Dairy Promotion and Research Board. A consumer issue is whether using taxpayers' dollars for promotional efforts is a good idea or not as well as whether it is an example of the crossover between government, industry, and media.

As we learned in previous chapters, the FTC is responsible for food advertising and industry competition. It does not distinguish between various claims and products (for example, whether a substance is a food or a drug), so there is this gray area of confusing policy whereby food labels are more closely watched or restricted than television commercials or magazine advertisements. Here is an example. A magazine advertisement can say that ketchup may reduce the risk of prostate and cervical cancers, but the label on the product will not say this even though ketchup contains cooked tomatoes that have the phytochemical lycopene, which is thought to reduce certain types of cancer. This brings us to the topic of **structure–function claims**, claims that are made about products by their producers and that are not regulated by the FDA. Health claims are fairly tightly regulated by the FDA, but structure–function claims can be made without FDA approval; for example, products can be said to "improve memory" or "build stronger bodies" without proof. Advertisers are careful to skirt the issue by not mentioning specific diseases, a fine distinction often lost on consumers. Here is another example. Milk contains calcium, which may reduce the risk of osteoporosis—this health claim and the nutrient content need FDA approval. But an advertisement that goes further and makes the structure–function claim that milk helps to promote bone health does not need FDA approval—the phrase "helps promote" is often the key and is considered an easy way out. Box 8.4 gives more examples of structure–function claims.

Box 8.3 Government Agencies Monitoring the Food Supply

Each government agency listed below deals with the food supply, is involved in consumer education, alerts the public to health concerns, and conducts research. Following is a very brief description of these agencies and their activities:

Centers for Disease Control (CDC): About one-fourth of the US population experiences a foodborne illness each year. The CDC monitors foodborne diseases, which are illnesses transmitted to humans through food and water. In homes, foodborne illnesses can be prevented by keeping a clean kitchen, avoiding cross–contamination, keeping hot foods hot, and keeping cold foods cold.

Environmental Protection Agency (EPA): The EPA is responsible for regulating pesticides and establishing water quality standards.

Food and Agricultural Organization (FAO): Part of the United Nations, the FAO has responsibilities that include international monitoring of pesticides.

Food and Drug Administration (FDA): The FDA is responsible for ensuring the safety and wholesomeness of foods processed and sold in interstate commerce, except for meat, poultry, and eggs (which the USDA monitors). The FDA also inspects food plants and imported foods. It cannot possibly sample all foods—it is a monitoring agency that sets standards—but it samples foods regularly and acts promptly when problems occur or when there is suspicion of a potential problem. The FDA is a part of the Department of Health and Human Services.

US Department of Agriculture (USDA): Enforcing standards for the wholesomeness and quality of meat, poultry, and eggs produced in the United States is the domain of the USDA.

World Health Organization (WHO): The WHO is an international agency that adopts standards on pesticide use and reports statistics on world food shortages.

Box 8.4 Structure–Function Claims

These product claims, which may be largely untested or not regulated by government, may be found in advertising:

- helps maintain body weight
- builds strong bones and teeth
- lifts your spirits
- slows aging
- improves memory
- boosts your immune system
- helps you relax so you can finally get some sleep
- promotes heart health
- reduces the risk of colds★
- promotes relaxation and good karma
- increases alertness
- enhances mood.

★This one is a borderline claim that has gotten some companies in trouble. A way around it is to mention the cold or flu season while using actors with red noses who are holding tissues and sneezing on each other and then let viewers draw their own conclusions. Actions or settings are less easily regulated than words.

The FTC does not have the resources to keep up with every US-based website offering products with health claims, and it certainly does not have the resources to keep up with foreign websites. Therefore, do not assume that law enforcement agencies can protect everyone from Internet food swindles or false claims.

Summary

Younger people want fresher foods and restaurants and grocery stores are responding to this move away from packaged and processed foods. This is an example of a change in food and water consumption in the United States, a process that has evolved since colonial times. Currently the top US beverage is water.

Coffee consumption was dropping considerably until it was reinvigorated in 1995 by Starbucks and its competitors. Many innovations in food (such as freeze-dried coffee) have their origins in military research (for example, the development of MREs, referring to Meals Ready to Eat).

The Food and Drug Administration (FDA) regulates bottled water as well as the safety of most foods, while the US Department of Agriculture (USDA) monitors the wholesomeness of meat, poultry, and eggs. The Federal Trade Commission (FTC) is active in food labeling and monitoring advertising.

Outbreaks in illnesses and deaths from contaminated human and pet foods have made many concerned about the safety of food supplies. Salmonella is the number one foodborne pathogen. Many frauds in the food and health industries exist, especially in the area of weight reduction as well as any product or service that promises a more attractive appearance.

The slow food movement (also called the "buy local" movement) is worldwide. It began in Italy as a reaction both to the increased use of fast food and to the toll that the spread of fast food was taking on unique and often more flavorful regional cuisines. Advocates of slow food emphasize local and fresh foods as alternatives to global internationalized foods.

In the typical family budget, food is the third most costly item, behind housing and transportation. Online grocery shopping is becoming more popular, with convenience being the main positive feature.

The debate is ongoing about the price and benefits of organically grown versus conventionally grown food. Sustainability of food and water sources is an important issue. Genetically altered foods are controversial because in many people's minds the process seems to go against what nature intended, although advocates of the value of genetically altered foods would point out that man has been altering nature for centuries through a variety of food production and agricultural practices. Irradiated foods are also met with skepticism. Some people think we have gone too far; others think we have not gone far enough. Starvation still exists on this planet, and advocates of genetically altered foods would suggest that higher crop yields and the reduction of hunger far outweigh worries about tampering with nature. Everyone agrees that as the world population grows, better methods of food production and land use are needed—the dispute is over the best way to do this.

KEY POINTS

1. The USDA MyPlate offers a guide for food choices and amounts. It encourages exercise.

2. Not all foods have labels, and not all labels are truthful.

3. It is difficult for consumers and even trained nutritionists to determine how many calories are in foods that they haven't prepared themselves. Many consumers think they are eating a low-calorie, healthy food in restaurants based on the name of the item, but many times that is not the case. Calorie information should be more readily available.

4. Weight and health effects and weight control are highly personal and complicated issues.

5. Bottled water guidelines are set by the FDA.

6. Drinking water comes from two sources: surface water and groundwater.

7. The FDA regulates what is considered an organically grown food. These foods usually cost 15 to 50 percent more than conventionally grown foods.

8. The largest grocer in the United States is Wal-Mart.

9. A number of government agencies monitor the US food supply; most important are the FDA and the USDA.

10. DNA matching (genetic testing) can be used to track tainted food, which has enormous health and legal implications.

11. Food allergies are rare, affecting about 2 percent of the adult population. Food intolerance, an adverse but not life-threatening reaction, is more common. Through trial and error, most people learn what foods their bodies will not tolerate.

KEY TERMS

additives	foods	pathogen
biotechnology	food stamp program	preservatives
boycott	genetic engineering	pull date
calories	GRAS List	quality assurance date
Delaney clause	loss leader	radio frequency identification (RFID)
end-of-aisle displays	nutrition	structure–function claims
expiration date	open dating	tie-ins
food allergy	organically grown foods	trans fats
food irradiation	pack date	unit pricing

DISCUSSION QUESTIONS

1. How have food preferences changed in the last 100 years? Give at least three examples.

2. What does the Delaney clause refer to? What does negligible or minimal risk mean?

3. Why do people buy branded bottled water? What government agency regulates bottled water?

4. What is your opinion of organic foods? Why have they grown in popularity? Are they worth the extra money?

REFERENCES

Abboud, L. (January 21, 2003). DNA matching helps track tainted meat. *Wall Street Journal*, p. B1.

Addicted to grease (May 2002). *American Demographics*, 56.

Buller, A. C. (July–August 2002). Bottled water: better than the tap? *FDA Consumer*, 14–18.

Callahan, P., and A. Zimmerman. (May 27, 2003). Price war in aisle 3. *Wall Street Journal*, p. B1.

Constant cravings (May 2002). *American Demographics*, 56.

Daly, K. (1996). *Families and time*. Thousand Oaks, CA: Sage.

de Lisser, E. (August 20, 2002). Is that $5 gallon of milk really organic? *Wall Street Journal*, p. D1.

December, R. (September 18, 2002). New miracle weight-loss product? Fat chance! *Wall Street Journal*, p. D7.

Diamond, J. (1999). *Guns, germs, and steel*. New York: Norton.

Friedman, M. (1999). *Consumer boycotts*. New York: Routledge.

FTC Press Release. (2015). Marketers of "fat burning" and "calorie blocking" diet pills to pay $500,000 for making deceptive weight loss claims. Available online at ftc.gov/news-events/press-releases/2015/02/ftc-sends.

Gifford, K., and J. Bernard. (2006). Influencing consumer purchase likelihood, *International Journal of Consumer Studies*, 30 (2), 155–163.

Heitmann, B. L., J. Kaprio, J. R. Harris, A. Rissanen, M. Korkeila, and M. Koskenvuo. (1997). Are genetic determinants of weight gain modified by leisure-time physical activity? A prospective study of Finnish twins. *American Journal of Clinical Nutrition*, 66, 672–678.

Hochschild, A. R. (1989). *The second shift: working parents and the revolution at home*. New York: Viking.

Honkanen, P., B. Verplanken, and S. Olsen. (2006). Ethical values and motives driving organic food choice, *Journal of Consumer Behavior*, 5 (5), 420–430.

Insel, P., and W. Roth. (2002). *Core concepts in health*, 9th ed. Boston: McGraw-Hill.

Junk-food nation (November 2001). *American Demographics*, p. 25.

Kilman, S. (February 2, 2002). A roast is a roast? Not in the new game of marketing meat. *Wall Street Journal*, p. A1.

Kowitt, B. (September 22, 2014). Waste not, want not. *Fortune*, p. 14.

Landro, L. (2002). The informed patient: knowledge is half the battle in avoiding infectious diseases. *Wall Street Journal*, p. C2.

Low-cal muffins: too good to be true? (October 2001). *Good Housekeeping*, p. 18.

Mariani, J. (1991). *America eats out*. New York: William Morrow.

McEachern, M., and G. Warnaby. (2006). Foodshopping behavior in Scotland: the influence of relative rurality, *International Journal of Consumer Studies*, 30 (2), 189–201.

McKay, B. (September 23, 2002). Fit to eat? PepsiCo challenges itself to concoct healthier snacks. *Wall Street Journal*, p. A1.

Morganosky, M., and B. Cude. (2000a). Large format retailing in the US: a consumer experience perspective. *Journal of Retailing and Consumer Services*, 7, 215–222.

Morganosky, M., and B. Cude. (2000b). Consumer response to online grocery shopping. *International Journal of Retail and Distribution Management*, 28 (1), 17–26.

Nassauer, S. (February 25, 2015). What's made from scratch? *Wall Street Journal*, p. D1.

Nassauer, S. (March 18, 2015). What if we all bought organic? *Wall Street Journal*, p. D1.

Parker-Pope, T. (January 14, 2003). That veggie wrap you just chowed down is more fattening than a ham sandwich. *Wall Street Journal*, p. D1.

Pollan, M. (2001). *The botany of desire*. New York: Random House.

Rai, N. (April 2013). Impact of advertising on consumer behaviour and attitude with reference to consumer durables. *International Journal of Management Research and Business Strategy*, 2 (2), 77.

Reynolds, L. P., M. Wulster-Radcliffe, D. Aaron, and T. Davis. (2015). Importance of animals in agricultural sustainability and food security. *Journal of Nutrition*, 145: 1377–1379.

Roxburgh, S. (2002). Racing through life: the distribution of time pressures by roles and role resources among full-time workers. *Journal of Family and Economic Issues*, 23 (2), 121–145.

Schor, J. B. (1992). *The overworked American: the unexpected decline of leisure*. New York: Basic Books.

Shape of biotech to come. (September 2, 2002). *Fortune*, p. 130.

Should companies be required to label genetically modified foods? (July 13, 2015). *Wall Street Journal*, p. R1.

Stipp, D. (January 20, 2003). Son of Spam. *Fortune*, p. 46.

Weiss, M. (April 2002). Inconspicuous consumption. *American Demographics*, 31–39.

Whitney, E., and S. Rolfes. (2002). *Understanding nutrition*, 9th ed. Belmont, CA: Wadsworth.

Whitney, E., and S. Rolfes. (2008). *Understanding nutrition*, 11th ed. Belmont, CA: Thomson.

Whole Foods Market (2014). Get to know responsibly grown. Available online at wfm.com/responsiblygrown.

Chapter

Health and Wellness Issues

The first wealth is health.

Ralph Waldo Emerson

LEARNING OBJECTIVES

1. Explain the complexity of the subject of health and wellness.

2. Discuss the reasons why fraudulent health claims are rampant.

3. List ways to reduce health care costs.

4. Discuss medical malpractice insurance issues.

5. Explain the market for cosmetics and the reasons people use them.

6. Discuss addictions, such as to alcohol and tobacco, and the related consumer issues of health, safety, advertising, and cost.

> ### CASE STUDY
>
> **Do You Have Insomnia or Not?**
>
> "Have you ever had nights when you feel like you barely slept, only to hear from your partner in the morning that you were actually out like a light? It turns out that many people are terrible judges of how much shut-eye they get. That is especially true for those who have insomnia. Many people with insomnia think they sleep much less than they actually do. They tend to misjudge how long it takes for them to fall asleep and how often they wake up during the night. Sometimes people can even mistake being asleep for being awake. . . . About 30% of American adults have symptoms of insomnia each year, according to scientific studies. And about 10% of the population has chronic insomnia, which is generally defined as having difficulty sleeping at least three times a week for three months or more. People with chronic insomnia also tend to feel tired, grumpy and foggy-headed during the day."
>
> Source: Andrea Petersen (July 14, 2015). "You May Be Getting More Sleep Than You Think." *Wall Street Journal*, p. D1.

Introduction

The last chapter focused on food and water issues, and this chapter extends the discussion by turning its attention to the general topic of health and wellness. Health is a more difficult topic than one would assume because "healthy is a very subjective definition," says Gene Cameron, vice president of marketing for Baja Fresh (Parker-Pope, 2003, p. D1). Health and body issues are important to study from a consumer economics standpoint because so much money is spent on health and body products, so much consumer protection legislation and regulation revolve around these issues, fraud is rampant, and, most important, individual and family health are critical. Subtopics to be covered include vaccines, brand-name versus generic drugs, cosmetics, and tobacco and alcohol use. The emphasis in this chapter is on legal drug use, not illicit drugs such as cocaine (the Harrison Act of 1914 prohibited the use of cocaine, morphine, and opiates for nonmedical purposes). Colorado and other states have loosened their rules on marijuana with considerations of who can grow it, who can sell it, and who can use it.

What is enough sleep and what is healthy are very subjective.

Throughout the twentieth century and into the present century, there has been an ongoing battle over the definition of what is a socially acceptable desire or habit and what is an addiction. The Eighteenth Amendment of 1919 (more commonly referred to as Prohibition) outlawed most alcohol use, with the purpose of eliminating or drastically reducing alcohol consumption. The amendment challenged the free market; it was protested by distillers, brewers, and importers and was supported by the American Medical Association (AMA), reformers, and religious groups. In the end, the experiment failed,

Prohibition began in 1919 and ended in 1933.

and the act was repealed in 1933 by the Twenty-First Amendment to the Constitution. Most of the enforcement efforts were directed at sellers rather than consumers, so Prohibition introduced a new kind of criminal—the bootlegger—the most famous of whom was Al Capone. It also forced otherwise law-abiding citizens into a position of circumventing the law, which made many people uncomfortable. There was a concern that if citizens were acting illegally in this area, they were more likely to ignore the law in other areas as well. After Prohibition, a few states continued to prohibit or control the sale of alcohol, but by 1966 liquor control became more a local control issue rather than a statewide or nationwide effort.

Life has gotten more complicated since the days of Al Capone and bootleg whiskey. Drugs, legal and illegal, have introduced a new set of health concerns. "Recent ads in newspapers and magazines claim that it's now legal to import drugs into the United States for personal use: In fact, some ads on the Internet and elsewhere claim that people can legally bring up to a 90-day supply of their prescription medications bought outside the United States home with them. Neither of these claims is true," says Ray Formanek Jr., editor of the *FDA Consumer* (October 2002, p. 2). Under the Federal Food, Drug, and Cosmetic Act, unapproved, misbranded, and adulterated drugs are prohibited from importation into the United States. This quote points out the interaction between the consumer, business, media, and government in the marketplace, as shown in the circular power model of consumerism; it also emphasizes the importance of the Internet in terms of obtaining drugs and information about both drugs and medical treatment. Health information sites on the Internet get an incredible amount of traffic (for example, the Mayo Clinic reports over two million visitors a month).

Due to the following, life improved during the twentieth century for most Americans:

- availability of vaccinations for childhood diseases
- fluoridation of drinking water
- safer workplaces, homes, and schools
- recognition of the severe health problems caused by tobacco use
- healthier mothers and babies as well as improved obstetric care
- increase in life expectancy
- control of infectious diseases
- improved sanitation.

It is assumed that the readers of this chapter have learned about the harmful short- and long-term effects of alcohol and drug abuse in previous classes; for individual health advice, they should consult their physician. This chapter begins with a discussion of wellness and well-being and ends with the government initiative called "Healthy People 2020."

Wellness and Well-Being

For millennia, humans have asked themselves, what is the good life? Answers to this perplexing question cannot be developed in any detail without reference to personal and collective consumption behaviors. Without consumption—at least at the basic level of air, water, food, and shelter—life ceases. (Mick, Pettigrew, Pechmann, & Ozanne, 2012, p. 3)

"Everyone knows the feeling of waking up after a long illness and suddenly, miraculously, feeling full of life again! Being anxious to dive back into things that have been neglected, and try new things, too. Not feeling isolated, powerless, or estranged anymore" (De Graaf, Wann, & Naylor, 2001, p. 231). Well-being and wellness are different. **Wellness** is the ability to live life fully with optimal health and vitality, encompassing physical, emotional, intellectual, spiritual, interpersonal, social, and environmental well-being (Insel & Roth, 2002). Thus, wellness is an expanded idea of health, going beyond just the absence of physical disease. It can be said to transcend health—for example, when individuals with serious illnesses or disabilities rise above their physical or mental limitations to live rich, meaningful, and vital lives.

Well-being is the state of being healthy, happy, or prosperous. Well-being is multifaceted and usually comes down to being mentally, financially, and physically well (Goldsmith, 2015; Xiao, 2015). The term *well-being*, then, is about someone's present health and his or her expectation and realization of a good life, which includes excellent health in the future. Well-being can be measured both subjectively and objectively. It can be a synonym for Quality of Life (QOL).

Subjective, individual well-being reflects both the extent to which people's needs are met and their perspective on the future. Understanding whether people are experiencing a high profile of well-being requires the close examination of their lives as well as their interpretations of their life experiences. (McGregor, 2010, p. 3)

Why do we study health, wellness, and well-being in consumer economics? The answer is as the opening quote to this section shows, life ceases without consumption—air, water, etc. Health is an asset; in fact, it is generally agreed that it is your greatest asset. "Some aspects of health are determined by your genes, your age, environment, and other factors that may be beyond your control. But true wellness is largely determined by the decisions you make about how to live your life" (Insel & Roth, 2002, p. 2). According to Insel and Roth, wellness is made up of six components or subtypes:

1. *Physical wellness.* Exercising, eating well, avoiding harmful habits, making responsible decisions regarding sex, and getting regular dental and physical care all contribute to keeping physically well.

2. *Emotional wellness.* Emotional wellness includes having the ability to share feelings and being optimistic and trusting.

3. *Intellectual wellness.* Curiosity, a sense of humor, openness to new ideas, a love of learning, and the capacity to question and to think creatively are all components of intellectual wellness.

4. *Spiritual wellness.* Being spiritually well includes both having a set of guiding beliefs, values, or principles that adds meaning to life and thinking beyond oneself.

5. *Interpersonal and social wellness.* Developing satisfying relationships is an important part of interpersonal and social wellness.

6. *Environmental or planetary wellness.* Environmental or planetary wellness includes an appreciation for and care of one's surroundings, both natural and man-made (and increasingly, personal health depends on the health of the planet).

According to the AMA, 90 percent of patients don't get good explanations of tests or treatments from their doctors.

Well-being is promoted by sensible behaviors such as paying attention to safety (wearing safety belts), eating well (good nutrition), and regularly exercising. Economists perceive that maintaining good health and safety is linked to personal behavior. The consumer of health care services is called the **principal**; the provider of health care is an **agent**. Apart from self-help (such as wearing seat belts), the consumer as principal needs to find the right agent—the right doctor or health services provider and health insurance provider.

CRITICAL THINKING

Do you ever return from a doctor's visit and realize all the questions you should have asked? Or have you ever forgotten what the doctor said? Two solutions are taking someone with you to take notes or bringing paper to take your own notes. Another is to go online after the visit if your physician offers online notes and results of tests. Patient advocates and medical professionals agree that patients need to become active advocates for their own care. Arming yourself with information and questions before the visit begins is a good start. During the exam, carefully frame the discussion about medical concerns. The American Medical Association (AMA) reports that 90 percent of patients don't get good explanations of tests or treatments from their doctors.

Preventive health care includes being careful while driving, maintaining friendships and families, taking time to exercise and play, using a buddy system when swimming, and having smoke alarms installed at home. Families are important socializing influences for teaching their children the do's and don'ts of safe behavior. Moderation is also important as a means to avoid overexertion and injury. Avoiding risk, another key economic concept, involves avoiding certain consumption behaviors such as heavy smoking and drinking.

Consumer health is an umbrella term encompassing the decisions that consumers make about health care, including products and services that they buy or that their insurance covers, and the decisions that they make about their lifestyle that affect health care needs. Because health decisions are often made in a hurry, time is involved as well as money and information. Health information is available through many media, and consumers like buying over the telephone or computer in their own homes because of the privacy it provides. But because of the personal or privacy issues involved, consumers who are gypped are less likely to complain or ask for a refund in this area of consumption than they are in less personal areas. The result is that many **quacks** (unscrupulous individuals specializing in medical or health swindlers) and quasi-legitimate products and programs continue to exist because of the lack of complaints. This is worrisome because not only is there a money and esteem loss, but also there may be a health loss because the consumer did not seek legitimate advice or treatment.

Fraudulent Health Claims vs. Science

Because health is so fundamental to our sense of well-being and people want to appear as well as feel healthy and well, people are susceptible to products and services that offer a healthy glow or appearance. From Abraham Maslow's perspective, health and cosmetic products and services meet the full range of needs (see Figure 9.1).

Self-
actualization

spas + clinics**

Esteem

hair-coloring kits*
plastic surgery

Belongingness and love

tooth whiteners, mouthwash, deodorants

Safety

safety razor, baby shampoo, toothpaste

Physiological needs

soap, shampoo, cough medicine

*For example, ads that say "I'm worth it."
**For example, ads that say "You have arrived."

Figure 9.1 Maslow's Hierarchy of Needs. This hierarchy includes examples of drugs or cosmetic products

Health frauds are perpetrated against all segments of the population, but some age groups are particularly vulnerable to certain types of frauds, such as the homeless in the Case Study on fraud and footwear. Teenagers are susceptible to acne cream, bust developers, and diet claims; the middle-aged group is prone to products offering wrinkle reduction and perpetual youth; and the elderly fall victim to fraudulent hearing aid schemes, medical quackery and gadgetry, and arthritis remedies. Usually the fraud victim loses time, money, and dignity. For example, consumers spend an estimated $2 billion a year on unproven arthritis remedies such as honey and vinegar mixtures, magnets, and copper bracelets—none of these remedies have been proven to offer long-term relief. Some products and treatments can cause serious harm and even death; many are expensive because health insurance rarely covers unapproved treatments.

> Consumers spend $2 billion a year on unproven arthritis cures.

Fraudulent health claims run the gamut from inflated claims about mouthwash to very serious life-threatening treatments. As noted in Chapter 7, a classic case arose in the 1960s when the Federal Trade Commission (FTC) greatly stepped up efforts to regulate television advertising, attacking the exaggerated health claims of Listerine mouthwash. Fundamental to a study of consumer behavior is the acceptance that there is always a market for products that will beautify or make consumers more socially acceptable.

CASE STUDY

Fraud and Footwear

"A group of doctors in Brooklyn subjected homeless people to unnecessary medical tests and equipment prescriptions so they could rake in Medicare and Medicaid dollars, prosecutors say. In exchange, the homeless people were given free shoes. Nine doctors and 14 others were charged with fraud in Brooklyn on Tuesday. Stephanie Clifford, the Times reporter who covered the indictment, told us more. 'Medicare and Medicaid fraud is pretty common in Brooklyn,' Ms. Clifford said, 'but the size and organization of this particular scheme was unusual.'"

Source: Tatiana Schlossberg and Andy Newman (April 1, 2015).
"New York Today: Of Fraud and Footwear." *New York Times.*
http://cityroom.blogs.nytimes.com/2015/04/01new-york-today.

The question is not why consumers buy health-related or appearance-related products, but why they continue to buy obviously questionable or fraudulent products. The simple answer is that successful fraud trades on false hope and trust in the wrong doctors or spokespeople. But as people become more educated and sophisticated, shouldn't they be more skeptical of especially improbable product claims such as "lose 10 pounds while you sleep"? What can be done? Perhaps the answer lies in encouraging people to be less gullible (easily deceived or duped) by being more scientific in their approach to consumption, such as asking for proof. Robert Park (professor of physics at the University of Maryland, frequent commentator on TV news programs, and author of *Voodoo Science: The Road from Foolishness to Fraud*) states:

> Of the major problems confronting society—problems involving the environment, national security, health, and the economy—there are few that can be sensibly addressed without input from science. As I sought to make the case for science, however, I kept bumping up against scientific ideas and claims that are totally, indisputably, extravagantly, wrong, but which nevertheless attract a large following of passionate, and sometimes powerful, proponents. I came to realize that many people choose scientific beliefs the same way they choose to be Methodists, or Democrats, or Chicago Cub fans. They judge science by how well it agrees with the way they want the world to be. (2000, pp. viii–ix)

He makes a strong case in his book that the media play a major role in promoting false health claims and that even the supposedly investigative shows or evening news shows have promulgated obviously fraudulent products. He says that if scientists can fool themselves and make mistakes, "how much easier is it to craft arguments deliberately intended to befuddle jurists or lawmakers with little or no scientific background? This is junk science." **Junk science** is a term for when there is little or no evidence or proof to support claims.

Health fraud trades on false hope. It promises quick results and easy solutions.

> ## CRITICAL THINKING
>
> ### Two Questions
>
> Why is it that some people faced with the same set of facts choose to believe and others choose to doubt? Why do some people need more proof than others? What are your answers to these questions?

To discuss the critical thinking questions, perhaps the answers have to do with life experience and the ability to discern patterns and accumulate observations, and some people are stronger at this than others. It should also be understood that not everyone desires a world that is predictable and measurable through scientific reasoning and testing; they prefer a little adventure and mystery. It is more fun to believe that a $100 tiny jar of moisturizer will cause wrinkles to vanish than to face up to the fact of being old enough to have wrinkles.

Science is systemized knowledge that is the object of study. To put it another way, "Science is the systematic enterprise of gathering knowledge about the world and organizing and condensing that knowledge into testable laws and theories" (Park, 2000, p. 39). When considering a new product or claim, scientists would apply two rules:

1. Expose the idea and/or result to independent testing and replication by other scientists.

2. Abandon or modify accepted facts, theories, or procedures in light of the new evidence.

Many inventors of new products or claims do not allow them to be tested by independent scientists or doctors, so one of the first rules of determining whether a new health or cosmetic discovery is legitimate or not is to find out what sort of testing was done and by whom. Box 9.1 lists the various words in advertising or labeling that might lead one to believe that fakery (or at least puffery) is at hand. A way to lessen the chance of people being taken in by false claims is to encourage **scientific literacy**, the promotion of science education in the schools and in the community. Park adds that what is needed is a broader scientific worldview, by which he means an understanding that we live in an orderly universe governed by natural laws that cannot be circumvented by magic or miracles.

In Box 9.1 it mentions that the consumer should beware of ads that use testimonials, especially full-page ads for such things as weight reduction and miracle cures. Here is an example from *FTC Facts for Consumers*: "My husband has Alzheimer's [disease]. He began eating a teaspoonful of this product each day. And now in just 22 days he mowed the grass, cleaned out the garage, weeded the flower beds and we take our morning walk again" (2003, p. 9).

To go back to the beginning of this section, the FTC continues to do everything it can to lessen misleading advertising, putting particular emphasis on advertising and products directed to children under the age of eight. For adults, a concern is the amount of fraudulent cures and products on the Internet along with the marketing of brand-name prescription drugs on television and in magazines. The ads on evening television and in magazines suggest that consumers ask their doctor for a brand-name drug the next time that they have an appointment. The problem is that these ads are designed for the general public and may not fit an individual's health status or symptoms. There is real potential for self-diagnosis, which most likely will be off the mark. The counterpoint to this is that someone may recognize symptoms in themselves for a disease like depression and know that there is help.

Box 9.1 Health Fraud Buzzwords and Scams

Look out for before-and-after photos, testimonials, limited supplies (so hurry!), and the following claims about a product:

- shrinks tumors
- improves sex life and cures impotency

- is an ancient remedy
- why the medical community is keeping this discovery secret
- is fast/safe/easy
- is guaranteed to work for everyone
- is amazing
- is a new product breakthrough
- is a miracle
- contains a secret formula
- is exciting
- is painless
- can help you sleep well every night and wake refreshed
- what primitive tribes can tell you
- will improve your popularity
- can end baldness forever
- is recommended by three out of four doctors.

CONSUMER ALERTS

Beware of health frauds about cures for cancer. Because a diagnosis brings feelings of fear and hopelessness, people will try just about anything. They are susceptible to exotic cures or remedies. Cancer is a name given to a wide range of diseases, and each requires different forms of treatment that are best determined by a specialist, a health professional trained in that field.

The FTC turns up hundreds of websites touting unproven cures or treatments for cancer. One site pushes more than 100 alternative cancer treatments that it claims are safe, effective, and nontoxic. Some of these sites are by medical doctors, so just because a product or treatment is endorsed by medical doctors does not mean it is safe. Types of cures include herbal teas and fish extracts—even electronic zappers. The FTC obtained "a $4.3 million judgment against BioPulse International Inc., for making unsubstantiated claims about two cancer 'treatments' it offered in Tijuana, Mexico. One of them, billed as 'hypoglycemic sleep therapy,' involved placing cancer patients in a series of insulin-induced comas over a seven-week period at a cost of nearly $40,000. Some patients, according to news accounts, died from their cancers soon after receiving the treatment" (Fleck, 2003, p.18).

> **CONSUMER ALERTS**
>
> Beware also of health care frauds involving HIV and AIDS. According to the FTC, although legitimate treatments can extend life and improve the quality of life for people with AIDS, there is no cure for the disease so far. People diagnosed with HIV, the virus that causes AIDS, may want to try untested drugs or treatments, but trying unproven products or treatments, such as electrical and magnetic devices and so-called herbal cures, can be dangerous and may cause HIV-positive individuals to delay seeking medical care.

Government Agencies and their Health Care Tasks

As the Consumer Alert shows, the FTC is one of the active government agencies engaged in guarding the public's health. Table 9.2 gives a partial list of key agencies and their main tasks. Figure 9.2 shows the different groups impacting one particular agency, the Food and Drug Administration (FDA). Two goals of regulatory agencies are to help people attain a high level of health at a reasonable cost and to protect them from being misled or taken in by outright fraud. Many issues surround the competency, credentialing, cost, and access to medical care.

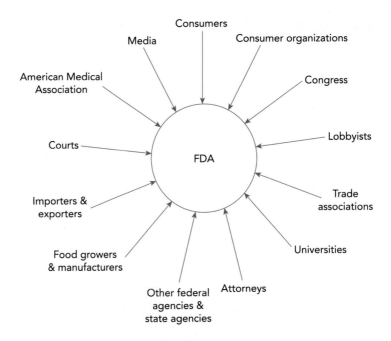

Figure 9.2 Groups Impacting the Food and Drug Administration

Human Development Index and Cost of Care

The United States has one of the most expensive health care systems in the world, and the costs are rising, yet we are not the healthiest. See Table 9.1 for the list of countries with the highest human development scores from the United Nations along with the Human Development Index (HDI) value and life expectancy at birth. For the HDI value, other factors come into play such as years of schooling and gross national income per capita, so it is not purely about physical health, but this goes along with our general definition of well-being as encompassing more than physical health.

> *Medical costs increased 10 to 15 percent in 2001, after averaging 5 to 6 percent for a decade. Hospital spending accounted for about 45 percent of increased health care costs in 2000. Unnecessary admissions and labor shortages are among the factors that make hospitals the primary driver of rising costs. Some hospitals have demanded increases of 40 percent to 60 percent for certain services. (Florida Blue State Edition, 2002)*

Health care premiums rise as medical costs and services rise. Hospitals are for the most part for-profit organizations that have to be enterprising to survive; unprofitable hospitals close totally or close down unprofitable services.

During the Obama Administration the Affordable Care Act was passed, and more Americans had access to health insurance. As this book went to press there was political debate about repealing or changing portions of the Affordable Care Act. Disagreements

Table 9.1 Human Development Index: Top Ten Countries

HDI rank	Country	HDI value	Life expectancy at birth (years)
1	Norway	0.944	81.5
2	Australia	0.933	82.5
3	Switzerland	0.917	82.6
4	Netherlands	0.915	81
5	United States	0.914	78.9
6	Germany	0.911	80.7
7	New Zealand	0.91	81.1
8	Canada	0.902	81.5
9	Singapore	0.901	82.3
10	Denmark	0.9	79.4

Source: http://hdr.undp. Org. table 1. Human Development Index and Components, 2013.

Table 9.2 Partial List of Government Agencies and their Health Care Tasks

All agencies are involved in some form of education or public outreach; beyond that, some of their main tasks and responsibilities are given below.

Agencies	Tasks/responsibilities
National Institutes of Health (NIH)	Research
Internal Revenue Service (IRS)	Taxes and tax policy regarding deductions
Environmental Protection Agency (EPA)	Environmental protection, cleanup and disposal of toxic waste, and protection of water supplies
Centers for Disease Control and Prevention (CDC)	Disease control, accident prevention, and the search for cures
US Department of Health and Human Services, the Surgeon General's Office, and state and county health departments	Help for ill people, policy setting, and oversight of the nation's public health
Occupational Safety and Health Administration (OSHA)	Monitoring of the nation's workplaces for potential health hazards
Food and Drug Administration (FDA)	Testing and regulation

about health insurance can occur at several levels, including in unions and in individual companies. In 2003, 17,500 employees of General Electric Co. (GE) went on a two-day nationwide walkout to protest higher out-of-pocket health costs. It was the first national walkout at GE since 1969, which shows that employees of GE do not lightly make the decision to go on strike. This also illustrates that even employees with health insurance provided by their employers have to pay for part of the coverage (the GE workers were protesting an average copay increase of $300 to $400 annually). In Chapter 14, there is more coverage on health insurance availability through employers (HMOs and so on), but here are eight general guidelines to follow to reduce health care costs:

1. Get good health care coverage from your employer. Find out about your health plan/program in terms of copayments, deductibles, and choice of physician. For example, find out if you can visit a non-network physician, and if you can, what the cost differences are between a network and non-network physician.

2. Use generic drugs instead of a brand-name drug. A **generic drug** is a lower-cost copy of a brand-name drug that becomes available after the brand-name product's patent expires, typically after 15 years or more. The usual cost is 30 percent less than the brand-name drug but is sometimes as much as 75 percent less. More information on generic drugs is given in the next section.

3. Try a mail-order program or shop around for the best price when you use a drug regularly.

4. Choose a physician who participates in your health plan/program when you are traveling. If you choose a nonparticipating provider, your deductible and coinsurance amounts may be higher. One of the biggest plans, Blue Cross/Blue Shield, has 400,000 providers in the United States who participate in the plans.

5. Ask how much it is going to cost you. Can the payments be stretched out?

6. Get free samples from the physician. Some prescription drugs are free at grocery stores or pharmacies or by mail. Your physician will know. This can be a free one-year offer or permanently free.

7. Comparison-shop for the best health care coverage at the best price if your employer (or your spouse's) does not offer health care insurance. One suggestion is to check group policies offered by universities, credit unions, clubs, associations, and other groups that may offer better deals than you could find buying insurance as a nonaffiliated individual.

8. Ask the pharmacist any further questions when getting a prescription filled. Pharmacists are an underused resource.

One of the basic tenets of consumer economics is trying to get the best product at the lowest cost (time and money), but when it comes to your health, perhaps this is not always the wisest course. For example, before agreeing to surgery, you should seek a second opinion; fortunately, most insurance companies will cover the cost of a second opinion. Peace of mind is worth a great deal.

Medicare Fraud

The earlier case study entitled "Fraud and Footwear" showed how homeless people can be taken advantage of in a Medicare and Medicaid scam. Frauds and scams drive up the cost of health care for all of us. The federal government has been working for years to reduce the money loss through Medicare fraud, and it instituted a volunteer program called the Senior Medicare Patrol sponsored by the US Administration on Aging. **Medicare** is the federal health insurance program for people age 65 or older and for many people with disabilities. It covers over 40 million Americans and is the nation's largest health insurance program; by 2030, this number will double, and there are concerns about how to keep this program solvent. Fraud prevention will help. Medicare is subject to a number of errors and abuses, partly because it is so large. Someone who gets Social Security at age 65 is automatically enrolled in Medicare, which has two parts: hospital insurance and medical insurance that helps pay for doctors' services, outpatient care, tests, home health visits, and other services. Medicare fraud, abuse, and billing errors, which together cost taxpayers $12 billion a year, are being investigated through the Senior Medicare Patrol by volunteers who are retirees (often retired medical doctors) looking into possible improper Medicare charges, based on tips from beneficiaries, or who serve as educators to other seniors about the potential for problems. As one example, after two days of training, volunteers worked one on one with beneficiaries to

Photo 9.1
Rising labor costs
drive hospital
bills up

Source: Thinkstock:
Jochen Sands

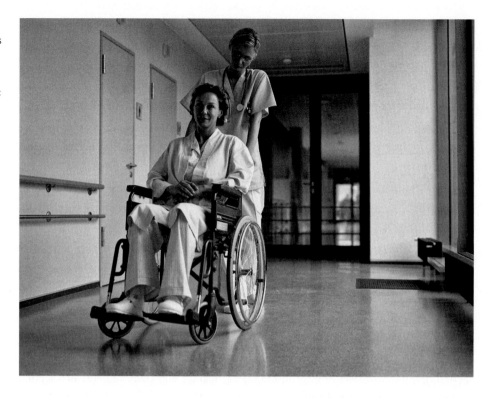

track down suspicious charges on the beneficiaries' monthly Medicare summary notices, or billing statements. Even when fraud is found, sometimes beneficiaries do not want to become involved in clearing it up, fearing bureaucracies and the time loss; volunteers can help with this, making it easier for fraud victims to come forward by showing them the ropes and helping with the paperwork. Other volunteers may be trained to do educational programs because in the long run the biggest gains may come from prevention of fraud, abuse, and error rather than fixing things after they occur.

What kinds of frauds exist? Examples of fraud are Medicare payments for people long since dead, reconditioned wheelchairs billed as new, saline solutions sold as painkillers, and bills for home health services never rendered. "Scam artists are really, really smart. There's a new gimmick every day," says Shirley Merner, state coordinator for Operation Restore Trust of Iowa, a Patrol project that has about 1,500 senior volunteers (Engstrom, 2002, p. R6).

Brand-Name Drugs and Generic Drugs

Drugs are chemicals other than foods intended to affect the structure or function of the body.

The Food, Drug, and Cosmetic Act defines drugs by their intended use: "(A) articles intended for use in the diagnosis, cure, mitigation, treatment, or prevention of disease . . . and (B) articles (other than food) intended to affect the structure or any function of the body of man or other animals" (Food, Drug, and Cosmetic Act, section

201[g][1]). A simpler way to say this is that **drugs** are any chemical other than food intended to affect the structure or function of the body (Insel & Roth, 2002).

Prescription drugs are obtained by a written instruction, usually from a physician, for the preparation and use of a drug. It is illegal to write your own prescription or modify an existing prescription from a doctor. Since drugs have side effects, undesirable reactions and interactions, consumers are given warnings on labels and in advertising. Nonetheless it is estimated that nearly 200,000 people die every year from adverse drug reactions, making it one of the leading causes of death. Most of the medications sold are for **over-the-counter (OTC) drugs** (nonprescription drugs) because most people choose to self-medicate or are treating minor illnesses or discomfort such as headaches, stomachaches, or pain relief with an analgesic.

According to the *FDA Consumer*, a bimonthly publication of the FDA, when the pain reliever acetaminophen was developed in the 1950s, it was only available under the brand name Tylenol. Today, acetaminophen can be found in many generic and store-brand versions such as Pamprin, Midol, and Anacin. Similarly, many drug products, both prescription and over-the-counter, have generic versions available. An estimated 44 percent of all prescriptions in the United States are filled with generic drugs. The biggest seller is aspirin, which is acetylsalicyclic acid; it is sold by nearly 500 companies and may be mixed or coated with other substances. Excedrin and Bayer are common brand names. In using OTCs, the potential for misdiagnosis is very high, resulting in side effects, hospitalization, overuse, overdose, lack of efficacy, and failure to get professional care. **Lack of efficacy** means that the pill or treatment fails to produce the desired effect or outcome.

Photo 9.2
In pharmacy, accuracy is very important

Source: Thinkstock: IPGGutenbergUKLtd

The biggest selling OTC drug is aspirin.

Drugs are continually being changed from prescription to over-the-counter (OTC) drugs. An FDA committee decides whether to approve or disapprove the change from one category to another; once approved, the agency is concerned about OTC labeling so that consumers know what they are buying, as well as any warnings. The FDA's purpose is to protect human health while at the same time providing freedom of choice in the marketplace—something that isn't always easy to attain. Public participation is sought, and this is happening more often as consumers take an active role in acquiring health information and taking care of themselves, although this is not without challenges. "Health care professionals are particularly challenged by a continuing puzzle regarding consumer health behavior: why do chronically ill individuals so often fail to follow doctors' orders?" (Makarem, Smith, Mudami, and Hunt, 2014, p. 457).

Given the possible savings, why doesn't everyone switch to generics? In an American Association of Retired Persons (AARP) study, 95 percent of respondents were aware of generics, but only 31 percent asked for them from their doctors ("Generics May Be 'Equivalent,' Cheaper, But Consumers Resist," 2002). About 28 percent of the respondents worried that the drugs would be less effective, of inferior quality, or in some other way different from brand-name drugs. As this section shows, this is not the case since generics must pass strict standards to earn FDA approval.

The way the approval process works for brand-name drugs is that companies develop new drugs and patent them, and in so doing, they earn the right to sell the drugs for a certain number of years. When the brand-name drugs near their expiration dates, manufacturers can apply to the FDA to sell generic versions. The Drug Price Competition and Patent Term Restoration Act of 1984 allows for this approval process. To summarize, generic drugs are safe, effective, and FDA approved (see Box 9.2). People can use them with total confidence, according to Gary Buehler, MD, director of the FDA's Office of Generic Drugs.

Imported Drugs

Safety Concerns. "With an unapproved drug, you can't be sure that it has been shipped, handled, and stored under conditions that meet U.S. requirements" (Meadows, 2002b, p. 19). Unapproved drugs that come into the United States carry innumerable health risks. The Internet, as well as increased travel (much of it between Mexico and the United States), has made it easier for unapproved drugs to come into this country. "We've found drugs that were stored in time containers and car trunks," says Daniel Hancz, a pharmacist with the Health Authority Law Enforcement Task Force (HALT) in Los Angeles (Meadows, 2002b, p. 18). Some criminals claim to have a medical background, and they not only sell drugs but also give injections illegally. Some of the drugs are very old, others have side effects, some cause death. Through the Food, Drug, and Cosmetic Act, the interstate shipment of any prescription drug that lacks required FDA approval is illegal, and interstate shipment includes importation. The FDA works with the US Customs Service. If a bag or package arouses suspicion, the FDA or the Drug Enforcement Agency (DEA) will be contacted. The US Customs Canine Enforcement Team inspects arriving international mail for illegal pharmaceuticals.

Box 9.2 Frequently Asked Questions about Generic Drugs (and FDA's Answers)

1. Are generic drugs as safe as brand-name drugs?

   Yes. The FDA requires that all drugs be safe and effective.

2. Are generic drugs as strong as brand-name drugs?

   Yes. The FDA requires generic drugs to have the same quality, strength, purity, and stability as brand-name drugs.

3. Do generic drugs take longer to work in the body?

   No. Generic drugs work in the same way and in the same amount of time as brand-name drugs.

4. Why are generic drugs less expensive?

   Generic drugs are less expensive because generic manufacturers don't have the investment costs of the developer of a new drug. New drugs are developed under patent protection, and the patent protects the investment—including research, development, marketing, and promotion—by giving the company the sole right to sell the drug while it is in effect.

5. Does every brand-name drug have a generic counterpart?

   No. Brand-name drugs are generally given patent protection for 20 years from the date of submission of the patent. This provides protection for the innovator.

6. If brand-name drugs and generics have the same active ingredients, why do they look different?

   In the United States, trademark laws do not allow a generic drug to look exactly like the brand-name drug, but a generic drug must duplicate the active ingredient. Colors, flavors, and certain other inactive ingredients may be different.

   Source: Adapted from *FDA Consumer,* September–October 2002, p. 24. For the sake of brevity, the key point of the answer is given; for additional information, go to FDA.

To summarize, there are several potential health risks with imported drugs:

1. Quality assurance concerns.
2. Counterfeit potential.
3. Presence of untested substances.
4. Risks of unsupervised use.
5. Labeling and language issues.
6. Lack of information.

Crossing of National Borders to Buy Drugs. Depending on currency exchange rates and other factors, sometimes prescription drugs are less expensive in other countries; strength or types of drugs or treatments may also vary. So, for example, in years past elderly Americans went on bus trips to Canada to save money on prescription drugs. It is estimated that tens of thousands of Americans were going across the border on buying trips or buying drugs online from Canadian pharmacies (Parker-Pope, 2002). There can be real cost savings because drugs such as Celebrex (for arthritis) and Tamoxifen (for breast cancer) were selling in Canada at less than half of American prices in US dollars (Parker-Pope, 2003). Another example is the cholesterol-lowering drug Zocor. In 2002, it cost $327.86 for a three-month supply from US-based drugstore.com, but at hometownmeds.com (based in Manitoba, Canada) the price was $189.55 (Parker-Pope, 2003). Depending on the drug and shipping charges, savings may be more or less than this. When a married couple is using a dozen drugs between them, the savings can be $300 or more a month, so it is worth shopping around. The US and Canadian government regulators are looking into increased online shopping behavior, and Canadian regulators are cracking down on unaccredited Canadian pharmacies that are staffed with unregistered pharmacists.

The FDA says people are taking a risk when they buy outside the United States, but not everyone sees it that way, including many physicians, congressmen, and senators. The concern according to *FDA Consumer* is that some of the drugs may be exact and some may not. Consumers report that one problem is that certain doses carried in the United States aren't always available or are sold in quantities that do not match their prescription quantity. The FDA does not have authority to approve drugs sold in Canada. Canada, which is cooperating with US authorities, is having to deal with some of the same regulatory issues, including their citizens buying from other countries over the Internet. Although this section has been primarily about Americans going to Canada, there are similar issues regarding Americans living in the Southwest going to Mexico to find less expensive drugs, and people in other countries traveling to neighboring countries around the world to save money. Crossing borders, physically or online, to buy drugs is an issue to watch, and more international agreements between countries in this regard are underway.

Doctors Online

"Almost 30% of doctors have their own websites, according to the American Medical Association" (Reagan, 2002, p. D4). This percentage keeps going up, and group practices are more likely to have websites than individual doctors. Websites or to-the-patient information delivery have several functions:

- provide information such as telephone numbers and office addresses
- attract new patients
- increase efficiency (for example, an online feature allows patients to fill out their medical history before a visit, thus saving time in the waiting room)
- announce availability ("We have flu shots available for $20 from October 1–November 15")
- provide test results to the patient.

Thorny online issues for physicians include whether they should respond to patients' email requests for information and whether they should post warnings (such as "The flu season has arrived"). Many patients would like more interaction with their doctors, but doctors who are already overworked may have a hard time responding to individual emails or keeping up-to-date information posted. Another issue is the privacy of email exchanges because messages sent through unsecured servers can be intercepted. Under the Health Insurance Portability and Accountability Act (HIPAA) of 1996, doctors can be fined for compromising the confidentiality of patients' records (Reagan, 2002). In spite of all this, the overall trend is toward more online consultations.

The bottom line is that what works on e-commerce sites may not necessarily work in health care issues because their highly personal and individualistic nature requires special thought and discretion. Clearly, there are ethical, technological, and cost issues to be worked out, but the trend is toward more doctors going online and toward developing a national system where patients, parents, and doctors can easily access health records, such as vaccination records of children, online. A national system would save lives and reduce pain and suffering because X-rays, tests, and other records could be sent immediately to offices, emergency rooms, and operating rooms—the wait or float time while records are being found and sent would be erased. When doctors close their offices, there will be no more announcements or rushes to get records because they will automatically be in the system—they will never be lost. It would also be a boon to the majority of people in this country who move around a lot or are traveling—their records could be accessed immediately, anywhere. Research is underway to build a worldwide system, or at least cooperative relationships among a number of countries so that people who travel abroad can be assured of their records being available when needed.

Biologics

Following a series of tragic deaths from tainted biological products, Congress enacted the Biologics Control Act in 1902. This law gave the FDA's Center for Biologics Evaluation and Research (CBER) authority to regulate biological products and ensure their quality. **Biologics** include vaccines, blood and blood derivatives, allergenic patch tests and extracts, tests to detect HIV and hepatitis, gene therapy products, cells and tissues for transplantation, and new treatments for cancers and arthritis (100 Years of Biologics Regulation, 2002). Key developments since 1902 include polio vaccine, measles vaccine, pertussis vaccine (for whooping cough), blood and plasma products, and the screening of the blood supply. A hundred years ago, the average American could expect to die by age 47. Whooping cough, flu, pneumonia, and diphtheria could kill whole families; if someone got cancer, he or she did not usually live for long. Today 4 out of 10 patients are alive five years after diagnosis, and we are nearing additional permanent cures. Life expectancy has greatly increased in the US to 78.9 years (see Table 9.1 for life expectancy rates in other countries).

Health Challenges

The main challenge is to find ways to reduce the five leading causes of death in the United States:

1. Heart disease (23.7 percent of total deaths).
2. Cancer (22.9 percent of total deaths).
3. Chronic lower respiratory disease (5.6 percent of total deaths).
4. Stroke (5.1 percent of total deaths).
5. Accidents (unintentional, 5.02 percent of total deaths).

Other challenges include ethical issues surrounding tissue transplants and research on gene therapy and the growing costs of health care and prescription drugs. Another challenge is reducing the cost of health care while expanding services to underserved populations—the young, the elderly, rural dwellers, and the poor.

Malpractice insurance (insurance doctors or clinics have in case they are sued by patients) is one of the things driving up the costs of health care and shaping the decisions doctors make about what specializations to go into and where to practice because malpractice insurance rates vary by specialization and by state. Many doctors pay over $100,000 a year for malpractice insurance. "An analysis by the American Medical Association finds that the escalating cost of medical-liability insurance is causing doctors to quit, relocate or abandon high-risk practices, creating a health-care crisis in 12 states," including Washington, Oregon, Nevada, Texas, Ohio, West Virginia, Pennsylvania, Florida, New York, New Jersey, Mississippi, and Georgia (Cummings, 2003, p. A4).

Doctors have staged rallies in several of these states. On January 1, 2003, West Virginia surgeons "[walked] out of four hospitals to protest the rising insurance premiums that are driving some to quit and others to abandon high-risk specialties such as obstetrics, some surgeries and trauma treatment" (Cummings, 2003, p. A4). Generally, malpractice insurance premiums are highest for obstetricians and orthopedic surgeons. As this book went to press, physicians were pressuring Congress to cap damage awards as one means of bringing down premiums (their payments to insurance companies).

Several powerful groups, including trial lawyers and patients' rights groups, oppose the doctors. These groups make the following two points:

1. Capping awards may not work (and may hurt consumers, especially families with young children who have had severe medical problems and face lifelong care and medical expenses).

2. The medical profession could do a better job of policing their own physicians since only a small percentage account for most of the malpractice suits. They would say here is a good opportunity to root out less-than-adequate doctors. They would also say that government boards could do a better job of reprimanding or taking licenses away from errant physicians.

The end of this is not in sight. Two of the proposals being considered are to limit noneconomic patient damages (such as legal and court fees) to $250,000 and to shorten the statute of limitations for filing complaints (Cummings, 2003). In a move toward political activism, in 2003 the AMA moved all of its leadership meetings to Washington to give doctors plenty of opportunity to lobby and influence representatives. From the consumer point of view, what it really comes down to is doctor availability, and there are very critical health concerns connected with this. Patients in primarily rural states have died because the nearest available specialist was six hours or more away. Why? The specialists moved to states with better malpractice insurance rates. This is a many-sided issue involving states, the federal government, the medical profession, attorneys and courts, patients' rights, and consumers' choices.

Another factor driving up the cost of health care is the nursing shortage. Nurses are now being offered signing bonuses, scholarships, more flexible hours, and significantly higher salaries than in the past.

Another substantial cost is the money poured into research and development (R&D), the search for cures. Pharmaceuticals commit a higher percentage to R&D than any other industry—it costs an average of $500 million to discover and develop a single new medicine. Of the thousands of compounds screened for medical potential each year, only a few will pass enough hurdles to get to the human testing stage and be approved by the FDA. If drug prices were lowered or more controlled, would it reduce R&D? Those representing pharmaceutical companies and researchers in the United States and Europe say yes, but those representing consumer groups are more likely to say no. Some consumer advocacy groups argue that the companies should plow more of their profits into R&D. The industry replies that this is not realistic, that price controls are harmful to innovation and discovery, and that cutting back on R&D would be harmful to patients in the long run.

One of the themes in this book is regulation, and when it comes to health this is widespread in terms of products and services. In the Critical Thinking example, a question arises of who regulates household cleaning supplies such as laundry detergent. The answer is that packaged-food products and cosmetics are required by the Food and Drug Administration to list their individual ingredients on their labels. Most household cleaning products aren't required to provide the same amount of detail.

CRITICAL THINKING

Health Challenge of Laundry-Pod Unintentional Accidents

What do you think is the best solution to the following problem?

"This past spring, Edward Bottei punctured dozens of laundry detergent packets using a chisel-shaped instrument to see what it took to burst them. The medical director of Iowa's Poison Control Center was seeking explanations for a mystery that has stumped toxicologists: Why some children who bit into laundry detergent packets get hurt so badly, including in some cases needing to be intubated to help them breathe. That question is one of many that poison-control experts have about so-called single-dose laundry detergent. Children have been sampling regular detergent for years without much harm. But young children who accidentally burst packets of concentrated detergent have been hospitalized at a rate of about one a day in the U.S. since the products were rolled out widely in 2012. While at least seven people have died after ingesting their contents, thousands of children experienced only minor symptoms."

Source: Serena Ng (July 1, 2015). "Laundry-Pod Dangers Stump Medical Experts." *Wall Street Journal*, pp. B1, B6.

Vaccines and Bioterrorism

To say the subject of vaccines and children has grown substantially since the last edition of this book would be a vast understatement. Public health educators, doctors, parents, talk show hosts, and local, state, and federal government agencies are involved in the protection debate.

Another area of concern is **bioterrorism**, which is the intentional spreading of disease-causing microorganisms or toxins. The emergence of new diseases or disease strains that have become resistant to antibiotics has made the possibility of bioterrorism more prevalent.

In the early twentieth century, many people died as a result of common infectious diseases and poor environmental conditions such as unrefrigerated food, poor sanitation, and air and water pollution. **Infectious disease** is defined as a disease that is communicable from person to person; the causes are invading microorganisms such as viruses and bacteria. These are different from **chronic disease**, which is a disease that develops and continues over a long period of time. Chronic disease is usually caused by a variety of factors, including lifestyle; examples of chronic disease are heart disease and cancer.

Bioterriorism threats in the twenty-first century have forced a reexamination of the nation's vaccine supply. Do we have enough vaccines? Vaccine shortages frustrate parents, patients, and doctors alike.

> *There are many reasons for the shortages. A major reason is the fact that there are relatively few manufacturers in the vaccine business. It's also difficult to make vaccines; from start to finish, a particular batch of a given vaccine requires roughly a year of production time. Unlike most drugs, vaccines are produced from living cells and organisms. Most require growing the immunizing agent, whether it's bacteria or viruses, in [a] production facility where growth conditions are complex. (Meadows, 2002a, p. 12)*

Of particular concern is the smallpox vaccine, a possible tool in the war on bioterror. In its recorded 3,000-year history, smallpox has killed hundreds of millions of people. The problem with the vaccine is that it causes life-threatening reactions in 15 of every million people vaccinated, killing one or two of them (Chase & Hitt, 2002). At highest risk of reaction are babies, pregnant women, people with the common skin rash eczema, and those with weakened immune systems. So doctors are wary to give the vaccine unless it becomes necessary, and government policy makers are tackling the issue of who should get the vaccine first. One idea favored by federal health officials was to offer smallpox vaccinations to the 500,000 hospital workers viewed as most likely to come in contact with patients with smallpox should there be a widespread bioterrorism attack (Chase & Hitt, 2002).

Several vaccines have been in short supply in the past, and these numbers and treatments are changing, so ask your doctor for the latest information specific to you and your family:

1. *Diphtheria, tetanus toxoids, and acellular pertussis (DTaP).* The DTaP supply has returned to normal and is used the most for children ages six weeks to six years.

2. *Measles, mumps, and rubella (MMR)*. The first dose in the two-dose MMR regimen is given between ages 12 and 15 months and the second between ages four and six years. Supply is now normal (this vaccine has been stockpiled since 1983).

3. *Chickenpox (varicella)*. Normally, the recommendation is one dose of varicella vaccine between 12 months and 18 months or at any age after 18 months if a child has not had chickenpox or the vaccine. When this book was written, there was a shortage that was soon to improve.

4. *Pneumococcal conjugate*. Infants normally receive a series of four shots, with the final shot at age 12–15 months. According to manufacturers, supplies were low until 2003.

5. *Tetanus and diphtheria toxoids for adults (Td)*. Tds are given as booster shots to adolescents and adults; supply levels are adequate.

A number of government groups, in particular the FDA and the CDC, are working together to ensure a steady supply of vaccines. Discussions are underway regarding how to speed up production and how to stockpile more vaccines. Check with your health care provider about whether you need any of these vaccines, as well as others such as flu (influenza) vaccines and hepatitis B vaccine (HBV) which protects against hepatitis B virus. Hepatitis B is spread through contact with blood and body fluids of an infected person. To access the recommended schedule of adult vaccines, ask your doctor.

Tanning

A different subject is a health issue that is, for the most part, under our control—how much or how little to tan. **Tanning** is the body's response to skin exposed to ultraviolet radiation (UV) from the sun. The darker side of tanning includes increased risk of skin cancer, eye damage, skin aging, and allergic reactions. Health problems can occur from using sunlamps and tanning beds, as well as from natural sunlight. If using artificial means to tan, the consumer should use goggles and other protective gear and should watch the timing carefully. The Food and Drug Administration (FDA) warns that if sunlamps are not properly filtered, consumers using tanning beds can get burned and have damage to their eyes and blood vessels.

Using a sunscreen appropriate to exposure and skin type is recommended. The consumer should also be careful about any possible reactions that may occur from the use of certain medications while being exposed to the sun.

Besides the physical problems associated with excessive tanning, consumers should be careful before signing contracts with tanning salons. Tanning salons often go in and out of business, so contracts may not be fulfilled. Individual questions about tanning salons, skin damage, and tanning from the sun should be directed to physicians.

Why do people spend time and money getting a deep tan given the negative health effects? Obviously, they do it to improve their appearance, but it goes beyond that.

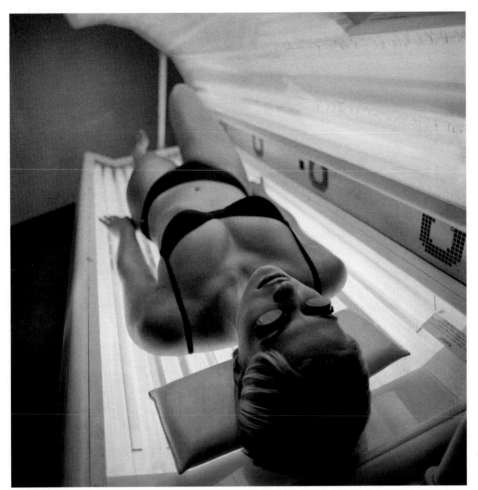

Photo 9.3
A woman lying on a tanning bed. Note that she is wearing protective goggles

Source: Thinkstock: Stockbyte

Getting a tan before going to the beach for the first time may provide freedom from ridicule—a motivator—although so many of the public know the dangers of tanning and burns this is changing. Some, in the cities, get a tan to look healthier at work especially if they are in the entertainment, political, or news business. Some wear makeup that gives the appearance of a tan. More children and adults are wearing hats and specially treated swim shirts and other protective gear while swimming.

In consumer theory, there exists a dimension of the want-satisfying nature of products described as **hedonism**, referring to the fact that many products and behaviors (such as tanning cosmetics or treatments) provide sensory benefits—in short, they taste, feel, look, or smell good to us. It is not difficult to understand why someone would want to escape a long, snowy winter to find the sun in the Caribbean or Hawaii.

Photo 9.4
Where would
you rather be this
winter?

Source: Thinkstock:
Kritchanut

Botox

Botox is a drug.

The Botox cosmetic (onabotulinumtoxinA) is a prescription medicine that is injected into muscles and used to improve the look of frown lines between the eyebrows and to improve the look of moderate crow's feet (around the sides of the eyes) in adults for a temporary period of time. Is botox a cosmetic, or is it a drug treatment? Botox is a drug by FDA definition. There are possible side effects from use. **Botox** is made from a toxin produced by the bacterium *Clostridium botulinum*. "When used in a medical setting an injectable form of sterile, purified botulinum toxin, small doses block the release of a chemical called acetycholine by nerve cells that signal muscle contraction. By selectively interfering with underlying muscles' ability to contract, existing frown lines are smoothed out and in most cases are nearly invisible in a week" (Lewis, 2002, p. 11).

> ### CASE STUDY
>
> **Botox and Men**
>
> "There are many ways in which it seems men and women couldn't be more different, and Botox is no exception. While women are looking to be wrinkle-free, men are not. 'About three-quarters of the women that come to see me [for Botox] are looking to be completely wrinkle-free,' said Dr. Norman Rowe, a New York City board certified plastic surgeon. It's a look that Rowe has dubbed

the 'Wall Street Wrinkle.' The name, he said, comes from the high percentage of male patients who work in finance. 'They really want to avoid looking overdone.' These left-behind lines, Rowe said, are seen by his patients as a 'badge of honor.' Rowe said that while the national average of men seeking non-invasive procedures is about 7 percent, his is nearly double that."

Source: G. S. Brown (March 5, 2015). "The Wall Street Wrinkle: It's How Men Like Their Botox." *ABC News Internet Ventures.* http://abcnews.go.com/Lifestyle.

The FDA approved the use of the drug under certain conditions. Drugs, including those used for cosmetic purposes such as botox, are subject to the FDA approval process. Part of the confusion is that the FDA regulates the products but not how they are used. Botox treatments have been given by nonmedical personnel, which is against the law. Sometimes, a doctor oversaw a clinic or gave his or her name to be used in advertisements, but the actual injections were given by nonmedical personnel such as cosmetics/spa workers or beauticians. Unauthorized people who are caught giving injections are arrested and charged.

Botox gained public attention because it was marketed to groups of people in a party setting. At the parties, adult men and women gathered, paid a fee, signed a consent form, ate snacks, and had drinks; then they were led off one by one to treatment rooms where they were sedated and the numbing treatments given (sometimes the numbing does not wear off easily).

Medical Devices, Treatments, and Procedures

Since the beginnings of recorded time, people have been experimenting with various devices and procedures to restore health. Even today, there are so many fake devices and procedures that it is difficult to put them into categories; many of them defy categorization because they claim to cure so many different kinds of ills. The best advice is that if it seems to be too good to be true, it probably is. Some products are harmful, and others are merely ineffective. As an example, do warmed-up fist-size stones placed on your back give long-lasting health results? What do you think? Is the treatment worth the $250 spa charge? Or, do you accept it as a temporary pleasant, comforting experience?

The FDA cannot keep up with every device, treatment, or product sold in the marketplace, especially those from foreign countries advertised on the Internet or those cooked up in someone's kitchen or formulated in someone's bathtub (like homemade soaps can be and sold at farmers' markets). The FDA tries to review products, especially those sold nationally, to see if they are effective and do not present unreasonable risk to patients. In short, not everything is thoroughly tested, and most medical devices are cleared only

CONSUMER ALERTS

Be careful when using health-related websites; not all are safe and reliable sites. When you are deciding about the worthiness of a site, consider the following:

- Who the source is.
- Where the information comes from, who wrote it or what institution stands behind it, and how old the information is.
- Why the source exists and what it is selling (avoid sites that sell or have testimonials as a sales gimmick, and avoid sites that offer easy or "natural" cures for serious, complex disorders).
- What the message is (look for names you know and trust, and remember that a fraudulent name can be very close to a legitimate source name).

through the premarket notification process, a less rigorous process. Examples of medical devices are contraceptives, defibrillators, lasers, heart devices, breast-imaging devices, wart removal systems, contact lenses, and weight-loss devices. The FDA website lists newly approved devices and procedures.

The FDA regulates prescription, OTC, and generic drugs as well as radiation-emitting products such as cell phones, lasers, microwaves, and mammogram machines. The 1993 Mammography Quality Standards Act was reauthorized in 1998 and is set to be revisited in the twenty-first century. Under this act, facilities are initially certified as meeting certain quality standards and then must continue to pass annual inspections. In 1994 a landmark Dietary Supplement Health and Education Act established specific labeling requirements, provided a regulatory framework, and authorized the FDA to promulgate good manufacturing practice regulations for dietary supplements. In 1999 the Food and Drug Administration Modernization Act mandated the most wide-ranging reforms in agency practices since 1918; its provisions included measures to accelerate review of devices and regulate advertising of unapproved drugs and devices. Examples of medical devices regulated by the FDA include pacemakers, contact lenses, and hearing aids.

The challenge of preventive medicine is to get people to focus on feeling better rather than looking thinner or making whatever other appearance change is desired. Many frauds in the health industries have their root in the promise of a more attractive appearance and an easy way to get it, which leads us into the next section on cosmetics.

Cosmetics

The FDA is the main regulator of cosmetics in the United States—it has its work cut out for it. The number of products grows every day, and there are 13,500 officially recognized cosmetic ingredients, according to the *International Cosmetic Ingredient Dictionary.*

Different types of cosmetics are marketed to different demographic groups around the world. In some countries, skin care is emphasized; in others, the emphasis is more on products that provide color to the skin and lips or a combination of skin care and color enhancement.

The 77 million baby boomers (Americans born between 1946 and 1964) are prime targets for anti-aging products, from facial creams to hand lotions. Over the past few years, sales of anti-aging products have been growing incredibly fast worldwide. Expensive cosmetics produced in France, Switzerland, and Japan can run as high as $500 an ounce for creams or serums infused with silk extract or gold particles. In a *Consumer Reports* study, the top performer out of nine anti-wrinkle brands was the lowest-priced cream selling for $18.99, which beat out competitive brands running as high as $335. So when it comes to cosmetics, "May the buyer beware." For example, be aware of deceptive packaging sizes for cosmetics.

CASE STUDY

Olay Skin-Care Products Packaging

"Proctor & Gamble Co. will change the packaging of some Olay skin-care products as part of a settlement with California Prosecutors, who had accused the company of misleading consumers by selling jars of face cream in packaging that was at times much larger than the contents. The company also agreed to pay $850,000 in civil penalties and costs. The civil protection lawsuit stems from an investigation that began in 2012, according to a spokesman for the district attorney's office in California's Riverside County, which was one of four counties that handled the case. Inspections of Olay containers and packages led to allegations that P&G was violating the states's so-called slack-fill law, which prohibits the use of oversize packaging to make products appear larger. Olay is one of P&G's biggest beauty brands, with sales of more than $2 billion globally."

Source: Serena Ng (July 8, 2015). "P&G Backs Off Puffed-Up Packages." *Wall Street Journal*, p. B1.

The Food, Drug, and Cosmetic Act defines **cosmetics** (products made to beautify the body by their external application) by their intended use. According to the act, cosmetics are "articles to be rubbed, poured, sprinkled, or sprayed on, introduced into, or otherwise applied to the human body . . . for cleansing, beautifying, promoting attractiveness, or altering the appearance (FD&C Act, section 20[i]). Among the products included in this definition are skin moisturizers, perfumes, lipsticks, fingernail polish, eye and facial makeup preparations, shampoos, permanent waves, hair colors, toothpastes, and deodorants, as well as any material intended for use as a component of a cosmetic product.

Famous name brands may be **aspirational products**, such as Chanel No. 5, meaning that consumers aspire to own them. A perfume or famous-brand cosmetic may fulfill a consumer's desire for acceptance, affiliation, esteem, achievement, prestige, and status. Another consumer may have no interest in what another individual or group thinks but may aspire to own a certain fragrance or cosmetic to fulfill a personal sense of happiness, beauty, or pleasure.

Companies try to satisfy different needs and may even position a product to fulfill several levels of needs. Thus, advertising for the same product may vary greatly from media outlet to media outlet. Depending on the **cues**—ads, signs, packaging, and other stimuli—the individual will respond positively, neutrally, or negatively. If there is a positive response, it is because the cue worked, that is, it somehow struck a nerve or fulfilled a drive. When no one responds, the marketers or product manufacturers have missed their target. Research studies show that when consumers purchase cosmetics, they pursue convenience, enjoyment, prestige maintenance, utility, and fulfillment, and experience a cancellation of a sense of uneasiness (Yoo, Hong, & Jung, 2006). If people are unsure about their appearance, cosmetics may be bought for reassurance, and the wise salesperson knows this.

A few years ago, manufacturers and advertisers tried to get most of the American adult population interested in applying a special foot deodorant to their feet on a daily basis, just as they apply deodorant under their arms. Consumers failed to pick up the cues because they didn't perceive foot odor to be an everyday kind of problem deserving their attention. This is a good example of consumers driving the marketplace—they will not buy a product if they do not perceive a need.

When it comes to cosmetics, some consumers are experimental, meaning they like to try new brands and products, whereas others are brand loyal, preferring the tried-and-true. In fact, the latter type gets quite upset when their favorite lipstick or scent is no longer available. Cosmetics companies play into both experimental and stick-to-it types with promotions or samples of new products coupled with a few conventional products. Samples, as a type of cue, create the perception of a want or a need. Once a sample is tried, a certain percentage of customers will buy a full-size product—if not for themselves, then for someone on their gift list.

Can a product be both a drug and a cosmetic? Yes, some products meet both definitions. For example, a shampoo is a cosmetic because it is intended to clean hair, but an antidandruff shampoo also contains a drug to treat dandruff, so it is both a drug and a cosmetic. Other examples of duo products are toothpastes that contain fluoride, deodorants that are also antiperspirants, and moisturizers and makeup that provide sun protection.

The FDA only regulates cosmetics after products are released to the marketplace; ingredients or products are not reviewed or approved by FDA prior to being sold to the public. If the FDA wishes to remove a cosmetic from the market, it must first prove in a court of law that the product may be injurious to users, is improperly labeled, or otherwise violates the law. The FDA inspects cosmetics manufacturing facilities, collects samples to check, and takes action through the Department of Justice. Foreign products may be refused entry into the United States.

Labeling

Personal care products can produce unwanted effects such as skin irritations and allergies. About 10 percent of the population has adverse reactions to cosmetics and toiletries ("The Hype in 'Hypoallergenic,'" 2002). Fragrance is the most common irritant, but emulsifiers and preservatives can also be irritating. One of the ways consumers can minimize adverse effects is to know their skin type and read labels. The drawback to suggesting that consumers read labels is that they would have to be chemists to understand many of the ingredients.

About 10 percent of the population has adverse reactions to cosmetics and toiletries. Fragrance is the most common irritant.

According to the FDA website, federal regulations require ingredients to be listed on product labels in descending order by quantity. Consumers can check the ingredient listing to identify ingredients they want to avoid. Based on the amount used, an ingredient such as water is usually found at the beginning of the product's ingredient list while color additives and fragrances (usually present in small amounts) are normally seen at the end of the listing. These rules apply only to products for home use; professionally used products are not required to have ingredient declarations. The FDA regulates the labeling directly on the product, and ads for cosmetics in magazines, in newspapers, or on television are monitored by the FTC.

Hypoallergenic Products

A common claim is that cosmetics are hypoallergenic. Consumers with sensitive skin are drawn to them, but in reality there are no federal standards or definitions governing the term *hypoallergenic*. What consumers find on a list of ingredients on the product label are ingredients that usually are compatible with sensitive skin, but there are no guarantees. Manufacturers are not required to disclose the components of fragrances, which (as stated earlier) are the most common irritants.

Organic Beauty: Natural or Environmentally Friendly Products

Just as there are organic foods, there are organic beauty products. Are they better? How much is hype? To be certified organic, a beauty product must contain at least 70 percent certified organic ingredients, which means they come from natural sources such as nuts, flowers, and fruits. They should be cultivated in pesticide-free soil and be free

Certified organic beauty products must contain at least 70 percent certified organic ingredients that come from natural sources such as nuts, flowers, and fruits.

of spraying. Regular and organic cosmetics are formulated to be irritation-free, but an individual may have a reaction. Differences may be found in scents, preservatives, colors, and emollients (oils, essential fatty acids). Organic products may not last as long as regular cosmetics with preservatives, so the rule of thumb is to use the product in a timely fashion and to throw out anything that smells, separates, or looks bad. There have been reports that organic cosmetics are more likely to have purity problems. Choosing organic or environmentally friendly products comes down to personal preference; they may be more compatible with both your skin and your politics than conventional products. Connected to this are concerns about the use of animals in product testing. Many consumers prefer cosmetics that do not use animal testing in research and development, so some companies put this on their label or manufacture whole lines of products in North America and in Europe that do not use animal testing.

Tooth Whiteners: Road to Glamour

It used to be that entertainers had to frequent a Hollywood dentist to get really white teeth, with the treatments being done over several weeks' or months' worth of appointments in the dentist's chair. But with new technologies and inventions, there are now more effective in-office dental treatments and home-based do-it-yourself kits. Is there a market? Yes—a whopping 93 percent of Americans worry about their teeth being yellow or stained according to a survey by Trident. The dental-bleaching business has gone from nearly nothing to billions of dollars in annual sales for oral care kits within the last few years. Sales for "tooth polishes" more than doubled in 2002, and Procter & Gamble alone had $1 billion in oral-care sales (De Lisser, 2003). Teeth darken with age, so treatments work best on those over 30 years of age and those with a history of coffee drinking and smoking.

Whiteners come in a variety of ways, including bottles, swabs, little brushes, strips, and tooth trays to collect the drool. Prices range from $15 to nearly a $1,000. Do they work? The answer is that it depends on the product and the person's teeth, as well as on how well the person follows the directions. Journalists and *Consumer Reports* have been testing the dental-bleaching products, and since these products are being perfected, it is best to continue watching for the best-performing products. To establish a baseline (what your teeth are like before treatment), a dentist can use a shade guide; then he or she can check your teeth to see how much they have whitened after the treatment is completed. While at the dentist's office, ask what treatment may be right for you. When looking at whitening toothpastes, look for the American Dental Association (ADA) seal of approval.

The point of this section is that consumers are always interested in new health or cosmetic products, especially ones that have the promise of enhancing their appearance. Different generations tend to focus on different parts of the body, such as shiny hair or whiter teeth. Fads come and go, but the fact that consumers want to improve their appearance is a permanent human condition.

Alcohol and Tobacco Consumption

Now the chapter turns its attention to the topic of potentially addictive behavior—alcohol and tobacco consumption. **Addictions** are habits that have gotten out of control, resulting in a negative impact on one's health that often spills over into other aspects of life such as personal relationships or the ability to do work.

Alcohol Consumption

Alcohol, a colorless, pungent liquid, is the intoxicating ingredient found in fermented liquors (Insel & Roth, 2002). The common use of the word *alcohol* refers to the intoxicating ingredients found in beer, wine, and distilled spirits (hard liquor); chemists would use the term *ethyl alcohol* or *ethanol*. A drink is an alcoholic beverage that delivers one-half ounce of pure ethanol. Examples are 5 ounces of wine, 12 ounces of beer, and one-half ounce of distilled liquor (80-proof scotch, rum, vodka, or whiskey). People have different tolerance levels, so it is difficult to determine what would be a moderate amount. The generally accepted definition of moderation is not more than one drink per average-size woman and two drinks per average-size man per day (Whitney & Rolfes, 2008). Alcohol consumption has both short- and long-term effects. The most horrifying long-term effects are those of babies born to mothers who abused alcohol, which is called **fetal alcohol syndrome**.

The federal government's Alcohol and Tobacco Tax and Trade Bureau (TTB) is responsible for protecting the American public by enforcing the provisions of the Federal Alcohol Administration Act (FAA Act) to ensure that only qualified persons engage in the alcohol beverage industry. It enforces laws regulating alcohol production, importation, and wholesale businesses and tobacco manufacturing and importing. TBB is responsible for enforcing the laws regulating:

- Alcohol Production, Importation, and Distribution
- Tobacco Manufacturing, Importation, and Operations
- Alcohol Labeling and Advertising
- Tobacco Products Advertising.

Why is alcohol abuse a consumer issue? Society pays a very high price for alcohol abuse, including the harm caused by drunk-driving accidents, homicides, suicides, and unintentional injuries, not to mention the health effects, insurance costs, lost workdays, and lower productivity. According to Whitney and Rolfe (2008, p. 238), "A drink is any alcoholic beverage that delivers ½ ounce of pure ethanol:

- 5 ounces of wine
- 10 ounces of wine cooler

- 12 ounces of beer
- 1½ ounces of distilled liquor (80 proof whiskey, scotch, rum, or vodka)."

Generally, wine and beer have less alcohol than distilled liquor, but the amount varies, and there are fortified wines and beer that have more alcohol than regular types.

The liquor industry has voluntary advertising guidelines, including self-imposed bans, but according to George Hacker, director of the Center for Science in the Public Interest's (CSPI) alcohol policies project, the ads for fruit-flavored alcohol drinks are luring millions of teenagers. He says, "Those ads put liquor brand names right in kids' faces" (Alcohol Ads Reaching Teens, 2002, p. 3A). An example is alcoholic lemonade; it has the same amount of alcohol as beer, but the alcohol taste is masked by the lemonade. Another product category appealing to young consumers is the "malternative" beverages, ads for which feature loud music and attractive young people laughing or dancing. In a survey taken by a polling firm for CSPI, an estimated 22 million teenagers— 3 out of 4 people ages 12 to 18—watch television after 9:00 P.M. on school nights when alcohol ads are typically run; furthermore, 6 in 10 teens could name a specific company or brand that advertises during that time. Another product aimed at young people is "zippers," fruit-flavored gelatin cups containing 12 percent alcohol, roughly the same amount found in a glass of wine. In 2002, "zippers" were sold in at least 20 states, and the Community Anti-Drug Coalition of America spoke out against them. Grocery stores were selling "zippers" without proper labeling, making it easier for underage drinkers to buy them. The packaging looked like the type of dessert packs that thousands of children eat every day, so parents were unaware of what their children were consuming.

About 30 percent of the American population is under age 21, but certain magazines that run alcohol ads draw a higher percentage of young readers.

Certain publications draw a higher percentage of young readers than others. For example, *Spin* magazine draws 48 percent of readers under the legal drinking age of 21, according to data used by ad executives. *Allure* has 44 percent underage readers, and *Rolling Stone* has 35 percent. Each of these magazines has alcohol ads, including products such as V. O. Seagram Co.'s Absolut Vodka (Wells, Burnet, & Moriarty, 2000).

Less than socially responsible ads have been removed from circulation, such as those showing people drinking while driving or boating. But in general, liquor ads show well-dressed young adults out as a group in an attractive setting having fun while drinking, so drinking is portrayed as a social activity. In reality, a lot of excessive drinking takes place behind closed doors at home, alone—not an appealing image.

Smoking, Nicotine, and Alternative Products

Since the last edition of this book, smoking-type methods and stores called "vape shops" devoted to stopping smoking or smoking in a different way or as the industry likes to say, "smoke-free alternatives," have escalated. Watch for government regulations on warning labels and child-resistant packaging on bottles of liquid nicotine used in electronic cigarettes. E-cigarettes are reshaping the industry, consumer, and government response.

Tobacco refers to the leaves of cultivated plants prepared for smoking, chewing, or using as snuff (Insel & Roth, 2002). Nearly 90 percent of adult smokers began smoking before the age of 18 according to the US Office of Adolescent Health. **Nicotine** is a poisonous addictive substance found in tobacco that is responsible for many of the effects of tobacco (Insel & Roth, 2002). It is addictive—three out of four smokers want to quit but find they cannot easily do that (Insel & Roth, 2002).

CASE STUDY

FDA and Vape Shops

"Tige Mercer quadrupled his income when he quit audiovisual freelancing to open Vape Atlanta, in this city's funky Little Five Points area. He expects his income to rise another 50% after he opens two more e-cigarette stores in nearby cities this summer. But federal regulations due to be unveiled this summer threaten to ruin his plans. Within the next two months, the Food and Drug Administration is expected to complete rules that would require federal approval for nearly all flavored liquid nicotine juices and e-cig devices sold in vape shops like Mr. Mercer's. . . . In April 2014, the FDA proposed rules that would require e-cigarettes, including liquid nicotine and devices, to be approved by the agency.

Source: Tripp Mickle (July 7, 2015). "FDA Cloud
Hangs Over Vape Shops." *Wall Street Journal*, p. B1.

Cigarette smoking contains many toxic and carcinogenic (cancer-causing) chemicals that affect both the person smoking and the people breathing in tobacco smoke in the nearby environment. The debate about the use of smoking and nicotine products often circulates around the issue of individual choice versus the rights of others and leads to discussions of how much should be regulated or banned. In various states there are initiatives or laws that limit or ban smoking in restaurants. Many campuses are smoke-free. Many states eliminated smoking outside state buildings, requiring employees to smoke at least 50 feet away from state office buildings and specifying that no benches or other seating or shelters would be made available. In the debate, consumers may disagree with one another (smokers versus nonsmokers). Generally consumer groups want more regulations because of the dangers inherent in secondhand smoke inhalation, and the industry (in it for the profit) wants fewer. Other issues include how much to tax smoking and nicotine products, use of age restrictions, health warnings on labels, and advertising. There are related product issues, such as candy cigarettes, which are a bad idea because they encourage children to imitate smoking behaviors. Should tobacco company advertisers be allowed to use cartoonlike characters in ads? How much risk disclosure is necessary on product labels and in advertising?

Many government groups actively set policies, taxation, and regulations on tobacco products. As one example, in 1995 the FDA declared cigarettes to be "drug delivery devices," and restrictions were proposed on marketing and sales to reduce smoking by young people. However, some consumer groups feel there are double messages because tobacco farmers are given crop subsidies (money from the federal government to grow or not grow crops) while at the same time consumption of cigarettes is taxed. They wonder why the government is supporting the industry that has so many devastating effects on the health of the nation—in the United States, more than 400,000 deaths a year are associated with cigarette smoking.

Nicotine products range from gums and chewing tobacco to bottled waters. Some are marketed as a smoking substitute (for example, you can drink when you can't light up on an airplane or in the office, or you can use tobacco as a way to lose weight). Others are marketed as a way to quit or reduce smoking. Nicotine addiction is considered a disease. The FDA has ruled that nicotine water is an unapproved drug under the Federal Food, Drug, and Cosmetic Act and therefore cannot be marketed without going through the approval process. The FDA has warned that nicotine lollipops and lip balm, which had been selling over the Internet without a doctor's prescription, are also illegal. Children were getting hold of the lollipops, lip balm, waters, and gums. Several groups, including the National Center for Tobacco-Free Kids, the AMA, and the American Lung Association, have joined together to ban nicotine water marketed to children.

Cigarette smoking is declining in the United States.

The percentage of US adults who smoke cigarettes is dropping. In 2002 the percentage was 23 percent, compared with 28 percent in 1984.

Healthy People 2020

The US government has had a national Healthy People Initiative for three decades that seeks to prevent unnecessary diseases and disabilities and to achieve a better quality of life for all. Looking forward, the Healthy People 2020 strives to:

- Identify nationwide health improvement priorities.
- Increase public awareness and understanding of the determinants of health, disease, and disability and the opportunities for progress.
- Provide measurable objectives and goals that are applicable at the national, state, and local levels.
- Engage multiple sectors to take actions to strengthen policies and improve practices that are driven by the best available evidence and knowledge.
- Identify critical research, evaluation, and data collection needs.

The federal government has a vital interest in the health of all citizens because a healthy population is the nation's greatest resource—the foundation of its vitality, creativity, and true wealth. Conversely, poor health is a drain on the nation's resources.

Summary

In the United States, the Food and Drug Administration (FDA) is the main regulator of health-related products and (as its name implies) of drugs. The emphasis in the chapter was on legal drugs, such as those gained by prescription or sold over the counter and online from legitimate sources. The Harrison Act of 1914 prohibited the use of cocaine, morphine, and opiates for nonmedical purposes.

Besides safety concerns, there are cost maintenance concerns because health care costs are skyrocketing; on average, they are increasing faster than most other areas of consumer expenditures. What consumers seek is the best health care at a reasonable price. Preventive self-help is one way to reduce costs, and another way consumers pay less is by using generic drugs. It is estimated that 44 percent of all prescriptions in the United States are filled with generic drugs. Issues in the twenty-first century include the continued search for cures and the issues surrounding vaccines, tissue replacement, fertility treatments, and research on gene therapy. The threat of legal action (malpractice lawsuits) has driven up the cost of providing health care, as have labor costs in general. About 30 percent of doctors post health information on their own websites, and the trend is increasing. More and more medical advice and information are being offered over the Internet, and there is a push to switch to e-records in the entire health industry. With this system, parents could look up their child's vaccination records online, and this type of information would also be beneficial to schools and universities.

Consumers should be aware of quality issues, and guidelines for determining them were given in the chapter. Cosmetics as well as alcohol and tobacco use were covered. There are many health care and cosmetic products that are fraudulent. The chapter presented different reasons for why consumers are so susceptible to this particular area of fraud (mostly false hope winning out over reason), why they may choose not to report fraud problems, and why they may choose to ignore science. Some products are classified as both cosmetics and drugs (for example, antidandruff shampoos).

National legislation to stop adult intake of alcohol (most specifically the Eighteenth Amendment to the Constitution passed in 1919 and repealed in 1933, more commonly referred to as Prohibition) has failed. The Federal Trade Commission (FTC) is the main regulator of advertising of alcohol and tobacco/nicotine products.

KEY POINTS

1. About 30 percent of Americans have symptoms of insomnia each year.

2. Consumer health is an umbrella term encompassing the decisions consumers make about their health care and lifestyle.

3. Many health care frauds exist. Be especially wary of suspicious cancer cures and HIV-AIDS cures. The FTC has clamped down on fraudulent treatments. Other government agencies, such as the FDA, TTB, and the CDC, are dedicated to protecting the public's health.

4. Health is your greatest asset.

5. Health care costs are rising significantly, and about 40 million Americans do not have health insurance.

6. Cigarette smoking is declining in the United States.

7. Congress enacted the Biologics Control Act in 1902, giving the FDA the authority to regulate biological products such as vaccines to ensure their quality.

8. Infectious disease is communicable from person to person; it is caused by invading microorganisms such as viruses and bacteria. One of the great advances of the twentieth century was a decrease in the percentage of deaths due to infectious diseases.

9. The top five causes of death in the United States are heart disease, cancer, chronic lower respiratory disease, stroke, and unintentional accidents.

10. Botox is a drug that is FDA-regulated.

11. When it comes to cosmetics, there are no federal standards or definitions of the term *hypoallergenic*.

12. Some cosmetics and scents are aspirational products, meaning consumers aspire to own them.

13. Debates on limiting cigarette smoking usually revolve around individual rights versus the rights of others. Many college campuses are smoke-free.

KEY TERMS

addictions	consumer health	junk science
agent	cosmetics	lack of efficacy
alcohol	cues	malpractice insurance
aspirational products	drugs	Medicare
biologics	fetal alcohol syndrome	nicotine
bioterrorism	generic drug	over-the-counter (OTC) drugs
botox	hedonism	
chronic disease	infectious disease	prescription drugs

principal   scientific literacy   well-being

quacks   tanning   wellness

science   tobacco

DISCUSSION QUESTIONS

1. Why would the size of packaging for a face cream become a concern of the US government? Which US government agency regulates cosmetics? How does it define cosmetics?

2. How long does it take before a patent usually runs out on an FDA-approved drug? Are all drugs available in generic form?

3. Why are people hesitant to use generic drugs?

4. How can a product be both a drug and a cosmetic? Give at least three examples of products that are both.

5. Why do chronically ill individuals so often fail to follow doctors' orders?

REFERENCES

100 years of biologics regulation (July–August 2002). *FDA Consumer*, 36 (4), 8–10.

Alcohol ads reaching teens (July 17, 2002). *Tallahassee Democrat,* p. A3.

Chase, M., and G. Hitt. (October 21, 2002). Ugly side effects of smallpox vaccine color terror plans. *Wall Street Journal,* p. A1.

Cummings, J. (January 14, 2003). Doctors' activism revives malpractice bill. *Wall Street Journal*, p. A4.

De Graaf, J., D. Wann, and T. Naylor. (2001). *Affluenza: the all-consuming epidemic.* San Franciso, CA: Berrett-Koehler Publishers.

De Lisser, E. (January 14, 2003). The cranky consumer works on its smile. *Wall Street Journal,* p. D1.

Engstrom, P. (September 30, 2002). Medical sleuths. *Wall Street Journal,* p. R6.

Fleck, C. (January 2003). Cancer and snake oil. *AARP Bulletin,* 18.

FTC facts for consumers: miracle health claims: add a dose of skepticism (2003). Washington, DC.

Generics may be "equivalent," cheaper, but consumers resist (July–August 2002). *AARP Bulletin,* 13.

Goldsmith, E. B. (2015). *Social influence and sustainable consumption.* New York: Springer.

Insel, P., and W. Roth. (2002). *Core concepts in health,* 9th ed. Boston: McGraw-Hill.

Lewis, C. (July–August 2002). Botox cosmetics: a look at looking good. *FDA Consumer,* 11–13.

Makarem, S. C., M. Smith, S. Mudambi, and J. Hunt. (Fall 2014). Why people do not always follow the doctor's orders: the role of hope and perceived control. *Journal of Consumer Affairs,* 48 (3), 457–485.

McGregor, S. (2010). *Well-being, wellness and basic human needs in home economics.* McGregor Monograph Series No. 201003. http://www.consultmcgregor.com.

Meadows, M. (September–October 2002a). *FDA Consumer,* 12–14.

Meadows, M. (September–October 2002b). *FDA Consumer,* 18–23.

Mick, D., S. Pettigrew, C. Pechmann, and J. Ozanne. (2012). *Transformative consumer research for personal and collective well-being.* New York: Routledge.

Park, R. L. (2000). *Voodoo science: the road from foolishness to fraud.* Oxford: Oxford University Press.

Parker-Pope, T. (October 22, 2002). The ins and outs of getting drugs (the legal kind) from across the border. *Wall Street Journal,* p. D1.

Parker-Pope, T. (January 14, 2003). That veggie wrap you just chowed down is more fattening than a ham sandwich. *Wall Street Journal,* p. D1.

Reagan, B. (October 21, 2002). Handle with care. *Wall Street Journal,* p. D4.

The hype in "hypoallergenic." (June 2002). *Consumer Reports*, 6.

Wells, W., J. Burnett, and S. Moriarty. (2000). *Advertising: principles & practice*, 5th ed. Upper Saddle River, NJ: Prentice Hall.

Whitney, E., and S. Rolfes. (2008). *Understanding nutrition*, 11th ed. Belmont, CA: Wadsworth.

Xiao, Jing Jian (2015). *Consumer economic well-being*, New York: Springer.

Yoo, C. J., S. T. Hong, and H. E. Jung. (2006). In-depth study on women's needs for makeup and consumption behavior of cosmetics products. *Journal of Korean Academic Society of Business*, 35 (1), 21–49.

Sustainability and Safety

Go to bed smarter than when you woke up.

Charlie Munger

1. Discuss sustainability issues, product life, and disposal decisions.

2. Explain the value of warranties and guarantees.

3. Discuss examples of products that may cause injury and harm.

4. Explain what the US Consumer Product Safety Commission does.

5. Know how to minimize susceptibility to frauds.

Potential Injuries from Teacups

"The Florida Department of Agriculture and Consumer Services, the U.S. consumer Product Safety Commission, and Urban Outfitters Inc., of Philadelphia, Pennsylvania, have announced the recall of about 11,640 units. The tea cups are mislabeled as microwave safe, if microwaved, the gold paint accents on the teacups can spark, posing a fire hazard. This recall involves four styles of 'Cheeky' six-ounce ceramic teacups. The cups have floral motifs with gold painted accents. . . . The recalled teacups were manufactured in China and sold exclusively at Urban Outfitters stores nationwide and online at UrbanOutfitters. com from August 2014 through January 2015 for about $16. Consumers should immediately stop using the recalled teacups and contact Urban Outfitters for instructions on returning the product for a refund. Consumers can contact Urban Outfitters at (800) 282-2200 anytime, or online at www.urbanoutfitters.com."

Source: Florida Department of Agriculture and Consumer Services (March 25, 2015). "Consumer watch." CW 2035.

Introduction

The previous chapter focused on health and wellness issues; this one covers a myriad of topics regarding the safety of consumer products and sustainability. These are important areas to cover because many consumer complaints arise from faulty products such as fire hazards caused by imported teacups in the introductory case and repairs that don't live up to expectations. Severe injuries or death can result, so safety concerns go beyond mere inconvenience and questions about restitution. The chapter focuses on how products are used after purchase, how they perform, and how they are disposed of. Hazardous materials, such as old paint and out-of-date medicines, should be disposed of responsibly.

Disposal decisions revolve around:

- *recycling* (re-using packaging or commercial practices such as companies recycling used tires)
- *converting* (in the home, finding new uses such as using old T-shirts as dust or car rags)
- *trashing* (throwing away)
- *trading* (example, trading in an old car for a new one)
- *donating* (to causes)
- *reselling* (examples are eBay, Craigslist, garage sales).

These disposal decisions involve emotions, learned practices, finances, product symbolism, and sustainability issues. There are over 70 definitions of sustainability, but most simply said, sustainability has to do with what is good in the long run for the environment and future generations.

Sustainable behavior is a multidimensional concept that includes behaviors such as conservation of natural resources through efficient use, recycling, purchase and use of green products, and other behaviors that preserve the natural environment including air and water quality. One means of promoting these desirable behaviors is the use of social influence, that is, the influence that people have over other people. Social influence is how one person or group affects another's opinions, attitudes, emotions, or behaviors (Goldsmith, 2015, p. 3).

In this chapter, public awareness of the hazards of everyday products is also discussed, as are the functions of the main consumer safety agencies that handle complaints. Can consumers be assured of safety? Yes, to a certain extent, but there is also "may the buyer beware." Federal and state agencies have recalled many products, ranging from lawn motors to toys, because of defects or potential safety hazards. Special safety regulations are applied to products for infants and children because child safety is paramount. Manufacturers should pretest toys, and parents should read product labels to determine if their child is old enough for a certain toy. Locking up household laundry detergent and chemicals, drugs, and firearms is also an important safety measure. Further, this chapter covers travel fraud and travel safety, including where to find sources of regular alerts about places of particular concern. If planning to travel or work abroad, this section

Photo 10.1
A school nurse tests a diabetic young boy's blood sugar

Source: Getty Images: Chris Fert

should not be missed. Keeping yourself and your money safe are part of the general topic of safety.

A recurring theme throughout the chapter is the importance of information gathering. For example, consumers should read and understand warranties. You may recall from Chapter 2 that the right to safety and the right to information are two of the four basic rights in President John F. Kennedy's Consumer Bill of Rights.

Consumer Product Use and Nonuse

Before we can talk about safety and repairs, we need to explore how goods are used or not used. You read that right. A lot of things that are bought are never used or only partially used. **Disposition** (disposal) of a product can occur before, during, or after its use. It is estimated that 30 percent or more of food brought into the home is disposed of before use. Millions of pounds of packaging are thrown out every year, and efforts are being made in the industry and in home-use to reduce this waste or convert the packaging into another use.

To put this discussion into a framework, consumer research typically deals with three processes pertaining to the use of goods and services (Jacoby, Berning, & Dietvorst, 1977):

1. Decision making.
2. Usage.
3. Disposal.

We discussed decision making (prepurchase, purchase, and postpurchase) in Chapter 6. This chapter explores the last two on the list, which are the least researched. Within these categories is the rather peculiar one of items or services that are bought and never used or rarely used. In an earlier chapter we talked about how foods are bought and never used, but other items include membership in health and fitness clubs, in-home exercise equipment, sports equipment, small kitchen appliances, vitamins and supplements, crafts, sewing machines, high-tech goods, personal care items (such as hair gel, aftershave, and perfume), and clothes. What have you got sitting around your house that you rarely or never use? It is estimated that about 50 percent of prescribed medicine isn't used (Makarem, Smith, Mudambi, and Hunt, 2014).

Underutilization is a condition where consumers use a product, but only to a small fraction of the extent to which they intended to use it (Trocchia & Swinder, 2002). Anger, embarrassment, and guilt may be associated with underutilization, or the buyer may simply have lost interest in the product or service. Interests change frequently regarding sports, foods, books, workout equipment or clubs, and video games. People may throw themselves into a new hobby or life change and buy everything associated with it such as $4,000–$10,000 bikes and then change their minds. For example, an individual may try to grow orchids, put in special growing lights, and in the process spend several thousand dollars and uncountable hours of work; when all the orchids die, he or she decides there must be an easier hobby. There may be concerns about physical injury or an illness may prevent or lessen use of workout gyms or equipment. Other life changes include changes in marital status, children, educational or career goals, or geographic location (snow skis aren't much use in Hawaii).

A product may disappoint as well—perhaps it is not as much fun or it does not smell as good or taste as yummy as hoped. The product or service may not transform the user into a popular or attractive person, as had been hoped. When it comes to in-home products, there are storage and maintenance issues as well. A waffle iron, for instance, may be too much trouble to haul out and clean after use, so a consumer may decide that a frozen waffle popped in the toaster is nearly as good and a lot less trouble than whipping up waffle mix, cooking, and cleaning up afterward.

Storage can be a problem and along with it is the possibility of compulsive hoarding or packrat behavior. **Hoarding** means to gather or accumulate. It may involve saving or hiding. There are television shows and documentaries devoted to the subject of compulsive hoarding behavior and in severe cases it can lead to injuries and death (for example, fires).

> *Compulsive hoarding is a serious problem for consumers, their families, and the communities in which they live. Consumers naturally form attachments to their possessions. However, at the extreme end of the attachment spectrum, these attachments can undermine a consumer's well-being. (Roster, 2015, p. 303)*

To summarize, many products and services are purchased and then rarely or never used and disposed of or stored in basements, barns or sheds, garages, attics, closets, and spare rooms. There are various reasons for underutilization or nonuse:

- *Sustainability or environmentally-oriented behavior.* Someone may throw out, exchange, or recycle conventional products in favor of organic or CSR products (certified as **corporate social responsibility**). An example of a CSR-certified product is canned tuna (De Magistris, Del Giudice, & Verneau, 2015).

  > *Corporate social responsibility (CSR) is an important concept to signify good business behaviors. Although there are different definitions of corporate social responsibility, CSR implies particular attention to ethical, social, and environmental implications of business. Business practices of corporate social responsibility include social, environmental, and economic dimensions." (Xiao, 2015, p. 81)*

- *Impulsiveness or compulsiveness.* One respondent in a survey said, "Even though I knew that the [high-heeled] shoes would hurt my feet, I bought them anyway" (Trocchia

& Swinder, 2002, p. 191). As another example, after a cooking demonstration in a store, someone may impulsively think he or she needs a special gadget or ingredient when the one already at home would suffice. If compulsive, the individual may feel they have to have every kitchen gadget available.

- *Sale purchases.* A sale purchase might be made at a promotion such as three T-shirts for $10 when only one is needed. If the purchase was inexpensive, people may shrug their shoulders and say, "Oh well, it didn't cost much, so if I get only a couple of wearings, that is okay."

- *Function problems.* Purchased items often have maintenance difficulties or disappointing results, and the buyer may have difficulties using the product (Trocchia & Swinder, 2002). Examples are food preparation devices such as grills, juice machines, lawn mowers, cosmetic/personal care treatments, and clothes that wrinkle easily or are difficult to care for (for example, requiring washing by hand and drying flat).

- *Ill-fitting or malfunctioning products.* After an item is purchased, it either doesn't fit or doesn't work.

- *Self-consciousness.* People are not comfortable using or wearing the product after buying it. The product is not consistent with their self-image or with other people's image of them. An individual may feel like an idiot wearing the item, or a child may say that the style is too young-looking.

- *Concerns about personal injury.* The use of new power tools or recreational equipment may engender safety concerns.

- *Loss of interest or enthusiasm.* Consumers may decide they don't need the product or service; examples include language tapes, humorous items or toys, and exercise equipment.

- *Lifestyle changes.* Soon after an item is bought, the consumer's lifestyle changes and the item is no longer necessary or desired. The person no longer feels attached to the product such as a souvenir from a vacation or an earlier time in his or her life.

It is true that businesses make money from products and services that are bought and never used, but nonuse is not good for repeat business. An unhappy buyer may spread bad word-of-mouth information, which further brings down sales.

> *Consumers are involved in networks of information. Certain situations such as a purchasing situation will evoke these networks and will awake consumer sensitivity to brands they like or dislike. (Goldsmith, 2015, p. 59)*

Money-back guarantees and generous return policies can reduce the number of disgruntled customers. Because of embarrassment or loss of interest, the consumer may not pursue getting a refund or returning a product, representing a waste of resources. Businesses and government agencies that handle complaints and recalls should do all

Photo 10.2 Two consumers shop for an expensive motorbike

Source: Getty Images: Don Mason/Fuse

they can to encourage use of products and services, and if the customer is not satisfied, they should do what they can to encourage redress. Presenting realistic views of products and services in the first place would reduce the incidence of nonuse.

Underutilization also points to the fact that consumer behavior is imprecise—mistakes occur. In order to save money and heartache (guilt, anger, or whatever), consumers need to try to lessen nonuse, perhaps by knowing themselves better and by spending more time on the decision end of the consumption process. Another remedy is to take advantage of the warranties and money-back or replacement guarantees (discussed next).

Warranties and Guarantees: Perceptions and Realities

In previous chapters, we've covered the importance of price and brand name in consumer decision making, especially in determining quality. National brands are perceived by many as better than private label or store brands. As examples, consumers may think that a Band-Aid from Johnson & Johnson, Inc. may be better quality than a store brand or that a name-brand sweater is better quality than a store-brand sweater. Other indicators of quality are country of manufacture and warranties. A lot of this has to do with perception: Would you think a camera or car from Japan is better than one manufactured in Russia? Do you think Egyptian cotton is better than Malaysian cotton?

Research indicates that the longer and more inclusive the warranty, the better the quality of the product is assumed to be (Boulding & Kirmani, 1993). A product with a five-year warranty is assumed to be better than one with a three-month warranty. But what happens if the company goes out of business? Regardless of length, the warranty may be worthless. Note the word *inclusive* because besides length, consumers need to know what is covered, that is, what types of repairs, replacement parts, and product conditions are included.

In order to sell products, marketers extol the virtues of goods such as an extended warranty. They have found that the more variables or attributes presented, the greater is the perception of reduction of risk, which is referred to as **attribute-based choices**. Warranties and guarantees are very important to risk reduction. One associates them with higher-priced items, but they can apply to less expensive ones. For example, a shampoo can be guaranteed to give satisfaction, or your money is refunded in full. Some clothing stores will allow returns at any time for any reason, and others are more selective, perhaps having a three-month-from-purchase return policy or no returns on sale items.

Besides manufacturers and stores, service businesses such as dry cleaners or home inspection businesses provide warranties or guarantees (a checklist is given in Table 10.1). To complicate things, attributes are not equally weighted. Price may be by far the most important attribute in a product purchase, or it may be quick service or brand name; for example, a person may prefer a certain brand of deodorant and will not buy any other at any price. On the other hand, a product line may be eliminated as too expensive. In a competitive market, one product maker will emphasize price as a dominant evaluative criterion in its advertisement, whereas a competitor will stress other aspects such as safety or warranties. Another example of attributes is features weighting. A person may want not only a safe car with a good warranty but also a car with automatic windows and air conditioning.

In economics, rational choice theory assumes a rational decision maker has well-defined preferences. Each option or alternative in a choice set is assumed to have a value to the consumer that depends on the characteristics of that option, and consumers are assumed to have sufficient skill to determine which options best suit their needs—they will

Table 10.1 Product or Service Comparison Checklist★

Evaluative criteria	Brand A (name)	Brand B (name)
Price		
Size/dimensions		
Country of origin		
Warranty/guaranty		
Repairs/service/refunds		
Reputation of company		

★Suggested rating system: 1 equals very poor and 5 equals very good.

maximize their value, getting the most for their money and needs. As we know from earlier chapters, rationality does not always exist. Consumers are said to have **bounded rationality**, meaning a limited capacity for processing information. What does this have to do with warranties and guaranties? In a word, *everything* because unless they are lawyers, consumers cannot possibly understand every word in a lengthy tiny-print warranty or guaranty, nor are they inclined to take the time to read it. What happens is that most make a **constructive choice**, which is a timely decision based on the situation at hand.

Many businesses now guarantee customer satisfaction with services. This may include free pizza if delivery does not take place in half an hour or a free lunch if not brought to the table in 15 minutes or less. These types of guarantees ensure that service is timely and increases customer satisfaction. Regarding warranties and guarantees, customer service is paramount. Not only does the product have to be fixed, but it also has to be fixed or replaced quickly by courteous employees, whether online, over the phone, or in person. So customer–employee interaction is important not only at points of sale but also during service encounters. Consumers respond well not only to pleasant people but also to pleasant environments while they wait, which is why car dealership repair shops have comfortable waiting rooms with snacks, reading material, and chairs for customers.

The role of competition was covered in previous chapters, and one way firms compete is through guarantees. For example, the United Parcel Service (UPS) competes with FedEx Corp. and the US Postal Service. In a move to erase the service gap between UPS and FedEx Corp., UPS rolled out money-back guarantees for US residential shipments in the lower 48 states. About 20 percent of UPS shipments go to homes (Brooks, 2002). Regarding the announcement, "The consumer is the winner," said Satish Jindel, a transportation consultant at SJ Consulting Group Inc., in Pittsburgh. "Now, if they know when to expect it, it tells them when to be ready" (Brooks, 2002, p. D2).

Extended Warranties and Service Contracts

When buying a new car, appliance, or computer, you may be offered an **extended warranty** or **service contract**, which provides repair and/or maintenance for a specific time period.

CASE STUDY

Federal Trade Commission: Differences

"But there's an important difference: a warranty is included in the price of an item; a service contract costs extra. It's an add-on that might not be worth the price. Some service contracts duplicate the warranty coverage that the manufacturer provides; some cover only part of the product; and some make it nearly impossible to get repairs when you need them. Here are a few factors to consider before deciding to buy a service contract:

- Is the Product Likely to Need Repairs?
- Does the Service Contract Really Provide Extra Coverage?
- How are Claims Handled?
- Who is Responsible for the Contract?
- Is There a Better Option?"

Source: Federal Trade Commission Consumer Information (2015). Available online at consumer.ftc.gov/articles/0240-extended-warranties-and-service-contracts.

The length of warranty may differ: For a small appliance, the warranty may be for 90 days; for larger, more expensive items, the length of warranty is longer. For example, new cars come with a manufacturer's warranty, which usually offers coverage for 12,000 miles or at least one year, or whichever comes first. A service contract would then extend the warranty and pick up either after 12,000 miles or after that first year. Many consumers buy a service contract for peace of mind, and this is how the contracts are marketed. But are they necessary? Service contracts cost extra and are sold separately; they give extra protection but are rarely worth the cost.

Photo 10.3
A couple buy a car together

Source: Thinkstock: Fuse

Statistics show that costly consumer products do not break very often within the one-to three-year period covered by service contracts. True flaws show up quickly and are covered by regular product warranties that should be included in the purchase price. Service contracts often exclude problems that are most likely to happen, and in many cases the warranties cost more than a repair or replacement would cost. If the car or appliance is sold, the service contract is probably ended because service contracts are rarely transferable to the next owner.

If you have a complaint about a service contract, you should follow the usual procedure of starting with the dealer first. The Federal Trade Commission (FTC) gets many complaints about service contracts. Although the FTC cannot represent you in a dispute, it wants to know if companies are not meeting their obligations. To let the FTC know what is going on, use the complaint form available at www.ftc.gov. The FTC enters fraud-related complaints and also Internet, telemarketing, and identity theft fraud information.

Consumer Complaints

Consumer complaints about food, products, restaurants, hotels, cars, music—you name it—are spreading rapidly through the Internet. Social media and product reviews have revolutionized the ability of consumers to complain to a wide audience. So, consumers are definitely complaining more. In addition, in a busier, faster world, consumers expect better and faster service. Forrester Research, a marketing research company, found in a survey that 84 percent of people wished companies would make it easier to complain (Higgins, 2002); since then, there is no question it is easier to complain in many ways. Top complaint categories include:

- auto
- home improvement/construction
- credit/debt
- retail sales
- services
- utilities
- landlord/tenant
- home solicitations
- Internet sales
- health products/services
- fraud: bogus sweepstakes and lotteries, work-at-home schemes, grant offers.

Companies are increasingly viewing consumer complaints not only as a good source of feedback but also as an opportunity to sell more products, which is called **cross-selling**.

If the person does not like a certain product, he or she may be given a refund or a coupon to buy another brand that the company sells. For example, if Unilever, which sells everything from Hellmann's mayonnaise to Dove soap, finds out someone doesn't like a taste or a fragrance, it suggests another one of its brands rather than lose a customer (Higgins, 2002).

Companies say they receive not only complaints but also compliments on toll-free lines and through the Internet.

> *In fact, offering a compliment may be the quickest way to get what you want. John Schachter of Arlington, VA, says he has received everything from free coupons to a transistor radio in the shape of a Tropicana orange, in return for praising products to the manufacturer." (Higgins, 2002, p. D4)*

Injuries

Each year about a quarter of the population is injured in some way and one in five Americans has some form of disability. Injuries can result from a variety of sources from falls or car accidents to workplace injuries. Everyone is at risk, but injuries are most common among men, minorities, and people with low incomes due to a variety of factors, including social, environmental, and economic. Table 10.2 shows US accident or unintentional injuries causing death in a given year.

Table 10.2 Accidents or Unintentional Injuries Leading to Death in the US

All Unintentional Injury Deaths

- Number of deaths: 130,557
- Deaths per 100,000 population: 41.3
- Cause of death rank: 4

Unintentional Fall Deaths

- Number of deaths: 30,208
- Deaths per 100,000 population: 9.6

Motor Vehicle Traffic Deaths

- Number of deaths: 33,804
- Deaths per 100,000 population: 10.7

Unintentional Poisoning Deaths

- Number of deaths: 38,851
- Deaths per 100,000 population: 12.3

Source: Centers for Disease Control and Prevention (CDC) "Deaths: Final Data for 2013, tables 9, 18." Available online at cdc.gov/nchs/fastats/accidental-injury.htm.

Besides loss of life, unintentional injuries are so common that they account for more years of potential life lost (which refers to the difference between an individual's life expectancy and his or her age at death) than any other cause of death (Insel & Roth, 2002).

Intentional injuries are purposely inflicted by oneself or by another person and include homicide, suicide, and assault. **Unintentional injuries** occur when no harm is intended, such as the result of falls, fires, or motor vehicle crashes. The fifth leading cause of death as well as the leading cause of death and disability among children and young adults is unintentional injuries. To lower injuries, engineers help by designing safety belts and safety-related products such as tamper-proof containers for over-the-counter (OTC) and prescription drugs, and law enforcement helps in these same areas by enforcing regulations and laws.

What causes most injuries? The answer is a combination of human and environmental errors. Slick roads, foggy conditions, defective tires, and undertow in the ocean are examples of environmental hazards. Human error involves the following:

- fatigue, stress, and sleep deprivation
- risk taking
- bad judgment
- distractions (such as children yelling, pets jumping around, cell phones ringing)
- drugs and alcohol
- smoking in bed
- improper or nonuse of safety belts, child safety seats, and air bags (since 1998, all new cars have been equipped with dual air bags for driver and front-seat passenger)
- nonuse of helmets and other safety equipment when on motorcycles, mopeds, and bicycles
- inattention (when driving, crossing the street, exercising).

Unintentional injuries occur primarily in three areas:

1. *In the home.* Accidents in the home involve falls, fires, poisoning (carbon monoxide poisoning is the most common type of poisoning by gases), suffocation and choking, and firearm use. Over 100,000 deaths and injuries are caused by firearms each year. To protect yourself in the home from unintentional injuries, remove or fix anything that causes tripping or falling, make sure smoke alarms and fireplaces work properly, use safety equipment, remove electrical cords in pathways, and store firearms appropriately.

2. *During leisure.* Injuries occur during leisure activities such as boating, swimming, and other sports, possibly due to lack of skill or proper equipment. In-line skating

accounts for more than 250,000 injuries a year in the emergency room (injuries to head and wrist are most common); scooter injuries account for 27,000 emergency room visits a year.

3. *At work.* Nearly four million Americans suffer disabling injuries on the job each year, and many die. Possible causes include falls, exposure to toxic chemicals and radiation, burns, cuts, back sprains, loss of body parts in machinery, and electrical shocks. Back injuries are especially common. Another common injury is **carpal tunnel syndrome**, which is compression of the median nerve in the wrist, often caused by repetitive use of the hands such as in cutting or using a computer; it is characterized by numbness, tingling, and pain in the hands and fingers (Insel & Roth, 2002). This can be prevented or lessened by changes both in behavior and in workstations, by the temporary wearing of a splint to stabilize the hand and wrist, and by surgery (in extreme cases). In the workplace, the main federal agency concerned with safety is the Occupational Safety and Health Administration (OSHA), created within the Department of Labor; it was established in 1970 through the Occupational Safety and Health Act.

Product Safety

Children are often the victims of injuries from consumer products. The government and the public want to lessen the severity and reduce the incidence of accidents, so the question is how to improve product safety. The answers lie in better-designed products, better labeling, removal of hazards and hazardous products, better industry standards, more government regulation (where necessary), and increased consumer/parental awareness. Another question concerns an appropriate number of regulations or warnings. How many accidents happen from lack of common sense and preparedness? In the case of children, how many accidents occur because of parental neglect or ignorance? The government is doing what it can. According to Inez Tenenbaum, former Chairman of the Consumer Product Safety Commission (2009–2013), "Today, the CPSC is stronger, more proactive, and better at protecting the consumer especially children" (Tenenbaum, 2014, p. 648).

Some hazards are known and some are hidden. For example, individuals would not know that a wheel is going to fall off a bicycle or that a pan on a stove would explode. They would also not know that someone's brakes on a car would fail and the car would plow through the front window of a restaurant, injuring customers. On the other hand, known hazards would include driving a faulty car and living in a house with a leaky roof.

Critics of safety regulations often state:

- *People should know better.* Consumers should look out for themselves. It is true that many injuries are the result of misuse of a product, an example being putting plasticware on the stove and cooking in it. These injuries can stem from ignorance, inexperience, and behavioral and environmental errors; examples of behavioral and environmental errors would be riding in a boat or playing golf during a lightning storm and surfing during a hurricane. Product manufacturers would say that behavioral and environmental conditions are beyond their control and that they should not be held responsible. Likewise, a product made for an adult that falls into the hands of a child (such as a prescription drug container left on the sink with the cap off) is primarily the responsibility of the supervising adult.

- *Too much government costs too much money.* Government-mandated safety standards cost manufacturers millions of dollars, and those costs are passed on to consumers.

- *Too much government puts too much power in the hands of a few at the top.* Power can corrupt, so it is better to not let a few make decisions that affect so many consumers.

- *Too many regulations limit freedom.* For example, in some states motorcycle riders have to wear helmets, but in other states it is optional. Motorcycle riders argue that it is their lives that are at stake, so if they don't want to wear helmets, they should not have to. Federal, state, and local governments have passed laws and regulations regarding safety, but how much is too much? All laws and regulations must be considered from several points of view, and the individual's right to freedom is one of them.

Risks and Factors in Product Safety: Consumer Product Safety Commission

What is an acceptable amount of risk? Everyone has to answer that question for him- or herself. Is one accidental death too many, or do we just assume that a certain percentage of the public will be injured or die every year from consumer products?

To find out how many injuries and deaths occur each year from consumer products, one turns to the National Injury Information Clearinghouse, which disseminates statistics and information relating to the prevention of injuries and deaths associated with consumer products. Where does the clearinghouse get its statistics and data?

- hospital emergency rooms
- health departments (from death certificates when consumer products were involved)
- victim interviews
- newspaper accounts
- reports from medical sources (in addition to hospital emergency rooms)
- consumer complaints and inquiries sent to the CPSC.

Who uses CPSC's injury data?

- consumer groups
- manufacturers and industry associations

- media
- educators, students, researchers, and attorneys.

What can we learn from the clearinghouse statistics? Studying clearinghouse statistics reveals a myriad of problems, including young children getting into problems by using consumer products. Box 10.1 gives a list of categories of consumer product-related statistics categories.

Consumer Product Safety: Toys, Baby Equipment, Sports Equipment

As Box 10.1 indicates, a lot of consumer product safety concerns revolve around infants and children. A large category of household consumption is in the area of toys, leisure or recreation or sports equipment, and baby equipment. The prime toy market is children between the ages of 2 to 11. American children are more diverse racially and ethnically than the adult population. According to Census 2000, two in five children (39 percent) under the age of 18 are part of a minority group; toy manufacturers are responding by adding Spanish-language Barbie websites and making phones and pull toys that use English and Spanish. Video games have expanded "toy" use into the teen years, with teen boys being heavy users, although 44 percent of the video game market is geared for children ages 12 and under (Fetto, 2002). According to the London-based market research firm Mintel, sales of toys in the "play sports" category, including foam sports equipment, have grown the fastest, followed by infant/preschool toys, ride-ons like mini-jeeps, activity toys, and dolls. Sales of plush toys have declined.

CONSUMER ALERTS

The US Consumer Product Safety Commission (CPSC) and the American Academy of Pediatrics have made recommendations for safe bedding practices for infants under 12 months of age. Among these are specific cautions on the use of soft bedding in cribs. Go to the CPSC website and consult with pediatricians for the latest information on crib safety.

Box 10.1 Categories of Consumer Products and Potential Hazards Related to Infants and Children

Toys

Nursery Products

Playpens

Asbestos Fibers in Children's Crayons

Sudden Infant Death Syndrome (SIDS)

Portable Youth Bed Rails

Hazards Associated with Children Placed in Adult Beds

Child Poisonings

Carbon Monoxide (CO) Poisonings

Electrocutions

Fires

Fires Caused by Children Playing with Lighters

Laundry Products

Fireworks

Sports and Recreation

Amusement Rides

Children's Playground Equipment

Trampoline-Related Injuries (Bounce Houses)

ATV-Related Injuries and Deaths

Helmets

Pool Alarm Reliability

Shopping Cart Injuries

Source: Adapted from the US Consumer Product
Safety Commission. Available online at cpsc.gov.

Toy-Related Injuries to Children

According to the CPSC, over 200,000 toy-related injuries are treated each year in US hospital emergency rooms. Males are more likely to be injured than females. Most of the victims (98 percent) are treated and released from the hospital. The most likely area of the body to be hurt is the head and face area, followed by the shoulders and fingers. Riding toys (including non-powered scooters) cause the most injuries. The most reported toy-related deaths among children younger than 15 years of age, according to the Consumer Product Safety Commission, are from doll accessories or toy figures (choking). Burn hazards are also a concern.

CASE STUDY

Monkey Toy Recalled

"The Florida Department of Agriculture and Consumer Services, the U.S. Consumer Product Safety Commission, and Giggles International Ltd., of Hong Kong, have announced the recall of about 13,000 monkey toys. The battery compartment can reach temperatures up to 230 degrees Fahrenheit, posing a burn hazard. The recall involves Giggles International Animated Sing-Along Monkey toys. The monkey is made of brown and beige plush material and is about 9 inches tall. . . . Consumers should immediately take the animated monkey away from children, remove the batteries and return the toy to any Cracker Barrel Old Country Store or contact Giggles International for a full refund."

Source: Florida Department of Agriculture and Consumer Services (February 18, 2015). "Recall: Giggles International animated monkey toy." CW 2030.

Advertising and Children's Products

Advertising plays a vital role in children's safety. Box 10.2 shows messages or images that should not occur in advertising because of potential harm to children. As mentioned in previous chapters, the FTC is the main regulator of advertising, and it works for the consumer to prevent fraudulent, deceptive, and unfair business practices in the marketplace and to provide information to help consumers spot, stop, and avoid them.

Box 10.2 Inappropriate Messages and Images in Advertising for Children

1. Displaying products children should not use. These products include alcohol, cigarettes, and drugs.

2. Showing adults and children using products in a way they shouldn't, which may be misinterpreted. For example, a "miniaturized" adult could be pictured in a toilet, refrigerator, washing machine, or dishwasher or a child might be seen alone in a swimming pool. Small children may imitate these behaviors.

3. Having young children play with toys and sporting equipment or drive ATVs that are only appropriate for teenagers and adults.

4. Showing children not being accepted by their peers if they do not use or own a product. Messages implying increased popularity are inappropriate. Showing children having fun with a product is okay, but showing mockery, bullying, or loneliness of nonusers or nonowners of a particular brand of toy, shoes, or clothing is not.

5. Picturing children eating less-than-healthy foods. Food advertising directed at children should show foods in the context of a balanced meal. If the food is a snack, it should be clear that it is a snack and not a meal; sugared and fast-food products are especially controversial. Food advertising on Saturday mornings has increased substantially over the last decade.

6. Showing items that do not perform as expected when a child uses them. An example would be an ad showing a boomerang that is thrown by an expert; the same boomerang would not work as well when a seven-year-old throws it.

Note: Advertisements during children's program hours such as Saturday morning and after school are heavily monitored, but increasingly children watch prime-time television (7:30–11:00 P.M.), so this places an additional responsibility on advertisers, marketers, and parents.

The regulation of advertising and marketing activities directed at children focuses primarily on the impact messages may have on children's health and safety and also on their values. In other words, physical harm is important, but so is personal and social development. Advertising in a sense is an educator and part of the child's socialization process since children between 2 and 11 years old spend more than 25 hours per week watching television and are exposed to almost 25,000 commercials per year (Weisskoff, 1985). As discussed earlier in the book, television is primarily a one-way process: The viewer sits and watches. Games and websites provide the opportunity for two-way interaction, so children are not only being exposed to advertising but may also be providing information that marketers can use. Parental guidance is suggested.

Vehicle Safety and Repair

The go-to government agency in the US regarding vehicle safety and recalls is the National Highway Traffic Safety Administration (NHTSA). The kinds of investigations, recalls, and complaints they handle have to do with vehicles, child restraints, tires, and equipment. They keep government statistics, including 11 children dying from heat strokes in cars in the first half of 2015. They say all these tragedies were 100 percent avoidable. Sometimes parents and caregivers worry about potential injuries to children that are very unlikely to occur and ignore the more likely danger of heat stroke in hot weather, for example. There is national alarm about this issue and substantial publicity about public action and police action in the case of a child locked or left in a car in unsafe conditions.

In 2015, the NHTSA reported that Fiat Chrysler must pay a record $105-million penalty because of car safety issues. The automaker admitted failures, agreed to federal oversight, paid fines, and agreed to some buy backs.

Regarding repair history, as a consumer you can enter a Vehicle Identification Number (VIN) to quickly learn if a specific vehicle has not been repaired as part of a safety recall

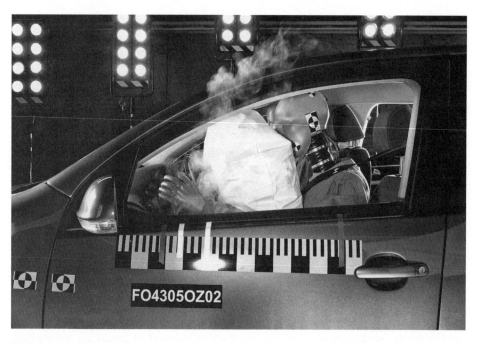

Photo 10.4 Air bag inflation. An air bag inflates in front of a dummy in the driver side of the car upon impact during a crash test

Source: Getty Images: fStop Images – Caspar Benson

in the last 15 years. The mission of the NHTSA is to save lives, prevent injuries, and reduce traffic-related health care and other economic costs by facilitating the development, deployment, and evaluation of safety products and systems. Among other things, this involves research into the science of crash avoidance to enable the development of safety-enhancing products. The agency works with the automobile industry and other technology companies. The goal of the agency is to demonstrate improved capability of collision avoidance systems, to ensure that systems are both effective and usable for consumers, and to provide a basis for understanding the benefits (for example, collisions, injuries, and fatalities that will be avoided).

In an earlier chapter, we covered automobile safety in the discussion of Ralph Nader and his book *Unsafe at Any Speed*, which condemned the auto industry's record on safety and brought about much-needed vehicle safety legislation. Since then, laws have been passed requiring the wearing of seat belts and the installation of airbags.

Recalls are expensive to a company, but not as expensive as bad publicity, loss of sales, lawsuits, and injuries or loss of human life. Likewise, government is charged to protect the welfare and lives of citizens. State governments register auto repair companies and resolve customer complaints. Repair shops have to follow certain rules, so if they are in trouble, they have to get back into compliance and then renew their licenses to operate. There are regulated and nonregulated complaints: Regulated complaints fall under the state's statutory authority to enforce, such as a repair shop's failure to fill out forms or other problems that are specifically listed in statutes; nonregulated complaints may cover car accessories, towing charges, and other things that may not fall under statutes. Across the country, millions of dollars are refunded to consumers each year through consumer divisions in state government. These divisions send in undercover investigators who take in a car that has been pre-checked for problems and then see if the repair shops find the correct problem and fix it at a reasonable price. If the shops add on extra charges or even go so far as to damage the car further and ask for more repair money, then they are in trouble.

How can you protect yourself from auto repair fraud? As mentioned earlier, enter the VIN to learn if a specific vehicle has not been repaired as part of a safety recall. Another way is to go to companies or car dealerships that have existed for a long time and have a reputation for good service and quality work (see Box 10.3). Complaint records can be checked through Better Business Bureaus (BBBs) and motor vehicle divisions in states, most likely under the main consumer protection agency.

One of the worst consumer frauds in the auto repair market is the black market in used auto parts. In this scam, auto parts are switched around, with used ones often being sold to the consumer as new auto parts. A particularly bad practice is the black market on

---

Box 10.3 Vehicle Repairs: Steps to Follow

1. Choose a reliable repair shop based on recommendations from family and friends. If you are unsure, check out the repair shop's complaint record with a BBB or local or state consumer protection agency.

2. Describe the symptoms of the car (what it is doing) when you take it in.

3. Get more than one estimate in writing if repairs are costly.

4. Do not allow work to begin until you authorize it and have an estimate.

5. Don't sign a blank repair order, and understand anything you sign.

6. Check your warranty—should the repairs be covered?

7. Pay by credit card if the bill is over $50 because if there is a defect or problem with the repair, payment to the credit card company can be withheld until improvements are made.

8. Keep copies of all paperwork.

9. Report complaints to your local or state consumer protection office.

Source: These steps have been adapted and modified from *The Consumer Action Handbook,* US General Services Administration, GSA Office of Communications, and Federal Consumer Information Center, 1800 F. Street, NW, Washington, DC 20405.

air bags, where used or damaged air bags are sold as new. Law officers in Florida made an arrest when a repair shop was putting cardboard in the slot for the air bag; if there was an accident, cardboard would fly out of the air bag compartment instead of an air bag. Auto safety and repair are not just about paying less or being cheated—they are about saving lives. Fly-by-night repair shops exist; in other words, someone does car repairs and also does other types of repairs, going from one business to another. This is a good example of getting what you pay for—someone without an established business is someone to avoid or at least to check out thoroughly.

Vehicle Warranties

Standard car warranties are for three years or 36,000 miles (whichever happens first) and cover manufacturer defects (labor and parts may be extra). To increase customer satisfaction and to encourage car sales, manufacturers are lengthening warranties and wrapping in new services, such as free car washes with each checkup and free donuts and cappuccinos in the service area waiting room. As may be expected, luxury car dealers offer more services than low-end dealers, including generous free loaner car policies, free wiper blade replacement, and 24-hour roadside service. Warranties that used to be limited to three years now go as high as five years for a Ford Focus and ten years for a Hyundai; Daimler-Chrysler introduced seven-year, 70,000-mile power-train warranties. Lengthy contracts are a way to distinguish brands. Whether they are a good idea or not depends on the features (likelihood that they will be needed) and the added price. Most are not transferable to a second buyer, so the original purchaser should decide whether or not to keep the car past five or ten years before buying an extended warranty. From the manufacturer's point of view, extended warranties can be moneymakers or they can be costly.

Consumers are more aware than ever before about the necessity for repairs because of the computer systems on dashboards of vehicles. Sometimes these systems malfunction, and the repair is not needed. This type of warning error wastes the consumer's and the dealer's time. However, usually these systems of blinking lights and warning signals are accurate and let the customer know when repairs are needed, so they are useful safety features. Unquestionably the warning systems have saved lives as well as time and money. Volvos are particularly well known for safety features.

For warranties to remain in effect, it may be in the contract that you must follow all the manufacturer's recommendations for routine maintenance, such as changing the oil and spark plugs and bringing the car in for routine maintenance checks. Keep records and receipts to prove this, although in most cases dealership service offices will keep records of work done on your car as well. There may be clauses in the contracts that say that taking your car to repair shops other than the dealership will not count.

According to a newspaper article, Alan Entin (a clinical psychologist in Richard, Virginia) says, "People who make heavy warranty demands may be seeking parental attention from their mechanics. It's 'Take care of me. You're bigger, you're stronger, you can make all things right in the world if you fix my car,' he says. The warranty represents approval or fixing from their daddy" (Spencer, 2002, p. D2). Entin's interpretation may seem reasonable or extreme depending on your point of view, but nevertheless the trend is toward more lengthy warranties. Box 10.4 explains how to get the most out of any car warranty.

Implied warranties are unspoken and unwritten and are based on the principle that the seller stands behind the product. Sold "as is" means there is no warranty—you buy the car and must pay for all repairs even if the car breaks down on the street outside the dealership lot. Some states prohibit "as is" sales; other states have lemon laws under which a consumer can receive a refund or replacement.

Box 10.4 Vehicle Warranties: How to Get the Most from Them

First:

- Keep up with the recommended maintenance schedule, especially oil changes.
- Fill out all the necessary paperwork, including service logs; save receipts.

When a repair is needed:

- Find out if other drivers have similar problems by make of car. Visit the National Highway Traffic Safety Administration (NHTSA) website for posted defect bulletins.
- If the dealer will not fix the problem when it is under warranty (to your satisfaction), appeal to the manufacturer by contacting the manufacturer's regional or national office. Ask for the consumer affairs representative or go to the company website for this information.
- If still unsuccessful, consider contacting other organizations (including www. autosafety.org) for legal advice.

After warranties expire:

- Ask the dealer if policy adjustments/extensions are possible. A free fix is possible if the manufacturer has told dealers to authorize repairs.
- If the warranty has recently expired and the service log shows that the repair problem started before the warranty ran out, then there is a possibility of a free or lower-cost repair.

Basic advice: Car dealers want return customers, so most will try to make the needed repairs in a timely fashion.

Buying a used car "as is" is risky business.

The Built Environment and Remodeling

The built environment continually changes through remodeling, which is a substantial consumer investment in time, energy, and money.

> *The built environment is not a static one or one that becomes without a great dedication of both physical and metaphysical resources. A building represents the needs of people, their vision, financial means, technical skills, permissibility, willingness, and the ability to integrate those resources and means into a physical environment. The process of a building becoming is one of alternation and influence of all these resources with the intent to provide more than existed before. (D. Goldsmith, contributing author, in* Social Influence and Sustainable Consumption, *2015, p. 161)*

Remodeling can range in price from a $25 can of paint to a $1,000,000 addition. A wide range of minor repairs or upgrades cost under $5,000, and the do-it-yourself market is huge.

With repairs and upgrades also comes the potential for fraud or at least disappointment with the quality of end results. An area of consumer complaints is home repair and renovations and related items, such as pool construction and anything else having to do with yards, garages, and outbuildings. Small claims courts are filled with these types of complaints, which pit the consumer against the contractor. Since in-ground swimming pools and kitchen remodeling can cost over $30,000, cases often go to higher courts. Similar to the advice for car repair, one should look for established businesses with good

Photo 10.5
House construction is expensive

Source: Thinkstock: blanscape

reputations, and the homeowner should be realistic in terms of the amount of time and inconvenience substantial renovations will cause; contractors should be appropriately licensed. See Box 10.5 for more steps to follow in home improvements.

Certain behaviors should draw your attention. Avoid contractors who come door to door, especially those in unmarked vans with out-of-state license plates—busy legitimate contractors wait for you to call them. Very low bids should also be a warning sign, as are exceptionally long guarantees. If you feel any kind of pressure to hurry and pay up front, then that is another warning sign. If you are considering having a home painted, for example, get two or three bids from local services and check references. Not only the price but the availability and quality of materials and workmanship should be compared. According to Beck (2002), to evaluate workmanship, ask previous customers about these four critical measures of the contractor's past work:

- on budget
- on time
- agreeableness (worked with homeowner)
- capability of finishing the job to the homeowner's standards.

In regard to evaluating sustainable designs, a resource is the National Institute of Building Sciences (Goldsmith, 2015). They point out that the six fundamental principles of sustainable building design are:

- optimize site potential
- optimize energy use
- protect and conserve water
- optimize building space and material use
- enhance indoor environmental quality
- optimize operational and maintenance practices.

CRITICAL THINKING

Remodeling and Sustainability

Should companies (such as appliance manufacturers) and governments (local, state, federal) offer discounts, rebates, or cost incentives for sustainable design such as the use of energy or water saving products or services? If so, how much would be an incentive for you if you were remodeling? Do you know of any discounts, rebates, or cost incentives in your community regarding the built environment?

> ## Box 10.5 Home Improvements: Steps to Follow
>
> - Choose a reliable contractor or company based on recommendations from family and friends.
> - Check your BBB or local or state consumer agency for information on contractors' licensing or registration requirements and complaint records (license requirements vary by state).
> - Get at least three written estimates, and remember that the lowest one may not be the best.
> - Get references and talk with people who have had work done by the contractor.
> - Contact your local building inspection department to check for permit and inspection requirements.
> - Get a complete written contract detailing work to be done, quality of materials, timetables, warranties, subcontractors' names, and total price of the job and payment schedules.
> - Do not pay completely up front, and try to limit your down payment. Don't make a final payment until you are satisfied.
> - Remember that you have cancellation rights (usually three business days) in home improvement contracts, meaning you can get out of the contract without penalty.
> - Pay by credit card because under most laws (in most cases) you have the right to refuse to pay the credit card company until any defects or problems are corrected.
>
> Source: These steps have been adapted and modified from *The Consumer Action Handbook,* US General Services Administration, GSA Office of Communications, Federal Consumer Information Center, 1800 F. Street, NW, Washington, DC 20405.

Home Improvement Professionals

Whom do you hire? Home improvement professionals vary by complexity of the project:

- *General contractors.* Those who manage all aspects of a project, including hiring and supervising subcontractors, are called general contractors.
- *Subcontractors or specialty contractors.* A subcontractor would install a particular product, such as staircases, cabinets, or bathroom plumbing fixtures.
- *Architects.* An architect designs homes, buildings, additions, and major renovations, especially those having to do with structural changes. A related specialty area is landscape architecture.

- *Designers.* People who have expertise in design and layout as well as space planning are called designers. For example, they may specialize in kitchens and baths, using contemporary or traditional designs, or they may do it all. Designers may work independently or with a firm, they may charge by the hour or by the project, or they may work for free if you purchase items from the company they work for.
- *Design/builder contractors.* A design/builder contractor oversees projects from start to finish. Some firms have architects on staff; others use certified designers.

Contracts are well advised and can range from a letter of agreement for a modest job to a full-blown contract. In each case, the who, what, where, and when as well as the cost of the project should be spelled out. The agreement should be clear, concise, and complete, including the contractor's or designer's name, address, phone, and license number. Keep all paperwork in one place, and at the completion of the project, the homeowner and the home improvement professional should do a walk-through, checking that everything was done to expectation and as agreed upon.

Where to Complain and Where to Find Help

First, try to resolve differences with the home improvement professional; if you are unsuccessful, then follow the other steps listed in the complaint section earlier in the book. Besides the usual sources of help, there are state and local builders' associations. The federal agency having the most to do with housing is the Department of Housing and Urban Development. The industry self-monitors to some extent. The National Association of Home Builders and any state associations would be the main groups interested in maintaining quality and good relations with the public. The FTC also investigates home improvement scams that are considered to be fraudulent, deceptive, or unfair business practices and would especially check false or misleading advertising.

If a home has construction defects, there are moves afoot called **right-to-cure laws** (laws stating that homeowners can allow a builder to correct problems before they take legal action) that have passed in California, Washington, Arizona, and Nevada and that are being considered in other states. Since this is a rapidly changing area, check the laws in your state before buying a home or hiring a builder for major home improvements.

Are home improvements good investments? It depends on several factors. If you rent out a house, then the monthly check from the renter can be considered a dividend. If you live in the house yourself, then it can be considered "imputed rent," which means you get to live in the house rent-free. A capital gain from housing on a national average is modest. The bottom line is that usually home prices do not outpace inflation once maintenance and remodeling costs are figured in, unless a person lives in a high-growth area. Another way people make money on houses is to buy the worst house on the block

Historically, kitchen and bathroom remodeling provide the greatest return at resale time.

and bring it up to comparable houses on the same street. A mistake (from a financial point of view) would be to upgrade the house so much that it is far grander than all its neighbors because usually this type of investment will not be regained at resale.

Another way to look at the value of home improvements from a consumer point of view is that the consumer will save money by adding on to a cheaper house rather than moving up to a much more expensive and bigger house. Staying in an existing neighborhood (if it is a good one) is usually cheaper than incurring the costs involved in buying and selling houses. Home improvements should not be made with an eye solely on resale unless the house is going on the market within a year because home improvements age (just like any other consumer product or service) and become worthless as time goes on. *Remodeling* magazine says that the most likely recoup on money spent on home improvements is 70 percent to 80 percent, assuming the house is sold within one year of making improvements. Kitchen and bath remodeling historically provide the best return at resell; for example, according to *Remodeling* magazine, you can get back 80 percent to 87 percent of what you spend on a kitchen upgrade. Perhaps how quickly remodeling ages is discouraging, but the biggest return on home ownership is the dividend discussed earlier, whether collected in rent or in the ability to live rent-free. Unless a homeowner is planning to sell soon, any remodeling should start with his or her needs first. A budget or spending plan may be set up to take care of short- and long-term goals. If you are doing it yourself, work safe and smart. Use safety goggles, and protect yourself from splashes, spills, falls, scrapes, dropped tools, and flying debris. Wear sturdy shoes (not sandals or slippers); add a dust mask (if sanding), work gloves, long-sleeved shirts, and so forth—in short, do what the professionals do.

Federal Aviation Administration

How safe are you when you fly? The Federal Aviation Administration (FAA), part of the Department of Transportation (DOT), is in charge of air safety for the general public and the aviation community, and it investigates unsafe aviation practices. According to the FAA home page, the DOT oversees consumer issues such as denied boarding, baggage, overbooking, and ticketing, as well as statistics on on-time performance, while the FAA is in charge of civil aviation safety, including developing safety regulations, certifying pilots, and compiling airport flight delay information. The Transportation Security Administration (TSA) is responsible for all modes of transportation. On the FAA website, there is a list of consumer rights and airline consumer obligations, including guides for traveling smart.

Travel

Numerous travel magazines and company and consolidators' websites exist to help cost-conscious consumers compare options. Travel bargaining is sometimes confusing and time consuming. US consumers were formerly used to a **one-price system** in which a hotel room or air flight was a predictable set price or within a slight range. Airlines differ on whether they charge for checked luggage or not. In summary, there are a lot more variables and consumer choice.

Another issue in the travel industry is the extensive amount of fraud or deception that exists—each year, travel moves up higher on the list of consumer complaints. The steps to follow to avoid being ripped off are similar to those for auto repairs and home improvements. When going out of the country especially, start with reputable, established travel agencies or tour companies. Make sure that you understand the terms of the contract, and remember that brochures are mostly marketing hype. Be wary of very low fares, sweepstakes wins, and off-season bargains (they may not be bargains if you have to endure hurricanes and closed museums). For example, one woman booked an August museum tour of Paris; on arrival, she found out that nearly every August the museum workers go on strike and the museums are closed. Watch out for paying in advance; if the trip is a long time away, you may want travel insurance. In some states, some travel agencies and tour operators have to be registered and insured, but in others there is less regulation. Contact the attorney general in your state or the one where the company is located to see if any complaints have been lodged. Foreign travel is especially susceptible to fraud and problems; again, the main protection is to deal with reputable companies.

Regarding travel safety, the governments of Australia, Japan, Denmark, Canada, Great Britain, and the United States regularly issue travel warnings. These are handy because they provide information pertaining to traveler safety. As a potential traveler to a certain country, it is difficult to tell from the news on television and in newspapers just how unsettled the country or region is or how much an infectious disease has spread, so travel warnings issued by governments are useful.

CONSUMER ALERTS

College students are especially susceptible to travel fraud. Beware of ads in student newspapers and flyers posted on campus for extremely inexpensive trips at spring break and holiday times such as ski trips. Students have been stranded in Mexico and the Caribbean without hotels to stay in or have been sent to extremely low-quality hotels. In Europe, students are approached at railway stations and sometimes led to shoddy hotels or, worse, mugged. Pickpocketing is much more common in Europe and other parts of the world than in the United States and Canada; there are fraudulent on-the-street ticket sales to Broadway and London plays. Group travel is usually safer than singles traveling alone, and groups can usually negotiate better prices. A tour guide or faculty member with a student trip can provide additional guidance and protection.

CONSUMER ALERTS

Be especially wary of a phone call, letter, text message, or email telling you that you have won a free or incredibly inexpensive trip. It is probably a trap. When you respond, the salesperson will want your credit card number as a way of confirming, but he or she could use this to build up charges for something you do not want. A typical scam is when your first night is free but subsequent nights are overpriced. Some offers do not include hotel taxes or service fees, transportation, or even basics like air conditioning and working televisions. One family with young children found themselves in Nassau in a very seedy, bug-ridden hotel; they had to pay to get a decent room in another hotel, and their "free" trip was ruined. Their return flight didn't leave for several days, so they were stuck. They had been had and they knew it. Protect yourself by being wary of great deals, do not be pressured into buying, ask detailed questions, get all information in writing before buying, don't buy part of the package, don't give credit card numbers over the phone, and don't send money by messenger or overnight mail. The best protection is to make travel plans on your own. Beware of all unsolicited offers.

Unordered Merchandise

The FTC has ruled on merchandise sent through the mail directly to the consumer who did not order the merchandise. Only two kinds of merchandise may be sent legally in this way (without the consumer's consent):

1. Free samples that are clearly marked as such (besides arriving in the mail, these may also be attached to newspapers).
2. Merchandise (such as address labels) from charitable organizations.

If you receive anything that does not fit these two categories, be wary—especially of opening unexpected packages, unlabeled packages, and packages with no return address or an unknown return address—but you have the right to keep whatever is in the package if it is clearly addressed to you, the occupant, and you should not pay anything. You can also simply return the package to the post office.

Summary

Sustainable consumption in terms of what lasts and consumer safety are central themes in this chapter. Good buying and disposal decisions and ownership tactics were covered. Even following all the tips and rules, consumers sometimes make mistakes and seek remedies or solutions. Sometimes bad purchases are buried in the back of closets or in the corner of basements or garages, only to be found when moving. Compulsive hoarding can be an issue for individuals, families, and communities (a fire hazard, for example).

Disposition (disposal) of a product can occur at any time, even before use. Warranties are included in the price of the product, while service contracts cost extra and are sold separately. Care should be taken before signing a service contract; often consumers pay for more protection than they need.

Home improvement scams are rampant. Investigating the credentials and past work of designers, architects, contractors and subcontractors, and other home improvement professionals can go a long way in reducing potential problems. Letters of agreement or contracts up front are imperative.

The travel market has its own set of scams, and travelers should be aware of dangerous areas prone to terrorist attacks and epidemics. There are many ways to reduce risks, the foremost including being informed before traveling, keeping aware of news and world events while traveling, changing itineraries when necessary, and using common sense. The FAA is in charge of airlines and airspace safety.

The safety of consumer products especially those designed for infants and children is very serious business and much of it falls under the purview of the Consumer Product Safety Commission. Most infant equipment injuries are caused by infant carriers and car seats. Riding toys, including unpowered scooters, are associated with more injuries than any other toy category for older children.

Americans are used to a one-price system for most things, meaning the sticker price is what they expect to pay at a grocery or discount store. However, bargaining and sliding price systems (price variation) are on the rise for certain categories like airplane tickets, car rentals, and hotel rooms. Careful shoppers also look for warranties, read labels, pay cash when feasible to save credit card fees, keep records and receipts, and file complaints or send letters or online complaints when necessary. The steps in the buying process are to find out all you can before buying, make sure the product or service, such as home remodeling, is truly needed, and then find the best reliable supplier at the best price.

KEY POINTS

1. Consumers strive to be more sustainable in their behavior. Even so, they underutilize products for a variety of reasons from impulse buying to changes in lifestyle and interests. The use of products influences the need for safety and repairs.

2. Warranties are useful, but in most cases service contracts are unnecessary. The Federal Trade Commission keeps a database of fraud-related complaints and enters them into the Consumer Sentinel, a secure online database available to law enforcement agencies.

3. The Consumer Product Safety Commission assembles consumer product-related statistics for child-related products and for other products such as fireworks, helmets,

and candles. They examine imported goods at ports. They are proactive at protecting consumers, especially infants and young children.

4. The Federal Trade Commission regulates advertising and especially monitors advertising aimed at children.

5. Travel prices are increasingly negotiable. More than one price exists for the same flight or the same hotel, and discount and frequent user programs are increasing.

6. Travel fraud, especially at holiday time and during spring break, is aimed at college students.

7. Before traveling abroad, government websites should be checked to find out if there are particular concerns or warnings.

8. Home improvement frauds are rampant. Right-to-cure laws set up a procedure for homeowners to give builders a chance to repair their homes before they file a lawsuit. Builder associations support these laws. The National Institute of Building Sciences is a resource for sustainable building design.

KEY TERMS

attribute-based choices	cross-selling	right-to-cure laws
bounded rationality	disposition	service contract
carpal tunnel syndrome	extended warranty	sustainable behavior
constructive choice	hoarding	underutilization
corporate social responsibility (CSR)	intentional injuries	unintentional injuries
	one-price system	

DISCUSSION QUESTIONS

1. What are the usual ways that consumers dispose of products? What is an example of a product that you have bought and rarely or never used? Describe the reasons why you underutilized the product.

2. Have you or a family member ever experienced car recalls? What happened as a result? What was the process and cost from knowing of the problem to the final repair?

3. Why is it said that information is the smart traveler's secret weapon? For safety purposes, what are some information sources that a traveler could use before and during travel?

REFERENCES

Beck, E. (2002). Get with the remodeling boom. *Home improvement: a great investment*. Available online at Lowes.com/investment.

Boulding, W., and A. Kirmani. (June 1993). A consumer-side experimental examination of signaling theory. *Journal of Consumer Research*, 11–23.

Brooks, R. (August 1, 2002). UPS guarantees home deliveries on time, following FedEx's lead. *Wall Street Journal*, p. D2.

De Magistris, T., T. Del Giudice, and F. Verneau. (Summer 2015). The effect of information on willingness to pay for canned tuna fish with different corporate social responsibility (CSR) certification: a pilot study. *The Journal of Consumer Affairs*, 49 (2), 457–471.

Federal Trade Commission Consumer Information (2015). Extended warranties and service contracts. Available online at consumer.ftc.gov/articles/0240-extended-warranties-and-service-contracts.

Fetto, J. (October 2002). Babes in toyland. *American Demographics*, 14.

Florida Department of Agriculture and Consumer Services (February 18, 2015). Recall: Giggles International animated monkey toy. CW 2030.

Florida Department of Agriculture and Consumer Services (March 25, 2015). Consumer watch. CW 2035.

Goldsmith, E. (2015). *Social influence and sustainable consumption*. New York: Springer.

Higgins, M. (August 28, 2002). "My cookies are crumbled": The art of consumer griping. *Wall Street Journal*, pp. D1 and D4.

Insel, P., and W. Roth. (2002). *Core concepts in health*, 9th ed. Boston: McGraw-Hill.

Jacoby, J., C. K. Berning, and T. G. Dietvorst. (1977). What about disposition? *Journal of Marketing*, 41, 22–28.

Makarem, S. C., M. F. Smith, S. Mudambi, and J. Hunt. (Fall 2014). Why people do not always follow the doctor's orders: the role of hope and perceived control. *The Journal of Consumer Affairs*, 48 (3), 457–485.

Roster, C. (Summer 2015). "Help, I have too much stuff!": extreme possession attachment and professional organizers. *The Journal of Consumer Affairs*, 303–327.

Spencer, J. (November 12, 2002). The best care deal around: never paying for repairs. *Wall Street Journal*, p. D1.

Tenenbaum, I. (Fall 2014). The US Consumer Product Safety Commission: a global leader in consumer product safety. *The Journal of Consumer Affairs*, 48 (3), 648–652.

Trocchia, P., and J. Swinder. (2002). An investigation of product purchase and subsequent non-consumption. *Journal of Consumer Marketing*, 19 (3), 188–204.

Weisskoff, R. (March 1985). Current trends in children's advertising. *Journal of Advertising Research*, 12–14.

Xiao, J. (2015). *Consumer economic wellbeing*. New York: Springer.

Chapter **11**

The Internet, Technology, and Identity Theft

Optimism is the faith that leads to achievement. Nothing can be done without hope and confidence.

Helen Keller

It was after midnight, and I was facing a ticking-clock real estate transaction. All I had to do was print 15 pages of a black-and-white contract, sign it and fax it back. Only halfway through, my printer ran out of ink—magenta ink! Thus began a chain reaction culminating in my nearly throwing the printer out the window. I ended up at Kinko's. We all have a printer story. They run out of ink at the worst possible time, or worse, nag us about running low on ink when there's plenty left. So how much would you pay for a printer that doesn't run out. Epson, the maker of my nightmare printer, has finally put an end to the horror of ink cartridges, at least for people willing to throw cash at the problem up front. The five new Eco-Tank series printers look like normal models, only they have containers on their sides that hold gobs and gobs of ink.

Wilson Rothman (August 5, 2015). The end of ink cartridges for printers, at last. Wall Street Journal, p. D1.

1. Discuss the role of the Internet, technology, and technical disruption on consumption patterns.

2. Explain the environmental impact of the Internet.

3. Define identity theft, biometrics, and privacy protection.

4. Describe how to do self-background checks.

5. Discuss the federal agencies involved in resolving identity theft.

6. List deceptions occurring online in regard to charitable giving.

Introduction

The last chapter dealt with sustainability, safety, and protection issues. This chapter continues along that same vein but emphasizes the growing consumer and privacy problems associated with new technologies (such as automated data collection) and the broad reach of the Internet. It also explores the new ways of handling security, such as verifying identities through biometrics. **Biometrics** refers to using people's unique physical traits (such as fingerprints) to verify identity. As examples, cellphones voice activated and laptops coming equipped with fingerprint readers so passwords aren't needed. In the future, biometrics will be used more for identification purposes.

This chapter also explores **technical disruption**, when something so new comes along it disrupts existing patterns of behavior and, in our case, consumer behavior. An example is when Uber was started by Garrett Camp and Travis Kalanick in 2009 and within a few years it was worth billions and rocked the taxi industry. Uber is an example of consumers in control, embracing change. Other examples are consumers wanting self-driving cars, ways to do medical monitoring without going to their doctor's office, and more home delivery of groceries and electronics from local stores and destination sites like Amazon. They want more say about products and services. They want services to be more efficient. They want more input about what is available on the Internet and want to be assured of safety. They are using the Internet more and more to perform information searches as well as to make purchases, to meet others, and to put their own messages and products online. A student told the author, "I go online before I shop to read what other people are buying and to see what is out there. Then I go to the mall."

Consumers want to be more directly involved and to be heard; they also want to control more of what they see and how they react. Part of this stems from the interactivity that the Internet (as a pull medium) provides, compared with the push medium of television and radio. Television is more passive, requiring little of the viewer but to watch and listen—think of local car salesmen screaming at you in television commercials. The Internet requires action. Knowing this, several television shows have Internet sites so that after a show is over, the viewer is directed to more information and conversation at the site. Thus, the shows are keeping the viewer more involved for a longer period of time and providing interactivity, such as the ability to vote on issues or download recipes or buy products.

As we all know, the Internet has opened up consumer choice and worldwide communication. These are great developments. Few among us can live without email and/or text messaging, or information searches via search engines such as Google or Yahoo. According to Harris Interactive, about 80 percent of Internet traffic begins with a search engine (Klaassen, 2006). Increasingly, students are using Google Scholar for research searches.

Although there are many positives, the darker side of the marketplace looms in the ease with which identity theft can take place and the deceptive practices and sales pitches aimed at children and gullible adults. It is more difficult than ever to be a careful consumer and to maintain privacy.

CASE STUDY

Case Study: Taxes and Identity Theft

"We live in an age of cyber-insecurity but I recently got a troubling reminder of the 'old-fashioned' risk of identity theft when I received the following email from my accountant: 'I am GREATLY concerned, your tax package arrived this morning and the envelope was completely opened when delivered to our office by the mailman. There were only 16 pages in the envelope and no W-2 or any other documents.' Panic was my initial reaction to knowing my and my wife's W-2s along with other sensitive and highly personal information, were floating around unchecked."

Source: Aaron Task (March 30, 2015). "Tax fraud and identity theft: how to protect yourself." *Yahoo Finance*. Available online at http://finance.yahoo.com/news/what-to-do-if-your-identity-has-been-stolen-170112261.html. Aaron Task is editor-at-large of *Yahoo Finance*.

Many of the surface mail and online mail problems stem from stealing, auction fraud, general merchandise fraud, and a wide range of email scams. The growth of the Internet has resulted in a need for new laws and governmental scrutiny. Another issue is the **digital divide**, which refers to how the Internet is not accessible equally by all; not everyone has the benefit of this new technology. It is another case of the haves and the have-nots.

Identity theft refers to someone using your name or personal information, such as your Social Security number, driver's license number, student identification number, credit card number or other account number, telephone number, or email or street address, without your permission. Identity theft involves more than a loss of immediate cash—it can destroy a person's credit score or financial or personal reputation, which may take months or years to reestablish. Steps to follow to prevent identity theft will be covered in this chapter, along with suggestions about what to do if it happens to you.

Media reports of stolen veterans' records, bank account numbers, college student records, and employee records are rampant. These may be stolen from computers by hackers. A **hacker** is a person who breaks into a computer—in-person or remotely. Break-ins can happen to computers in your home, workplace, or businesses you patronize. In recent years there have been massive break-ins in government files and in stores such as Target. Besides stealing files, hackers can corrupt files through the use of computer viruses and can use password detection software to steal people's identities. Hackers generally steal passwords first and then break into computers to obtain personal information. So identity theft can happen to individual consumers or to hundreds of thousands of consumers through mistakes, mishaps, and fraudulent behavior.

Before addressing the safety issues, first we will look at how consumers are using the Internet: Who buys what, when, and where online? We'll also discuss trust issues related to buying online and the use of online personal shoppers. Then we will delve into the subject of biometrics as it relates to security.

Areas ripe with trust issues are charitable giving and political campaign donations. How do you separate legitimate charities from the quasi-legitimate or fraudulent charities? Although giving to charities can be done in person, over the phone, or through the mail, more and more charities are using the Internet as their primary form of solicitation, so

The US Federal Trade Commission reports that in recent years, identity theft has been at the top of consumer complaints.

Photo 11.1
Online shopping is the fastest-growing category of consumer buying

Source: Thinkstock: Tetsuo Morita

charities are included at the end of this chapter. Online donating was heavily used in recent presidential campaigns.

The Internet: Consumption Patterns

Online commerce is a major driving force in the worldwide economy. From the consumer point of view, buying online offers convenience and selection: Websites are open 24/7, products and prices can be easily compared, and an immediate purchase can be made. Online shoppers tend to live in more affluent income households, and millennials, those consumers aged 18 to 34, remain the key age demographic for online commerce, spending more money online in a given year than any other age group. In the first quarter of 2014, 198 million US consumers bought something online, according to comScore's quarterly State of Retail Report. Men are more likely than women to make purchases on mobile devices (Smith, 2015).

> Most of the US population age 15 and above made an online purchase in the last year.

Not all is positive; here are several common complaints about online shopping:

- product return policies
- quality of merchandise
- slow or poor customer service
- refund and billing pursuits
- privacy, security, and trust issues
- complex or difficult-to-navigate websites.

Consumers process a lot of information from a variety of sources such as media, families and friends, work colleagues, coupons and promotions, in-store presentations, personal experiences, online product reviews, and other social influences. The directionality of social influence can be seen in Figure 11.1, which begins with an invention or innovation.

Consumers cite past experience as the number one influencer when buying, so a proven brand name, store name, or website is a powerful factor in repeat buying behavior. Having brand names on websites was found to be an important influence on purchase decisions for consumers (Kim & Shim, 2002).

Access to the Internet as well as actual use varies significantly by country (the digital divide referred to in the Introduction section to this chapter), and the gap is changing so rapidly that in a book such as this, reporting too many statistics would be foolhardy since the numbers will be outdated immediately. This chapter will offer an overview and research results that indicate not only what is but what is predicted to come. The focus, therefore, is not so much on the numbers, percentages, or specific equipment but on trends of usage and the consumer issues involved.

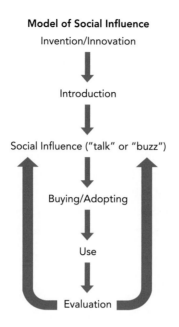

Model of Social Influence

Figure 11.1 Social Influence Model

Source: Elizabeth B. Goldsmith (2015). *Social influence and sustainable consumption*. New York: Springer, p. 20.

Research indicates that use of the Internet is based on several factors:

- household income
- age
- gender
- country
- education level.

Regarding Internet users, one general trend is that the higher their income and the higher their education level, the more they use the Internet. Many early studies showed that men were heavier users of the Internet than women, but more recent studies show that both men and women are heavy users, although they may be accessing different websites and using the Internet slightly differently in communicating with friends and in shopping. As mentioned earlier, men are more likely to purchase using their mobile devices than are women. In regard to shopping, both men and women shop online, but they may shop for different product categories and for different reasons. Internet shoppers tend to be younger than conventional in-store shoppers or mail-order catalog shoppers. Take, for example, the Saks Fifth Avenue store chain. Shoppers on the Saks website are "on the average about seven years younger than the typical Saks customer and spend more per transaction" (O'Connell, 2007, p. B2). According to a Television Bureau of Advertising-sponsored media study on where adults are most likely to learn about products or brands, it found that those younger than 55 are heavier users of the Internet than older persons. Young people are heavy browsers. Because browsing activity often does not result in an immediate purchase but does result in a future purchase, companies try to encourage consumers to stay online or to come back for another visit. Interestingly, when it comes to actual purchasing, older Internet-savvy shoppers were more likely to purchase online than younger shoppers (Sorce, Perotti, & Widrick, 2005).

Perception of product price is especially important to older shoppers (Loke & Chan, 2007). One in four mobile shoppers in the US is over the age of 55 (Smith, 2015).

To reach all consumers, many print magazines have online versions to attract younger audiences who do not want to pay for subscriptions. The return rate of magazines (those on store shelves that go unsold and go out of date) is over 50 percent. Most magazines (such as *Consumer Reports*) and newspapers have online versions as well as print versions. Some have dropped their print versions, and some stores, magazines, and newspapers only have an online presence.

The Internet is just one player in the information world but is a growing one. Besides magazines and newspapers, other sources of brand and product information are television and radio as well as word of mouth. Depending on the particular study, sometimes newspapers come before magazines in terms of consumers learning about products or brands. But the main message is that the younger the age group, the more likely they will be to choose the Internet over other types of media.

In a study of the 25- to 34-year-old age group with Internet access, 78 percent shopped online in the past month (*How America Shops & Spends*, 2006). Comparing the 1990s to today's shopping pattern, there is a gradual lessening of shopping in malls—resulting in "dead malls"—and a rise in shopping in neighborhood stores and shopping online. To combat this trend, malls are encouraging cinemas, entertainment, activities such as fashion shows, outdoor concerts, extended hours, and restaurants or food courts to give more reasons for consumers to come to the mall. The popularity of malls varies by time of year, climate, location, and available alternatives. The Internet, of course, is a convenient alternative.

In the *How America Shops & Spends* study, here are the ways consumers used the Internet (from highest to lowest):

- doing shopping-related activities
- researching goods and services
- buying something on the Internet
- buying something locally after checking it out on the Internet
- buying an item after checking local stores for that product.

This consumer research focusing on 25–34-year-olds showed that the main category they searched was electronics, such as types of cameras; other categories of interest included computers, home and garden equipment, sports and outdoor equipment, and clothing and accessories.

Search Engines

When you go online to buy a wedding gift, the bridal registry or department store will supply a list of gifts for $50 and under or for $50 to $100. You have encountered a personal shopper or search engine. **Search engines**, and by this is meant web search engines, are software systems designed to search for information on the World Wide Web (www). They are intelligent agent programs that scan the Internet and compile the information they are asked to locate in a format convenient for users. In other words, they aggregate information from various databases and recommend or list choices. Sometimes what appears at the top of the lists are the most commonly chosen or most authoritative sources, but other times they are paid placements, which are text ads targeted to keyword search results, or paid inclusion, which involves a fee structure (paid by the store or company) commonly used in shopping comparison sites. So what is at the top of the list may or may not be the wisest choice in terms of accurate information and the best price. Search engine companies make money from paid advertising and data collection.

Table 11.1 lists the top ten most popular search engines at the time this chapter went to press. The main breakthroughs on search engines occurred in the 90s and since then they have been perfected and companies merged. In the 2000s, Google became prominent. Dominance varies by country; in South Korea and Russia, for example, there are other leading search engines.

> Google is the leading search engine worldwide.

Table 11.1 Top Ten Search Engines by Estimated Unique Monthly Visitors

1. Google: 1,100,000,000
2. Bing: 350,000,000
3. Yahoo! Search: 300,000,000
4. Ask: 245,000,000
5. AOL Search: 125,000,000
6. Wow: 100,000,000
7. WebCrawler: 60,000,000
8. MyWebSearch: 60,000,000
9. Infospace: 24,000,000
10. Info: 13,5000,000

Source: eBizMBARank (August 2015). Available online at ebizmba.com/articles/search-engines.

Online Auctions

Looking for a signed baseball glove or a wooden sled from 1930? An Internet auction may be the place for you. Since it appeared in 1995, this has been a fast-growing phenomenon in the Internet marketplace. The most famous is eBay. "The key to eBay's success is trust among buyers, sellers, and the company that facilitates the auctions" (Awad, 2007, p 378). And, it keeps getting bigger. In 2015, eBay opened new sections on its site for Sotheby's Auctions. This means there are items $1,000 to $50,000 and up for sale. The number of eBay's 155 million monthly users keeps increasing (Isaac, 2015).

The global flea market has items going from dollars to millions of dollars, from kitchen gadgets to yachts. Prohibited auction items include counterfeit goods, illegal drugs, guns, and government IDs such as passports. Usually individual sellers offer one item at a time, although companies unload large amounts of unsold merchandise. Typically the seller sells items at the price of the highest successful bid. The seller may set a minimum acceptable price. The bidding closes at a scheduled time, and the highest bidder wins. Afterward, the seller and the buyer communicate to arrange payment and delivery. This describes person-to-person sales, but there can also be business-to-person sales.

Buyers may pay by credit card, debit card, personal check, cashier's check, money order, cash on delivery, and escrow services. Credit cards offer buyers the most consumer protection, and typically this is the form of payment that business-to-person sales want, but person-to-person auctions often do not. The main choices for paying for online purchases are:

- PayPal
- credit cards
- money orders
- cashier's checks.

Table 11.2 Typical Online Auction Categories

- Smartphones and tablets
- High-end clothing and accessories (designer purses, jewelry)
- Art and musical instruments
- Sports and fitness equipment
- Antiques and collectibles
- Home furnishings and electronics
- Travel packages/hotels
- Cars

Some sellers use an escrow fee arrangement in which the buyer pays 5 percent of the cost of the item. The escrow service accepts payment from the buyer by check, credit card, or money order; the service releases the money to the seller after the buyer receives and accepts the merchandise. This offers more protection to the buyer but slows up the transaction process. Another option is for the seller to agree to send purchases COD (collect on delivery) and the buyer to pay when the item is received.

The Federal Trade Commission (FTC) receives complaints about auction fraud, and most complaints center on sellers:

- They do not deliver the goods as advertised.
- They deliver something far less valuable.
- They do not deliver on time.
- They fail to disclose relevant information (cracks, missing pieces, etc.).

Buyers can protect themselves by identifying the seller, checking the seller's feedback rating, and reviewing comments supplied by previous buyers. They should also know products and prices and should establish a top price and stick with it, avoiding getting caught up in bidding fever. Find out about payment options, payment of shipping and delivery fees, and return policies before bidding. Know all you can about the site itself. What protections does it offer buyers?

Sellers can protect themselves by providing accurate information, dealing with a reputable site, responding quickly to potential buyers' questions, contacting the highest bidder immediately, and shipping the merchandise as soon as possible. They cannot sell illegal goods or place shill bids or false testimonials. Sellers increase sales by offering photos of items.

CONSUMER ALERTS

Beware of shill bids that are put there either by the sellers themselves (using made-up names) or by friends or relatives of the seller. Many people have been caught doing this. It is a technique used in live auctions as well as auctions where a seller's friend bids against potential buyers, driving up the price, and then the friend backs out at the last minute. There are also shill testimonials available online and in print. These made-up testimonials usually relate to product performance.

CONSUMER ALERTS

Be aware of damaged goods, and watch for words such as *refurbished*, *flood sale*, *close-out*, *discontinued*, and *off-brand*. Take special caution when buying electrical or mechanical goods.

Security and Trust

In order to buy online in the **marketspace** (the Internet realm in which buying and selling take place) a consumer must be able to have **trust** in (reliance on) the process. The issue of trust is described this way:

> *Trust is the psychological status of involved parties who are willing to pursue further interactions to achieve a planned goal. A trading party makes itself vulnerable to the other party's behavior; in other words, both parties assume risk. In the marketspace, sellers and buyers do not meet face to face. The buyer can see a picture of the product but not the product itself. (Turban et al., 2000, p. 86)*

The buyer must trust not only the seller but also the e-commerce infrastructure and environment. Can someone look in on the transaction and take information away from it? Security mechanisms can help solidify the trust between buyer and seller in the marketspace,

Trust is also a basic expectation of brands—customers are more likely to buy brand names than unknown products online. According to an article in *Advertising Age*, "When we ask consumers to tell us about those they believe are the best 'best brands,' the No. 1 attribute mentioned is 'it's a brand I trust.' Trust is the foundation for building relationships and for sustaining loyalty. Trust is critical when you introduce new ideas, products and benefits" (Keller, 2003, p. 28). According to this same article, trust was severely eroded with all the corporate scandals, including bloated chief executive officer (CEO) compensation, in 2002 and the continuing downturn of the economy in 2003. Not only did these factors affect stock valuations, but they also eroded people's confidence in business. In a survey, 6 in 10 people believed that the scandals resulted in a loss of trust that would take a long time to restore (Keller, 2003). Regulation is part of the solution, but businesses, through sound practices, must make a conscious effort to build trust.

In Chapter 2 on consumer movement history, we discussed the rise of antitrust legislation. The Internet has made the application of these laws even more important. One case in point is the worldwide practice of downloading or pirating copyrighted music without paying fees. A study found that many students felt downloading music was an acceptable act and that the majority of people were doing it (Siegfried, 2006). The legalities surrounding downloading are complex and involve competition laws and intellectual property laws in addition to antitrust and antimonopoly laws.

Since 2000, companies have faced serious penalties for not being careful with consumer information. Privacy-related regulations include the following:

- Sarbanes-Oxley Act
- Gramm-Leach-Bliley Act
- Fair Credit Reporting Act
- Health Insurance Portability and Accountability Act (HIPAA)

Customer service and legal compliance are critical to the success of an online business. According to Charles Hofacker, author of *Internet Marketing* (2000), trust is essential in facilitating exchange, and consumers need three kinds of trust before buying:

1. Trust in the mechanics of the selling process.

2. Trust in the fairness and integrity of the specific people involved.

3. Trust in the firm or institution and its ability to fulfill its delivery promise.

The benefits of shopping online are that the Internet is always open—7 days a week, 24 hours a day—and comparison shopping is easier. Good deals, convenience, and selection abound, but how do you make sure your online shopping experience is safe? Here are some rules to follow when buying online:

- *Use secure connections and websites.* Computers come with browsers installed, and you can program them to filter secure and insecure sites.

- *Shop for known brands with known companies.* You should also determine companies' refund and mailing policies.

- *Keep passwords private.* The most secure passwords use a combination of numbers, letters, and symbols that have nothing to do with other parts of your life; in other words, avoid mailing addresses, phone numbers, and birthdays.

- *Pay by credit card.* When you pay by credit card, your transaction is protected by the Fair Credit Billing Act. In fact, this is usually the only way you can pay online, so it should be automatic. More and more sites are allowing payment with checks and bank accounts. These transactions are covered by the Electronic Funds Transfer Act.

- *Update virus program.* Run an updated virus scanner and legitimate spyware scanner weekly.

- *Keep a record.* You should maintain a personal record of purchases by printing a copy of any transaction.

- *Read the company's online privacy policy.* The policy should disclose what information is being collected about you and how the company may use the information. As mentioned before, opt out of having your information passed on to others whenever possible.

Children as Online Consumers

The Federal Trade Commission offers specific information on how to protect your child's personal information against theft. Related to this is the Computer Decency Act (CDA), which added some safeguards to Internet access, but content on the Internet is still difficult to control. As a counterpoint, there are issues of free speech. But most everyone agrees that children need to be protected from pornography and other inappropriate images and messages. Before delving into Internet issues regarding children, let us first discuss children as consumers in general.

Children are consumers of breakfast cereals, toys, games, entertainment, clothes, snack foods, technology, and sports equipment and exert a great deal of influence on family purchases such as vacations and cars. More than half of US children are playing video games by the time they are five years old, and many are doing so as young as ages two and three. You may or may not agree with the following sentiment: "Childhood in recent decades has been defined . . . by parents who see their job as building self-esteem, by soccer coaches who give every player a trophy, by schools that used to name one 'student of the month' and these days name 40" (Zaslow, 2007, p. W1).

Parents and children are often seen as partners in consumerism. "Moms want the best for their children and that includes teaching them to realize that they have the power to make their own choices and decisions—and these decisions count!" (Coffey, Siegel, & Livingston, 2006, p. x). Children are exposed to brands on the Internet, on television, and in a variety of other ways. Brands that are used in childhood are often preferred in adulthood, and this knowledge makes children a target for marketers. For example, Home Depot has workshops for parents and children to build birdhouses or other small items, and during the workshops the children wear orange Home Depot aprons. This is both cute and purposeful—the brand and the store are being mentally imprinted.

One study found that children were influenced by brand names and what the brands represented, so massive marketing campaigns by clothing and athletic shoe companies such as Tommy Hilfiger, Nike, and Adidas are undertaken (Zollo, 1999). In this study, two-thirds of teens interviewed associated "cool" brands with quality; they assumed that a marketing campaign message of "cool" meant that the brands were of high quality, that the two characteristics go together. At any age, the meaning of quality is not easy to define, but characteristics of quality may include durability and superior features.

Children as young as 4 years may have made their first independent purchase, although 8 is a more likely age (McNeal & Yeh, 1993). Consumers 8 to 18 years old spend over $30 billion a year on electronics, food and beverages, toys, clothing, entertainment, and personal care.

It is during the preadolescent years, ages 8 to 12, that buying really takes off and purchasing behaviors are established. Countless media messages about consumption bombard children, parents, and teachers.

The Federal Communications Commission (FCC) regulates children's TV programming to make sure that children are not deceived by advertising, but this is not so easy to do because children watch television more times than on Saturday mornings. Generally, the TV ads aimed at children are for toys, food, games, and clothing. The Internet is largely unregulated, so if children are online, it is likely they are exposed to messages and images that parents would consider inappropriate. There are millions of personal blogs (daily accounts of people's lives) that are unregulated, which raises ethical issues about censorship in the home as well as in the greater society. **Censorship** is an attempt to control or the act, process, or policy of control. In the case of children, what might need to be censored are inappropriate materials (such as pornographic, offensive, hate, and other potentially dangerous materials) plus the solicitation of children for information about their parents, their families, or themselves. Possible approaches include training children how to be careful, getting parents involved, installing blocking software, and having government and Internet providers take steps to protect children.

The Children's Online Privacy Protection Act (COPPA), enforced by the FTC, requires commercial website operators to get parental consent before collecting personal inform-ation from children under the age of 13; this act also allows teachers to act on behalf of a parent during online school activities but does not require them to do so. Many school districts have adopted acceptable use policies to educate parents and children about both Internet use and issues of online safety, privacy, and parental consent, cautioning about the use of children's full names, addresses, and telephone numbers. Teachers are encouraged to notice the websites students are using and to steer them away from ones asking for personal information. Violators of COPPA should be reported to the FTC.

Strong encryption means the ability to achieve unbreakable confidentiality. Parents can put filters on messages coming into the home on their home computers, thus limiting what content can be viewed by their children. Monitoring software will allow parents to view their child's activity on the computer. Some employers may use filters to screen what employees can see and do on work computers. Following are some tips for parents from www.secureflorida.org:

1. Create rules for Internet use in the home.
2. Know what your kids are doing online.
3. Use the Internet with your kids.
4. Don't allow solitary surfing.
5. If you agree to let your child meet an online buddy in person, go with them.
6. Don't rely solely on technology as a substitute for you.

Environmental Impact of the Internet

There is no doubt that the Internet has an impact on the environment, but no one has measured the full impact mainly because it is changing so rapidly and is so profuse. The best that we can do is to provide estimates. The obvious sorts of impact have been in the areas of reduced use of paper, problems involved with equipment disposal, and decreased use of electricity. As one example, consider the movement of money. Payment systems in the paper world involve cash, checks, vouchers, coupons, and stamped and mailed credit card statements and bills. All this paper is saved in the digital world of e-commerce, which has the same look and feel and should be at least as secure as paper transactions. Electronic financial transactions should be properly encrypted, meaning security is embedded in the transactions.

Discussing the environmental impact of the Internet is important because issues about the natural environment such as global warming and the destruction of the rain forests have grown massively in the public's awareness. Environmental impact is of worldwide concern. The United States is particularly of interest because it leads the world in energy consumption, representing 24 percent of the world's primary energy consumption (Caruso, 2003).

"Moving businesses online and marketing by pixels instead of packages, e-commerce can reduce the need for such wasteful products as printed catalogs, telephone books, newspapers, and magazines" (Sui & Rejeski, 2002). Other areas of environmental impact include shipping, warehouse space, and employee productivity. Electronic purchasing and inventory have made the recording of the buying, selling, and storing of goods and services much more efficient, but it is difficult to say how much energy is saved. For example, in some cases more fuel is used because half-filled delivery trucks are sent so that a company can back up its promise of rapid delivery. Less warehouse space may be needed, or all the warehousing may be done in one central place rather than in scattered storage facilities. More people working at home would seem to indicate a reduction both in travel (meaning less fuel) and in the need for outside office space (meaning less energy), so one would assume that more teleworkers would indicate less stress on the environment.

Using less paper would indicate less stress on most resources; for example, less wood would be needed for paper products and less energy would be used in processing the wood into paper. E-commerce has also affected the packaging and display of products. If products are sold online, that reduces the need for packaging and displaying products and for driving to the store to see the products. Internet billing and direct depositing use less paper and envelopes. To conclude, the full extent of the environmental impact from use of the Internet (versus other forms of getting information, conducting business, and buying and selling products) is yet to be determined.

Biometrics

As covered in the Introduction section, biometrics refers to the use of one's unique physical traits to verify identity. Consumers like the speed and the convenience and mostly they like not carrying a lot of cards around. "One day soon, it may not matter that you lost the house key or can't find all five documents required to renew your driver's license, Instead, you'll need just your fingerprints for identification. That's the future painted by a number of companies that are touting fingerprints as the preferred way to use biometrics" (Keeton, 2007, p. B4). Although this quote is from 2007, we are still talking about it and making progress. Someday written signatures and identification cards will be used so rarely that at a store register or bank only a fingerprint will be used. And, of course, banking can be done by taking photos of checks and sending them online. It is a continuum more than an end state.

In Japan, the use of biometrics is common on cell phones, at bank automated teller machines (ATMs), and for point-of-purchase credit card purchases. Hotels are coming along on this as well. Home Depot stores in Canada and the United States are selling keyless door entries, and so are car manufacturers around the world. Fingerprint sensors have been used for many years at universities for dormitory or cafeteria entrance by students and at companies where security is important for entrance by employees. One manufacturer of biometric devices has a sensor that reads below the fingerprint to living tissue, which is harder to fake with a piece of tape or some other substitute.

Airports, laboratories, and border patrol stations are experimenting with biometrics. Law enforcement already uses them. One of the problems is the vast amount of data. Imagine managing a fingerprint database of over 320 million Americans; then imagine doing this for the worldwide population of over seven billion.

Are there privacy issues? Yes, there are. Barry Steinhart of the American Civil Liberties Union (ACLU) says that "the use of biometric identification raises legal privacy issues, particularly if a big database were used for national drivers' license or ID-card program. In the worst case, the government could use personal information to keep tabs

Photo 11.2
How do you keep laptop information private?

Source: Getty Images: Colin Anderson

on innocent citizens" (Keeton, 2007, p. B4). Surveys of Americans show that most are comfortable with biometric identification and that they like the convenience of not carrying keys or cards or remembering passwords.

In addition to fingerprint scanners, there are eye readers (referred to as retinal scanners), which have people look at a sensor that causes a garage door to open or makes something else happen. Other biometrics include facial analysis, speech analysis, body odor analysis, and signature analysis, but currently fingerprint analysis leads the way for identification. "The reason is the one in a billion chance that two people will have the same fingerprint" (Awad, 2007, p. 441). The main goal of using biometrics would be to make identification hacking or spoofing more difficult, which makes biometrics a safe and secure identity tool. Biometric methods should be used in combination with other security methods. For example, to enter a secure area an individual would need to supply a password, enter a code, and provide a fingerprint.

Identity Theft and Privacy Protection

The advent of the Internet has opened up the possibility for more ways to seize another's identity and stores in consequence have to put more privacy protections in place. New distribution channels such as retail channels have changed how to reach consumers and do business with them. Multichannel retailing refers to using more than one channel to sell merchandise and deliver it. The practice is not really new. An example is Sears, which opened its first store in 1925, decades after it launched a successful paper catalog.

Models of decision making that are based on economic considerations of utility, value maximization, and scarcity predict that consumers would evaluate the utility provided by each offering and choose the option that provides the maximum utility. Choice is narrowed by these considerations. Consumers want the best product at the lowest price with the maximum return or benefit; they also want ease of use, which leads to the increased use of credit cards and the Internet as modes of purchase (as opposed to in-person cash transactions where identity theft is not a problem). No one is identified, the cash is exchanged, and that is the end—there is no paper trail. This is the starting point in our discussion. Times have changed, and the frauds have kept pace.

As defined in the Introduction section to this chapter, identity theft refers to someone using your name or personal information, such as your Social Security number, driver's license number, credit card number or other account number, telephone number, or street address without your permission. Essentially the identity thief is stealing your identity for personal gain, such as claiming a refund (as in the following Case Study) or using the information to open up credit accounts or bank accounts, take out loans, place long-distance calls, or make major purchases. Identity theft can result in the loss of money and the loss of reputation. An example of the latter would be the loss of a good credit rating.

CASE STUDY

Claiming Someone Else's Tax Refund

"Robert Scott Jack took precautions most people never dream of to prevent tax identity theft. Mr. Jack, a retired federal cybersecurity expert in Alexandria, Va., who now works as a consultant, shunned online tax-preparation programs that store data on the Internet. He researched the security features of different software programs and opted for a packaged – not downloaded – product. He checked the package for signs of tampering before loading it into his secure home computer. Yet soon after he tried to electronically file his federal tax return through TurboTax on Feb. 14, the company told him it had been rejected because someone already had filed using his Social Security number. 'I was disappointed and frustrated,' Mr. Jack says."

Source: Laura Saunders (March 1, 2015). "Invasion of the tax snatchers." *Wall Street Journal*, p. B7.

Privacy is a state of an individual or group which keeps information about their lives and activities from public consumption. It means to not be bothered by unwanted intrusions such as unsolicited sales calls. The right to privacy is recognized by federal and state laws in the United States and by the laws of many other countries. Box 11.1 gives a list of some federal privacy legislation. The question is how much government regulation is necessary. Some degree of regulation and authority is necessary, but not at the expense of individual freedoms and civil liberties. In the long run, the best defense against unwanted scams and other intrusions is through using self-regulation and discretion and by being aware, making wise choices, being careful about participation, learning about security, knowing legal rights, and seeking redress.

According to Mason et al. (1995), ethical issues can be categorized in several ways:

- *Privacy*. The collection, storage, and dissemination of information about individuals all impact privacy. A question in this category would be: What information about oneself should one have to reveal in order to get a product or service?

- *Accuracy*. Accuracy involves the authenticity, fidelity, and accuracy of information collected and processed. A question in this category would be: Who is to be held accountable for errors in information?

- *Property*. The ownership and value both of information and of intellectual property are property issues. A question in this category would be: Who owns the information?

- *Accessibility*. The term *accessibility* refers to the right to access information and the payment of fees to access it. Questions in this category would be: Who is allowed access to information? Should I be afraid to give information that may be sold, used, or revealed in an inappropriate manner? Research reveals that this issue comes up again and again and is one of the main reasons people refuse to buy over the Internet.

Box 11.1 Main Federal Privacy Legislation

Privacy rights are built into many state and federal laws. Here is a list of representative federal privacy legislation acts:

Privacy Act of 1974. This act prohibits the government from collecting information secretly, or if it is collected, it must be for a specific purpose.

Privacy Protection Act of 1980. This act provides protection of privacy in computerized and related documents.

Electronic Communications Privacy Act of 1986. This act prohibits citizens from intercepting data communications without authority.

Computer Matching and Privacy Act of 1988. This act regulates the matching of computer files by state and federal agencies.

Video Privacy Protection Act of 1988. This act protects privacy in picture transmissions.

Fair Health Information Practices Act of 1997. This act sets a code of fair information practices.

Consumer Internet Privacy Protection Act of 1997. This act requires prior written consent before a computer service can disclose information about subscribers.

Federal Internet Privacy Protection Act of 1997. This act prohibits federal agencies from disclosing personal records from the Internet.

Communications Privacy and Consumer Empowerment Act of 1997. This act protects online commerce in terms of privacy rights.

Data Privacy Act of 1997. This act limits the use of personal information and regulates spamming.

Children's Online Privacy Act of 1998. This act, an amendment to the Internet Tax Freedom Act, requires companies to verify a person's age before showing online material that could be harmful to minors. This can be done through credit cards or access numbers.

Internet School Filtering Act of 1998. This act attempts to limit access to inappropriate material by controlling federal funds and grants to school and libraries. Schools provide blocking software.

USA PATRIOT Act of 2001. This act attempts to unite and strengthen the United States by providing appropriate tools required to intercept and observe terrorism. It also expands government law enforcement powers, especially with regard to the Internet.

Federal Legislation

The Identity Theft and Assumption Deterrence Act of 1998 makes it a federal crime if someone "knowingly transfers or uses, without lawful authority, a means of identification of another person with the intent to commit, or to aid or abet, any unlawful activity that constitutes a violation of federal law, or that constitutes a felony under any applicable state or local law." A Social Security number is considered a means of identification, as are credit card numbers. The penalties are stiff: A conviction of identity theft carries fines and prison sentences of up to 15 years, and states have passed laws related to identity theft as well.

Many federal government agencies are involved in educating the public about identity theft and hunting down criminals. The following agencies are particularly important in the fight to protect personal information:

- *US Department of Justice.* The Justice Department and its US attorneys prosecute federal identity theft cases.

- *Federal Bureau of Investigation (FBI).* The FBI investigates cases connected with bank fraud, mail fraud, wire fraud, bankruptcy fraud, insurance fraud, fraud against the government, and terrorism. According to their main webpage "A stolen identity is a powerful cloak of anonymity for criminals and terrorists . . . and a danger to national security and private citizens alike. For the FBI, identity theft is nothing new. We've been dealing with criminals faking IDs for decades, from check forgers to fugitives on the run. But the threat is more pervasive and the scams more sophisticated than ever, including new online elements." Source: Federal Bureau of Investigation (2015). "Identity theft." Available online at fbi.gov/about-us/investigate/cyber/identity_theft.

- *Secret Service.* The Secret Service investigates financial crimes involving identity theft, usually cases involving substantial dollar loss. The main headquarters is in the Washington, DC, area but there are field offices as well.

- *US Department of the Treasury.* The Treasury Department has a financial crimes division that specializes in identity theft problems.

Identity Theft: Methods and Protections

Skilled identity thieves have a number of methods to gain access to personal information (see Box 11.2). Box 11.3 shows how the thieves use the personal information they obtain. No one can prevent identity theft entirely, but you can minimize the risk by doing the following:

- Watch credit card statements, and order a copy of credit reports from each of the three major credit bureaus (Equifax, Experian, and TransUnion).

- Be careful with the following items: checkbooks, pay stubs, receipts with credit card numbers, credit cards, ATM cards, driver's licenses, and health insurance cards

Photo 11.3 A thumb or fingerprint is one of the most reliable methods of identification because everyone's prints are different

Source: Thinkstock: lestyan4

(especially those with Social Security numbers). If you think you are safe because you have never lost any of these or put them in the wrong hands, think again. Anyone processing your credit card or taking information about you can turn around and sell that information to a fraud ring. Be especially cautious when traveling.

- Use hard-to-figure-out passwords or passphrases on credit card, bank, and phone accounts.
- Secure personal information at home if there are roommates. At work, be watchful of people who are in and out doing remodeling or repairs.
- Secure personal information at work.
- Update virus protection software regularly on computers.
- Never click on hyperlinks sent from strangers or download unknown files.
- Take special care with laptops, and log off when finished.
- Take mail with checks and personal information to the post office instead of putting it in unsecured mailboxes.
- Delete personal information using a "wipe" utility program to overwrite the entire hard drive when disposing of a computer.

Self-Background Checks

There is an upsurge of interest in background checks, both personal background checks and those by outside parties such as employers, who hire a corporate background-screening agency such as LexisNexis Risk Solutions (employers can do this once consent is provided on the application form). LexisNexis Risk Solutions has information from government public records and some courts and can do employment and education verification, such as finding out if someone really graduated from Harvard or Stanford.

What is the first step in a self-background check? Googling yourself is a beginning, but it is not enough—you should order your credit report. This can be obtained by going to www.annualcreditreport.com or by contacting credit-reporting agencies such as Experian, TransUnion, or Equifax. Under a 2004 federal law, consumers have access to these reports, those by LexisNexis Risk Solutions, and others. The credit-reporting agencies keep records on your credit history as well as personal information such as previous addresses. A free annual credit report is available from them and is required by federal law at the phone number given or the website www.annualcreditreport.com. Another place to check is www.ssa.gov. Through this website, you can check your Social Security earnings and find out if anyone has been using your number. For example, someone else could be working under your Social Security number.

Box 11.2 Identity Theft Prevention

"Identity thieves steal your personal information to commit fraud. They can damage your credit status and cost you time and money restoring your good name. To reduce your risk of becoming a victim, follow the tips below:

- Don't carry your Social Security card in your wallet or write it on your checks. Only give out your SSN when absolutely necessary. Even if doctors' and dentists' offices ask for this number you usually do not have to give it.
- Protect your PIN.
- Watch out for 'shoulder surfers.' Use your free hand to shield the keypad.
- Collect mail promptly.
- Pay attention to your billing cycles.
- Tear up or shred unwanted receipts, credit offers, account statements, expired cards, etc., to prevent dumpster divers getting your personal information.
- Don't respond to unsolicited requests for personal information in the mail, over the phone or online.
- Install firewalls and virus-detection software on your home computer.

> ● Check your credit report once a year. Check more frequently if you suspect someone has gotten access to your account information."
>
> Source: Adapted from "Prevent and report identity theft," US Government Web Portal (2015). Available online at usa.gov/topics/money/identity-theft/prevention.shtml.

Photo 11.4
Protect yourself against identity theft

Source: Thinkstock: Creatas

Box 11.3 How Identity Theft Information is Used

Following are eight ways that identity thieves may use personal information:

1. They call your credit card issuer while pretending to be you and ask to change the mailing address on your credit card account. The imposter then runs up charges on your account. Because your bills are being sent to the new address, it may take some time before you realize there's a problem.

2. They open a new credit card account using your name, date of birth, and Social Security number. When they use the credit card and don't pay the bills, the delinquent account is reported on your credit report.

3. They establish phone or wireless service in your name.

4. They open a bank account in your name and write bad checks on that account.

5. They file for bankruptcy under your name to avoid paying debts they've incurred under your name or to avoid eviction.

6. They counterfeit checks or debit cards and drain your bank account.

7. They buy cars by taking out auto loans in your name.

8. They give your name to the police during an arrest. If they're released from police custody but don't show up for their court date, an arrest warrant is issued in your name.

> Source: Federal Trade Commission (September 2002).
> "Theft: when bad things happen to your good name," p. 4.

When filling out information cards in person or over the computer, choose the opt-out option as a way to reduce the number of people and organizations that receive personal information about you. Use work phone numbers and addresses whenever possible. You can notify the three major credit bureaus that you do not want personal information about you shared for selling or promotional purposes.

CONSUMER ALERTS

When it comes to identity theft, the most victimized age group is 18–29. This is due to:

1. Transient nature.

2. Prevalence on the Internet.

3. Simple naivety.

Recourse for Victims of Identity Theft

Here are steps to follow if you are a victim of identity theft:

1. Report first to your financial institutions (banks and credit card companies).

2. Report the fraud to your local police immediately.

3. Contact the fraud department of the three credit reporting bureaus.

4. File a complaint with the FTC. This can be done online. The FTC does not bring criminal cases but can help victims by providing information to assist them in resolving the financial and other problems that can result from this crime, and reporting this information can help law enforcement officials track down identity thieves and stop them.

CONSUMER ALERTS

The elderly are prone to frauds such as telemarketing, contests ("You have won!"), and medical identification theft. For example, according to the FTC, an identity thief can use personal information to get medical care or services. The elderly are especially likely to have identity theft problems when they are in nursing homes or assisted living centers. Seniors are vulnerable because they tend to have good credit, they are less likely to use their cards often, and they are unlikely to request their credit reports from credit bureaus. Their lack of use makes them easy targets. The cardholder's name can be used to open bank accounts, to forge checks, and even to take out bank loans for cars. Seniors' relatives can look out for them by lowering their credit card limit to $300 or $500; relatives should also be familiar with the security policies at any residential facility. Besides relatives, police department detectives can look out for the elderly and give talks on what to notice. Nursing homes and assisted living centers should do background checks on potential employees before hiring them.

Charities: When Giving Helps and When it Hurts

As noted in the Introduction section of this chapter, many charities are moving toward the Internet as their main way of advertising what they do and for soliciting donations. Charities can be legitimate, quasi-legitimate, or outright fraudulent. Americans donate billions of dollars a year to the 400 largest charities in the United States. Curiously, low-income people are often more generous donors than wealthier people; some speculate this is because they can more easily relate to those in need.

Box 11.4 The Ten Largest US Charities Ranked by Income

1. YMCA of the USA
2. United Way
3. Catholic Charities USA
4. Goodwill Industries International
5. The Salvation Army
6. American Red Cross
7. Food for the Poor
8. The Nature Conservancy
9. Boys & Girls Clubs of America
10. Habitat for Humanity

Note: The order on this list may change slightly in any given year.

For many years, the Salvation Army received the largest donations, but following the September 11, 2001, disaster, donations to the American Red Cross skyrocketed. These are both legitimate charities and illustrate that events and crises affect giving patterns.

An estimated over $2 billion a year falls into the hands of fraudulent solicitors. The problem is there are so many charities that it is difficult to sort the good ones from the bad ones. There are hundreds of thousands of charities vying for your contribution, and new ones join their ranks every year. How do you make good choices? Your first thought should center on the causes or charities you believe in because your donations should be a reflection of your values and principles. This will narrow the field. The next guide should be how the charity ranks on the basis of how efficiently its dollars are spent. For example, the American Red Cross ranks consistently high in the percentage of its income that goes directly to programs to help those in need. *Money* magazine regularly reports the rankings of charities; other magazines, Better Business Bureaus (BBBs), newspapers, state government consumer protection agencies, and consumer watchdog organizations also offer lists and rankings. Go online and investigate the charity itself; all large charities have websites with information.

> ### CONSUMER ALERTS
>
> Look out for fraudulent middlemen representing real charities or churches. For example, they may say "buy this raffle ticket and the proceeds will go to the Red Cross," but the person pockets all or some of the cash.

The surest way to avoid fraud is to know about the charity and its activities, so ask questions about how money is used (make sure most of it gets to those who are in need), and be sure the money will be spent where you want it spent. Do you want it to go to terrorist causes that blow up buildings? Do you want your hard-earned money to go to fake religious leaders for building their mansions or for adding to their fleet of luxury cars? Sometimes the surface organization seems okay, but the money is funneled to other organizations, people, and causes that you would not normally support. Box 11.5 provides a charity checklist to ensure that your donation dollars benefit the people and organizations that you want. Be especially wary of charities or persons you do not know who ask for donations over the Internet.

Special care should be taken when giving large donations, especially those made through trusts and wills. Donations of this sort should not be made without legal and tax advice from professionals.

Box 11.5 Charity Checklist

1. Ask for written information. Do not go by what is said on the telephone or in email. Be especially wary of unsolicited emails with sad stories from foreign countries.

2. Ask for identification. If the solicitor refuses, call the local authorities.

3. Call the charity back to find out if the caller was legitimate.

4. Watch for similar-sounding names. The fraudulent name may differ by only one word from a legitimate charity's name.

5. Be skeptical about being pressured to pledge money. Be wary if anyone says that you or someone in your family has already pledged money.

6. Ask how the donation will be spent.

7. Find out how much of the donation is tax-exempt or tax-deductible if there are special events or tickets. If tax deductibility is important to you, ask for a receipt showing the amount of your contribution and stating that it is tax-deductible. For security reasons, pay by check. Beware of any solicitor insisting on cash.

8. Discourage employers from pushing employees or schools from pushing schoolchildren to donate to charities. Donations should be by individual choice, not by force.

9. Be wary of any gifts or sweepstakes offers connected with a contribution. To be eligible to win, a donation is not necessary (depending on state regulations).

10. Be wary of people who gather money at street corners or at traffic intersections; they may or may not be legitimate.

11. Be wary of fraudsters operating immediately after a crisis. They prey on your sympathy.

12. Let the attorney general, your local consumer protection office, and the FTC know of any organization that is making misleading solicitations.

CONSUMER ALERTS

For years, common consumer fraud relied on the victim's desire to help organizations and individuals. The way it works is that you are first led to feel sorry for the charity or source; then it evolves into not only charity fraud but also mail and investment fraud. A particularly enduring and costly one is a proposal that asks individuals to assist government officials in transferring "tied-up" funds by establishing accounts in their country. The offer claims you can earn millions as a percentage of the money you help transfer into new accounts. For example, you provide a bank account where they can deposit millions of dollars that the Nigerian government has "tied up" in bureaucracy. Initially, the proposal states that you need not invest any money up front. However, as time passes, you begin receiving letters or faxes stating that the Nigerian government has snagged the transaction of depositing money into the account you set up; then they ask you to provide your own money to complete the transaction, stating that afterward "millions" will be deposited into your account. Victims have been known to pump thousands of dollars into this scam. US postal officials believe that this type of mail fraud has cost victims more than $100 million a year.

Source: Florida Department of Consumer Services website (January 22, 2003).

Summary

Technical disruption involves new technologies coming along that change the way we do things. They push societies and economies in new directions. For example, Uber was started in 2009 and it rocked the taxi industry. The end result is still not in sight. Online buying is another example of a technical disruption. It offers convenience and selection, with the main negatives being security and potential for fraud. The Internet has revolutionized the shopping experience and information searches. From the sellers' point of view, hard-to-reach populations are no longer difficult to reach. Companies are often multi-channel retailers.

Consumer information processing is fundamental to the study of consumer economics. Greater access to information should lead to greater confidence in decision making and more choices for consumers. The downside to greater access is greater exposure to identity theft. In short, technology brings with it new opportunities and challenges for regulators, consumers, and marketers. Google is the number one search engine.

In terms of demographics, Internet customers tend to be younger than the usual in-store customers, but older online shoppers are often more likely to actually purchase. The Internet is a pull medium, meaning there is interactivity between the consumer and the Internet. The Internet requires action; it is less passive than watching television or listening to radio.

The Identity Theft and Deterrence Act of 1998 made it a federal crime for someone to steal your identity. The Internet creates numerous problems in the area of privacy, identity protection, sales, and children's issues. The risk to privacy can be minimized if the buyer trusts the mechanics of the selling process, the fairness and integrity of the people involved, and the firm or the institution and its ability to deliver as promised. This chapter showed how to conduct a self-background check to find out what information is out there about you. The USA PATRIOT Act of 2001 confers extra powers on the executive brand of government, especially in regard to the Internet. This act unites and strengthens America by providing appropriate tools required to intercept and obstruct terrorism.

KEY POINTS

1. More consumers are using the Internet for prepurchase and purchase activities.

2. Biometrics such as fingerprints and retinal scans are being used more frequently for identity purposes.

3. Search engines are used by consumers to locate and compare products.

4. Identity theft has challenged the trust among consumers and between consumers and markets and can lead to a loss of money, reputation, and time. It is a worldwide problem, and in the United States it is a federal crime.

5. Children are at risk on the Internet due to predators and fraudsters who take advantage of them.

6. The spread of the Internet has an environmental impact, and the extent of this impact is being studied.

7. Under a 2004 federal law, consumers can perform self-background checks, which begin with ordering free credit reports.

8. People are buying more electronics than anything else on Amazon, and groceries are selling better than expected.

9. Men are more likely to make purchases on mobile devices than women.

KEY TERMS

biometrics	identity theft	strong encryption
censorship	marketspace	technical disruption
digital divide	privacy	trust
hacker	search engines	

DISCUSSION QUESTIONS

1. How is the subject of the consumer-in-control movement related to the Internet?

2. Why are children particularly vulnerable when it comes to the Internet? What steps can be taken to lessen the risk?

3. Why are the elderly often victims of identity theft?

4. What federal agencies are involved in monitoring the Internet?

REFERENCES

Awad, E. M. (2007). *Electronic commerce from vision to fulfillment*, 3rd ed. Upper Saddle River, NJ: Pearson Prentice Hall.

Caruso, G. (2003). *United States: environmental issues.* Energy Information Administration. Available online at eia.doe.gov/emeu/cabs/usenv.html.

Coffey, T., D. Siegel, and G. Livingston. (2006). *Marketing to the new super consumer mom & kid.* Ithaca, NY: Paramount Market Publishing, Inc.

Federal Trade Commission (September 2002). Theft: when bad things happen to your good name, p. 4.

Goldsmith, E. (2015). *Social influence and sustainable consumption.* New York: Springer.

Hofacker, C. (2000). *Internet marketing*, 3rd ed. New York: John Wiley.

How America shops & spends (2006). Newspaper Association of America.

Isaac, M. (March 17, 2015). EBay set to open new section on its site for Sotheby's auctions. *New York Times.* Available online at http://bits.blogs.nytimes.com/2015/03/17/ebay-set-to-open-new-section-of-site-for-sothebys-auctions.

Keeton, A. (April 12, 2007). Fingerprints give a hand to security. *Wall Street Journal*, p. B4.

Keller, E. (February 24, 2003). To regain trust, faking won't do. *Advertising Age*, p. 28.

Kim, Y., and K. Shim. (2002). The influence of Internet shopping mall characteristics and user traits on purchase intent. *Irish Marketing*, 15 (2), 25–34.

Klaassen, A. (2006). *Search marketing fact pack 2006.* New York: Crain Communications, Inc.

Loke, Y. J., and W. Y. Chan. (2007). Seasoned and potential Internet shoppers: a multinomial logit analysis. *Applied Economics Letters*, 14, 43–47.

Mason, R. O., F. M. Mason, and M. J. Culnan. (1995). *Ethics of information management.* Thousand Oaks, CA: Sage.

McNeal, J., and C. Yeh. (June 1993). Born to shop. *American Demographics*, 34–39.

O'Connell, V. (April 20, 2007). Park avenue classic or Soho trendy? *Wall Street Journal*, pp. B1–B2.

Rothman, W. (August 5, 2015). The end of ink cartridges for printers, at last. *Wall Street Journal*, p. D1.

Saunders (March 1, 2015). Invasion of the tax snatchers. *Wall Street Journal*, p. B7.

Secure Florida, Best practices for parents and online safety. Available online at www.secureflorida.org.

Siegfried, R. (2006). Student attitudes on software piracy and related issues of computer ethics. *Ethics and Information Technology*, 6, 215–222.

Smith, C. (February 23, 2015). The surprising facts about who shops online and on mobile. *Business Insider.* Available online at www.businessinsider.com/the-surprising-demographics.

Sorce, P., V. Perotti, and S. Widrick. (2005). Attitude and age differences in online buying. *International Journal of Retail and Distribution Management*, 33 (2/3), 122–133.

Sui, D., and D. Rejeski. (2002). Environmental impacts of the emerging digital economy: the e-for-environment e-commerce. *Environmental Management*, 29 (2), 155–163.

Task, A. (March 30, 2015). Tax fraud and identity theft: how to protect yourself. *Yahoo Finance.* Available online at http://finance.yahoo.com/news/what-to-do-if-your-identity-has-been-stolen-170112261.html.

Turban, E., J. Lee, D. King, and H. M. Chung. (2000). *Electronic commerce: a managerial perspective.* Upper Saddle River, NJ: Prentice Hall.

Zaslow, J. (April 20, 2007). The most-praised generation goes to work. *Wall Street Journal*, p. W1.

Zollo, P. (1999). *Wise up to teens: insights into marketing and advertising to teenagers.* Ithaca: NY: New Strategist Publications.

Chapter **12**

Being a Better Consumer of Housing and Vehicles

A comfortable house is a great source of happiness. It ranks immediately after health and a good conscience.

Sydney Smith

LEARNING OBJECTIVES

1. Define consumer unit and describe a typical unit's expenditures.
2. Explain the pros and cons of owning versus renting housing.
3. Explain the different types of home mortgages.
4. Discuss change points in people's lives and their effect on consumption.
5. Discuss the cost of utilities.
6. Explain the pros and cons of leasing versus owning vehicles.
7. Discuss buying vehicles and what deceptive practices to avoid.

Introduction

Companies are fiercely competing for the Millennials' dollars. "There are eighty million millennials in America alone and they represent about a fourth of the entire population, with $200 billion in annual buying power. They have a lot of influence over older generations and are trendsetters across all industries from food to fashion" (Schawbel, 2015). How to sell cars and homes to them is complicated because they aren't very influenced by advertising, they review blogs before making a purchase, and they value authenticity over surface polish. Millennials refer to those born between 1981 and 2000.

Wise consumers of any age need survival tips for navigating the higher priced items of houses and cars and for understanding the ups and downs of the real estate market. Because homes and cars are the most visible high-ticket items that most consumers own, this chapter is devoted to how to become better consumers of both.

Housing is the number one budget item for most people, followed by transportation.

In the typical family's budget, housing represents 34 percent and transportation represents 18 percent, followed by food at 13 percent. Thus, housing is the most expensive item for most consumers. There are costs attached to these major categories such as the average US household spends over $1,200 a year on auto insurance. The pie chart in Figure 12.1 shows a typical family budget.

Since Chapter 10 covers repairs (such as vehicular repairs and home improvements), the emphasis in this chapter is on the prebuying and purchasing part of these investments, starting with the decision of whether to buy or rent housing. In 2015, the average rent across the US was $1,231 a month; in certain areas it was triple that number (Glink, 2015). There are not enough apartments in high demand cities.

Figure 12.1 Typical Household of Consumer Unit Budget

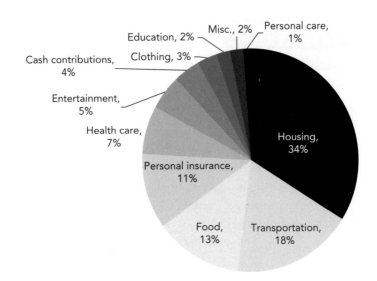

To provide context and historical perspective, it should be noted that "[no] century began with as much promise for change as the twentieth. The automobile and airplane, motion pictures and radio, the electric light and appliances, bottled soft drinks and canned soups, all so prosaic and common at the end of the century, were the new wonders of 1900" (Cross, 2000, p. 17). Can the same be said for the twenty-first century? What developments bode well for our future? One trend discussed in this chapter is the growth in home technology, in particular home monitoring systems. About 67 percent of Americans own their homes, and home equity accounts for 23.5 percent of household net worth. These percentages and many others in the chapter, including those in the pie chart, come from the Consumer Expenditure Survey reported by the Bureau of Labor Statistics.

According to the Bureau, the terms *household* and *consumer unit* are used interchangeably for convenience. The definition of a **consumer unit** is members of a household related by blood, marriage, adoption, or other legal arrangement; a single person living alone or sharing a household with others but who is financially independent; or two persons living together who share responsibilities for at least two out of three major types of expenses (food, housing, and other expenses). In the United States, the average number of persons in a consumer unit is 2.5 with 1.3 earners, and they have two vehicles.

With ownership comes responsibility and the need to make lasting choices. Before buying, nearly everyone rents, so the chapter begins with a discussion of renting and leasing. In the second half of the chapter, we'll discuss the pros and cons of leasing and buying vehicles and the traps to avoid.

Leasing and Renting Housing

Advantages of Leasing vs. Renting

Millions of students sign their first leases while in college. Leases may be difficult to get out of, so caution is advised. There are month-to-month leases, school-year leases, and yearly leases. Landlords give financial incentives or make improvements to keep the same renters year in and year out. **Rent** is payment for the use of property. Most students will continue to pay rent for the first few years out of college with the intention of eventually buying housing. A great advantage of renting is that it is a temporary arrangement; you pay month to month so that money is not tied up. Even with this advantage, some people are buying homes at a younger age because low mortgage rates make buying more affordable than or just as affordable as renting. As one 24-year-old said, "Why pay $1,000 a month for a small apartment when I can own a townhouse for the same price and then have something to sell when I move on?" But one has to make these

Photo 12.1 Young adults struggle to keep up with rent or mortgage payments with huge student loan repayments

Source: Getty Images: Jupiterimages

decisions while weighing other parts of one's financial life. For example, a 33-year-old Atlanta hospital administrative assistant bought a $150,000 condominium whose $1,473 monthly mortgage and carrying charges she could easily meet, but trouble came after moving in. The problem was she already had about $40,000 in credit card debt and student loans, and then spent another $5,000 for bedroom and dining room furniture. She ended up in credit counseling to get things straightened out (a subject that is discussed in the next chapter). *Single women represent 11 percent of all home buyers.*

Renting has become a more attractive option since the second edition of this book. People are marrying later, having children later. Money saved on housing can be invested in stocks, bonds, retirement, education and mutual funds, and/or spent for travel and other desirables. An advantage to owning is that mortgage tax deductions give a slight break to homeowners, but that may not be enough to say it is smarter to own than to rent. Renting usually involves a **security deposit**, which is a payment required by the landlord in advance to cover wear and tear of the unit and (as the name implies) to secure a unit for the renter. Most typically this is one month's rent on top of writing a check for the first month's rent, so a renter would probably pay $1,800 to move in if the rent was $900 a month plus the security deposit. There may also be a refundable or nonrefundable pet fee or deposit to take care of cleaning carpets and so forth when the renter moves out. Many landlord–tenant disputes are over the return of the security deposit at the end of the renting period.

Another part of renting is the signing of a **lease**, a legal document between the renter and the landlord describing the rights and responsibilities of both. Part of the lease is a clause about **subleasing**, which will describe what is or is not allowed and under what circumstances. Subleasing means the property can be leased by the original tenant to another person or persons.

Landlord–Tenant Disputes

Disputes between landlords and tenants are common, especially in college towns. Before moving in, renters should take photos showing the condition of the rental unit, especially focusing on any damaged or substandard areas that may come into dispute later. If the landlord promises repairs such as re-tiling a bathroom or re-carpeting, get that promise in writing. Upon leaving the unit, if it has been kept clean and undamaged, the tenants have the right to expect a prompt return of the security deposit. Tenants should give ample notice of vacating (usually at least a month) in order for the landlord to inspect the unit and line up another tenant. If there is a dispute about the return of the security deposit or the conditions of subleasing, the tenant should try first to work something out with the landlord or leasing agent. If this does not work, most campuses offer free legal services to students to try to resolve issues such as landlord–tenant disputes, and you can locate this service through university student services. Another alternative is small claims court.

CONSUMER ALERTS

Before signing a lease, do the following:

- Review its contents in order to know what you are signing.
- Look for features such as time and conditions. Is it a one-year lease or a month-to-month lease? Are you liable for damages and what kind?
- Look over the property. How well maintained are the grounds and the interiors? Are there newer appliances?
- Find out about subleasing. Is there a fee for the privilege of subleasing?
- Remember that landlords are not bound to anything they promise orally. If a landlord makes an oral promise, ask that it be written into the lease.
- Final advice: Write everything down.

CONSUMER ALERTS

A common problem is bait-and-switch regarding the quality of the apartment rented. For example, two students may look at a model apartment in a large complex in the spring and sign a lease to rent a similar apartment in the fall. When they arrive in the fall, their apartment is not of the same quality as the model apartment they were shown. Perhaps the carpet is not new, or the apartment has not been repainted; if it is furnished, the furniture may be broken and so forth. As mentioned in the text, the students' first step is to try to resolve the issue with the landlord. Are there other apartments? Will the landlord agree in writing to fix the problems immediately?

Photo 12.2 Photos of apartments don't always live up to the reality

Source: Thinkstock: Franck-Boston

Home ownership

Minorities, immigrants, and single people are buying homes in record numbers.

As mentioned in the Introduction, owning a home is often referred to as the American dream. We have sentimental songs like Stephen Foster's "Home Sweet Home" that extol the virtues of home. Can you picture this as "Apartment Sweet Apartment"? According to the US Census Bureau, record home ownership rates are taking place. Half of all Americans live in the suburbs, and nearly three-quarters (73 percent) of households are owner occupied.

When buying a home, what do most people want? Usually the answer for a middle-income US family is a single-family detached house with three or four bedrooms, multiple bathrooms, central heating and air conditioning, an up-to-date kitchen, a two-car garage, and a yard. With higher income comes the desire for a three-car garage for the extra car or for the storage space. One of the biggest changes in homes has been the increasing size of kitchens. According to the Census Bureau, from 1950 to 2004 the average size of the kitchen increased 216 percent, while the home itself increased only 72 percent in size. Consumers not only want spacious kitchens but also may specify the type of countertops, floors, backsplashes, and appliances.

The typical buyer of a new house spends $11,800 on improvements in the first year.

A starter home may be a manufactured home, a townhouse, half of a duplex, a condominium, a small home in a new development, or a house that needs fixing up. Some people, especially dual-income couples, skip the starter home phase and head straight for the three-bedroom, two-bath house in the suburbs or a deluxe condominium. "Minorities, immigrants and single people are buying homes in record numbers. They have transformed the housing market over the past 10 years and will likely be leading the charge in the decade to come" (The New "Starter" Home, 2002, p. 53).

Larger homes usually mean the purchase of more furniture as well as higher utility bills and property taxes, so size and location of the home have financial implications beyond the home's price. "Credit counselors say that new homeowners often get into financial trouble by spending too much after they move in. The typical buyer of a new house lays out $11,800 for home improvements in the first year, according to Harvard's Joint Center for Housing Studies."

Another development is adding more technology, including "green" technology, to homes. This ranges from compact fluorescent light bulbs to high-tech laundry equipment to home monitoring systems using cameras, cell phones, and computers. "The market for home-monitoring systems is expected to grow from $91 million in 2007 to $400 million in 2012, according to Parks Associates, a Dallas research firm" (Goodloe & Jurgensen, 2007, p. P6). Real estate agents can use the monitors to check who is looking at a house. Homeowners can use the monitors to turn on air conditioning so that the house is cool when they return after work or to see if their children got home safely from school; they can also watch renovations from afar. Costs can range from a monthly fee to a start-up package of over $15,000; these systems are sold by big-box stores or individual installers who customize home monitoring or security devices. The technology is being promoted by telephone, electronics, contracting, security, and computer companies—the more indispensable the devices, the better. It is easy to see how consumers get hooked on technology so they can be anywhere and see what is going on at home. You no longer have to worry whether you left a door unlocked or not: you can see if you did. On the joys of home monitoring systems, here is one example: "For some, it's pure escapist. Zach Glenwright spends most of his day editing video for a local news station. But every 30 minutes or so, he takes a break on this work computer to check on a camera of his own, monitoring the squirrels and birds in the backyard of his home in York, Pa. 'It's kind of like watching a TV show,' says the 25-year-old" (Goodloe & Jurgensen, 2007, p. P6).

Life Change Points and Consumption

The discussion of people going from renting to owning a home is a good example of a visible change point in people's lives. It is a signal of settling down and putting down roots. Other change points in people's lives include going to college, getting married, having children, getting a first professional job, moving, and retiring. These all usually involve increased expenses.

Marriage or having a first or second child, or even getting a dog, often signals the need for owning rather than renting. Families, friends, and work colleagues may help celebrate transitions with moving-in parties, baby showers, wedding showers, house warming parties, and retirement parties, which involve presents for the changing family and/or household needs. Since life changes involve the spending of money, media and business are well aware of this and try to capitalize on it by sponsoring bridal shows or giving free sample gift packs at marriage license bureaus and at maternity wards in hospitals. The thinking is that free magazines; free Tide, Secret, or Pampers samples; or discount coupons given at the right moment can set the mood for future sales. Condé Nast, publisher of *Bride* and *Modern Bride*, estimates that US newlyweds spend a combined $70 billion in the first year after marriage on their households. Consumers buy more in their first six months of marriage than a settled household does in five years (Ellison & Tejada, 2003). Consider the following:

> *Corporate marketers say certain points in life make consumers especially vulnerable to sales pitches, with the soon-to-be married often being the most susceptible. It's a time when they aren't just choosing a marriage partner but also are making brand decisions about toothpaste, detergent and appliances that could last even longer. Unless a couple has been living together for years, wedding represents a moment when two sets of habits and brand preferences meet and usually only one survives. "Newlyweds," says James Stengel, global marketing officer at Procter & Gamble Co. in Cincinnati, "are in some ways the ultimate consumer." (Ellison & Tejada, 2003, p. B1)*

Newlyweds are the ultimate consumers.

Change points surge at certain times of the year. For example, graduations and weddings peak in June. Also, one-fifth of wedding proposals occur in December, causing a huge spike in advertising in January bridal magazines; these ads are not just for wedding gowns and bridesmaid dresses but for vacation destinations, household goods, shampoos, cosmetics, fragrances, and cars. American List Counsel, a marketing firm, gathers names of newlyweds from county clerk's offices and photographers, and sells the names to marketers, including realtors. "Newlywed names 'are like gold,' says Pete Hunsinger, president of Condé Nast's bridal group" (Ellison & Tejada, 2003, p. B3). House sales peak in the summer because people with children want to be settled before the new school year begins, so movers can charge more in the summer than they can during the rest of the year.

Homes as Investments

Technically speaking, housing is considered a consumer good, not a pure investment; however, most people think of their homes as an investment. It is a consumer good because the house is typically used by the owners. Homeowners typically stay in their homes for eight years, which is longer than most people hold shares of stock. Even with all that said, real estate investments are compared to investing in stocks. This is important to do to gain perspective, even though they are not truly equivalent. As former Federal Reserve Board Chairman Alan Greenspan said, "The transaction costs of homes are very high. You can't readily sell a home without a very large cost, and perhaps more importantly, you have to move. The type of underlying conditions that creates bubbles [is] very difficult to create in the housing market" (*The Freddie Mac Reporter Fact Book*, 2002–2003, p. 17).

Home values in recent years have had their ups and downs. Location, as always, matters greatly.

Home values fell nationally during the depression of the 1930s but held up well for much of the rest of the twentieth century and into the twenty-first century until the Great Recession of 2009. Home values dipped considerably in that year, and only in 2014 and 2015 did they start climbing back to pre-2009 prices in much of the country. Over the last 50 years, home values have gone up on average 4 percent per year compared to stocks at 7 percent per year, so some would say stocks are better investments but, again, that differs by individual stocks. Diversifying is the key to a more steady state as stocks, bonds, mutual funds, individual retirement funds (IRAs), and real estate values and prices fluctuate.

In looking back, when the economy took a slight dip from 1999 to 2003, real estate held its value because of low mortgage rates and actually increased considerably in value in places such as Greenwich, CT, Washington, DC, and Southern California. In fact, the housing market was so good that an article in the *Wall Street Journal* said, "Forget watching the stock market. The best—maybe the only—game in town these days is the remarkably resilient real-estate market. Last year alone, amid all the bad news, home prices still rose by 7% nationally—and some economists believe things will be almost as strong this year" (Fletcher, 2003, p. W1). What followed this article was a slowing down of the real estate market. In most areas of the United States in 2006 and 2007, there were more sellers than buyers, and many homes were sitting on the market for six months or more. Real estate values declined, leveled off, or kept pace with inflation. At the same time, property insurance and taxes skyrocketed in many parts of the country, making real estate investing less attractive. The practice of flipping houses to make quick profits (popular from 2000–2006) slowed; extravagant remodeling jobs were also reconsidered in terms of their added value at resale time. So land and/or a home may or may not be a good investment depending on the time, the location, taxes, and interest rates. Realtors and wise buyers study the national economy as well as the local market when comparing house values. The takeaway from this is that the real estate market cycles and a boom will be followed by a downswing or a more stable period when values do not rise sharply.

Renting vs. Buying homes: Time Factor

The longer you stay in a house, the more you will benefit from the ability to live rent-free and the less you need to worry about short-term price dips. "Over seven or eight years, you can be pretty sure that buying a house will financially dominate renting," according to Chris Mayer, a real estate professor at the University of Pennsylvania's Wharton School (Clements, 2003, p. D1).

If you will be living in an area for less than three years, it may be wiser to rent than to buy.

But if your time horizon is shorter than that, what should you do? The shorter the time horizon, the more risk there is, so more care should be taken in choosing the type of housing and the location. As a general rule, condominiums and high-end houses should be avoided because during market downturns these are hit harder than middle-income single-family homes. The cutoff point is three years, so if you are going to be in an area less than three years, renting may be a better option from a financial standpoint. The reasons are the high expenses involved in buying and selling the house (including closing and financing costs) and the possibility that the home will not rise significantly in value in a short amount of time. Of course, an area where housing prices are soaring would be an exception to this. Homes can be an **illiquid asset**, meaning they are difficult to sell readily to get the cash. It is not unusual for homes to take more than a year to sell; if they are vacant during that time, the homeowners are paying the mortgage, property taxes, and upkeep expenses, while at the same time paying rent or mortgage payments in the new location.

As stocks declined in the early 2000s and real estate rose in value, scam artists shifted their attention to the real estate market. Newlyweds can be a target since they are new to the housing market. State and federal regulators reported a decided increase in complaints regarding time-shares and other types of real estate investments, including land in places like Texas. One scam was the promise of oil on land in Texas, the basic pitch being that because of unrest in the world, Texas oil was going to be worth more. As readers of this book know, geopolitical situations and the economy change, and fraudsters take advantage of conditions to prey on fear and uncertainty. Whether for personal use or as a way to build wealth, real estate investments should be carefully scrutinized. Ask yourself if the seller is legitimate (established) and if the price is reasonable. In general, investigate before you invest. The best way to protect yourself is to remember, as always, "If it sounds too good to be true, it probably isn't." Does the offer pass the sniff test?

Decision Points

Readiness to Buy

After years of renting, individuals want to own. The main reason first-time home buyers give for looking for a home is that they are tired of paying rent, according to the National Association of Realtors, so the first determinant of readiness to buy is the feeling that it is time to buy. When asking people why they want to buy, the second most-cited reason is tax advantages, and the third is a desire for a larger place. Box 12.1 gives other reasons why someone may prefer buying over renting.

Owning a home has several advantages, including the most basic—supplying the need for shelter. A home is an investment as well, offering an opportunity to build equity; when someone buys, he or she hopes the house will go up in value. Emotional reasons include the need to lay down roots, pride, an opportunity for self-expression, security, and a sense of ownership.

Financially, how does someone determine how much house he or she can afford? Several formulas exist to determine readiness to buy: The simplest is the 2.5 times rule (some lenders would say 3 times is more realistic so try that formula too), which gives a person a general idea of the maximum amount he or she could spend. To calculate this, multiply the annual household income by two and one-half; for example, a person earning $40,000 a year could afford a $100,000 house.

A typical down payment is 10 to 20 percent of the purchase price, so for the $100,000 house, a person should save up $10,000 to $20,000 before seriously looking to buy. Ads for new developments will often say no money down; in that case, the person would

Box 12.1 Pros and Cons of Renting and Buying Housing

	Renting	Buying
Pros	Extras like swimming pools	Pride of ownership
	Few responsibilities	Tax deductions
	No yard work, no repairs	Equity building
	Feeling of not being tied down	Feeling of community
	Close neighbors offering security	Ability to borrow against equity
	Problems handled by manager	Improved credit rating
	Utilities possibly included	Garage and/or yard possibly included
		More space
Cons	No tax deductions	Feeling of being tied down
	Transient neighbors	Down payment
	Inability to make many changes	Closing costs
	No pets policy	Repair bills
	Not much storage	Yard work
	Rent increase with little notice	Property taxes
	Inability to build equity	Homeowners' association dues
	Lack of washer/dryer	Money tied up

Table 12.1 The Mortgage Application Process

The mortgage application process can be sped up by having:

- a legal description of the property and the price
- income, recent pay stubs
- real estate background: what was owned or rented before
- liquid assets: cash, checking and savings accounts, bank statements, insurance policies, and other proof
- personal information about the borrowers: social security number, addresses

not need a down payment, although it is usually a good idea because there are more choices and a higher down payment will diminish how much is owed.

Mortgages, loans to purchase real estate in which the real estate serves as collateral, are what remains after the down payment is subtracted from the purchase price. Lenders

Table 12.2 The 28/36 Qualifying Rule

	28 Qualifying Rule	36 Qualifying Rule
Monthly Income	$4,000	$4,000
	× 0.28	× 0.36
	$1,120	$1,440

such as banks can help a person determine how much house he or she can afford. Lenders estimate mortgages based on the down payment and the buyer's ability to handle monthly payments of **PITI**, which stands for principal, interest, taxes, insurance. Another method for determining whether one is ready to buy or not is the 28/36 qualifying rule: Monthly gross income is multiplied by 0.28 (28 percent) or 0.36 (36 percent) to show the monthly range of PITI that lenders would consider appropriate.

For example, if someone had a $4,000 monthly income, the person could afford a mortgage of between $1,120 and $1,440 per month, assuming the person does not have large amounts owed on cars or on credit cards. The lender will look at the person's total **net worth** (assets minus liabilities) to determine how much he or she can afford. **Assets** are what is owned; **liabilities** are what is owed. The 2.5 times rule and the 28/36 qualifying rule are conservative starting points (see Table 12.2).

An online tutorial that helps consumers determine if they are ready for home ownership and that provides descriptions of the mortgage process and options is available from Freddie Mac. Through a congressional charter in 1970, **Freddie Mac** was established to work with mortgage lenders to help people get lower housing costs and better access to residential home financing. Because of Freddie Mac, more people have access to better home financing and lower monthly mortgage payments, the goal being to make housing more accessible and affordable to a wide range of Americans.

Housing Types

The two main housing types are unattached single-family dwellings and multiunit dwellings such as duplexes, townhouses, condominiums, and cooperatives. **Condominiums** and townhouses are homes attached to one another: You own a unit, but you and your neighbors share common areas such as swimming pools and lobbies. Condominiums can be found anywhere but are most often associated with beaches, ski areas, golf courses, theme parks, and other types of resort, retirement, or recreational areas. The monthly maintenance or repair fees for common areas collected from owners of townhouses or from condominium owners are called **homeowner's fees**. **Cooperative apartments** are similar, except you own shares in the building as a whole, with the right to lease a certain unit. Cooperative apartments are found mostly in big cities such as Boston and New York City. **Manufactured housing** includes units that are fully or partially assembled in a factory and moved to the living site.

Housing Quality

Regardless of housing type, care should be taken in assessing housing quality—availability of services, zoning laws, school zones, and covenants. Potential buyers should inquire about **home warranties**, which provide additional protection for the buyer, and **home inspections**, which assess the condition of the home. States vary in how much is disclosed to the potential buyer before or at **closing**, the meeting in which real estate is transferred from seller to buyer. States also vary in how much is paid by the seller and how much is paid by the buyer at closing in terms of fees and add-ons; many of these can be negotiated before going into the closing. An anxious seller is more likely to pick up extra costs and fees than a seller with many potential buyers. **Defect-disclosure forms** that describe the condition of the home are required in some states, and termite inspections are required in others. Before purchasing, find out what the rules are in your area. Realtors should be up front about a home's or a neighborhood's defects, but they are usually paid commission by the seller and therefore are more likely to be working in the seller's interest. Many realtors, however, take the long-term view and realize it is equally important to have satisfied buyers who either may hire them again to buy or sell a house or who may give good word-of-mouth publicity to other potential buyers and sellers. The majority of homes are sold by realtors, although this percentage may be declining slightly for a number of reasons, including the use of the Internet. More homeowners are using the Internet to sell their houses, and more buyers are searching online on their own, at least initially.

One would assume a new home bought directly from the builder would not require a home inspection, but today hiring inspectors for new housing is becoming more and more common. The potential buyer hires the home inspector and pays the fee. Investing in real estate is very much about the old adage that "you get what you pay for"—using highly recommended realtors and inspectors, and buying well-built houses pay off in the long run.

Mortgages

This section provides a quick overview of the main types of mortgages. Here are three hints when shopping for a mortgage:

1. Educate yourself. Current interest rates are reported in the newspaper and over the Internet, and mortgages are available locally and over the Internet.
2. Know your lending institution.
3. Visit websites providing home buying information.

Most people get a fixed-rate, fixed-term, fixed-payment loan, which is usually carried for 15 or 30 years and is called a **fixed-rate conventional mortgage**. When mortgage rates are low (and they were ranging from 3 to 4 percent when this chapter went to press), this is a good choice because the housing costs are known, budgeting is easier, and the mortgage rate is set. If mortgage rates increase sharply, more people consider **adjustable-rate mortgages (ARMs),** which allow the interest rates to fluctuate within a range that is based on changes in the economy. Usually with ARMs, less is paid initially—as much as 2 percent less (a teaser rate) than with fixed-rate conventional mortgages—so ARMs may be a good option for people starting out as new hires or as newlyweds, assuming their incomes will build. At preset intervals, the ARM would be revisited and go up or down within a range.

Mortgage seekers can get mortgages either online or at mortgage companies, banks, or credit unions. A home buyer can negotiate with the lender (online or in person) rather than assuming a published rate is final. If a person has a good credit rating, the amount may be reduced.

Sometimes, the seller offers help with financing. Potential buyers should weigh all the financial options and the state of the economy at the time of purchase.

If mortgage rates drop considerably (at least two percentage points) after the house is bought, then the homeowner can look into refinancing. For example, if the mortgage was 9 percent and the current fixed-rate conventional mortgage is at 5 percent, it would be worthwhile to look into refinancing. The problem is that this change involves paperwork, time, and fees, so the homeowner will have to weigh the costs and the benefits of changing to a different mortgage. Usually refinancing makes the most sense if the homeowner is planning to stay several more years in the same home.

Predatory Home Mortgage Abuses. Most people get their homes financed through legitimate mortgage companies or banks, but as with anything involving money (and in this case, large sums of money), the potential for fraud is enormous. May the borrower beware! **Predatory lending** lures people into loans they really can't afford, usually by borrowing against the equity in their homes or a relative's home. The predatory practice could involve a new mortgage or a home equity loan on a home that is already owned. Consumers' rights in this regard are partially protected by the Home Ownership and Equity Protection Act of 1994, and consumer advocates would like to strengthen this act to provide further protection, which would include wider regulation of the high-interest subprime lending market where predatory practices are common. Here are five warning signs of predatory lenders:

1. Advertising "we give credit to anyone" or "poor credit, no problem."
2. Rushing the person to sign immediately.
3. Asking for a large fee up front to see if the potential homeowner qualifies for a loan.
4. Offering an unusually low mortgage rate compared to the general market.
5. Offering small monthly payments with a large balloon payment at the end.

Older people and low-income people are prime targets for predatory home mortgage sellers. Many people do not understand that they could lose their homes if they do not keep up payments. Loan origination fees are part of the problem; these may run as high as 10 to 25 percent of the total loan amount (versus a more typical lender fee of around 2 percent). Advocacy groups such as the American Association of Retired Persons (AARP) have successfully represented homeowners in suits against mortgage lenders in New York, West Virginia, and Washington, DC. For copies of settlements, go to the Federal Trade Commission (FTC) website. Freddie Mac provides information on predatory lending. Examples are given in Table 12.3.

Mortgage Pitfalls and Fraud Potential. Once individuals own a home and start building equity, they may take out a second mortgage, a home equity line of credit, cash-out refinancing, or a reverse mortgage (the latter is discussed in a later section). Each financial instrument has pitfalls, the main one being that all forms of home equity borrowing leech value from the home. Here are the main types:

- In a second mortgage, a person pays a fixed rate of interest (usually around 5 or 6 percent) for a set amount of money repaid over 5 to 10 years to finance a single project such as renovations.

- The **home equity line of credit** carries a variable interest rate (usually around 4 percent, but it varies, so investigate current rates) and allows the homeowner to borrow up to a set amount. This can work well to finance home improvement projects.

- Cash-out refinancing allows the homeowner to replace the first mortgage with another, perhaps larger, loan and pocket the difference. The drawback here is that a person may be starting over with a new 30-year loan.

Table 12.3 Beneficial Lending Practices and their Predatory Potential

Lending practice	Benefit	Predatory potential
Higher-than-market interest rates	Enables relatively risky borrowers to obtain credit	Can financially ruin borrowers who lack financial capacity to repay the loan with its excessive interest rate
Ability to refinance	Enables borrowers to take advantage of lower interest rates	Can invite loan flipping, resulting in high loan fees and unnecessary credit costs
Prepayment penalties	Provides borrowers with lower rates	Can prevent borrowers from refinancing or can unnecessarily drive up loan balance (as penalties are financed as part of a new loan)

Source: *The Freddie Mac Reporter Fact Book 2007*, McLean, VA, p. 25.

These are the basic types, but there are new combinations being offered, including a combination of a first mortgage with a home equity line of credit. One of the features is that the credit line automatically increases as the borrower pays down the mortgage and the home's value grows.

The main advantages of home-based loans are that they offer low interest rates and that the interest paid is usually deductible from income tax. Rates are usually tied to the prime rate and move up when the prime rate increases.

Here is an example:

> *Chris Englin, an executive recruiter who lives near Seattle, took out a home equity line from Wells Fargo when she refinanced her $200,000 mortgage in December. Ms. Englin says her loan officer suggested the credit line when she mentioned she needed cash to buy a half-interest in a 24-foot fishing boat. Taking out the home-equity line "was really easy," she says. "We did the whole thing by e-mail." (Simon, 2003, p. D1)*

The main drawback of home equity loans is that the home is at risk if the person does not keep up with the monthly loan payments. Before taking out a home equity loan, the homeowner should ask some questions:

1. Do I really need the money?
2. Is there a minimum or maximum monthly payment?
3. What is the annual percentage rate? Is it set or adjustable? (If rates are low, a set rate is usually a better choice.)
4. Are there any annual fees or transaction fees?
5. How long is the loan for?

See the Consumer Alert below for further advice.

Fraud—through advertisements on television, high-pressure telephone sales calls, and door-to-door salespeople—abounds. The elderly are often targeted because they have built up so much equity in their homes yet may be cash poor. The best way to go about this is to apply for an equity loan through a local credit union or bank or at least to talk with a loan officer, which provides a sense of baseline amounts and terms. Do not sign anything unless it is completely understood. Home equity lines of credit, refinancing arrangements, and second mortgages may carry closing costs, fees, points, and taxes that may total up to 10 percent of the loan, so a $40,000 loan could end up costing an additional $4,000—and this is with a legitimate business.

Reverse mortgages pay the homeowner, usually an elderly person, in monthly advances or through a line of credit. Reverse mortgages convert home equity into cash with no repayment required for as long as the borrowers live in their homes. The main drawback is that the homeowners are taking value away from their home, so when they move elsewhere or die, the home equity for them or their heirs is reduced. It is prudent to consult an attorney, an accountant, or another financial advisor before taking out a reverse mortgage. As mentioned in an earlier chapter, in 1969 the Truth in Lending Act became a federal law as part of the Consumer Protection Act. It requires disclosure of a truth-in-lending statement on consumer loans, including mortgages. The consumer has to know the total cost of credit, such as the annual percentage rate and other specifics of the loan. The law was updated in 1980 as part of the Depository Institutions Deregulation and Monetary Control Act.

Discrimination and Redlining. Discrimination is an act based on prejudice or bias. In housing, it means that someone may not be treated fairly in terms of renting, buying, or financing. The following federal agencies, collectively known as "the agencies," are concerned that some prospective buyers and other borrowers may be experiencing discriminatory treatment in their efforts to obtain loans:

- The Department of Housing and Urban Development (HUD)
- The Department of Justice (DOJ)
- The Office of the Comptroller of the Currency (OCC)
- The Office of Thrift Supervision (OTS)
- The Board of Governors of the Federal Reserve System (the "Board")
- The Federal Deposit Insurance Corporation (FDIC)
- The Federal Housing Finance Board (FHFB)
- The Federal Trade Commission (FTC)
- The National Credit Union Administration (NCUA)
- The Office of Federal Housing Enterprise Oversight (OFHEO).

Redlining is a type of discrimination that is prohibited by law. It refers to the practice of drawing a line around an area that signifies that the area will not receive the same treatment as other areas regarding financing (redlining can also exist for insurance and credit). Typically state laws protect consumers from being discriminated against regarding housing and financing; however, there are exceptions, such as private clubs and religious organizations. There have been many lawsuits about discriminatory practices, including retirement-living developments that have tried to keep out younger occupants. The Home Mortgage Disclosure Act requires the lenders to report where they make loans. No loans may be available in certain locations, usually low-income or crime-ridden areas; if loans are available, they may be significantly overpriced. Box 12.2 lists the protections against discrimination that the Equal Credit Opportunity Act (ECOA) and the Fair Housing Act (FHA) offer. These acts cover purchasing and refinancing homes as well as making home improvements.

CONSUMER ALERTS

Banks are aggressively marketing home equity lines, but they are not for everyone:

- They make the most sense for short-term loans (two or three years) for things such as home improvements.
- If money is needed for a longer period of time, the borrower should seek fixed-rate loans.
- Pay attention to the interest rate, and compare rates. One source is Bankrate.com, a consumer finance website. The best home equity line may be from the same lender as the mortgage lender because usually banks look favorably on someone they already know and have a relationship with.

Lenders cannot discourage an individual from applying for a mortgage or reject an application due to race, national origin, religion, sex, marital status, age, or support from public assistance, but it is legal for lenders to factor in a person's income, expenses, debts, and credit history. Stable employment is also an important factor in how a lender will evaluate an application. When a mortgage is denied, the lender has to give specific reasons. Before applying for mortgages, potential home buyers should check their credit reports and have any errors corrected; credit bureaus are required to investigate any errors in dispute.

CONSUMER ALERTS

If you or someone you know has been discriminated against, complain to the lender; then check your state consumer affairs department or attorney general's office to see if the creditor has violated state laws. Many states have their own equal credit opportunity laws. If a mortgage application is denied, the lender must provide the name and address of the appropriate government agency to contact. Another option is suing the lender in federal district court—you can sue as an individual or join others to file a class-action suit. Another source for advice is the National Fair Housing Alliance. You can file a complaint with the US Department of Housing and Urban Development (HUD) in Washington, DC, and HUD will investigate the complaint and determine if there is reasonable cause to believe the Fair Housing Act has been violated.

Box 12.2 Protections against Mortgage Discrimination

The Equal Credit Opportunity Act (ECOA) and the Fair Housing Act (FHA) protect against discrimination when an individual applies for a mortgage to purchase or refinance a home or to make home improvements.

Under ECOA, discrimination is prohibited in any aspect of an applicant's credit transaction based on the following:

- race or color
- religion
- national origin
- sex
- marital status
- age (provided the applicant has the capacity to contract)
- applicant's income derived from any public assistance program
- applicant's exercise, in good faith, of any right under the Consumer Credit Protection Act (the umbrella statute that includes ECOA).

Under FHA, discrimination is prohibited in all aspects of residential real estate-related transactions:

- loans to buy, build, repair, or improve a dwelling
- sale, brokering, or appraisal of residential real estate
- sale, brokering, or appraisal of residential real estate
- sale or renting of a dwelling
- borrower's race or color
- borrower's national origin
- borrower's sex
- borrower's familial status (defined as children under age 18 living with a parent or legal guardian, pregnant women, and people with custody of children under age 18)
- borrower's handicap.

Source: Adapted from FTC Facts for Consumers,
Mortgage Discrimination, at www.ftc.gov.

Utilities: Costs and Environmental Impact

Since the first edition of this book, there has been a tremendous energy-saving, pro-environment push, with earth-friendly products and ideas showing up everywhere. Specially designed products and programs can cut energy bills and decrease greenhouse gas emissions by up to 30 percent. When it comes to going green, a lot of people are jumping on board on the home front and also nationally by supporting policy changes.

In the typical household, the utilities, including electricity, natural gas, and water, take about 5 percent of the housing budget. Sometimes telephone services are included in estimate lists of utilities, but because of the variety of new phone systems, most of them are not tied to home use. Consumers have choices of energy suppliers (including natural gas suppliers) in most states, and these choices include a local private or public utility company or a cooperative. Water comes from local water agencies; the main government protection in this area comes from the Environmental Protection Agency (EPA). Costs as well as services should be compared.

When looking at national averages, the highest utility cost is for residential space heating at 33 percent, followed by water heating at 15 percent; next comes space cooling at 10 percent. Of course, in warm climates the space cooling can run higher on a yearly basis than heating bills. Small appliances, such as small motors, electric knives, and sewing machines, use very little energy and won't affect utility bills much one way or the other. Appliances, devices, and lights that are large and left on for long periods of time use more energy than appliances that are turned off and on and only used for a few minutes (for example, a blender uses far less energy than a refrigerator).

To address the new ways people cook and the reduced spaces in which they live, appliance manufacturers are developing refrigerators that are multifunctional. Combination washer/dryers, which are rare in the United States, are common in Europe, and other multipurpose appliances are in development.

Energy Smart is a government program that requires appliance manufacturers to label the energy use of new appliances so the consumer will know how much energy the appliance uses in a typical year. A growing number of appliances and systems in the home are said to be getting smarter by communicating with each other, ascertaining workloads, and so on. Microprocessors and computer networking have made these connections possible; for example, new washing machines can measure how heavy a wash load is and how soiled the clothing is and then react accordingly. The majority of new large appliances have some type of electronic device that makes them smarter— appliances can be put on timers that will have them run during off-peak energy times for energy savings and potential money savings. As another way to reduce utility bills, most utility companies or government energy offices have inspectors or auditors who will provide free home energy audits so that homeowners can learn how to save energy costs in their specific house.

In the long run, though, "There isn't a silver bullet," says David Garman, the US Energy Department's assistant secretary for energy-efficiency programs. "There isn't a single 'gee whiz' technology that changes everything. You usually have to try to do a lot of little things to achieve energy savings" (Moore, 2001). That said, builders and architects are working on this concept to the point that energy savings with fluorescent lighting and tankless water heaters can be as much as 75 percent compared with those in conventional homes. Saving on utilities while saving the environment is a good example of the crossover between consumerism and environmentalism (discussed in Chapter 2). Environmentally friendly building practices, spurred by home buyers' values, the cost savings derived from greater energy efficiency, and pressure from environmentalists, have become increasingly popular in the custom building industry. The good news is that the United States is more than 2.5 times more energy efficient today than in the 1970s (Yergin, 2015, p. C2).

Vehicles

> **CASE STUDY**
>
> ### Tesla Model S
>
> "The introduction of the Tesla Model S in 2012 was a very impressive engineering and marketing feat. But the rechargeable lithium-ion battery that powers the car was originally invented in an Exxon laboratory during the energy crisis of the 1970s, when it was thought that oil was about to run out."
>
> Source: Yergin, D. (August 22–23, 2015). "The Next Energy Revolutions." *Wall Street Journal*, p. C2.

Innovation in cars, as well as in houses, is what we expect. Thomas Edison, who was always ahead of his time, spent a great deal of time trying to develop an electric car.

Houses are expensive but cars are too. The average transaction price for a new vehicle set a record at $31,262 in August 2015, according to TrueCar.com, up 3.2% from 2014. The leading five car companies in that month were Chrysler, Ford, Honda, Nissan, and Volkswagen. The **transaction price** includes the price of the vehicle, discounts, add-ons, taxes, and license fees. Daniel Gilbert (2006) says that cars might seem like good purchases because of their lasting value, but actually cars experience depreciation (a loss of value, especially right after purchase) and slowly deteriorate. This is in comparison to homes, which generally (except in a housing recession) see **appreciation** (an increase in value). That said, most of us need cars, so questions revolve around which ones to buy, how to maintain them, how long to keep them, and whether to lease them or not. Do you want a hybrid or not? How do you feel about fuel efficiency and the environment? How important are added safety features? Will a less expensive car bring as much satisfaction as a more expensive car?

There is no question that a vehicle that runs well is useful and enjoyable and that vehicles are needed to get you where you want to go. Some consumers also get great satisfaction from owning, collecting, showing, and restoring cars. This discussion goes back to the beginning of the first chapter, which explored the connection between happiness and consumption. If ever there was a purchase category where this is true (or not), it is vehicle ownership. Have you had good or bad experiences when purchasing cars? The following section begins with an exploration of leasing as an option.

Leasing Vehicles

Pros and Cons

Leasing a vehicle is a contractual arrangement with terms concerning the monthly payment, security deposit, and condition of the vehicle upon return. The price may be negotiable. Basically a lease means you are renting a car, usually for three years for 36,000 miles. It is estimated that about 30 percent of new cars are leased, with some consumers leasing a new car every three years. There are several *advantages* to leasing:

- Less money is needed up front. A low down payment or no down payment is needed; the car can be leased with a security deposit (similar to renting an apartment). During promotions and in competitive markets, the security deposit may be waived.
- Monthly payments may be less than the payments when a car is bought.
- There are no worries about getting a trade-in or having to personally sell the car.
- The lease may be paid by an employer or may be a tax deduction if the owner owns a business that uses the car.

- Some consumers deduct leasing charges as a legitimate business expense. People in businesses such as real estate where having a fairly new and presentable car is an asset may find that leasing is a good option.

There are also *disadvantages* of leasing:

- The vehicle isn't owned, so it is not an investment or an asset with a return.
- Extra charges may be added when the vehicle is turned in; for example, if more than the recommended mileage has accrued or repairs are needed beyond average wear, the lease agreement may not cover those expenses.
- Insurance costs for leasing a car may be higher than for owning a car.

Before leasing, read the contract thoroughly; focus on the number of miles recommended, and determine if that number meets your needs. Contracts are usually written for 12,000–15,000 miles per year, which was figured as reasonable given that the average car is driven 15,100 miles per year; however, with commutes getting longer, it is expected that the average mileage will increase. To figure total cost, a leaser should find out what the additional per-mile charge is for going over the minimum.

When reading the contract, be alert to other charges such as conveyance, disposition, and preparation fees. If there was a trade-in allowance, make sure the contract includes it.

Types of Leases

Not all leases are created equal. There are three main types:

1. *Closed-end or "walk-away" lease.* In a closed-end lease, the leaser returns the vehicle at the end of the lease period (usually three years) and pays only for additional miles or repairs.
2. *Open-end or finance lease.* The leaser pays the difference between the expected value of the leased vehicle and the amount for which the leasing company sells it in an open-end lease. There may also be an end-of-lease payment.
3. *Single-payment lease.* A single-payment lease allows the consumer to obtain a discount on the vehicle rental agreement if certain standards are met.

Consumer rights and responsibilities regarding leasing vehicles are given in Box 12.3.

CONSUMER ALERTS

A lease covering 12,000 miles a year is typical, but big names in the luxury car business are pushing low-payment leases to spur consumer traffic. Many of these deals allow motorists just 10,000 miles of driving a year before severe penalties occur. Here were two options for a BMW 325i three-year lease:

Lease Miles	Monthly Payment
10,000	$299
15,000	$321

If mileage was exceeded by 5,000 miles/year, the penalty charge was $3,000. If the cost was added at the time of the lease (up front), the 5,000 extra miles/year would be $792 (White, 2003). To win at this game, the driver should be realistic about the average number of miles that will be driven and pick the best option.

CONSUMER ALERTS

When leases first became available, some consumers did not understand that they were renting a vehicle rather than owning it outright, so when it came time to get a new model, they did not understand that they could not sell it or get any money back—in fact, they most likely owed money. Others have been less than happy at the extra add-on charges when they brought the vehicle in for a new one. Still other consumers felt pressured to buy from the same dealership and found there were financial penalties involved in switching manufacturers, making them feel locked in to the same make for years—the only choices being a new color and updated features. On the other hand, some consumers have found a type of car they want and get it over and over again, and the leasing process makes this process easy.

Vehicle Preleasing and Prebuying: Information Search

Before leasing or buying a car, many consumers take a spin around the Internet. A search reveals makes, models, and features such as color choices, upgrade packages, and dealer locations. Some individual dealers have put their whole inventory online; so in addition to information from the manufacturer, you can get specific information from the lot down the street. Before leasing or purchasing, most consumers want to test-drive a few cars to get a sense of how they feel and fit, but as a first step, it is hard to beat an online search. Of course, websites vary. Some provide much-needed information, and others are more heavily into marketing and sales without the necessary concrete information. The best ones give energy-use figures and 360-degree photo tours of the interiors, including zoom-in features so that the dashboard and engine can be examined.

Box 12.3 Know Your Rights and Responsibilities When Leasing Vehicles

The federal Consumer Leasing Act gives you the right to information that helps you understand and negotiate your lease. When you lease a vehicle, you have these rights:

1. To use it for an agreed-on number of months and miles.

2. To turn it in at lease end, pay any end-of-lease fees and charges, and "walk away."

3. To buy the vehicle (if you have a purchase option).

4. To take advantage of any warranties, recalls, or other services that apply to the vehicle.

Your responsibilities include the following:

1. To pay excess mileage charges when you return the vehicle.

2. To pay excess wear charges when you return the vehicle.

3. To make substantial payments if you end the lease early.

Source: Adapted from *Keys to Vehicle Leasing: A Consumer Guide* from the Board of Governors of the Federal Reserve System, Washington, DC 20551.

Buying Vehicles

Pros and Cons

The main advantage of buying is that you own the vehicle—it is an asset. Up-front costs include the cash price or a down payment, taxes, registration and other fees, and other charges. A drawback is that the monthly loan payments are usually higher than monthly lease payments because the total cost includes interest and other charges, and if you end the loan early, there may be fees. Future value will be determined by the condition of the vehicle and the vehicle's market value at time of sale or trade. Another drawback is that a lot of money can be tied up in car payments that could be spent or invested elsewhere. Advantages to owning versus leasing include no limits on the number of miles driven and no charges for excessive wear. Once the car is paid for in full or at the end of the loan term, there are no further loan payments. Being debt free is a positive feeling and a goal many people hope to attain.

Photo 12.3
Car sales go up
and down with
the general
economy

Source: Getty
Images: Bill
Pugliano

New Cars

Information Gathering. Besides researching cars online, another option is to read *Consumer Reports, Popular Mechanics*, and *Motor Trend* for car ratings, service, and safety. Information gathering of this sort can be pleasurable and useful since a new car is a major purchase, second only to a house in terms of expense. Once the make and model have been selected, here are some other suggestions:

- Do comparison shopping at area dealerships or through online services or buying services such as the American Automobile Association (AAA). Buy only from reputable dealers or services. Complaint records are available from state and local consumer protection agencies and the Better Business Bureau (BBB).

- Shop in advance for the best financing option. Local or online credit unions and banks often offer better interest rates than dealerships.

- Test-drive cars to get a sense of how they handle and whether they fit your size, shape, and driving behavior. Get price quotes from several dealers. If buying from a dealer, test-drive the specific car you are going to buy; do not test-drive a substitute car or one that is coming in next week. If you order a car from a dealership, test-drive it before buying it.

- Read the "Buyer's Guide" sticker required to be displayed in the window of the car.

- Don't buy on impulse or when you are pressured by salespeople.

- Negotiate the price. Dealer profit margin is usually between 10 and 20 percent. The difference may be between the manufacturer's suggested retail price and the invoice price. The **invoice price** is the manufacturer's initial charge to the dealer (in other words, what the car cost the dealer). The **sticker price** or **suggested retail price** is the price of the car, including options, transportation charges, and any "market adjustments." Look at the total price, not just the monthly payment.

- Find out if the manufacturer is offering rebates.

- Remember that buying off the lot may bring the lowest price because that is in-stock inventory that has to move, but ordering a car from a dealer or service will get the desired features and will omit the ones not cared about. Volume, especially the cars sitting on a dealer's lot, tends to drive down prices.

Sales Techniques. A common sales technique is to polish up cars and put them under flattering lights in showrooms. A second one is to encourage the buyer of a new car to become a loyal repeat customer, and there are several ways of doing this, including offering good dealer repair services (with free donuts in the waiting room). Another sales technique is for the salesperson to build a relationship with the buyer. As a first step, the salesperson calls recent buyers to find out if they are satisfied with their car. But some salespeople go further than that. Joe Girard, known as the "world's greatest car salesman" (how is that for puffery), says the secret of his success was getting customers to like him. He did this by sending every one of his more than 13,000 customers holiday greeting cards every month (Happy New Year, Happy Thanksgiving, etc.), and each card had the same printed message: "I like you." Joe explained, "There's nothing else on the card, nothin' but my name. I'm just telling 'em that I like 'em" (Cialdini, 2001, p. 152). Joe had learned that flattery worked. We tend to believe praise, and we like the people who give it (Cialdini, 2001).

Another sales technique involves pressure. This can work selling cars (new and used) and houses. If the salesperson can convince potential buyers that this is the one and only car or house for them, that is a very hard pitch for buyers to resist. Making the buyer feel special (smart, unique, and forward-thinking) is a strong sales ploy.

Used Cars

There's nothing like that new-car smell. Buying a new car has a lot of allure: It's brand new and it's all yours; nobody has abused it. You can get the vehicle equipped just the way you want, and you get the full factory warranty. But hold on. Your best deal could well be a late-model used car. The used-car market has changed dramatically in the past few years. To start with, today's new cars—and the used cars—are simply made better. Overall quality and durability has increased as US manufacturers pushed hard to catch up to imports. A second factor is the rise of leasing. New used-car superstore chains also are making it easier than ever to buy, with huge inventories and no-haggle shopping (Money Essentials, 2015).

As a potential buyer of a used car, the first step is to figure out how much you can afford, and the next step is to narrow the choices by going online, researching the frequency of repair and maintenance costs on the models, knowing sellers, and checking the US Department of Transportation's Auto Safety Hotline (1-800-424-9393) to find out about recalls. Average prices can be located in *Edmund's Used Car Prices* and *Kelley Blue Book*, as well as other guides and websites. For paying, there are two options: pay in full or finance over time. Financing will be more costly than paying cash because of the interest and other loan costs. Annual percentage rates (APRs) are usually higher and loan periods shorter on used cars than on new ones.

Where do you find used cars? Choices include new car dealers selling trade-ins, used-car dealers specializing locally in used cars, and dealers such as CarMax who have huge national inventories. One option to consider is buying a certified pre-owned car backed by a warranty from a dealership. Find out how many years or miles the warranty protection covers (some go as high as six years or 100,000 miles). Previously leased cars are usually well-maintained. There are also rental car companies, friends, relatives, coworkers, and strangers selling cars on the side of the road or out of driveways. The FTC Used Car Rule requires dealers to post a buyer's guide in every used car they sell. Note: this rule applies only to dealers, specifically to dealers that sell six or more cars a year. There are fewer protections (if any) when buying from friends or private sellers. Be especially careful of private sellers since generally they are not covered by the Used Car Rule; they sell cars "as is." Box 12.4 shows parts of the Buyer's Guide.

States vary on whether dealers can offer cars "as is—no warranty." State divisions of consumer services will know the laws in your state and can also tell you about state requirements regarding implied warranties, warranty of merchantability, and warranty of fitness for a particular purpose (for example, whether a dealer is liable if he or she

---

Box 12.4 Buyer's Guide for Used Cars

If a car is bought from a dealer, the Buyer's Guide must tell you whether the vehicle is being sold "as is" or with a warranty, as well as what percentage of the repair costs a dealer will pay under the warranty. Remember to do the following:

- Get all promises in writing.
- Keep the Buyer's Guide for reference after the sale.
- Check out the mechanical and electrical systems on the car as well as any other major problem areas.
- Ask to have the car inspected by an independent mechanic before you buy.

Source: Adapted from *Buying a Used Car: A Consumer Guide from the Federal Trade Commission*. Bureau of Consumer Protection, March 2002, p. 3.

says a car can haul a trailer and it turns out that it can't). You need to find out whether the used car has a full or limited warranty and what the warranty covers. Before buying, the purchaser has the right to see a copy of the dealer's warranty. According to the FTC, warranties are included in the price of a product, but service contracts cost extra and are sold separately. As discussed in Chapter 10, service contracts provide extra protection at a price, and it is questionable whether a service contract is needed. Many used-car service contracts only last 90 days, so the time limit should be noted as well as what it covers.

What is truly necessary is to have a used car inspected by an independent mechanic, particularly if the used car is being purchased from a private seller.

To summarize, take these steps before buying a used car:

1. Examine the car yourself in daylight. Research the make and model, and know prices and the seller.
2. Test-drive the car over varied road conditions.
3. Inspect the car's maintenance record. Check with the dealership or the previous owner if the current owner's record is incomplete.

After the purchase, any problem should be worked out first with the dealer (see Chapter 4); the last step would be small claims court (if the amount falls within the dollar limit in a particular state). Suspected fraud should be reported to the state or the FTC. To file a complaint or to get information on consumer issues, go to www.ftc.gov.

Photo 12.4
A salesman hands a couple the keys to their new car at a car dealership

Source: Thinkstock: Wavebreakmedia

Lemon Laws

Some states have **lemon laws**, which allow owners of new vehicles that repeatedly break down to get their money back or get the car replaced. For example, the lemon law covers cars and trucks that are sold in Florida to transport persons or property. This includes recreational vehicles (other than living facilities, meaning permanent homes), demonstrators, and leased vehicles. It does not cover off-road vehicles, large trucks, and motorcycles. For information, one would call the Florida Department of Agriculture and Consumer Services and in other states similar government agencies.

Rules vary by state regarding how many miles the car was driven, how long the person has had the car, and the amount of repair problems that exist. Mainly, what is the defect and what are the problems with repairs and warranties. A common rule of thumb is whether the car has been out of service for 15–30 days within the first 12,000 miles/12 months; another is whether the car has been in the repair shop four or more times during the first year of ownership. The procedure to get the money back or to replace the car is called **revocation of acceptance**, which must be in writing and is usually handled between the buyer and the seller. Customers suspecting they have a lemon should follow a number of steps, including contacting their state or local consumer protection office, giving the dealer a list of symptoms, keeping repair order copies, and contacting the manufacturer as well as the dealer. Most states require dealers of used cars to label cars that have been returned as lemons so that future buyers know the car has had problems.

CONSUMER ALERTS

A common fraud involves moving water-damaged cars (from floods) to another state, drying them out, and selling the cars to unsuspecting consumers. A mechanic inspecting the engine will find this out. Stolen cars are another potential problem when purchasing from private sellers. There is also the problem of dealers posing as private individuals. To avoid this problem, look at the title and the registration to determine whether the seller is the registered owner of the vehicle. Remember that private sellers have less responsibility than dealers to disclose defects.

CONSUMER ALERTS

When it comes to cars, all sorts of financial frauds can occur. In a real case in an unnamed state, the attorney general sued a dealership for damages and penalties under the state's Deceptive and Unfair Trade Practices Act, according to courthouse records. The lawsuit alleges that a car dealership sent promotional mailings to residents promising (among other things) it would pay off their trade-ins; instead, customers were obliged to pay off their former vehicles themselves, were enticed into unfavorable financing agreements, and were denied the promised discounts. Customers filed complaints with the attorney general's office. This is an example of a classic bait-and-switch scheme in which customers are lured in (the bait being the paying off of the trade-in), and once they are there, the switch takes place.

Unfair Vehicle Pricing

When buying a car, one of two unfair price-setting practices may be used:

- *High-balling.* The term **high-balling** means that a high amount is offered for a trade-in, but the extra amount is made up in an increased new car price. It is possible that car owners would be better off selling their old car themselves rather than going through the dealer.
- *Low-balling.* The term **low-balling** refers to a very low price being quoted, but there are add-on costs at the end that drive the final price up.

On a more minor level, some dealers add on extra frills at the end that buyers don't want, such as vinyl racing stripes or floor mats. This may have nothing to do with whether there is a trade-in, so this practice is not necessarily high-balling. Buyers should mention that they do not want these extras; by doing so, they can either save hundreds of dollars when they are removed or use them as part of the negotiation. The best advice is to know the fair market price for new vehicles and for trade-ins—a little knowledge goes a long way in the car business. Because many people dislike the haggling part of car buying, they use auto brokers or car-buying services, or they go through dealers that offer a no-haggling car-selling method.

Summary

The Bureau of Labor Statistics, through its Consumer Expenditure Survey, provides a picture of American consumption habits, noting that there are typically two cars per household or consumer unit and that housing makes up the major part of the typical budget. Renting was suggested as a preferred alternative to owning if a person is staying less than three years in an area; the exception to this would be if home prices are rising rapidly, making owning a more viable option. A benefit to buying is that homeowners receive tax deductions for interest on mortgage and property taxes. The American dream is still to own a house, with 67 percent of American households owning their own house. Housing represents 34 percent, transportation 18 percent, and food 13 percent of a typical budget.

Many federal agencies listed in this chapter are concerned that some prospective home buyers and other borrowers may be experiencing discriminatory treatment in their efforts to secure loans. Redlining is illegal.

Environmentally friendly building practices reduce the cost of utilities and are examples of the crossover between consumerism and environmentalism. There is a growth in home monitoring systems; one of their benefits is that what is happening in and around a house (such as renovations) can be watched from afar. A significant change has been in the average size of the kitchen: It increased 216 percent from 1950 to 2004 while the home itself increased in size only 72 percent.

People's lives go through change points that accelerate consumption, including the desire to own a home and buy new furnishings and appliances. Buying a house is the single most expensive purchase most people make, and a house is their most visible asset. There are a number of ways to determine how much house a person can afford, two of the most common being the 2.5 times rule and the 28/36 qualifying rule. More millennials are choosing to rent, putting off home ownership.

To pay for improvements or to get cash, four financial instruments based on home ownership include the second mortgage, the home equity line of credit, cash-out refinancing, and the reversible mortgage. Fraud potential and other problems, such as losing one's house or paying too much in fees, are rampant. The Truth in Lending Act, a federal law enacted in 1968, provides some protection. The lender must disclose in a truth-in-lending statement the total cost of a consumer loan, including a mortgage loan.

The discussion of the pros and cons of leasing cars and buying new and used cars included a number of steps to follow to avoid being fleeced. The Federal Trade Commission works to prevent fraudulent, deceptive, and unfair business practices involved in leasing and buying vehicles. Some states have lemon laws to cover new cars with repeated repair problems in the first year of ownership or the first 12,000 miles. Vehicle sales techniques include the use of flattery and praise because repeat business is sought.

KEY POINTS

1. A lease is a legal document. Vehicles or homes can be rented/leased.

2. Appreciation means the increase in a home's value.

3. Mortgages are loans to purchase real estate. Rates can be compared online, and mortgages can be negotiated online.

4. Net worth is calculated as assets minus liabilities. Lenders will look at net worth before loaning money for a house because they are trying to determine a person's ability to pay the mortgage.

5. Car leases are typically for 12,000 miles per year, and if the driver goes over that amount, there are financial penalties. Some luxury car dealers are offering teaser rates

for 10,000 miles to attract customers. The average car is driven 15,100 miles per year. A down payment may be required.

6. Buyers of used cars should hire their own independent mechanic to inspect the car they are interested in buying.

7. When shopping for used vehicles, consumers should consider buying a certified pre-owned vehicle backed by warranties.

8. Car buyers should be aware of unfair pricing practices such as high-balling and low-balling.

9. Dealer profit margins on new cars are usually between 10 and 20 percent.

KEY TERMS

adjustable-rate mortgages (ARMs)	high-balling	mortgages
appreciation	home equity lines of credit	net worth
assets	home inspections	PITI
closing	homeowner's fees	predatory lending
condominiums	home warranties	redlining
consumer unit	illiquid asset	rent
cooperative apartments	invoice price	reverse mortgages
defect-disclosure forms	lease	revocation of acceptance
discrimination	leasing	security deposit
fixed-rate conventional mortgage	lemon laws	sticker price
Freddie Mac	liabilities	subleasing
	low-balling	suggested retail price
	manufactured housing	transaction price

DISCUSSION QUESTIONS

1. Why have corporate executives called newlyweds the ultimate consumer? And why are their names like gold? How do companies get lists of newlyweds' names?

2. What are the pros of renting versus owning? What are the reasons people give for buying a home?

3. What are the pros and cons of leasing vehicles? What is the typical financial arrangement for a lease?

4. What does the transaction price of a vehicle purchase include?

REFERENCES

Buying a Used Car: A Consumer Guide from the Federal Trade Commission. Bureau of Consumer Protection, March 2002, p. 3.

Cialdini, R. (2001). *Influence: Science and practice*, 4th ed. Boston: Allyn and Bacon.

Clements, J. (February 5, 2003). Bubble? What bubble? Housing isn't that pricey, so go ahead and buy. *Wall Street Journal*, p. D1.

Cross, G. (2000). *An all consuming century.* New York: Columbia University Press.

Ellison, S, and C. Tejada. (January 30, 2003). Young couples starting out are every marketer's dream. *Wall Street Journal*, pp. B1, B3.

Fletcher, J. (January 31, 2003). How's your town doing? *Wall Street Journal*, p. W1.

The Freddie Mac Reporter Fact Book 2002–2003. Freddie Mac Corporate Communications, McLean, VA.

The Freddie Mac Reporter Fact Book 2007. Freddie Mac Corporate Communications, McLean, VA.

Gilbert, D. (2006). *Stumbling on happiness.* New York: Alfred A. Knopf.

Glink, I. (July 15, 2015). Top 10 priciest U.S. cities to rent an apartment. *CBS News.* http://www.cbsnews.com/media/top-10-priciest-us-cities-to rent-an apartment.

Goodloe, K., and J. Jurgensen. (April 21–22, 2007). Remote control. *Wall Street Journal*, p. P7.

Keys to Vehicle Leasing: A Consumer Guide from the Board of Governors of the Federal Reserve System, Washington, DC 20551.

Money Essentials (April 8, 2015). Buy a new car or a used car? *Money.* http://money.cnn.com/magazines/moneymag/money101/lesson 17.

Schawbel, D. (January 20, 2015). 10 new findings about the millennial consumer. *Forbes.com.* www.forbes.com/sites/danschawbel/2015/.

Simon, R. (January 29, 2003). Getting a two-fer on a home loan. *Wall Street Journal*, pp. D1–D2.

The new "starter" home. (October 2002). *American Demographics*, 53.

White, J. (February 10, 2003). Low lease price on luxury cars may cost you. *Wall Street Journal*, p. B1.

Yergin, D. (August 22–23, 2015). Power up. *Wall Street Journal*, p. C1.

Yergin, D. (August 22–23, 2015). The next energy revolutions. *Wall Street Journal*, p. C2.

Part **4**

Consumers in the Financial Marketplace

Chapter 13

Banking, Debt, and Credit Issues

Money is like an arm or a leg—use it or lose it.

Henry Ford

LEARNING OBJECTIVES

1. Identify the three steps in the financial management process.
2. Explain budgets, net worth statements, and the role of taxes.
3. Describe banking and savings strategies and scams.
4. Discuss financial planner credentials and fees.
5. Explain credit, common pitfalls, and consumer rights.
6. Explain bankruptcy and how to avoid it.

It's news we've heard before: Online banks are the way of the future. Online banks seem to have it all: relatively high interest rates, stellar customer service, low fees, and the added bonus of 24/7 access to your finances with the click of a button. Still, online banking isn't for everyone, and the line between the two is becoming blurred as more banks ramp up their web presence to compete. To help you decide, we tapped Richard Barrington, a senior financial analyst at MoneyRates.com, to break down the pros and cons of keeping your cash in a traditional versus an online bank. Security: This is one issue that scares many people away from taking their banking online, but Barrington said it shouldn't. Even traditional banks have all your financial information stored in a big data center that could be vulnerable to hackers. "Data theft is a very real risk these days, but, unfortunately, as a consumer, it doesn't come down to whether you choose to bank online." He said. If you choose an online bank backed by the FDIC, you'll be covered for losses up to $250,000 just like any other bank customer (use the FDIC's Bank Find tool to be sure). And, of course, remember to avoid doing any online banking on a public or shared Wi-Fi connection, since that's when your information can be most easily intercepted.

Source: Megan Durisin (May 6, 2013). "Here's Why Online Banks Are Better than Traditional Banks." *Business Insider*, Available at http://www.businessinsider.com/online -banks-vs-traditional-banks-2013-5.

Introduction

"Financial knowledge is an essential component in financial decision making: however, knowledge is insufficient to ensure responsible financial behavior" (Tang, Baker, & Peter, 2015, p. 376). Economic decisions are made by individuals, households, and families, mainly in their roles as consumers and owners of privately held goods and services such as houses, cars, college, and retirement plans. It takes money to have these things, and this section of the book explores how consumers can make the most of the money they have through saving and wise planning. As the paragraph opening quote shows, financial knowledge is important but it needs to be coupled with responsible financial behavior.

We discussed the connection between happiness and consumption in preceding chapters. Someone living in poverty (defined as a US family of four earning less than $23,050 in 2015) will get a boost from more money, but studies show that once you go further up the income scale, the connection between income and happiness is less clear. One reason may be **nexting**, meaning that when people buy or attain something, their minds are already thinking of the next purchase or goal. Those with considerable financial wealth do score slightly higher on the happiness scale, but what appears to make most happy is not the actual amount of money but what they do with it or plan to do with it. Daniel Gilbert, author of *Stumbling on Happiness*, says, "Our brains are made for nexting and that's just what they'll do. When we take a stroll on the beach, our brains predict how stable the sand will be when our foot hits it and adjust the tension in our knee accordingly" (2006, p. 8). Saving is all about nexting. You save in order to have more money to spend or invest or give away.

In this chapter, we will also go over steps to financial success as well as common pitfalls and frauds related to finances. Throughout the life cycle, we spend, save, borrow, and lend. As one ages, the goal is to become more of a saver and a lender in order to build financial wealth and maintain stability. This chapter introduces the topic of personal finance and shows how it fits into life plans. **Personal finance** is an umbrella term that covers the spending, saving, investing, and protecting of financial resources. Financial planning is a lifelong process.

According to former Federal Reserve Chairman Alan Greenspan, "Making informed decisions about what to do with your money will help build a more stable financial future for you and your family" (Ip, 2003, p. D3). Consumers are besieged by investment schemes and quasi-legitimate financial schemes on television and over the Internet. To counteract these negative information sources, the Federal Reserve has stepped in with public service announcements and a website with links to dependable financial information sources.

The goal of this chapter is to make readers more aware of how money can be more successfully managed (including where to go for help) and, in so doing, increase life satisfaction. Most consumption requires money—to get in the consumer game, one needs money or something worth trading. An individual's or family's standard of living and future financial stability hinge on the ability to accumulate, save, invest, protect, and spend money wisely. Consider the weekend expenses in the case study of one active family with four soccer-playing boys.

CASE STUDY

The Jones Family of Folsom, California

"Like most parents, Steve and Siobhan Joes of Folsom, Calif., will do just about anything to support their children's passions. But the Joneses are the parents of four talented, soccer-crazed boys, which means that life can get a little bonkers. Take a four-day weekend this summer. It starts at 5 a.m. on Friday when Steve, a 47-year-old senior network engineer at Intel, and his 14-year-old son, Rhys, set out in their rental car on a 10-hour drive to San Diego for the latest big tournament. Before Rhys hits the field, Siobhan, 43, a part-time elementary school teacher, has piled her three younger boys—Kye, 13, Taine, 11, and Bryn, 9—into her 2009 Honda Pilot for their own tournament three hours away in Santa Cruz. They'll sleep in a rented Airstream trailer. (Left at home: the family's creaky minivan.) On Saturday and Sunday, Siobhan scurries among the eight games played by Taine's and Bryn's individual teams. (Kye's team, mercifully, has the weekend off.) Meanwhile, Steve watches Rhys play three games, then drives the eight hours from San Diego to Santa Cruz, where all six jam into the Airstream's four sleeping berths. After a pit stop to ride the roller coasters on the Santa Cruz Beach Boardwalk, they got home Monday at midnight—exhausted, happy, and (after shelling out for lodging, car rental, gas, meals, and amusement park tickets) $2,000 poorer. And that's just one weekend."

Source: Paul Keegan (October 2015). "The Bills Footing." *Money.com*, p. 72.

Personal finance takes place on the home front within the ups and downs of the general economy, and as covered earlier in the book, the ways consumers spend, save, and invest affect the way the economy cycles, so there are many interchanges between households and the greater economy.

Photo 13.1 Raising children can be expensive

Source: Thinkstock: Dejan Ristovski

Financial Management Process

The Joneses' situation in the case study may sound extreme, but the challenge of balancing sports and finances is not unusual. It shows that money management is very individual and changes with family or household type. Steve's $126,000 Intel salary sounds like a lot, but he says the family barely makes ends meet. So, budgeting and meeting expenses are not so simple.

On the surface, money management should be a no-brainer—you work, you earn money, you save, and you build an independent financial life. Over a million personal bankruptcies are filed each year, indicating that this set of tasks is not so easy to accomplish. As further evidence, credit card debt is at an all-time high, and a small percentage of consumers are keeping up with their monthly bills. The number of loan defaults and home foreclosures were at level highs in 2008 and 2009, and when this book went to press, the number of foreclosures had finally started decreasing. Overall, it is still safe to say that more and more people are having trouble making ends meet.

As college students, you are in a uniquely positive position to begin a lifetime habit of good money management. The bottom line is being responsible, being a wise consumer, and handling income and expenditures in a prudent manner by avoiding debt and putting your hard-earned money where you want it to go, where it will do the most good. It is not only about helping yourself but also about helping others. Personal finance is a process involving three steps:

1. Awareness and setting financial goals.
2. Creating and activating financial plans.
3. Evaluating and revising plans: moving forward.

Step 1: Awareness and Setting Financial Goals

First of all, the individual has to be aware of their money and financial assets and goals. How much do I have? How much do I want? What do I want? What is most important? The first question financial planners should ask a client is "What are your financial goals?" In other words, "What are you saving for—a primary residence, a comfortable life, a vacation home, a secure retirement, or the private school or college education of children? What are you striving for?" Your answers may involve short-range goals such as paying bills each month. As mentioned in Chapter 1, goals are end results, things worth striving for, things to be achieved. Goals are based on **values** (principles that guide behavior), **attitudes** (likes and dislikes), and **resources** (sources of wealth) and are affected by **decision making** (process of making a choice between two or more alternatives). Idealism is a value, and a sample behavior associated with idealism is the choice that more students are making to be active in their communities—many students

Table 13.1 The Setting of Financial Goals

Time	Example of a goal	Estimated cost	Priority*
Short-term (less than two months)	1 _____	$ _____	_____
	2 _____	$ _____	_____
Intermediate (2 months to 1 year)	1 _____	$ _____	_____
	2 _____	$ _____	_____
Long-range (1 year or more)	1 _____	$ _____	_____
	2 _____	$ _____	_____

*In each category, select a or b (a = 1st priority, b = 2nd priority).

have a tradition of volunteering to help others. According to US Census Bureau data, the number of people aged 16 to 24 engaged in volunteer work is rising significantly. "For a lot of my friends from college and high school, the buzz word is finding your passion," says Sean Smith, age 24, a University of Notre Dame graduate and Peace Corps volunteer (Shellenbarger, 2006, p. D1).

Table 13.1 provides a space for you to fill in your own financial goals based on time—short-term, intermediate, and long-range goals—along with estimated prices and a place to rank their priority. People in their forties may have the following long-range goals: (1) to provide a college education for two children, (2) to move to a better house, (3) to buy a vacation home, and (4) to retire at age 65. Not all of these goals will be held as equally important, which is where prioritizing comes in. Financial planners (to be discussed later in this chapter) help people make informed decisions about their financial future.

So the first step in the financial process includes setting and prioritizing goals and (on the basis of those goals) creating and implementing plans. To be successful, goals should be flexible, action oriented, specific, and realistic. Financial goals are affected by risk, the possibility of experiencing loss or harm. Examples of risk are income risk (loss of income), investment risk, personal risk (health and safety), status risk, time risk, liquidity risk, interest rate risk, and inflation risk. Several of these were discussed in previous chapters, but as a recap, inflation is a rise in prices and liquidity refers to how readily something can be turned into cash. Everyone varies in the amount of risk they can handle, which is referred to as risk tolerance. In regard to time, the longer one has until money is needed (the time horizon), the more chances or risks can be taken. Plans involve setting a course of action and then making decisions about what to do, such as continuing at the same pace, expanding (earning more, spending more, investing more), cutting back (saving more), or choosing an entirely new course of action.

Step 2: Creating and Activating Plans

In this step, plans are made and actually carried out. Individuals make calls, go on appointments, open up a savings or brokerage account, or put a 20 percent down payment on a house. Flexibility at this stage is important because plans may need to change due to circumstances. For example, 17 houses may need to be looked at before the right one is found, and then the desired one may be more expensive, requiring a reworking of the budget. At this step, there will be gains and losses, and learning takes place that will affect future decisions.

CRITICAL THINKING

Choosing an Internship

Shanna is torn between two internships. One is with a big-box retailer and the other with a small local store. The local store will allow her to stay in her college town where her rent is already paid, so it is the easy choice. The downside is that it will probably not lead to a full-time job. The big-box retailer will mean she will have to find somewhere to stay in another location for several months, but it may more likely lead to full-time job offers and exposure to more training. To activate her plan, she is doing company research and interviewing with the two internship positions. If you were Shanna, what else would you do or what else would you consider when making an internship plan?

Step 3: Evaluating and Revising Plans: Moving Forward

This step involves looking back at how the plans went. Did they succeed or fail? Was the success total or partial? Evaluation is probably the least attractive of the steps, but in many ways it is the most important: people learn what works and what doesn't. Personal comfort level with risk is reassessed. Every day, some level of assessment takes place, but a more formal once-a-year evaluation of financial plans is recommended. This usually takes place when people are filing taxes and have W-2 forms and other records of earnings and expenditures in hand. At the end of the evaluation, they reset their course by going back to step one and asking themselves, "For next year, what do I want to accomplish, what goals do I want to achieve, and what plans do I need to make?"

A deeper life evaluation may take place at the change points (discussed in the last chapter) such as graduations, weddings, and births of children. Another evaluation point may occur around a significant birthday such as age 30, 40, 50, or 60. The evaluation may not take place right on the birthday but in the surrounding years. For example turning 30 years old can involve an evaluation anywhere from age 29 to age 32. People often look back on the last decade of their lives and evaluate how it went. Career exploration is common between the ages of 20 and 29, and it is not until the ages of 45 to 54 that median income peaks. Self-evaluation involves an assessment of career, education, and personal and family progress.

Budgets and Net Worth Statements

If you don't know your net worth or where your money is going, you need to find out.

A budget is a financial plan based on income and expenditures in a month. To develop a budget, one needs financial records that show consumption (for example, bank and credit card statements) and organized paperwork. Budgets show how much money is flowing in (earnings, dividends, gifts) and how much is flowing out (rent, expenses). Budgets have **fixed expenses** such as rent and **variable expenses** such as food and entertainment. In the last chapter, net worth was defined as assets minus liabilities; net worth statements are useful because they give an overall picture of financial worth, and lenders and creditors use them to determine whether to extend credit. Box 13.1 gives a budget and Box 13.2 gives ways to stretch paychecks further. To summarize, a **budget** consists of a monthly estimate of income and expenses. Box 13.3 gives an example of a net worth statement. You can do budgets and net worth statements yourself or with the help of a financial advisor. A negative net worth is not unusual for college students, but your goal should be to get on the plus side (having more assets than debts).

Savings

We all need cash for small immediate needs and savings for longer-range needs. Savings provide a safety net and are also helpful for putting together money for future needs such as a down payment on a house. Savings provide a sense of comfort and security, so they are useful from an emotional and fiscal point of view. Traditionally, an **emergency fund** of three to six months of salary set aside as savings is recommended as a financial goal; these funds should be kept in a liquid interest-bearing account such as a money market fund, short-term certificates of deposit (CDs), or a savings account. During recessionary times with higher-than-usual unemployment, six or more months' salary is recommended for extra cushioning in case of job loss or other major setbacks or expenses, such as unexpected auto or home repairs or medical bills.

Americans save 4 to 5 percent on average of disposable income per year, a rate much lower than is found in most other industrialized countries. Some would say the savings rate is in the negative zone, meaning more money is being spent than is brought into the household: for example, someone owes more for his or her mortgage and credit cards each month than he or she brings home in income.

Savings accounts in banks and credit unions earn interest that is compounded continuously. The **Truth in Savings Act** requires financial institutions to reveal the annual percentage yield (the amount of interest earned on a yearly basis expressed as a percentage), fees charged, and information about rules regarding maintaining a minimum balance.

Box 13.1 Budget: Tracing the Flow of Income and Expenses

A budget is made up of cash inflows and cash outflows, usually figured on a monthly basis.

Cash Inflows

Net salary	$
Interest or dividends from savings accounts or investments	$
Financial aid checks, scholarships	$
Gifts	$
Other sources of income★	$
Total of Cash Inflows	$

Cash Outflows

Housing (rent or mortgage payment)	$
Utilities (electric, water, cable TV)	$
Child care, educational expenses, tuition and books	$
Cellphone	$
Auto payments	$
Gasoline, auto repairs	$
Gifts	$
Food (including restaurant expenses)	$
Clothing	$
Credit card payments	$
Entertainment	$
Medical/dental/prescriptions	$
Personal care	$
Pet care	$
Savings	$
Other expenses	$
Total of Cash Outflows	$
Subtract outflow total from inflow total to determine what is left over at the end of a typical month.	$

★Example: Josh, a college junior, gets $1,000 a month to live on from his mom while he is in college. His biggest expense is a combination of rent and utilities (he shares an apartment with a friend), followed by food. She pays for his tuition and books, and he drives an old used car that is paid for. He noticed friends coming over and eating all his food, so he put an end to that. When he eats out, he goes for the cheap all-you-can-eat places. Josh eats at his mom's house when he can. In exchange, he mows the yard and takes care of the pets when his mom travels. He had jobs in high school but is currently not working.

Box 13.2 Stretching Paychecks Strategy

"According to a recent CareerBuilder survey, 19 percent of workers at all salary levels were unable to make ends meet during the past year. Sixty-five percent of all workers said they're in debt." Here are suggested strategies to stretch dollars further:

1. Budget monthly, not annually. Expenses fluctuate.
2. Make budgeting easy by using your bank website or Mint.com.
3. Cut unnecessary expenses.
4. Find creative ways to save.
5. Set savings goals. Even if only $20 a month.

Source: Debra Auerbach (October 11, 2015). "Your paycheck can go further with 5 easy strategies." *Tallahassee Democrat*, p. 4E.

CRITICAL THINKING

Importance of Balance Sheets

A **balance sheet** perspective on financial success is constructive (what a family saves, owns, and owes) according to Ray Boshara and William R. Emmons (2015). They suggest efforts early in life to build saving and assets. How healthy is your balance sheet?

One of the best ways to build savings is to automate savings through payroll deduction or transfers from a checking account to a savings account. Young adults in their twenties and thirties should be developing an overall savings and investment plan and putting together an emergency fund. They may also have very high child care expenses (see the Critical Thinking exercise), and child care can cost much more than college tuition.

CRITICAL THINKING

Soaring Child Care Costs

Can you believe that the cost of sending a single child to a day care center can cost more than a home mortgage payment or rent? *As a young parent, what would you do?* Read the following: "American families are having a tough time catching a break, thanks to stagnant wages and an uneven recovery. But a less-known issue may be playing an even bigger role: child care costs.

This expense is now a major stress on many American families, given that only a handful of cities meet the Department of Health and Human Services' affordability threshold for the service – 10 percent of family income – and that child care costs more than college tuition in 33 states and the District of Columbia. That's according to a new report from the Economic Policy Institute. The issue increasingly isn't a problem only for low-income families but also for middle-income and even upper-income Americans, given that the median household income peaked in 1999. 'In 500 out of 618 budget areas, child care actually exceeded the cost of rent. It was so shocking, given that rent is considered one of the major expenses in a family's budget,' said Elise Gould, a senior economist at the EPI who wrote the report with Tanyell Cooke."

Source: Aimee Picchi (Oct. 6, 2015, 12:01 A.M.). "The shock of soaring child care costs." MONEYWATCH. http://www. cbsnews.com/news/the-shock-of-soaring-child -care-costs/

By the ages of 40 to 50, a goal should be to increase savings by holding on to money and making it grow. Middle-age adults should be saving for retirement based on estimates of how much they will need per year. Older adults are interested in receiving dividends from their investments and trying to make their savings last and, in some cases, leaving a legacy.

Taxes

In 1789, Benjamin Franklin said that in this world nothing is certain but death and taxes. The Internal Revenue Service (IRS) relies on citizens to report their income and file tax returns on time. Table 13.2 gives a list of providers as well as products and services including the category of tax preparers. **Taxes** are payments of money to federal, state, and local governments. Each level of government has various methods of taxation. For example, sales taxes on items such as autos, clothing, and furniture are set by state and local governments. Another example of a tax is an **excise tax**, which is collected from the manufacturer of a product. You pay an excise tax every time you purchase a gallon of gasoline; these taxes are considered regressive taxes, meaning they take a smaller share of people's income as their income grows. The majority of state and local taxes are regressive—they tend to hit low- and middle-income earners harder than higher-income individuals.

The federal income tax is progressive: The more you make, the more you pay. Income taxes are taxes on income, which includes salaries, wages, interest from savings accounts and other investments, commissions, and tips. Both individuals and businesses pay taxes. For individuals, the most-used forms are Form 1040 and Form 1040A. Throughout the year, it is important to keep good records of expenditures, including charitable

Box 13.3 Net Worth Statement

Net Worth: Assets − Liabilities = Net Worth	
Assets are what a person owns, and liabilities are debts (what is owed).	
Step 1: Figure out **Total Assets**.	
Current Assets	
Checking accounts	$
Money market or savings accounts	$
Cash value of life insurance	$
Investments	
Stocks, bonds, mutual funds (estimated worth)	$
Individual retirement accounts	$
Employer retirement accounts	$
Other Assets	
Worth of house, other real estate	$
Value of car, appliances, computers	$
Jewelry, collections, equipment	$
Other belongings such as furniture	$
Add together each category to get **Total Assets**.	$
Step 2: Figure out **Total Liabilities**.	
Current Liabilities	
Credit card bills	$
Medical/dental bills	$
Car payments	$
Other	$
Total Current Liabilities	$
Long-Term Liabilities	
Mortgage	$
Student loans	$
Other	$
Total Long-Term Liabilities	$
Add together each category to get **Total Liabilities**.	$
Step 3: Subtract **Total Liabilities** from **Total Assets** to determine **Net Worth**.	$

contributions, because you may be able to itemize **deductions**, which are expenses subtracted from income before figuring out the amount of taxes owed. A simpler form is Form 1040EZ, often used by college students because it is most appropriate if someone is single or married but without dependents or a lot of money. All forms are available online from the Internal Revenue Service (IRS). The greatest percentage of federal income dollars is spent on human resources that include payments to Social Security, Medicare, and other retirement programs. The greatest amount of federal income comes from individual income taxes (what is paid in).

For a citizen to not pay taxes is cause for fines or various penalties, including jail sentences. **Tax avoidance** is a legal money management strategy to reduce one's taxes through such investments as tax-deferred individual retirement accounts (IRAs) or charitable donations, which are allowed under the tax code and should be properly documented. Before making or selling an investment such as a house or a stock or bond, the tax consequences should be considered. A well-trained financial planner, realtor, banker, or stock broker should be able to assist in these matters. Most people want to pay what they owe and not a penny more. **Tax evasion** is illegal because of the methods involved, such as not paying taxes or not reporting all income. Box 13.4 gives a list of nonprofit and government organizations that can help with money management, including how to manage debt.

Banks Changing

CRITICAL THINKING

How Might Banking Change?

No more paper money by 2043? "In at least one Texas bank and one Ohio credit union, 3D video banking is currently undergoing testing. . . . Three dimensional video banking is similar to a consumer video conference with a bank representative – only in this case, the executive looks like a living, breathing person sitting across from you. Thanks to theater surround sound, the representative also sounds as if they're in the same room. And since the consumer is interacting with a real person and not an automated hologram, the experience apparently isn't much different than the real thing." What do you think of no paper money? What do you think of 3D video banking?

Source: Geoff Williams (Sept. 20, 2013). "Our financial future: how banking and money will change." US News and World Report, http://money.usnews.com 4/16/2015 10:33 A.M.

This is the era of mobile banking. The modern financial marketplace has several features, including electronic banking, 24/7 access to accounts, automatic teller machines

(ATMs), electronic transfer of funds, stock-brokerages offering checking and savings accounts (including money market funds), banks offering investment services, and deregulation. Overall, in recent years there has been more easy access to money and a crossover of services that has benefited consumers with more competition between banks. There may be some confusion as to who to pick to do business with along with the issues of privacy, safety, and security. For example, today neighborhood banks offer mutual funds and other types of investments that are not protected by the **Federal Deposit Insurance Corporation (FDIC)**, which is government insurance of bank or savings and loan (S&L) accounts (up to $250,000 per account). Offerings that are not FDIC-protected are subject to risk, which confuses some elderly consumers who assume that everything offered by a bank is insured. Credit unions are insured by the National Credit Union Administration.

FDIC insures bank accounts up to $250,000 per account.

Bank Products and Issues

Banks and brokerage firms offer CDs with a maturity of at least seven days, with penalties on early withdrawals. CDs, a type of **time deposit**, are usually safe ways to store money from seven days to several years. The longer the money is deposited and the larger the amount is, the higher the interest rate offered. After the CD reaches maturity (the designated period of time has passed), the CD can be cashed in or rolled over to a new CD, hopefully at a higher rate. Banks compete for CD business, and rates are compared in newspapers or can be found by going online or making phone calls or visiting banks in person.

Table 13.2 Financial Services Providers and their Products and Services

Financial services providers	Typical products and services
Accountants	Budgets, advice, preparation of tax returns and audits, financial planning
Attorneys	Lawsuits, estate plans, trusts, legal matters regarding adoption or divorce, bankruptcy, wills, mediation, dispute resolution
Banks, credit unions, savings and loans (S&Ls)	Checking accounts, share and savings accounts, money market accounts, CDs, loans, safety deposit boxes, ATMs, debit and credit cards, trusts
Brokerage firms (financial counselors)	Online or in-person stock purchases or sales, bonds, mutual funds, money market and asset management accounts (including checking accounts), mortgages, IRAs, financial planning
Credit counselors	Debt management, credit consolidation, budgets, 24-hour hotlines (sometimes free, sometimes sliding-scale fees), bankruptcy issues
Financial planners	Fee- and commission-based financial planning services (budgets, investments, life insurance, mutual funds)
Insurance companies	Annuities, retirement plans, sales of insurance
Real estate companies	Housing and land sales, investments, rentals
Tax preparation services	Income tax returns, tax advice

Box 13.4 Nonprofit and Government Organizations with Information on Wise Money Management

Consumer Action. This national consumer advocacy organization directs consumers to complaint-handling agencies and offers educational materials.

Consumer Counseling Centers of America, Inc. These centers offer free and low-fee counseling and services to help people manage their debts.

Consumer Federation of America. This is a pro-consumer advocacy and educational organization.

Debtors Anonymous. This national 12-step organization is dedicated to helping people overcome debt problems.

FDIC Money Smart News (online newsletter).

National Foundation for Credit Counseling. This network of 150 member agencies at 1,300 locations offers educational programs on money management, budgeting, credit, and debt counseling, including help with arranging debt-repayment plans.

National Institute for Consumer Education. This professional development, training, and research institute promotes personal finance education in workplaces, communities, and schools.

CONSUMER ALERTS

Although banks usually exercise good judgment, there are exceptions. Is your bank selling your secrets? In 1999, US Bancorp allegedly sold information on 930,000 account holders to a telemarketing firm called MemberWorks, which then pitched these customers "trial memberships" for a variety of services such as phones and discount travel. Even though some people said no to these offers, their accounts were charged anyway (the bank received a commission). Allowing these kinds of withdrawals without the customers' permission is illegal and resulted in lawsuits totaling $6.5 million. Selling information is legal, so to stop it customers must tell banks to keep their dealings confidential (Stirland, 2001).

Money market accounts are a type of account that offers a higher rate of interest than most checking or savings accounts. Many require a minimum balance to be maintained.

Checking accounts are offered by banks, and share accounts are offered by credit unions. Legislation is underway to streamline this process, which used to take up to five days per check. Photographing checks from home or the office and sending online directly to banks is saving businesses and consumers a lot of time and money.

Photo 13.2
People use credit cards due to convenience of use

Source: Getty Images: Frank van Delft

Banks or credit card companies offer **debit cards**, which are issued to allow customers access to their funds electronically in places like grocery stores, and **smart cards** (also called **chip cards** or **stored value cards**), which may be worth $25 or $100 and can be used for placing phone calls or buying gifts (as in gift cards). Please note that many gift cards are never redeemed. If you have some, use them.

CONSUMER ALERTS

Under the Electronic Fund Transfer Act (EFTA), if there is a mistake or unauthorized withdrawal from a bank account through the use of a debit card or other electronic fund transfers, the person must notify the financial institution of the problem or error not later than 60 days after the statement containing the problem or error was sent. If someone uses your debit card without your permission, you can lose from $50 to $500 or more, depending on when you report the loss or theft. If you report the loss within two business days after the discovery of the problem, you will not be responsible for more than $50 of unauthorized use. The longer you wait to report the loss, the higher the amount you could lose. If you do not report an unauthorized transfer or withdrawal within 60 days after your statement is mailed to you, you risk unlimited loss.

CONSUMER ALERTS

Be careful in selecting a **personal identification number (PIN)** for use in ATMs and other forms of cash management. Usually you are better off using the one assigned to you by the bank, but if you select one yourself, don't make it too easy. A number like 1111 and one too easily traced to you (like your street address number, telephone number, or birth date) would be examples. Never keep the PIN with your card—memorize it. When using an ATM, be careful of your surroundings and take your receipt. If the ATM card is lost or stolen, report it immediately to the financial institution. Watch out for ATM charges, especially if you use your bank card in another bank's machine. On the plus side, ATMs have made it possible to get cash any time and nearly anywhere, including abroad, reducing the need to carry traveler's checks and large sums of cash.

CONSUMER ALERTS

ATM thieves target customers in a variety of ways according to the Florida Division of Consumer Services website. A new scheme works like this. The ATM customer attempts to make an ATM withdrawal, and there is a malfunction, resulting in the card being held by the machine. An official-looking sign posted on the machine reads, "If for any reason your card gets stuck, punch in your PIN." The customer does as instructed, but the card is not returned. Later the customer learns money has been withdrawn from his or her account. Police investigators believe that the suspect inserts some type of plastic sleeve into the card slot and then waits for a customer to use the machine. When a customer arrives, he or she inserts the ATM card and keys in the PIN. Investigators believe the suspect may be using binoculars to watch the victim enter the PIN; then after the customer leaves, the suspect retrieves the card and starts making withdrawals. The advice to consumers is that if an ATM malfunctions, report it immediately to bank officials. In addition, ignore all signs, no matter how official looking, and report all suspicious-looking persons or vehicles in the ATM vicinity to the bank and the local police department immediately.

Deregulation of Banking

With deregulation, there are different rules and more players in the financial market. For consumers, the good news is that the Depository Institutions Deregulation and Monetary Control Act of 1980 opened up competition: New forms of banking emerged, including banks without main offices or branches, which became even more popular with the advent of the Internet in the 1990s; new services opened up as well, and mergers took place more readily. So to recap regarding money and savings, with deregulation consumers have benefited by having more choices of financial institutions, including commercial banks, savings and loans, credit unions, and brokerage firms. Consumers should take advantage of this by comparing interest rates, features, risk, and convenience.

> ### CONSUMER ALERTS
>
> Several steps can be taken for safety when you do online banking:
>
> - Make sure that your bank uses Secure Socket Layer (SSL) encryption technology or another such system.
> - Look for a liability guarantee against late payments and fraudulent activity.
> - Make sure you have the ability to regularly log on to your account and see what is happening.
> - Secure your system with antivirus software and a firewall program.
> - Pick a hard-to-trace PIN.

Money Laundering and Terrorist Financing

Since this chapter is about global as well as personal financial issues, it would be remiss not to address the issue of global problems regarding money laundering and terrorist financing. In the United States, the Bank Secrecy Act (BSA) requires all national banks to file a Suspicious Activity Report (SAR) when they detect certain known or suspected violations of federal law or suspicious transactions related to a money-laundering activity or a violation of the BSA. There are a number of systems, controls, and rules too lengthy to go into here in regard to BSA and SARs, but generally speaking, movements of money in amounts over $5,000 are likely to be noted. Bank employees are trained to coordinate and maintain compliance. Under section 326 of the USA PATRIOT Act, every bank adopted a customer identification program. To learn more, go online to the Comptroller of the Currency Administrator of National Banks in the US Department of Treasury. Other countries have similar money movement detection policies through their departments of the treasury or a related department.

Financial Planner Credentials and Scams

A **financial planner** looks at a person's or a family's total financial picture, helps that person or family define and prioritize goals, and then works out a plan to achieve those goals. Once the plan is in place, the financial planner may help implement or manage the plan, prepare tax returns, discuss investments, and obtain insurance coverage. A financial planner is really an asset manager, who is different from a financial counselor who tries to organize and reduce a client's debts.

Regulations and Credentials

Financial planning requires involvement and commitment from everyone in the family or household in order to succeed. Individuals availing themselves of financial planning help are trying to gain control over their money and move in a better financial direction. Over 500,000 people in the United States call themselves financial planners. This is an industry that is largely unregulated; hence the phrase "may the buyer beware" applies. The amount of regulation varies and is carried out by states, by credentialing associations, and by the Securities and Exchange Commission (SEC). It is not possible for the SEC to send investigators and auditors to visit every person claiming to be a financial planner, and better ways to regulate the industry are under discussion. That said, there are many financial planners who are legitimate and well trained. The most recognized credential is **Certified Financial Planner (CFP)** because of the rigorous examinations, the required three years of practical experience, and the code of ethics. New planners receive experience from established CFPs; nationally, there are more than 40,000 CFPs (Hoffman, 2003). Other credentials are Chartered Financial Consultant (ChFC) and the Personal Financial Specialist (PFS).

Often certified public accountants (CPAs) have taken the exams and are also CFPs—this is a strong set of credentials. After individuals check for these types of credentials, then they would interview two or three potential financial planners before final selection. The more that is known about the planner, the better. Recommendations from several people whom you trust and a careful questioning of the financial planner's way of working should help screen out the fraudulent ones. The Consumer Alert below gives other clues.

How much do financial planners charge? Most charge by commission (from financial products sold) and/or an hourly fee. An initial consultation may be free. For example, Andy Claybrook, a CFP in Franklin, Tennessee, is a fee-only planner who used to charge $135 an hour (Hoffman, 2003). Others charge a flat fee, such as $300, to do a net worth statement and write an initial plan; still others charge commissions on products they sell, such as mutual funds and life insurance. Charles Schwab and other brokerage houses may offer financial planning online or in person for free or at a reduced cost (such as $99) if a person has an account with them—especially a sizable account.

If going with a CFP, generally it is accepted that the fee-only advisor brings the least-biased advice (Clements, 2003). The CFP may charge a yearly fee of 1 percent to maintain your records and update your investments once they are set up. With this setup, the advisor has an incentive to manage money wisely because as the portfolio grows, the advisor will make more money. As might be expected, the more work CFPs do, the more they will charge. Through commissions, advisors make their money by selling life insurance, mutual funds, or other investments that will pay them a commission. A lot of planners like the flexibility and the income derived from the combination fee and commission method. What it boils down to is matching the client's needs with what is being offered, whether it be help with a particular problem that needs immediate attention (such as an impending divorce or sudden job loss) or more long-term planning. Some planners specialize in a certain type of client (widow, doctor, entertainer, executive, small-business owner) and may not want to work with other types of clients.

Divorce Planners: A Type of Financial Planner

A **certified divorce planner** is a specialist who is trained to focus on who gets the assets in divorces and who works alongside attorneys who handle legal documents and child custody issues. Divorce planners help couples divvy up retirement accounts and stock options, divide up businesses, calculate alimony payments, and decide who keeps the primary house and vacation home.

CONSUMER ALERTS

Rapport, setting, websites, and materials give an indication of how a financial planner operates. Do the materials look professional or amateurish? Is the office nice but not over the top? Are calls returned promptly? Does the financial planner really listen? How long have they been in business in the same location? Remember that the courts are filled with horror stories about judges, bankers, relatives, and personal friends who acted as financial advisors and robbed others of everything they have. Be wary, be cautious, start small, and keep your eyes open. No matter which financial planner is selected, make sure to obtain a written estimate of what services are to be expected and at what price; then check records of purchases.

Free Financial Seminars and "Get Rich" Books

A popular mode of communication about financial matters involves free seminars at hotels, schools, universities, churches, and libraries that are given by financial planners, stockbrokers, insurance agents, and motivational speakers. The worth of these has to do with who is sponsoring the talk or seminar and who is the speaker. Be wary of direct mailings or advertisements in newspapers offering free financial talks—in some cases, the quality of information is suspect, and in others the "free" seminar is really a sales presentation. There is nothing wrong with a sales pitch as long as it is clear from the beginning that is what the seminar is about. Scams occur when seminars are given in public places that are followed up by high-pressure in-home one-on-one sales talks for a product or service.

A more dependable source of financial information is available from employers who offer it as a perk. For example, companies such as Honeywell, Dell, Pitney Bowes, and Procter & Gamble pay for reliable financial services specialists to help executives prepare their taxes and set up estate plans and to help lower-ranking employees with college savings plans and retirement planning, including offering 800 numbers they can call for advice. The basic financial planning help may be one-on-one meetings or full-day seminars. The reasons employers are doing this is because of the growing role that workers assume in managing their personal finances and the knowledge that financial worries take employees' attention away from their work. As the 401(k) and 403(b) savings accounts for retirement and benefit plans become more employee controlled, workers are forced to make investment decisions that were normally made by higher management. About 28 percent of workers receive financial planning advice through their employer, and the percentage is climbing (Higgins & Simon, 2003).

Regardless of source or sponsor, realize that no one speaker or author has the key to financial success; if that person did, he or she would be on a yacht enjoying it and not sharing financial secrets with the public. A speaker or author who supports diversification (a variety of investments) and is not selling any one way to get rich, such as buying options or investing in foreign real estate, is on the right track. Television programs on money management as well as in-person talks can be enjoyed as long as one realizes that a personal viewpoint is being given and that this perspective is one among many. These shows are mostly about entertainment. The best advice is tailored to individuals based on their circumstances and goals as well as changes in the economy and the financial marketplace, which is why the one-on-one consultations or 800 numbers are beneficial. Because there are so many changes in tax rules and in investments (including real estate), books and advice quickly become outdated. Few things are more worthless than a five-year-old "how to get rich" book.

Credit, Loans, and Debt Warning Signs

Researchers have found that debt stress for short-run debtors is more than twice that of long-run debtors (Shen, Sam, & Jones, 2014). In other words, debt stresses people out and how long the debt lasts has an effect. Short-term debt can pack a wallop: People can get in trouble when they borrow money through the use of credit and loans. The "buy now, pay later" philosophy is ingrained in American society. Credit can be used for luxury items or for longer-term investments such as educational expenses.

The difference between using credit to purchase luxury products and using it to finance an education is that the former usage is more consumption-oriented, while the latter is more investment-oriented. The commonality is that both incur long-term financial obligation, or consumer debt. Although the growth of consumer credit has contributed to the expansion of the US economy and raised the quality of life for millions of American consumers, it also has brought about extensive consumer debt (Lee & Lee, 2001/2002, pp. 25–26).

Photo 13.3
More students are starting to use credit cards, generating more debt

Source: Getty Images: UpperCut Images

A study by Eun-Ju Lee and Jinkook Lee (2001/2002) found that consumers who approved of using credit for luxury purchases had more credit cards and greater credit card debt than consumers who disapproved of using credit for such purchases, but they found this was not the case for using consumer debt to finance education. So they concluded that "learn now and pay later" is a reasonable credit choice for most consumers but that people should beware of "buy luxury now and pay later" since this strategy tends to lead to more serious financial burdens on households. Another reason that using credit to finance education is a sounder choice is because higher education significantly enhances future earning potential, so borrowing money for educational purposes can be viewed as an investment.

The cost of using money is called **interest**. The rate of interest is determined by supply (amount of money lenders are willing to lend) and demand (amount of money borrowers are willing to pay). Interest rates are expressed as percentages (for example, 4 percent per year). You are a receiver of interest when you have a savings account that pays interest, and you are a payer of interest if you use a credit card or take out a student loan. Interest rates do not exist in a vacuum; they respond to changes in other parts of the financial market or the economy, so they may change daily or weekly. Naturally, when people borrow, they seek the lowest interest rate with the best terms.

Convenience is the main benefit of credit. **Credit cards**, which came into being in 1973, are used to purchase something or to get cash now with the promise of future payment. The typical cardholder carries 8 to 10 cards. Credit cards are also useful for identification purposes, rebates, emergencies, and purchases of big-ticket items.

Credit cards began in 1973.

A number of laws, most notably the Consumer Credit Protection Act of 1968, have been passed to reduce the problems with and confusion about consumer credit. The laws make several stipulations:

- You cannot be denied a credit card because you are a single woman.
- You can limit your risk if a credit card is lost or stolen.
- You can resolve errors in your monthly bill without damage to your credit rating.
- You cannot have credit shut off just because you've reached age 62.

The main drawback is overextension—people overuse credit and go into debt. Other problems include loss of cards, loss of privacy, and loss of financial freedom as money becomes more and more tied up in past purchases and interest payments.

CONSUMER ALERTS

Use caution when signing for a loan or acting as a cosigner. As a cosigner, if the borrower defaults, you will have to repay the loan. Not only would you lose money, but also failure to pay promptly will affect your credit rating.

Loans are sums of money lent at interest. A person considering taking out a loan should consider the source, the interest rate, and the terms, including the repayment schedule and any fees or penalties. Loans can be divided up into two types: by the reason for the loan (education, furniture, cash) and by the repayment schedule (monthly or yearly). Loans come from universities, stores, car dealerships, brokerage firms, banks, S&Ls, credit unions, consumer finance companies, sales finance companies, and life insurance companies. With the Internet, applying for a loan has never been easier, but that also causes problems because although applying is easy, paying up is another matter. A **cosigner** agrees to repay the loan if the borrower does not (defaults). Property such as a car, recreational vehicle, or boat used to secure a loan is called **collateral**. **Liens** are legal rights to take and hold property if the person with the loan does not pay up. When the loan is paid off, the liens are removed. When someone buys a house, a title search will reveal if there is a lien on the property, and the buyer will not purchase the house until the liens are cleaned up. A mortgage is a lien against a house.

Different types of loans such as mortgages, home equity loans, and car loans have been covered in previous chapters. The main thing to focus on is the annual percentage rate (APR), known as the interest rate; for example, the APR could be 8 percent a year or 12 percent a year—obviously the lower, the better. Most students are familiar with car or student loans. Regarding education loans, upon graduation, students should schedule an exit counseling session with their lender or university financial aid office to determine their rights and responsibilities and to set up a repayment schedule. Choices are going to include stretching out payments over 10 years or having higher payments and getting them paid off faster; there will also be choices about how soon the repayment begins. Some people never pay off their student loans, and lenders are getting more aggressive about getting their money back (sooner or later). In some cases, lenders can get their money back when a person starts getting Social Security—they go through a process to remove a part of the Social Security payment each month until the student loan is paid off. Recent graduates should review loan statements, and if they could have trouble making payments, then the lender should be contacted and a new repayment schedule developed.

Credit and Consumer Rights

A good credit rating (paying off student loans promptly is part of this) is important for a number of reasons, including the fact that potential employers may check your credit history before hiring you and landlords may check it to see if they would be wise to give you a lease. Sometimes things happen in the system that can cause credit problems, so credit records should be checked. The FTC enforces credit laws and protects your rights to obtain, use, and maintain credit; it cannot guarantee that everyone will get credit but can require businesses to be fair and equal in their treatment of customers and their resolution of disputes.

> ### CONSUMER ALERTS
>
> Is it possible to be turned down for a new credit card because you have no balance on another card because it is paid off each month? Yes. Lenders like people who borrow wisely and pay their bills; however, too much financial discipline can be a negative from their point of view because their goal is to make money off you in finance charges. Is this fair for consumers? No. If you still want a card, one option is to spend a moderate amount on the current card each month and make smaller repayments. After six months, reapply, and you should get a new card, which you can then pay off each month. Or you can forget this credit card company and try another.

Consumer reporting agencies (CRAs), more commonly known as **credit bureaus**, have files that contain information about your income, debt, and credit payment history as well as information on whether you have been sued or arrested or have filed for bankruptcy. A **credit score** is given that includes all this information plus assets, length of employment, and length of living in one place. Negative events such as bankruptcies or failure to pay bills impact heavily on the credit score. There are two types of credit scores:

1. As this book went to press, Fair Isaac Corporation was considering a new metric which would aid people with weak credit. In other words, it would give them a better chance of getting credit than past metrics. Traditionally, the **FICO score** developed by the firm Fair Isaac is the score most widely used by lenders and is also the one you have to pay to see (the three credit reporting centers all provide a FICO score to lenders). FICO scores range from 300 to 850, and a score below 500 is considered subprime, which means it may be hard to get loans or very high interest may be charged because a subprime borrower is considered more of a risk than someone with a high FICO score. The median score is 623, so someone with a score above that is preferred by lenders such as mortgage lenders; a score over 750 is considered a very high score, and anything above 800 is unusual. FICO scores are often checked by employers before they hire someone, so it is a good idea to get your financial house in order before job hunting. How consistent and reliable individuals are at paying their bills and loans is a major factor in the score. FICO scores tend to go up and down slowly because they reflect many years of consumption, payments, and financial patterns. Students who have dealt strictly in cash or whose parents paid all the bills may not have a FICO score, but employers will not hold that against them if they realize that is the case.

2. Other scores available for free use factors that are similar to (but not the same as) those used by FICO. These scores are available online from such companies as FreeCreditReport.com and eLoan.com. However, in exchange for the free score, you may get emails from e-loan companies or other financial services.

Below are the three main credit reporting centers:

Equifax Information Service Center
PO Box 10596
Atlanta, GA 30348-5496
www.econsumer.equifax.com

Experian Consumer Assistance Center
PO Box 2104
Allen, TX 75013
www.experian.com

Trans Union LLC Consumer Disclosure Center
PO Box 1000
Chester, PA 19022
www.transunion.com

> ### CONSUMER ALERTS
>
> Each credit bureau keeps a separate file on each person with information supplied to it by creditors. It is possible for one of the reports to have serious inaccuracies that could damage credit while the other two would not have the error in the file. So if there are problems, some experts suggest getting copies from all three bureaus. If everything is going okay, then a check may not be necessary, or it may be prudent to receive a copy of your credit report each year from one bureau to check for errors and to make sure you have not been a victim of identity theft. If there is a mistake, contact the credit bureau in writing or online and explain the situation. The way to raise a FICO score is by paying down your current account balances and by paying bills on time.

Your credit rights are protected under the Fair Credit Reporting Act (FCRA), which is designed to ensure that CRAs furnish correct and complete information to business when evaluating your application. According to the FTC, under FCRA your rights are as follows:

- You have the right to receive a copy of your credit report.
- You have the right to know the name of anyone who received your credit report in the last year for most purposes and in the last year for employment purposes.
- Companies that deny your application must supply the name and address of the CRA.
- You have the right to a free copy of your credit report when your application has been denied.
- If you disagree with the accuracy of information, you can file a dispute with the CRA and the company that furnished the information. Afterward, you should receive a summary explanation of the settling of the dispute.

Your credit rights are also protected under the Equal Credit Opportunity Act (ECOA), which prohibits credit discrimination. According to the FTC, under ECOA your rights are as follows:

- You cannot be denied credit based on your race, sex, marital status, religion, age, national origin, or receipt of public assistance.
- You have the right to reliable public assistance that is considered in the same manner as other income.
- If you are denied credit, you have a legal right to know why.

According to the FTC, your credit rights under the Fair Credit Billing Act (FCBA) and the EFTA establish procedures for resolving mistakes on credit billing and electronic fund transfer statements, including the following areas:

- Charges or electronic fund transfers that you—or anyone you have authorized to use your account—have not made.
- Charges or electronic fund transfers that are incorrectly identified or that show the wrong amount or date.
- Computation or similar errors that have been made.
- Failure to reflect payments, credits, or electronic fund transfers properly.
- Failure to mail or deliver credit billing statements to your current address (as long as that address was received by the creditor in writing at least 20 days before the billing period ended).
- Charges or electronic fund transfers for which you request an explanation or documentation, due to a possible error.

Most credit laws apply to open-ended credit (up to a maximum such as $5,000 or $10,000), revolving charge accounts such as department store accounts, and overdraft checking accounts. The EFTA applies to ATMs, debit transactions, and other electronic banking transactions.

To take advantage of consumer protection laws regarding incorrect charges, the person falsely charged must first write to creditors to straighten things out. The letter should be sent by certified mail, return receipt requested, so the person has proof that the creditor has received the letter; copies of sales slips and other documents should be included. The sender should keep a copy of the dispute letter.

College Students, Banks, and Credit Cards

Money is increasingly digital with online-only banks and apps. Credit card companies target students before their freshman year in college and hit them again before graduation and again when they get their first full-time jobs. Confirm that online banks and credit card companies are legitimate. The Federal Deposit Insurance Corporation (FDIC) has information on this.

CONSUMER ALERTS

A person's liability for lost or stolen credit cards is limited to $50. If this happens, notify card issuers promptly upon discovery of loss. Most companies have toll-free numbers and 24/7 service. Companies will instruct on the next steps to be taken (if any).

Debit cards, ATM cards, and stored value cards are other options that students can use. A growing number of colleges now give students identification cards that can be used to buy everything from books to pizza, with the school getting a share of the revenue. Alumni cards are also being used by schools as a source of revenue.

Debt Collectors and Creditor Rights

Debts are what is owed. Examples of debts are bonds, notes, mortgages, and other forms of paper evidencing amounts owed and payable on specified dates or on demand. A debtor is a person who owes money. If a debtor does not keep up with debts (such as not keeping up with car payments) or if there has been an error in the record or account, a debt collector may call. A debt collector is any person other than the creditor who collects debts. Lawyers can be debt collectors. The Fair Debt Collection Practices Act (FDCPA) prohibits debt collectors from using unfair, deceptive, or abusive practices while collecting debts. According to the FTC, these are your rights under the FDCPA:

- Debt collectors may contact you only between 8:00 A.M. and 9:00 P.M.
- Debt collectors may not contact you at work if they know your employer disapproves.
- Debt collectors may not harass, oppress, or abuse you.
- Debt collectors may not lie when collecting debts, such as falsely implying that you have committed a crime.
- Debt collectors must identify themselves to you on the phone.
- Debt collectors must stop contacting you if you ask them to in writing.

Solutions to Credit Problems

Your credit record or report influences your purchasing, getting a job, renting or buying a house, and buying insurance. Negative information can stay on a report for seven years and bankruptcy for ten. Any problems paying bills should be reported at once to creditors and a modified payment plan worked out. In other words, be up front about problems and take care of them before creditors turn to debt collectors. Creditors want the money even if it takes a long time; it costs them money to hire debt collectors, and that's an expense they want to avoid. People who have been turned down for credit may get desperate and fall for credit card scams. See Box 13.5 for advice on how to avoid scams.

Box 13.5 How to Avoid Credit Card Scams

- Beware of television or radio ads for "easy credit."
- Beware of the phrase "Anyone can qualify for a major credit card, even bankrupts!"
- Look out for calls to a "900" number for a credit card. This call may not be toll-free and may not result in a credit card. The FTC has found that calls can run from $2 to $50 or more.
- Watch out for credit repair companies or clinics. There are no tricks or short cuts—only time and consistently paid bills will repair damaged credit. If someone advertises help consolidating debts into one check instead of several, find out how much has to be paid and for how long.

Credit Counseling Services

After a person tries everything to straighten out credit problems, an alternative is to turn to credit counseling services such as the National Foundation for Credit Counseling or the Consolidated Credit Counseling Service. They have offices throughout the United States and offer websites and toll-free 24-hour hotlines. Services may be free or low cost. How can they afford to operate for free or with low fees? The answer is that they are supported by local businesses and banks that want to help consumers be fiscally responsible and by foundations and groups such as the United Way. Also universities, military bases, credit unions, employers (through employee assistance programs) and housing or community authorities may offer free or low-cost money management or credit counseling services. Counselors look at the bills and try to arrange repayment plans that are acceptable to the people with credit problems and to their creditors. This may mean debt consolidation or the formation of a debt repayment plan. The Federal Consumer Information Center (1-888-878-3256) offers publications on credit counselors and debt management as well as checklists of questions to ask when choosing a counseling agency.

CONSUMER ALERTS

Women have often had trouble establishing a good credit history—a record of how bills were paid—because they have made name changes due to marriage and because creditors would report accounts shared by married couples in the husband's name only. Women should make sure all relevant information in the credit bureau's file is in their name. The credit bureaus should be informed of any changes in names and in marital status, including getting married, separated, divorced, or widowed.

Who has financial or credit problems? Nearly everyone has experienced a bounced check or problems with electric or telephone bills, but credit counseling services are primarily for people who really have gotten in over their heads. The average customer at the National Foundation for Credit Counseling is a woman, is 35.4 years old, is married (or has never married) with children, has low to middle income, and owes several thousand dollars to over ten creditors. How do you know when things are getting out of hand? This typical profile provides a few indicators, such as having dependents and several creditors. There are other signs:

- Routinely fighting about money with a spouse or partner.
- Being continually anxious about money, never feeling there is enough, or worried about spending what is available.
- Having an inability to save, feeling that spending is out of control, seeking instant gratification through shopping, or rationalizing purchases (such as the tenth pair of running shoes).
- Having no idea where money goes and not balancing a checkbook or looking at statements.
- Living paycheck to paycheck, usually running out of money before the next paycheck.
- Being turned down for credit cards.
- Bouncing checks regularly and having problems with bank accounts.
- Having trouble paying the rent and car payment.
- Having to regularly borrow money from family members and friends.
- Paying only the minimum each month on credit cards and never paying them off completely.
- Not wanting to hear about money problems and using avoidance.
- Having a history of falling into debt, getting out of debt, and falling back into it.
- Having an attraction to people who have money problems as kindred souls.
- Having to have the best of everything (such as the most expensive set of golf clubs or a showy car) even if it is not affordable.

Debt and Relationships/Self-Worth

Debt affects relationships. In a magazine article, a 31-year-old registered nurse revealed that she owed $57,000 and was afraid to tell her fiancé. When she told him, it turned out he had $27,000 in debt, so they postponed the wedding. Later, they disagreed about money; for example, he bought a new car instead of paying his bills. Eventually they broke up. Since then she has been paying off her debts each month and so far has reduced it by $5,000. Her goal is to be debt free in three years (Orman, 2001). In the same article, another woman, age 34, who was in debt set a financial goal to save for a down payment for a house and eventually wanted to start a family. She gained control of her finances by paying off three credit cards, which changed the dynamic between her husband and her for the better, and she reported they don't argue as much about money anymore.

Self-worth is a system of thoughts and feelings concerning or focused on self. Research indicates that self-worth is a driving force in people's perceptions of their financial situation and spending behavior. In an article on self-worth and finances, the relationship was explained this way:

> Some people spend because they have low self-worth. This spending helps them feel better about themselves, at least momentarily. On the other hand, some people engage in excessive spending behavior and feel guilty, thereby diminishing their self-worth. The positive and significant relationship between self-worth and financial satisfaction is an important finding that has significant implications for educators and financial advisors. (Hira & Mugenda, 1999, p. 220)

Bankruptcy

"The Great Recession revealed the financial vulnerability of millions of U.S. households" (Sherraden & Grinstein-Weiss, 2015, p. 1). Even in tough economic times, a person should try everything possible before resorting to **bankruptcy,** which is a form of legal recourse open to insolvent debtors. A debtor would petition a federal court for protection from creditors and arrange for the liquidation of assets. The bankruptcy rate is about 1.4 million Americans a year, and the number is rising. Some of it is caused by credit overextension; other times it is caused by health crises, business failures, job losses, divorces, accidents, and natural disasters. Usually the debtors are under stress and unable to think clearly about the ramifications of bankruptcy, which remains on credit reports for up to ten years. The person may get out from under debt but will be unable to buy a car, rent an apartment, or buy a house and may not be able to get a job or do other things most people take for granted. Over 25 percent of employers look into credit backgrounds before hiring, especially for jobs involving money and accounting such as retail, bank, and management positions (on an employment application, the potential employee authorizes the employer to do background checks, which can include checking credit records).

Options

Most bankrupt individuals want to choose Chapter 7 of the federal bankruptcy code, but because of changes, most bankrupt individuals are steered to Chapter 13. **Chapter 7 bankruptcy** is known as "Straight Liquidation Chapter," because in return for eliminating debts, the debtor agrees to turn over nonexempt assets and pay as much as possible to creditors. However, the way it usually goes is that there are no nonexempt assets to sell, so creditors receive nothing. Exempt items differ by state but usually include houses, tools of trade, cars, and farm animals. Chapter 7 bankruptcy is popular because if it is granted, the court erases all dischargeable debt. In this situation, assets are turned over to an appointed trustee who will sell the assets to pay debts, making partial payments to creditors. Usually the first one to be paid is the attorney who handles the bankruptcy, and it is suggested that people hire an attorney for these cases. Costs include attorney fees, a filing fee, and trustee fees.

Another choice is **Chapter 13 bankruptcy**, which allows debtors to repay some of the debt they owe, and in return they get to keep most of their property; usually this type of debtor is a person with regular income. Through a court-approved plan, the debtor pays back some of the debt, and this looks better on the person's future credit report. Under Chapter 13 bankruptcy, the debtor retains some assets, and debts have to be paid within five to seven years. States differ about what assets the debtor may keep. People may hide such assets as jewelry, cars, or boats at relatives' and friends' houses, but the courts are quite shrewd and try to determine whether the debtor has given an honest accounting of assets and liabilities before final decisions are made.

Bankruptcy, then, represents an issue with several sides to it. Sometimes the debtor may have been fiscally irresponsible and may be bilking creditors and lenders; in other cases, the debtor has been through an unfortunate set of circumstances, such as ill health or an injury, and the laws are there to protect him or her from being harassed or unfairly treated. In recent years, Congress has considered bankruptcy legislation that would make declaring bankruptcy more difficult and might also include education requirements (similar to traffic school for drivers with traffic tickets). Repeated or serial bankruptcies are not uncommon, and stopping the cycle for the debtors' sake and their families' sake, as well as for the sake of the economy and of creditors, is a goal. Ultimately, the cost of bankruptcy is passed down to the people who pay their bills and are responsible through higher interest rates, more credit charges, and higher taxes. Somewhere along the line, someone has to pay for other people's misfortunes and mistakes.

Steps to Follow

When people declare bankruptcy, they file petitions and schedules with the clerk's office of the federal bankruptcy court. In the petition, there will be a list of assets, income sources, liabilities (including lists of creditors and amounts owed), and living expenses (including number and ages of dependents). Proof will be needed in the form of deeds, mortgages, tax returns, credit card bills, medical bills, savings records, and loan papers. The process will take from four to six months to complete. One of the positive aspects is that debt collectors stop calling until things are settled, giving people breathing space. Attorneys also provide a buffer zone because debtors can refer creditors to them. Lenders may show up during the court case and will talk to the debtors and their attorneys immediately after the case ends, trying to get their money first. Attorneys do the following:

- Advise the person of rights and options in bankruptcy.
- Complete the forms (or have someone in their office complete the forms) and file them.
- Attend the "First Meeting of Creditors" with the debtor (this is also called the 341 meeting).
- Represent the debtor in the courtroom.

A trustee is appointed by a US trustee, who works for the Department of Justice, and administers the case but cannot give legal advice. The trustee's job is to ensure that the debtor and creditors (people, banks, institutions, and stores to which the debtor owes money) are treated in accordance with the rules and procedures established in the US Bankruptcy Code. Even though people go bankrupt, they still have to pay taxes, alimony, child support, property settlements, and student loans. A judge decides disputes, and usually debtors only see a judge if someone objects to their case.

Government's Role in Consumer Finances

Throughout this chapter, the government's role as defender of consumers' rights, regulator, law setter, holder of hearings, and mediator has been emphasized. The government also has a role in providing financial education; examples of this were mentioned earlier and include public service announcements and the website of the Federal Reserve. Since the 1970s, financial and credit rights have been at the forefront of the consumer movement. As this chapter has shown, there are many agencies and laws regulating the use of credit. The leading agency is the FTC, which works for the consumer to prevent fraudulent, deceptive, and unfair business practices in the marketplace and to provide information to help consumers spot, stop, and avoid scams. Complaints against all kinds of creditors can be filed with the Department of Justice, Civil Rights Division, Washington, DC 20530.

CONSUMER ALERTS

People file for bankruptcy with the idea of being free from debt, but as noted in the chapter some debts (such as student loans) are not dischargeable—they keep going. Also, a Chapter 7 bankruptcy only eliminates past debt, debt owed before the filing, so debtors are not absolved from future debt. They have to keep paying rent, telephone, electricity, and water bills or face losing services or being evicted even while they are in the process of filing for bankruptcy.

An example in the chapter of government legislation aiding consumers and the banking business is the legislation being considered by Congress as this book went to press that would give electronic check images the same legal weight as paper checks. Instead of couriers arriving at bank branches to pick up checks to be processed, the checks would be sent electronically—this makes so much more sense in terms of time efficiency, cost-effectiveness, and gasoline savings. Technology in e-finance is one of the fastest-growing areas of e-commerce.

Besides federal agencies and Congress, state agencies and legislators also work to protect consumers. Each state has usury laws that limit how high an interest rate pawnbrokers and other lenders can charge. State attorneys general can prosecute creditors who have violated state equal credit opportunity laws, and in state governments, the office of the attorney general has the muscle to stop anti-consumer practices.

Summary

Research indicates that self-worth, financial beliefs, behavior, and satisfaction are linked. Reaching financial goals requires setting realistic targets and creating a plan to reach them; the best strategy is to set short-, medium-, and long-term goals and to build savings. The sum that Americans save, as a percentage of their disposable income, has fallen sharply in recent years. Most of our federal tax dollars go to human resources. When it comes to taxes, money management, and investments, seeking financial advice will help, but the quality of financial advice varies. With the deregulation of financial institutions in 1980, the market opened up, mergers happened, and more choices were available to consumers. Banks are offering products such as mutual funds that are not backed by the FDIC, and this is confusing to some investors who thought all bank products and services were secure and backed by the federal government.

Online banking, a fast-growing use of the Internet for bill paying and account checking, is more popular than online auctions or stock trading. The chapter covered a number of ways to make sure that your online banking is conducted in a safe way and that your liability is limited. Streamlining bill paying saves time and reduces clutter.

There are few controls or regulations for financial planners. The Certified Financial Planner (CFP) is the most recognized certification. Many different situations, such as significant changes in lifestyle or marital status, can trigger the need for professional help. Certified divorce planners are financial planners who specialize in dividing assets in divorce cases.

The three main consumer reporting agencies (CRAs), which are also known as credit bureaus, keep credit scores and records. Credit is used by many consumers to finance educations, buy houses, remodel homes, and buy cars. A number of acts ensure that consumers are given equal access to credit and are treated fairly. The list of uses for credit scores is growing and includes auto and homeowner insurance companies; every lender looks at credit scores to gauge the likelihood of customers' future claims and then sets their premiums accordingly. More employers are using credit scores to screen job applicants, and landlords use them before renting. A credit score may be the earliest indication of an identity theft problem. Credit counseling is recommended for people with credit or bill-paying problems. If the problems cannot be solved, an alternative is filing for bankruptcy, which is a form of legal recourse open to insolvent debtors; the two main types of personal bankruptcy are Chapter 7 and Chapter 13 bankruptcy.

KEY POINTS

1. Financial management is a three-step process.

2. A balance sheet reflects what is saved, owned, and owed. In recent years, Americans have been saving 4 to 5 percent of disposable income on average each year.

3. An emergency fund is recommended as a fallback in case of job loss or other major setbacks.

4. With deregulation, money markets opened up and consumers had more choices because of increased competition.

5. Four main kinds of financial institutions are commercial banks, credit unions, brokerage firms, and savings and loan associations.

6. Under the old check-processing system, paper checks took five days to go through the system and were handled more than 15 times. In the new online and electronic systems checks can go through immediately.

7. Online banking and online tax forms for the Internal Revenue Service offer convenience.

8. Progressive taxes (for example, income taxes) and regressive taxes (for example, taxes on gasoline) have different impacts on the population. Tax avoidance is legal, but tax evasion is illegal.

9. There are over 500,000 financial planners in the United States.

10. Consumer credit can be used for a variety of reasons, including financing education and buying luxury items. Financing education is an investment in human capital.

11. A credit score is a key factor in determining access to credit as well as the interest rate a person may be charged. The FICO score is the credit industry standard. FICO scores, which range from 300 to 850, allow lenders to rank loan applicants according to the likelihood they will repay on time.

12. Federal law sets procedures for correcting inaccurate information on credit reports.

KEY TERMS

attitudes

balance sheet

bankruptcy

budget

certified divorce planner

Certified Financial Planner (CFP)

Chapter 7 bankruptcy

Chapter 13 bankruptcy

chip cards

collateral

consumer reporting agencies (CRAs)

cosigner

credit bureaus

credit cards

credit score

debit cards

debts

decision making

deductions

emergency fund

excise tax

Federal Deposit Insurance Corporation (FDIC)

FICO score

financial planner

fixed expenses

interest

liens

loans

nexting

personal finance

personal identification number (PIN)

resources

smart cards

stored value cards

tax avoidance

taxes

tax evasion

time deposit

Truth in Savings Act

values

variable expenses

DISCUSSION QUESTIONS

1. Are you pleased or disappointed with your financial situation? What steps are you taking to get on sounder footing? What are your short-, medium-, and long-range goals? Why does financial planning require flexibility?

2. Why is it true that it is never too soon or too late to start working on improving a financial situation?

3. What is your potential liability if your debit card is lost or stolen? What is your potential liability if your credit card is lost or stolen? In either case, what should you do first?

REFERENCES

Boshara, R. and W. Emmons. (Spring 2015). Balance sheet perspective on financial success: Why starting early matters. *The Journal of Consumer Affairs*, 49 (1), 267–298.

Clements, J. (February 19, 2003). Finding a financial adviser who won't sneer at your little nest egg. *Wall Street Journal*, p. D1.

Gilbert, D. (2006). *Stumbling on happiness*. New York: Alfred A. Knopf.

Higgins, M., and R. Simon. (February 12, 2003). Getting stock picks from your boss. *Wall Street Journal*, p. D1.

Hira, T., and O. Mugenda. (1999). The relationships between self-worth and financial beliefs, behavior, and satisfaction. *Journal of Family and Consumer Sciences*, 91 (4), 214–220.

Hoffman, E. (February 2003). Want some outside advice? *AARP Bulletin*, p. 26.

Ip, G. (May 20, 2003). New role for Greenspan: pitching financial advice. *Wall Street Journal*, p. D3.

Lee, E., and J. Lee. (2001/2002). Credit choices: an examination of consumer approval for the financing of luxury items and education. *Journal of Consumer Education*, 19/20, pp. 25–34.

Orman, S. (September 2001). Your net worth? Priceless. *O Magazine*, pp. 66–70.

Shellenbarger, S. (June 26, 2006). Doing well vs. doing good: parents struggle with their grad's idealism. *Wall Street Journal*, p. D1.

Shen, S., Sam, A., and Jones, E. (Fall 2014). Credit card indebtedness and psychological well-being over time: empirical evidence from a household survey, *The Journal of Consumer Affairs*, 48(3), 431–456.

Sherraden, M. and Grinstein-Weiss, M. (Spring 2015). Creating financial capability in the next generation: an introduction to the special issue. *The Journal of Consumer Affairs*, 49 (1), 1–12.

Stirland, S. (October 2001). Is your bank selling the world your secrets? *Good Housekeeping*, pp. 229–30.

Tang, N., Baker, A., and Peter, P. (Summer 2015). Investigating the disconnect between financial knowledge and behavior: the role of parental influence and psychological characteristics in responsible financial behaviors among young adults. *The Journal of Consumer Affairs*, 49 (2), 376–406.

Chapter 14

Insurance and Investment Issues

Money is like promises—easier made than kept.

Josh Billings

LEARNING OBJECTIVES

1. Explain the purpose and types of insurance.

2. Describe the parts of insurance contracts.

3. Explain the purpose and different types of investments.

4. Describe frauds and scams involved in insurance and investments.

5. Discuss government agencies that look out for insurance and investment frauds.

CASE STUDY

Millennials on Investing

"Despite the blessings of youth—I'm 24 years old, with limber joints and without mortgage payments—I am aware that we have something of a retirement crisis on our hands. You can't miss it if you watch sports on TV, where financial-services pitch themselves to worried middle-aged men. I can't miss it either when I call home. My parents are in fine shape, thank goodness, but like any other self-respecting late-50-something professionals, they are gaming out survival plans for so many improbably scenarios. And, it didn't take a lot of days on the job for me to notice that my employer was lowering its match on employees' 401(k)s, leading to grumbling among some of my older co-workers, who saw their defined-benefit plans end in 2010. The boomers, we're told might be going bust. But what—if I may be so millennial—about me?

Source: Jack Dickey (October 27, 2014). "I'm 24. I Just Retired and I Never Want to Do It Again." *Time*. p. 40.

Introduction

Insurance (risk management) and investments are little-understood yet important parts of our lives from beginning to end.

In long-term investing, such as saving for retirement, consumers need to consider the financial risk of return on their financial assts. Risk tolerance is an important concept in economic research and financial planning (Xaio, 2015, p. 206).

This chapter explains the basic forms of insurance and investments as well as the most common fraud problems. Since this is an ever-evolving area, readers need to keep abreast of changes in the general economy and the legislation that affects financial products and services. For example, I can state the fact that on October 20, 2015 one area bank offered 1.5 percent interest on Certificates of Deposit (CDs) if someone invested $1,000 with them for one year, but is that really useful across time and across the globe?

"Consumers have more power to influence and be influenced by the marketplace than ever before due to increased connectivity" (Goldsmith, 2015, p. 84). The Internet brings with it increasing choices along with increasing opportunities for fraud. Since large sums of money are involved in insurance and investments, the attraction to swindlers is easily seen—swindlers go where the money is. But let's say you are a cautious person and unlikely to fall victim to obvious fraud. Why should you care? Insurance fraud alone can inflate your premiums as much as 30 percent, according to the National Insurance Crime Bureau. Whether you fall victim directly or not, you pay for the insurance fraud that involves others because the cost is passed on to all consumers.

The chapter begins with a brief overview of the purpose of and types of insurance because this type of fraud cannot be explained until the reader understands the way insurance works. Specifics on the different types of insurance will be given, leading to a discussion of consumer rights and responsibilities. After the insurance section, the chapter turns to a description of different types of investments and the connected frauds.

Is there one surefire way to get rich? The answer to this is no. A basic principle in economics is that the greater the expected return on investment, the greater the risks associated with it. Before putting money into either insurance or investments, read this chapter and then investigate further.

Insurance

Purpose

Insurance is a financial arrangement between individuals and insurance companies *to protect* against loss or injury, and it provides peace of mind. This protection can be for a house, a business, a boat, recreational vehicle, or an automobile, and also protection from possible liability claims. Another purpose is that some types of insurance, such as whole life insurance, can be used as a form of investment. By buying insurance, individuals are trying to protect themselves, their families, and their assets such as homes, businesses, and cars. Insurer American International Group Inc. (AIG) estimates that high net worth individuals in the US pay about "$5 billion in annual insurance premiums but says that only about 20% of them are adequately insured" (Binkley, 2015, D3). **Premiums** are payments to insurers typically made monthly or yearly.

> Insurance, a financial arrangement between consumers and insurers, is for protection.

College courses in insurance usually fall under the category of risk management, and they are taught in business school. Individuals take out policies (contracts). The policies include agreements, **exclusions** (items not covered), conditions, deductibles, and endorsements (amendments or additions to the basic policy). An example of an exclusion would be exempting claims stemming from nuclear explosions or radioactive fallout. State Farm, one of the nation's largest auto and residential insurers, changed its car insurance policies to exclude such claims in the wake of heightened awareness of terrorism and the realization that there was no specific language in its existing contracts regarding nuclear-related claims. In light of this, letters were sent to millions of auto policy holders saying that nuclear blasts and radioactive damage are not normal road hazards, whether the incidents are accidental or intentional, and in so doing, the company clarified that cars damaged by nuclear incidents are not covered.

Deductibles are amounts policy holders pay toward a loss before insurance coverage begins. If there is a loss or injury, the insurer pays up after the deductible is met.

Insurance is sold through agents in person, over the telephone, or online. Auto insurance is one type of insurance that is increasingly being sold online. **Exposures**, such as driving, are sources of risks; **perils** are events such as car accidents that cause financial loss.

The buying of insurance can be thought of as a process beginning with awareness of need, moving through analysis, then action (including purchase), and ending with evaluation. Insurance policies should be revisited at least once a year—and more often when there are significant lifestyle changes. One kind of thing that could change, for example, is peril exposure, such as when a consumer takes up skydiving or starts traveling extensively.

CASE STUDY

Julie Macklowe about Insuring Couture Clothes

"Julie Macklowe and her husband Billy take care that their homes and belongings are insured. Ms. Macklowe assumed that her wardrobe, an impeccable collection that spans from this season's Valentino and Dior Haute couture to Chanel track suits, is covered by her homeowners' insurance, until she recently asked her insurance agent. 'I checked. It totally does not cover it,' says Ms. Macklowe, a former hedge-fund manager and founder of the beauty brand Vbeaute. A designer day dress can cost several thousand dollars—haute couture costs six figures . . . The options for apparel insurance have been limited . . . A clothing collection valued by its owner at $1 million would cost about $3,000 a year to insure, depending on the risks to the clothes, according to AIG."

Source: Christina Binkley (Sept. 3, 2015). "New Insurance for a Fashion Disaster (Not That Kind)." *The Wall Street Journal*, D3.

An insurer can turn down an applicant. If this happens, the applicant can ask the insurer why he or she was denied coverage and request a copy of personal medical information. The individual denied insurance can try other companies and check with the state department of insurance to find out about rights and responsibilities.

Automobile Insurance

Many states (but not all) require auto insurance. Since not all states require auto insurance, it is possible to get in an accident with an uninsured motorist, so what you may want to have is **uninsured motorist coverage**, which pays for bodily injury caused by an uninsured motorist, a hit-and-run driver, or a negligent driver with an insolvent insurer. A driver may be underinsured as well. In the case of an accident, whether or not a claim is paid depends on the insurance of the two drivers who were legally liable, any agreements between the people involved, the amount of damage, and the amount of maximum limit on the policies.

Photo 14.1
He found a low insurance rate for his car!

Source: Thinkstock: m-imagephotography

CONSUMER ALERTS

Protect yourself when buying insurance online by doing research. Determine which insurance coverage best fits your needs; then shop around for companies, premiums, and coverage. In order to sell insurance in your state, the company and the agent must be licensed. Remember that security is important—protect your personal information, taking extra precautions when paying with credit cards. Keep detailed records, get all rate quotes, and print out forms and information. You should receive a copy of new policies within 30 to 60 days of purchase. If you do not, contact the company immediately.

In the last chapter, it was stated that banks and other institutions are crossing lines by adding more and more types of financial products. Similarly, there is a new twist in car insurance: In order to control cost, some insurers have their own chain of one-stop auto claims centers. Customers make an appointment and bring in their cars, and the company takes it from there.

Regarding the differences between states in auto insurance coverage required, in Louisiana you must have liability coverage, which pays for property damages or personal injury for which the driver is legally responsible. No-fault insurance (after an auto accident, each party collects from his or her insurer) is available in only a few states; no-fault insurance policies are rife with fraud, and motorists are paying too much for limited coverage. There are several types of insurance:

- *Bodily injury liability.* Coverage of bodily injury liability pays for serious and permanent injury or death to others when you cause an accident involving your automobile.

- *Collision.* Collision coverage pays for repair or replacement of your vehicle if it collides with another vehicle or flips over or crashes into an object, regardless of who causes the accident.

- *Comprehensive.* Comprehensive coverage pays for losses from incidents other than a collision, such as fire, theft, windstorm, vandalism, or flood.

- *Uninsured or underinsured motorist.* Coverage for uninsured or underinsured drivers pays for bodily injuries to you, your family members, and any other person occupying your covered vehicle if the injuries are caused by the negligence of others.

- *Medical payments.* Another type of coverage pays for medical expenses for accidental injury up to the limit of your policy.

- *Towing.* Coverage can be added to basic auto insurance for towing and road service.

There are additional kinds of auto insurance, but they tend to be for unique situations. The point is that auto insurance is something that individuals buy on their own (not through an employer) and that the states vary in what they require. Following are some factors that affect premiums:

- *Driving history.* A driving history includes past accidents and traffic violations.

- *Type of vehicle.* Premiums are impacted by the vehicle's model, year, and value.

- *Gender and age.* Insurance companies typically charge higher premiums for males under the age of 25.

Photo 14.2 Two drivers argue after a minor accident

Source: Thinkstock: monkeybusiness images

- *Territory.* Where you drive and where you keep your car influence premiums. Urban drivers typically pay more than rural drivers; for example, insurance is higher in New York City than it is in rural areas of Wyoming or North Dakota.

Ways to reduce premiums include having a good driving record, being a nondrinker and nonsmoker, driving low-profile automobiles, getting older, raising your deductible, and getting good grades (this last one depends on insurer). Box 14.1 lists the typical types of insurance frauds related to autos.

Box 14.1 Types of Fraud Schemes and Scams Related to Auto Insurance

Agent sliding. The term *agent sliding* refers to an agent selling a consumer optional coverage or services without his or her full consent.

Deceptive claim. An example is when an accident victim files a claim for lost wages and medical bills following an accident, and investigators find out that the injury was preexisting and had nothing to do with the accident.

Fictional theft. When a policy holder files a phony claim for a stolen luxury car when the car is actually hidden in storage or at a friend's house, that is fictional theft.

Repair shop rip-off. An example of a repair shop rip-off is when an owner of a repair shop offers to inflate the damage estimate as a favor, and the dishonest owner of the vehicle submits the inflated claim.

Understatement of risk. A dishonest applicant lying about the number of miles frequently driven per year in order to get a lower premium is an understatement of risk.

Note that some of these scams and schemes are caused by the insurer and some by the consumer.

CONSUMER ALERTS

When applying for auto insurance policies, individuals must disclose past tickets or accidents, otherwise individuals risk policies being cancelled, leaving them without coverage. Applicants must also be truthful about the number of drivers in their family. An insurance company can cancel the policy if the driver has been in three or more accidents in a three-year period; failure to make premiums can also result in cancellation. As with any other major purchase, individuals should shop around. Investigate how companies are rated. If you receive phone calls after an accident, it could be someone trying to involve you in a fraud scheme.

Credit Insurance

Credit insurance is one of the lesser known forms of insurance. It protects a loan or mortgage on the chance that a person cannot make the payments. Usually it is optional, meaning the lender will not demand it. The Federal Trade Commission (FTC) says it is against the law for a lender to deceptively include credit insurance in your loan without your knowledge or permission. There are four types of credit insurance:

1. *Credit disability insurance.* A credit disability insurance policy pays off all or some of your loan if you become ill or injured and can't work.

2. *Credit life insurance.* A credit type of life insurance pays off all or some of your loan if you die.

3. *Credit property insurance.* Credit property insurance protects personal property used to secure a loan.

4. *Involuntary unemployment insurance.* Insurance coverage for involuntary unemployment makes loan payments if you lose your job through no fault of your own, such as a layoff.

Several of these credit insurance types are covered by other kinds of insurance an individual may already have, such as health or auto insurance, so before buying credit insurance, he or she should check this first. Alternatives, such as life insurance instead of credit life insurance, may make more sense. Before buying credit insurance, find out about these issues and the length of loan, as well as the usual issues about insurance such as coverage, cost of premiums, and ratings of companies.

Homeowners' (Property and Liability) Insurance

Homeowners' insurance helps pay to repair or rebuild your home and to replace personal possessions lost to theft, fire, storm, or other disasters. Most states do not require the purchase of homeowners' insurance but may require it for specific purposes (for example, liability insurance if you have a swimming pool). **Property insurance** pays for losses to homes and personal property due to theft, fire, vandalism, natural disaster, or another cause such as trees falling on houses. **Liability insurance** pays for losses from negligence resulting in bodily injury or property damage to others for which the policy holder is responsible; all homeowners' policies provide liability coverage. From a consumer point of view, the main thing is to have replacement-cost coverage. If the home or apartment is destroyed by fire, a person wants to replace the contents, and if the dwelling was owned, replacing the structure should be covered as well. There are a variety of forms. The most popular of all policies for homeowners that cover the basics is HO-3; HO-4 is for renters. Policy seekers look for a match between what they need and what the policy covers while keeping costs to a minimum. If a person owns only a beat-up bicycle, a three-year-old computer, and clothes, renters' insurance is probably not necessary. The more valuable the possessions are, the more insurance is needed. To save money, homeowners and renters should raise the deductible, use security systems and smoke detectors, not smoke, and take advantage of available discounts such as those offered to groups.

Liability may be related to homes, autos, situations involving bodily injury, libel (a written, printed, or pictorial statement that damages a person by damaging his or her character or reputation), or other damages caused by the insured.

There are three red flags that may prevent an insurer from covering a home:

1. Water claims.
2. Wind/hail damage.
3. Burglaries.

The insurance industry has been cracking down on houses with a past. The message from the insurer is "It is not you—it is your house."

Policies usually cover the basics, but for extras such as jewelry, furs, and expensive computers, a person may need additional coverage that can be obtained as an **endorsement**, an addition to an insurance policy. "The truth is that homeowners insurance can be very limited in protecting valuable possessions. It's common to encounter special clauses that exclude fine art and antiques, or that cap payments on losses. . . . Standard policies also rarely protect against common causes of loss to fine art, like water damage and breakage" (Whitehouse, 2003, p. D2). Decisions about insurance should hinge on how losses are reimbursed. Some insurers use a method that gives replacement value minus depreciation. Usually sentimental value is not included, so the policy holder has to decide how much coverage is appropriate. Cost is going to vary by part of the country; for example, in coastal areas of Florida, endorsement or additions for breakables like china are going to be higher than in Utah. Box 14.2 gives a list of typical insurance frauds related to homeowners' policies. An **adjuster** is a person who determines the amount of claim, loss, or damage payable under a contract and should be properly licensed. If there is a loss, insurers require that you notify them immediately.

CONSUMER ALERTS

If a housing unit is vacant for 30 days in a row, it may be considered abandoned, and insurance coverage may halt. If you are going to be gone for longer than 30 days, check your policy. A house-sitter or someone checking your property regularly, including police, may take care of this problem. Also some policies do not cover floods or other disasters, so if you live in a flood-prone area, you may need extra insurance or you can take your chances.

> ### Box 14.2 Types of Insurance Fraud Related to Homeowners' Policies
>
> *Arson for profit.* Financially strapped homeowners who intentionally set fires to destroy property in hopes of collecting insurance claims are committing arson for profit.
>
> *Duplicate policies for profit.* When consumers buy multiple policies on the same house or property (such as a piece of jewelry), hoping to collect from more than one company when the item is destroyed or lost, that is use of duplicate policies for profit.
>
> *Fictional theft.* A fictional theft includes exaggerating the value of missing items.
>
> *Unlicensed public adjuster.* It is illegal to use a public adjuster who lacks a license and who solicits distraught homeowners during claims settlement after a disaster. The trick would include the homeowner paying more than 10 percent of the settlement and paying the money upfront.
>
> Note: Some of these insurance frauds are caused by insurers and some by consumers.

Health Insurance

Of all the types of insurance, health insurance is the most costly and the most vital. Understanding who health care consumers are and how they are changing is a primary concern of health insurance companies, hospitals, nurses, doctors, pharmaceutical companies, government policy makers, and the media. Health care is one of the nation's largest industries, and insurance is a big part of it. Some of the issues related to health insurance include the rapid rise of health care spending, the diversity of health care consumers, the Internet's growing importance to health care, the growing use of alternative medicine, the aging of the population, the deinstitutionalization of medical care, the growth of outpatient care, and the change in attitudes toward disability, mental health, psychiatry, and even death.

Health care costs are rising steeply, which is affecting the cost of insurance. On a yearly basis, health care costs are increasing 20 percent faster than the general inflation rate, and the cost of prescription drugs is rising more than 20 percent per year. People can have no insurance, private health insurance, or government-linked or managed care insurance through employers. Increasingly, employers are cutting health care benefits or raising deductibles so that employees pay more before health insurance kicks in. Private health insurance (meaning that not obtained through an employer) is very expensive, and consumer difficulties generally fall into the categories of cost-related issues, communications-based problems of convenience, and serious medical concerns.

Health care costs are rising steeply.

A main problem that people report having with their health care plan is payment or billing for services. Another major problem is that more than half of all Americans are not satisfied with the availability of their doctors and the amount of information they receive in an office visit.

The majority of Americans are at least partially insured under governmental or managed care plans. An example of managed care is a health maintenance organization (HMO). Employers with at least 25 employees have to offer an HMO choice. In the past, a lot of people were dissatisfied with managed care, but recent polls show the public is discontented with "the system" but not with their own health care plans. So despite a general atmosphere of frustration with the health care industry and with hassles with insurance companies, a Harris Interactive survey found that two-thirds of Americans gave their plan a grade of A or B, three-fourths said they would recommend their plan to someone who is healthy, and 68 percent would recommend it to friends or family with a serious or chronic disease.

Medicaid is a *state-run program* that provides hospital and medical coverage for people with low income and little or no resources. **Medicare** is the *federal health insurance program* for people age 65 or older and for people with certain disabilities. Medicare has four parts:

1. Hospital insurance (Part A).
2. Medical insurance (Part B).
3. Medical Advantage (Part C).
4. Prescription drug coverage (Part D).

A whole industry has sprung up helping seniors to qualify, and often it is aided by children who are doing asset transfers for sick parents (see Box 14.3). This is a form of defrauding the government if the elderly person is not actually poor. Therefore, guidelines are being looked into so this is not so easy to do. It is also unfortunate that people feel they have to do this to take care of sick parents—better solutions need to be found.

Box 14.3 Common Red Flags Regarding Medicare Fraud

Look out for people who say the following:

- I represent Medicare.
- I have free service or equipment.
- I need your Medicare number or Social Security number.

- I want to tell you how you can get more out of Medicare.
- I offer free tests, exams, or consultations.

Also beware of people who pressure you to buy Medigap insurance or who use scare tactics as well as those who show up at your front door or call you over the phone.

Doing any of the following is illegal:

- billing for services not rendered or equipment not received
- billing twice for same services
- misrepresenting a diagnosis or the place of diagnosis to get a higher payment
- falsifying documents
- soliciting, offering, or receiving kickbacks, bribes, or illegal rebates
- seeking to defraud Medicare or the government in any way other than those previously mentioned.

Disability Income Insurance

Disability income insurance pays benefits to policy holders when they are incapable of working; it can be for temporary or long-term disability and typically pays 60 to 80 percent of their paycheck. Most people get this coverage through employers, but someone can buy it as an individual (for example, if a person is self-employed or owns a small business). The policies have an elimination period, meaning a period of time that must elapse before insurance begins. Obviously, it is linked to employment, so this type of insurance does not make sense for retirees or other nonworkers. Social Security also has disability insurance. In **workers' compensation**, money is paid if a disability is due to illness or injury received on the job. If someone becomes disabled, there are a variety of options: Benefits usually go to the injured or ill person, but there are situations in which the benefits go to the spouse or underage children if the person dies.

Employers and unions sometimes offer disability income insurance, and if it is offered at a low cost or for free, it should be considered, especially if one travels to high-risk parts of the world or if one performs high-risk work. Even desk work can bring injuries such as carpal tunnel syndrome, so a case could be made for every worker to have disability income insurance and/or workers' compensation. To keep premiums low, an employee should reduce coverage time, pay a high deductible, lower the monthly benefit, and lengthen the elimination period.

Life Insurance

In the United States, 70 percent of adults have life insurance policies.

About 70 percent of US adults have life insurance policies. **Life insurance** is a contract between a policy holder and an insurer that says what sum will be paid to beneficiaries on the insured's death. These can be bought on your own or through employers; some employers offer, for example, a free $100,000 policy as a perk. Most new policies are bought by people between the ages of 25 and 44, often when they have children, because life insurance is a protection for survivors. Other reasons people have life insurance are to protect or make a more secure life for a surviving spouse or an aging or disabled relative, to protect a business and business partners, and to leave money to a charity or a cause. College students without dependents generally don't need it, but if an employer provides it at a low cost or for free, this is a benefit to consider.

How much is needed depends on life circumstances such as age, income, and number and ages of children. One rule of thumb is the five to seven times rule; for example, a person earning $30,000 a year should have life insurance in the range of $150,000 to $210,000. Someone with several young children who is the main support of the family needs more than someone whose children are grown.

The two main types of life insurance are term (for a fixed time such as five or ten years) and whole (with a savings feature). With term, protection expires when the contract expires, so an individual with five-year term insurance would have to renew it to keep it going. Term is considered pure protection; in other words, it only offers insurance and does not have a savings feature. It costs less than whole life insurance and is therefore recommended by most personal financial experts. Whole life insurance offers savings but at a very low rate of interest; most investors could make better money elsewhere. Policies should be reviewed every few years and changed if there are major life changes such as a marriage, a divorce, the birth or adoption of children, a new house, a different employer, a promotion, retirement, or an empty nest.

> ### CONSUMER ALERTS
>
> **Churning** is an illegal practice of encouraging insureds (consumers) to switch policies in order to generate commissions. Insurance agents make commissions when consumers purchase a policy, especially a whole life policy. When switching policies is not in the best interest of the client and is done solely to generate more commissions, this is considered churning, a practice disdained by the legitimate insurance industry. Multimillion-dollar class-action suits about churning have been brought by bilked policy holders.
>
> If an agent offers to replace your old life insurance policy, which has a high cash value, with a new and "better" one, carefully review the premium schedule, benefits, and restrictions on benefits, such as preexisting conditions. Also, if a

life insurance pitch comes at a time when there is no apparent need to change insurance coverage, such as a marriage, a new child, or a similar life change, be cautious. Do not buy insurance from a door-to-door salesperson or sign blank insurance claims forms.

Long-Term Care Insurance

Long-term care (LTC) insurance provides benefits for nursing home, assisted living, or in-home care not covered by Medicare insurance as well as for other types of long-term care. For example, a severe auto accident at age 40 could lay a person up for several months, and LTC insurance could help with the bills. Most people buy LTC insurance with the intention of using it in old age.

CRITICAL THINKING

Is Long-Term Care Insurance Worth It?

Consider the following paragraph and respond to the title above. Yes or no? Explain your answer. "People used to buy long-term-care insurance because they were scared. Now it is the policies themselves that are keeping buyers awake at night. The coverage—which pays for some or all of the costs of nursing homes, assisted-living facilities and home health care for people unable to take care of themselves—has been coming under fire. Premiums have been rising, fewer insurers are selling the product, and new research is questioning whether many people need it. More than two-thirds of individuals 65 and older will require some kind of long-term care, according to experts. The median annual cost for a private nursing-home room is $91,250 and round-the-clock home care can top $170,000."

Source: Leslie Scism (May 2-3, 2015). "Long-Term-Care Insurance: Is It Worth It?" *The Wall Street Journal*, B7.

Most LTC policies have the same basic features, such as covering Alzheimer's disease. There may also be coverage if you can no longer perform two of the following activities of daily living:

- bathing
- being continent
- dressing
- eating
- transferring from one location to another
- using the toilet.

The policies pay for a certain amount of care. The most important feature is the dollars paid per day that the policy will cover toward eventual care, but the problem is that these costs keep going up, and no one knows if and when they will need assisted living or other help. People buy LTC insurance because the high cost of care could wipe out any savings they have accumulated. Policies range in cost depending on the age of the person and the coverage offered. The older you are, the more expensive LTC insurance becomes because it is more likely that you will actually access it. Policies may have riders (add-ons). One of the most important riders is a compound-inflation option; this is a desirable feature because costs keep going up as the years pass.

Who sells LTC insurance? Many insurance agents sell it, but they vary in their skills and credentials. A person seeking a policy should look for an agent who specializes in LTC insurance. The younger you are when you purchase it, the lower the premiums will be. Medicare or private health insurance does not cover all aspects of long-term care. Medicaid covers long-term care, but an elderly person has to "spend down" assets to at or near the federal poverty level in order to qualify. Another problem is that Medicaid-approved facilities have to be used, which narrows the choices, some of which may be far from families and friends. Women are especially vulnerable because they outlive men by an average of seven years and are more likely to need LTC insurance or other arrangements.

> **CONSUMER ALERTS**
>
> LTC is a fairly new form of insurance, and regulations between states vary widely. Low-income people can rarely afford it and may be better off putting money into current health care or other investments. In the case of LTC insurance, the company will have to last a long time. If the insurer goes bankrupt, you could be left with little or no coverage.

Rare Forms of Insurance

The previous sections listed some of the major kinds of insurance that consumers buy. If things weren't complicated enough, some insurers are offering hybrid products that combine life insurance, annuities, and long-term-care benefits (Scism, 2015). This may not be a bad thing because usually putting policies together with the same insurer can result in better services and lower premiums: definitely something the consumer should look into if they are pleased with their current insurance agents/companies. *The guiding principle is do not over-buy insurance.* Consumers probably don't need the following rare forms of insurance.

- *Private mortgage or mortgage life insurance.* It would be better to pick other forms of investing or add on to existing life insurance policies rather than take out a new mortgage or life insurance policy.

- *Service contracts and extended warranties.* These are usually both unnecessary and too expensive (these were described in previous chapters).

- *Separate policies versus riders.* When a rider is added to an existing policy, it usually costs less than buying a whole new policy; a new boat or motorcycle, for example, could be added to an existing policy.

- *Flight insurance.* Statistics show an individual can fly on an airline every day for 26,000 years before that person would be involved in a plane crash, and even then the odds are in that person's favor that he or she would survive.

- *Short-term (cash value) life insurance.* If a policy holder does not keep cash value (whole life) insurance for a long time, the policy is a waste of money.

- *Life insurance for children.* Children do not have debts or dependents, so they do not need life insurance.

- *Cancer or other disease-specific insurance.* Unless the specific disease runs in your family, you don't need insurance coverage for it. Conventional health insurance will cover most illnesses and diseases.

- *Add-ons to homeowners' insurance.* Insurance for such things as "family protection" is unnecessary for most individuals. This type of insurance covers victims of home invasion, child abductions, and stalking threats, and it pays medical bills, consulting, and other expenses (but not ransom payments). A wealthy high-profile person may need this, but for most people this is unneeded insurance.

- *Short-term medical coverage.* Under the federal COBRA law, an employee's old insurance policy can follow him or her (if his or her employer has 20 or more employees) for about 18 months after the end of employment, but there is a catch—the person has to pay the whole premium, so the cost of coverage is high. A single healthy person may pass on short-term medical coverage after a job that has insurance coverage ends, but someone with a family may go ahead and get it. The idea is that buying employer-based insurance should be less expensive than having the former employee buy it in the open market as a private individual. This may or may not be the case, so a former employee should comparison-shop.

What to buy and what to pass on both refer back to the beginning of the chapter and the discussion of matching insurance to a person's needs and not paying for protection that is unnecessary. In terms of overpriced insurance, studies show that the poor pay more for goods and services, mostly due to a lack of creditworthiness indicated by low credit scores (Lee, 2002). That puts the poor in a disadvantaged position in the financial market, including the area of insurance. Policy makers and regulators continue to evaluate how the poor are affected in the financial market and are on the lookout for discrimination, including procedures such as redlining (not providing services in certain areas) addressed in the previous chapter.

Consumer Rights and Responsibilities

Rights

Consumers have these rights:

- to choose insurance companies and agents
- to obtain fair quotes for coverage
- to receive policies in a timely manner
- to receive proper and timely investigations of claims
- to receive payments for repairs or whatever is necessary
- to buy policies free of unfair discrimination due to age, gender, occupation, marital status, national origin, or physical handicap (for example, a handicap that does not impair someone's ability to drive)
- to file complaints
- to receive copies of all forms and applications signed by the applicant and insurer.

Responsibilities

Consumers are responsible for doing the following:

- evaluating their needs and choosing the policy or contract that meets those needs
- shopping around and comparing costs and services
- watching for exclusions and limitations
- investigating insurance salespeople's credentials, and finding out about licensure
- reading policies or contracts and understanding what is covered
- keeping insurance policies and records at home, and keeping copies in safe deposit boxes or with a trusted friend or attorney
- telling beneficiaries about the kinds and amounts of health and life insurance owned and where policies are kept
- reviewing coverage periodically to make sure it is still meeting needs
- being truthful when applying, and disclosing pertinent information
- contacting the insurance company or agent immediately after auto accidents
- keeping up with premiums and reviewing all bills.

Scams and Frauds

Remember the line "Oh, what a tangled web we weave, when first we practice to deceive"? The insurance industry is rampant with scams and frauds. Insurance scams are more subtle than the snake oil salesmen of old and thus more difficult to root out. The frauds in the financial area feed on greed and fear rather than the need for a quick cure sought from patent medicines and weight-reduction pills. In financial fraud, victims are susceptible to things they do not understand and fall prey to promises of large returns on their money. The area of insurance is particularly vulnerable because it is a subject few like to think about or discuss. The chance that something bad will happen—illness, disability, theft, destruction, death—makes it easier to perpetuate fraud. The sources for much of the following information are the state departments of insurance and the Coalition against Insurance Fraud Report. The next section covers scams by companies, and the section after that discusses how customers defraud companies.

Company Scams

Most agents are reputable professionals who have been trained in their area of expertise; they take classes and pass tests to be licensed. But there are **rogue agents** who are not associated with established companies and who are engaging in illegal activities. They will sell insurance and pocket the premiums, and when people try to file a claim, they find out they have been had—there is no policy and there is no money. Naturally the industry wants to root out rogue agents and drive them from business because they give the whole industry a bad name.

One trick is for an agent to drain the cash value of one policy to buy a new policy with the same insurer. Another fraud is called failure to forward premiums: An insurance agent convinces a consumer to pay each premium by a check written directly to the agent or to pay in cash; the agent then pockets these payments, leaving the consumer without coverage.

Understatement of risk or "clean sheeting" is another type of fraud. In this case the agent omits pertinent health information from a consumer's application to make a sale that might not otherwise meet the insurance company's risk management requirements.

Overselling refers to selling too much insurance to one individual. For example, in a testimony at a National Association of Insurance Commissioners (NAIC) meeting in Atlanta in March 2003, an Alabama attorney said that an elderly woman with a house worth $19,000 had 17 homeowner's insurance policies on it—far too much coverage for the modest house. He said that she would sign anything that was put before her and that unscrupulous agents took advantage.

Consumer Frauds

One survey reports the following: Nearly one in four Americans say it is acceptable to defraud an insurance company, according to a survey by consulting firm Accenture Ltd. The results appear to confirm the worst suspicions of insurance companies, which say fraudulent claims are costing them—and honest policy holders—billions of dollars a year.

According to the survey (Oster, 2003), there are at least three kinds of fraud that consumers engage in:

1. Overstating the value of a claim to an insurance agency.
2. Submitting claims for items that aren't actually lost or damaged.
3. Submitting claims for personal injuries that did not occur.

Why do people do it? Nearly half of the survey respondents said it was because people could get away with it; others said that people needed the money or that they paid too much to insurance companies and thought it was their due. The study subjects said it was important that insurers track down deceptive claims. Another study found that "four out of ten Americans have tried to pad an insurance bill to cover the deductible" (Solomon, 2003, p. 234).

Another type of fraud is applicant fraud. In this case, the applicant provides false information to a life insurance company to obtain a lower premium or to prevent the application from being rejected.

Another fraud called deceptive claims happens when a financially strapped consumer files false claims on credit disability and health insurance policies after staging an accident and exaggerating a preexisting injury—in other words, they are faking it. Insurance companies have investigators who can prove fraud by filming claimants with bad backs hauling lumber out of trucks or working out in gyms. One of the reasons that states got rid of or altered no-fault auto insurance is because people would fake their own accidents (purposely run into a tree, have a friend's car nudge their car) and claim huge repairs, emotional damage, or medical expenses. Along these same lines, people have faked accidents such as slipping and falling in a theme park or at a hotel and tried to sue the park or hotel. The use of more security cameras has diminished these types of cases.

Role of State Departments of Insurance

Insurance is largely regulated by states. The objectives of state regulators are to protect consumers and to help maintain the financial stability of the insurance industry.

Consumers should find out how their company is rated. Consumers residing in states that set minimum standards for coverage and limit how high premiums can go tend to have better protection. If a person is turned down for health insurance, he or she can investigate state requirements for obtaining a policy of last resort, and anyone with low income should find out if he or she qualifies for Medicaid.

Investing

Purpose

The chapter switches gears now away from insurance to the subject of investment. Most simply stated, **investment** is the commitment of funds (capital) to long-term growth, and the purpose of investing is to build and maintain wealth. People invest to feel more secure or comfortable in retirement or in midlife and to acquire funds for vacations, for children's educations, and for homes. Investing should be based on goals; it is an important means for getting ahead, keeping ahead of inflation, and becoming independent and self-supporting.

Guiding Principles

Concerted attempts at investing start after people have stabilized their lives, meaning they have a job, they can meet basic life needs, and their debt is under control. Retirement plans through an employer or individually through individual retirement accounts (IRAs) are forms of investing. Nearer the end of careers, investors are interested in making the most of income and estate tax planning but as the following quote shows this isn't so easy.

> Income and estate tax planning has been remarkably difficult for the past decade, inhibited by an ongoing series of temporary rules and important tax planning provisions that are perpetually scheduled to phase out or about to sunset. Due to the never-certain-for-long environment, many clients (and even their planners) have struggled to engage in effective long-term income and estate tax planning. (Kitces, 2013, p. 10)

A guiding investment principle is that the sooner you start, the greater the return (money needs time to grow) and that even a modest start (like $20 a week in a savings account) is better than no start at all. In investing, one assesses risk and return.

As stated in the Introduction to this chapter, the higher the risk is, the greater the chance for return. Taking financial risks in your youth makes more sense than taking risks in old age when you have fewer years to recover from loss; when you are young, your income keeps growing and you can replace lost income from poorly performing investments. How you feel about risk is called risk tolerance. Following is a widely used risk assessment question from the Federal Reserve Board Survey of Consumer Finances (SCF):

> Which of the following statements comes closest to the amount of financial risk that you are willing to take when you save or make investments?
>
> 1. Substantial financial risks expecting to earn substantial returns.

2.   *Above-average financial risks expecting to earn above-average returns.*

3. *Average financial risks expecting to earn average returns.*

4. *No financial risks.*

There are no completely risk-free investments and one's reaction to risk affects future investment behavior (Gamble & Johnson, 2014). For example, government bonds and savings accounts may guarantee principal but may fall behind in keeping up with inflation. Because the principal is guaranteed, these are considered safer investments compared with investments such as stocks when much or all of the principal can be lost. Utah State University professor Jean Lown, in an article in the *Journal of Consumer Education* (2001/2002), suggested that educators can help investors adopt a more realistic view of risk tolerance and investment selection based on a time horizon (for example, the number of years until retirement) for financial goals. Further, she says that **volatility** (the ups and downs of a security or a commodity or of the stock market itself) should be of little concern to the long-term investor. A person needs to do the following to be a successful investor:

- keep perspective, staying in through the ups and downs
- keep investing, even with small amounts
- believe in the growth of business (stocks and corporate bonds) or the strength of government (bonds).

Some investments provide interest or **dividends**, which are distributions of money from companies or government to investors. Most typically, dividends are paid twice a year and can come from stocks or bonds. Sometimes stocks and bonds can be bought in such a way (usually directly, such as bonds from the federal government) that there are no fees for transactions; other times there are fees that vary greatly. Charges for transactions should be weighed against services rendered and probable returns. A consideration in investing is the tax implications of certain types of investing, such as tax-deferred retirement savings plans and municipal bonds or municipal bond funds.

CONSUMER ALERTS

Every investment has advantages and disadvantages—there are no "magic" investments that fit all of the people, all of the time. There is little hope of more than average returns without extraordinary luck or knowledge and, of course, risk. A realistic approach works best, basing investments on goals, acceptable levels of risk, personality, and a time horizon (how many years until the money will be needed). Knowledge is power, so find out everything you can about a potential investment from reliable sources.

Another guiding principle is that investors should use **diversification**, meaning the spreading of money over several categories of investments such as bonds, blue-chip stocks, small and large companies, foreign shares, real estate, and real estate investment trusts. In this way, an investor will have a balanced **portfolio**, a combined set of holdings to increase diversification and to reduce risk. At any given time, some of the holdings will be in favor and some will be out of favor, but in the long run this strategy, rather than putting all one's money into a single investment, should work. To summarize, the least risk is involved in cash, government savings bonds, money market funds, and CDs; the most risk is associated with speculative investments such as options, commodities, and junk bonds. The Securities and Exchange Commission (SEC) is a good source for information about investing wisely and avoiding fraud. In the next sections, the most widely used types of investing, along with potential frauds and scams, are discussed.

Types of Investments and Income

Stocks

As noted in the Introduction, more than half of Americans own stock. **Stocks** represent ownership in a company. For example, if you own one share of Microsoft stock, you own part of Microsoft. Is the stock market rational (meaning reasonable, predictable)? The answer is no—it rises and falls, and it is very difficult to predict how well an individual stock will do. It is useful to know a company's financial history and future prospects as a guide in choosing well. The best advice is to buy and hold, ride out the ups and downs, invest in quality companies, and keep transaction (buying and selling) costs low. Over the last 50 years, stocks have far exceeded inflation, but in the short run investing can be risky.

Most stocks are called **common stock**, which refers to shares or units of ownership in a public corporation such as NetFlix, Apple, or Coca-Cola. You can buy stock online or in person through brokerage firms such as Charles Schwab, Ameritrade, or Merrill Lynch, or you can buy stock directly from the company. One of the values of having a broker is that you have someone with whom to discuss your investment choices and to create a financial plan. To invest directly in a company (called a **direct investment plan**), go to the company website and look for investor relations. You could then purchase a certain number of shares of stock for a set amount of money or set up a payroll deduction so that $50 a month goes into buying shares of that particular company's stock. Over 1,000 companies (including most of the larger ones such as McDonald's) offer direct investment plans. Another choice is a **dividend reinvestment plan (DRIP)**, which also eliminates the need for a broker (who will charge a fee called a commission to buy or sell a stock). DRIPs allow dividends to be automatically reinvested in additional shares purchased directly from the company.

Investors may engage in **socially responsible investing**, meaning they invest in stocks that directly express their values. For example, they will not invest in companies that are involved in practices they do not believe in, such as making alcohol or tobacco products, or that have unfair labor practices, such as using child labor. They seek to influence corporate decision making by including social and ethical criteria in their investment choices.

CONSUMER ALERTS

Millions of dollars' worth of consumer lawsuits, for everything from faulty cell phones to stock fraud, are filed each year, but consumers are not always aware that money is owed to them. More than half the people who are eligible for compensation never follow up: often this is because the compensation is so low, like $25 per person for a lot of paperwork. Fraud happens when companies charge substantial finder's fees (money to find out if you should be getting a consumer lawsuit settlement) when in reality you can check yourself for free.

Bonds

Bonds are investments involving the lending of money. If you have a bond for a corporation, you have lent money to that corporation (to build a new factory, for example). Bonds can be for corporations or for state, local, or federal government (as in US savings bonds). They can be a significant part of a diversified investment portfolio. "Direct bond purchases can address major issues confronting retirees better than alternative investments such as providing retirement income, moving to a retirement home, leaving a legacy, etc." (Huxley & Tarrazo, 2013, p. 99).

When the stock market took a downturn in 2008 and 2009 and many saw a decline in their 401(k)s (Blanchett, 2013, p. 46), many investors switched to bonds for these reasons:

- They are considered safer than stocks.
- In many cases, the rate of return is guaranteed.
- There may be the added benefit of biannual dividends paid to the bondholder, so the bonds serve as a source of income.

Government bonds are more secure than corporate bonds. Bonds from corporations are rated, and these ratings should be used as a guide. The two types of US savings bonds are Series EE and Series I. For information about these, go to www.savingsbonds.gov. You can buy bonds online directly from the government, or you can buy savings bonds at local banks or through your employer.

Photo 14.3
Businessman
analyzes growth

Source: Thinkstock:
Ridofranz

Mutual Funds

American investors are increasingly turning to mutual funds to save for retirement and other financial goals. **Mutual funds** are groups of investments. Over 100 million Americans own mutual funds, mostly in their retirement accounts through their employers and in their IRAs. There are over 7,000 mutual funds of stocks and bonds from which to choose. If you buy one share of a mutual fund such as Capital Growth Fund, you are buying a small amount of several different holdings and spreading your risk, which is a positive feature of mutual funds. Funds come in different types such as growth, international, and value. Growth funds are the largest category and focus on stocks that have the potential for large capital gains. The name of the fund implies the type of fund that it is; for example, the Capital Growth Fund would be a growth mutual fund. In 2001, rulings were passed calling for more alignment of fund names with fund holdings and requiring funds to include after-tax return data. Since each fund has to have a unique name, the names can get creative: the Rydex Velocity 100 Fund, the Columbia Thermostat Fund, the Amidex Cancer Innovations and Health-Care Mutual Fund. Investors purchase fund shares from the fund itself or through a broker for the fund.

There are several advantages:

- *Affordability.* Some funds set relatively low dollar amounts for initial purchase and subsequently monthly purchases, or both.
- *Diversification.* Spreading investments across a wide range of companies and industry sectors is advantageous to the investor.

- *Liquidity.* Funds can be redeemed for cash, although there may be fees and charges at redemption time.
- *Professional management.* Money managers research, select, and monitor funds.

Disadvantages include the following:

- Front-end or management fees.
- Taxes.
- Lack of control (managers choose what stocks are in funds, not investors).

Mutual funds are also not guaranteed or insured by the Federal Deposit Insurance Corporation (FDIC) or any other government agency—even if bought at a bank. A person can lose money investing in mutual funds, and past performance is not a totally reliable indicator of future performance; however, past performance is one factor to consider because it shows a pattern over time. The SEC offers a Mutual Fund Cost Calculator to compare the costs of owning different funds before an individual makes a purchase. Another source for mutual fund information is Morningstar.com.

CONSUMER ALERTS

Investment con artists thrive during times of uncertainty. Low-interest rates and poor investment returns in conventional markets drive risk-taking consumers to look for something other than traditional investments. They are looking for excitement and want to be part of the action, which includes investing in defense industries. Do not play this game. Protect yourself:

1. Do not talk with aggressive cold callers promoting investments in mutual funds; foreign currencies; precious metals such as gold, platinum, and silver; or oil and gas schemes.

2. Ignore tips about tiny companies with great growth potential, especially those involved in war industries or bioterrorism.

3. Contact state securities regulators or check with the National Association of Securities Dealers (1-800-288-9999) when you suspect fraud.

4. Request written information about investments. Promotions with the word *safe, secure,* or *guaranteed* are usually rip-offs.

5. When it comes to investing, being rash and feeling pressured are warning signs—don't do anything in a hurry. Use common sense, and do not succumb to confusion and fear.

Real Estate

Real estate refers to a piece of land and everything related to it, including houses, landscaping, and fencing, plus the right to the airspace above and the earth below (with limits, of course). In Chapter 11, we covered how to be a better consumer of housing and included advice on buying homes. This chapter discusses real estate more from an investment angle. About 70 percent of American households own their own homes, which is a type of **direct investment**; other examples include owning apartment buildings, raw land, and other houses. One of the main disadvantages of real estate over other types of investments is illiquidity, meaning it is difficult to turn it quickly into cash. **Indirect investments** refer to investing with a group of investors to own **real estate investment trusts (REITs)**, apartment buildings, or office buildings. REITs are traded on the major stock exchanges, so you can buy a share in them the same way that you can buy a share in a stock or mutual fund.

REITs are sold through stock brokerage firms or over the counter and are listed in the *Wall Street Journal* and other financial news sources. One of the main advantages is the pooling of money with others to buy a bigger investment than one normally could alone. Another advantage is the professional management aspect, meaning one could invest in apartments without having landlord worries. With any investment, however, there is both a risk of loss and tax consequences.

Owning a primary residence has tax advantages, but the tax advantages of second homes and vacation homes are less attractive. **Time-shares** are apartments, units, or homes with several owners that are normally used for vacation purposes.

CONSUMER ALERTS

Do not buy time-shares or vacation homes without investigating all the costs, rules, fees, taxes, and resale terms. Many people have had trouble selling time-shares and wish they had rented instead of tying up their money. Consumers are more satisfied if they purchase time-shares in companies with cooperative arrangements across the country because this opens up more choices of places to visit and the types of available units. Remember that all buildings age—the brand-new model time-share unit will not look so good after a few years of wear and tear.

CONSUMER ALERTS

REITs fluctuate with the ups and downs of the market and with the quality of the investment. While some parts of the country are having marvelous success with new office buildings and shopping malls, others are overbuilt, so care should be taken in selecting REITs. REITs are traded publicly on the New York Stock Exchange.

Franchises

Another form of investing is franchises. A **franchise** is a right to operate a business and sell the franchisor's products or services in a given area. This may or may not be an exclusive right; in other words, you could be the only franchisee at a certain intersection or the only one in a whole city. Arrangements are formalized in a franchisee agreement, a contract between the franchisee and the franchisor. Television infomercials and advertisements in newspapers suggest there is easy money to be had in franchises, and being your own boss. Although franchises can be legitimate (such as a franchise for a McDonald's or a Subway restaurant), many are investments with little or no guarantee of success. If you have never heard of the franchise before, this is a warning sign to slow down.

Benefits. The benefit to this type of arrangement is that investment risk is reduced by being associated with an established company. Also the franchisor will often grant the right to use the company name for a limited amount of time and provide assistance, initial training, marketing, and so on. There will probably be ongoing technical support and training.

Loss Potential. The downside of being associated with an established company is that the franchisee has to conform to its standards and is essentially giving up a lot of individual control. In exchange for the name and the services, the franchisee will have to pay both fees, such as an initial franchise fee, and other expenses, for rent, building and equipment, signs, insurance, and licenses (this can run from thousands of dollars to several hundred thousand dollars). Over time, the franchisee will pay royalty payments to continue to use the name. The startup costs are very high, and since most businesses fail in the first two years, many people lose money.

Responsibilities. Before investing, potential franchisees should consider their goals, abilities, and experience and determine how much this investment is going to cost as well as the current strength and potential growth of the parent company. Is the product or service in demand? What is the competition like? For example, a common type of franchise is a janitorial service franchise. Before investing, find out how businesses, schools, and government agencies in your area hire janitorial services. If you had a franchise, would there be a demand for it? How much are locals willing to pay? Often figures given by franchisors are national and may be far higher than what you could charge locally.

Before attending a franchise exposition, investors should know how much they have to invest and what type of business is the best for them. Before investing, the franchisee should get a copy of the franchisor's disclosure document. Under the Federal Trade Commission (FTC) Franchise Rule, a potential franchisee must receive the document at least ten business days before being asked to sign any contract or paying any money to the franchisor. Things to look out for include business background, litigation history, bankruptcy, costs, restrictions, terminations, training, advertising, current and former franchisees' experiences, earnings potential, and financial history. Besides doing research, potential franchisees should talk with attorneys with franchise experience, accountants, banks, the local Better Business Bureau (BBB), government departments that regulate the particular business (provide licenses), and the FTC before investing. A bank or other financial institution can give an unbiased view of a franchise. If ever there was an area where the phrase "investigate before you invest" is true, it is in the franchise industry.

All That Glitters: Precious Gems, Metals, and Collectibles

Diamonds are the most regulated gems and the ones most likely to hold their value; they come from several countries including Botswana, Russia, and Canada. Canada's diamond mines have strict environmental guidelines and pay miners well. Some jewelers say people won't care about origin, but Oren Sofer, a New York wholesaler, says, "If you can put water in a bottle and sell it under a brand name, then trust me, you

Over a third of Americans collect something.

Photo 14.4 One of the costly items a young couple might buy is a diamond ring

Source: Thinkstock: dolgachov

can brand a diamond. It just takes time" (Baglole, 2003, p. B1). Consider as examples Swiss watches, Idaho potatoes, and French champagne —we associate certain products with places, but with other products, location is unimportant. How do you know the diamond is from Canada? Each diamond comes with a certificate of where it was mined, cut, and polished, and the certificate has a serial number engraved by laser on the diamond. A microscopically laser-engraved polar bear is sometimes put on larger Canadian diamonds.

Rubies are mined in Burma; sapphires come from Tanzania, Madagascar, and Sri Lanka. The gems are flown into Thailand, where they are sorted and treated before export.

The most precious metal available to consumers is platinum, followed by gold and silver. Gold is produced primarily in Russia and South Africa and can be purchased as gold coins, gold certificates, gold mutual funds, bullion accounts, and stock shares in existing companies. People have lost and gained fortunes from investing in diamond and gold mines—it is not for amateurs. The price of precious metals usually rises when inflation rises and falls when inflation falls, but international events can disturb this. International incidents tend to drive up the price of gold, but it fluctuates widely. Before investing in precious metals, an investor should know the current price per ounce and the market's ups and downs during the last several years.

Over a third of Americans collect something. Collectibles include everything from books to stamps, coins, athletic shoes, lunch boxes with cartoon characters on them, and priceless antiques. In collectibles, knowledge is crucial, and this includes trusting one's source or dealer. There is no substitute for education and knowledge of prices and quality. Special care should be taken when buying valuables at auctions or over the Internet (see the next section). Generally speaking, gems, metals, and collectibles should be purchased primarily because the owner likes them or could use them and secondly as an investment.

Online Investing

The Internet has opened up a whole new world of investment opportunities—some legitimate and some not. Many of the schemes are the same as have been played out for centuries, only in a glossy new format. Beware of promoters who make their companies look like venerable, established Wall Street firms, and look out for the usual promise of high profits in short amounts of time. On the Internet, you may find a website asking you to submit personal financial information such as income level, bank accounts, Social Security numbers, and other personal information. Read the site's privacy policy and consider the source, but never give PINs, account information, or Social Security numbers. Before putting money in offshore investments, get a second opinion and learn about the tax implications.

Retirement Sources of Income Including Social Security

For most Americans, retirement support comes from several sources such as Social Security; private, employer-sponsored (401ks), or government pensions or retirement plans; and personal savings and investments such as Individual Retirement Accounts (IRAs). "How much do I have?" and "how much income can I expect per month?" are typical questions.

> *Valuing a 401(k) or IRA initially does not seem like a difficult exercise. Unlike assets such as paintings, homes, or cars (e.g., your IRA is worth $62,549.23). Using this dollar value to define the value of the account is an approach we will call the "Balance" method. This is the most common technique used to value IRAs and 401(k)s within a financial planning context. (Blanchett, 2013, p. 49)*

Social Security (from the US government) is the primary source of retirement income for many beneficiaries, and one in four US households has someone getting monthly income from Social Security, but not everyone who receives Social Security is retired.

You qualify for benefits when you work and pay Social Security taxes, and you earn credits toward Social Security benefits. There are also family benefits where spouses and children are eligible and benefits for divorced spouses if the marriage lasted at least ten years. The divorced spouse must be 62 or older and unmarried. If you stop working before earning enough credits to qualify for benefits, the credits remain on your record and if you return to work you can add more credits. You have to pay in enough to qualify for receiving benefits. The best way to find out more about your individual situation is to contact www.socialsecurity.gov or go to the local Social Security Office.

Ninety-six percent of American workers are covered under Social Security (others including federal workers or military may have their own retirement programs). Traditionally Americans started receiving partial benefits at age 62 (if they chose to do so) and full Social Security at age 65, but in recent years the eligible age for full benefits has been sliding up from 65 to 67, depending on date of birth. If born in 1937 or earlier full retirement age is 65. If born from 1943–1954 then full retirement age is 66. Those born 1960 and later reach full retirement age at 67.

According to the Social Security Administration, increases in the number of projected beneficiaries per 100 workers will rise to 32 in 2020 and 39 in 2030.

Annuities

A common myth is that once one saves for retirement, the need for financial planning is over—nothing could be further from the truth. While people are retired, investments have to keep growing to keep up with inflation. Often when nearing retirement, people consider **annuities**, which are contracts in which the insurer promises the insured a series of periodic payments and are a type of investment which provides investors with tax-deferred growth. Annuities do not limit how much can be contributed each year and can be purchased directly from insurance companies or indirectly from stock brokers. They come in several forms, including fixed annuities that guarantee fixed payments for life or a specific number of years, and variable annuities, which provide returns based on the performance of the assets in the annuities; there are different payout options, from lump sums to more periodic sums. Fixed annuities are invested in financial securities that pay a fixed interest rate, such as certificates of deposit, bonds, and treasury securities (safe investments), but money in variable annuities is more likely to be put into stocks and mutual funds. An investor could put money into both fixed and variable annuities and thus spread the risk and return.

Fixed annuities are being sold in record numbers as baby boomers retire and can be an especially good hedge in a volatile market; still confusion, fraud, and deception are rampant. Consumers should use caution before buying annuities, making sure they understand what they are getting, what the amount of risk is, and how much it is going to cost. Annual expense fees vary by product. The major disadvantage of annuities is illiquidity, meaning money is locked in for a long time.

Investment Swindles

Investment swindles abound because people are drawn to high and quick returns on their money. They fall victim to various schemes and scams that can be nationally or internationally based.

Certain catchy phrases should be warning signs:

- "This is a once-in-a-lifetime opportunity."
- "Learn the secret of the wealthy."
- "Quickly invest now in this low-risk short-term offer."
- "Only a few will be invited to participate."
- "Get in on the ground floor."
- "You are assured of [list of products such as display racks for greeting cards or vending machines for candy]."
- "This is approved by [a celebrity or a doctor or the IRS] and is IRA approved."
- "The market is moving, so don't be left behind."

You will notice from this list that many financial scams sound a lot like the come-on phrases used in weight-loss scams. Swindlers (also called con artists and fraudsters) prey on the same emotions of fear, greed, and excitement, and even though they cheat people out of their money, they often advertise in legitimate sources such as *USA Today* and campus newspapers.

CONSUMER ALERTS

Be wary of the sales pitches and products sold on infomercials, which are a half-hour or longer, as well as radio and television commercials for gold, real estate, and other forms of investing. If it sounds too good to be true, it probably is. Common techniques are endorsements by actors and actresses (many of whom later regret getting involved), by motivational speakers, and by "satisfied" past investors.

Multilevel Marketing Plans

Pyramid schemes or **multilevel marketing plans** are ways of selling goods and services through distributors. The plans promise that if someone signs up as a distributor, he or she will receive commissions both from his or her own sales and from those of people who are recruited to become distributors. The FTC cannot tell anyone which plans are legal and which are illegal—you must decide for yourself—but it does say that if a plan offers to pay commissions for recruiting new distributors, consumers should watch out. Most states outlaw this practice, which is called **pyramiding**. It is legal to pay commissions for retail sales of goods or services but not for recruiting of new distributors. Why are states so cautious about pyramiding? In the past, plans such as these invariably collapsed when new distributors could not be recruited—the people who began the scam (at the top of the pyramid) often benefited, but the late recruits lost their money. An example of a pyramid scheme was one in which an "investor" gave $100 to become a member, and the money was passed on to the president of the scheme; then the investor had to sign up two more people and collect $100 from each of them. After ten people were recruited, the investor would become a president and form a new pyramid. The problem was finding new recruits to keep the money flow going. Unfortunately, pyramid schemes exist worldwide. Box 14.4 gives a list of tips to help consumers avoid pyramid schemes.

Box 14.4 FTC's Seven Tips to Avoid Pyramid Schemes

Consider these tips before investing in multilevel marketing plans:

1. Avoid any plan that includes commissions for recruiting additional distributors. It may be an illegal pyramid.

2. Beware of plans that ask new distributors to purchase expensive inventory. These plans can collapse quickly—and also may be thinly disguised pyramids.

3. Be cautious of plans that claim you will make money through continued growth of your "downline"—the commissions on sales made by new distributors you recruit—rather than through sales of products you make yourself.

4. Beware of plans that claim to sell miracle products or promise enormous earnings. Just because a promoter of a plan makes a claim doesn't mean it's true! Ask the promoter of the plan to substantiate claims with hard evidence.

5. Beware of shills—"decoy" references paid by a plan's promoter to describe fictional success in earning money through the plan.

6. Don't pay or sign any contracts in an "opportunity meeting" or any other high-pressure situation. Insist on taking your time to think over a decision to join. Talk it over with your spouse, a knowledgeable friend, an accountant, or a lawyer.

7. Do your homework! Check with your local Better Business Bureau and state attorney general about any plan you're considering—especially when the claims about the product or your potential earnings seem too good to be true.

Ponzi schemes are a kind of pyramid scheme with enticing come-ons that promise to make huge profits from a small investment in a very short time (Figure 14.1). They are named after Charles A. Ponzi, a dapper five-foot-two-inch Italian immigrant who in 1920 raked in an estimated $15 million in eight months by persuading tens of thousands of Bostonians that he had unlocked the secret to easy wealth (Darby, 1998). Ponzi claimed to have found a way to profit by speculating in international postal-reply coupons, a form of prepaid return postage used in foreign correspondence. The first round of investors made money, and at the height of his success, Ponzi had offices from Maine to New Jersey, but later recruits lost everything, and half a dozen banks crashed. The problem was that there was no actual investing going on, just a shuffling of money from new investors to old ones. Ponzi was offering 50 percent interest in 90 days (later he shortened the investment period to 45 days), so it's no wonder people joined up, but these kinds of returns should raise any thinking person's suspicions.

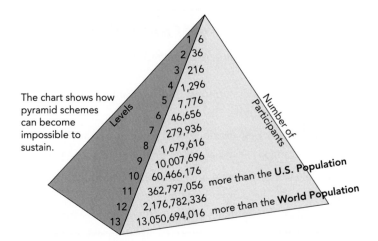

Figure 14.1 Ponzi Scheme

Courtesy of the US Securities and Exchange Commission.

Some modern-day Ponzi swindlers explain losses by telling people that investments went sour; other times the swindlers just disappear. Ponzi schemes involve the idea that something is for sale, whether it is coupons, foreign real estate, or racehorses. Legitimate multilevel plans involve the selling of actual products, such as clothing, home furnishings, cookware, and cosmetics that one can see and examine in person. These plans involve in-home or at-workplace sales that do not differ too much from conventional store sales, other than the fact that sellers are given incentives of free products or deep discounts on products and that any money they make is based on commissions rather than salaries (for the most part). Examples of legitimate multilevel plans are Avon and Amway; as a customer, you can purchase the merchandise, as opposed to pyramid or Ponzi schemes where you walk away with nothing and you have to endure the hassle of trying to recruit new members.

Ways to Avoid Swindles

The main ways to avoid swindles are to use common sense and to ask questions—research is by far the best protection. Find the investment that meets your needs and goals; then shop around for companies and choices, double-checking the source and the seller. It is important to keep detailed records. Avoid high-pressure tactics, and seek advice from attorneys, accountants, and banks as well as government agencies and consumer watchdog organizations. Do not be taken in by television infomercial hype or late-night commercials when your sales resistance may be low. The FTC is a leader in alerting the public to investment fraud. Box 14.5 gives a list of some types of fraud to avoid.

Box 14.5 Investment-Related Frauds to Avoid

Coupon scams

Get-rich-quick and self-employment schemes

Gifting clubs

Hoaxes aimed at the elderly or minority groups

International lottery scams

Investment schemes involving rare coins or stamps

Chain letters*

At-home medical billing scams

Online investment opportunities

Invention patent scams

Publishing of your own book (for a price)

Work-at-home schemes

Learn-at-home schemes

Note: Check out the source and the company's background, and talk with previous owners or investors (in addition to the ones the company recommends).

*These are violations of the mail fraud statute and can carry fines and prison sentences. Report any chain letter (especially those involving money schemes or threats) to the US Postal Service if the letter was received in the mail because the government will go after the starters of the letters—not the recipients.

Summary

Insurance is purchased to protect. Investments are bought to build or preserve wealth. This chapter provided a start toward understanding insurance and investments as well as the possible deceptions. Those who wish to stay ahead of inflation (rising prices) need to invest, but they also need to protect what they have.

Nearly all insurance is sold through agents. The trend is to buy insurance over the Internet. Group plans usually cost less than plans sold to individuals. Health insurance is the most expensive and the most vital, yet with growing costs many individuals and their families do not have health insurance. Employers are the main source of health insurance.

Today more and more employees are being asked to make investment decisions, and consumers are actively looking for ways to invest so that their money grows and lasts for their lifetime. Investments are used to build or maintain wealth; they involve risks and returns, and they should be based on goals. A guiding principle is that the greater the risk is, the higher the potential return. Diversification refers to reducing the risk by spreading investments around to different categories such as bonds, blue-chip stocks, small and large companies, mutual funds, real estate, and real estate investment trusts. Stocks represent ownership in a company; bonds are loans to the government or to companies.

Other forms of investing such as real estate, real estate investment trusts, franchises, gems, precious metals, collectibles, and annuities were also discussed in the chapter. When the world becomes less stable, investors often rush to buy precious gems and metals (especially gold), but careful investors have an accurate knowledge of current and past prices and ride out the ups and the downs. Although there are legitimate investment opportunities for precious metals, this area tends to be risky and is inappropriate for beginning investors.

Multilevel marketing plans are a way of selling goods or services through distributors—some are legal and some are illegal. Pyramiding, a type of multilevel marketing wherein most people lose money except for the people who started the plan, is prohibited. The Federal Trade Commission and the Securities and Exchange Commission are sources of information on investments and ways to avoid frauds. The FTC works for the consumer to prevent fraudulent, deceptive, and unfair business practices in the marketplace; the SEC works specifically to prevent investment fraud.

KEY POINTS

1. The primary purpose of insurance is protection. Most health insurance comes from employers or government programs such as Medicare and Medicaid.

2. Not everyone needs life insurance, but those who do usually have dependents.

3. Term insurance is less expensive than whole life insurance.

4. Life insurance needs increase in midlife and decrease in old age.

5. Life insurance policies cannot be cancelled because of an insured's poor health.

6. Credit insurance protects a loan or mortgage if a person cannot make payments.

7. Homeowners' insurance pays to repair or rebuild a home and to replace personal possessions.

8. Long-term care insurance provides for nursing homes, assisted living, hospice, and in-home care.

9. The purpose of investing is to build and maintain wealth, and successful investors are in it for the long term.

10. Historically, stocks have gained in value more rapidly than bonds and most other forms of investing.

11. There is no one miracle or fool-proof investment that fits everyone all of the time.

12. Pyramid investment schemes, a type of speculation, are illegal; Ponzi schemes are a type of pyramid scheme.

KEY TERMS

adjuster	disability income insurance	indirect investments
annuities	diversification	insurance
bonds	dividend reinvestment plan (DRIP)	investment
churning		liability insurance
common stock	dividends	life insurance
deductibles	endorsement	long-term care (LTC) insurance
direct investment	exclusions	
direct investment plan	exposures	Medicaid
	franchise	Medicare

multilevel marketing plans	property insurance	stocks
mutual funds	pyramiding	time-shares
perils	real estate	uninsured motorist coverage
Ponzi schemes	real estate investment trusts (REITs)	volatility
portfolio	rogue agents	workers' compensation
premiums	socially responsible investing	

DISCUSSION QUESTIONS

1. If current age and employment rates continue, there will be fewer working Americans to support the nonworking older adult population in the year 2020. What may be done to make the Social Security system more viable?

2. The famous philosopher George Santayana (1863–1952) said, "Nonsense is so good only because common sense is so limited." Considering this saying, why do you think so many people fall prey to scams and frauds? List five financial phrases or scams that attract investors.

3. Why do people have collections? Do you or any of your friends collect anything? If so, what is it, and how did the collection start? How can someone tell if a collectible is correctly priced?

REFERENCES

Baglole, J. (April 17, 2003). Political correctness by the carat. *Wall Street Journal*, pp. B1, B3.

Binkley, C. (September 3, 2015). New insurance for a fashion disaster (not that kind). *The Wall Street Journal*, D3.

Blanchett, D. (2013). How much is your 401(k) worth? *Journal of Personal Finance*, 12(1), 46–71.

Darby, M. (December 1998). In Ponzi we trust. *Smithsonian* magazine.

Gamble, K., and Johnson, B. (2014). How prior outcomes affect individual investors' subsequent risk taking. *Journal of Personal Finance,* 13 (1), 8–37.

Goldsmith, E. (2015). *Social influence and sustainable consumption.* New York: Springer.

Huxley, S. J. and Tarrazo, M. (2013). Direct investing in bonds during retirement. *Journal of Personal Finance*, 12(1), 98–134.

Kitces, M. (2013). Financial planning implications of the American Taxpayer Relief Act of 2012, *Journal of Personal Finance*, 12 (1), 10–45.

Lee, J. (2002). The poor in the financial market: changes in the use of financial products, institutions, and services from 1995 to 1998. *Journal of Consumer Policy*, 25, 203–31.

Lown, J. (2001/2002). Educating consumers about investment risk. *Journal of Consumer Education*, 19(20), 1–8.

Oster, C. (April 8, 2003). Car insurers get into the repair business. *The Wall Street Journal*, p. D1.

Scism, L. (May 2–3, 2015). Long-term-care insurance: is it worth it? *The Wall Street Journal*, B7.

Solomon, M. (2003). *Conquering consumerspace.* New York: AMACOM.

Whitehouse, K. (March 6, 2003). Is that Picasso covered by your home insurance? *Wall Street Journal*, p. D1.

Xaio, J. (2015). *Consumer economic well-being.* New York: Springer.

Part **5**

Emerging Consumer Issues and the Global Perspective

Chapter **15**

Issues, Ethics, and Globalization

An economist is an expert who will know tomorrow why the things he predicted yesterday didn't happen today.

Evan Esar

LEARNING OBJECTIVES

1. Describe the four drives impacting consumer behavior.

2. Explain globalization and the need for a global perspective.

3. Explain the blocks to more sustainable consumer behavior.

4. Discuss the need for consumer and financial literacy.

CASE STUDY

What Drives Consumer Decisions?

"As Madison Avenue focuses more intently on trying to influence consumer behavior, one of the world's largest agencies is starting a unit that will tap into research from academics in the field as well as the work of its own employees. Draftcb, owned by the Interpublic Group of Companies, is opening what it is calling the Institute of Decision Making, devoted to finding out more about the instinctual ways that consumers behave along with the rational and emotional ones. The unit will concentrate on emerging fields like behavioral economics and neuroscience. The institute is getting its own leader from inside Draftcb, which works for advertisers like Del Monte Foods, S.C. Johnson, Kmart and Miller Coors . . . The institute has formed ties with assistant professors of marketing and psychology at Stanford and the Haas School of Business at the University of California, Berkeley." (Note: Draftcb, is now called FCB.)

Source: Stuart Elliott (June 29, 2010). "A Quest to Learn What Drives Consumer Decisions." *The New York Times*, NYTimes.com 4/22/2015 12:32 P.M.

Introduction

We've covered a lot of issues in this book. This concluding chapter focuses on the economic beliefs and behaviors of consumers from sustainable and global perspectives. There is no question that our measurement of consumer behavior, specifically decision making, is rapidly changing. More data are being collected and analyzed at the immediate point of sale. Anticipated behavior is also measured. Polls showed that holiday shoppers in 2015 were going to buy 46 percent of their presents online. Brick and mortar stores to compete were coming up with new strategies such as interactive shopping where more consumers could participate beyond browsing. One example was to let customers try on cosmetics themselves, allowing them to give themselves facials at aisle sinks. The question is why someone would come to a store versus the ease of buying online? Retailers from grocery stores to luxury clothing stores have known for a long time that the longer the shopper stays in the store the more they will buy so having comfortable chairs are a plus along with interactive experiences. Here is another example of consumer behavior. Consumers will go out of the house to get coffee. They will go to Starbucks or Dunkin' Donuts versus making coffee at home. Why? Going out for ice cream is considered a treat versus opening up the home freezer and scooping out ice cream. *Probably one of the reasons is that as social beings we want to be around others.* What is changing are the means and modes and significant questions arise about the worth and use of new technology (E. Goldsmith, 2015).

Another change is that the products and the foods we crave are considerably different than our tastes 40 years ago when there were no flat-screen TVs or Chipotles. The scope is much wider. Consumers seek luxury brands acquired cross-border (Chung, Youn, & Lee, 2014). Consumer economics as a field of study has to advance and move with the times. Controversy and concerns about the planet have always been part of consumer economics and the future holds more of the same. E-commerce has had the effect of eliminating geography or distance from the consumer–market exchange. Making decisions and choices after careful consideration of every possible course of action is not possible, so how do consumers narrow their selection and in the process avoid as much fraud as possible? Unfortunately protecting themselves in the marketplace has become more difficult. The saving grace is that "our brains have a unique structure that allows us to mentally transport ourselves into future circumstances and then ask ourselves how it feels to be there" (Gilbert, 2006, p. 262). In addition, "With a little detective work, a pencil, and a good eraser, we can usually estimate—at least roughly—the probability that a choice will give us what we desire" (Gilbert, 2006, p. 260).

Ethics were introduced earlier in the book, and they underlie consumer decisions about courses of action. To review, ethics is the study of the general nature of morals and of specific moral choices made by individuals within the context of the larger society. According to the Better Business Bureau's Consumer Code of Ethics, ethics are evidenced in education, truthfulness, honesty, integrity, courtesy, and sensibility. The BBB promotes, develops and encourages an ethical marketplace.

The essence of modern consumer economics is its eclectic approach. This chapter begins with a description of four drives that affect consumer behavior and then uses these drives as an organizing principle for the rest of the chapter. One of the drives, the drive to bond, is linked with gifting behavior; the subject of gift cards (an established phenomenon) is covered. Another drive, the one to learn and make sense of the world and ourselves, is tested when it comes to selecting a phone service and the add-on equipment and services, so the practical application of this drive, that of trying to make sense of a purchase plan, is included in this chapter. Next, the chapter moves on to discussions of global and environmental perspectives, which are so blended together that often they are difficult to differentiate. An example is the use of pesticides, which is of worldwide concern. In the United States, we ban the use of certain pesticides that are acceptable in other parts of the world, and vice versa, so because food is imported and exported globally, there are real differences among nations about what is acceptable and safe.

The chapter wraps up with a retrospective on the book and the consumer movement in general. What have we learned? Where are we going? Even though consumer fraud has been with us since the beginning of trade and exchange, there are always new wrinkles, new swindlers, and new issues. By this time in the course and the book, you should be far less gullible.

Four Drives Impacting Consumer Behavior

We talked earlier in the book about consumer behavior, and following is some additional information on the subject and the organizing principle of four drives developed by Paul Lawrence and Nitin Nohria, two Harvard-based researchers. They concluded that the way we act is a result of the conscious choices we make, often based on our ethics. These choices are fueled by an internal battle among four drives (Lawrence & Nohria, 2002, p. 5):

1. The drive to acquire objects and experiences that improve our status relative to others.

2. The drive to bond with others in long-term relationships of mutual care and commitment.

3. The drive to learn and make sense of the world and of ourselves.

4. The drive to defend ourselves, our loved ones, our beliefs, and our resources from harm.

Drive to Acquire

The drive to acquire is crucial to the understanding of consumerism and was addressed in Chapter 1 in the discussion of needs versus wants. This section provides further evidence of this drive: When subjects are given the choice of living in two worlds, in which prices are the same, but in one they earn $90,000 and their neighbors earn $100,000 versus another in which they earn $110,000 but their neighbors earn $200,000, they are more likely to choose the former situation. Such behavior is at odds with standard utility-maximizing models of human behavior—in absolute terms, subjects would be better off earning $110,000 instead of $90,000" (Lawrence & Nohria, 2002, p. 66). What this experiment suggests is that humans compare themselves to others and care about relative status. It sheds light on such concepts as competition, ambition, envy, and status. This is part of the general concept of social influence—we notice others, they notice us (E. Goldsmith, 2015).

In an earlier chapter, we discussed prospect theory, developed by Daniel Kahneman and Amos Tversky in 1979 as an alternative to expected utility theory. What they found was that people frame outcomes or transactions in their minds, affecting how they behave and what they expect to receive. Prospect theory has been used to explain various gambling and betting behaviors; for example, even though the odds are very poor, consumers go ahead and bet or gamble anyway. In short, consumers aren't always rational, they engage in risky behaviors, they have a drive to acquire even if the odds are not in their favor, and their behavior is not always consistent. For example, someone could be conservative in stock market investments but regularly play the lottery.

Connected with the drive to acquire is the desire to use something we have paid for. This reluctance to waste a purchase is called the **sunk-cost fallacy**, a decision-making bias. An example given in Michael Solomon's book *Conquering Consumerspace* is that if there is a sudden snowstorm that makes it dangerous to go to a big football game, the person who paid for the ticket will more likely brave the storm and go than the person who was given a free ticket. The person who paid—in other words, who sunk money into the ticket—is more determined to go.

As consumers, we are always weighing wins and losses, taking chances, and comparing costs and benefits. Our goal is to improve our well-being (Xiao, 2015). The theory of mental accounting indicates that decisions are influenced by the way a problem is framed, meaning how it is posed, so purchases should not be looked at solely in terms of price but also in terms of circumstances or conditions. For example, someone may not balk at paying $70 for a haircut in a fancy salon but might object to that price at a Cost Cutters or Walmart Supercenter. How can this be? Why do we react this way?

Money is, in and of itself, inert. But everywhere it becomes empowered with special meanings, imbued with unusual powers. Psychologists are interested in attitudes toward money, why and how people behave as they do toward and with money, as well as what effect money has on human relations (Furnham, 2014, p. 2).

As an example of the drive to acquire, employees may be perfectly happy with 5 percent raises until they find out that their colleagues received 7 percent raises; then they will want to know why the difference exists, but probably no explanation will appease them because they have a bad taste in their mouth. This reaction illustrates that drives are not always positive—they can lead to personal unhappiness, unsettling comparisons, and unproductive consequences. Reward systems cannot always live up to expectations.

The drive to acquire is counterbalanced with other drives such as the need for more time, specifically family time. Many people report being more pressed for time than ever before, and they are actively seeking solutions to be less pressured, resulting in growth in the interest in prepared foods and in yoga and other relaxing or stretching forms of exercise. About a third of Americans report always feeling rushed. Consider the Atherton, California lifestyle of Ron Johnson in the case study.

CASE STUDY

Ron Johnson, Former Executive of Target, Apple Stores, and JCPenney

Consider the busy lifestyle of the founder of an e-commerce startup called Enjoy in Silicon Valley. "Most mornings, Ron Johnson rises just after 4 A.M., without the use of an alarm clock, and sets off on a five-mile run . . . Johnson has a desk with a computer on top of it, but he almost never sits there, and although he carries an iPhone, he mostly gestures with it. In my time with him, I never once saw him even glance at the screen. 'Anytime you're going to your phone, it's a withdrawal from a relationship,' Johnson says. 'The team needs to feel your presence, your concentration, your interest.' Johnson, 56 has found that he can be efficient this way, so much so that on most days he heads home around 3 p.m. Family matters to him . . ."

Source: Max Chafkin (November 2015). "Redemption of Ron Johnson." *FastCompany*, pp. 112–113.

Drive to Bond

Relational Issues. Social relationships contain a mix of both competitive and cooperative elements (E. Goldsmith, 2015; Lawrence & Nohria, 2002). Self-interest is not the only motivator—caring about others (extended family, friends, communities, the world) and a sense of fairness serve as counterbalances. Acts of selfless generosity or altruism, such as giving to charities, returning found wallets, helping strangers with flat tires, and doing volunteer work, abound in human affairs. The drive to bond also refers to the drive to seek experiences. The experience of studying and working in another society and culture transforms individuals and has a multiplier effect that extends to their communities and their own countries on their return. The needs both to acquire and to bond cannot be underestimated, and the benefits in terms of improving global understanding are enormous. Cellphones help us bond in remote places, make plans, connect.

CRITICAL THINKING

Cellphone Pricing Issues

If ever there was an industry that ranks high on the list of complaints, this is it. Advances in cellphone technology and deregulation brought more consumer choice but also more consumer confusion. The problems with cellphones (updating, repairs, and pricing of services) is an on-going battle that nearly all individuals and families face. Have you or your family had difficulty with cellphones? Describe and connect this to the drive to bond. How do cellphones help us bond?

The drive to bond is part of what it means to be a consumer because we, as consumers, wonder how other consumers are faring, and we care about their rights as well as our own. How does what we do on a daily basis affect others? What skills do we need in an ever-changing society to preserve and enhance not only our own lives but the lives of others? Furthermore, on the subject of the drive to bond, customer loyalty, which is the bonding of customers to companies, is fundamental to such firms as Ben & Jerry's, whose Waterbury, VT, factory pumps out over 200,000 pints of ice cream each day.

Gifting and Gift Cards. An example of the drive to bond is the experience of giving and receiving gifts. **Gifting** is a symbolic act of voluntarily bestowing and occurs in nearly every culture as a means of celebration. "Each American on average buys about six birthday gifts a year—about one billion gifts in total. Business gifts are used strategically to define and nurture professional relationships, to the tune of more than $1.5 billion per year" (Solomon, 2003, p. 204). Other gifting occasions include Hanukkah, Christmas, anniversaries, Easter, weddings, Mother's Day, Father's Day, and graduations. If you are a reader from another country, supply your own list of typical gifting occasions and behaviors; for US readers who have traveled extensively, you may supply your own memories of gifting and celebrating in other countries. A US visitor to Italy celebrated her birthday in Venice and the usual cake and singing happened, as are typical in the United States, but the difference was that the restaurant turned the lights off so the candles would show and that everyone in the restaurant joined in the singing.

Gift cards were the number one gift preference in 2015. They are enormously popular because of the choices they provide. Many are never redeemed meaning the store or company keeps all the money. What often happens is that customers leave a little money on the gift cards and the stores keep that money. As a piece of advice, if you buy an $18.99 item from a $20.00 gift card and the store clerk offers you the change, take it because the likelihood is that you couldn't find another item for a dollar or less or

Photo 15.1 Shoppers are driven by events such as birthdays or traditional celebrations such as Christmas

Source: Thinkstock: funstock

that you would forget about it and the card would expire or get mislaid. A significant problem is that people forget about cards or lose them.

The sale of gift cards totals over $100 million a year and is a significant source of revenue for retail companies. Besides making 5 percent to 10 percent of value stored on gift cards that are never spent, stores also profit because a customer with a card often spends over the amount, paying more. For example, with a $25 gift card, someone might spend $30 and pay the extra $5. It may get them in a store they would normally never go in.

Drive to Learn and to Make Sense of the World and Ourselves

A simple way to say this is that "I want to know." I want to know what is going on and what I should do. Consumers often go online to read product reviews as a way of learning before purchasing. The drive to learn is inherent in consumer education, and a section on that can be found near the end of this chapter. The second part of that drive, the need to make sense of the world and of ourselves, is covered in the section on obtaining a global perspective.

Drive to Defend

Defending is complicated but one wants to defend oneself from bad purchases, from being ripped off. Buying insurance is a way to protect and defend. Other examples are defending against identity theft and protecting privacy. "Apple chief executive Tim Cook has warned that there will be 'dire consequences' if technology companies do not protect the privacy of their users" (Armstrong, 2015, p.2).

Development of a Global Perspective

Technological and distribution advances are shrinking the distances in the world, with the Internet and communications technology making it possible for global businesses to operate at far less cost in time and money than ever before.

New global markets have led to more affluence and more competition worldwide. The major competitors in the global market come from Australia, Europe, Asia, and North America, and the largest economies in the world are found in the United States, Japan, and Germany. **Globalization** refers to the distribution of goods and services worldwide, with most consumer goods eventually becoming universally accepted. This is different from the term **global perspective**, which is a philosophy, a way of thinking, a type of ethics—it delves into moral choices we all make. According to one source, "[A global perspective] entails the challenging of materialism and commercialism and an examination of one's role as citizen. It further includes global ethics" (Erasmus, Kok, & Retief, 2001, p. 116). The global perspective encourages and appreciates local small businesses, including home-based businesses, as well as the balance, creativity, and job opportunities

Photo 15.2 The world is becoming more urban with large metropolitan areas spreading throughout the globe

Source: Thinkstock: leonello

they bring to the world economy. Even the bigger companies are increasingly expected to put money and support back into the communities that purchase from them or where their headquarters are located. People are feeling that those who generate profits have more of an obligation, a **social responsibility**, to do something worthwhile with at least some of those profits. To be truly socially responsible or to engage in social marketing, companies must address the needs of the masses as well as the needs of the few and balance individual quality with societal and environmental quality. For example, it does not work to give money to charities while at the same time polluting the streams and rivers that run past the homes of the recipients of those charities—a more complete view of corporate responsibility is needed.

To go back to the concept of globalization, a large-scale economy is beyond the purview of one person or one company, although James Bond and superpower movies would lead us to believe that there are wealthy, power-hungry individuals out there who would like to rule the world. One of the leading management experts in the world, Peter Drucker, says,

> When we talk about the global economy, I hope nobody believes it can be managed. It can't. There is no information on it. But if you are in the hospital field, you can know hospitals. If you were to parachute into some strange place and make your way to the lights in the valley, you would be able to identify the correct building as the hospital. (2002, p. 49)

Photo 15.3 Founder of TOMS Shoes, Blake Mycoskie, arrives at TOMS for Target Launch Event at The Bookbindery on November 12, 2014 in Culver City, California

Source: Getty Images: Valerie Macon

CASE STUDY

TOMS Story: An Example of a Socially Responsible Company

"In 2006, American traveler Blake Mycoskie (http://www.twitter.com/blake-mycoskie) befriended children in a village in Argentina and found they had no shoes to protect their feet. Wanting to Help, he created TOMS, a company that would match every pair of shoes purchased with a pair of new shoes given to a child in need. One for One. Realizing this movement could serve other basic needs, TOMS Eyewear was launched. With every pair purchased, TOMS will help give sight to a person in need. One for one . . . We give in over 60 countries. We've given 10 million pairs of shoes to children in need, teaching us 10 million lessons . . . .150,000 had had their sight restored . . ."

Source: "About TOMS," http://www.toms.com/about -toms. 7/30/2014.

No one can completely manage the global economy, but a single person, an expert, can know how a specific industry or area of business operates. This is not to say that there are not some extremely powerful individuals and pervasive businesses such as Amazon, Apple, Facebook, and Microsoft. The largest foundation in the world is the Bill & Melinda Gates Foundation. According to its website, simple values are at the center of the foundation's work:

- All lives—no matter where they are being led—have equal value.
- To whom much is given, much is expected.

The Bill & Melinda Gates Foundation is an example of one of the greatest challenges, which is knowing what information to access in order to make sound decisions. Who to believe? What to buy or not buy? The global economy has opened up the world to limitless possibilities. Customers are changing and distribution systems are changing, and the effects on technology and competition are immeasurable. Drucker says,

> Under e-commerce, delivery will become the one area in which a business can truly distinguish itself. It will become the critical "core competence." Its speed, quality, and responsiveness may well become the decisive competitive factor even where brands seem to be entrenched. And no existing multination and altogether very few businesses are organized for it. (2002, pp. 57–58)

There are limitations; for example, haircuts, manicures, and massages still require the personal touch, and most brides would like to try on a wedding dress (or several of them) before making a purchase.

Consumer Terrorism

Consumer terrorism refers to a variety of activities conducted by individuals or groups whose purpose is to disrupt the marketplace. It includes making threats and deliberately spreading misinformation and fear, as well as actually tampering with products. Product tampering is a form of bioterrorism that can cause great harm to individuals (such as those made ill by tampered-with foods or drugs) and can ruin or temporarily cripple companies. The wise company immediately addresses any problems with its products by alerting the public and by handling recalls and rebates efficiently. The increased use of surveillance cameras in stores and in factories should reduce product tampering.

Another form of consumer terrorism is tampering with websites, company data, and personal computers through computer viruses. There are many cases in the news about hackers accessing company and government records and stealing consumers' identities.

Stealth Marketing

Global marketing strategies come and go, but one with lasting power is called **stealth marketing**, the provision of a unique service or product in a way that is not too public. Rather than being overt in offering a new product or service, in stealth marketing the company's intent is to "come in under the radar" by introducing something new without it being too obvious to competitors. Once a marketing plan is established, the company may keep new offerings or changes under wraps until it is time to launch. Stealth is used as a tool to gain competitive advantage.

In the public's mind, mainstream marketing is often thought of as being obvious, pushy, slick, and pressured and as being highly publicized in magazines and newspapers (for example, celebrity-filled product launches for fashions, perfumes, or restaurant chains). Stealth marketing is the opposite of this. Stealth marketing is not illegal, nor is it fully developed, but it is a consumer issue involving protection and awareness.

Location Marketing

One of the newest twists in consumer privacy is location marketing which engages mobile app users in the context of their daily lives using **location-based marketing (LBM)**. A company can use the location technology and push notification capabilities in customers' smartphones to learn more about them, such as where they are and what they are doing. The company's goal would be to get their targeted message to the right person at the right time. Some consumers find this irritating or intrusive, others welcome the personalized messages.

Sustainability and Consumerism

Sustainability and environmental awareness are at the forefront of consumer behavioral economics. The relationships between environment and economics can be looked at

Photo 15.4 Environmental concerns such as global warming are spurring "green" consumerism
Source: Thinkstock: Romolo Tavani

from a variety of perspectives. The specialization in economics that focuses on these relationships is called **ecological economics**, with a particular emphasis in changes in **natural capital**, which consists of natural resources and ecological systems. "Natural capital is defined as the whole endowment of land and resources available to us, including air, water, fertile soil, forests, fisheries, mineral resources, and the ecological life support systems that make economic activity, and indeed life itself, possible" (Harris, 2002). In ecological economics, changes in these realms are viewed as important as changes in human-made capital. The gross national product (GNP) measures human production. The quality of our lives is a combination of the state of the environment and the social issues of family, well-being, health, education, and harmony. "The economic indicators, such as the GNP, which measure how well the society is doing, are essentially measures of how rapidly resources are being used up—converted to economic product. The more economic the product, the 'healthier' the economy and, by implication, the society. Is that good, you ask, on a finite planet to place a premium on the maximum rate of using up resources?" (Harman, 1998, p. 123).

"Sustainability has many dimensions: behavioral social, economic, legal, technological, and material" (D.S. Goldsmith, 2015, p. 168). **Sustainable development** would mean not using up natural resources or endangering ecosystems. One author states that sustainable development is "economic development that provides for human needs without undermining global ecosystems and depleting essential resources" (Harris, 2002, p. 28). Although it may seem like a contradiction in terms, abundance and affluence bring new forms of scarcity— "scarcity of natural resources, of fresh air and water, of arable land, of the waste-absorbing capacities of the natural environment, of resilience of the planet's life-support systems, of spirit-renewing wilderness. . . . The 'new scarcities' are of course also related to population growth, which in turn is a consequence of improved sanitation and public health measures" (Harman, 1998, p. 125).

Because of pervasive smog worldwide, the people today in many locations are aware of the effects of production, transportation, and consumption on the environment. As mentioned earlier, many consumers feel that business has a social responsibility to look out for the quality of the environment as part of the consumer–market exchange. Wal-Mart even has sustainability experts on its headquarters staff. Green advocate Amanda Freeman, a founder of VitalJuiceDaily.com, says that "social responsibility is hot this year as well, so everyone is trying to be less consumption-oriented and more cause-oriented" (Puente, 2007, p. 2D). Consumers have a responsibility to consume in environmentally friendly ways and to engage in recycling behaviors.

According to South African authors Alet C. Erasmus, Martha Kok, and Arda Retief, "Consumer behavior of the Western world can generally be described as materialistic. . . . Driven by economic principles, the retail environment encourages and even promotes a materialistic value system. Although many consumers will deny being materialistic, every day consumer related behavior in the Western world unfortunately bears testimony of the opposite" (2001, p. 116).

They also say that a global perspective results in an appreciation for voluntary simplicity and conservation and a respect for past and future generations. **Voluntary simplicity** refers to a conscious effort to live more modestly, with fewer possessions and at lower consumption levels. Erasmus, Kok, and Retief (2001) call for decisions to be based on these types of considerations, of the effect on interactive environments, rather than with a passion for consumption. Does anyone really need a 17-bedroom, 20-bathroom house? Many are calling for a "mind shift" away from indiscriminate consumption to a socially conscious and environmentally responsible consumer behavior where the consumer is regarded as a citizen (McGregor, 1998a, 1998b, 1999). "Voluntary simplifiers range from senior citizens who downsize their homes to young, mobile professionals who don't want to be tied down to their possessions . . . clearly, most mainstream consumers are not about to give up their Prada bags any time soon. However, many of us are overwhelmed by the profusion of stuff out there" (Solomon, 2003, p. 248). Voluntary simplifiers believe that once their basic needs are met, there is no reason to keep consuming on top of that—they do not believe that more is better.

The word *environment* can refer to so many things, from energy alternatives to air quality to use of fuels to water quality. There is also the consumer right to a healthy environment. As mentioned in Chapter 2 on the history of consumerism, President John F. Kennedy, inspired by Rachel Carson's book *Silent Spring*, was an early advocate for better environmental protection. The Consumer Federation of America (CFA)—one of the most active consumer organizations advocating for a cleaner environment—believes that we must all reduce, reuse, and recycle more. The main government agency regarding environmental control is the Environmental Protection Agency (EPA).

The manufacture of packaging involves raw materials such as wood, energy, and water. First, when making packaging materials, there can be an awareness of the negative effect of certain manufacturing procedures on the environment and a consideration of redesign and acceptable alternatives. A next step could be eliminating unnecessary packaging, such as double and triple layers of packaging. Have you ever noticed how much packaging you throw out? Biodegradable and recyclable packaging could be alternatives. **Biodegradability** means that packaging material will decompose naturally through biological processes; in homes, packaging could be recycled for another use.

Another way to look at the environment–consumption interchange is to consider the environmental costs of producing goods from cradle to grave (from inception to disposal). How much electricity, raw materials, water, and gasoline (for transportation) are used? New methods and materials are needed, as is support for consumers when they are offered more environmentally friendly goods. Consumers have to be informed about the larger part they play, and education is one of the keys to making informed decisions (more on this in a later section).

The discussion of caring about the environment harkens back to the beginning of the book when values (individual or collective beliefs that are considered desirable), standard of living, and quality or quantity of goods and services were introduced. Values and standards of living impact economic life in the home. This approach is part of a far greater concept: life satisfaction (including the concept of buying wisely). This is in direct contrast to the concept that consumption just happens. On the contrary, consumption is far more complex and involves a set of behaviors, presumptions, and perspectives, including a global, environmental, or citizen-oriented approach.

All of us are at risk in terms of consumption. For example, we can select a sandwich with bean sprouts, spinach, or peanut butter that has been infected or drink an infected milkshake. It is estimated that a third or more of the American population get sick each year from poorly prepared or handled food. From a global perspective, one of the growing concerns is how much food is imported from countries such as China and India that do not have the sanitation and pesticide rules regarding farming that are common in other nations. As mentioned earlier, this is a two-way street—infected food has been produced, exported, and circulated in more developed nations including the United States.

Although most of us would agree that to live more sustainably is a good idea, there are the following barriers to more sustainable consumption behaviors:

- demographic factors
- external factors (existing buildings and infrastructures)
- economic factors (costs and benefits)
- social and cultural factors
- internal factors (motivations and values)
- environmental knowledge (awareness and education)
- attitudes
- emotional involvement (feelings of denial, helplessness) (adapted from D.S. Goldsmith, 2015, pp. 156–157).

Progress may be slow and incremental. Shifting environmental beliefs and practices is monumental.

Consumer and Financial Literacy

By reading this book, you have experienced consumer education and improved your financial acumen. The goal of consumer education is to provide a broad range of people with the information, technology, and confidence needed to give them a sense of control over their decisions. Formal **consumer education** (knowledge about today's marketplace) in grades K–12 varies by state but is usually part of several courses in high schools; colleges vary in what they offer as well. Batty et al. (2015) used an experimental design to evaluate a set of standardized financial education lessons delivered to fourth and fifth graders in two school districts. Here is their analysis:

> *We find that even a relatively brief program results in knowledge gains that persist one year later. While measuring financial behaviors in this age group is challenging, students exposed to financial education have more positive attitudes about personal finance and appear more likely to save. These results show that younger students can learn financial topics and that learning is associated with improved attitudes and behaviors which, if sustained, may result in increased financial capacity later in life. (p. 69)*

To summarize,

> **Consumer education** *is concerned with the skills, attitudes, knowledge and understanding that individuals need to cope in an increasingly complex marketplace. Adding to the complexity is a growing recognition of accommodating the needs of multicultural and multilingual learners. (Allison & Rehm, 2007, p. 8)*

> *Consumer education aims to protect consumers, inform them, promote an understanding between buyer and seller, and contribute to society as a whole, including providing a sense of economic well-being and fair play. The consumer experience relies on trust and dependability. (Goldsmith & McGregor, 2000, p. 126)*

Consumer education curricula require a three-prong attack:

1. *Consumer decision making.* External and internal factors affect consumer decisions as well as the stages of the decision-making process.
2. *Resource management.* Goal setting, personal finance, buying skills, technological developments, and conservation are all part of resource management.
3. *Citizen and government participation.* Both individual citizens and their government as a whole need to have an awareness of economic conditions and to make legislative changes.

In modern consumer economics, there is an intense relationship among economic, social, and geopolitical forces that focuses on how market forces operate and how individuals and families make choices in a complex society and a diverse economy. Consumer education has its challenges in terms of getting students at all levels to identify needs, allocate resources, and recognize the harsh reality of scarcity. Some needs are going to go unmet; in the process of determining who gets what and who is left out of the loop, there are issues of equity, justice, and fairness. These all fall under the subject of economic education as well as the more general category of character education. Discussions such as these are not for the faint of heart or the perfectionist, but these issues should be debated with many sides represented. Legislators and governors constantly struggle with how to disburse tax dollars in a fair and effective way. Should budget money go to border control, space programs, or consumer protection? No matter which way they turn, some program will have to do with less than in the past in order that other programs or new programs can thrive—growth requires hard choices. Consumer education straddles family and consumer sciences and other subjects within the social sciences such as economics, so it sometimes falls through the cracks when money is being disbursed and programs set up.

"Financial well-being is a multifaceted concept that transcends both traditional financial literacy and the broader notion of financial capability" (Drever et al., 2015). According to the Consumer Financial Protection Bureau, financial well-being entails having control over one's finances day-to-day and month-to-month, having the capacity to absorb financial shocks, being on track to meet financial goals, and having the financial freedom to make choices that allow one to enjoy life (Consumer Financial Protection Bureau, 2015).

The majority of high school seniors taking financial literacy tests fail to comprehend basic subjects such as banking products, credit cards, taxes, savings, and investments (Mandell, 1998). Further, the National Council on Economic Education has said that most high school students and adults score failing grades on their understanding of basic economics. A multi-prong approach is suggested.

Besides teaching these types of courses in school settings, it is clear that adult outreach programs are needed in consumer economics, including e-consumerism. Extension programs and Internet resources are available to those outside school environments. Consumer educators see their role as encompassing both the formal and informal learning environments. As more and more people become lifelong learners and because consumerism is a lifelong process, it makes sense that this topic transcends age and income groups.

Consumer Economics Retrospective

How far we have come. As an example, the television of the twentieth century is not the television of the twenty-first century with apps. Apps are available for watching your favorite movies, shows, and live sports. Apple TV has a Siri Remote, a new interface, and the App Store where there are games and apps that completely change what you expect from your big screen. It all adds up to change and televisions are only a very small part of the wave of the future.

The goals of this book were to inform and inspire. A modern boutique hotel has a saying: When you call down to the front desk, the first thing the receptionist says is, "How can I inspire you today?" As we have traced the unfolding of consumer economic thought, we concentrated on economic thinking while keeping the welfare of the individual, family, community, and the planet in mind. In assessing economic issues, it is important to remember that what we are seeing today has a history.

As we have traced the theories guide us on the right road. One of the fundamentals of economic theory is that we all experience scarcity while at the same time we are surrounded by abundance. We have much to choose from and no matter how rich we cannot own or consume everything.

It is difficult to fully appreciate the development of economic thought as applied to consumerism without an examination of a variety of ideas and viewpoints. The Consumer Power Model of consumer economics (introduced in Chapter 3) showed the interaction among various components such as the media, consumers, businesses, the government, and consumer organizations. In that same chapter it was noted that consumers want useful, safe, environmentally sound products at fair prices, and they also want selection. In this process of sorting information and acquiring, we also learned about the less noble aspects of consumerism, namely, frauds and scams, which both have a history and tend to repeat themselves in new and "improved" forms. Where money is involved, fraud and deception are never far behind. As positive counterpoints, the concepts of citizenship, consumer advocacy, and regulatory action were introduced.

Summary

Companies and consumers are connecting across the physical and digital worlds. Underlying this are four human drives: the drive to acquire, the drive to bond, the drive to learn, and the drive to defend. Thinking and caring about others relate to the drive to bond as well as the drive to learn and make sense of the world and of ourselves, and the example of the Bill & Melinda Gates Foundation was given. A global perspective is a way of thinking, a philosophy, in which local small businesses are appreciated and seen as part of the worldwide economy. Ethics and citizenship are important considerations in the interchange between environmentalism and consumer behavior, and choosing wisely with an eye to future generations takes present consumption into a higher realm, that of thinking of others besides oneself. This requires a shift from individual consumer rights to an awareness of collective human responsibilities. The underlying principles of a global perspective require a mind shift to the greater good, to an awareness of a greater role.

KEY POINTS

1. Globalization refers to international marketing and exchange, the distribution of goods and services worldwide.

2. The global perspective includes global ethics and consideration of others.

3. Consumer terrorism refers to activities whose purpose is to disrupt the marketplace.

4. Stealth marketing, engaged in to gain competitive advantage, refers to targeting an audience or market without being too obvious about it.

5. No one person or company manages the worldwide economy.

6. Educating consumers about the long-term effects of consumption, including environmental impact and sustainable development, is part of building a global perspective.

7. Through work, internships, and study abroad or exchange programs, along with volunteering, there are ways to get involved in international consumer and environmental issues.

KEY TERMS

biodegradability

consumer education

consumer terrorism

ecological economics

gifting

globalization

global perspective

location-based marketing (LBM)

natural capital

social responsibility

stealth marketing

sunk-cost fallacy

sustainable development

voluntary simplicity

DISCUSSION QUESTIONS

1. How important is gifting to you? Do you think there is too much or too little emphasis in our society on gifting and celebrating holidays? For your holiday gift, how would you feel about someone donating a goat to a family in an African village? Explain your answers.

2. Why would a company use location-based marketing? Can you give an example of a Smartphone App that uses location-based marketing?

3. Although most would agree that sustainable behavior is a good thing, what are some of the reasons it is slow to be adopted?

REFERENCES

Allison, B., and M. Rehm. (2007). Teaching strategies for diverse learners in FCS classrooms. *Journal of Family and Consumer Sciences*, 99 (2), 8–10.

Armstrong, A. (February 13, 2015). Tim Cook: cyber privacy is a 'life and death' issue, *Telegraph*. http://www.telegraph.co.uk/finance/11412625.

Batty, M., Collins, J. M. and Odders-White, E. (Spring 2015). Experimental evidence on the effects of financial education on elementary school students' knowledge, behavior, and attitudes. *Journal of Consumer Affairs*, 49(1), 69–96.

Chung, K., Youn, C., and Lee, Y. (October 2014). The influence of luxury brands' cross-border acquisition on consumer brand perception. *Clothing and Textiles Research Journal*, 32 (4), 219–234.

Consumer Financial Protection Bureau (2015). *Financial well-being: the goal of financial education report*. Iowa City, IA: Consumer Financial Protection Bureau.

Drever, A., Odders-White, E., Kalish, C., Else-Quest, N., Hoagland, E., and Nelms, E. (Spring 2015). Foundations of financial well-being: Insights into the role of executive function, financial socialization and experience-based learning in childhood and youth. *Journal of Consumer Affairs*, 49 (1), 13–38.

Drucker, P. (2002). *Managing in the next society*. New York: St. Martin's Press.

Erasmus, A., M. Kok, and A. Retief. (2001). Adopting a global perspective in the discipline consumer science. *Journal of Family Ecology and Consumer Sciences*, 29, 116–23.

Furnham, A. (2014). *The new psychology of money*. London: Routledge.

Gilbert, D. (2006). *Stumbling on happiness*. New York: Alfred A. Knopf.

Goldsmith, D.S. (2015). Sustainably managing resources in the built environment. Guest book chapter in *Social influence and sustainable consumption* (author: Elizabeth Goldsmith). New York: Springer.

Goldsmith, E. (2015). *Social influence and sustainable consumption*. New York: Springer.

Goldsmith, E., and S. McGregor. (2000). E-commerce: consumer protection issues and implications for research and education. *Journal of Consumer Studies and Home Economics*, 24 (2), 124–27.

Harman, W. (1998). *Global mind change: the promise of the 21st century.* San Francisco, CA: Berrett-Koehler Publishers.

Harris, J. (2002). *Environmental and natural resource economics.* Boston: Houghton Mifflin.

Lawrence, P., and N. Nohria. (2002). *Driven: how human nature shapes our choices.* Cambridge, MA: Harvard Business School.

Mandell, L. (1998). *Our vulnerable youth: the financial literacy of American 12th graders.* Jump$tart Coalition for Personal Financial Literacy.

McGregor, S. (1998a). Reinterpreting economic theory in a global reality. *Journal of Family and Consumer Sciences,* 90 (3), 35–40.

McGregor, S. (1998b). Towards adopting a global perspective in the field of consumer studies. *Journal of Consumer Studies and Home Economics,* 22 (2), 111–19.

McGregor, S. (September 1999). Globalizing consumer education: shifting from individual consumer rights to collective human responsibilities. Proceedings of the 19th International Consumer Studies and Home Economics Research Conference, pp. 43–52.

Puente, M. (December 11, 2007). Oh, you shouldn't have—really! *USA Today,* p. 1D.

Solomon, M. (2003). *Conquering consumerspace.* New York: AMACOM.

Xiao, J. (2015). *Consumer economic wellbeing.* New York: Springer.

Index